PLAGUES UPON THE EARTH

THE PRINCETON ECONOMIC HISTORY
OF THE WESTERN WORLD

Joel Mokyr, Series Editor

A list of titles in this series appears in the back of the book.

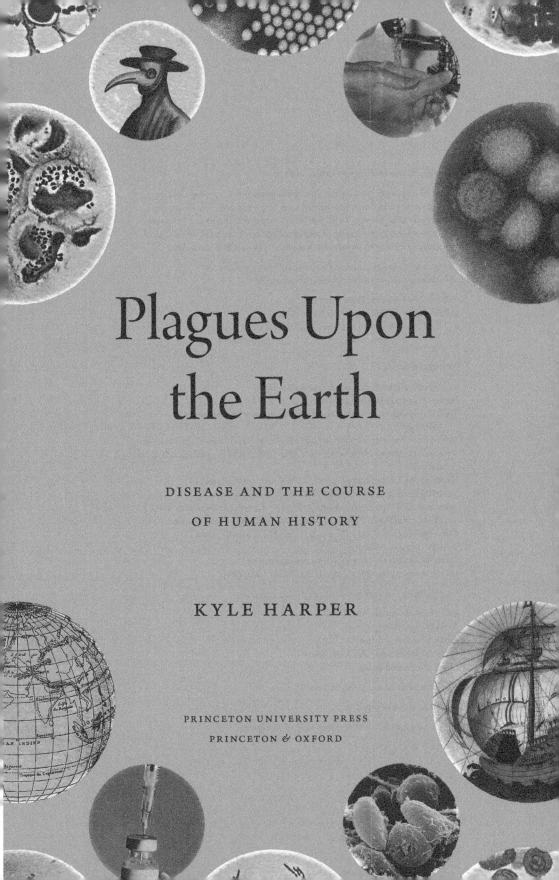

Plagues Upon the Earth

DISEASE AND THE COURSE OF HUMAN HISTORY

KYLE HARPER

PRINCETON UNIVERSITY PRESS

PRINCETON & OXFORD

Published by Princeton University Press
41 William Street, Princeton, New Jersey 08540
6 Oxford Street, Woodstock, Oxfordshire OX20 1TR

press.princeton.edu

Library of Congress Cataloging-in-Publication Data
Names: Harper, Kyle, 1979– author.
Title: Plagues upon the earth : disease and the course of human history / Kyle Harper.
Description: Princeton : Princeton University Press, [2021] | Series: The Princeton economic history of the western world; 46 | Includes bibliographical references and index.
Identifiers: LCCN 2021012798 (print) | LCCN 2021012799 (ebook) | ISBN 9780691192123 (hardback) | ISBN 9780691224725 (ebook)
Subjects: LCSH: Epidemics—History. | Plague—History. | Disease and history. | BISAC: HISTORY / Social History | MEDICAL / Infectious Diseases
Classification: LCC RA649 .H274 2021 (print) | LCC RA649 (ebook) | DDC 614.4/9—dc23
LC record available at https://lccn.loc.gov/2021012798
LC ebook record available at https://lccn.loc.gov/2021012799

British Library Cataloging-in-Publication Data is available.

Editorial: Rob Tempio, Matt Rohal
Jacket Design: Karl Spurzem
Production: Erin Suydam
Publicity: James Schneider, Amy Stewart
Copyeditor: Ingrid Burke

This book has been composed in Arno

Printed on acid-free paper. ∞

Printed and bound in Great Britain by Clays Ltd, Elcograf S.p.A.

10 9 8 7 6 5 4 3 2 1

For Sylvie, August, Blaise, Max, and Michelle

This new world may be safer, being told

The dangers and diseases of the old;

For with due temper men do then forgo,

Or covet things, when they their true worth know.

There is no health; physicians say that we

At best enjoy but a neutrality.

And can there be worse sickness than to know

That we are never well, nor can be so?

—JOHN DONNE, *AN ANATOMY OF THE WORLD* (1611)

TABLE OF CONTENTS

PLAGUES UPON THE EARTH

Introduction

MICROORGANISMS AND MACROHISTORY

ONE OF THE CHIEF BLESSINGS of living in the modern world is supposed to be that the risk of dying from an infectious disease has become vanishingly small. The nuisances of modern civilization are a small price to pay for the good fortune of being alive at a time when our germs have been brought to heel. We can grudgingly resign ourselves to the inevitability that cancers, chronic diseases, or degenerative disorders will catch up to us someday. We moderns die of old age, of overabundance, of cellular malfunction . . . but not plagues and poxes. Until, that is, a new pestilence has the temerity to disrupt our daily lives, here and now.

More than we are apt to remember, even in the shadow of a pandemic, the world we inhabit thoroughly presupposes the subjugation of infectious disease. Consider, if you are privileged enough to live in a developed society, a routine morning. It starts with a walk across a cold (but easily disinfected) tile floor to deposit roughly one hundred grams of stool in a gravity-powered flushing device. A few liters of water, carrying nine trillion or so bacteria, are whisked away for treatment. A thin, two-ply tree product minimized contact between your waste and your hands, but for good measure you wash them anyway, using soap containing mild antibiotic compounds. In the shower you douse your whole body with gentle disinfectants, and then apply a jelly loaded with an aluminum compound to waylay the malodorous bacteria in your underarms.[1]

When you walk into the kitchen, you open a refrigerated box and feel the 40°F air rush out—just cool enough to slow the decay of the dead fruits, vegetables, and animals inside. You grab (on a weekend morning, perhaps) some slices of slaughtered pig, tightly wrapped in an impermeable sheet of cellulose that keeps bacteria and oxygen out. Using one of the very oldest technologies, you light a fire—or at least twist a knob that does it for you—and heat your meat until it is around 150°F, and the microbes hanging all over it are good and dead. When you drink a glass of water, the fact that it has been mildly chlorinated upstream of your faucet relieves you of any need to worry that you will contract a ghastly intestinal disease. And should you pour yourself a glass of cow's milk, you can be assured that any microbial stowaways were exterminated in a process developed by the father of germ theory himself, Louis Pasteur.

Belly appeased, you leave the house owned by the bank that made you a thirty-year loan on the safe bet that you will be alive long enough to pay the money back. You depart through a door that is sealed to keep out rodents, mosquitos, and other carriers of pathogens. Perhaps you load your kids (on average, just over two of them) into the van, taking them to a school where they spend more than a decade sponging up knowledge for a future they fully expect to see. Thankfully, it is safe to put your darlings in a building with hundreds of other humans because they have immune systems artificially primed by vaccines to withstand a whole array of half-forgotten diseases. You accept, and bear gracefully, the seasonal colds and sore throats that are the price of existence on a crowded planet.

Our whole way of life depends on the control of infectious disease. But the dominance of *Homo sapiens* over its microbial enemies is astonishingly recent. Throughout most of human history, pathogens and parasites held the upper hand. Infectious diseases were the leading cause of death into the twentieth century. There have been about ten thousand generations of humans so far. For all but the last three or four generations, life was short, lasting on average around thirty years. Yet this average is deceptive, because life in a world ruled by infectious disease was both short *and* uncertain. Infectious diseases came in steady drips and in massive unforeseen waves. The control of infectious disease thus did more than double the average human lifespan. It changed our most basic expectations about suffering and predictability.[2]

Humanity's control is not only recent. It is also incomplete, in at least two senses. First, it is geographically uneven. In large parts of the world, infectious diseases remain an everyday threat. The freedom from fear of pestilence is a privilege not uniformly shared around the planet—an insidious fact whose history this book seeks to retrace. Second, our control of infectious disease is fragile. The tools we possess to mitigate the risks of infectious disease are many and clever, but they are also imperfect. Meanwhile, the evolution of new threats not only continues but accelerates, as human numbers rise and as we put pressure on natural ecosystems. For a parasite, there is now more incentive to exploit humans than ever. We do not, and cannot, live in a state of permanent victory over our germs. Eternal vigilance is the price of liberation from infectious disease, but interruptions are inevitable, not anomalous.

The COVID-19 pandemic has been a painful reminder of this vulnerability. A history of infectious disease can help us understand why such an outbreak was bound to happen—and why there will be another pandemic after this one, and then another. It can also prepare us to see that infectious diseases continue to affect our lives profoundly, in ways that are both visible and invisible. The danger of disease shapes our personal routines, everyday environments, and unspoken assumptions about life and death. It also permeates our relationship to the planet and to each other. The history of disease is the history of migration and power, of poverty and prosperity, of progress and its unintended consequences. In short, our history as a species is inseparable from our strange and intimate connection with the parasites that have stalked our journey every step of the way.

The Contours of History

This book is a study of infectious disease in human history. Infectious disease is a state of impaired health caused by an invader—a pathogen, a parasite, or, more colloquially, a germ (chapter 1 explores these terms in more rigorous detail). The severity of infectious disease runs the spectrum from mere annoyance to existential threat. Our pathogens fall into five big

biological groups (or taxa): fungi, helminths, protozoa, bacteria, and viruses. Fungi are all around us but usually only pose a severe threat to the
health of the immunocompromised. Helminths are worms, some of our
oldest parasites. Protozoa are single-celled microorganisms that cause sin-
ister diseases like malaria. Bacteria are also single-celled organisms, but,
unlike protozoa, they lack an organized nucleus. They are responsible for
many of our worst afflictions, including plague, tuberculosis, cholera, typhus, and typhoid fever. Viruses are infectious agents stripped down to
the essentials; they replicate themselves by inserting their genetic code
into the machinery of the host's cell. Viruses cause smallpox, measles, yellow fever, influenza, polio, AIDS, the common cold, and COVID-19.[3]

Every organism on earth, from the simplest bacterium to the blue
whale, is exploited by parasites. In nature, the rules of parasitism—what
determines the parasites that any organism will suffer—are governed by
ecology and evolution. Consider our closest surviving relative, the chimpanzee. Chimps have the parasites they have because they live in equatorial forests, eat a range of plants, insects, and small monkeys, and exhibit
certain social habits and behavioral traits. Their parasites will change over
time, in response to the natural ups and downs of chimpanzee populations, and the continuous cycle of emergence and extinction among microbes. Chimpanzees have a natural history, insofar as they have evolved
as a species and have existed for a few million years. But they do not have
a history in the way we usually mean "history." Their societies do not have
cumulative culture-driven change over time. Chimps one hundred thousand years ago lived essentially the same way that chimpanzees live today.
They used the same simple tools and ate the same menu of forest foods.
Chimps one hundred thousand years ago would have suffered from a set
of diseases not so different from what their successors face today.[4]

By contrast, humanity's diseases result from the interplay of ecology,
evolution, and a third term: history. Our dispersal across the globe, the
transition to sedentary lifestyles and agriculture, the rise of cities, the
growth of overland and overseas networks, the takeoff to modern economic and population growth, and so on, have reshaped the ecology
and evolution of our germs. Humans today practice lifestyles that would
have been unrecognizable a century ago, much less one hundred thousand years ago. Because of this history, we also have a disease pool our

ancestors would not recognize. When *Homo sapiens* evolved, some two hundred to three hundred thousand years ago in Africa, the vast majority of the pathogens we suffer today did not yet exist. Even ten thousand years ago most of our pathogens had not yet emerged. There was no tuberculosis, no measles, no smallpox, no plague, no cholera, no AIDS, and so on. In that sense, our deadly disease pool is an artefact of our history. We are apes who learned to master fire, domesticate plants and animals, conquer distance, build machines, and tap fossil energy. We live like no other ape, and in consequence we have a brood of parasites unlike any of our relatives in the animal kingdom.

The goal of this book is to tell the story of how we have acquired our distinct disease pool and what it has meant for us as a species. It is a history in which we are part of nature, rather than apart from it. The rules of ecology and evolution still apply to us, but our history influences ecology and evolution in uniquely powerful ways. On this reckoning, disease-causing microbes, in all their glorious particularity, are historical actors, and it is worth the effort to get acquainted with the most influential among them. Yet the emergence, incidence, and consequences of disease, in individuals and populations alike, are always inseparable from a wider array of social and environmental factors. The central theme of the book is thus simple. Human history shapes disease ecology and pathogen evolution; disease ecology and pathogen evolution in turn shape the course of human history. Our germs are a product of our history, and our history has been decisively patterned by the battle with infectious disease.

To understand how our progress as a species has created the distinctive human disease pool, we must commit ourselves to seeing the world through the "eyes" of our germs. From a parasite's perspective, a human is simply a host. Our parasites' goals are not to harm us per se, but to pass on their genes to future generations. In a basic sense, it is obvious why humans are such irresistible hosts. Thanks to technological innovation, we are very good at extracting energy from the environment and turning it into human cells. Consider just our sheer numbers. Other great apes have global populations up to a few hundred thousand. There are now nearly eight billion of us. Just as robbers steal from banks because that is where the money is, parasites exploit human bodies because there are high rewards for being able to do so.[5]

Of course, it is not only our immoderate numbers but almost everything about the way we live—how we use nature, how we congregate and connect—that shapes our disease ecology. The book is organized around four transformative energy revolutions. The first such revolution—the mastery of fire—long precedes the emergence of *Homo sapiens*, although human evolution is entirely dependent on this primordial technology. Fire allowed our ancestors to disperse out of Africa and settle from the equator to the arctic. Humans have the extraordinary capacity to occupy virtually every niche on Earth. This versatility exposed our ancestors to an unusual variety of potential pathogens and also created important differences in the disease burden faced by different human societies. Physical geography plays an important role in infectious disease. For instance, tropical regions have borne—and continue to bear—the heaviest burden of disease. This inequity in the disease burden between human populations is one of the really distinctive features of our species, and it is shaped by geography. But the extent, nature, and consequences of the uneven disease burden have changed over time, as the entanglements of ecology, power, and disease have been continuously reshaped throughout our history.[6]

The second energy revolution was the invention of farming. Starting around ten thousand years ago, in different foyers across the globe, human societies learned to control the reproduction of preferred species of plants and animals. As farming spread, human numbers soared, and the result has been a virtually unceasing acceleration of parasite evolution. Farming also created a novel and intimate ecological relationship between humans and other animals. One of the goals of this book is to revise the familiar story in which our farm animals were the definitive source of new diseases. That story is not so much wrong as incomplete. Cross-species transmission of microparasites is pervasive in nature. We now understand that most human diseases originate from wild animals—for instance, from bats and rodents. Our domesticates—cows, pigs, sheep, horses, camels, and so on—have more often been an evolutionary bridge than an ultimate reservoir of human pathogens. What permanently changed with farming, then, was humanity's place in the broader web of animal life—and animal disease (see figure 0.1).

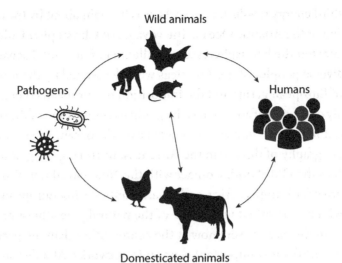

FIGURE 0.1. Disease webs: pathogens transmit between different
species. Pathogens have varying degrees of host specificity,
and they can adapt to new hosts.

Agriculture also required ancestral hunter-gatherers to trade their
mobile ways for a permanent address. In turn, the sedentary lifestyle
created ecological niches for germs that flourished in the unique waste
environments surrounding human settlements. Diarrhea and dysentery
became more formidable problems for human health in the first millennia of farming. Yet, agriculture did not immediately spawn most of the
so-called crowd diseases, caused by respiratory pathogens that require
large, dense populations to sustain permanent transmission. Only later,
with bronze and iron metallurgy, the domestication of donkeys and
horses, and the rise of true cities and large empires, did more and more
respiratory pathogens (like the agents of measles and smallpox) enter
the permanent human disease pool. Civilizations in the Bronze and Iron
Ages also became more interconnected, and long-distance networks
allowed diseases to circulate across Europe, Asia, and Africa during this
period. Great killers like tuberculosis and malaria diffused across the
Old World, while the most peculiar and most explosive of the ancient
diseases—bubonic plague—took advantage of the worldwide network
of rats that human progress had unintentionally constructed.

A third energy revolution, of sorts, was brought about by the regular crossing of the Atlantic Ocean. The voyages of Christopher Columbus reconnected the hemispheres after millennia of near total separation. The diverse peoples of the Americas were devastated by the introduction of European germs and the imposition of European colonization. Equally deserving of attention is the gradual reunification of the tropics, as equatorial germs migrated westward over the ocean. The result was a new geography of disease in the Americas, mirroring the gradients of health in the Old World. Contact with the New World was also transformative for Europe, Africa, and Asia. Atlantic-facing European societies, which were gifted with some of the naturally healthiest environments on the planet, were now at the center rather than the periphery of the world's most important economic networks. At a decisive moment of global history, these societies weathered the "general crisis" of the seventeenth century, whose biological dimensions are sketched in chapter 9. The breakthrough to modern growth and good health was achieved not because the old diseases whimpered out, but because human societies (and stronger states) adapted, even in the face of more daunting, and increasingly globalized, biological challenges.

The fourth energy revolution was the harnessing of fossil fuels. Eons of congealed sunlight stored underground as coal (and later oil and gas) provided energy for the Industrial Revolution. The Enlightenment and modern empirical science promoted economic growth, as well as greater control over infectious disease. Positive feedback loops between science, technology, education, population expansion, and state power created the regime of modern growth. But the negative health feedbacks of modern growth have also been extreme and have shaped health disparities both within and between societies. Steamships and railroads fueled the circulation of deadly diseases, and over the last two centuries, as human numbers exploded, new diseases have emerged continuously. At the same time, scientific knowledge of infectious disease has grown, and the capacity of states to control threats to human health has vastly expanded too. Modernity is not a one-way street to human supremacy over nature, but a kind of escalating ratchet, in which humans have gained a remarkable but unstable advantage over an ever-growing number of parasites.

The distinctive human disease pool is thus a byproduct of our success as a species. And in turn, the trajectory of human history has been deeply influenced by the patterns of infectious disease. The population dynamics of other animals are shaped by their parasites, but there is nothing really comparable to the way that variations in the disease burden in space and time have imprinted on human history. This book tries to capture this two-way story. Our germs are a product of our history. And patterns of endemic disease (that is, a disease permanently established in a population) and epidemic disease (a disease that suddenly increases in prevalence, often with high mortality) have stamped our history.[7]

Infectious disease has shaped the course of human history in myriad ways. The most basic channel through which pathogens have shaped our past is demography, the population-level processes of birth, marriage, and death. Up to the twentieth century, most people died of infectious disease, so it is hard to overstate the relationship between patterns of infectious disease and the structures through which societies reproduce themselves. Mortality patterns shape fertility patterns, marriage systems, and educational investment. In turn, population dynamics affect everything from the incentives for technological innovation to the processes of state formation and decline. Beyond that, diseases have played a pervasive role in the power dynamics between societies. The history of disease has been integral to the history of war, migration, imperialism, and slavery. This book tries to bring a historical sensibility to these patterns, recognizing that, very often, both the distant and recent effects of infectious disease fold in upon one another in unpredictable ways.[8]

One of the major patterns of human history has been what we will call the paradox of progress. Very often, technological advance generates negative feedbacks for human health. From an ecological perspective, this pattern is not in fact paradoxical at all. Our success as a species has been a boon for our parasites, which are trying to accomplish the same biological ends as you or I: acquiring chemical energy that can be metabolized to do the work of replicating genetic information. The timescales of these negative feedbacks vary: sometimes they are slow and insidious, other times they come in the form of violent shocks. Populations absorb, respond, and adapt to these challenges in various ways. Human societies have always sought to understand and control their disease environments, and we should recognize that modern biomedical science and public health are dramatically successful extensions of humanity's long quest for good health.

To see this history in full requires us to operate on big scales—both geographically and chronologically. Inevitably there are tradeoffs in writing this kind of history. The book spans a few million years and covers the entire planet. It thus surrenders any pretext of adequate detail. The hope is that what is lost in granularity will be recouped in insight if we can start to see a little more clearly some of the broad patterns that have shaped the particular experience of different human societies. My own past work has focused on the history of the Roman Empire, which was struck by a series of deadly pandemics, one possibly caused by an ancestral form of the smallpox virus, another certainly caused by the bubonic plague. This work left me with a sense of big, important questions left unseen when we only zoom in, and never out. Why did the Roman Empire suffer giant pandemics at all? Why these diseases and why then?[9]

Such questions cannot be answered if we stay inside the usual lines. The history of disease simply does not conform to the way professional historians partition the past, along geographical and chronological boundaries. The history of human disease is a planetary story, and we try to keep a global perspective on health from start to finish. There is an analogue in the choice of which infectious diseases we choose to highlight. Sometimes histories of disease have been seduced by the drama of a few glamorous germs (like smallpox and plague). The allure is obvious, but such a view is blinkered. It represents the perspective of European societies looking back on a few dramatic chapters in the history of northern populations, a sort of latitudinal bias. Not only does such a narrative leave out the earthy reality of much of our struggle as a species—shaped by worms, biting bugs, dirty water, human and animal feces—it distorts the place of the great epidemics in history and makes them all the more difficult to understand.[10]

A planetary perspective also helps to untangle the relationship between disease and globalization. The term *globalization* is often used loosely; it calls to mind images of contemporary corporate capitalism in a borderless world. But globalization is more than that, and it too has a backstory. Globalization is a major theme in the history of disease, because transportation technologies and human movements have repeatedly intersected the evolution and transmission of infectious diseases. Seen from the perspective of planetary disease ecology, the history of globalization spans at least six distinct phases:[11]

- Prehistoric globalization. Starting around five thousand years ago, the domestication of the horse and invention of wheeled transport intensified long-range human connection and allowed more rapid dispersals of infectious disease.
- Iron Age globalization. From about three thousand years ago, the rise of massive territorial empires and the organization of transcontinental trade drew the societies of Asia, Europe, and Africa into regular contact.
- Peak Old-World globalization. Around one thousand years ago, prior to trans-Atlantic and trans-Pacific shipping, Europe, Asia, and Africa were linked by vibrant overland networks of exchange as well as by Indian Ocean commercial circuits.
- The Columbian Exchange. Just over five hundred years ago, long-distance sailing reconnected the hemispheres, marking the beginning of true planetary globalization.
- Fossil-energy transport. In the nineteenth century, steamships, trains, and automobiles started to release humans from dependence on foot, horse, and wind for transportation, leading to increases in trade, migration, and urbanization.
- The age of the jet plane. Over the last three generations, rapid airborne transportation has made distance virtually irrelevant as an epidemiological barrier.

It also needs to be stated at the beginning that this book is a history of infectious disease, which is not the same thing as a history of health. Human health is a multidimensional phenomenon, shaped by interrelated biological, social, and cultural factors. It is true that before the twentieth century, especially, infectious diseases were a primary determinant of human health, and they were always the leading cause of death. But nutrition, gender, social status, age, and other environmental factors affected patterns of health and disease, including infectious disease, in the past as they do now. It is also important to recognize that there is no ideal or entirely transparent way to measure human health, especially as we journey deeper into the past. Throughout the book I try to draw on a range of indicators that can help us understand the experience of health and the burden of disease: from skeletal records to estimates of crude death rates (a standard measure of how many people per one thousand die in a given year) to average life expectancies. To be sure, none of these are perfect ways to measure the more complex phenomena we are often striving to grasp, but they do offer us insights into changing patterns of health and disease that would otherwise remain hopelessly obscure.[12]

The final chapters of the book explore what the economist Angus Deaton has memorably called the Great Escape, the process in which modern societies became vastly more prosperous and in which the average human lifespan more than doubled. The control of infectious disease is a lynchpin of the Great Escape. Economic growth and dramatic reductions in the burden of infectious disease are deeply intertwined and ultimately share the same two root causes: the advance of scientific knowledge and the empowerment of states capable of protecting public health. This is a miraculous achievement. And yet, an ecological view of human history can add depth to a purely self-congratulatory narrative of progress. The negative feedbacks of growth have often been grim, especially for societies less prepared for the shock of new diseases. The homogenization of global disease pools in the age of steamships and railroads, paradoxically, contributed to enormous global divergence in wealth and health, creating gaps that have narrowed but still not been closed.[13]

We can see the control of infectious disease that we have achieved as part of a recent and novel experiment in human planetary domination. However, our dominance may be more tenuous than we would like to believe. For a moment in the mid-twentieth century, it seemed as though human progress would render infectious diseases a thing of the past. Emboldened by antibiotics, vaccination, and insecticides, our species went on the offensive. The smallpox virus, one of our cruelest enemies, was wiped off the face of the earth by a global health crusade. But progress stalled. The negative feedbacks of growth have continued to operate. New infectious diseases have continuously emerged. Old foes are developing resistance to antibiotics. Climate change is starting to upset ecological balances. We will never go back to the past, in which our ancestors were essentially helpless in the face of a threat they did not understand. But there is no guarantee that the extent of control we have achieved is permanent. Parasites adapt to the new environments we create, and unforeseen biological disruption has been, and continues to be, one of the great sources of instability in human civilization.

Evidence Old and New

There is a conspicuous reason why few historians since William Mc-Neill, whose 1976 book *Plagues and Peoples* is a landmark and an inspiration, have tried to tackle the big history of infectious disease. Historians have an occupational attachment to evidence, especially written evidence: medical texts, government statistics, historical chronicles, and so forth. The further back we venture into the past, the thinner the record becomes, and the harder it is to use, especially if we are trying to determine what diseases really mattered. The challenge of retrospective diagnosis—identifying real diseases behind historical accounts of infection and sickness—is pervasive and profound. For example, until recently, historians hotly debated the biological agent of the Black Death, caused by a disease with a fairly distinct clinical presentation (bubonic plague, identifiable by the hard globes of pus that extrude from infected lymph nodes). This controversy highlights the serious challenge of understanding the biology of disease in former times.[14]

This book draws on a rich body of work in medical, environmental, and economic history that has helped us understand the role of infectious disease in the human past. But its claim to novelty rests in part on the effort to draw from a new source of knowledge: genomes. Genomes are the instructions encoded in the DNA (or, in the case of some viruses, RNA) of an organism. The code is written with molecular "letters"—long strands of nucleic acids—handed down from parents to offspring during reproduction (whether sexually, as with worms and some protozoa, or asexually, as with bacteria and viruses). These sequences are enormous in length. A human genome has three billion units (or base pairs); a viral genome might have tens or hundreds of thousands of base pairs, a bacterium a few million. Genome sequencing technologies are machines that take pieces of the DNA molecule and "read" the code, chemically deciphering the order of the letters that make up a strand of genetic material. Over the last decade or so, the speed of genome sequencing has increased, and its cost has tumbled, thanks to technologies known as high-throughput sequencing that can process millions of fragments of DNA simultaneously. Consequently, the amount of genetic data that has accumulated is staggering.[15]

Genomes are passed from generation to generation, with slight variations in the code that arise due to random mutations. These differences are a way to trace an organism's ancestry. In much the same way that your DNA, analyzed by a commercial ancestry company, can tell you certain facts about the population history of your forebears, the genomes of the microbes that infect us hold important clues to their past. The mountains of genetic data that are piling up thus constitute a potentially massive archive of evolutionary history. Chapter 1 further explores the implications of this new evidence, but suffice it to mention here two ways that high-throughput sequencing has been transformative. First, it has dramatically expanded the potential of genome-based *phylogenetics*, or the study of evolutionary family trees. Second, it undergirds the growing field of *paleogenomics*, which analyzes fragments of ancient DNA recovered from archaeological samples. These terms are a mouthful, and we can call them, colloquially, "tree thinking" (phylogenetics) and "time travel" (paleogenomics). Tree thinking will help us understand the evolutionary history of our germs: how old they are, where they came from, who their relatives are, and so forth. Time travel, when it is possible, lets us know what pathogens made our ancestors sick at specific points in the human past.[16]

This new evidence is exhilarating, but, as always, the rush of fresh information brings its own kinds of uncertainties; often the most impressive thing we learn is the breadth of our ignorance. This is more than the conventional gesture of intellectual humility or academic hedging of bets. The sheer novelty of the methods, and the rapid pace at which they are moving, mean that every month brings important new evidence and insights, revised chronologies and geographies of disease. Paleogenomics and genome-based phylogenetics are fields on the move. What we think now may seem obsolete in the near future. That is all to the good. Thucydides wrote his famous history as a "possession for all time." Our aims are rather more circumscribed. It will be enough to explore how these new kinds of evidence are starting to deepen our understanding of the relationship between human history and pathogen evolution.

This book aspires to practice what the biologist E. O. Wilson called consilience, the joining together of knowledge from different domains to form a unified explanation. It is a work of history that draws heavily from both biology and economics. It tries to weave together the social sciences and natural sciences, but its concerns are resolutely humanistic. The history of infectious disease can teach us about who we really are. We are primates—clever, voracious primates—who have taken over the planet, and, like any organism, we have parasites that constantly evolve in response to the circumstances we present them. This history reminds us that we are one species whose health is ultimately indivisible. When I started this project, I had hoped that a new history of infectious disease might encourage us to appreciate the dangers we still face collectively. COVID-19, of course, has changed the stakes and made it self-evident that infectious diseases retain the capacity to upend our lives. We know we are living through something historic, and at times it can feel like we are living in history, in the past. The story of disease can help us understand how we came to be where we are, and possibly help us decide where we want to go.[17]

PART I

Fire

1

Mammals in a Microbe's World

The Mightiest Living Beings

In 1877, a colleague sent Charles Darwin an academic journal with an unusual series of photographs. Taken by the German scientist Robert Koch, they were the first photographs of bacteria ever published. Darwin's correspondent realized the importance of what he was seeing. They were "the least but also perhaps the mightiest living beings." Darwin recognized it too. "I well remember saying to myself between twenty and thirty years ago, that if ever the origin of any infectious disease could be proved, it would be the greatest triumph to Science; and now I rejoice to have seen the triumph."[1]

In 1882, just weeks after Darwin died, Koch made public his sensational discovery of the bacterium that causes tuberculosis. The idea that microscopic, particle-like forms of life might exist and cause disease had long floated around the margins of respectable science. Over the course of the nineteenth century, the tide turned. Scientists—some of their names hallowed, like Koch and Louis Pasteur, and others little remembered, like Agostino Bassi and Casimir Davaine—built an irresistible case for what we retrospectively call germ theory. As the evidence continued to accumulate, the old consensus, the idea that disease was caused by filth or by deadly vapors in the atmosphere known as miasma, crumbled. Koch's discovery of *Mycobacterium tuberculosis* was an especially poignant moment, laying bare the counterintuitive truth that such a tiny life-form could cause such vast human misery. The notion that infectious diseases have microscopic agents with their own motives was ascendant only in Darwin's dying days. But his theory of evolution, the great unifying explanation of all life, is the foundation for understanding the pathogens that cause human disease.[2]

In Darwin's lifetime, increasingly powerful microscopes helped to facilitate the mental revolution that germ theory required. We are now living through an equally radical sea change, in which the ability to observe the genomes of microbes thanks to new sequencing technologies helps us to perceive how utterly pervasive and diverse they are. They have been here far longer than we have—from the beginning of life on earth—and, odds are, they will be here long after we are gone. It is thrilling if also humbling to learn that our story inserts itself as a minuscule chapter in a much vaster and much older struggle between hosts and parasites.[3]

It's a microbe's world. We're just living in it.

Defining Basic Terms

We experience disease as a medical phenomenon: naturally, we think of germs as things that make us sick. From nature's perspective, though, we are hosts, not patients, and they are parasites. They are rewarded and punished according to how well they succeed in sending their genes into future generations. Our parasites have evolved wildly different strategies and abilities to do so. Some use poison, some use disguise. Some are aggressive, some are ingeniously subtle. Yet every one of them is the product of natural selection. In the well-known words of the biologist Theodosius Dobzhansky, "nothing in biology makes sense except in the light of evolution." Ultimately, the driving logic in the history of infectious disease is ferocious and unforgiving Darwinian selection.[4]

Darwin's theory provides the framework to answer questions about the patterns of human disease in both the past and the present. Why are some diseases, and many of our oldest ones, adapted only to the tropics? Why do humans have such an array of diarrheal diseases? Why did smallpox and measles emerge along with large-scale empires, and why did those same viruses fail to establish in small-scale societies like those on remote islands? What made bubonic plague so deadly? How does the influenza virus so often outsmart our vaccines? Why is HIV so insidious? No answers make sense except in the light of evolution.

Our germs have no intentions or consciousness. We can anthropomorphize them for the sake of simplicity—we speak of them "trying" to do things like evade our immune system or adapt to new circumstances. That is fine, so long as it is understood that evolution is a blind, physical process that rewards those individuals whose traits are most effective at transmitting genes to succeeding generations. The pathogens that seem exquisitely designed to exploit our body and its defenses are simply the winners of past contests. And as with a stock portfolio, the past is no guarantee of future success.

Let us begin by acquainting ourselves with humanity's enemies. Evolution furnishes the logic of taxonomy, or the biological classification of organisms. Over the last generation, the tools of taxonomy have changed radically, especially for microbes. Consider that, before genomic data became widely available, the family trees of microbes had to be pieced together by observing their characteristics. For obvious reasons, it is hard to observe microbial organisms directly. In consequence, a whole array of criteria and chemical tests were devised as aids to classification. Gram-staining is maybe the most familiar; this technique involves a dye that will soak into the cell walls of some bacteria and turn them a violet color. Gram-staining captures something fundamental about bacterial physiology (whether or not a certain kind of sugar is used in the cell wall—a matter of great interest to your immune system as well). But compared to genome sequencing, such tests are limited and slow, what the abacus is to the supercomputer.[5]

Genome sequencing has revolutionized microbial taxonomy. It has also underlined the fact that the preponderance of the world's biodiversity is microbial. It is now possible to see more clearly the place of our disease-causing microbes in the tree of life and to view them against the backdrop of a much bigger invisible world. Most of the planet's microbial inhabitants are indifferent to us, and many of them are even helpful, playing an essential role in ecosystems and in our bodies. Microbes are everywhere—around, on, and inside us. We are far more porous and permeable than we had ever thought, but only a tiny sliver of the earth's microbes would or could do us harm. Recognizing this diversity can help to sharpen some fundamental questions, like "What is a pathogen?" and "What is a parasite?"[6]

The word *pathogen* is a modern English coinage derived from two Greek roots meaning "to cause to be" and "disease." Simply stated, a pathogen is an organism that causes disease. The term is a handy and helpful way of describing certain phenomena in nature. Pathogens form a category much like "creatures that fly," which encompasses birds, bees, bats, butterflies, and a rare fish or two. These organisms are defined by what they do rather than genetic relatedness. But unlike winged creatures, what pathogens do, by definition, is affect other organisms in a particular way. Moreover, flying creatures dependably fly. Many pathogens, by contrast, are rank opportunists, only causing disease under certain circumstances. It would be better to say, then, that a pathogen is an organism *capable of* causing disease in another organism.[7]

The word *parasite* derives from an ancient Greek term referring to a person who eats at the table of someone else. A parasite is an organism that lives at the expense of another, taking energy from its host and causing at least some level of harm. Often, the word *parasite* in vernacular English is reserved to denote macroscopic parasites such as worms. But the bacteria and protozoa that exploit us meet the textbook definition of parasite, even if English usage has never caught up. What about viruses? The idea that viruses are parasites grates against the etymology of the term, because viruses do not "eat" (i.e., perform metabolism). Even though viruses are more like hijackers than thieves, in most other senses, viruses fit the definition of a parasite. Sometimes the word *microparasite* is used to distinguish microbial parasites from worms. There is not perfect consistency in English usage, in part because the concepts behind the words are slippery. We will use *pathogen* to mean any organism that can cause disease, and *parasite* to mean any organism, macroscopic or microscopic, that exploits a host.[8]

Pathogen is a medical term. *Parasite* is an ecological one, which is to say that it describes something fundamental about the place of organisms within the flow of energy through the environment. In nature, organisms either produce their own food or take it from others. Producers are *autotrophs*, organisms like plants and some bacteria that use energy from the sun or chemical compounds to make their own food. The rest of us are *heterotrophs* who acquire energy from producers—or from other consumers who have taken it first. Parasitism is functionally similar to predation; the host is a kind of prey. As E. O. Wilson put it, "Parasites, in a phrase, are predators that eat prey in units of less than one." In simple terms, parasitism is a strategy for taking the essentials of life from another organism. Parasites are simply heterotrophs like us, in search of energy and materials to do the work of reproducing their genes. By looking at it this way, you can see yourself a little more clearly from their perspective. You are an organized bundle of refined energy, essential elements, and machinery for making proteins: an irresistible target.[9]

Parasitism is a strategy that has arisen countless times through different evolutionary pathways in the 3.5 billion years during which life has existed on earth. Precisely *because* the strategy has evolved repeatedly, our parasites form an unruly and biologically diverse cast of characters. Collectively, our parasites are more like what ecologists call a guild, a group of unrelated species that share an ecological resource or territory. The human parasite guild has numerous species as members, but there is not even remote agreement about how many organisms cause human disease. One standard and often cited catalog of human pathogens includes 1,415 species. A more recent and systematic survey identified 1,611. Oddly enough, there is only about 60 percent overlap between these lists, so the number of unique pathogens identified between them is 2,107. Yet the Global Infectious Diseases and Epidemiology Online Network (GIDEON), a standard database of infectious diseases created for clinicians, lists 1,988 bacteria alone that have been found to infect humans. More than one thousand of these are not in either of the other lists, meaning the total surpasses three thousand, and this tally surely understates the number of organisms that could infect humans.[10]

Why is there so much uncertainty about how many organisms cause disease in humans? The simple reason is that most of the species in the tallies cited above are fundamentally unimportant as pathogens of humans. Most organisms *capable* of causing disease in humans do so rarely. They only infect humans incidentally and transiently, but as human populations have grown, and genome sequencing has become more common, these rare and ephemeral infections get caught, cataloged, and counted. Consider an example drawn from the genus *Mycobacterium*. One study counted sixty-four different species in this genus as pathogens of humans. Another study found twenty-eight. If you asked a global health expert concerned with human well-being, she would probably say that there are five medically important species of *Mycobacterium* (including the bacteria that cause tuberculosis, leprosy, and Buruli ulcer). The other species can infect humans and cause disease, so, strictly speaking, they can be human pathogens. But it is relatively meaningless to include the other species in any count of human pathogens.[11]

What we would truly like to know is how many major identified species of human pathogens there are. Of course, every one of these terms is complicated; there is even debate over what constitutes a species, let alone what makes a pathogen a *human* pathogen. And where should we draw the line regarding what constitutes a *major* human pathogen? There is a lot of ground between a species that infects only a handful of humans each year and one like the bacterium that causes tuberculosis, which is responsible for about ten million new cases annually. Although drawing a line to determine what counts as major is both difficult and arbitrary, it is helpful to distinguish between organisms that are a burden on human populations and those organisms that *can* infect us but do so only sporadically. If we apply a rough, simple filter—counting only species that have been known to cause at least fifty thousand deaths in one year, or are estimated to account for five million or more cases of disease in one year—then there are about 236 species that we could consider major pathogens of humans (see the appendix).[12]

The definition of what makes a species a *human* pathogen is also more ambiguous and interesting than it might first appear. Some microbes do specialize in the exploitation of us. They have gone all-in on a human-only strategy, relying on continuous circulation among human hosts for evolutionary survival. Others are more promiscuous, capable of exploiting a wider range of hosts. Such generalist strategies are common in nature, because it is often prudent for parasites to keep their options open. When a disease is caused by a pathogen whose primary reservoir is a non-human animal, it is known as a *zoonosis*—literally, an "animal disease." Often, these infections are dead-end ventures for the parasite, the human host serving as the graveyard of the germ and all its direct descendants. However, some zoonotic diseases—like the Ebola virus—can spread from human to human and trigger epidemics. And, to make matters even more complicated, some essentially human pathogens are known to be able to sustain infections in animal populations. Leprosy is a good example; it is caused by a human-adapted bacterium that also has animal reservoirs in species such as red squirrels, armadillos, and nonhuman primates. Thus, specialist and generalist parasites fall along a spectrum, with gradations in the middle. As we will see, one of the major themes in the history of infectious disease is the unusual number of pathogens that have narrowed their host range to focus on exploiting us alone.[13]

Our pathogens fall across five taxa or evolutionary groups: viruses, bacteria, protozoa, helminths, and fungi (see figure 1.1). With all due respect to mycology, fungi do not figure much in the rest of this book. It is true that a great many of them (more than four hundred different species) *can* infect humans, but they tend to be nuisances (like athlete's foot) or secondary to other infections that compromise the immune system. Although drug-resistant or highly pathogenic fungi are a potential threat, fungi have yet to exert a major influence on the course of human history (except indirectly, as plant diseases, which are discussed in chapter 11). Prions, also, are a type of infectious agent that merit consideration. Prions are tiny infectious particles that cause neurological disease (like kuru or variant Creutzfeldt-Jakob disease). Prions are misfolded proteins that recruit other proteins to take the same misshapen form. The accumulation of these particles can rapidly progress to severe, usually fatal, disease. But prion diseases triggered by infection are surpassingly rare, and their historical import has been negligible, as far as we know. Hereafter we leave them aside. By contrast, viruses, bacteria,

TAXA OF MAJOR SPECIES OF HUMAN PATHOGENS

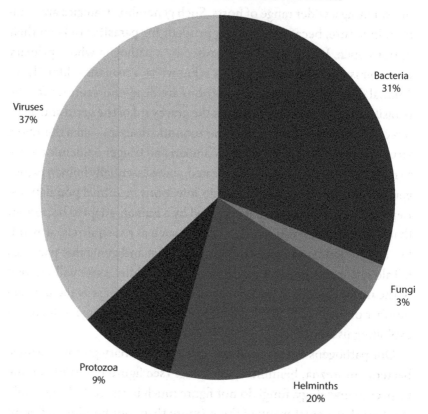

Bacteria
31%

Viruses
37%

Fungi
3%

Protozoa
9%

Helminths
20%

FIGURE 1.1. Taxa of major identified species of human pathogens.
See the appendix for complete checklist.

protozoa, and helminths have all played major roles in our past. We will consider the biological basics of each of these four groups in turn.[14]

Viruses are entities that exploit hosts by simplifying matters as far as possible. Viruses are little more than strands of nefarious genetic code enclosed in organic armor (see figure 1.2). A virus, in Peter and Jean Medawar's famous definition, is nothing more than "a piece of bad news wrapped up in protein." Viruses do not steal energy or nutrients because they do not have the capacity for metabolism. They do not make anything on their own. They break into our cells and use our machinery to replicate themselves. Hence, humanity has failed to reach consensus on

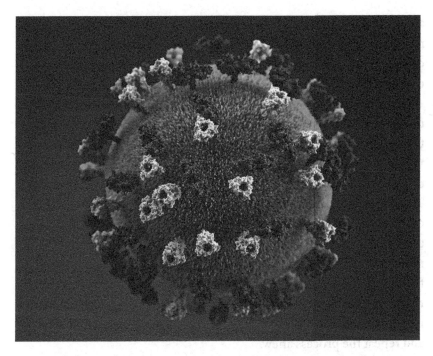

FIGURE 1.2. Viruses are tiny infectious entities that insert themselves into host cells and use the host's cellular machinery to replicate. CDC/Allison M. Maiuri, MPH, CHES: Public Health Image Library #21074.

the basic question of whether viruses should be considered alive. Viruses have some of the properties of life. They are types of replicating nucleic acid that evolve through Darwinian selection. But viruses accomplish replication with a minimum number of their own parts.[15]

Historically, some of humanity's worst enemies (smallpox, measles, yellow fever) have come from the ranks of viruses. Viruses have given us some of our oldest (herpes) and some of our newest (AIDS, COVID-19) afflictions, some of our most fearsome (Ebola) and most underappreciated (rotavirus) enemies. The diversity of viruses bespeaks their tremendous evolutionary success. They are the most abundant entity in the biosphere. They infect every kingdom of life. Viruses that infect bacteria are known as bacteriophages (or simply phages), and low-level molecular struggle between viruses and bacteria is going on all around us, all the time. Viruses of higher organisms are less plenteous but still almost beyond comprehension in number. The diversity of mammal viruses can only be estimated, and the number of species is probably north of forty thousand. The eighty-seven viruses that are a significant burden on human health constitute an infinitesimal slice of all viral diversity.[16]

The simplicity of a virus is mesmerizing. Measles virus, for instance, manages to be among the most contagious pathogens known, yet it has the ability to code only eight proteins. The protein shell protecting a viral genome (known as a capsid) is often composed of only one or two different kinds of protein, repeated in elegant symmetrical patterns. These structures manage to guard the viral genome, attach to receptors on host cells, shuttle the genome through the cell membrane and into the cytoplasm (the crowded goop inside a cell), and disassemble at the right moment to release the viral nucleic acid. The viral genome must then insert itself into the cell's replication process so that the host's own machinery for synthesizing proteins and nucleic acids instead makes new copies of the viral parts. These copies must then assemble, escape, and repeat the process anew.[17]

Like guests who come to a party empty-handed, viruses have to exploit their hosts. Bacteria, by contrast, are more enigmatic (see figure 1.3). Bacteria are single-celled organisms, unambiguously alive. Compared to (most) viruses, they are huge. They have complicated, quilt-like cell walls. Inside, there is no nucleus holding the DNA, which floats freely in the cytoplasm, like a tangled thread in a water balloon. A bacterial genome can encode, on average, a few thousand proteins; unlike viruses, bacteria synthesize proteins, so their need for energy and nutrients is constant. Bacteria occupy every imaginable niche on the planet. Most of them are free-living, inhabiting the environment. Only some of them are parasitic, and very few of these are pathogenic to humans, although these bacteria tend to receive the most press. There are about seventy-three bacteria among major human pathogens—out of maybe a trillion bacterial species on earth. To imagine bacteria primarily as pathogens is about as fair as thinking of human beings as mostly serial killers.[18]

At this moment, if you are of average size, there are maybe 3.8×10^{13} bacteria living on and in you (although the number fluctuates with the bowel cycle, because fecal matter is loaded with microbial passengers).

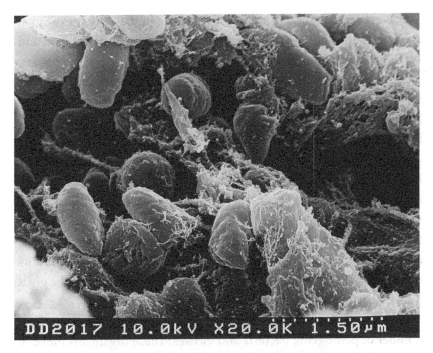

DD2017 10.0kV X20.0K 1.50μm

FIGURE 1.3. Bacteria are single-celled organisms without an organized nucleus.
Only a subset of bacteria are parasites. National Institute of Allergy and Infectious
Diseases (NIAID); NIH; Rocky Mountain Laboratories: Public Health Image
Library #18159.

You are made up of human cells and bacterial cells in roughly equal
number. Your bacteria colonize your skin, mouth, nasal mucosa, armpits, gut, and nether regions. These bacterial companions, collectively
known as the human microbiome, are integral to human health. Our
digestive system relies on them. They play an important role in our
overall immune strategy, because they have a vested interest in keeping out the competition. In times of health, there is harmony between
us and our microbiome. But the peace is fragile. Some helpers only
need the slightest chemical signal to turn savagely hostile, and many
of them are dangerous if they trespass into the wrong tissue. When we
at last shuffle off this mortal coil, and cease to provide energy and
nutrients, they unceremoniously make use of what they can scavenge
from us. The line between pal and parasite is thin indeed.[19]

Bacteria cause some of the most fearsome human diseases—such as cholera, diphtheria, typhoid, typhus, scarlet fever, leprosy, yaws, and syphilis. Two of the worst diseases in human history by almost any measure, bubonic plague and tuberculosis, are bacterial in origin. Yet the differences between these two killers underscore the diversity of bacteria. Bubonic plague is caused by the bacterium *Yersinia pestis*. This huge bacterium has acquired an array of virulence factors that make it a formidably versatile pathogen, and yet it is really a parasite of rodents, incapable of sustained transmission between humans. We are immaterial to its evolutionary trajectory (as hosts anyway—our impact on rodent ecologies is another matter). By contrast, as we will see, the tuberculosis bacterium is exquisitely honed to take advantage of us, and it has evolved remarkable abilities to manipulate and exploit its natural habitat, the human body. Tuberculosis is arguably *the* great human disease.[20]

Because of our distinctive history, humans have acquired an unusual number of pathogenic bacteria and viruses. These organisms move in Darwinian hyperdrive, and they have responded with alacrity to the opportunities offered by our expansion. By contrast, protozoa and helminths evolve more slowly. They are complex organisms. Our protozoa and helminths are enemies in deep evolutionary time. In quantity, the number of these organisms faced by humanity is not totally dissimilar from what chimpanzees encounter, although, even in these taxa, humans seem to have a larger number of pathogens and to suffer an unusually heavy burden of disease due to them.[21]

Protozoa are single-celled organisms (see figure 1.4). They differ from bacteria in having a nucleus to contain their genetic material. In the tree of life, they are closer to complex organisms like animals. Most protozoa are free-living, peaceable creatures, but a few have evolved parasitic lifestyles. Sometimes these lines are blurred. For example, the amoeba responsible for dysentery is a cyst-forming intestinal parasite that usually exists in an asymptomatic carriage state; with the right triggers, however, it can transform into a vicious pathogen. Only twenty-one protozoa are major human pathogens, and yet they manage to account for a disproportionate share of human suffering.

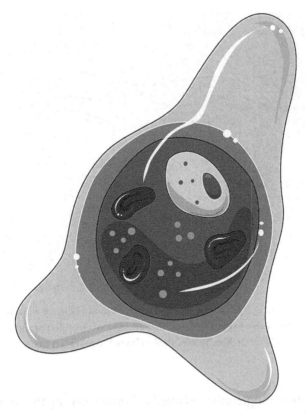

FIGURE 1.4. Protozoa, like the plasmodium shown here, are
single-celled organisms with a nucleus. Protozoan parasites often
have complex life cycles. Servier Medical Art: CC BY 3.0.

The most devastating protozoan infections are transmitted by biting
insects. The various forms of leishmaniasis that lurk in tropical climates are caused by vector-borne protozoa. Sleeping sickness is a devastating disease in Africa transmitted by tsetse flies. Protozoa also
cause malaria, a closely related group of diseases almost without equal
as an influence on human history. The complex life cycles of these
organisms make them unlike anything in the viral or bacterial world.
The malaria parasites pass through manifold stages of life as they move
through the mosquito and the human body. The protozoa that cause
malaria in humans are closely related to parasites of apes, but they have
crossed over to humans, as we will see, in the relatively recent past. They

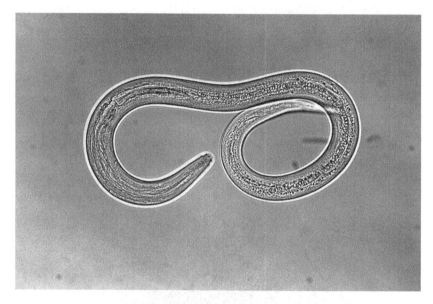

FIGURE 1.5. Helminths, like the hookworm shown here, are animals, often visible to the naked eye. They are some of our oldest parasites. CDC/Dr. Mae Melvin: Public Health Image Library #1513.

are primate pathogens that adapted to humans during the course of our history.[22]

Finally, humans are infected by a number of helminth parasites. *Helminth* is simply the Greek word for "worm," and in fact the category is really a catch-all that includes roundworms, tapeworms, and flukes (see figure 1.5). Helminths are invertebrate animals, macroparasites visible to the naked eye. Although some stages of their life cycle are accomplished externally, our worms must ultimately exploit us to run their life's course. Helminths have large genomes and relatively long generation times. In consequence, they evolve far more slowly than microscopic parasites. There are no emerging infectious diseases caused by worms. Our helminths are ancient. Their closest relatives live in our closest relatives, chimps and gorillas. Our worms are our primate parasites, an ape problem that we made worse by coming down from the trees and later by the agricultural ties that bind us so closely to the soil. It is easy for people in wealthy countries to underestimate the importance of parasitic worms as a burden on human health. Helminths loom large in the World Health Organization's list of neglected diseases, and over a billion humans currently suffer from these debilitating and stigmatizing infections.[23]

In sum, humans have parasites falling into the same taxa as any other mammal. But, as we will see in the coming chapters, our adversaries are unusual in their number, their narrowness, and their nastiness. In other words, we have lots of germs, many of them are adapted to exploit us, and an unnerving number of them cause severe disease. This book will try to explain this predicament as the result of our sudden and dramatic success as a species. Our history inserts itself rudely and unexpectedly into the ongoing and ceaseless evolutionary contest between hosts and parasites.

Fortunately, we are the evolutionary heirs of some ancient and truly ingenious biological mechanisms to fend off our unscrupulous microbial enemies.

Evolution, Virulence, and Immunity

When Darwin developed his theory of natural selection, he imagined evolution unrolling on geological timescales: the way a glacier sculpts a valley or weather beats on a rock, so time molds one species into another. Such was the conventional wisdom for over a century. But in the late twentieth century, our understanding of evolution started to change, thanks in no small part to the continuing study of the Galápagos finches that Darwin himself had observed on the voyage of the *Beagle*. It turns out that evolution works far more quickly than Darwin imagined. The finches of the Galápagos evolve on timescales we can observe. In 1983, for instance, a year with superabundant rainfall, a species of vine with tiny seeds overran the flora of Daphne Island. The birds with the smallest and pointiest beaks were suddenly, and starkly, advantaged. Their genes rapidly spread. Selection for traits can happen over the course of years or decades, not just eons. And Darwin's finches are exemplary, not exceptional. They are a privileged case of the paradigm that the biologist John Thompson has called "relentless evolution."[24]

What is true for large and complex species like Darwin's finches—the fact that evolution is relentless—is even more relevant for microbes. Because every generation is a chance at evolution—an opportunity for genes to mutate or variants to spread—microorganisms are playing the game on a deliriously rapid timescale. Among the different taxa of parasites that exploit humans, viruses are the evolutionary pacesetters. They evolve with unmatched gusto. Viruses have both the fastest replication cycles and the highest mutation rates of any kind of organism, which means that nature is constantly trying new genetic arrangements. A single host cell infected with poliovirus can produce ten thousand new virus particles in the space of eight hours. The error rates vary from virus to virus, but in some small viruses they are as high as one mistake in every one thousand base pairs (the "letters" that make up the genetic code). Most organisms have genomes with proofreading machinery that, like a good copy editor, stops errors from happening. But many viruses lack this restraint, in effect dialing up their mutation rate. There is an evolutionary method to their madness. The sloppiness is strategic, because the shape-shifting can help viruses escape immune recognition. Many viruses skate so close to the edge of fatal sloppiness that some antiviral therapies work by dousing cells with a chemical that slightly speeds up the mutation rate. With just a little nudge, the viral replication process starts to spit out molecular gibberish.[25]

Given such error rates, there could be a new genetic variant in every single replica of the virus, or, more likely, a mutant in every one hundred or one thousand copies. Consider rhinoviruses, important agents of the common cold. A rhinovirus genome has about 7,200 base pairs. The error rate every time the genome is copied has been estimated at one mutation per one thousand or ten thousand base pairs, so *most* copies are mutants. There are billions of them inside you during the course of a single infection. The virus you catch from your sniffling child, and the one you accidentally cough toward a coworker a few days later, are likely to be ever so slightly genetically different. This swarm of closely related but slightly different variants has been called a *mutant cloud* or a *quasispecies*. The diversity that arises even in the course of a single infection confounds our categories and stretches our language.[26]

It is no wonder then that the virologist Vincent Raccianello has called viruses "simple Darwinian machines." In the course of an infection, each variant of an individual species of virus is competing with all the other variants to pass its genes to future generations. Most mutations either do nothing or cause miserable failure. But on rare occasions, a small change in the viral genome will do something like alter the shape of a protein in such a way that suddenly the offspring of *that* mutant are more efficient at attaching to a receptor on our cell, or slipping into the host nucleus, or doing some other piece of viral business. The progeny of that mutant then have an advantage over their brethren and ruthlessly exploit the advantage to send their genes into future hosts. Viruses experience a fast and furious version of survival of the fittest.[27]

Like viruses, bacteria can evolve through random mutations, although bacteria are less sloppy in copying their genomes. They acquire mutations faster than we do primarily because their generation times are shorter, measured in hours rather than years. But bacteria have other evolutionary tricks. Bacteria regularly sidle up to one another and swap entire genes in a process called bacterial conjugation. Often considered a kind of "sex for microbes," bacterial conjugation is not really a form of sexual reproduction; rather, it is an exchange of genes that affects the recipient directly. Sometimes bacteria absorb wheels of genetic information, known as plasmids, from other bacteria. Sometimes viruses deliver a payload of genes from one bacterium to another. These mechanisms, known collectively as horizontal gene transfer, bypass the randomness of genetic mutation. If mutation is like monkeys at a typewriter, occasionally turning a nice phrase by accident, horizontal gene transfer is cutting and pasting from the great books. Horizontal gene transfer is integral to the history of infectious disease, because it turns out that the genes most often swapped between organisms are those that affect virulence. There is a kind of public library of virulence genes out there, helpful for living the lifestyle of a parasite.[28]

Throughout the book, we borrow the term *relentless evolution* to emphasize that evolution is pervasive, constant, and fast. Microbial evolution is also high stakes, full of daunting challenges and intricate trade-offs. We must always remember that our pathogens, however dastardly they seem, are not *trying* to make us sick. We will understand their perspective a little better if we recognize two fundamental challenges faced by every microparasite: surviving the host's immune system and transmitting between hosts. To be successful—that is, to pass its genes into the future—a parasite has to find its way to the next host, while surviving the inevitable onslaught from the current one.

Although to a parasite you are an exploitable package of energy, elements, and cellular machinery, these biological treasures are well guarded. Our bodies are armored with an elaborate system of natural defense—our immune system—which tries to regulate who can enter and who can colonize. Although our exceptional history as a species has fueled the rapid and recent evolution of our microbial enemies, the immune system that forms our basic biological defense against them is a legacy of our vertebrate inheritance, shared with the fishes of the sea, the birds in the sky, and four-legged creatures on land. The architecture of the human immune system is imponderably ancient, and it remains remarkably versatile and effective.[29]

The immune system is a three-tiered network of defense comprised of physical barriers, innate responses, and adaptive mechanisms. Some of our common metaphors for the immune response—like activating, kicking in, turning on—vastly understate the extent to which immunity is always operational. It regulates our relationship with the microbial world at all times. Whereas alarms, sirens, and gunshots might only sound during an actual bank robbery, steel vaults, surveillance cameras, and armed security guards provide round-the-clock protection. So, too, the immune system never rests from its duties to protect our precious resources. And there are infinitely more parasites than bank robbers on the prowl.

Our first line of defense is comprised of the barriers that separate our bodies from the dangers that surround us. Our surfaces are covered with skin and mucosa that buffer sterile tissue from contamination. Although the tough layer of dead, keratinized cells that comprises the outer layer of our skin is important for immunity, the mucosa are even more so. Each human has 400 m² of mucous membrane facing the world. Mucus is full of antibodies and enzymes that break down common microbial components. Thus, from the moment a foreign cell reaches this perimeter, it is washed in generic antimicrobial compounds. Chemical warfare at the vulnerable interface between our bodies and the external environment is constant.[30]

If a pathogen breaches our first tier of defense, it should expect an immediate attack from the innate immune system. Innate immunity is an ensemble of proteins and cells that form a rapid response unit to microbial invasion. The basic principles of innate immunity are shared even with invertebrates (creatures lacking a backbone, such as insects). Over time, organisms that could recognize intruders quickly and efficiently possessed a major biological advantage. Many pathogens have highly conserved elements—biochemical parts that their ancestors, and their ancestors' ancestors, used to accomplish the basic tasks necessary for a microbe, like building a cell wall or a protein coat. The innate immune system quickly recognizes fats or carbohydrates on cell surfaces that are out of place in human blood or tissue. Innate immunity, in a sense, is the evolutionary memory of hundreds of millions of years of battle between hosts and parasites.[31]

The chief virtue of the innate system is its speed. In a game of margins, speed is everything. The battle between infection and immunity will often be decided by quantity and timing. Pathogens seek small tactical advantages—a loophole, feint, or disguise that creates a margin of opportunity—enabling them to multiply before the immune system catches up. Conversely, the strategy of innate immunity is containment rather than clearance. The proteins and cells deployed by the innate system hope to control the threat while simultaneously calling in the slower but more sophisticated weaponry of the adaptive—or specific—immune system. Innate immunity is as much an alarm system as a counterattack, and its chemical sirens summon the heavy artillery of the adaptive immune system.

The adaptive immune system is nearly five hundred million years old; it is a lynchpin of vertebrate success, one of the great inventions in the history of evolution. Adaptive immunity is the vertebrate answer to the unfathomable variety of microbial life. It would not be biologically possible to keep billions of cells at the ready to respond to each and every possible pathogen, so vertebrates have evolved an ingenious solution. In essence, our adaptive immune system can build proteins and cells specifically designed to respond to a particular invader. Using principles of modular design, the adaptive immune system is able to customize proteins and cellular receptors in almost infinite variety to keep pace with the diversity and evolutionary speed of the microbial world.[32]

The proteins made by the adaptive immune system are known as antibodies. They are bespoke molecules, custom designed to attach to particular molecules on particular pathogens. Antibodies are made and secreted by B cells (so called because they mature in the bone marrow). The adaptive immune system also uses modular principles to build highly specific T cells (so called because they mature in the thymus). All viruses, and some bacteria and protozoa, spend much of their time *inside* our cells. The immune system needs to know from the outside if any funny business is going on behind our own cell walls, so our cells have the ability to let the immune system know when they have been compromised; our cells take degraded pieces of pathogen proteins and carry them to the surface, where they are displayed on receptors that bind to T cells. T cells read the distress signal and destroy our compromised cells.[33]

The adaptive immune system is destructive and a danger even to ourselves. Hence, it is controlled by an intricate regime of checks and balances. B cells and T cells require stimulation and verification, a kind of double-key system. The adaptive system takes longer to rev up than the innate system, but if the mechanisms of innate immunity are able to maintain control long enough for the adaptive system to respond to infection, the chances of clearance are good. As an infection recedes, a general de-escalation ensues. But the adaptive system possesses the remarkable ability to "remember" an infection, keeping on hand B cells and T cells that have been effective against the pathogen. This immune memory allows the adaptive response to move into action even more rapidly if the intruder returns. Immunological memory is how vaccination works, giving the body winning combinations the way gamers trade cheat codes. The memorized codes are kept at the ready, and the immune system will make quick work of the invaders in cases of reinfection—unless the pathogen can somehow change its appearance.

While the architecture of our immune system is extraordinarily ancient, the human genome has continuously evolved in response to the threats posed by disease-causing microbes. The immune system is controlled by a vast symphony of genes, and whenever genetic variants confer a biological advantage to the human host, those genes are (all else being equal) more likely to be passed on to future generations of humans. In fact, infectious diseases have been a particularly powerful force in driving natural selection, even in the recent past. In the words of a group of geneticists, "Pathogen-imposed selective pressures have been paramount during human evolution." Yet here we should strike a balance between the excitement of discovery and caution. As we will see in later chapters, sweeping population-level differences in immunity have sometimes been invoked in histories of disease, even without strong evidence. In many cases, the functional importance of variants in protecting against specific diseases is not understood. But with the ceaseless accumulation of genetic data, and the snapshots of recent evolutionary history provided by ancient DNA, our knowledge is expanding fast. While a few examples of pathogen-driven evolution in human populations have long been known or hypothesized (such as the advantage conferred by certain red-blood-cell traits against malaria), the list is growing. For instance, familial Mediterranean fever, an autoinflammatory disease, has been linked to genetic variants that arose because they confer some protection against the plague. Other recent studies have traced the remorseless influence of tuberculosis on the human genome. It is likely that a stream of revelations lies in the near future, helping us trace the imprint of deadly diseases on the human genome in once inconceivable detail.[34]

For pathogens, our immune system is simply a feature of the environment. They have adapted solutions that allow them to survive and replicate even in the most hostile territory, and those parasites that are effective in subverting or evading host immunity are more likely to pass on their genes. But all parasites face a second, equally basic, conundrum: how to get from one host to the next before the first host either develops immunity or dies.

Transmission between hosts is a tricky business, and there are only a few well-trodden routes. Five of these pathways have been of major importance for infectious diseases affecting humans: skin contact, sexual intercourse, biting insects, plus entry via the gastrointestinal and respiratory tracts. The first two are used by a relatively limited number of parasites. Soil-transmitted helminths, for instance, are picked up through the bare skin of the unshod. Among sexually transmitted diseases, syphilis and AIDS have been the biggest burden on human health. But the striking paucity of such parasites suggests that it is hard to evolve the mechanisms that allow successful transmission. Sex is infrequent enough (on average) that a microbe must have the ability to survive inside one host long enough to make it to the next, which is hard to do.[35]

Vector-borne diseases are transmitted by arthropods—that is, animals with exoskeletons, such as ticks, fleas, lice, midges, biting flies, and, above all, mosquitos. As we will see, some of history's most devastating diseases—bubonic plague, yellow fever, typhus, and malaria—have adapted to use this route of transmission. To be successful, a pathogen that depends on a vector must be able to navigate at least two immune systems, which is no small task. But if it can successfully do that, the payoff is splendid: direct entry into the warm, vulnerable tissue and blood of a new host. As we will see, mosquitos constitute the most important group of disease vectors; the ecology of mosquitos thus becomes a primary fact in the ecology of human disease.[36]

Most of our pathogens enter via the gastrointestinal or respiratory tract. They take advantage of the fact that we must eat, drink, and breathe, and that we dependably exhale and defecate. The entire GI tract, from mouth to anus, is the site of intense conflict between our body and would-be invaders. Similarly, the respiratory route from the tip of the nostril to the depths of the lung is traveled by an array of bacteria and viruses. Both of these fields of exposure feature extensive mucosal boundaries to fend off unwanted intruders, but both are used by some of our most tenacious enemies.

The solutions that parasites have devised to meet these challenges are many and cunning, and they are often devastatingly harmful to us. The term *virulence* is used to describe the harm that a pathogen does to its host. Harm to the host is a side effect of the many functions that must be performed for a pathogen to usher its genes into the future. Survival requires them to do the things that pathogens do—enter, attach, hide, subvert, hijack, reassemble, escape, steal, and so on. Usually, the traits of the pathogen that cause us harm are those designed to evade, confuse, or misdirect the immune system. Often, the actual harm we experience is caused by the immune response itself.

Like the word *pathogen*, the concept of virulence is helpful, but its precise meaning can be a bit elusive. It looks at the relationship between pathogen and host entirely from the host's perspective. It collapses the enormous variety of evolutionary mechanisms and strategies pursued by pathogens into the single category of "harm." But it captures something essential and important about pathogens—especially, perhaps, human pathogens. Nature furnishes plenty of examples of virulent animal disease (think of Ebola virus laying low chimpanzee populations, or rinderpest virus ripping through herds of cattle with depraved indifference). But humans seem to suffer from an unnatural number of acute, virulent diseases, and to see how this came to be, we have to appreciate the complex tradeoffs faced by any parasite.[37]

Parasites depend on their hosts and, for purely selfish reasons, they may benefit by limiting the damage they do to their victims. Imagine the parasitic lifestyle as an ongoing embezzlement scheme (where bilking money translates into genetic success). The best strategy might be one that is restrained enough to avoid detection by not bankrupting the victim. From a selfish perspective, the best strategy is not always the most harmful in the short run. This is the pathogen's dilemma, and it is fundamental to the evolutionary history of infectious disease.

The last decades have witnessed a radical shift in our understanding of the evolution of virulence. Until the late twentieth century, the prevailing dogma was that infectious diseases reliably evolved to become less virulent or even avirulent. Older diseases, it was thought, had evolved toward a stable equilibrium with their hosts, causing them little harm. Newer diseases were simply in a state of temporary imbalance. But this perspective is flawed and underestimates the complex tradeoffs present to a parasite. There are evolutionary rewards for being effective at subverting immunity and propagating within a host, which in turn correlate with virulence. We will explore important historical examples in which newer, nastier strains of a germ replaced its meeker rivals, as seems to have happened with the smallpox virus, for instance.[38]

The only guarantee is that parasites have a biological incentive to pass on their genes. In general, this should incentivize our parasites to do three things: (1) be highly transmissible between hosts and (2) cause a long-lasting infection in the host, while (3) causing as little harm as possible to the host. The perfect pathogen would be extremely transmissible, cause a chronic infection, and do little damage to the host's health. Human alpha-herpesvirus 1, the cause of most cold sores, is pretty close. But the tensions between these incentives are obvious. In general, it is hard to be transmissible or persistent without doing damage to the host. Mechanically, the same traits that allow a pathogen to gather in huge numbers in a cough droplet, or to congregate so thickly in the blood as to be picked up by a biting insect, or to accumulate in the genital mucosa, require the pathogen to subvert our immune response, which is likely to do harm.[39]

The constraints on virulence only apply if the current host actually belongs to the reservoir species that the pathogen depends upon for its evolutionary survival. The absence of evolutionary tradeoffs helps to explain why zoonoses, animal diseases, can be so virulent for humans: because we are not the true reservoir host. The pathogens that are adapted to other vertebrate species, particularly mammals, have evolved mechanisms to survive immune systems similar enough to ours that they can sometimes do so with devastating efficiency. For instance, bats are the natural reservoir of the rabies virus. Before the development of antiviral treatment, rabies infection was uniformly lethal. And yet, it is effectively nontransmissible between humans. Rabies virus would thus have the worst evolutionary strategy conceivable—extreme virulence and zero transmissibility—*if* it relied on human hosts, which it does not.[40]

In general, parasites have strong evolutionary incentives to find any tactic or trick that enhances transmission. Some of the tactics nature has discovered are diabolically clever. The latent phase of many pathogens—exemplified by the ability of vivax malaria to persist in the liver in relatively quiescent form—is a means of modulating replication to increase the chances of transmission. Even the relatively harmless herpesvirus infection lurks in a latent stage, but explodes into cold sores when stress weakens the host's immune system. Some parasites with complex life cycles are transmitted in an innocuous larval stage and only develop into virulent pathogens once they reach preferred sites inside the host. One microworm knows to come out of the inner depths of your body and swim to the blood of your extremities just as night falls, when you are most likely to be bitten by a mosquito.[41]

Anything that helps a parasite transmit between hosts *despite* harming the host will contribute to its evolutionary advantage. Pathogens with the ability to form hardy spores or to survive in the environment, even for a limited time like the smallpox virus, can be more virulent than if they relied entirely on direct transmission. Above all, vector-borne parasites enjoy many evolutionary advantages, including assisted access to sterile tissue or blood and the ability to disperse even from victims who lie dying. The number of unapologetically horrid diseases that rely on the transport services of an insect vector is telling.[42]

Luckily, it seems to be difficult for pathogens to evolve successful strategies that prolong infection: our immune systems are just very good at finding intruders. Most infections are acute (short and fast) rather than chronic (long and slow). But the organisms that have solved this conundrum and do cause chronic infection—for example, the bacteria that cause tuberculosis, syphilis, and leprosy; the hepatitis C virus; and HIV—do so through extraordinary modulation of the human immune response. They are terrifyingly effective but fortunately rare.

Evolution is relentless, and our invisible enemies are ceaselessly tinkering with new strategies to pass on their genes, even as we continually change the environment to which they must adapt. Imagine the rise of humanity as the planetary spread of a warm, nutrient-rich, well-defended host environment—a strange mixture of allure and danger—and you begin to see the world through the eyes of a pathogen.

Decoding Evolutionary History

In 1976, the same year that William McNeill published *Plagues and Peoples*, a Belgian microbiologist named Walter Fiers did something extraordinary. He sequenced the genome of a small virus. It was a scientific milestone, the first complete genome of any organism to be sequenced. Yet, for decades, taking strands of nucleic acid and chemically reading the sequence of "letters" was a plodding and expensive undertaking. It was almost twenty years before a complete bacterial genome was sequenced. The Human Genome Project took thirteen years, about $1 billion, and a massive worldwide collaboration to map the human genome. But over the past decade or so, advances in high-throughput gene sequencing—which allows millions of strands of DNA to be decoded simultaneously—have changed the equation.[43]

The implications for the study of history are immense. Biology is an inherently historical discipline, and genomes are its archives. In the words of Stephen Jay Gould, "evolutionary biology is the primary science of history." As we noted in the introduction, genomes can be exploited as a record of evolutionary history in two distinct but complementary ways: "tree thinking" (phylogenetics) and "time travel" (paleogenomics). Phylogenetics, or tree thinking, is the study of evolutionary relationships. A phylogeny is a family tree—a way of representing the historical relationships between groups of organisms as the branches of a tree that spread apart when time moves forward, or converge (toward the trunk) when time moves backward. Tree thinking can tell us a lot about history, and not just the history of microbes. For instance, the phylogeny of primates reveals that *Homo sapiens* is most closely related to chimpanzees, more distantly to gorillas, and even more remotely to monkeys. Of course, humans and chimpanzees last shared a common ancestor six to nine million years ago, and this kind of giant timescale is a reflection of the pace of mammalian evolution. Because microorganisms evolve quickly, their phylogenies are of relevance on much shorter timescales.[44]

Genome-based phylogenetics is a field that has flourished amid the proliferation of data generated by high-throughput sequencing. It is, in fact, a field whose computational methods and tools are still being refined, but already, the ability to use massive data sets to place microbial species in the tree of life is yielding fresh historical insights about when, where, and whence (that is to say, from what animal pathogen) our pathogens emerged. Phylogenies can give us a sense of when pathogens emerged thanks to a kind of analysis known as the molecular clock. Molecular clocks estimate the time it has taken for genetic differences to accumulate. Consider a crude analogy: Imagine that you are copying Shakespeare's *Hamlet* by hand once a day (what is called the generation time) and every day you accidentally copy one letter in error (the substitution rate), uncorrected in subsequent copies: "To be or got to be." After ten days, there are ten differences between the latest version and the original. If you only have a much later copy of *Hamlet*, and then counted one hundred differences between it and the original, you could treat the differences as an estimate of time: that copy was made one hundred days after the original.[45]

This analogy oversimplifies molecular clock analysis. Generation times (how long it takes to make a copy) and substitution rates (how often a "letter" or nucleotide is changed) vary across species. The rate of change can also vary over time, as do population sizes. Errors may become saturated, or they can get weeded out by natural selection. And it is important to underscore that molecular clocks only *estimate* how long ago two sampled groups shared a common ancestor. Historians have a rather ingrained preference for precise dates, and tree thinking can sometimes do no better than broad estimates. If you said there is a 95 percent chance that Alexander the Great was king of Macedon in the first millennium BCE, you would fail high school history. But if it could be demonstrated that the measles virus emerged on that timescale, it is a meaningful result that helps to narrow down the context for the evolution of a major human pathogen. We must remain aware that molecular clock dates still shift around with the inclusion of new evidence or use of different models. In general, we should take them as broad estimates that are nonetheless "useful in placing bounds on when pathogens emerged and diversified."[46]

Tree thinking can also sometimes furnish otherwise irretrievable information about where an organism emerged. When the evolutionary tree of a microbe can be situated in space, it offers clues about the geography of disease. To take a notable example, Europeans started crossing the Atlantic Ocean from the late fifteenth century, and when they did, regular contact inaugurated the massive biological chain reaction known as the Columbian Exchange. We know for a fact that organisms like horses and pigs were introduced from the Old World to the Americas. But because pathogens are invisible to the naked eye, phylogenies are tremendously helpful in tracing the microbial dimensions of the Columbian Exchange. Phylogenies resolve questions about the Old World origins of malaria, yellow fever, and other important diseases.[47]

Finally, tree thinking can tell us about the animals that served as hosts to the ancestors of our germs. Phylogenies help us see our disease-causing microbes within the bigger tree of life. As we will see throughout this book, these relationships between human and animal disease are pervasive, and it turns out that they are more complex than we used to believe. For example, when McNeill wrote, it was known that human and bovine tuberculosis were closely related, and it was reasonable to suppose that humans contracted TB from cows. As it turns out, bovine TB evolved from human TB, meaning we got our cows sick and not vice versa. These cross-species connections are integral to the ecology of disease, and tree thinking is quickly unveiling their hidden history. Motivated in part by the experience of recent health crises (like the coronavirus outbreaks and Ebola epidemics), interest in animal disease has been growing, as has a much broader hunt for microbes that cause disease in other species. Much has been learned, and the near future is likely to be full of interesting and unexpected discoveries.[48]

If tree thinking is one way to use genomes as a kind of biological archive, *paleogenomics*—what has been called genetic time travel—is equally revolutionary for historians. Paleogenomics (sometimes also called archaeogenetics) is the study of ancient biomolecules. If you want to have your personal genome sequenced, you will likely swab some saliva and ship it off. The dead cannot do that, but they often have remnants of DNA preserved, for instance, in the petrous bone in the base of the skull or in the pulp cavities of their teeth (the former has proven fertile ground for finding ancient human DNA, the latter a rich source of pathogen DNA). If enough microbes were swimming in the blood when a person died, the microbes' genetic remains might be left behind in the skeleton. Paleogenomics is the retrieval and study of these archaeological molecules.

Ingenious efforts to sequence the DNA of archaeological pathogens were already underway by the 1990s, but these early forays suffered from

various technical challenges—notably, contamination. Tantalizing results were published but not replicated. Refined lab protocols, new ways
of probing for small fragments of target DNA, and, above all, data-rich
methods enabled by high-throughput sequencing have allowed the field
of paleogenomics to take off. In 2010, five ancient human genomes were
published. The next year, a complete ancient pathogen genome was
published for the first time. Over the next few years, in the words of
David Reich, a leader in the field of using ancient DNA to study human
population history, "whole-genome analysis of ancient DNA went into
hyperdrive." The data are now flooding in faster than ever.[49]

Time travel is an extraordinary tool for studying the past. Ancient
DNA has been called "an evolutionary photo album": we can look *directly*
at ancestors instead of having to infer things about ancestors from their
descendants. (This is analogous to dusting off old photographs of
Grandpa and Grandma instead of lining up eight cousins and trying to
imagine what their grandparents looked like.) Ancient DNA can provide
direct identification of the biological agents of past disease, occasionally
ending doubts about retrospective diagnosis. The longstanding debate
over the cause of the Black Death was definitively resolved by ancient
DNA evidence from plague cemeteries, which fingered *Yersinia pestis* as
the guilty microbe. In other cases, ancient DNA has implicated pathogens that were unsuspected in major disease events; there is now genetic
evidence that a strain of paratyphoid fever had a hand in the decimation
of New World peoples following the arrival of Europeans.[50]

We are still in the early days of paleogenomics. The technical protocols and even ethical standards of the field are still in formation, and
there are still important limitations and blind spots. One obvious weak-
ness is the lack of material from RNA viruses, many of which are important human pathogens. Although ancient human DNA research has
broadened to include much of the globe, Europe is still egregiously
overrepresented in the study of ancient pathogens. Another ever-
present issue is the sheer unlikelihood that ancient biomolecules are
preserved. The historian Michael McCormick, who has done as much
as anyone to bring the natural sciences into the study of the human past,
captured the conundrum, reflecting on the recovery of the bubonic
plague bacterium from the skeletons of ancient victims: "It is essential

to grasp that DNA molecules begin decaying as soon as an organism dies, and that today's best aDNA labs succeed in extracting authentic human DNA from only a fraction of their samples even in temperate climates, which are less inimical to DNA preservation; for reasons that are presently unclear, authentic pathogen aDNA is considerably more difficult to recover. Given the amount of contaminating DNA from the environment, the low survival rate of relatively abundant human DNA and the less abundant bacterial DNA originally present in an infected human's blood, detecting plague today from minute blood traces in 1,500-year-old dental pulp seems an almost miraculous signal of its presence at the moment of death." In sum, the molecular evidence—like the traditional written evidence—is patchy and unevenly preserved in both time and space. The temptation to treat the evidence we have as though it were genuinely representative (more formally known as ascertainment bias) is an ever-present challenge. No less than the familiar documents that historians have always drawn from, the scientific record must be used critically as we strive to write narratives of the microbial past.[51]

If there has been one basic takeaway from tree thinking and time travel so far, it is that many of our pathogens are younger, and have more eventful evolutionary histories, than we might have imagined. Relentless evolution means that as we have changed the way we live, our microparasites have responded with adaptations to take advantage of new opportunities. The human disease pool is not just a product of our history as a species. It is, to a large extent, a product of our *recent* history. And yet the beauty of evolution is that the past, even the distant past, always remains, constraining and shaping the present. Evolution acts on what exists in the present, and what exists in the present is a product of genetic successes in the past.

A Tiny Twig

Darwin believed that the Galápagos Islands, with their barren, craggy aspect and abundance of reptiles, had taken him back closer to the origins of life. "We seem to be brought somewhat near to that great fact—that mystery of mysteries—the first appearance of new beings on this earth." But it was not the visible organisms he collected and cataloged that take us back to the first appearance of life on Earth. The ancestors of mammals are only three hundred million years old. Vertebrates in general are a little over five hundred million years old. Bacteria, by contrast, have been here for about 3.5 billion of the 4.5 billion years that the earth has existed. Viruses have been infecting them almost from the start and, in turn, bacteria have evolved sophisticated defense mechanisms against viruses. *Homo sapiens* has existed for the last 1/10,000th of the evolutionary contest between hosts and parasites.[52]

The grandeur of Darwin's theory is that it helps us understand that we are, however distantly, related even to the pathogens that cause us harm. To quote Gould again, we are a "tiny twig" on life's tree. The human struggle against infectious disease is an extension of the universal competition that is life. We enter the contest with a standard-issue vertebrate immune system, even as our parasites start from an inheritance handed down by billions of years of evolution. Yet we should not take for granted how strange—how unnatural, in a sense—the human disease pool is. Our parasites are extraordinary in their number, narrowness, and nastiness. They exist because we exist, or, more specifically, because of our unique history. It is a history that extends back millions of years to the savannas of Africa—and the invention that first sparked an ongoing story of ecological transformation.[53]

2

Prometheus among the Primates

THE TAÏ RAINFOREST IN CÔTE D'IVOIRE in West Africa is a small, lush remnant of the once vast wet forests that stretched across the equator. It is thick with life. The forest is home to elephants, pygmy hippos, leopards, and western chimpanzees (along with about ten species of monkeys, including red colobus monkeys, a favorite snack of the chimps). Today one of the major groups of western chimpanzees, totaling maybe twenty-five to fifty thousand animals, lives in this forest (see figure 2.1). In contrast to the eastern chimpanzees made famous by Jane Goodall, which inhabit a mosaic of savanna woodland, these are jungle chimps. The Taï chimps are famous for their facility with tools, which they make to hunt and to crack nuts. The western chimps are endangered, threatened by habitat loss, human poachers, and the big cats that prowl the forest. But some of their worst enemies are microscopic.[1]

In May 1999, one of the Taï forest chimpanzees came down with a cough. Sneezing, labored breathing, loss of appetite, and severe lethargy followed. The affliction spread, and soon a full-blown epidemic was underway. In one group of chimps, closely observed by scientists since the 1980s, the morbidity rate was 100 percent—that is, every single individual fell sick. Worse, the mortality rate was 19 percent, meaning nearly one in five of these chimps succumbed to the disease.

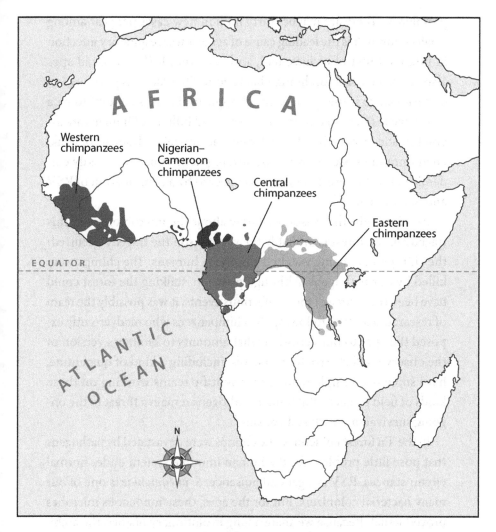

FIGURE 2.1. Map of chimpanzee populations.

It was a tragic demographic blow for a population already under pressure to survive.[2]

The pathogens that caused the outbreak were identified. The Taï chimps were struck with a double infection, caused by a common human virus and an opportunistic bacterium. The first culprit was respiratory syncytial virus (RSV). This virus is a universal human pathogen. Even with modern surveillance, it is hard to estimate its global prevalence. There are maybe thirty million new cases per year among small children. It is the leading cause of acute lower respiratory infection in infants. Most of us have had, and survived, RSV. The dead apes also carried a common human bacterium, *Streptococcus pneumoniae*. *S. pneumoniae* is the quintessential opportunist. It is content to be a peaceable resident in our upper airways, and billions of humans are asymptomatic carriers. But the bacterium can also take advantage of weakened immune systems and cause severe pneumonia. The deadly epidemic in the Taï forest in 1999 was triggered by a combination of RSV and *S. pneumoniae*.[3]

Paradoxically, the reason we know about the microbiology of this tragedy in the forest is probably the very reason the tragedy occurred: the chimps were being watched closely by humans. The chimps were killed by our pathogens. Although poachers stalking the forest could have been the source of these infectious events, it was possibly the team of research scientists following the chimpanzees who inadvertently exposed the apes to our germs, in what amounts to biology's version of the observer effect. Stricter protocols, including a kind of quarantine, have since been implemented by scientific teams working on these kinds of field projects. But human pathogens remain a threat to the ongoing survival of our closest cousins.[4]

In the Taï forest epidemics, the chimps were devastated by pathogens that pose little problem for the human immune system under normal circumstances. RSV is a general nuisance. *S. pneumoniae* is one of our many bacterial colonizers. But for the apes, these innocuous microbes proved lethal. Because we share a long evolutionary history, the architecture of our immunity is similar. Our germs are potentially dangerous to chimps, and theirs are dangerous to us, precisely because pathogens that have solved the puzzle of our immune system can apply the same molecular tricks across the species boundary. And cross-species transmission is unpredictable. A germ exploring a new kind of host has not had to reckon with the evolutionary tradeoffs between transmission and virulence. In other words, if a microbe's natural host is the chimpanzee, humans have been irrelevant to its evolutionary success so far. Germs have a selfish interest in their natural host's survival, but in spillover species, that selfish restraint is missing.

In fact, the germs that made the leap to the chimps were so virulent that their biological failure was almost immediate. From the microbe's perspective, we could think of the Taï forest epidemic as a local extinction event. The species crossover was a fast and furious evolutionary experiment. The individual viruses that gave it a try among the chimps are gone, their genes unreplicated, their pedigree ended like a lineage without an heir. Of course, this failure is unsurprising. Experiment and extinction are the perpetual drama of evolution. There are billions of species of viruses on the planet, and only a handful of them are permanently established among chimpanzees. Around twenty-eight viruses have ever been identified in chimps, and many of these are in fact human viruses that have transiently infected chimpanzee populations. Chimps are the natural host of only a few viruses, and these are, on the whole, relatively benign.[5]

From the chimp's perspective, we harbor a disturbing number of parasites. Hundreds of viruses infect humans, and eighty-seven viruses are a major burden on human health. Stranger still, humans are the main or exclusive reservoir host for most of these viruses. Many of them are acute, virulent, and specialized in us. In short, our chimpanzee cousins, who live in the jungle, eat raw monkey for breakfast, never bathe, and make a habit of chewing on their own feces, endure only a fraction of the viral diversity that we do. Among primates, we, not our forest-dwelling relatives, are the ones who are unusual.[6]

Chimpanzees have an evolutionary past. Their numbers rise and fall, but without runaway trends. Chimps today live more or less like chimps of yesteryear; consequently, they get sick and die in the same way their ancestors did. Humans, too, have an evolutionary past, but we also have a history full of fast, cumulative, culture-driven change. The essential reason we have history on these terms is because of technology, which, in turn, is a product of our big brains. The propulsive force of human history has been the promethean spirit of innovation that drives technological progress. Yet we must avoid any misleading dualisms— humans have culture, but we are part of nature. We have technology, but that technology is used to extract energy, increase our populations, and transform environments for our benefit. We have a distinctive ecological history, but this distinctiveness does not exempt us from the rules of parasite ecology and evolution. So we should start by trying to understand how biologists think about the patterns of parasite ecology and evolution for other species, including our great ape relatives, and then tracing our distinctiveness to its prehuman origins.

Principles of Parasitism

Ecology is the study of the relationship between organisms and their environment, including their relationship with the physical environment and with other living creatures. Central to ecology is the movement of energy through ecosystems. Put simply, ecology asks of any organism what it eats and what eats it. We would never study any other species without attending to these fundamental questions, and we would be flattering ourselves to think we were so different. Human history is a branch of primate ecology that gets a little out of hand.

Parasite ecology is the study of hosts, parasites, and their environments. Every ecosystem is rife with parasitism, but some creatures suffer more than others, and the study of parasite ecology tries to discern patterns. Why does the honeybee have more than seventy known parasites? Why do some species of fish have hundreds of parasites? Why do some animals seem to have far fewer?[7]

Ecologists often measure parasite burden by the standard of "parasite species richness"—a simple count of the number of parasite species that have been observed to infect a particular host. Such a measure is obviously imperfect. Parasite species richness is sensitive to the intensity of surveillance: host organisms that have been closely studied are more likely to have more parasites observed. Still, this distortion can be controlled for, and it is not insuperable. More fundamentally, parasite species richness does not measure the prevalence or virulence of the germs that infect a host. Having a few really nefarious germs might be biologically worse than having a lot of weak or rare parasites. But prevalence and virulence are nearly impossible to measure in any consistent way in wild animal populations. So, parasite species richness is commonly used as a practical way to assess parasite ecology.[8]

Some general principles govern the ecology of parasitism. In broad terms, anything about a host species that enables parasites to be more successful in passing their genes to future generations can correlate with higher levels of parasitism. In practice, the host's (1) physiology/behavior, (2) demography, and (3) geography strongly influence the level of parasitism it will suffer. Because transmission is such an intricate challenge for all parasites, host characteristics that make it easier or harder for parasites to transmit from one host to the next have an enormous bearing on levels of parasitism.

(1) Features of host physiology and behavior influence levels of parasitism. Body size matters in a highly predictable way: larger hosts have more energy and nutrients for parasites to exploit and more habitats to invade. In general, larger animals have more parasites. Ranging behavior also matters. Hosts that cover more space in the course of a day are exposed to more pathogens. Greater habitat diversity also means a greater number of parasites. Sexual promiscuity is a factor, too, because contact increases the opportunities for transmission, and the predicted relationship between sexually transmitted diseases (STDs) and promiscuity has been found in nature. In short, physical or behavioral traits that make an organism a more appealing host translate into higher levels of parasitism.[9]

(2) Population structure is fundamental to patterns of parasitism. Living in large and dense groups is an obvious, and maybe the most important, risk factor for high levels of parasitism. The reason is simple: parasites have to transmit between hosts, and when there are more individuals living in closer contact, it is easier for a parasite to reach its next victim. For similar reasons, larger groups can sustain more virulent pathogens. Close and frequent contact between hosts enhances the odds of transmission and thus lowers the chances of a parasite's extinction. But it is not just about the raw numbers. An important finding of parasite ecology is that the network structure of a group matters. For instance, primates that break into smaller, modular groups suffer lower parasite burdens than expected, suggesting that such fragmentation interrupts the transmission of pathogens. Therefore, it is not just the sheer number of individuals within a group but also the manner in which they interact that provides the evolutionary environment for parasites.[10]

The effect of group size is most pronounced at the extremes. For instance, it may not matter too much whether a primate lives in a group of a dozen or a few dozen individuals, because so many other factors can overwhelm the importance of group size at such a modest level of difference. The largest primate groups (excluding those of humans) consist of only a few hundred members. Birds and bats, by contrast, can live in colonies of thousands and tens of thousands of individuals, and some rodents, too, live in large groups. On these larger scales, the effect of group size becomes drastically more important. As genome sequencing has given us more insight into the circulation of parasites in wild animal populations, it has become apparent that birds, bats, and rodents are important reservoirs of many pathogens, especially viruses. In a sense, humans have taken the intense sociability of primates—lengthy parental care, complex food sharing, social grooming, and so forth—and combined it with group sizes beyond the scale of what any other mammal has attempted.[11]

(3) As in real estate, location is everything. The host's zip code is as important as its behavior and group size. Fundamentally, primate species that live nearer the equator suffer from higher parasite burdens. This pattern is mirrored among human societies. It is important to understand why living nearer the equator is a microbiological hazard. The most important pattern of global biodiversity is known as the latitudinal species gradient: the observation that there is substantially more biodiversity near the equator. Energy is the primary reason: more solar energy means more life. And, because repeated ice ages have intermittently wiped the higher latitudes clean of nearly all life, the biodiversity found around the equator is also more ancient. The diversity of parasites in the tropics is simply a version of a more general pattern that holds across all kinds of life.[12]

Closer to the equator, there is more overlap in the ranges of different species, which means more chances to cross between host species. The tropics lack the cold winters that, in temperate latitudes, suppress parasite transmission. The effect of latitude is especially pronounced for vector-borne diseases. Biting insects are more abundant in hotter climates without hard frosts, and year-round warmth allows uninterrupted cycles of transmission to be sustained. The tropics are thus a zone of stark tradeoffs. More primary energy from the sun produces more food, but it also fills the air with bloodsucking bugs bearing deadly parasites.

In sum, these basic principles of parasite ecology help to explain why primates in general, and especially great apes like chimpanzees, make appealing hosts. Chimps are big-bodied. They are highly social. They range widely relative to other primates. And they live near the equator. So it is unsurprising that our closest relatives have more identified parasites than any other primate (this is true even when we attempt to control for the fact that we also study them pretty intensely, given our kinship). What is striking, though, is how the chimpanzee germ pool compares to ours in size and composition. The anthropologist Charles Nunn maintains a database of primate parasites in the Global Mammal Parasite Database. For most species of primates, only a dozen or so parasites have ever been found. Around eighty-nine unique species of parasites have been identified at some point in chimpanzees. It should be mentioned immediately that many of these infect chimpanzees only rarely or sporadically, and an inordinate number—especially of the viruses and bacteria—are really human germs that have transiently affected chimpanzee populations.[13]

If we compare the proportions of the four most important taxa of parasites—helminths, protozoa, bacteria, and viruses—that affect chimps and humans, the differences are obvious (see table 2.1). Yet, we must hasten to emphasize that we are not comparing apples to apples, because the list of human parasites includes only major pathogens, and if we included every pathogen that has ever been found to infect humans, the differences would be far more stark (in particular, the number of viruses would be increased for humans). Moreover, if we excluded from the count of chimpanzee parasites those pathogens that actually specialize in humans, most of the bacteria and many of the viruses would disappear, making the differences more striking still. In short, as crude as this thought experiment is, it strongly suggests that relative to humans, a much larger proportion of the overall chimpanzee germ pool is comprised of worms and protozoa, whereas bacteria and viruses are comparatively less important.[14]

TABLE 2.1. Parasite Taxa in Chimpanzees and Humans

	Parasite taxa			
	Helminths (%)	Protozoa (%)	Bacteria (%)	Viruses (%)
Chimpanzees	29	30	8	33
Humans (major)	21	9	32	38

Comparison with animal parasites also suggests that humans harbor an uncommon number of pathogens with a restricted host range. In other words, an unusual array of parasites specializes in us. Most of the viruses that infect primates are not particular about their host species. They tend to be extreme generalists, adapted to infect a wide range of different hosts. Such pathogens are rapidly changing evolutionary gamblers, jacks of all trades, masters of none. Yet many of the helminths that infect primates are well adapted to specific hosts. They have evolved with their host species in deep time. Every primate has a worm—or worms—of its own. The protozoa are a mix of generalists and specialists. Vector-borne protozoa tend to be host specific, whereas protozoa that rely on direct transmission between hosts are able to infect a wider variety of species. Protozoa that pass via feces on the forest floor cannot be too fussy about their next target.[15]

Overall, the contrasts between the parasites of humans and nonhuman primates are arresting. Of course, it is utterly impossible to control for the human proclivity to study ourselves. We are the most observed, examined, and analyzed animal, by an incalculable margin. The raw comparison with humans is thus only impressionistic. But in the summation of Nunn and his coauthor Sonia Altizer, "Even those primate species that have been particularly well studied in terms of infectious diseases . . . reportedly harbor only a tiny fraction of the diversity of parasites infecting contemporary human populations. Furthermore, whereas the greatest diversity of parasites reported from wild primates is captured by helminths and protozoa, which are commonly linked with chronic infections and vector-borne or fecal-oral transmission, the majority of modern-day human pathogens are bacteria, viruses, and fungi, many of which cause acute infections and are often associated with contact-based transmission."[16]

And yet, even if our primate relatives confront a small number of pathogens, by human standards, we should not underestimate their importance. Primate demography is stamped by the effects of infectious disease. Among wild chimpanzee populations, infectious diseases are the leading cause of death. In one study of chimpanzee mortality, collating data from three populations, infectious diseases accounted for at least 36 percent of all deaths, with unknown illnesses accounting for another 18 percent. (Violence was the next leading cause, at 15 percent; predation amounted to another 8 percent; accidents caused 3 percent.) In reality, of course, mortality patterns are highly unstable. As in human populations, the role of infectious disease mortality is volatile, rising and falling in time. The arrival of new diseases can alter the landscape suddenly and with terrific fury. Chimpanzees, for example, have been decimated by catastrophic epidemics of the Ebola virus. Infectious diseases are a potent and unpredictable force in the population dynamics of our great ape cousins.[17]

And here, in the realm of large-scale population dynamics, is where ecological comparisons between ourselves and other animals, primates especially, can be most revealing of all. The most successful primate species, ourselves excluded, number a few hundred thousand individuals. Most have far fewer than that, numbering in the thousands or tens of thousands at most. Why are there not millions of chimpanzees? Why is there no other cosmopolitan primate, sprawling over several continents? Why is it not a world full of gorillas or gibbons?[18]

The basic answer is that, in nature, all populations of animals are regulated. The flow of energy through ecosystems ensures that rates of population change are controlled by density-dependent mechanisms. As a population grows, energy availability (i.e., food) declines. Or other organisms—namely, predators and parasites—are more able to take energy from successful species. Access to energy promotes reproduction, whereas food shortages choke fertility and ramp up the death rate. In other words, more food means more offspring, more survival, and, thus, population growth. Meanwhile, changes in the level of parasitism and predation drive the mortality rate. If there are more parasites or more predators, then the

FIGURE 2.2. Thomas Robert Malthus (1766–1834), an English priest and social thinker, whose ideas on human population presage ecological theories of population regulation. Mezzotint by John Linnell, 1834. Wellcome Collection (CC BY 4.0).

mortality rate will increase. Populations are regulated insofar as these mechanisms are density dependent, their relative force waxing and waning in response to changes in the size of the animal population itself.[19]

The availability of food is the most basic and probably the most powerful density-dependent mechanism regulating population. This mechanism is at the heart of the model of human populations described by the English cleric and theorist of human populations Thomas Robert Malthus (1766–1834; see figure 2.2). His landmark *Essay on the Principle of Population*, first published in 1798, presents an essentially ecological theory of the regulation of human numbers. As Darwin recognized, it applies just as well to animal populations. The main difference is that most animal populations are adapted to relatively narrow ecological niches. Primates are exquisitely adapted to the foods available in their native habitats. For example, chimps have digestive equipment perfectly honed to the forest, with its variety of fruits, leaves, bugs, and small monkeys. They have evolved to be good at finding energy in the competitive and unforgiving environment where they live. But they are also, for that reason, confined there and powerfully limited by the food available in their habitat.[20]

Predation and parasitism also work by density-dependent mechanisms. A species that experiences population increase becomes more attractive prey, and predators often have a decisive part in regulating animal populations. Parasites, too, take advantage of larger and denser populations, and they act to keep animal numbers in check. Volatility in the mortality rate, attributable to epidemic disease, is a brake on long-term growth in animal populations. We can easily imagine that there were sharp spikes in primate mortality, such as those caused by the Ebola virus and other nonhuman pathogens in recent times, throughout the past. Short-term swings, and long-term stability, are probably characteristic of the demographic dynamics of many of our relatives in the animal kingdom. What looks like volatility on short timescales may be a guarantee of population equilibrium in the long run.[21]

Even a species as clever as the chimpanzee is constrained by insuperable natural limits. The chimp is utterly dependent on the food it can win from the tropical forest, and for that very reason, it is condemned to endure the numerous parasites and savage predators that haunt its native habitat. Chimpanzee populations may oscillate, or shift to new equilibria as conditions (like the climate) fundamentally change, but they never experience breakaway growth. In that there is nothing unusual or unexpected. Their strange hominin cousins, on the other hand, contrived a technology that loosened some of those constraints, launching an unparalleled experiment in population growth and parasite evolution that continues to this day.

Mastering Fire

A European missionary recorded an old myth told by the indigenous peoples of the Paraguayan Chaco, in the dry interior of South America. There was a time when humans had no use of fire. One day, a hungry hunter was eating snails in a swamp, when he saw a bird also gathering snails and piling them up. A thin column of smoke lifted from the pile. The curious hunter went to investigate and found that the bird was cooking snails. He ate one and, savoring the taste, resolved never to settle for raw food again. He stole the fire, and his tribe collected wood to keep the flame alive. They began to cook all their food. The bird was angry and sent a thunderstorm with fearsome lightning, but it did no good, and the bird was left to eat raw food. Thunderstorms were an enduring reminder of the animal's anger, but henceforth humans alone controlled fire.[22]

Countless societies have myths explaining the origins of fire. In ancient Greece, Prometheus stole fire from Zeus and taught its use to humankind. It is commonplace in such myths that fire is divine, or that it came from the sky. Often birds are said to have taught humans the secrets of procuring and producing fire. The arrival of fire is always a great transition, a passage from a primitive to a more fully human state. In the words of the anthropologist James Frazer, "In spite of the fantastic features which distort many of them, the myths of the origin of fire probably contain a substantial element of truth, and supply a clue which helps us to grope our way through the darkness of the human past in the unnumbered ages which preceded the rise of history."[23]

Other animals, including our primate relatives, employ technologies—using sticks to rustle ants from a hole, for instance. But none of these meager tools can compare with the power of fire. The control of fire is an energy technology contrived by hominin ingenuity, the first energy revolution in our history. In effect, all later technologies of consequence presuppose our use of fire. Agriculture requires fire to clear forests and fend off wild animals, and farming certainly became more productive once human societies learned to use fire to forge metal tools like plows.

Industry requires fossil fuels, the combustion of fossilized sunlight congealed in coal and hydrocarbons to provide energy for our machines. The mastery of fire is the primordial technology, the origin of our unique abilities as ecological engineers.

Among the planets of our solar system, only Earth has fire. It is a remarkable feature of the world we inhabit that solar energy captured by plants and converted to biomass can be released by combustion. Thank photosynthesis. Plants build organic compounds that can burn, *and* they load our atmosphere with the oxygen necessary for combustion. Our species alone has tapped the transformational potential of fire as a means of unlocking energy. In the words of the environmental historian Alfred Crosby, "When our ancestors learned to make knives and axes of stone, they were only producing extensions of their puny teeth and fingernails. In contrast, when they learned to manipulate fire, they were doing something truly unprecedented."[24]

Insofar as many of the ancient myths imagine that the mastery of fire lies within human history, rather than before it, they are wrong. The control of fire is actually older than our species. There was not a time when humans did not control fire—in fact, the evolution of modern humans was shaped by the control of fire. Fire was a prerequisite of human evolution. No fire, no us.[25]

The common ancestor shared by humans and chimpanzees was chimp-like. It lived in the forest. It loved to eat fruit and hang from trees. It walked on its knuckles. It almost certainly lived in social groups, small by modern human standards but large by the measures of the animal world. Around four million years ago, australopithecines ("southern apes") evolved in Africa. Australopithecines are the ancestors of the genus *Homo*. These apes walked upright and had modestly larger brains (about 450 cm^3) than chimpanzees (350–400 cm^3). Upright bipedalism was a crucial evolutionary adaptation. But australopithecines were still manifestly ape-like: small climbers with big mouths and forceful jaws. In the words of primatologist Richard Wrangham, "If they still lived today in some remote area of Africa, we would find them fascinating. But to judge from their ape-sized brains, we would observe them in national parks and keep them in zoos, rather than give them legal rights or invite them to dinner."[26]

The emergence of *Homo erectus* some two million years ago was an evolutionary watershed. Distance running, extensive tool making, and cooperative hunting made this hominin more recognizably like us. And it is no coincidence that *Homo erectus* also tamed fire. The archaeological record for the origins of controlled fire remains sparse and ambiguous. Control was probably learned haltingly, by degrees. The earliest credible evidence for fire comes from a *Homo erectus* site in Kenya dating to 1.5 million years ago. From around one million years ago, the evidence for the use of fire becomes less ambiguous and more widespread. It will not be surprising if archaeological discoveries continue to push the origins of controlled fire back closer to the emergence of *Homo erectus.*[27]

The best evidence for the origin of fire is in fact indirect, in the very bones of *Homo erectus*, which point to transformational changes in the diet and lifeways of early hominins. *Homo erectus* had little teeth and a weak jaw. Its mouth had a tiny aperture, like ours, not the gaping maw of an ape. Its bite was nothing impressive. Its stomach and colon were small compared to a chimp's digestive organs. *Homo erectus* was tall, upright, and big-brained ($870–950$ cm^3). Its body was better suited for running than climbing. In all, these dramatic evolutionary changes suggest that *Homo erectus* had adapted to a radically altered diet. *Homo erectus* had learned to cook.[28]

Cooking helped *Homo erectus* extract energy from plants and meat more efficiently, and it widened the range of food sources that *Homo erectus* was able to consume. Heat denatures protein, gelatinizes starch, and (unless you overdo it) softens food. Cooking outsources some of the work of digestion to fire and makes the conversion of food into energy more efficient. This revolutionary application of fire drove biological evolution in our ancestors. Our small mouths, tiny teeth, puny jaws, and diminutive digestive system require us to use fire. The control of fire is a cultural technology, learned and passed down from generation to generation; it is not something we can do instinctually or with our own body parts. Yet making fire is so universal and so deeply embedded in culture that our biology has come to depend upon it.[29]

The control of fire changed our digestion and diet, which had cascading effects. The brain of *Homo erectus* evolved, growing to more than three times the size of a chimpanzee's. The extra energy acquired from cooked food was instrumental in the evolution of larger brains. The brain is an energy sink. It consumes 20 percent of the basal metabolism of *Homo sapiens*. It also helped that we now spent less energy on our smaller digestive system. The digestive organs are energy intensive, so by outsourcing some of the hard work to fire, *Homo erectus* was able to cut its costs and devote the savings to extra brainpower. Cooking was instrumental in the rise of a distinctly brainy species. To the extent that our cognitive abilities make us human, we are a creature born of fire.[30]

Fire has been called a "species monopoly" of humans. It is an ecological trump card. When our ancestors first learned to keep the flames alive, it tilted the balance of power in nature. One intimate correlate of this new advantage was registered in the behavior of *Homo erectus*: this species slept on the ground. The great apes sleep in trees. Large male gorillas are sometimes brave enough to snooze on the forest floor, but our primate relatives prefer some distance between themselves and whatever hunts in the dark. A chimpanzee can make a nice bed in the forest canopy with military efficiency. But our *Homo erectus* ancestors left the trees and learned to spend the night in the protective glow of the fire's light. Despite the tingling fear we still feel in the face of large animals, fire made predators a negligible factor in human population dynamics. The warmth, security, and mystic peace you feel around the campfire have been instilled by almost two million years of evolutionary advantage given to us by the flames.[31]

The monopoly on fire also accentuated the importance of meat. Our ancestors did not become hunters in one single transformational moment. After all, chimpanzees will hunt and eat meat. But it is a small part of their diet, which remains dominated by fruit and bugs. Chimps have been observed to kill a monkey, quickly gobble the soft innards such as brains and intestines, and then toss away the bones, fur, and muscle, which is full of tough connective tissue and therefore hard to chew and digest. Chimps are not built for dedicated carnivory. True carnivores, like canids, have stomachs with extremely acidic environments designed to break down flesh slowly. Primates have stomachs with moderate acidity, made to move plants through expeditiously. Humans, from this vantage too, are a strange breed. Our digestive equipment is actually less formidable than an ape's, being smaller and faster moving, with a less acidic stomach. But our tastes, and our metabolic needs, program us to lust for meat.[32]

As our ancestors' dependence upon hunting deepened, it reshaped patterns of social organization. The intimate trust of the night watch, the greater sharing of meat from giant kills, and a more pronounced sexual division of labor all tightened the bonds of hominin society. It seems likely that *Homo erectus* was the first ancestor to practice any form of medical care, tending the sick and aiding recovery from disease. Some anthropologists think that *Homo erectus* had rudimentary language, even if early hominins have left no traces of a symbolic imagination comparable to that of *Homo sapiens*. The cognitive and social world of *Homo erectus* remains elusive, maybe beyond recovery. What were these ancestors like? Would they have seemed human-like? If one showed up sick on your doorstep, would you take her to the veterinarian or the doctor? Very likely the latter.[33]

We can only wonder if they feared death, or what they thought as they looked up at the stars, but we know that our *Homo erectus* forebears soon did something unmistakably familiar to us. They wandered. *Homo erectus* groups migrated out of Africa and occupied Asia and Europe. Other primates can push the edges of their habitats or disperse to new territory, but with *Homo erectus* a single species went intercontinental. The energy revolution had fueled population growth, and that growth quickly spilled over into migration. Brains, tools, and the use of fire empowered ancestral hominins, giving them the versatility to exploit new food sources across three continents. *Homo erectus* had the human-like capacity to adapt to unfamiliar ecological niches. More than a million years ago, our predecessors had already started to burn their way across the planet. The dispersal of *Homo erectus* across the Old World foreshadowed the geographic boundlessness of *Homo sapiens*. This geographic versatility is one of the truly distinctive facts of our kind—and its implications for disease ecology would turn out to be profound.[34]

We cannot know what the disease environment of *Homo erectus* was like in precise detail. We can reasonably presume that the germs faced by our ape-like ancestors were broadly similar to those of tropical primates in general and chimpanzees in particular. The last common ancestor of chimps and humans would have been pestered by worms and surrounded by protozoa, some picked up from the bloodsucking insects that buzzed in the air and some from the forest floor. Dangerous viruses, often traded with other jungle-dwelling monkeys and apes, lurked in the lush tropical surroundings, and occasionally these virulent pathogens decimated the population of our ape ancestors. Their numbers were contained by their relatively specialized diet, their fearsome predators stalking in the night, and their tropical parasites.

The rise of *Homo* was something new. Big brains, better tools, and the control of fire relaxed our ecological dependence on a narrow range of foods, and it rendered predators virtually irrelevant. But progress also offered novel opportunities for our parasites. The intensification of social bonds facilitated parasite transmission. Demographic growth surely provided more exposure to pathogenic organisms. Larger body sizes meant more room for invaders. Broader habitat ranges and wider ecological diversity were risk factors for new infectious diseases. In sum, given what we know of their lifeways, the pathogen load of our early hominin ancestors—and this is of course speculative—would have started to approach that of human hunter-gatherers. Already, our intrepid ancestors had set off on a course that would create a uniquely dynamic relationship between population, technology, and microbial evolution.

New Niches, New Germs

How might the expansion of *Homo* have changed the disease environment of our ancestors? We cannot directly observe the health environment of extinct relatives that lived a million years ago. But tree thinking can shed light on the formation of a distinctly hominin disease pool. Sometimes there are faint traces of an eventful past. Humans, for instance, serve as host to two herpes simplex viruses. All primates seem to have one herpes simplex virus; humans alone are cursed to carry two. One of them (HSV-1) is as old as the split between our ancestors and chimps; it primarily causes lesions in the mouth. The second, bonus species (HSV-2, the cause of genital herpes) was acquired around 1.6 million years ago by a now extinct *Homo* ancestor, who contracted the virus from chimpanzees and subsequently handed it down to hominin descendants until it reached us.[35]

In the case of the disease known as schistosomiasis, tree thinking, along with archaeology, helps us piece together an example of how the new ecological frontiers exploited by *Homo* fostered the evolution of a deadly human parasite. East Africa has been an especially fertile source of ancient fossils, and not a few of the "missing links" of hominin evolutionary history have come from the region. On the eastern shores of Kenya's Lake Turkana, for instance, our Pleistocene ancestors found a green landscape crossed with rivers and teeming with life. In recent years, at a place near the ridge known as Koobi Fora, archaeologists found a dense assemblage of stone tools and animal bones. Around 1.95 million years ago, these traces of our past were fortuitously buried in an episode of rapid alluviation. More than 2,600 artifacts and some 1,000 fossils of animal bone have been recovered. These finds transport us back to the world of early *Homo erectus*, and they reveal that our distant ancestors had already learned to fish.[36]

The assemblage of bones found at Koobi Fora exhibits telltale signs of the work of a hominin hunter. The bones have the unmistakable marks of butchery. The tools were manufactured from nearby basalt sources. The remains reflect such a variety of creatures—from the ancestors of wild pigs to crocodiles—that only a hominin could be behind them. The leftovers on the cutting floor underscore the skill and versatility of early *Homo* as a hunter. But the most striking feature of the site is the sheer number of catfish and turtle bones. Catfish are plump and delicious; frequently trapped in shallow pools, they are easy prey. Turtles are bundles of rich meat in a hard wrapper, wanting only a tool to be unshelled. Hundreds of specimens from Koobi Fora suggest that *Homo erectus* looked to the waters for food and found a feast waiting to be had.

Aquatic resources have been instrumental in hominin expansion, and *Homo erectus* already had the body and technological prowess to catch fish, kill turtles, collect snails, and otherwise exploit the potential of rivers and lakes to provide food. Ethnographic comparison underscores that human hunter-gatherers often rely on such resources. The fire myth from the Paraguayan Chaco is revealing: an exasperated hunter turned to the water for snails to relieve his hunger. Indeed, aquatic resources are often a lifesaver toward the end of cool or dry seasons, when animals are lean, before the fields and forests have bloomed again. Fish are also highly nutritious, packed with micronutrients necessary for brain development. The bigger brains of *Homo erectus* were paid for in part by the riches hidden under water.[37]

The lifeways of *Homo erectus* drew us into tighter relations with the shoreline. This kind of ecological versatility also meant exposure to new disease environments. The deeper reliance on aquatic resources helps to explain the relationship between humanity and the devastating waterborne parasites that cause schistosomiasis. Our species has a revealing relationship with these unusually burdensome helminth parasites, and this relationship took shape on a time horizon of tens to hundreds of thousands of years ago. Our ancestors came to the shore to fish, and they left with worms.

Schistosomiasis is one of the most important diseases of humanity. If you are unfamiliar with this affliction that sounds like a tongue-twister, you are fortunate. Schistosomiasis infects some two to four hundred million people around the world today. Few diseases have exacted such a heavy toll over such a remarkably long timespan. Schistosomiasis is also known by the names bilharzia, red-water fever, and snail fever. It is caused by blood flukes, or flatworms, in the genus *Schistosoma* ("split body"; see figure 2.3). The disease came to the sudden attention of Europeans during Napoleon's Egyptian campaign. The worms that cause schistosomiasis were identified in 1851, when Theodore Bilharz, a German doctor, was posted to the Kasr-el-'Ain Hospital in Cairo. In his first eighteen months, Bilharz carried out some four hundred autopsies. He found bodies full of worms. In his words, "As helminths in general and those who attack humans in particular are concerned, I think Egypt

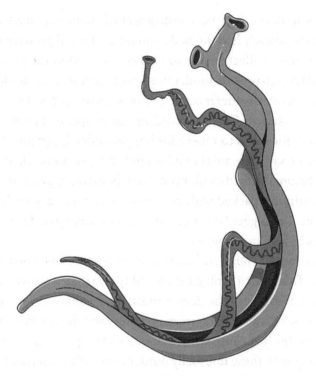

FIGURE 2.3. Schistosome parasite, adult male and female living
in copula. Servier Medical Art: CC BY 3.0.

is the best country to study them." Through his microscope, he discovered a worm with "a flat body and a twisted tail." With more than a hint
of Orientalism, he imagined that his discoveries amounted to "a few
leaves of a saga as wonderful as the best of the Thousand and One
Nights."[38]

Bilharz was about to be even more enthused. The first of these worms
he had seen was a male. He soon found "samples of the worm which
harbored a grey thread in the canal of their tails. You can picture my
surprise when I saw that a trematode [a flatworm] projected out of the
anterior opening of the canal." These worms within the worms are in
fact the females, whose eggs are fertilized while she is living inside the
male. Schistosomes reproduce sexually inside their definitive host (a
definitive host, in contrast to an intermediate host, is where parasites
with complex life cycles reach their adult or mature stage). Bilharz did not

fully unlock the complex life cycle of the worms that he found, but through his microscope he found the parasitic agent of this horrific disease.[39]

Schistosomes are parasites with an intricate strategy. Their principal habitat, where they spend most of their adult lives, is in the veins around our bladder or intestine. There, males and females live "in copula," the female inside the male. The females are prolific, laying hundreds of eggs a day. The worms are perfectly content in these conditions. They have evolved to disguise themselves from our immune system, in part by wearing our own molecules on their outside as camouflage. An adult schistosome worm can live inside its human host for

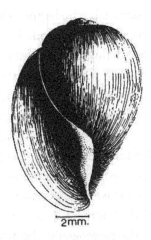

2mm.

FIGURE 2.4. *Bulinus* snails, widely distributed in freshwater habitats, are the intermediate hosts of schistosome parasites. Credit: *Koedoe* 10 (1967): Figure 1. CC BY 4.0.

more than a decade. But the eggs must quickly find their way out. The eggs are armed with a spine, a blade-like appendage used to cut themselves out of our veins. They bore into the bladder or intestine and thence pass from the human body in blood-stained urine or feces. In some regions where schistosomiasis is endemic, the bloody urine caused by these parasites has been considered a rite of passage not unlike menarche.[40]

Once excreted, the eggs have to hope that they are washed into a body of fresh water. There the eggs hatch, and swimming larvae go off in search of snails to call their home for a time. The life cycle of all species of *Schistosoma* worms is completely dependent on two hosts: a definitive host, such as humans, and an intermediate host, always a freshwater snail of the genus *Bulinus* (figure 2.4). Different species of *Schistosoma* worms are adapted to different *Bulinus* snails, and the distribution of these snails around the planet is the primary factor determining the geography of schistosomiasis. Inside the snail, the parasite undergoes asexual reproduction and spawns a second larval form. A single infected snail can shed tens of thousands of larvae. These creatures have a forked tail that enables them to swim. They attach to mammals who happen to be in the water, drinking, cooling themselves, or hunting for food. The larvae penetrate directly through the skin of the definitive host and enter the bloodstream. Then they pass through the lungs and liver of the host before reaching their goal in the veins around the bladder or intestine, where they live and mate for years, starting the cycle over again.[41]

There are twenty-two known species of *Schistosoma* parasites, and all of them are obligated to pursue the multistage lifestyle with a snail intermediary and a mammal in the role of definitive host. Three of the schistosome species are major parasites of humans, and another five can infect humans. *S. japonicum* is an Asian species of the parasite. It is an extreme generalist, the most versatile of the schistosomes, infecting a wide range of mammals besides humans. *S. mansoni* and *S. haematobium* are African species, specializing in humans, even if they are able to infect other hosts incidentally. These two African species cause the greatest burden of disease today. One of them, *S. mansoni*, was dispersed to South America in the sixteenth century via the slave trade, and it adapted to snail hosts in the New World tropics. It remains endemic there still.[42]

Because it is a parasitic disease caused by long-term infection, schistosomiasis takes various clinical courses. The most direct danger is presented by the army of eggs that bore their way out of our veins, damaging blood vessels en route to escape. Most species of schistosomes inhabit the veins around the intestine, and thus cause bloody diarrhea. One species endemic to Africa, *S. haematobium*, infects the veins around the bladder and exits in bloody urine, hence "red-water fever." Schistosome infection causes anemia and malnutrition, and our inflammatory immune response risks further health complications. The parasite stunts the cognitive and physical development of its host. Long-term infection can also critically damage the kidneys, intestines, lungs, and liver, progressing to fatal disease. In short, these free-swimming, forked-tailed worms that disguise themselves in order to have never-ending sex in our veins and prolifically lay eggs with a bayonet on the end cause a disease altogether just about as ghastly as one might expect.[43]

Before the advent of genome sequencing, it was customary to say a few words about the early history of schistosomes as known from traces in Egyptian mummies and scattered mention in early Chinese medical texts (in the history of medicine, this combination is the surest confession of near ignorance). We could say that the disease was very old, but we knew precious little about its real history. Now, molecular evidence has thrown light onto the history of a parasite whose biography was previously nothing but shadows. It is possible to build a family tree of the *Schistosoma* genus by untangling the relationships between its species. The genetic distance between the different branches of the family can be measured, and the order in which they branched off can be established. With a molecular clock, a date can be approximated for various points in the evolutionary history of these parasitic organisms. Such dates are only estimates—but they have revolutionized our ability to understand the evolutionary past.[44]

Schistosomes emerged as parasites of mammals sixty to seventy million years ago, in Asia. At first they probably infected rodents, because rodent schistosomes are the deepest branch of the tree. Around twenty million years ago, *Schistosoma* shifted hosts, acquiring the ability to infect ungulates (hoofed mammals). The Asian species *S. japonicum*, with more than forty known hosts, is most closely related to this early branch. The generalist form of the parasite is thus older than the more specialized species known today. Schistosome parasites probably moved from Asia to Africa with the dispersal of ungulates some twelve million years ago. In Africa, schistosomes infect a wide variety of rodents and ungulates as well as some nonhuman primates. It is possible that ancestral forms of schistosomiasis afflicted our distant primate ancestors, in the millions of years prior to the split between chimpanzees and humans. Like other mammals, any time our ape-like ancestors went to the lake or river in search of a drink, they were exposed to the dangers of this parasitic infection. But the family tree of *Schistosoma* suggests there was no special relationship between this parasite and our primate ancestors.[45]

In the last few hundred thousand years, the African schistosomes experienced a radiation, rapidly diversifying in response to evolutionary opportunities. There is every reason to believe that hominins played a major role. Humans are the dominant host among the African branches of *Schistosoma*. Several species that infect ungulates are derived from more ancient branches that feature human specialists. Thus, schistosomiasis is another example of a zoonotic disease that adapted to humans from wild hosts, and which we in turn have transmitted to other animals. Whether it was early *Homo sapiens* or one of our recent hominin ancestors, a large-bodied ape, splashing around in lakes and rivers looking for fish, turtles, and snails, was an irresistible evolutionary opportunity for the worms.[46]

Evolution has adapted these parasites to their human hosts in profound and intimate ways. To take one example, schistosome worms have circadian rhythms that are responsive to the habits of their host. The larvae are shed from the snail intermediary into the water at various times of day, depending on the routines of their definitive host. Schistosomes adapted to humans have evolved an atypical pattern, shedding larvae during the middle of the day, when humans are most likely to be found looking for food. These remarkable adaptations were the unintended product of Darwinian selection, chosen for the simple fact that parasites with effective traits were more likely to pass on their genes to future generations. Once hominins started exploiting aquatic resources more intensely, parasites that adapted to steal energy from these big, crafty creatures living along the waterways of the African savanna were rewarded handsomely.[47]

The deep history of *Schistosoma* is thus full of contingency across multiple timescales. A bolt of lightning sparked a fire, and some clever apes learned to control it. Their brains grew. They learned to fish, and they harvested the nutrients derived from aquatic food. The waters in which they swam were full of worms that had been brought to East Africa more than ten million years before. Some of the worms were able to pierce the skin of these ancestral hominins. Over time, random mutations made the worms even more insidious thieves of the energy and nutrients that circulated in the blood of those fish-, snail-, and turtle-eating hominins. And today, hundreds of millions of their descendants still suffer from schistosomiasis.

It is unsurprising that such an ancient infection was caused by a helminth parasite. Worms are a common problem for tropical primates.

And yet, already in prehistoric times, the ecological versatility and de-mographic success of *Homo* had provided the context for an unusually virulent and specialized worm. The story of schistosomiasis is just one poignant example of a major human disease that adapted to our ances-tors in the deep evolutionary past. We were already a strange host spe-cies, perhaps even before we were *Homo sapiens*. And the subsequent history of this parasitic worm was shaped by the course of human social development. Much later, the rise of irrigation agriculture played into the hands of our water-borne parasites. The Nile Valley and the Fertile Crescent, where vast floodplains were turned into farms, became sprawling zones of endemic schistosomiasis infection. Rice-paddy ag-riculture in Asia was an incalculable gift to swimming parasitic worms. Almost every increment of human progress also advanced the interests of the schistosome parasites.

The incidence of schistosomiasis expanded in step with human population growth and ecological transformation, right up to the twen-tieth century. Finally, brutal deworming campaigns (such as those that were launched by Chairman Mao in China in the 1950s) and medical interventions have stemmed the tide and started its rollback. But be-fore these radical reversals, in effect the only check on this remorseless parasite was its evolutionary dependence on particular snails. Schisto-some parasites dispersed wherever there were humans living in prox-imity to the *Bulinus* snails that are competent as intermediate hosts. The limits of schistosomiasis were traced by the presence, or absence, of the right snails.[48]

This geographic distribution is a final way in which the contingencies of evolution reverberate throughout human history. The reason why schistosomiasis ravaged one society, and not another, had everything to do with what snails happen to colonize their respective territories. The burden of schistosomiasis was disproportionately heavy in the lower latitudes and throughout Asia because of purely exogenous geographic facts. Schistosomiasis is a paradigmatic example of a geographically un-even disease, its distribution decided by something as utterly fortuitous as the distribution of snails in the freshwater environments of the world.

The worm is, in more ways than one, a fluke.

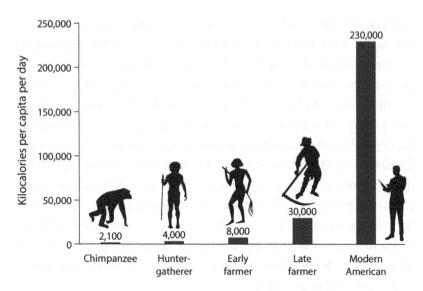

FIGURE 2.5. Humans consume energy via metabolism and combustion, and energy consumption has increased through technical innovation.

Energy, Ecology, and History

The emergence of *Homo* marked the beginning of our career as a host organism unlike anything else on the planet. In many ways, the control of fire and evolution of bigger brains provided our hominin ancestors unprecedented leverage over nature. It gave them access to a much wider array of food sources, and it gave them the upper hand over predators. But our cognitive prowess and early technologies were of little use against our invisible enemies, and the new lifeways of hominin ancestors also played to the advantage of our parasites.

From an ecological perspective, humanity's success at capturing energy is the central thread of our distinctive history. Humans consume energy through metabolism and combustion. The ability of human societies to capture, transform, and exchange energy through cumulative organizational and technological adaptations makes us different from other great apes. Following the historian Ian Morris, we can call this progressive capacity "social development," and we can measure it in simple terms by energy consumption (figure 2.5). Consider that an adult male chimpanzee expends about 2,100 kilocalories per individual, per day. The earliest humans already used about 4,000 kilocalories per person, per day. The inhabitant of an early farming society used about 8,000 kilocalories of energy per day. A farmer in the late preindustrial period consumed about 30,000 kilocalories per day. Today, the average American uses 230,000 kilocalories of energy per day, some 2,000–3,000 of it consumed as food. To look at human energy consumption in another way, in a developed society today, every individual consumer is the rough ecological equivalent to a herd of gazelles.[49]

Humans have experienced an unusually dramatic history because of social development, and yet the principles of parasite ecology and evolution never cease to operate. As humans have spread to every niche on the planet, slashed and burned landscapes, settled into sedentary habitats, tamed a few favored animals, learned to cross continents and oceans, and constructed giant cities, we have changed the ecological prospects for our pathogens and potential pathogens. Ecologically, humans are a global primate that spreads like a weed, lives like a rat, and consumes like a plague of locusts. In time, we have acquired the pathogen load to match.

3

Where the Bloodsuckers Aren't

Before the Fall

In histories that span the length of our journey as a species, the transition from hunting and gathering to farming has an awful reputation. It has been called "the worst mistake in the history of the human race," or "history's biggest fraud." On this view, agriculture enabled massive inequality, and it undermined human health by lowering the quality of our diets and exposing us to new infectious diseases. This reputation is not totally undeserved. The transition to farming did lead to steeper forms of hierarchy and spawn vicious new germs. But seeing agriculture as a fall from grace threatens to obscure what really came before. We spent 95 percent of our history as hunter-gatherers, taking our food from the wild instead of planting it or herding it. This long period of our past cannot be glossed over in a history of disease.[1]

Infectious diseases shaped human history already during the Pleistocene. (A brief note on chronological terms: the Pleistocene is the epoch of repeated ice ages spanning from about 2.6 million years ago to 11,700 years ago. The *late* Pleistocene refers to the last 130,000 years of that epoch. The Pleistocene came to a close with the arrival of the warmer Holocene epoch. Because farming originated near the beginning of the Holocene, the Pleistocene is also the period of the past when all humans on earth were hunter-gatherers.) As we will see, reconstructing the disease burden faced by ancestral hunter-gatherers is far from easy, but tree thinking can help us to see that some major diseases adapted to humans well before the domestication of plants and animals. We need to be wary of a myopic preoccupation with directly communicable and acute diseases. Macroparasites like worms, pathogens capable of causing chronic infection, and pathogens that relied on animal hosts all weighed on our ancestors' health. Above all, vector-borne diseases already constituted a major burden in early human societies.[2]

The alluring idea that the transition to agriculture was a loss of innocence distorts the role of infectious disease in the deep past. It also underestimates the enduring legacy of the Pleistocene in the development of later patterns of health and social development. During the Pleistocene, *Homo sapiens* spread over six continents, occupying every habitable niche between the equatorial rainforest and the arctic tundra. Every hunter-gatherer society faced two basic ecological problems: how to get enough energy, and how to survive the threats of parasitism. But the balance of these two basic challenges varied enormously in different environments. It is an elemental fact that pathogens evolved to transmit within small, scattered, and mobile populations are unevenly distributed around the globe. To see why, we have to think like a germ. Hopping from one hunter-gatherer to the next is no simple feat, but an ingenious way to do so is by hitching a ride from a bloodsucking insect. The geography of biting bugs has intimately shaped the history of earth's only global primate.[3]

The Rise of *Sapiens*

Homo erectus was human-like—an intelligent, bipedal, highly social hominin, adaptable enough to spread across three continents. Meanwhile, evolution continued throughout the Pleistocene, and evidence of various descendants of *Homo erectus* both within Africa and across Eurasia are found in the fossil record. The most familiar of these offshoots, excluding ourselves, are the Neanderthals, who lived from about four hundred thousand years ago until about thirty-five thousand years ago in the Near East and Europe. Other representatives of the genus *Homo* (such as the recently discovered Denisovans) occupied Asia all the way to its eastern shores. Hominin numbers were never very large, but the various children of the genus *Homo* successfully adapted to a wide range of the earth's habitats.[4]

Homo sapiens evolved in Africa some two to three hundred thousand years ago. Whether our emergence was gradual or sudden remains murky, but our brains got substantially bigger. All 7.8 billion of us alive today are descended from a tiny number of big-brained ancestors who lived in the savannas of Africa. Yet the line from early *Homo* to modern humans was anything but straight and simple. In the middle to late Pleistocene, the Old World was crisscrossed by distinct but related hominin offshoots, all of whom went extinct except for us. In fact, modern humans did not just overlap with these other types of human—we interbred with them. Some human populations still carry the genes of this admixture; for instance, some genomes still bear small amounts of Neanderthal or Denisovan DNA. Early humans undoubtedly also swapped germs with our now-extinct relatives. An important strain of human papillomavirus 16, for instance, seems to have been acquired by our ancestors from other hominins who had left Africa, and the diversity of this cancer-causing virus in human populations today is a legacy of these Pleistocene escapades.[5]

Homo sapiens also probably hastened the demise of the other branches of *Homo*. The arrival of humans in Europe, for instance, was followed by the relatively abrupt end of a long Neanderthal tradition on the continent. By about thirty-five thousand years ago, we were the only hominin game on earth. The hominin family has been aptly compared to a braided river, its streams overlapping, combining, and running dry until only one rivulet still runs—us.[6]

The oldest branches of the human family tree split within Africa, where there is the greatest genetic diversity between human populations. The rest of humanity is a subset of the groups who left Africa— branches from branches. The timing, nature, and itinerary of the human migrations remain in question. Increasingly, it appears that there was more trial and error, over a much longer period, than once believed.

Humans might have been in the Levant almost two hundred thousand years ago, very near our origins. We were in Arabia by at least eighty-five thousand years ago. Human fossils in South Asia might go back as far as seventy thousand years. But these seem to have been tentative and ultimately failed expansions. So far, nothing has upended the basic narrative that humans exploded out of Africa around fifty thousand years ago. Bands of hunter-gatherers now explored from Europe to Australia and established a lasting footprint across the entire Old World.[7]

The first humans, like *Homo erectus*, were exclusively hunter-gatherers, using stone-based technologies complemented by fire to extract energy from a variety of environments. Early humans thrived in the tropical savannas of Africa. In the late Pleistocene, a corridor of continuous grassland—what has been aptly called *savannahstan*—stretched from Africa to central Asia. The familiar environment stretched out like a mother road for human dispersal. But our species quickly adapted to a range of opportunities. Humans followed *Homo erectus* in learning how to exploit aquatic resources, and migrants hugged the shores of the Indian Ocean, traversing the unbroken mangrove highway along the coastal lowlands. Other bands of humans pushed the limits of northern expansion, hunting big game across northern Europe and Asia. By twenty thousand years ago, the first humans had crossed Beringia and started the peopling of North America, again exploiting marine environments as well as terrestrial ones in a vast open land.[8]

Technological development in the Pleistocene was slow but not immaterial. Fire and stone tools remained primary technologies. Maybe the most important advances came in projectile technology, such as the invention of the bow and arrow, sometime in the last one hundred thousand years. Archery helped to drive the advance of our species across the planet and might have given us a decisive advantage over other hominins. The domestication of our faithful hunting partner, the dog, helped too. Enterprising humans also made progress in transportation technology, particularly boats. Evidence for early seafaring by humans continues to be discovered. Our Pleistocene ancestors took easily to the water, and no longer was human travel bound by the distance we could

swim. Moreover, in the twilight of the Pleistocene, a number of populations in Africa and East Asia learned to make pottery. In all, even the
modest technological advances of the Pleistocene pushed human expansion around the globe and fostered growth in human numbers.[9]

Humanity's most remarkable achievement during the Pleistocene
was to disperse across the planet. Our adaptability made us both successful and wondrously diverse. Human diversity has its roots in this
great global scattering, as early societies separated and adapted to very
different environmental niches. At the same time, all human hunter-
gatherer societies share important structural similarities, grounded in
the requirements of extracting energy from wild food sources. Hunter-
gatherers all live in small, relatively (but not completely) egalitarian
societies with oral cultures. They have low population densities, by
modern standards. Stone tools, animal parts, and the control of fire
comprise the basic technological package. There is little accumulation
of wealth, and almost by definition per capita incomes are close to the
subsistence level. The vast diversity of hunter-gatherer lifeways are variations on these common themes.

Because of these essential similarities in technological development
and social organization, there is a tendency to pass by the Pleistocene
quickly in the search for the origins of human inequality. Jared Diamond, for instance, frames the question of how some societies became
technologically powerful and wealthy as the "basic problem of history."
His book *Guns, Germs, and Steel* provides one of the most influential
geographical theories about the origins of human inequality. In his view,
modern civilizations built directly on the geographical good fortune of
their remote ancestors. Some hunter-gatherer societies were lucky
enough to live in territories blessed with an abundance of plant and animal species that were susceptible to domestication. Relatively few
plants, and even fewer animals, have the right biology to allow domestication. The fortunate hunter-gatherers who were living on top of these
species became the first farmers, and their descendants had an insuperable head start.[10]

Diamond calls the beginning of the Holocene "the starting line"—
implying that all Pleistocene hunter-gatherers had reached the same

level of technological development and that only what came after shaped the rise of inequality. Ian Morris, in his long-term history of human social development, is one of the only historians who has asked whether this claim is true. He comes to the same conclusion as Diamond, which is that the origins of inequality between human societies are to be found in the rise of agriculture. At the end of the Pleistocene, "Each band foraged and hunted, roaming over huge areas as plants ripened and animals came and went. Each must have known its territory intimately and have told stories about every rock and tree; each had its own art and traditions, tools and weapons, spirits and demons." But ultimately, "far more united the little bands of humans scattered from Britain to Siberia . . . than divided them."[11]

We can agree that geographic factors shaped the rise of agriculture, and that the transition to farming was enormously consequential. And yet, we do not have to diminish the importance of Pleistocene differences for the lone surviving branch of *Homo*. Some of the first meaningful divergences between human societies might not be found in how they lived but, rather, in how they died.

Dying in the Pleistocene

When the British Navy Captain John Ross, searching for the Northwest Passage, made contact with the Inughuit people of Greenland in the year 1818, it came as a thorough surprise to this arctic population. They had believed they were the "only inhabitants of the universe, and that all the rest of the world was a mass of ice." Inughuit is a self-designation, meaning the "great and beautiful human beings," for the people that have often been called the "polar Eskimo" by Europeans and Americans. The Inughuit live in the far north of Greenland, between the seventy-fifth and seventy-ninth parallels. Even by Inuit standards, the Inughuit are up there. They are the northernmost human society. "They live in a region of eternal ice and snow, are hemmed in by glaciers, and can not therefore leave their locality and have no regular communication with other portions of the world." The Inughuit were, and still are, among the most isolated populations on the planet.[12]

The Inughuit inhabit the arctic tundra, which means they will never see a tree. For four months of summer, the sun never sets. For four months of winter, there is endless night. In January and February, the average temperature is −22°F. The Inughuit have adapted to this frigid world and, until recent times, they spent much of the winter inside sunken stone houses lighted by crude stone lamps that were fueled by moss and whale blubber. They lived in tiny, mobile, widely dispersed camps. Their society was loosely organized around nuclear family units. There were no chiefs, and consensus had to reign. Robert Peary, the American explorer, started to visit the Inughuit in the 1890s. He could only admire their ingenious methods of survival: "In powers of endurance, in certain directions, they are probably not surpassed by any other known race, and in their ingenuity and the intelligence displayed in making use, to the fullest extent, of every one of the few possibilities of their country which can assist them to live and be comfortable, they are, in my opinion, ahead of any other aboriginal race."[13]

Despite their remarkable adaptation to the arctic environment, the Inughuit always lived on the knife's edge of bare subsistence. Before regular contact with the outside world, the Inughuit were hunters living on a diet comprised almost entirely of meat. Hunting was by far most productive in the spring and autumn, and meat had to be stored. Every year brought two seasons of hunger, and the long, dark winter was inevitably the most perilous. In times of true shortage, they resorted to desperate measures. "Strangulation of both boys and girls younger than 3 or 4 years occurred, in order to save them from slow starvation due to lack of milk from the mother (or a substitute nurse) or from lack of food when the father died."[14]

When Captain Ross made contact with the Inughuit in 1818, he was struck by their vigor and health. "They seemed to have no diseases among them, nor could we learn that they died of any complaints peculiar to this or any other country. We saw no deformed persons among them, nor could we find out that there were any." Overall, he thought "they seemed happy and contented." Peary's expeditions in the 1890s carried out the first census of the Inughuit. In 1892, the population was 243. Peary believed that, prior to his visits, the population had been stationary. "Nature's balance between the population and the food-producing capabilities of the country had been established for generations." But in his own time, the birth rate ordinarily exceeded the death rate, and the population fluctuated. Epidemics of typhoid, influenza, and tuberculosis, introduced by European whalers and explorers, took a heavy toll in 1880, 1895, 1901, 1909, and 1920. Sometimes 10–15 percent of the entire population was lost in a single year. Even so, the Inughuit were able to offset these losses and achieve net demographic growth in the decades of early contact.[15]

The Inughuit are an example of a hunter-gatherer society that survived into modern times. Ten thousand years ago, every human on earth was a hunter-gatherer. By five hundred years ago, only 1 percent of humans were hunter-gatherers. And today, only a tiny sliver of that 1 percent still subsists without agriculture. For most of our history, we were hunter-gatherers. And yet it is hard to write definitively about most of this history for the obvious reason that writing was not invented until rather late in the game. One common resort has been to label everything that happened before the past five thousand years or so as *prehistory*, allotting it to anthropologists rather than historians to study. But human history does not begin with the rise of civilizations that have kindly left us documentary traces. Especially in the quest to understand the role of infectious disease in our past, the lingering divisions that assign the study of primates to the biologists, hunter-gatherers to the anthropologists, and civilization to the historians will lead us astray.[16]

In the absence of written documents, then, how can life—and death—in the Pleistocene be approached? The conventional routes are archaeology and ethnographic observation. But both have their limits. Most infectious diseases do not leave a mark in the victim's skeleton, and because DNA degrades, paleogenomics has not so far been able to illuminate the disease environment of the earliest humans. Ethnographic observation of modern-day hunter-gatherers is more promising but also full of perils. Even modest contact with modern industrial and agricultural societies introduced new technologies (like metal hunting instruments) and new germs (like tuberculosis). For instance, from the

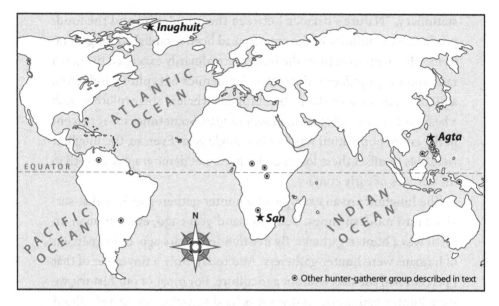

FIGURE 3.1. Map of hunter-gatherer populations discussed in text
and with reported life expectancy data in table 3.1.

moment western adventurers made landfall on the coasts of northern
Greenland, the Inughuit were exposed to pathogens that had evolved
over millennia of farming and urbanization. Moreover, remnant hunter-
gatherer populations tend to inhabit ecologically marginal or extreme
environments. These societies held out against farmers because they live
in hard and unwelcoming lands that defy the plow. No present-day
hunter-gatherer society is a Pleistocene time capsule.[17]

Despite these important caveats, anthropologists have shown how
much can be learned from close study of the ecological dynamics of
hunter-gatherer societies that survived into modern times. The sheer
diversity of ecological circumstance is itself a fact of prime importance.
Consider briefly two hunter-gatherer groups living in conditions almost
inconceivably different from the Inughuit (figure 3.1). First, take the San
of the central Kalahari. The Kalahari Desert of southern Africa is an
upland savanna with a continental climate, alternating between extreme
heat and freezing cold. The short rainy season brings about 400 mm of
rain, but the rest of the year is dry. The landscape is parched. Humans
are the only primate that can survive under these conditions, for a

simple reason: they acquire water from roots buried underground. Enduring some of the hottest summers on earth, the San people survive by using sticks to dig up moist roots.[18]

The San are a short-statured people who speak a click language. They are culturally and genetically distinct from the majority Bantu populations that surround them. The San subsist by hunting some fifty different animals, including various antelopes like eland, kudu, gemsbok, and steenbok. They rely on ten major plant foods and dozens of minor ones. Their technology is simple—spears, bows and arrows, and traps to hunt game. The San live in small, itinerant camps of about ten families. Even in the most densely occupied stretches of the Kalahari, population densities are low—around 0.055 people per square kilometer (the equivalent of eighteen people inhabiting Manhattan Island). Like the Inughuit, the San people live in simple and relatively egalitarian societies. Unlike the Inughuit, they consider the sun an evil force that shrivels life. It certainly prevents meat from being stored for long, so a successful hunt results in an immediate feast.[19]

The San are adapted to survive in the arid savanna. But like the Inughuit, they face lean times even in good years. The end of the dry season, in September and October, is grueling. "All the trees and grasses wither; every part of the Kalahari turns brown and barren." The margin for error is thin. The San lived in precarious equilibrium in a forbidding environment. Yet the very features that made the Kalahari forbidding also served to buffer the San from some of the lethal diseases that lurked in the richer landscapes all around them. Diseases like malaria were absent from an arid land inhospitable to mosquitos. Although there were reports of epidemics in the past—of smallpox, chickenpox, polio, and other diseases—none were witnessed under close observation. In the twentieth century, average life expectancy at birth for the San was estimated at 39.78 years, remarkably long for a preindustrial population. The average annual growth rate under these conditions was 1–2 percent. Like the Inughuit, the San achieved demographic growth under daunting ecological circumstances.[20]

Consider another hunter-gatherer society closely observed in modern times: the Agta of the Philippines. The Agta are short-statured people who live on an isolated peninsula of Luzon Island. The climate is tropical. The Sierra Madre mountains create a physical barrier separating the Agta from the population centers of Luzon, but the Agta have had interaction with farming societies for centuries. They are remote, but not completely isolated. Until the 1960s, the Agta subsisted by traditional hunting and gathering. But unlike the Inughuit or the San, the Agta are surrounded by food. The forest is a stocked pantry of edible plants and bushmeat—deer, wild pigs, and monkeys. The mangrove swamps and coral reefs along the coast teem with aquatic resources. The Agta are experts at using fire to drive game out of the forest and toward men hiding in ambush or women waiting on the beach below. "In the 1950s the Agta could secure as many as 20 pigs or deer in a single drive." The warm and wet tropical forest abutting the ocean offers an abundant supply of energy waiting for these hunter-gatherers.[21]

Yet the Agta were one of the unhealthiest human societies ever observed. The crude death rate (a commonly used measure that expresses a population's mortality rate in terms of the number of people per one thousand who die each year) was 42.7, astoundingly high by any standard of comparison. Life expectancy at birth, during the phase when the Agta lived entirely as hunter-gatherers, was 24.3 years. Illness and disease were constant. Why such misery?[22]

The answer lies in the infectious disease environment. Infectious diseases accounted for 50 percent of the known deaths, and the western anthropologists who studied this population suspect that virtually all of the "unknown" deaths were caused by infectious disease, so that in reality up to 86 percent of mortality may have been due to infectious disease. The Agta are pervasively infected with parasitic worms. Malaria is endemic. Gastroenteric and respiratory infections abound. And modern diseases like tuberculosis and measles have struck, too. In short, the Agta seem to suffer the entire gamut of infectious diseases that a human society can bear.[23]

Any estimate of life expectancy in hunter-gatherer societies should be taken with a grain of salt. There is no government to collect vital information. Ages are almost always guesstimates. The San of the central Kalahari, for example, only count up to three and the Inughuit only count to five, which makes it rather hard to know how old people really are. Infant deaths are underreported. And the period of observation is

TABLE 3.1. Hunter-Gatherer Life Expectancy

Society	e_0	Source
Efe	16	Migliano Vinicius, and Lahr 2007
Mbuti	16	Migliano, Vinicius, and Lahr 2007
Aeta	17	Migliano, Vinicius, and Lahr 2007
Aka	17	Migliano, Vinicius, and Lahr 2007
Ju/'hoansi	17	Harpending and Wandsnider 1982; Kelly 2013
Casiguran Agta	21	Headland 1988; Kelly 2013
Batak	24	Migliano, Vinicius, and Lahr 2007; see also Eder 1987 and Kelly 2013
San Ildefonso Agta	24	Early and Headland 1998
Asmat	25	Van Arsdale 1978; Kelly 2013
Hiwi	27	Hill, Hurtado, and Walker 2007; Kelly 2013
Dobe Ju/'hoansi	30	Lee 1979; Howell 1979; Kelly 2013
Hadza	33	Blurton Jones 2016
Ache	37	Hill and Hurtado 1996
Kade (San Kalahari)	40	Tanaka 1980; Kelly 2013

often short—measured in years or sometimes decades. Thus, snapshots are easier to obtain than long-term data sets. But the sheer diversity is a striking fact, and it is a finding that is supported by a range of observations from around the globe (see table 3.1).[24]

Life expectancy among hunter-gatherers spanned a wide spectrum. The societies with a life expectancy at birth lower than twenty years were pushing the outer limits of what any human society can sustain without going extinct. The groups with lowest life expectancies tended to be rainforest hunter-gatherers. They are naturally short-statured humans adapted to life in tropical forests; they respond to their high-mortality circumstances with fast life histories—early marriage for women and short birth intervals. Yet other hunter-gatherer groups, such as the Hadza of eastern Africa or the Ache of South America, enjoy much greater longevity, with average life expectancy reaching well into the thirties. Because the sample is skewed toward tropical and subtropical populations, it may even understate the sheer demographic diversity of hunter-gatherer societies in the past.[25]

The hunter-gatherer lifestyle has a reputation for being healthy. By necessity it entailed lots of exercise and a varied diet high in protein and fiber. Constant movement limited exposure to human and animal waste.

Even though population density varied widely among hunter-gatherers, it was radically lower than in later agricultural societies, which meant that the so-called crowd diseases—that is, directly transmissible respiratory infections causing acute disease—were not a standing threat. Hunter-gatherer societies were indeed often better nourished and had a lower infectious disease burden than agricultural societies. But that is a strange, or at least limited, standard of comparison. Next to our closest ape relatives, for instance, human hunter-gatherers are heavily diseased. In one metastudy, infectious diseases accounted for 54 percent of all chimpanzee deaths; among human hunter-gatherers, infectious diseases were responsible for 72 percent of all deaths.[26]

The challenges of measuring the impact of infectious disease among modern hunter-gatherers can hardly be overstated. As noted among the Agta in the Philippines, over 70 percent of deaths were due to unknown causes, "usually reflecting people's answers that the deceased took sick and died." Yet the anthropologists who studied them argue that infectious diseases really accounted for 85 percent of all deaths. To make matters more complicated, the effects of malnutrition and infectious disease are synergistic and often impossible to segregate. Parasitic infection by worms, for example, can rob the body of nutrients and render it vulnerable to hunger or to coinfection by other pathogens. Although precision is scurrilous, the impression that infectious diseases were responsible for most deaths is nonetheless overwhelming.[27]

In all, modern hunter-gatherers have suffered a heavy but highly variable burden of infectious disease. Can we extrapolate from present-day hunter-gatherers to Pleistocene populations? How different would the picture look if all exposure to modern diseases were removed? These are hard questions. We will never have certain or complete answers. But tree thinking can help us see that many of our infectious diseases predate the rise of farming and that, unsurprisingly, our oldest pathogens share biological features that allow them to survive in small, mobile societies. And, for reasons inseparable from their modes of transmission, these diseases are also some of the most unevenly distributed afflictions on the planet. The notorious infectious diseases that evolved in the millennia after the transition to agriculture tended to be geographically indiscriminate, because they are caused by viruses and bacteria that pass directly between humans. But many of humanity's ancient enemies rely upon, and are therefore limited by, the bugs that shuttle them from victim to victim.[28]

Pleistocene Pathogens

What kinds of infectious diseases afflicted our Pleistocene ancestors? To frame it differently, what kinds of parasites possessed the evolutionary characteristics to survive in a world where all members of *Homo sapiens* lived in small, scattered, non-sedentary groups? Fundamentally, a parasite had to (1) establish a long-lasting infection, (2) rely on nonhuman animal reservoirs, (3) find an efficient means of transmission among hosts living in low-density populations, or (4) pursue some combination of these strategies.

Among pathogens that cause long-lasting infections, helminths are prominent; unsurprisingly, worms are among our most ancient and enduring parasites. Many of our worms have speciated with us and co-evolved with us over millions of years, an inheritance from our time as tropical primates. They were certainly with us as we started to wander the globe. Whipworm, for instance, is an ancient human disease, and its family tree confirms its migration out of Africa with *Homo sapiens*. Similarly, the most important species of hookworm (*Necator americanus*) is a legacy of the Pleistocene dispersal. Other important worms, by contrast, such as roundworms, may have developed later—a product of animal domestication during the Holocene.[29]

Apart from schistosomiasis, most of our worms rely on one of the simplest routes of transmission: the ground. Whipworms and hookworms live in the intestines and rely on us to excrete their fertilized eggs, which hatch and spend their larval stage in the soil. In living memory, soil-transmitted helminths have been a serious burden on human health even in places like the U.S. South and southern Europe, although economic development, deworming campaigns, and sturdier footwear have mostly eliminated the threat. Intestinal parasites rob their victims of protein and iron, causing morbidity and malnourishment. They weaken their victims and render them far more vulnerable to other infections. Quietly and relentlessly, intestinal worms have been exploiting us from the beginning.[30]

Some viruses and bacteria also cause persistent infection or use a latent phase to prolong infection. We have already mentioned examples such as the herpes simplex viruses and papillomavirus. Other herpes viruses are also likely very old: cytomegalovirus, for example, is prevalent in human populations, but it tends to be extremely avirulent. Although varicella-zoster virus (VZV), which causes chickenpox and shingles, would seem to have the qualities necessary to persist in Pleistocene populations, molecular clock dating suggests that it is a spawn of more recent times. Similarly, bacteria that cause prolonged infection seem to have emerged only later. Tuberculosis appears to be a creature of the Holocene, and so do the agents of diseases like syphilis and yaws. The bacterium that causes typhoid fever *might* have emerged in the later Pleistocene; capable of establishing a latent infection in the gall bladder, the germ could have survived in small populations. On the whole, relatively few viruses and bacteria have actually evolved the capacity to cause chronic infection. Of those, only a small number cause severe disease, and it seems that these pathogens emerged only in our more recent past.[31]

Pleistocene hunter-gatherers would also have suffered from a variety of zoonotic diseases caused by microbes that did not rely on human hosts for their evolutionary survival. Some of these cross-species infections would have been sporadic, the human host providing an immediate dead end, as in a rabies virus infection. Others may have been capable of human-to-human transmission and caused transient epidemics. The recent Ebola epidemics are an instructive model. Fruit bats are thought to be the true reservoir host of Ebola viruses, which reached human populations via chimpanzees killed and butchered by bushmeat hunters. Ebola can transmit between humans. Even with strong public health interventions, the virus has managed to cause troubling epidemics of a severe disease that then retreats and lurks in wild animal hosts. Pleistocene hunters had extensive opportunity to come into contact with animal pathogens. Although these incidents have left no easy traces

TABLE 3.2. Major Vector-Borne Diseases

Vector	Human-adapted diseases	Zoonotic diseases
Fleas		Plague
Ticks		Lyme disease
		Rocky Mountain spotted fever
		Crimean-Congo fever
Lice	Typhus	Sleeping sickness
	Relapsing fever	Chikungunya virus
Mosquitos	Malaria	Yellow fever
	Dengue fever	
	Lymphatic filariasis	
	Rift Valley fever	
	West Nile virus	
Other hematophages	River blindness	Chagas disease
		Leishmaniasis

for us to follow, it is altogether likely that short-lived disease outbreaks have been a part of our past all along.[32]

Ultimately, the burden of disease in the Pleistocene was disproportionately due to a special class of pathogens that solved the evolutionary challenge of transmitting between hosts by adopting a daring gambit: vector-borne transportation (see table 3.2). Vector-borne transmission is a high-risk, high-reward strategy. The challenges are daunting. A microbe must learn to survive not one but two hostile immune systems and evolve all the molecular tools required to do so. Often, it must have a chemical repertoire that moves it from one part of the vector's body to another, from the guts to the needle-like proboscis. The pathogen must accept utter dependence on the vector. It must submit to all the idiosyncrasies and limitations of its transport vehicle. The diurnal rhythms, the seasonal preferences, the environmental constraints of the vector now become like properties of the pathogen itself. But the rewards are magnificent. The pathogen is a hidden payload on a vehicle aimed for the target with pinpoint accuracy. Better still, the pathogen can hope to be smuggled directly into vulnerable blood or tissue, bypassing the formidable outer barriers that protect the host. It is no wonder that some of the craftiest diseases in the world use blood-sucking bugs as their intermediaries.[33]

Among all the bugs that have become the unwitting vehicles of microbial pathogens, none can match the outsized impact of the

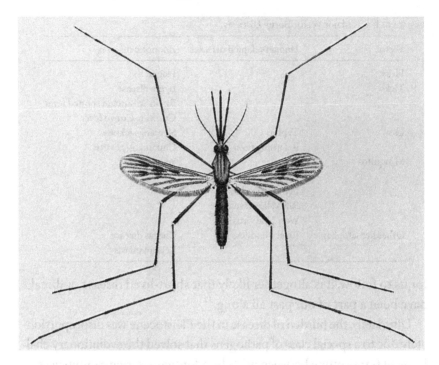

FIGURE 3.2. Mosquitos, including the genus *Anopheles*, pictured here, are the deadliest animals in the world. CDC/Dr. Darsie: Public Health Image Library #17325.

mosquito. Mosquitos are vampires with wings (see figure 3.2). In the words of the English writer and physician Havelock Ellis, "If you would see all of Nature gathered up at one point, in all her loveliness, and her skill, and her deadliness, and her sex, where would you find a more exquisite symbol than the mosquito?" Mosquitos evolved in the age of dinosaurs and have flourished ever since. There are more than 3,500 species of this remarkable creature on earth. "As a larva, the mosquito feeds and navigates in water. As an adult, she walks on water as well as land. She flies through the night air with the aid of the stars. She not only sees and smells but also senses heat from a distance. Lacking our kind of a brain, she nevertheless thinks with her skin, changing direction, and fleeing danger in response to myriad changes in her surroundings."[34]

Mosquitos hit on one truly brilliant evolutionary idea: thieving blood just when it is needed most to supercharge reproduction. Male mosquitos live relatively boring insect lives, mainly feeding from nectars and rotting fruits and vegetable matter, just another contender in nature's crowded hunt for sugars. Only females take blood meals, and only to nourish eggs. First a female mosquito mates with a male, storing his sperm. Then, at the critical moment when vertebrate blood will make the biggest difference for her genetic success, motherly mosquitos risk everything to steal it.[35]

The blood heist itself is an amazing feat. Following contrails of carbon dioxide that lead to her mark, the female mosquito lands and starts probing. Once she reaches her target, she inserts her tube-like needle, as flexible as a plumber's snake, into the skin. She pokes a dozen or more times until she hits her mark. The proboscis itself is moistened with compounds that anesthetize the victim's skin and deter coagulation. For a tense minute or two, she pulls blood into her gut, taking on several times her own weight, as much as she can carry and still fly. She has stolen a valuable liquid full of energy and free metals. Engorged, she unsteadily makes her getaway, desperate for the nearest vertical plane to land and recuperate, as her body digests the meal and keeps only what is needful for her precious eggs.[36]

Each precise mechanism in the feeding process is finely tuned by evolution and constantly under the judgmental eye of natural selection. The same is true of every step in the mosquito's four-part life cycle. Mosquito eggs float on water and are laid in batches of hundreds. Even though they will mature and hatch in only a few days, mosquito eggs are a helpless, appetizing treat, and so mosquitos are fussy about the kind of watery environments they choose. Some species can tolerate a little salinity, others cannot. Some are fine with flowing water; others need the perfect stillness of a pond. Some mosquitos are intent on laying eggs in a tree hole; others are adapted by natural selection to take advantage of the water that gathers in human-created environments like discarded rubber tires. The most deadly mosquito in the world makes devastating use of the tiny pools of rainwater gathered in the etch of a hoofprint—an evanescent but safe harbor for the hatchlings. A mosquito's life is usually short, and its entire life cycle can repeat itself in as little as a few weeks.[37]

It is easy to underestimate the power of vector-borne diseases, especially in parts of the world where bloodsucking arthropods are a nuisance on summer nights rather than an existential threat. We have sealed and screened them out, poisoned whole landscapes with insecticidal sprays, drained the pools, puddles, and swamps where they breed. Modern life as we know it rests on a giant, centuries-long project of vector control, though the victory has been partial at best. Human history has been shaped, profoundly, by vector-borne diseases and the patterns they have imprinted on our societies. Particularly in the tropics and subtropics, where the absence of winter frosts allows year-round reproduction, vector-borne diseases have been and remain a primary fact of life and death. And although most mosquitos have rather broad tastes—feeding indiscriminately on diverse mammals like diners at an all-you-can-eat buffet—a few have evolved a strong predilection for human blood—or, rather, natural selection has programmed them to detect and follow the chemical signatures of human scent. As it happens, this preference makes a handful of species woefully efficient vectors of disease in the tropics.[38]

During our ancestral hunter-gatherer past, when human societies were small, strewn lightly across the landscape, and always on the move, vector-borne diseases were of disproportionate consequence. No early disease was as important as malaria. It is "cumulatively the deadliest of the human infectious diseases." If we think in truly global terms, and in deep time, we find no other affliction that has exerted such influence on the species. It is "the mother of fevers," "the king of diseases." Malaria is an insidious force. In the words of one twentieth-century crusader against the disease, "It is a tolerant and self-perpetuating parasitism which aims to enslave rather than destroy the populations which succumb to it. The victims ordinarily come to some sort of terms with their inveterate enemy, making an annual sacrifice of their youth to obtain for the old a certain tolerable freedom from attack." Malaria is devastatingly powerful—and yet finicky, particular, even eccentric in its malignant patterns.[39]

The word *malaria* comes from Italian, meaning "evil air." Malaria is one name for what is actually a group of distinct diseases caused by related species of protozoan parasites in the genus *Plasmodium*. All of these diseases follow a similar, complex life cycle that is responsible for the characteristic sign of the disease: intense, regular waves of fevers and chills (hence, intermittent fevers in historical texts are usually identified as forms of malaria). In the words of an antimalaria cartoon distributed to U.S. soldiers during World War II (written by Dr. Seuss, no less), the disease "can make you feel like a combination of a forest fire, a January blizzard, and an old dish mop." All forms of malaria depend on mosquito vectors from a single genus, *Anopheles*. But the different plasmodium species that infect humans evolved independently. The most recently evolved of the major human malaria species, *Plasmodium falciparum*, is also the most violent. *Plasmodium vivax*, by contrast, is both the most widespread and most ancient human malaria parasite. It is without question a legacy of our hunter-gatherer past.[40]

The environmental dimensions of malaria were understood, however vaguely, centuries before the microparasite was discovered and the riddle of its reliance on the mosquito was solved. The earliest Greek, Indian, and Chinese medical records describe intermittent fevers that were sensitive to ecological conditions. The *Atharva Veda*, among the oldest texts of Sanskrit literature, classified intermittent fevers by their period—quotidian (every twenty-four hours), tertian (every forty-eight hours), or quartan (every seventy-two hours). The Indian doctors observed that the fevers came and went with the rains, in giant seasonal undulations. And they pointedly observed that some places were more cursed than others, held inexplicably in the grip of the fevers.[41]

The same ultimate causes—its complex life cycle and dependence on the anopheline vector—have resulted in both malaria's success and its exquisite sensitivity to environmental conditions (see figure 3.3). The parasite has both a sexual and an asexual reproductive stage. The sexual forms of the parasite are ingested by a mosquito taking a blood meal, and the sexual phase of reproduction unfolds inside the mosquito. In the mosquito's gut, the male and female parasites fuse to become in essence a seed factory with a tail, burrowing into the wall of the mosquito's stomach. There, each little malaria cyst incubates thousands of living seeds; once the cyst ruptures, these seeds find their way to the salivary gland of the mosquito, where they wait to be injected into the next human victim. This sexual phase can take two to three weeks. Because

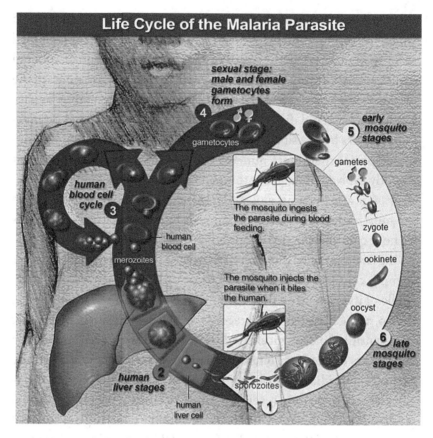

Life Cycle of the Malaria Parasite

sexual stage: male and female gametocytes form

4

gametocytes

human blood cell cycle 3

human blood cell

merozoites

early mosquito stages 5

gametes

zygote

ookinete

oocyst

6 late mosquito stages

The mosquito ingests the parasite during blood feeding.

The mosquito injects the parasite when it bites the human.

human liver stages 2

sporozoites

human liver cell

1

FIGURE 3.3. The plasmodium life cycle in malaria. National Institute of Allergy and Infectious Diseases (NIAID): Public Health Image Library #18161.

the anopheles mosquito only lives a few weeks, the window is narrow, and the timing must be almost perfect.[42]

Once in the human bloodstream, the living seeds are not yet ready to go to work. They must first travel to the liver, for a preparatory period. Crucially, *Plasmodium vivax* takes weeks to mature in the liver. Further, the vivax parasite can enter a dormant phase, "sleeping" for weeks or even several years. This drawn-out liver phase is a crucial adaptation underlying the transmission of *Plasmodium vivax*. In temperate climates, it allows vivax malaria to persist through the winter, when mosquito populations are knocked down. Malaria can suddenly break forth the following spring, like an evil tulip, reappearing in the blood just as the mosquitos buzz again. The ability of vivax malaria to relapse after months or years was also indispensable for continuous circulation among thinly scattered hunter-gatherer groups. Because there are no animal reservoirs, a continuous chain of infection must be maintained among humans, and the parasite's ability to lie low in the liver kept it from extinction in our deep past.[43]

Inside the liver, the parasite undergoes a metamorphosis into a nutrient thief specialized in the burglary of red blood cells. There are more than two hundred species of *Plasmodia* in the world, infecting a broad array of vertebrates. All of them are characterized by their focus on exploiting red blood cells. Red blood cells are the vertebrate's way of transporting oxygen to the body's tissues by binding it to an iron-rich protein molecule called hemoglobin. When malaria parasites burst forth from the liver, they are machines designed for one purpose: to find red blood cells, dock onto their surface, and sneak through. Once inside the red blood cell, they have found an unguarded cupboard of nature's most valuable nutrients. The parasite multiplies in a rapid, clocklike progression, in a predictable cycle that takes a day or two, until the cells rupture and the spawn burst forth to hunt for more red blood cells. The telltale paroxysms of malaria are timed to this cycle of hundreds of millions of cells bursting in unison, like a synchronized movement in some macabre waltz.[44]

Malaria can only be transmitted by anopheles mosquitos, and only certain varieties of those. There are nearly five hundred species of *Anopheles* around the world. Up to a hundred or so are competent vectors of human malaria, and around forty of these are truly significant vehicles of the parasite. "It seems remarkable that the world's most devastating disease is completely dependent on one sex of just some species of one genus of fly." The ecological intricacy of malaria comes from the environmental requirements of the plasmodium parasite itself, the biting habits and breeding habitats of the mosquito vector, and the elaborate timing of it all. The result is a mosaic of disease unlike anything else in nature. "Everything about malaria is so moulded by local conditions that it becomes a thousand epidemiological puzzles. Like chess, it is played with a few pieces but is capable of an infinite variety of situations."[45]

The malarial diseases wrap around the globe in overlapping zones. The falciparum zone, where the worst form of the affliction dominates, straddles the equator. A mixed zone, in the tropics and subtropics, is infected by both *vivax* and *falciparum*. And from the edges of the subtropics through the temperate latitudes, vivax malaria can lurk in the right environments. The local geography of malaria is determined by the territorial extent of particular anopheline mosquitos. For instance, long after the mosquito vector had been discovered, European experts were befuddled by the problem of "anophelism without malaria," the puzzle of regions rife with mosquitos but spared the ravages of the disease. The explanation proved to lie in the distribution of individual species. In northern Europe, the species *Anopheles atroparvus*, which prefers brackish waters, is the main vector, terrorizing coastlands and fens, whereas a few miles inland other mosquitos prevail, and malaria recedes in significance. In Southeast Asia, one *Anopheles* species might succeed another geographically as tidal plains give way to upland valleys and rising mountains. The patterns of malaria are correspondingly intricate.[46]

Today malaria is considered a tropical disease, and it continues to devastate human societies unfortunate enough to remain under its spell. It is true that falciparum malaria has always been a disease of the tropics and subtropics. And even vivax malaria is a more potent force in warmer and wetter climates. But we will misunderstand its history if we do not appreciate that its geographic reach was once much vaster than it is today. Vivax malaria was pushed back in Europe over the last several centuries. Landscape drainage reduced its scope. The mass-scale distribution of quinine, an antimalarial agent derived from the bark of the cinchona tree, helped stem malaria's tide. And then, in the early twentieth century, intentional mosquito control eradicated malaria from Europe. But throughout the warm Holocene, malaria cast a much longer shadow over the globe. The Soviet malariologist A. J. Lysenko's famous map of malaria around the world is a snapshot of the disease's former sway (figure 3.4).[47]

Too often, vivax malaria has been overshadowed by its evil cousin, *falciparum*, which draws most of the attention and nearly all of the biomedical research funding (97 percent at one count). To a certain extent that is understandable, for as we will see, *Plasmodium falciparum* is a

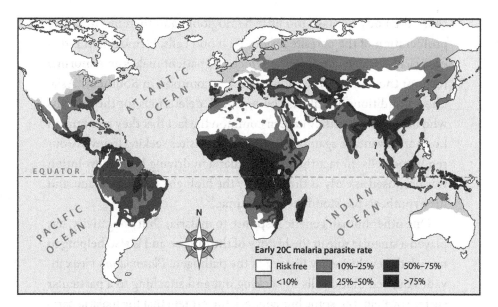

FIGURE 3.4. Distribution of malarial disease in the early twentieth century, following
Lysenko and Semashko 1968.

uniquely diabolical parasite. But to cast vivax malaria as the kinder and
gentler face of malaria is a mismeasurement of one of humanity's great
foes. Vivax malaria is not "a benign and rarely fatal disease" but, rather,
"one that can lead to severe disease and death." It exacts a heavy toll on
societies where it becomes established. It robs families of their children
and migrants of their dreams. When it does not kill, it weakens, and
leaves its victims for other germs to finish off. Those it does not kill it
stunts, impairing growth and development, including cognitive development. In short, the parasite affects entire societies when they fall into
its grip.[48]

The long, antagonistic history of humanity's relationship with malaria is written all over our genes. An unusual number of congenital
blood disorders persist in the human genome because they confer some
advantage against malaria parasites. The most extraordinary of these is
the sickle-cell trait, which evolved in response to falciparum malaria. It
is far from unique, however. Glucose-6-phosphate dehydrogenase deficiency is a genetic condition that causes chronic anemia but also buffers
against malaria. Beta thalassemia is a group of blood disorders that

cause the body to make too little hemoglobin and thereby choke the proliferation of the parasite inside red blood cells. Hemoglobin E disease is a heritable condition in which the patient makes an abnormal form of the hemoglobin molecule. It is common in Southeast Asia. These conditions are, all else being equal, deleterious for the humans who bear them. But they have in common the fact that they give human hosts an advantage against plasmodium parasites seeking to invade our red blood cells. In fact the role of malaria in driving human evolution was proposed as early as the 1940s by the biologist J. B. S. Haldane, and his hypothesis has stood the test of time.[49]

One other human genetic response to malaria, Duffy negativity, has played a singular role in the history of the disease and is also helping to unlock the evolutionary history of the pathogen. *Plasmodium vivax* invades our red blood cells by seeking out and attaching to a particular surface protein. But some humans lack the protein that the malaria parasite uses to grab hold and pull itself inside. The attempted invasion is stymied. This genetic trait is highly advantageous and, unlike in the aforementioned blood disorders, there are no hidden costs to pay.[50]

The absence of the crucial receptor protein is known as Duffy negativity. This genetic trait is the product of natural selection. At some point in the past, a child was born with a gene that blocked the synthesis of the Duffy protein. The chemical receptors of *P. vivax* scratching to get into his or her red blood cells were thwarted. As this child's band roved in search of food, mosquitos awaited in pools and puddles. Other children were bitten and fell sick, suffering the violent cycle of fevers and chills. Malaria robbed their blood of nutrients. Even if they survived, anemia stunted their development. Many of them were infected repeatedly, year after year. Their bodies bore the trauma permanently. But the child without the receptor was untouched. He or she grew up healthy and strong and had many children, who also carried the lucky gene.[51]

The global distribution of Duffy negativity is an artefact of human evolutionary history. But this example of natural selection at work seems to have occurred only in the later Pleistocene. In most of western and central Africa, the trait is effectively universal. People of European,

Asian, and indigenous American descent, by contrast, have the receptor and are susceptible to vivax malaria. The reason for this stark geographic contrast in the human genome is that Duffy negativity arose in our human homeland, Africa, but only *after* groups of ancestral humans had successfully migrated out of Africa and founded new populations around the globe. The evolution of resistance in the form of Duffy negativity is among the starkest examples of recent positive selection— Darwinism at work—across human populations.[52]

Vivax malaria is relatively rare (though far from absent) across most of Africa today, but the near universality of Duffy negativity in large parts of the continent suggests that the disease had a deep significance in its history. For a long time, though, the closest known relatives of *P. vivax* were malaria parasites that infected primates in South Asia, and it was believed that the vivax parasite must have evolved from a parasite whose host was an Asian monkey. However, in recent years, a previously unknown species of the malaria parasite, more closely related to *P. vivax*, has been discovered among the great apes of central Africa. This finding (which is a good example of how broader sampling of animal pathogens can reshuffle the inferences to be drawn from family trees) coheres with the evidence of the human genomes, and suggests that Africa is indeed the evolutionary cradle of *P. vivax*.[53]

Molecular clock estimates place the origins of *P. vivax* between 70,000 and 250,000 years ago. As humans dispersed out of Africa in the late Pleistocene, they carried malaria with them in their blood. Across South Asia and the tropical Pacific, the parasite found a welcoming climate and suitable anopheles vectors. It was in short order the most pervasive vector-borne disease specialized in humans in the Old World. Unfortunately, the migrants who carried malaria out of Africa left just too early to take advantage of the Duffy negative gene, which spread across Africa and reached fixation by about forty-two thousand years ago. As *P. vivax* lost ground in its land of origin, it flourished in human blood virtually everywhere else where the climate was warm enough to sustain it. But in a fateful turn of good luck, the parasite failed to make the passage across Beringia. Although the New World is home to plenty of anopheles mosquitos that are competent malaria vectors, the

Americas were free of the disease until it was exported across the Atlantic following the voyages of Columbus.[54]

Vivax malaria was born as a disease of hunter-gatherers. The use of a flying, biting bug as intermediary meant that this germ did not have to wait for the rise of farming to exploit us in extraordinary ways. Further, the latency period of *P. vivax* in the liver and its ability to relapse after years of dormancy adapted the parasite to circulate in low-density populations. By its nature, though, this disease is geographically discriminatory, disproportionately afflicting those in warm and wet climes. The evolutionary strategy that has supported its career as one of the most effective human pathogens has also been one of its chief ecological constraints.

Malaria is a particularly important infectious disease that adapted to humans in the Pleistocene, but it is far from alone. We should consider a handful of other vector-borne scourges already infecting humans in our hunter-gatherer past.

Beyond Malaria

In 1877 in Amoy (Xiamen), China, Patrick Manson started counting the tiny parasites in the blood of patients suffering from the disease that was then known as elephantiasis. Manson was born about as far away from China as possible, in the north of Scotland. After earning his medical degree at Aberdeen, he looked for adventure and spent the better part of his career in the service of the Chinese Imperial Maritime Customs. Amoy had become a treaty port in the aftermath of the First Opium War (1839–42). Manson was twenty-seven when he moved to what he called a "superlatively dirty" entrepôt on the southeastern shores of China. Clinical practice in the local Baptist missionary hospital gave Manson free reign to explore an array of tropical diseases. Manson himself cut an imperial figure, with the look of "a British hunting squire" (figure 3.5). He was destined to become the "father of tropical medicine."[55]

All of that lay in the future, though, when the unknown, thirty-three-year-old Manson started counting parasites. The worm that causes elephantiasis, more properly called lymphatic filariasis (the name means

FIGURE 3.5. Sir Patrick Manson. Etching by A. W. Turnbull. Wellcome
Collection (CC BY 4.0).

"disease caused by the thread-like worm that lives in the human lymphatic system"), had been discovered in the years before Manson's
research. Manson made two intriguing observations under the microscope. First, the same patient's blood might be at one time saturated with
the microparasites and at other times seemingly clear of infection. Second, there were simply too many of them in the bloodstream to imagine
that they could then mature into the adult phase of the worm inside the

human. It was physically inconceivable. Some phase of the life cycle, where these embryos were "nursed," was missing. Manson developed a hunch. "As the embryo parasite lives in the blood it is likely that the first step in its development and towards freedom will be given it by something that abstracts the blood. Thus, then, the privilege will be confined to a very limited number of animals—the blood-suckers."[56]

Only in retrospect does the logic seem obvious, that germs could be transmitted by insect vectors. Koch had just announced his discovery of the tuberculosis bacterium (in 1882), and the revelation of vector-borne transmission was a crucial extension of nascent germ theory. Manson's hunch was one of the greatest in the history of medicine, and he sought to test his hypothesis. Manson's Chinese gardener, Hin-Lo, suffered from lymphatic filariasis; Manson had no qualms about asking him to serve as an experimental subject. Manson put Hin-Lo in a shed overnight, inside a room with an open screen. After Hin-Lo was covered with mosquitos, the screen was closed. They fed on his blood and flew to the safety of a wall to digest their meal. Here another servant captured the engorged mosquitos and trapped them in glass jars. Manson dissected these mosquitos in the coming days. His hunch was confirmed when he not only found them teeming with lively microfilariae but also observed the maturation of the parasite into its larval form. Manson did not connect all the dots immediately (for a time he imagined that the mosquito carried the germ to water, whence humans ingested the parasite), but the mosquito as an intermediary of a major human disease was experimentally confirmed.[57]

There are still more than forty million cases of lymphatic filariasis today, despite major success in pushing back the disease over the course of the last generation. After malaria, it is the most prevalent vector-borne disease on the planet. Yet it seems fair to say that lymphatic filariasis is virtually invisible in western consciousness. There is still not a single book dedicated to its history. A long-lived, languorous worm that causes brutal disfigurement in its victims but is limited to the tropics, the source of lymphatic filariasis is almost the precise opposite of the glamorous germs that have caused explosive plagues in the developed world. Lymphatic filariasis is classified as a neglected tropical disease because of the imbalance between its global importance and the limited biomedical attention it receives. It has been just as neglected by students of history and global society. Lymphatic filariasis may be the most neglected of the neglected diseases.[58]

Lymphatic filariasis is caused by a nematode, a pale, filament-like worm. There are actually three species of nematode that cause lymphatic filariasis, but one of them, *Wuchereria bancrofti*, is responsible for over 90 percent of human cases. The parasite is transmitted by an unusually wide range of mosquitos across five genera (*Anopheles*, *Aedes*, *Culex*, *Mansonia*, and *Ochlerotatus*). Its distribution is limited by the presence of mosquitos but also by the effects of climate on the parasite's reproductive cycle, which is squelched below 71°F. The mosquito ingests a microfilaria, a miniature version of the worm that is really an embryo inside a shell. It takes the worm ten to twelve days inside the mosquito to lose the shell and grow into a larva. The larvae saturate the mosquito's saliva and hope to be injected into warm, human blood. Then the nematode begins one of the most extraordinary parasitic careers known to nature.[59]

The worm that causes lymphatic filariasis makes its home the human lymphatic system, our slow-moving vascular network of waste disposal. The lymphatic system is heavily patrolled by our immune cells, but this brash worm is undeterred. The larvae migrate through the lymphatic vessels to a lymph node, generally in the lower half of the body. Here they mature into adults, over the course of a year, and they might live in our lymphatic vessels for a decade. They grow to a length of two to four inches, they mate, and the female spawns thousands of microfilariae, which spread to the bloodstream. Manson had noted the curious fact that sometimes the blood of a patient swarmed with miniworms, whereas other times it seemed clear. In fact the microfilariae keep a daily schedule. During the day they swim to our deep veins. At night they come out, moving into our peripheral bloodstreams. Because many mosquitos generally start to bite around dusk, this is a savvy move. Near the skin, the worm eggs have a better chance of being taken up by a mosquito's slurping proboscis.[60]

The most visible symptom of lymphatic filariasis is the disfiguring swelling that makes a human limb look and feel like an elephant's leg.

The worm also has a tendency to cause gross enlargement of the scrotum of male victims, burdening sufferers with a medicine-ball-like appendage hanging between the legs. A parasitic worm capable of persisting for a decade can cause a whole range of complications for human health. The parasite more often robs than kills. It debilitates, disfigures, and disables. The stigma of the disease takes a psychological toll. But it is physically dangerous, too, particularly when the worm dies. The hyperinflammatory response, when the dead worms lose their disguise and our body wages full-on war against the intruders, is itself harmful. And secondary bacterial infections from the dead worms are threatening as well.[61]

The symptoms of lymphatic filariasis are occasionally described in ancient medical texts, especially in Asia. (In the Greco-Roman medical tradition, elephantiasis refers to leprosy, and filariasis is notably absent.) But the historical record for lymphatic filariasis becomes richer when Europeans started traversing the Indian and Pacific Oceans. Tomé Pires was a Portuguese drug-maker sent to South Asia from 1512 to 1515, in the first days of European expansion. He was struck by the prevalence of lymphatic filariasis in southwest India. "Many people in Malabar, Nayars as well as Brahmans and their wives—in fact about a quarter or a fifth of the total population, including the people of the lowest castes—have very large legs, swollen to a great size; and they die of this, and it is an ugly thing to see. They say that this is due to the water through which they go, because the country is marshy." Over the centuries, there is an almost unbroken line of testimony for the disease from merchants, soldiers, and medical attendants.[62]

The written evidence for lymphatic filariasis only takes us back so far, but the worm's genome holds clues to its evolutionary history. Its family tree helps to ground the biography of the pathogen in time and space. Lymphatic filariasis emerged in Southeast Asia, a little over fifty thousand years ago. From there it was carried by bands of humans dispersing across the Pacific. It also radiated across South Asia. As some point, it reached Africa, and from there was carried to the New World during the age of the slave trade.[63]

Lymphatic filariasis is therefore another lasting legacy of the hunter-gatherer past. It is a truly human disease in that its evolution was

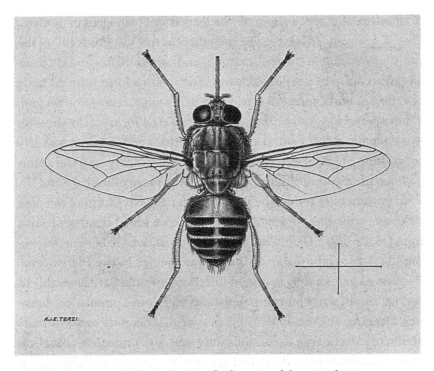

FIGURE 3.6. *Glossina*, the tsetse fly, the vector of sleeping sickness.
Wellcome Collection (CC BY 4.0).

dependent on the wandering ways of our species. The emergence of the parasite virtually coincided with the arrival of *Homo sapiens* in Southeast Asia. Like vivax malaria, this vector-borne disease, capable of establishing chronic infection, was able to sustain itself even among bands of hunter-gatherers. In short, lymphatic filariasis is another tropical disease of Pleistocene origins.

Three other vector-borne diseases can be described more briefly, but they illustrate evolutionary variations. Whereas malaria and lymphatic filariasis are both human diseases, in that we are their parasites' only host, many vector-borne diseases are relative generalists, able to infect a wide variety of animals. African sleeping sickness is a familiar example. The disease is caused by the protozoan *Trypanosoma brucei*, a slender, single-celled parasite with a tail it uses to swim in the blood. The tsetse fly is its vector (see figure 3.6). *Trypanosoma brucei* is actually a complex of closely related species, two of which are major pathogens of humans. First, *T. brucei rhodesiense* can be thought of as the "savanna form" of the parasite; it is endemic across southern and eastern Africa and it causes an acute course of sleeping sickness. The savanna form is broad in its selection of hosts, infecting a wide range of animal reservoirs. Second, *T. brucei gambiense* can be thought of as the "river form" of the parasite; it is endemic across central and western Africa and it causes a slowly progressing course of infection. Humans are the primary reservoir of this pathogen, but even the river form can infect a range of animal hosts.[64]

In evolutionary terms, the human-preferring river form of sleeping sickness (*gambiense*) is younger than the more broad-ranging savanna form (*rhodesiense*). *Gambiense* might have specialized in humans following the demographic expansion of our species in the Pleistocene. Because it causes a long course of infection, it would have been able to survive among early human populations with lower population densities. Sleeping sickness is a vicious disease that takes its name from its ability to infect nerve tissue and cause severe neurological complications. It has often been described as one of the quintessentially ancient diseases of humans that the first migrants out of Africa left behind. Indeed, the parasite is dependent on its vector and therefore confined to the tsetse fly belt across sub-Saharan Africa (see figure 3.7).[65]

Sleeping sickness may have exerted its greatest influence on human history through its effects on animal health. *Nagana* (an Anglicized form of a Zulu word) is the name of the animal form of the disease. Nagana has helped to preserve Africa's rich diversity of large game because the disease is so deadly to domesticated species. The giant tsetse belt stretching from one end of the continent to the other made it harder for humans to replace native biodiversity with domesticated livestock. African societies developed a range of ingenious responses to elude the damage of nagana, including bush clearance and transhumance strategies that moved livestock while dodging tsetse infested areas. This fragile "ecological equilibrium with the wildlife ecosystems and their associated diseases" was destroyed in the context of modern imperialism, when brute programs of development imposed by European powers exacerbated the burden of sleeping sickness for humans

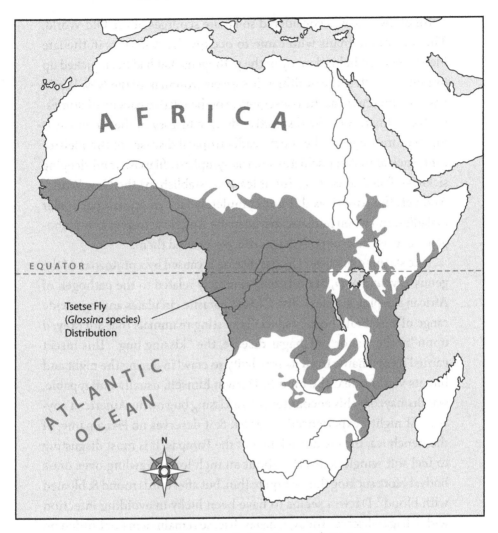

FIGURE 3.7. Map of tsetse fly (*Glossina* species) distribution.

and animals alike. Nagana confounded the imperialists; one British administrator bemoaned it as the "greatest curse which nature has laid" on Africa. The deep and enduring effects of the tsetse fly on African development have been rigorously explored by modern economic historians, who have argued that the presence of this single combination of vector and parasite contributed immensely to the low population density that is a major theme of African history.[66]

All of the diseases considered so far are scourges of the Old World. The intrepid humans who came to occupy the Americas in the late Pleistocene left behind many of the pathogens that had been picked up by humans. Often, the healthier disease environment of the New World has been presented as the consequence of the relative paucity of domesticated animals. But the distinctive disease history of the Americas is much more ancient. The most deadly tropical diseases of the Pleistocene, such as malaria, schistosomiasis, lymphatic filariasis, and sleeping sickness, failed to cross to (or at least to establish in) the New World. And yet, the Americas did not completely lack their own particular maladies, and when humans arrived in the American tropics new pathogens such as the agent of Chagas disease awaited them.

Like sleeping sickness, Chagas disease is caused by a protozoan of the genus *Trypanosoma*, but it is only remotely related to the pathogen of African sleeping sickness. The Chagas parasite circulates among a wide range of vertebrate hosts, especially nesting mammals that are preyed upon by the vector of Chagas disease, the "kissing bug." This insect earned its nickname from its proclivity to crawl in during the night and bite its victims near the mouth. Darwin himself, usually unflappable, was dismayed by his encounter with a kissing bug on his American voyage. "At night I experienced an attack & it deserves no less a name, of the Benchuca, the great black bug of the Pampas. It is most disgusting to feel soft wingless insects, about an inch long, crawling over one's body; before sucking they are quite thin, but afterwards round & bloated with blood." Darwin seems to have been lucky in avoiding infection with Chagas disease. Today, Chagas disease remains a major burden on human health, infecting up to ten million people in the Americas.[67]

Finally, the protozoa of the genus *Leishmania* are also ancient vector-borne parasites, some of which were present in the New World as soon as humans arrived. More than twenty different species of *Leishmania* can infect humans and cause a range of diseases, from skin ulcers (cutaneous leishmaniasis) to the dangerous acute infection known as *kala-azar* or black fever (visceral leishmaniasis). Humans are not the main reservoir of these parasites, which can infect a broad range of rodents, canids, bats, and other mammals. *Leishmania* parasites are transmitted by two different groups of sand flies: an Old World variety and a New

World type. Sand flies are small, blood-sucking insects that thrive in hot climates and can withstand semiarid conditions. Leishmaniasis remains an important disease in the tropics and subtropics, and, given its many animal reservoirs, it would have confronted early humans even as they wandered out of Africa and occupied the tropics and subtropics in both hemispheres.[68]

Disease and Pleistocene Demography

By the end of the Pleistocene, there were maybe ten million humans alive on earth. By comparison, there have been at a given time no more than perhaps a million to two million chimpanzees; in any case, the total is nowhere near ten million. What accounts for our demographic success? The ultimate answer is relatively straightforward: our promethean intelligence. The control of fire, and our big brains, let humans extract energy from an astonishing variety of ecological niches. We are the only cosmopolitan ape; even in the Pleistocene we were living on six continents. Human dispersal was an energy bonanza underwritten by human ingenuity and ecological adaptability. Fed by this energy, human numbers experienced staggering growth.[69]

At the same time, we should not be blinded by our demographic success and fail to ask why there were ten million humans, not more or less. To ask how humans became the prolific primate is only to address half the question. In fact, trying to answer why there were *only* ten million humans by 10,000 BC might be the more difficult task.

Hunter-gatherer societies observed in modern times exhibited annual growth rates of 1–2 percent, even in some of the most forbidding environments on the planet. Among the Inughuit, the San of the central Kalahari, and the Agta, births exceeded deaths. The pattern would probably be accentuated if we had better representation from hunter-gatherers in the temperate latitudes where agricultural societies came to dominate. These rates of growth would not have been sustainable in the long run—or for very long at all. At such rates of growth, humans should have overrun the planet before the end of the Pleistocene. If there were only ten thousand humans in 75,000 BC, at a sustained 1 percent rate of growth, there would have been 8^{284} humans by 10,000 BC. Despite the image of hunter-gatherer populations living in harmony and balance with nature, their vital rates actually seem tuned to produce runaway human population growth.

Traditionally, historical demographers smooth over the problem by claiming that human societies experienced virtually zero growth in the long run. Although such a mathematical sleight of hand balances the books, it leaves unexplained the discrepancy between observed rates of short-term growth among hunter-gatherer societies and the reality of near zero growth in the long run. As the most perceptive scholars of hunter-gatherer demography have noted, the problem is that by observing extremely short snapshots of hunter-gatherer population history (determined by the funding and research agendas of anthropologists), we are underestimating the dynamism of hunter-gatherer demography.[70]

We are a boom and bust species, and we have been from the beginning. During the Pleistocene, when *Homo sapiens* migrated to new environments, the abundance of food and extremely low population density would have fueled higher rates of reproduction and lower rates of death. As populations reached the carrying capacities of their new environments, fertility would have slowed in response. Moreover, death rates would have responded to changing conditions and controlled demographic oscillations.[71]

As Malthus realized, human numbers are constrained by the food supply. When populations grow, pressure on the food supply reduces per capita energy availability. The megafaunal extinctions that have followed human expansion are an example of the carnage that results from humanity's demographic exuberance and demands for energy. The consequence of such pressure might be outright starvation. But more often, food shortages increase mortality through secondary mechanisms, like violence: scarcity is the mother of conflict. War and social disorder are the sequelae of hunger and poverty. In hunter-gatherer societies, territorial conflict has been one outcome of greater competition for limited food sources.[72]

Food, though, is not the only factor that controls population. Disease, too, plays a powerful role in human demography. It conspires with food shortage to weaken and kill humans: starvation and infectious disease are synergistic. Disease is also density-dependent because population growth facilitates transmission between hosts. Germs spread more easily where there is more contact between individuals. New diseases can also arise more frequently when there is more contact with zoonotic pathogens; more virulent pathogens can be sustained by larger populations. Thus, populations may increase for a time, but then these movements can be stalled or reversed by infectious disease.[73]

As human bands bravely dispersed over the globe, their numbers were controlled by these forces. New energy horizons fueled expansion, as more food was converted to more people. Humans filled virgin lands. But energy availability and parasites checked demographic expansion. As human numbers increased, pressure on the food supply slowed or even reversed our growth. In addition, our demographic success was probably interrupted by epidemic waves; even if these were smaller than what lay in store for the future, they were nonetheless consequential for hunter-gatherer population dynamics. In the words of Nicholas Blurton Jones, an anthropologist who has studied the demography of the Hadza and called attention to the paradoxes of hunter-gatherer demography, "perhaps we have been wrong about epidemics in a world of hunters."[74]

Humanity's Pleistocene expansion was not a steady advance toward ten million. Based on comparisons with hunter-gatherers observed in modern times, we have just as much reason to believe that our early population history was characterized by a sawtooth pattern of delirious growth followed by abrupt crashes, from which we started the climb again. The reason there were not billions of humans in the Pleistocene is because we did not have the technology to harvest enough energy to feed ourselves, especially against the backdrop of climate fluctuations, and because our parasites would have feasted on us first. Humans clawed their way across the planet; fueled by the energy rush of taking over naïve ecosystems, our numbers soared. But scarcity and disease struck back, cutting down our ancestors without pity. Short-term observations of hunter-gatherer societies give the false impression of stability. In reality, the experience of humanity in the Pleistocene was probably already a premonition of our ecologically volatile future.

Pleistocene Diversity

The Pleistocene dispersal set in motion different histories of infectious disease. It is a stark fact that the most oppressive diseases of our hunter-gatherer past were also geographically uneven. At the start of the Holocene, human groups already faced different pressures and different opportunities. As we will see in the next chapter, human ingenuity was able to overcome the challenge of energy scarcity far more readily than the problem of infectious disease. In other words, with the rise of agriculture, it was possible for human societies to expand food production, even as we remained mostly helpless against our invisible enemies. And the turn to farming would conjure a whole new cast of human pathogens—more explosive and less geographically constrained than anything our ancestors had faced so far.[75]

PART II

Farms

4

Dung and Death

Diseases That Count

In 1788, a London doctor named William Black published a broadside on the medical establishment. His book had a grandiloquent title, worthy of his ambition: *A Comparative View of the Mortality of the Human Species at All Ages; and of the Diseases and Casualties by which They Are Destroyed or Annoyed.* Black may have been the first person ever to make a serious attempt to understand how every person on the planet would die. And though he is long since forgotten, a footnote even in the history of medicine, the thrust of his critique is as powerful now as it was in the late eighteenth century: the attention devoted to various diseases is rarely in proportion to their actual significance.[1]

Black based his arguments on the London Bills of Mortality—one of the oldest running series of data on mortality by cause. It confirmed what his experience as a doctor had taught him. Unglamorous fevers and humble diarrheas were so ordinary and pervasive as to be uninteresting, yet they caused the greatest burden of suffering. These afflictions fell disproportionately on the young. Walter Harris, a doctor writing a few generations before Black, had published a book on the acute diseases of infants. He knew it would be an uphill battle to convince his readership that the subject was interesting. "Children, and especially sick Infants offer nothing for a clear Diagnostick, but what we can

collect from their moaning Complaints, & their uncertain Idiom of fro-
wardness; wherefore, very many Physicians of the best Vogue, have
often declared to my self, what unwilling Visits they made to Sick, but
especially New born Children; hoping little from these Notices for the
unridling of their Maladies."[2]

I will admit my own incredulity, many years ago, when I asked a medically trained historian what would have been the greatest killer in the
Roman Empire and received his answer: diarrhea. It seemed incongru-
ous that one of history's most powerful civilizations was helpless against
loose stool. Of course, this suggestion was only an informed guess. We
have no Bills of Mortality from the ancient world. But, once we are alert
to it, the weight of this burden feels palpable. Consider the famous Stoic
emperor, Marcus Aurelius. He and his wife Faustina had fourteen
children, only two of whom certainly survived their parents. Because we
happen to have some of the emperor's letters, we occasionally glimpse
the fevers and diarrheas that laid low so many of their offspring. Their
case was extreme, but not completely out of the ordinary.[3]

Black was ahead of his time. His noble (if crude) attempt to count
causes of death worldwide came to fruition in the late twentieth century.
In the early 1990s, the World Bank commissioned a review and assessment of priorities for global public health investments. This work gave
rise to an effort to assemble comprehensive estimates of morbidity and
mortality by cause for the entire planet, a project that became known
as the *Global Burden of Disease*. In 1990, diarrheal diseases were the
second leading source of disease burden (closely behind only lower
respiratory infections) in developing regions. Respiratory infections
and diarrheal diseases were far and away the two largest causes of death
among children. Even now, after three decades of progress, diarrheal
diseases account for one of every ten child deaths. Some germs are
good at stoking fear and generating headlines. Meanwhile, diarrheal
infections take their toll without much fanfare. Black's basic insight
remains as true as ever.[4]

In wealthy societies today, we are left to endure the unpleasant remnant of what we belittlingly call "stomach bugs." For much of the world,
and much of our past, diarrheal disease has been far more than a

temporary indisposition. Although nature is full of parasites that exploit animal intestines, humans have accumulated a truly extraordinary number of pathogens that invade our bodies along with the food and water we consume. Why do human beings suffer so much mayhem in the gastrointestinal tract? The answer has everything to do with the history of how our species feeds itself—with the transition from hunting and gathering to farming, and all the lifestyle, environmental, and evolutionary changes that this transition entailed.

The rise of farming in the early Holocene was first and foremost an energy revolution, as humans learned to make rather than just take their food from the environment. More than that, the rise of farming was a critical moment in the history of the planet. Humans are uniquely crafty ecosystem engineers, pitilessly altering biodiversity for our narrow benefit. The human impact on nature was already evident in the Pleistocene, especially in its increasingly dynamic last phases. But the domestication of plants and animals was a turning point, when humans started to influence the evolutionary history of a vastly wider range of creatures, great and small. In driving the evolution of a select number of preferred plants and animals through domestication, we also created new environments. This created unintentional but cascading evolutionary impacts on a range of other creatures, including microbial ones, not least of all those that thrived in our guts.[5]

This chapter is devoted to an indelicate subject that the historian James Webb has called humanity's "oldest ecological problem": diseases that spread via fecal matter. It is a chapter that is usually missing in big histories of infectious disease. In the traditional story, the rise of farming was the crux of a great epidemiological transition in which our lightly diseased hunting and gathering ancestors invented agriculture and immediately paid a price in the form of new diseases contracted from their farmyard animals. We have already emphasized that this story underrates the legacy of the Pleistocene in the formation of a distinctly human disease pool. And now we will add further texture to the story by trying not to pass in too much haste from the invention of agriculture to the rise of cities and the "crowd diseases" that followed. In between lies a story about humanity's search for food and the byproducts of our new, stationary ways of extracting energy from domesticated plants and animals.[6]

Long before there were cities, there were sedentary settlements—villages and small towns—where humans lived permanently and in close proximity to domesticated animals. This new lifestyle created a new ecology, unique in all of nature, and resulted in the fundamental problem of living amid fecal waste. New diseases traveling the fecal-oral route took advantage of these evolutionary opportunities. Because intestinal pathogens could thrive (almost) anywhere that humans built durable settlements, the diseases they cause have been more geographically indiscriminate, causing sickness and death at all latitudes. These diseases also proved more explosive than our Pleistocene pathogens, as our rumbling insides turned into roaring epidemics. The next chapter turns to cities and the diseases of the human respiratory tract, but here is an effort to give excrement its due in the story of human health.

Neolithic Evolutions

The Pleistocene epoch was cold and unstable, characterized by dramatic swings of climate change. Slight changes in the Earth's orbit, and cycles in the tilt and spin of the Earth around its axis, altered the amount and distribution of solar energy reaching our planet. These complex and overlapping cycles created a seesaw of glaciation and deglaciation that radically affected life on the ground for hunter-gatherers. Human populations adapted in response to environmental stimulus, dispersing across the planet, advancing and sometimes retreating, all the while seeking food from wild plants, animals, and fungi.

The Last Glacial Maximum was a brutally severe Ice Age that peaked around 24,500 BCE and then relented, gradually, for ten thousand years. Human populations swelled. From around 14,000 BCE the great melt accelerated. Population growth was brisk but then interrupted by a reversal known as the Younger Dryas. For more than a millennium, starting around 10,800 BCE, the earth's climate plunged back into Ice Age conditions. Swaths of the temperate latitudes were frosted over and rendered uninhabitable. In other regions, the resilience of human societies in the face of this challenge is evident. One particular culture, known as the later Natufian, thrived in the Near East during the Younger Dryas. The Natufians lived in permanent or quasi-permanent settlements along the edges of grasslands and forested steppes in the Levant. They hunted the great herds of gazelle that passed through in summer and cultivated the wild grasses of the upper Euphrates valleys. When confronted with a changing climate, they experimented with control and storage of food production. The Natufians edged close to the brink of the energy breakthroughs that would give rise to full-blown farming societies, and they were certainly not alone.[7]

Around 9600 BCE, the great defrosting known as the Holocene epoch was launched. The warm and stable Holocene climate epoch is our familiar home. Human populations expanded, and, in turn, energy extraction intensified. Some societies must have hit Malthusian walls; populations grew until food ran short. Other societies did what the economic historian Ester Boserup described as intensification: they innovated and adapted. Agriculture was born in the interplay of population growth, pressure on resources, and human ingenuity.[8]

If fire was the technology that made us human and fueled our colonization of the planet, then farming was the technology that kick-started the last 5 percent of our history as a species and set us on the path to accelerating social development. The archaeologist V. Gordon Childe famously called the origins of agriculture the Neolithic Revolution. The Neolithic Revolution is one of those historical ideas that has proven indestructible, even though a lot more is known now than when Childe coined the term. The rise of agriculture happened independently at least a dozen times, so it should be *revolutions*, plural (see figure 4.1). And it was a "revolution" that unraveled across a few millennia, in stages, so it was more evolutionary than revolutionary. Regardless, the domestication of plants and animals was an energy breakthrough.[9]

Agriculture is a way of harnessing the photosynthesis of digestible plants to convert sunlight into people. Because grains like wheat, rice, and maize (corn) have fed, and continue to feed, most of the world's population, we might think of humans as clever primates who figured out how to capture solar energy from a few species of grass with big

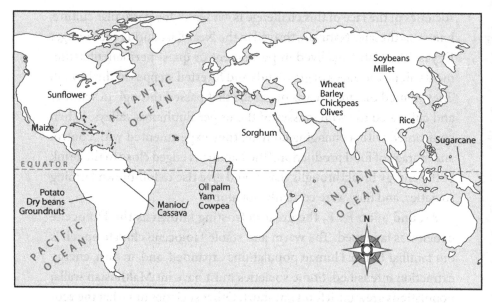

FIGURE 4.1. The origins of domestication (see Denham et al. 2020, Kantar et al. 2017, and text for sources).

seeds. At the dawn of the Holocene epoch, when agriculture started to spread, there were something like ten million humans—awfully successful for a primate, but hardly a premonition of what lay over the horizon. Today, there are almost eight billion of us, virtually all fed by farmers.[10]

Domestication is the complex process of genetic manipulation that brings a wild species under human control. It was not discovered in a single "eureka" moment of inspiration. Rather, domestication arose gradually and unintentionally, as an extension of foraging practices rather than a radical break from them. Our ancestors, without understanding the genetic mechanisms, selected traits like bigger seeds, loss of seed shattering, and synchronized ripening in grains; and greater docility in animals. Storage, food processing, and even, in some cases, sedentism preceded farming. Wild grains were collected and consumed for millennia prior to domestication. Because humans can easily digest seeds but not leaves, bark, stalks, and so on, it is in our interest to convert entire landscapes over to crops that capture energy in forms we can metabolize efficiently. Grasses have proven the most reliable way of turning sunlight into something we can eat. And because domesticated animals can often digest plant byproducts that we cannot, animal husbandry and farming have gone hand in hand (at least in the Old World).[11]

The first center of plant domestication was in the Near East, probably in the upper reaches of the Euphrates River valley (see table 4.1). By 9000 BC wheat had been domesticated, and rye and barley were not far behind. In South America, beans (8000 BC), squash (8000 BC), quinoa (6000 BC), maize (7000 BC), and potatoes (6000 BC) were brought under human control. In China, rice was domesticated before 6000 BC, and possibly much earlier. Rice was domesticated again in South Asia (6000 BC). In Africa, sorghum was domesticated very early (arguably as early as 8000 BC), and pearl millet (2500 BC) was also a local domesticate.[12]

The domestication of animals was also a process of genetic engineering that brought select species under human control (see table 4.2). Dogs were domesticated in the Pleistocene, complementing our hunting lifestyles. New forms of agricultural and pastoral subsistence emerged in the Holocene, accompanied by the familiar suite of major animal domesticates. Sheep and goats led the way, with cows and pigs close behind. "The foremost prerequisite of successful domestication must have been a reduced fear of humans, enabling reproduction in conditions that would normally elicit strong stress reactions (for example, confinement, human proximity, and crowding)." Once tamed, domesticated animal populations were shaped via selection by farmers and herders for other desired traits, such as body size. It was a fateful quirk of global biogeography that the Old World was more abundantly supplied with animals that were potentially tamed and economically valued. In the Americas, only two birds (the turkey and a kind of duck), the guinea pig, the alpaca, and the llama were brought under human control.[13]

The expansion of food production enabled by the domestication of plants and animals was the prerequisite to the rise of civilization, if we define that term to mean complex societies with specialization, states, cities, armies, and information technologies like writing. Scholars like Childe were confident that agriculture marked a crucial step in the march of civilization—no farming, no cities, no Shakespeare, no Newton, and so on. Today, scholars are probably more inclined to agree with the

TABLE 4.1. Timing and Geography of Major Plant Domestications

Crop	Years before present	Region	Cultivated hectares (millions, 2012)	References
Wheat	10,000	Fertile Crescent	217	Tanno and Willcox 2006; Brown et al. 2009
Maize	7,000	Mexico	177	Piperno and Flannery 2001; Cruz-Cárdenas et al. 2019
Rice	9,000	China	163	Choi et al. 2017; Li et al. 2006
Soybeans	7,500	China	107	Li et al. 2013; Sedivy et al. 2017
Barley	8,500	Fertile Crescent	49	Morrell and Clegg 2007
Sorghum	10,000	Africa (Sudan)	38	Morris et al. 2013
Cotton	5,000	South Asia, Near East, Americas	34	Brite and Marston 2013; Renny-Byfield et al. 2016
Millet	10,000	China	31	Lu et al. 2009
Dry beans	8,000	Peru	29	Piperno and Dillehay 2008
Sugarcane	7,500	Tropical Southeast Asia	26	Grivet et al. 2004; Denham 2013
Sunflowers	6,000	Eastern North America	25	Smith 2014
Groundnuts	9,000	Peru	25	Dillehay et al. 2007
Manioc/Cassava	10,000	South America	20	Rival and McKey 2008; Lombardo et al. 2020
Potatoes	9,000	Andes	19	Spooner et al. 2005
Oil palms	5,000	Africa	16	Kiple 2007
Chickpeas	11,000	Levant	12	Kerem et al. 2007
Coconuts	3,000	South Asia, Southeast Asia	12	Gunn et al. 2011
Cow peas	4,000	Africa	11	Xiong et al. 2016; Kouam et al. 2012; D'Andrea et al. 2007
Olives	6,000	Levant	10	Besnard et al. 2013

Source: Adapted from Kantar et al. 2017.

TABLE 4.2. Timing and Geography of Major Animal Domestications

Species	Years ago	Region
Dog	by 15,000	Eurasia
Sheep	11,000	Southwest Asia
Goat	10,500	Southwest Asia
Cow	10,300	Southwest Asia
Pig	10,300	Southwest Asia
Cat	9,500	Southwest Asia
Humped cattle	8,000	South Asia
Pig	8,000	East/Southeast Asia
Llama	6,000	South America
Horse	5,500	Central Asia
Donkey	5,500	North Africa
Alpaca	5,000	South America
Water buffalo	4,500	South Asia
Bactrian camel	4,500	Central Asia
Chicken	4,000	East/Southeast Asia
Dromedary	3,000	Southwest Asia
Duck	1,000	East/Southeast Asia

Source: After MacHugh, Larson, and Orlando 2017.

Note: New World species highlighted.

historian Donald Worster: "agriculture should be seen, not as a great leap forward, but as our species blundering into disaster."[14]

Why has the reputation of agriculture become so tarnished? Hunter-gatherers live lightly on the land. They move with the seasons and eat a varied diet rich in proteins and fibers. They live in relatively egalitarian bands, without private property and without too much sexual angst. Even allowing that this is a romantic caricature, the contrasts with agrarian society are stark. Farmers impose their selfish will on natural landscapes. Farmers are more sedentary, chained to the plot of land from which they eke out their subsistence. They are condemned to repetitive and backbreaking labor for which their only reward is a monotonous, if steady, diet of carbohydrates. Inequality, organized violence, rigid sexual rules to control the inheritance of property, and environmental degradation follow. Agriculture arose out of, and then amplified, some of our most brutish and competitive qualities as a species. Shakespeare seems like a small consolation.[15]

There is universal agreement that farming was an unmitigated disaster for human health; humans sought more calories and came away with less nutritional variety, harder work, and more germs. The best evidence for the decline of human health in the early Neolithic is etched in the skeletal record. The wear and tear of repetitive, grinding agricultural labor is scoured into the bones of farmers. Moreover, their teeth reveal the effects of a narrower and less nutritious diet, more dependent on carbohydrates. Certainly, the bones of farmers are shorter, a sure sign of declining health. Achieved stature is a complex trait influenced by both genetic and environmental factors, including nutrition and the burden of infectious disease. Farmers generally stood several centimeters shorter than hunter-gatherers, thanks to some combination of reduced access to protein and a harsher disease environment. Unfortunately, though, only a few infectious diseases (like tuberculosis) leave diagnostic signatures in the skeletal record. Most acute diseases do not leave a trace at all, quickly overrunning their human victims. Whether farmers were nutritionally deprived, fighting infection, or (as seems most likely) both, their bones broadly confirm that they were less healthy than the hunter-gatherers they replaced.[16]

To understand the deep history of infectious disease is to account for how the rise of farming revolutionized the environment for our germs. In the conventional narrative, the Neolithic Revolution fostered the rise of nastier and more numerous infectious diseases in two principal ways: density and domesticates. First, farming increased population densities and thus facilitated the rise of crowd diseases like measles, smallpox, and whooping cough. Second, domesticated livestock were the source of new diseases. In the words of a study published in the journal *Nature*, "The rise of agriculture starting 11,000 years ago played multiple roles in the evolution of animal pathogens into human pathogens. Those roles included both generation of the large human populations necessary for the evolution and persistence of human crowd diseases, and generation of large populations of domestic animals, with which farmers came into much closer and more frequent contact than hunter/gatherers had with wild animals."[17]

Tree thinking and genetic time travel are helping to revise this conventional story, which took shape in the pregenomic era. Insights from genomics are refining what we know about the chronology as well as the ecological setting of pathogen evolution. Importantly, the rise of agriculture did not immediately spawn the crowd diseases—or at least these diseases did not easily establish themselves in early farming societies as permanently endemic diseases. Many of the pathogens that cause the crowd diseases are respiratory viruses, and they are products of later history, following the rise of metal technologies and complex states. The villages and towns of the early Neolithic were not big enough to sustain continuous chains of transmission. The millennia between the invention of agriculture and the emergence of large-scale civilizations cannot be smudged over. Such a view gets both the history and the biology wrong.

We also need to revisit the claim that domesticated animals were *the* source of novel human diseases. There are often close biological relationships between the pathogens that cause human and veterinary diseases. When McNeill wrote *Plagues and Peoples*, the best science of the day suggested that such animal pathogens had "leaped" or "crossed the species barrier" to become human pathogens. This theory found its way into Alfred Crosby's *Ecological Imperialism* ("pox viruses oscillated back and forth between humans and cattle to produce smallpox and cowpox. . . . When humans domesticated animals and gathered them to the human bosom—sometimes literally, as human mothers wet-nursed motherless animals—they created maladies their hunter and gatherer ancestors had rarely or never known."). And in Diamond's *Guns, Germs, and Steel*, the germs of the title are evolutionary spinoffs from domesticated animals.[18]

It is an oversimplification to see the farmyard as the source of novel human pathogens. Although human health and animal health are deeply intertwined, our farm animals are not the ultimate reservoir of most new human diseases. More importantly, wild animals—birds, bats, rodents, and primates—have been and remain the main evolutionary source of new infectious diseases. Yet we must not remove domesticated species from the picture, because they have often been an evolutionary bridge between diseases of wild animals and human infection, a proximate source even if not an ultimate one. The fact that we have brought our domesticates together in unnatural ways—in big, dense, sedentary populations—is part of this ecological puzzle. In short, the importance of domestication was not just that we "gathered these animals into the human bosom," and thereby caught their germs. Rather, we reconfigured the broader human-animal ecosystem.

So if the crowd diseases became established in human populations thousands of years after agriculture, and farm animals were not the only source of new diseases, then was the Neolithic Revolution really such a catastrophe for human health? The answer is still a qualified yes. But to see why, we have to turn our eyes to an array of rather obscure pathogens, away from the celebrity germs with flashy names that usually get all the attention. The pathogens that cause smallpox, measles, bubonic plague, and so on are lavishly studied in histories of disease. Meanwhile, shigella, campylobacter, rotavirus, amoebic and bacillary dysentery, and typhoid and paratyphoid fever sound like forgotten answers from a college biology test. Rarely do these killers get a paragraph, much less a chapter, in the classic histories of human disease. Yet, for millennia, these have been quiet, persistent killers.

From the start, farming required a new kind of habitat, what has been called the *domus*. The Latin word for household, *domus*, is the root of the word domestication. The essence of the *domus* is permanent habitation. The sedentary lifestyle, based on a permanent homestead, created a novel environment for microbial parasites. As with the Neolithic Revolution more generally, we probably need to imagine the rise of the *domus* as an evolutionary process, with roots that stretch all the way back to the Pleistocene. Some bands of hunter-gatherers had started to live in quasi-permanent settlements—for example, in spots rich in aquatic resources. Such populations already faced some of the ecological challenges of sedentary life. The rise of farming, then, was an inflection point, a moment of no return that ultimately engulfed the mass of humanity in stationary modes of subsistence. When we gave up the everlasting hunt for food and gained a fixed address, we domesticated ourselves.[19]

The most basic ecological problem faced by humans living in large, immobile groups is waste disposal. "Our foraging ancestors feared with good reason their body wastes, which is why they trudged off into woods and bushes to do their business at a safe distance from cave dwellings and encampments. They understood that they were capable of despoiling their habitat. And when the woods and bushes became full of their wastes, they moved on." From the first experiments in sedentary life right up to the great cities of the Industrial Revolution—and still, tragically, in many parts of the world today—the question of how to get rid of fecal matter has been a primary question of human health. And, to the extent that animals had a new role in the history of disease during the early Neolithic, it was not so much because humans were butchering, breastfeeding, or breathing the same air as their livestock. Rather, it was due to the fact that farmers were suddenly surrounded by steaming piles of animal dung.[20]

The fecal-oral route is one of the busiest thoroughfares of disease transmission. Along with the respiratory tract and, to a lesser extent, our genitalia, the digestive canal is one of our most vulnerable fronts of exposure to the outside world. We have to get nutrients and energy in and waste out, and parasites try to exploit these great necessities every step of the way. Traveling from the waste of one host to the mouth of the next is a tried and true strategy.[21]

In the developed world, sanitation infrastructure and cultural norms have created distance between humans and their excrement. The household toilet is a private portal into the sprawling subterranean circuitry quietly gathering our collective muck. "Several times a day, we sit astride (or stand in front of) a section of the largest and most expensive environmental infrastructure in the world—the vast underground systems of sewers and wastewater treatment plants that are a defining feature of the developed world." In underdeveloped societies, diseases that rely on fecal-oral transmission remain a great hazard. The burden of these diseases always falls hardest on children, whose immune systems are still developing and whose hygienic habits, as any parent can readily attest, are the most dubious.[22]

Sanitation engineers use a handy list of the five Fs to summarize the pathways of the fecal-oral route: fluids, food, floors, fingers, and flies

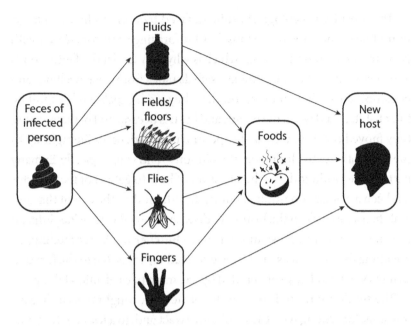

FIGURE 4.2. Sanitation engineers use the handy list of five *F*s to understand
fecal-oral transmission: fluids, food, floors, fingers, and flies.

(figure 4.2). The contamination of drinking water by feces is probably
the most important conduit of infection, because it is hard to keep waste
from seeping into sources of fresh water. Food, floors, and fingers are
easily exposed to feces, especially when the household does not have
piped water. And if there is an unheralded villain in the history of infectious disease, it is the humble housefly, *Musca domestica.*

We need to spend some time reflecting on this creature, because its
evolutionary history is so closely connected with human domestication.
The housefly seems designed to spread germs from feces to mouths. Its
natural breeding environment is dung, and its preferred diet is our own
food. It vomits and defecates with total abandon. It has a sturdy immune
system that stands up to pathogens. It is staggeringly prolific and thrives
in human dwellings that provide unintended shelter. *Musca domestica*
is the epitome of a *commensal* species (from Latin roots meaning "sharing a table"), one of those creatures—like mice, rats, sparrows, and
bedbugs—that has evolved to live in the crevices and shadows of human

settlements. The Neolithic Revolution was a gift to these noisome insects, one which they have not repaid kindly.

Aside from the housefly, the main characters in this drama are mostly bacteria. Agriculture does seem to have given us new worms, as farmers' feet trekked through soils loaded with eager helminths. There are also important viruses and protozoa that use the fecal-oral route. But the transition to agriculture was a heyday for bacteria. Bacteria are pervasive in the environment and versatile in their strategies for acquiring energy and nutrients. Many of them have learned to survive by adapting to exploit the solid waste of animal life. When humans created the unique ecosystem of the *domus*, and ravaged the globe to replicate this ecosystem, it brought us into a more intimate relationship with the microbes that make a living from excrement. And unlike the Pleistocene diseases that required vector-borne transport, fecal-oral pathogens are not nearly as geographically picky. They are almost as cosmopolitan as we are, able to thrive wherever humans settle down and defecate.

After fire, farming is the most consequential technology developed by human societies. The Neolithic Revolution is the story of how *Homo sapiens* came to manipulate entire landscapes for its own benefit through the domestication of plants and animals. The unintended consequence was that humans found themselves surrounded by a new, seething world of invisible enemies also eager to adapt to these domesticated environments. The enormous burden of diarrhea in human history is a case of Darwinian response to human transformation of the landscape.

Houses, Houseflies, and Germs

The prehistoric village known as Abu Hureyra sat on a shelf overlooking a sweeping bend in the Euphrates River, in what is now northern Syria. Here, in the very beginning of the Holocene, a group of hunter-gatherers built a settlement where they stayed year round, living off the wild game and plants amply supplied by the fertile valley. Intense cultivation fostered the domestication of wild grains, and Abu Hureyra became one of the earliest farming sites in the world. After a lull, a second phase of occupation saw a dramatic expansion of the village, with farming now complemented by animal husbandry, goat- and sheep-rearing. At its height, the village was home to some five thousand people, making Abu Hureyra one of the largest settlements known from the early Neolithic. For all practical purposes, Abu Hureyra was a Neolithic town.[23]

The people of Abu Hureyra lived in family dwellings. Hundreds of rectilinear buildings with multiple interconnected rooms were tightly packed inside the village, which was apparently unwalled. The houses were made of mud bricks, produced on site, and wooden beams. The walls and floors of the houses were plastered and painted. Even in ruins, at a distance of thousands of years, the interiors of these homes give archaeologists a sense of domestic comfort and upkeep. Just outside the door, however, is a different story.

In the words of the excavators, "the floors of the houses were usually clean. . . . The spaces around the outside of the houses, on the other hand, were choked with animal bones, charcoal and ashes from fires, charred plant remains, and other debris. Evidently, most of the preparation of food took place outdoors, and much domestic rubbish was deposited there. The smell of rotting organic matter and human waste would have been strong indeed. The contrast between interior cleanliness and exterior squalor was sharp—an enduring feature of settlements in Southwest Asia, as in Europe until recent times."[24]

Settlements like Abu Hureyra were a novel kind of ecosystem. In the words of James Scott, the rise of the *domus* witnessed "an unprecedented gathering of sheep, goats, cattle, pigs, dogs, cats, chickens, ducks, geese." This human-orchestrated gathering was also an irresistible temptation to other, uninvited species able to exploit the web of warm bodies and stored food. Commensal animals like rats and mice, pigeons and sparrows, are perfectly suited to live in the nooks and crannies of human-altered habitats, and humanity's success has been an evolutionary dream for the brood of creatures preadapted to thrive in the kinds of environments we created for them.[25]

The Neolithic village was also a historic aggregation of human and animal waste. We hardly need to observe that Neolithic houses lacked running water or sewage systems. Perhaps humans took care of necessities at some distance from the settlement, as hunter-gatherers often do, but the evidence suggests otherwise, and there was no controlling the bodily functions of the farm animals living right outside anyway. It was not long before farming societies learned the usefulness of feces as fertilizer. The dried dung of domesticates was also a major source of fuel, furnishing heat and light. Neolithic settlements were truly something novel. At least wild herd animals stay on the move and at intervals achieve some distance from their own filth. But as humans became sedentary, we also became the only social large-bodied mammal to be permanently surrounded by its own muck, like a colony of rodents but on a grandiose scale. And if that were not enough, we encircled ourselves with stationary herds of giant domesticated mammals. The Neolithic village was the single greatest accumulation of interspecies scat in all of nature.[26]

Inevitably, fecal matter found its way into human mouths. Fields and floors were easily contaminated and allowed the passage of particulates from one orifice to the next. Fingers were a major conduit of transmission in societies without ready access to running water or sanitary paper and where standards of personal hygiene were most likely underwhelming. Fluids—namely, water—were perhaps the most important source of contamination. Excrement can seep into groundwater, where it returns above ground through shallow wells. Or it can drain into the same streams and pools whence drinking water is drawn. Even today, clean water is the most important, and often the most elusive, health resource of all.

The fifth F of the sanitary engineers is the fly. *Musca domestica* is an underappreciated piece of the Neolithic package (figure 4.3). The housefly is one of several important commensal insects, along with the human body louse and the grain weevil. As its very name implies, *Musca domestica* is uncannily evolved to live in and around the human house. The remains of houseflies do not preserve well archeologically, and so the housefly has received less attention as a commensal species than rats and mice. But it is clear that the housefly adapted to the human household in the early Neolithic and dispersed along with agriculture to thrive wherever humans laid down permanent settlements. Because it eats our food, the housefly is the most absolutely literal example of a

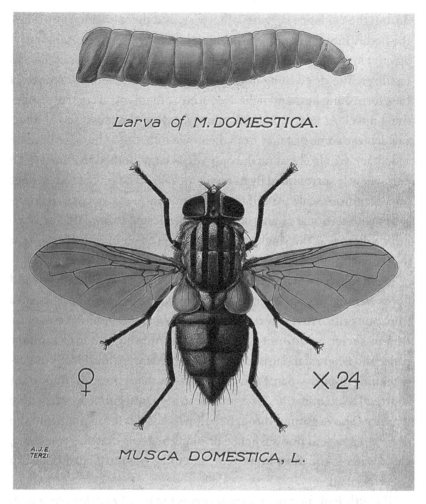

FIGURE 4.3. *Musca domestica*: the ultimate commensal. Drawing by
A.J.E. Terzi. Wellcome Collection (CC BY 4.0).

species that "shares a table" with us. Its history and biology are thus a
paradigm for understanding the unintended reverberations of human
ecological fashioning.[27]

There are more than five thousand species of fly in the family Muscidae. For tens of millions of years, they have been happily biting animals
and scavenging environments across the planet. Remarkably, the
housefly is the most successful representative of this ancient family. We

have made it a planetary superstar. Yet its evolutionary origins are obscure. *Musca domestica* is globally distributed today, but the housefly may have originated in Egypt. It probably evolved from an ancestor that exploited the feces of hoofed mammals. It was preadapted to take advantage of the unique concentration of food and feces in human villages. Even for a fly, *Musca domestica* has an impressive suite of immunity genes that protect it in septic environments. The rise of farming provided these dung-loving flies a never-ending feast.[28]

The habits and physiology of the housefly combine to make it an insidious vehicle of bacterial transmission. The housefly can reproduce in almost any decaying organic matter, but its preferred breeding matrix is feces. The female can smell an opportune place with her antennae, and she will lay eggs in the warm and moist environment provided by almost any putrefying medium. A fly can lay 150 eggs at a time and will do so up to half a dozen times in her life. If possible she will find feces in the sunlight and bury the eggs inside. They incubate for at least eight hours, at most two days, before hatching. The larvae burrow deeper into the fermenting dung and eat. They will molt three times and grow rapidly before pupating. The pupae shove their way to the surface, and the adult flies emerge from the waste that has been their sustenance and shelter, ready to spread their wings and search for food.[29]

It is not just what they eat—*our* food—that makes flies dangerous to us; it is also their uncommonly rude table manners. The adult housefly has tremendous visual acuity but modest powers of smell. It compensates with "restless, inquisitive behavior," and a strong instinct to aggregate, so that once a food source is found, the swarm descends. The fly has tasting organs on its hairy feet that can detect sugar and trigger the proboscis to descend. Flies love the foods that we do, but they cannot chew. Their proboscis is only good for lapping and sponging liquids. Yet the fly has the ability to salivate on solid foods in order to liquefy them. Flies feed to bursting. Then, they regurgitate liquid from their proboscis, mix it with their salivary juices, and suck it into their intestines. This frequent "vomiting" is part of the digestive process, but the fly also defecates with astonishing regularity—as often as every five minutes.[30]

The housefly carries bacteria on its exterior and in its digestive organs. "It is common knowledge that the hairy body, the tarsi with their sticky tenent hairs and corrugated plantas, the wings, and grooved proboscis all provide hideaways for microbial stowaways." Pathogens can also multiply inside the insect and then escape either in the vomit or excrement of the fly. A single fly can harbor millions of bacteria. "*Musca*, like *Anopheles*, should be recognized as one of the most deadly genera of animals." The creature is also cosmopolitan, able to survive the winter in any stage of its life cycle. In the temperate latitudes, though, its numbers oscillate with the seasons, declining with cold weather. In the tropics and subtropics, the housefly is abundant year-round.[31]

The association of flies with human disease was sensed long before modern science. The ancient Greeks worshiped a form of Zeus as the protector against flies, and the Roman encyclopedist Pliny the Elder knew of a religious tradition in which the gods could be invoked against a pestilence brought on by swarms of flies. It was proverbial in Russia: "fly in April, dead child in July." The famous seventeenth-century English physician Thomas Sydenham noted that "if swarms of insects, especially house-flies, were abundant in the summer, the succeeding autumn was unhealthy." By the eighteenth century, medical authorities regularly suggested a link between flies and outbreaks of dysentery. The German physician Christian Paullini suspected that "when you say that dysentery was going about then in nearby places, it is as if the fly had settled on the excrements or the corpses of infected men, and had carried the contagious fluid from these sources which it was able to transfer easily to another."[32]

In modern times, the crusade against the housefly became a cause célèbre for the sanitary movement. *Musca domestica* was rebranded as "the typhoid fly." Public health campaigns instilled a sense of dread in the minds of the public. The Boy Scouts launched a national effort to install window screens, targeting disease-bearing flies. The rise of the motor car, and the decline of the horse stable, were an unforeseen boost to fly control. Along with rats, mosquitos, and sparrows, flies were one of the targets of China's Four Pests Campaign, launched in the 1950s. Continuous advances in sanitation, sewage, and hygiene ultimately

rendered the fly merely a nuisance in the developed world, at last liber-
ating much of humanity from the menace of the housefly as the bearer
of deadly disease.[33]

But in the millennia between the rise of farming and the crusades of
the last century, the housefly was an unwelcome carrier of pathogens
looking to find their way from feces to mouth. Like many of the microbes the fly shuttles, this winged beast is an underappreciated avatar
of humanity's prowess in transforming environments.

Agents of Intestinal Turmoil

Although diarrhea and dysentery were leading causes of death until recent times, it is harder than you might imagine to find good clinical
descriptions of these universal scourges, particularly in the era before
antibiotics and rehydration therapies. The pervasiveness of severe gastroenteric disease seems to have shrouded it in anguished silence. There
are exceptions, like Dr. Benjamin Rush's *Inquiry into the Cause and Cure
of the Cholera Infantum*. Rush was a signer of the Declaration of Independence, a beacon of the American Enlightenment, and a proud Phila-
delphian. He was also the first titan of the American medical establishment. His 1794 book drew on the latest insights from across the Atlantic
as well as his own clinical experience. It is a vivid record of how a prac-
ticing physician grappled with the problem of infantile and childhood
diarrhea in an age when human societies remained mostly helpless
against such afflictions.[34]

Traditionally, cholera was the generic name for diarrheal disease (not
to be confused with the deadly new disease of the nineteenth century,
initially called Asiatic cholera, which eventually took over the term).
Rush knew cholera infantum as perennial summertime visitor. In Philadelphia, the disease was called simply "the vomiting and purging of
children." In the south, in places like balmy Charleston, its deadly work
commenced as early as April or May. In the north it predictably started
a month or two later. Rush observed that the intensity of the seasonal
wave was controlled by the weather—hot years were deadly years. The
disease was especially cruel to children in their first two years of life.[35]

The onset of the disease was marked by vomiting, diarrhea, and fever. Then the telltale signs of dysentery appeared: "The matter discharged from the stomach and bowels is generally yellow or green, but the stools are sometimes slimy and bloody." Patients endured terrible pain. "The children in this stage of the disorder, appear to suffer a good deal of pain. They draw up their feet, and are never easy in one posture. The pulse is quick and weak. . . . The disease affects the head so much, as in some instances to produce symptoms not only of delirium, but of mania, insomuch that the children throw their heads backwards and forwards, and sometimes make attempts to scratch, and to bite, their parents or nurses." William Black, in London, made similar observations. "Infants scream lamentably, and cannot be appeased; they contract and draw up their legs to the belly, are restless, sometimes costive; but often there is concomitant diarrhoea and green feces, vomiting, flatulent explosion."[36]

As the disease progressed, life ebbed away from its victims. "Such is the insensibility of the system in some instances in this disorder, that flies have been seen to alight upon the eyes when opened, without exciting a motion in the eyelids to remove them." Although some patients succumbed within days, more often the grueling struggle lasted weeks. "Where the disease has been of long continuance, the approach of death is gradual, and attended by a number of distressing symptoms. An emaciation of the body, to such a degree as that the bones come through the skin, livid spots, a singultus [hiccupping], convulsions, a strongly marked hippocratic countenance [a hollow, emaciated look], and a sore mouth, generally precede the fatal termination of this disorder."[37]

Before the rise of germ theory, doctors and medical writers did not see their world in terms of specific disease-causing agents. We think of fever or diarrhea as symptoms, whereas premodern societies thought of them as diseases. Even today, without expensive testing in a laboratory, it can be hard to pinpoint the cause of a diarrheal disease. So there are only two ways that we can gain a sense of the specific pathogens that likely caused diarrheal disease historically. One is through comparative data gathered from contemporary societies where diarrheal disease remains a major cause of mortality. The other is through genomic methods—tree thinking and time travel—that give us glimpses of the evolutionary background of these pathogens.

Only in the last decade, with global surveillance and advanced genomics, has the relative importance of various pathogens been reliably measured. The Global Enteric Multicenter Study, completed in 2013, was the largest-ever study of the global diarrhea burden. It looked at the huge variety of microbes that can cause diarrheal disease, including viruses (especially rotaviruses, adenoviruses, and noroviruses), bacteria (e.g., species belonging to the genuses *Shigella*, *Campylobacter*, and *Escherichia*), and protozoa (*Entamoeba histolytica*). This roster includes generalists as well as specialists adapted to humans. The effects of some are relatively mild, those of others uniformly severe, and those of many others in between. For instance, rotaviruses have been so ubiquitous that nearly every child is infected in his or her first few years even in developed societies (until recently, anyway, since an effective vaccine has become widely used). Deaths are relatively rare where children are well nourished and fluid replacement therapy is readily available. In poor countries, rotaviruses are the leading cause of diarrhea-related mortality.[38]

Our digestive tract and its excreta are an ecological context for these pathogens. The earth is full of microbes, especially bacteria, that live off the hard work of higher organisms, competing for the substantial amounts of energy available in waste matter and dead bodies. Because digestion is inefficient, leaving at least half the chemical energy of food unabsorbed, its byproducts are a biological treasure, rich in energy. The energy packaged in our blood and tissue is fiercely protected by the immune system, but the energy in our waste is more or less there for the taking outside the mucosal barrier. Many bacteria have adapted to this environment; most of them are in fact commensal or symbiotic, part of the normal flora of a healthy human gut. They live in peace with us but wrestle each other for access to scarce resources. Among organisms living in this ecosystem, pathogens are the exception rather than the rule.[39]

Yet fecal-oral pathogens are not uncommon in nature. We are hardly the only animal suffering bouts of loose stool. Some of the pathogens that cause diarrheal disease are not adapted to humans specifically.

Rotaviruses are a prime example. This genus includes nine different species of virus. *Rotavirus A* is the most common species infecting humans, but it also infects a wide range of birds and mammals. Rotaviruses are genetically diverse. Humans regularly contract new strains from animal reservoirs, and we have presumably been doing so for thousands of years, probably even before the transition to agriculture. Rotaviruses are generalists, and their strategy has been tremendously successful. With the rise of dense, dirty human settlements, we provided these zoonotic pathogens an irresistible environment that has drawn them in upon us to the point that rotavirus infection became an almost universal experience for human beings.[40]

Other important germs that cause diarrheal disease are specialists in humans. The genus of bacteria known as *Shigella* is exemplary. These pathogens are named after Kiyoshi Shiga (figure 4.4), a Japanese scientist who discovered these bacteria in the 1890s. Shigella bacteria cause shigellosis, or bacillary dysentery. Dysentery is a generic term for an inflammatory disease of the intestines. Although any diarrheal disease can be dangerous when its victims are physiologically stressed or malnourished, bacillary dysentery is in another category, as perilous as any major infectious disease. To contract a case of bacillary dysentery was to be sentenced to a grueling trial, guaranteeing at least a brush with death.[41]

Shigellosis belongs on any register of dangerous diseases. In the late twentieth century, there were 165 million cases of shigella infection each year globally, and more than one million deaths annually. Bacillary dysentery is probably the cause of many of the fatal diarrheas characterized by the discharge of blood and mucus that are described in the medical traditions of the world. In preindustrial societies, infant mortality was often above 30 percent, the lives of one in three newborns taken before the end of the first year. Bacillary dysentery likely played a leading role in such a grim harvest. The risks of infection were heightened at the time of weaning, and the transition away from mother's milk to water and solid foods not only broke access to protective maternal antibodies but brought exposure to new pathogens. In some environments, nearly all adults may have survived infection as children and therefore acquired

FIGURE 4.4. Kiyoshi Shiga (1871–1957), who discovered shigella
bacteria in 1897. Wellcome Collection (CC BY 4.0).

immunity. But the disease is not a respecter of age, and adults also suffered a heavy burden of bacillary dysentery.[42]

Traditionally, there are four recognized species of shigella bacteria.
In reality, though, the name *Shigella* and the very concept of such a
genus are maintained only to keep up appearances, for the sake of convention. (The poor human brain struggles to keep up with the complex
evolutionary relationships that have been revealed by bacterial genomics.)
Remarkably, it has become clear that *Shigella* bacteria are really strains
of the well-known bacterium *Escherichia coli*. In the developed world,
E. coli bacteria are still notorious as agents of "food poisoning": you hear
about this species on the news when an outbreak forces a recall of

something in your refrigerator. *E. coli* has many faces, and it has been called "a paradigm for a versatile bacterial species." It may have emerged with the rise of mammals tens of millions of years ago. Its natural home is the mucus layer of the large intestine of mammals or reptiles. It is a harmless resident of the healthy gut, colonizing infants soon after birth. Most strains of *E. coli* are not dedicated pathogens. But the four species of shigella are variants of *E. coli* that have acquired molecular tools that commit them to a more violent way of life.[43]

Shigella bacteria are deadly offshoots of *E. coli* that have given up the crowded and competitive mucus to seek energy and nutrients in our own cells lying just below. The epithelial layer of cells that line the intestines are interspersed with specialized sentinel cells that try to engulf invaders and warn the immune system. Shigella wants to be found by these guardians and then "eaten" by our innate immune cells, which are known as macrophages. Shigella is an intracellular parasite, exploiting the inside of our macrophages. In fact, once on the inside, Shigella props up the niche that it has taken over, making zombies of our own cells while the bacteria multiply furiously.[44]

The bloody and clumpy stool that the victim discharges is loaded with infectious bacteria in search of the next host. Shigella has an astonishingly low infective dose (or inoculum). Whereas it may take an inoculum of ten thousand individual bacteria for a normal intestinal microbe such as most *E. coli* to establish a successful infection in a new host, as few as ten shigella bacteria can spell doom for the next victim. The potential to transmit so efficiently is one of the evolutionary trademarks of shigella, a prerequisite for its brutality as a pathogen. It spreads easily in fluids. Houseflies have also been repeatedly confirmed as an important mechanism of diffusion. The role of water and flies both contribute to the seasonal patterns of bacillary dysentery, which are imperfectly understood. The disease tends to be worse in the heat, or when there are extreme deficiencies or excesses of rain.[45]

Dysentery was endemic as well as epidemic in past societies. Where established, it was part of the background of infectious disease, coming and going in predictable annual waves. But it also spiked into epidemic proportions whenever conditions allowed, especially where sanitary conditions deteriorated. Dysentery has been an adjunct of war. Sir John Pringle (1707–82), the "father of military medicine," was a crucial figure in the study of dysentery and carefully observed its patterns of transmission. "The contagion passes from one, who is ill, to his companions in the same tent; and from thence perhaps to the next. The foul straw becomes very infectious. But the great source of infection are the privies, after they have received the dysenteric excrements from those who first fall ill." And even for a seasoned medical veteran, the disease was repulsive: "Towards the end, when the bowels begin to mortify, the faetor is cadaverous and intolerable."[46]

The shigella bacteria are, in evolutionary terms, young. The various strains of shigella evolved from *E. coli* repeatedly and independently. These events happened in the recent past, in one case only a few hundred years ago. The key fact of shigella evolution is that these strains adapted to specialize in the infection of humans. Two genetic changes were critical. First, all shigella bacteria have acquired a suite of virulence factors that enable them to invade human cells. Second, the *Shigella* genome has lost an enormous range of genes that became superfluous once the strain had dedicated itself to becoming a human parasite. Most bacteria are the microbial equivalent of Swiss Army knives, with a whole array of genes that equip them for the diverse challenges and opportunities they might encounter in a range of hosts. But these tools are costly to maintain and operate, and as shigella adapted to humans, it shed genes for tools that had become extraneous. The germ became leaner and meaner, dedicated to the environment of the human cells lining the intestine. One group of geneticists has called precisely this pattern of genetic reduction "the Neolithic revolution of bacterial genomes."[47]

The Neolithic Revolution intermingled human and animal excrement as never before. Shigella bacteria are exemplary of the evolutionary response, but they are not alone, and we could as well have focused on fellow microbial travelers along the fecal-oral route. Rotavirus, entamoeba, cryptosporidium, giardia, campylobacter, and other intestinal pathogens took advantage of the new ecosystem of waste to spread their genes. In the wake of farming, we became the fecal-oral host par excellence, and the problem of human diarrhea took on its outsized proportions. And yet, in one of nature's endless twists, the most deadly disease that invades via the intestines is not really a diarrheal disease but a fever that starts in the guts and grips the rest of the body from the inside out: typhoid.[48]

Typhoid, the Great Gut Fever

On January 6, 1833, a twenty-four-year-old laborer arrived at the Hospital La Pitié in Paris. Six weeks earlier he had moved to the city in search of work. He came full of vigor, of "strong, robust aspect," with a ruddy complexion and red hair. He presented at the hospital with excruciating abdominal pain, chills, and loss of appetite. After a day he was no better, and his mental state was intermittently delirious. Over several days, the doctors gave him a series of bloodlettings, but his face remained flushed. He was given emetics and vomited bile. His ears rang, and his nights were sleepless.[49]

After almost two weeks, he developed spots on his skin, characterized by red pimples. His condition grew worse, the delirium more regular, his aspect hollow. Tremors, coughs, and pain became relentless. His pulse grew weak. The end was obviously near. "Cheeks red, excessively sunken; pupils dilated; eyes not fixed, but nearly so; moves arms freely and with comparative ease; not the least rigidity in the limbs; hears and understands better, attempts to answer, but speech unintelligible." Four weeks after admission, the young man's misery ended.[50]

Two days later, Pierre Charles Alexandre Louis dissected the corpse. Louis was one of the great "morbid anatomists" of the nineteenth century, for whom the patient's dead body was a way to understand the nature of disease. (He was also a pioneer of evidence-based medicine— trusting clinical data over received dogma—and an important critic of blood-letting.) Louis took apart the internal organs of the dead patient and subjected them to his austere glare. The protracted struggle had left the man's body the worse for wear, but only one organ showed really horrific carnage: the small intestine. The small intestine is where food is absorbed. It is thus one of the most vulnerable frontiers between the sterile tissue of the human body and the seething world beyond. The

FIGURE 4.5. Ulcerated small intestine, photographed by Budd himself. Typhoid infection damages lymphoid tissue in the intestine. Wellcome Collection (CC BY 4.0).

immune system patrols intensely here, especially in a few dozen zones of lymphatic tissue known as Peyer's patches. In the dead man's intestine, these patches looked ulcerated and patently diseased. Clearly, something terrible had happened here.[51]

Louis had seen it all before. The ulcerated lymphatic tissue of the small intestine is a particular sign of the disease known as typhoid fever (see figure 4.5). *Typhoid* means "like typhus," and the name is confusing. *Typhus* is Greek for "smoky" and refers to the sufferer's dimmed mental condition. Typhus and typhoid are very different diseases. Typhus is a vector-borne disease transmitted by lice; it is only known from about 1500 CE onward. Typhoid fevers are ancient. They are caused by strains of the bacterium *Salmonella enterica*. They spread via the fecal-oral route and invade the intestine. But for centuries typhus and typhoid fevers were conflated in European medicine, because they were the two most important continuous fevers in the early modern world (as opposed to "intermittent fevers," like malaria). Typhus and typhoid caused similar outward symptoms. The anatomical work of Louis, which carefully identified the diseased small intestine as a sign of typhoid, was crucial to the differentiation of the two diseases in the 1830s and 1840s.[52]

Louis was an inspirational mentor, and one of his devoted acolytes was an English doctor, William Budd. It was Budd's destiny to unravel the epidemiology of typhoid fever. Budd's father was a doctor, and so were six of his nine brothers. He followed in his father's footsteps as a country physician in Devonshire, but his horizons had been expanded by a four-year apprenticeship in Paris under the tutelage of the anatomist Louis, where Budd learned firsthand the importance of the intestinal pathology of typhoid fever. He contracted the disease himself and narrowly escaped with his life.[53]

Every year in the mid-nineteenth century, typhoid fever accounted for some fifteen thousand or more deaths in Budd's England, "a population equal to that of a considerable city every year swept into the grave by a single and . . . perfectly preventable plague." But it was not just the number of victims. It was the raw suffering. "No one can know," Budd wrote, "what they really imply who has not had experience of this fever in his own home. The dreary and painful night-watches—the great length of the period over which the anxiety is extended—the long suspense between hope and fear, and the large number of the cases in which hope is disappointed and the worst fear is at last realised, make up a sum of distress that is scarcely to be found in the history of any other acute disorder." Budd devoted himself to unlocking its mysteries: "Having been by accident thrown much in the way of this fever, I have long felt that it is impossible to bear a part in the calamities of which it is the source, without becoming possessed with a burning desire to devote the best powers of the mind to the discovery of means by which such calamities may be prevented."[54]

In Budd's lifetime, the prevailing view of typhoid fever held that it was a miasmatic disease, a deadly emanation generated by waste matter. Typhoid fever was thus a disorder of the environment, not an entity spread by direct contact between humans. Budd's insight was that this dichotomy between contagion and environmental causation was an illusion. Typhoid fever required a contagious element, and the unsanitary environment was the medium of its transmission.

Budd's remoteness from the centers of power and population worked to his advantage. In a metropolis like London, it was hard to disentangle the swirl of diseases and trace their exact causes. But in the country, patterns were clearer. Budd practiced in North Tawton, a village of 1,200 souls in Devonshire. He knew every inhabitant by personal acquaintance, and he was the only doctor for miles. Fortune had put him in position to be an epidemiologist *avant la lettre*.[55]

The sanitary conditions of rural Devonshire were deplorable. There was no sewage system. Budd could count on one hand the households wealthy enough to afford a covered drain. Among the "great bulk of the inhabitants, there was nothing to separate from the open air the offensive matters which collect around human habitations. Each cottage, or group of three or four cottages, had its common privy, to which a simple excavation in the ground served as cesspool." To make matters worse, nearly every house kept a pig, "one of whose functions was to furnish manure for the little plot of potatoes which fed man and pig alike. Thus, often, hard by the cottage door there was not only an open privy, but a dungheap also."[56]

Budd's observation was compelling: the muck was a permanent feature of human settlement in the English countryside, but typhoid fever was absent most of the time. Therefore, the environment had no power to generate the disease on its own. The "privies, pigstyes and dungheaps continued, year after year, to exhale ill odours, without any specific effect on the public health." However, these same conditions "had but too great power in promoting its spread when once the germ of fever had been introduced." And in July 1839 the germ arrived.[57]

Budd treated hundreds of patients in the outbreak that followed, and he minutely recorded the patterns of transmission. The conclusion became irresistible: typhoid fever was contagious. Budd deduced that fecal discharge was the medium of transmission. His lessons in Paris had prepared him for this insight. He realized that typhoid fever was, essentially, a fever whose "specific character" was infection of the small intestine. Budd knew that the folds of the intestine made it one of the body's most important surfaces, and he came to think of typhoid as a sort of pox of the bowels. And he concluded that "the contagious element by which it is mainly propagated is contained in the specific discharges from the diseased intestine."[58]

Budd died in 1880, the very year the typhoid bacillus was first isolated. Typhoid fever is caused by a strain of the bacterium *Salmonella enterica*. Like *E. coli*, salmonella bacteria live in the public consciousness of the developed world today mainly as a cause of food poisoning. *Salmonella enterica* is like *E. coli* in other ways too. Both are pervasive in nature as colonists in the guts of animals, and both can contaminate human food and water and cause usually nonfatal diarrhea. And both have spawned offshoots that are more deadly versions of themselves, specialized in the infection of humans.[59]

S. enterica is an abundant species, and the language required even to speak of the diversity of this successful bacterium is intimidating. There are more than 2,600 known varieties of it, distinguished by slight differences in the molecules on the surface of the cell. Most forms of *S. enterica* are considered nontyphoidal, for the obvious reason that they do not cause typhoid fever. When these strains that cause food poisoning invade the lining of the human small intestine, they immediately start a ruckus. Within a day, the bowels are agitated by the inflammatory immune response, a massive brigade of immune cells deployed to repel the invader. After a brief and sometimes explosive infection in the intestines, resulting in diarrhea, the germ is typically cleared from the body within a few days. These infections are still relatively common, even where hygiene and sanitation are good, simply because salmonella is so widespread and formidable.[60]

At least 5 of the 2,600 strains of *S. enterica* are something altogether more severe. These strains are the agents of enteric (that is, intestinal) fever. They are parasites specialized in the exploitation of humans. These five deadly offshoots of *S. enterica* are known (rather unimaginatively) as *typhi, sendai,* and *paratyphi A, B,* and *C.* Strictly speaking, only *typhi* causes typhoid fever; the others cause paratyphoid fever, which is close to being a distinction without a difference because they are all invasive enteric fevers with similar properties.[61]

The typhoidal strains are stealthy, careful not to trigger an immediate inflammatory response. Instead, they penetrate the specialized immune cells meant to guard the intestinal barrier and thereby sneak inside the immune system. The Peyer's patches or lymphoid tissue of the intestine are ulcerated during the prolonged infection, but already S. enterica has deepened its invasion, quietly spreading to the lymph nodes, liver, spleen, bone marrow, and gallbladder. This disseminated infection is what makes typhoid fevers systemic and dangerous. Fortunately for us, few pathogens have been able to adapt anything like this strategy, using the fecal-oral route to invade via the intestine and become a systemic infection. A typhoid infection subjects the patient to a long battle, lasting for weeks. Before antibiotics, case mortality rates may have been around 10 percent. Those who survived had a long recovery, during which they remained infectious.[62]

The stool of a typhoid patient is packed with infectious bacteria. And typhoid has an unusual property allowing convalescents to continually shed massive numbers of bacteria in their feces for months. The bacteria have evolved the ability to colonize the gallbladder, and can travel thence via bile into the intestines. A small percentage of victims recover but become healthy carriers, chronically shedding typhoidal bacteria in their stool for years. The case of Typhoid Mary in early twentieth-century New York is notorious. A chronic carrier can excrete 10^6–10^{10} bacteria in each gram of stool—so maybe thirty billion pathogens a day, each hoping to find its way into the mouth of the next victim. The ability to enter this carriage state, probably facilitated by the bacterium's ability to build protective biofilms, is an evolutionary adaptation, a trick selected because it helped the species propagate its genes.[63]

The lifestyle change from a generalist intestinal parasite that infects a wide range of animals into a human pathogen that causes invasive disease has occurred a number of times throughout history. Promiscuous strains of this low-grade intestinal parasite are stewing throughout nature, hopping from animal to animal. They are swapping virulence elements and trying new strategies constantly. Most of these are immediate Darwinian failures. Some are probably transiently successful, and the genetic diversity that we know is probably only a partial snapshot of what now exists and what has ever existed. But a handful of invasive experiments have proven wildly successful and persist to the present.[64]

The germ of typhoid fever proper is the most widespread and probably the oldest of all the major typhoid strains. Molecular clock dating suggests that it evolved in the late Pleistocene or possibly the early Holocene. Although the boundaries of possibility are still rather wide, they might be narrowed down with continued research. If typhoid fever emerged in the later Pleistocene, it would be a fascinating example of how a fecal-oral pathogen could have arisen before fully fledged agricultural sedentism; perhaps the carriage state was crucial in allowing the bacterium to persist in low-density populations. If the typhoid fever germ turns out to have been a creation of the early Neolithic, it will be unsurprising. Certainly the spread of dense, waste-filled habitats played right into the hands of this nefarious pathogen.[65]

Tree thinking and genetic time travel have also helped to elucidate the evolutionary history of the strain known as *paratyphi C*. In the early Neolithic, humans were infected with generalist strains related to *paratyphi C*. The closest relative of the human strain is a generalist version of the bacterium that is commonly found in pigs. *Paratyphi C* emerged as a human specialist, probably in Europe, around the time of pig domestication. Here, then, is a germ that adapted from livestock to farmers, among agriculturalists living much like the villagers from Budd's rural Devonshire: surrounded by their pigs and the inevitable brew of human and animal filth. This strain is relatively rare today, but it may have been much more prevalent in premodern times. It has been found in archaeological samples from Europe from the Middle Ages. More intriguingly still, this strain was recovered from an important mass grave in Mexico that was the resting place for victims of one of the epidemics of the postcontact period. This finding implicates paratyphoid fever in the mortality of New World peoples after the voyages of Columbus.[66]

Because the symptoms of typhoid fever are vague and variable, its history is hard to trace in the written record. But there is every reason to believe that between the rise of agriculture and the triumph of modern sanitation, *S. enterica* was one of the great scourges of humanity. The verdict of the great nineteenth-century medical historian August Hirsch is judicious: "There are still a good many indications, more or less ambiguous, of the general diffusion of the disease in former times as well; and those, taken along with the experiences of the present, justify the conclusion that typhoid takes a leading place among those acute infections which bear the pronounced character of ubiquitous diseases."[67]

Where typhoid fever was endemic, the disease contributed to infant and childhood mortality. Unfortunately, acquired immunity to typhoid is weak and very transient, so a recovered patient can contract it again. The disease was often lethal for migrants from the country to the city, like the twenty-four-year-old worker who arrived at Hospital La Pitié only six weeks after coming to Paris. And as Budd observed, the disease was a fearsome but sporadic presence in the countryside. It roved from town to town, village to village, and might be absent for years before reappearing in epidemic form. These patterns were probably as ancient as the disease itself.[68]

Typhoid fever went into decline in the later nineteenth century in societies that had started to control infectious diseases. Sewers were probably the most important early factor. Running water and handwashing habits hastened the demise of the germ, as did the control of houseflies with screens and waste management. The filtration and then chlorination of water were the death knell of the bacterium in the developed world. Globally, the elimination of typhoid fever is nowhere in sight, and still today there are twenty-five million cases and two hundred thousand deaths each year from a disease that Budd, a century and a half ago, rightly called "a perfectly preventable plague." We can grant the last word on this disease to the humane and perceptive country doctor who did so much to illuminate its causes: "The members of the great human family are, in fact, bound together by a thousand secret ties, of whose existence the world in general little dreams. And he that was never yet connected with his poorer neighbour, by deeds of charity or love, may one day find, when it is too late, that he is connected with him by a bond which may bring them both, at once, to a common grave."[69]

Boom and Bust

The millennia of the early Holocene were eventful ones in the biological history of our planet, a time when the expansion of human societies came to imprint far more drastically than before on the evolution of pathogens, plants, and animals. The traces of this revolution are legible in our own genomes, as well as those of our crops and livestock, our parasites, and our uninvited guests such as flies and rodents. And, excitingly, there is a lot still to be learned about this phase of our past, particularly now that genomics can complement and enrich traditional archaeological research.

Anthropologists and archaeologists have long debated the role of population pressure in stimulating the transition to agriculture, and on balance the case is strong for seeing the intensification of food production as an outgrowth of demographic expansion and the ensuing resource strain. In this view, hunger is the motivation for innovation. Among the many good reasons to see farming as humanity's answer to the tension between population growth and energy limits is this: the breakthrough to agriculture fostered demographic transformation. The archaeologist Jean-Pierre Bocquet-Appel has proposed characterizing the changes as the Neolithic Demographic Transition. Farmers had access to more calories and converted their gains to population growth. Fertility rose. Women were able to have more children. They started earlier and, most importantly, gave birth at shorter intervals. Women in agricultural societies were sedentary, and the energy they saved by not having to carry newborns was reinvested in higher fertility. It is simply easier to care for multiple children in a house than on the march. Infants were weaned earlier, accelerating reproduction.[70]

The Neolithic Demographic Transition has to be reconstructed from human skeletal remains. In the centuries after domestication, skeletal populations studied by archaeologists get "younger": a higher proportion of burials are children between five and nineteen years old. The altered distribution, it is argued, mirrors an entire population that skewed younger, because both fertility rates and mortality rates had increased. There was also population growth. In net terms, agricultural societies may have grown up to twenty-five times faster than hunter-gatherer societies. But in the long run, fertility and mortality returned almost to equilibrium, and growth rates, averaged out over the course of centuries or millennia, remained scarcely above zero, at 0.1–0.2 percent.[71]

Such long-term averages conceal short-term volatility. In the Holocene, as in the Pleistocene, near zero growth was the cumulative result of unstable cycles of boom and bust. In recent years archaeologists have suggested one ingenious proxy record for the waves of expansion and collapse following the Neolithic Revolution: the distribution of total radiocarbon dates recovered from archaeological finds. In essence, this provides a crude count of how much organic stuff was reshaped by human intervention. The stark pattern that emerges is, unsurprisingly, wild oscillation: soaring growth and staggering retreat. What accounts for these patterns remains unknown, though infectious disease is an obvious suspect.[72]

One of the greatest consequences of the Neolithic Revolution, perhaps, was to amplify temporal variations in the burden of infectious disease. As we have emphasized, hunter-gatherers must have sometimes experienced transient epidemics. But such outbreaks were perforce small in scale. As farming spread, populations became bigger and denser, creating more opportunity for both the emergence and transmission of infectious diseases. Although the novel respiratory diseases that we will consider in the next chapter heightened the potential explosiveness of epidemic mortality, some of the fecal-oral diseases whose evolutionary history we have traced (such as dysentery and typhoid fever) could also have detonated sudden, powerful mortality events.

One area in which the study of ancient DNA has already considerably deepened our knowledge of the early Neolithic is in the study of human genetic history. The demographic pulse of the Neolithic Revolution is apparent in the genetic success of farming populations. There has been a classic debate over whether the spread of agriculture was a "demic" or "cultural" diffusion—that is, whether farming populations replaced hunter-gatherers or hunter-gatherers adopted farming technologies. The pendulum has swung back and forth, and the truth clearly involves some mixture of both. But as ancient DNA has come to loom large in the debate, the demic explanation has found strong support. The early to middle Holocene witnessed major demographic movement and expansion, as farmers used their superior energy technologies to multiply. One of the clearest findings in human population history is that our past is marked not by timeless fixity but repeated episodes of upheaval. Migration, mixture, and displacement are hallmarks of human expansion.[73]

Take Europe as an example. In Europe, hunter-gatherer genomes were largely, but not completely, replaced by a first wave of farmers arriving from Anatolia and spreading northwest. Ancient DNA has also allowed the clear identification of a second tidal wave in Europe, several millennia later, of Indo-European speakers from north of the Black Sea. Generation after generation, both the technologies *and* the genes of farmers crept outward. The story is echoed in East Asia and Africa and perhaps elsewhere. One of the truly open questions at the moment is to what extent infectious disease played a role in these early displacements. Might the first farmers have carried, in their guts and feces, microbes that hastened the decline of hunter-gatherers with whom they came into contact? Time will tell.[74]

It is worth cautioning ourselves again that the history of infectious disease rarely conforms to tidy chronological schemes. The Neolithic Revolution itself played out in stunningly diverse ways across the planet, spreading into new environments over the course of thousands of years. It made some of our old, hunter-gatherer diseases—from vivax malaria to soil-transmitted helminths—worse. Some of our classic gastroenteric diseases emerged even before agriculture. Those caused by zoonotic pathogens would have already afflicted hunter-gatherers. During the early Neolithic, before large cities, respiratory viruses probably emerged and caused explosive epidemics, even if population densities remained too low for them to become human specialists. Nevertheless, the early Neolithic was a turning point in human history when our species came, irreversibly, to inhabit the sedentary *domus*, and thereby created a new ecosystem where fecal-oral diseases could evolve and flourish. Because writing lay far in the future, this transformation has not left behind any documentary traces. But thanks to tree thinking and genetic time travel, we can start to give this chapter of our past its rightful place.

Our intestines might be the first to agree that farming was our "worst mistake." This new technology allowed humans to transform environments in ways that triggered severe negative feedbacks. In the early Neolithic, the paradox of progress played out in the bowels of the first farmers. In the next wave of technical advance, brought on by metals and more complex forms of social organization, the scene of the action moved from our guts to our lungs.

5

The Sneezing Ape

The Measles Paradigm

In 1846, a carpenter with a cough arrived at the port of Tórshavn in the Faroe Islands. The Faroes are volcanic spits of land poking out of the far northern Atlantic Ocean (see figure 5.1). In 1846 these islands were one of the healthiest places on earth. Thanks to the cold climate and relative isolation from the populous mainland, average life expectancy was nearly forty-five years. The carpenter, a native of the Faroes, was returning from a visit to Copenhagen, Denmark. There he had contracted a virus, which he now carried home in his chest. He had the measles.[1]

The Faroes had not seen the measles virus since 1781. Its reappearance was dramatic. Over the course of five months, approximately 6,000 of the islands' 7,800 inhabitants were infected. More than a hundred died. Then the pathogen ran out of new victims and the chain of transmission was extinguished, done in by its own violence. The measles virus again disappeared from the Faroes.[2]

The measles epidemic on the Faroes is of unusual interest because the Danish government, the distant sovereign over these tiny islands, dispatched an observant young doctor named Peter Panum to the scene. His vivid report (much like Budd's study of typhoid) is a landmark in the history of epidemiology—the study of the population dynamics of infectious disease. By tracking the epidemic from house to house and

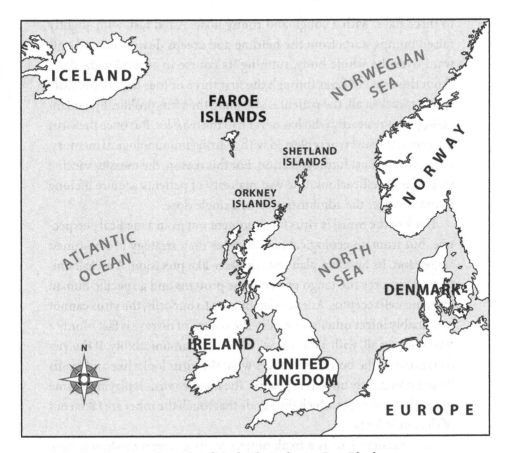

FIGURE 5.1. Map of North Atlantic showing Faroe Islands.

village to village, Panum was able to prove that the infection spread by contact. And he observed the phenomenon of acquired immunity, noting that the disease ignored the island's oldest residents. Anyone infected in the previous visitation, over six decades before, was spared in this round.[3]

The measles virus is among the most contagious human pathogens. It is spread via airborne transmission or infectious droplets, expelled from the lungs of a coughing or sneezing patient. It can linger in the air for a few hours, hoping to be inhaled by a new host. Measles invades via our respiratory tract. Once an infection is launched, the virus suppresses our initial immune response. The patient then experiences fever for two to three days, with a cough and runny nose. A red rash with slightly raised bumps starts from the hairline and creeps downward and outward over the whole body, running its course in around eight days. From the onset of fever through the first three or four days of the rash, about a week in all, the patient is shedding the virus prolifically, endangering anyone nearby who has never had the measles. But once the virus is cleared, the survivor is blessed with a strong immunological memory, protecting against future infection. For this reason, the measles vaccine is supremely efficacious. The vast majority of patients acquire lifelong immunity after the administration of a single dose.[4]

Think of the measles virus for a moment not from a medical perspective, but from an ecological one. It relies on a strategy of fine-tuned aggression. Its invasion plan rests on laser-like precision. A measles infection requires the tango of two virus proteins and a specific human immune-cell receptor. Adept at latching onto our cells, the virus cannot sustainably infect other mammals. The course of disease is fast—only a few weeks in all, with a narrow window of communicability. If the victim recovers, the body remembers what the virus looks like and snuffs it out immediately upon reexposure. The measles virus is playing a game of very hot potato, in which the hands that touch the tuber are taken out of the circle forever.[5]

The measles virus is a freak of nature. Its emergence should have failed miserably and quickly. What happened to the virus on the Faroe Islands—five months of heedless violence followed by hasty extinction—would have been the fate of the measles virus entirely if it had evolved to infect any other mammal. It would also have been the fate of the virus if it had emerged much earlier than it did in human history. The measles virus has a critical population threshold of around 250,000; if it is introduced to a human settlement with fewer susceptible hosts, it will burn through them quickly, careening toward its own extinction. Measles exists because we exist—or, rather, because we built certain kinds of social organizations capable of allowing a virus like measles to sustain transmission in a vast, interconnected network of human lungs. Measles is the ultimate crowd disease.[6]

The measles virus is one particularly stark example of the way that microbial evolution and human social development became intertwined in new ways in the later Holocene epoch. Acute respiratory diseases are a distinctive feature of the human disease pool. They are also, to a large extent, a byproduct of social processes set in motion by metal technologies; the domestication of donkeys, horses, and camels; and the rise of cities. But we will see that other kinds of pathogens also took advantage of continued human growth. We can count falciparum malaria—a vector-borne disease so violent that it is a bit like a crowd disease transmitted by mosquitos—as a kind of spinoff of the spread of metallurgy. Chronic respiratory infections such as tuberculosis and leprosy also now truly came into their own, their careers unimaginable apart from the dynamism of human social life in this period.

More than a generation ago, William McNeill called attention to the "confluence of the civilized disease pools" as the main feature of this era. In his version of events, the rise of agriculture had created disconnected foci of infectious disease, isolated in the various hearths of civilization; then, in the later Holocene, these discrete disease pools came into contact with explosive effect. This story captures something important about the role of trade and transportation in scaling up the dimensions of health crises. But ultimately its model of pathogen evolution is too narrow, too heavily weighted toward the exchange of a few species of germs acquired from a small number of domesticated animals. We will try to see, a little more panoramically, how the changes in human populations during this period shaped the emergence, establishment, and circulation of pathogens.[7]

This chapter covers the transformational period of history spanning from about 3000 BC to AD 500, encompassing what are conventionally known as the Copper, Bronze, and Iron Ages. Those labels work for much of Eurasia, but not at all for the Americas, where complex societies developed without metallurgy. They work only in a qualified way for sub-Saharan Africa, which bypassed the Bronze Age and leapt headlong into the Iron Age. Although this chapter is inevitably focused on the Old World, one goal is to highlight the interconnections between Europe, Asia, and Africa during this period, and their long-term importance for the future of human health. The donkey, the horse, and the camel contracted distance over land, while improvements in sailing and the mastery of the monsoons shrank distance over water. In consequence, human populations came to be networked in ways unseen in the more distant past.

This chapter in the history of infectious disease challenges us to think about scale: about the fine-tuned connections between matters of time and distance at play in the transmission of disease, and their larger implications for the evolution, establishment, and circulation of pathogens. What makes a virus like measles so fascinating, from the perspective of nature, is the way that its acute nature and aggressive strategy—its short temporal scales and utter dependence on the human host—presupposes the success of human societies in creating big, dense, interconnected populations. New technologies of agrarian production, of violence, and of transportation allowed human societies to take on new scales in this period. The diseases we will explore were evolution's response to our grandiose projects of aggregation.

Scaling Up: The Material Background

By 4000 or 3500 BC, agriculture was thousands of years old. Over five millennia had transpired since the first humans domesticated plants in the Near East. Farming had radiated outward from its core regions. But the classic crowd diseases—measles, smallpox, mumps, diphtheria, whooping cough, and a host of other, less virulent respiratory infections—were not yet fixtures in the human disease pool. Tree thinking and time travel have helped us see that the career of these human pathogens had not yet meaningfully begun. The reason is simple: there were no crowds in the early Neolithic. With marginal exceptions, the first farmers lived in villages. Big city life, and big city death, were things of the future.[8]

The scale of early Neolithic society was limited by technology. Agricultural surpluses were meager, and the ability of those in power to extract and wield surpluses was modest. But technological advances from the later fourth millennium BC enabled dramatic changes in human social organization. Metallurgy was of prime importance. Smiths learned to use new materials and to control higher temperatures. Humans had been smelting copper for centuries, but the addition of tin to make bronze was a breakthrough that spread toward the end of the fourth millennium. Bronze, much harder than anything that had been available before, let smiths make stronger tools and more ferocious weapons. The Bronze Age dates to circa 3300 BCE in much of Eurasia.[9]

In the wake of the Neolithic, human expansion was facilitated by the domestication of transport animals: donkeys, horses, and camels. Donkeys were domesticated first, in Africa, and their steady diffusion throughout the Old World should not be underestimated. Donkeys were invaluable farm laborers, and their ability and endurance as pack animals allowed agricultural goods to be borne to markets, fostering specialization and urbanization. The fourth millennium BCE then witnessed the domestication of the horse. Where, exactly, this momentous event happened remains debated, with the Pontic-Caspian steppe being the leading possibility. DNA, as well as archaeological evidence, puts the domestication of the horse around 3500 BCE. The arrival of the horse did more than add milk, meat, and traction power, although it did all of that too. Overland transportation was freed from the limits of human bipedalism. The horse more than doubled the speed of transport, and it multiplied the distances that could be traveled and freights that could be hauled. By accelerating and intensifying human movement, horses also altered the ability of germs to travel. The domestication of the horse was an epidemiological fact of the first order, and it was soon followed by the domestication of camels, with the Bactrian camel tamed before 2500 BCE and the dromedary by at least 1000 BCE. The hardiness of the camel added new itineraries of long-distance connection across arid central Asia and dry parts of east and central Africa.[10]

Other fundamental innovations soon followed—notably, wheeled transport and writing. Faster transport and greater freight capacity facilitated trade. Writing enabled communication over longer distances and thereby expanded the scale of human networks. These cascading innovations were mutually reinforcing, because metal resources were regionally disparate and conducive to specialized production. Social differentiation also created demand for aristocratic luxury goods, making long-distance trade in precious commodities lucrative for merchants.

The most consequential byproduct of these technical innovations, though, was the emergence of bigger cities and more complex social organizations like states and empires. Metals, transport animals, writing, and wheeled transport expanded the organizational capacity of human societies. One notable byproduct of this enlarged social capacity was large-scale irrigation in the great riverine societies that blossomed in Egypt, the Near East, the Indian subcontinent, and China. Larger agricultural surpluses fueled urbanization, as well as social differentiation. Writing was intimately tied to taxation and trade from the very beginning: states and merchants needed the written word for records, accounts, and contracts. Warfare grew in scope and intensity. In short, it became possible to coordinate and control human behavior on an unprecedented scale.

We can measure the growth of human social complexity through two proxy measures: urban populations and imperial territory sizes. These numbers are crude but useful indexes of social scales. Consider the largest cities at thousand-year intervals. In the early Bronze Age, around 3000 BC, the largest city in the world was Uruk (which may have peaked a century or so earlier). Located in Mesopotamia, Uruk was the main center of Sumerian civilization, home of one of the earliest Bronze Age states. Its population has been estimated to be around forty thousand. At the time, there were only a handful of cities with populations over ten thousand; all of these were in the Fertile Crescent, and thus they probably already formed a single disease environment.[11]

A millennium later, in the middle of the Bronze Age, little had fundamentally changed. There were now a few cities with around forty thousand inhabitants, all of them still in the Fertile Crescent. Only by the late Bronze Age, around 1000 BC, had the biggest cities noticeably grown. Egypt, also, had become a major foyer of urbanization. Its capital, Thebes, had grown to 120,000, and Babylon, in present-day Iraq, was not far behind. Over the next millennium, iron technology became widespread, and the largest cities grew by an order of magnitude. By the first century BCE, Rome was the first city to encompass a million residents. South Asia and East Asia had also developed major centers of population, like Chang'an in China. Imperial Rome at its height would

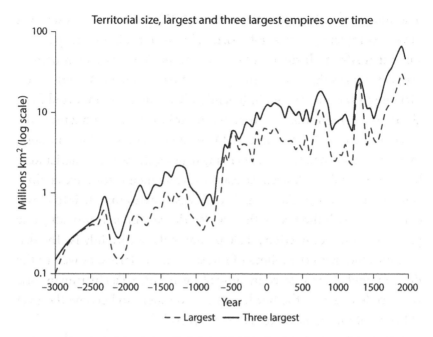

FIGURE 5.2. Territory of largest and three largest empires over time
(see Taagepera 1978a, 1978b, and 1979).

not be equaled in Asia until Tang times (AD 618–907), and no city in
Europe would reach this scale again until London circa 1800.[12]

The territorial scope of the world's largest empires is another measure
of the expanding human capacity for social organization. Consider the
estimated surface area controlled by the largest empire, as well as the
three largest empires combined, at hundred-year intervals from the early
Bronze Age to the present (see figure 5.2). Again, the Bronze Age witnessed material growth starting from almost zero, followed by a jump
during the Iron Age. The peak Iron Age empires established a new plateau that held for about a millennium. The Mongol Empire lunged ahead
again, and then the seaborne empires of modern times achieved a scale
that is unlikely to be surpassed, as long as humans are bound to this
rock.[13]

A full reckoning with this period must include Africa within the
frame of the picture. Sub-Saharan Africa was, in the words of John Iliffe,

in a "unique position of partial isolation." The great Sahara desert was never a completely impassable barrier, but its forbidding prospect ensured that African history had its own tempo. Yet Africa's remoteness was far from absolute, and in this period, it was shrinking. Whether iron metallurgy was discovered independently in Africa or imported from abroad is a contentious question, but regardless of the path it took, the onset of the Iron Age was fateful. Over large swathes of the continent, there was no Bronze Age. And in many regions, there was no agriculture before iron, which "allowed Africans to create their distinctive civilization." It also brought Africa and its disease environments into closer connection with the rest of the Old World. Smallpox is probably one product of this connectivity. Falciparum malaria certainly is. The disease profited from the felling of forests to make farms, as well as the denser populations allowed by agriculture in Africa. Falciparum malaria soon spilled beyond the borders of the continent to become *the* great affliction of the tropics across the Old World.[14]

Cities, states, and empires created new environments for the emergence, establishment, and circulation of human diseases. Transportation technology drew the ends of Europe and Asia into closer contact and increasingly connected Africa into an Old World system. In the Iron Age, the silk roads became a permanent relay system connecting the Mediterranean with the river valleys of China. Humans mastered the monsoon winds and made the Indian Ocean a zone of vibrant exchanges. The camel was tamed and caravan routes opened the interior of Africa. This pulse of globalization facilitated the easy transmission of germs across the continents and registers as one of the decisive chapters in the microbial unification of the world.[15]

Acute Respiratory Disease: Bats, Rats, and Us

Your body needs oxygen. Just as fecal-oral diseases exploit the fact that we have to eat and drink, respiratory diseases exploit the fact that we have to breathe. Because it is such a massive field of exposure to the outside world, the respiratory tract is an appealing target for parasites. The lungs' alveoli, where gases are exchanged, themselves create a surface area that is equivalent to the size of a tennis court. But targeting the respiratory tract is a tricky business. The entire zone is heavily guarded by the immune system. Transmission requires spreading via aerosols, droplets, or fomites (contaminated surfaces), so unless the potential hosts are bunched closely together, most progeny of a respiratory pathogen will never make it from the lungs of one victim to the next. Moreover, most respiratory pathogens cause acute disease: a fast and furious competition against the host's immune system, which creates a tiny window of time for transmission.[16]

In short, life is hard for lung-jumpers. Respiratory infection is rarer in nature than it might seem, judging from the experience of the average modern human. We have, by great ingenuity and strenuous effort, eliminated or controlled the really dangerous respiratory infections. But even today we trudge through a childhood full of sniffling and sneezing, and endure an adulthood marred by frequent coughs and colds. We should not be misled by this experience into believing that there is anything biologically normal about our condition. It is a strange artefact of civilized existence. Consider that no major human respiratory pathogens are known to be of primate origin (with the possible but far from proven exception of leprosy, a chronic infection with a natural history still being deciphered). By contrast, monkeys and apes are highly susceptible to human respiratory germs, and our diseases pose a serious threat to our primate relatives. We are the sneezing ape.[17]

Tree thinking and time travel are starting to illuminate the evolutionary history of our respiratory pathogens, and the general impression is that these germs evolved more recently than once believed. Farming did not immediately give rise to the crowd diseases. For one thing, there were not many true crowds in the early Neolithic. Moreover, the domestication of farm animals was not a one-off chance to come into contact with their germs. Rather, it created a perpetual and ever-widening interface for relentlessly evolving animal pathogens to move between hosts. The implications go beyond revising the chronology of human diseases, and encourage us to reimagine the interplay of evolutionary and social processes that did eventually generate the repertoire of familiar respiratory ailments.

The cross-species transmission of pathogens is pervasive in nature, and it has affected humans—like every other animal—from the beginning. Any time a predator eats its prey, it is exposed to blood and body parts that are teeming with strange and potentially dangerous microbes. The same has always been true of human hunters dressing and butchering game. Host-switching experiments were common, but they were usually dead on arrival. Most pathogens could not survive the human immune system, and if they did, they could not transmit to a new human host. However, those microbes that were able to replicate inside humans and transmit to a new host risked being *too* successful, immobilizing or killing us too quickly and thus failing to establish a continuous chain of human infection. Especially when population densities were low, and social groups were small, new acute diseases were likely to burn themselves out rapidly—like the measles outbreak on the Faroe Islands.

The spread of agriculture allowed human populations to grow, and so it increased the total exposure of our species to all the potential pathogens out there in the world. Already in the early Holocene, then, the number of pathogens invading human bodies must have increased, even though populations were too small to sustain the permanent circulation of the most violent diseases. It is also evident from the archaeological record that human land use, and presumably population growth, dramatically accelerated in the late Holocene, widening our exposure to new germs. Particularly from the fourth millennium BC onward, in much of Eurasia, humans also developed new forms of social organization and connectivity. When novel diseases experimented with the human host, they now had a better chance of avoiding rapid extinction, both because the number and scale of cities had increased and because the networks linking them in a vast human metapopulation thickened. In all, germs like measles and smallpox established *later*, but circulated *faster*, than once believed.[18]

We can delve further into the evolutionary history of the measles virus as an example of how we came to accumulate an array of acute respiratory diseases. The measles virus belongs to the genus *Morbillivirus*. The closest relative of measles is the Rinderpest virus, a pathogen that causes "cattle plague," an exceptionally destructive disease of cattle.

Rinderpest virus—which became an urgent global problem in later times, as we will see—has the distinction of being only the second pathogen, along with smallpox, that humans have intentionally driven to extinction. In turn, the closest relative of measles virus and Rinderpest virus is known as *peste des petits ruminants* virus (PPR virus), which infects goats and sheep. It too is highly contagious and dangerous to farm animals. The measles virus, then, might seem to conform to the traditional story: humans domesticated animals and contracted horrific new diseases from their herds. The truth is far more interesting.[19]

Consider the deeper history of the entire genus *Morbillivirus*. In the past few years, genomic data have created a richer picture of the evolutionary tree of these viruses. A huge number of previously unknown "cousins" of the measles virus have been found by screening bats and rodents for pathogens. The entire genus *Morbillivirus* seems to have evolved from a group of ancestral viruses that infect a range of rodents and bats. Many of these viruses dispersed globally from somewhere in Africa only a few thousand years ago. And even though these viruses are wild rodent pathogens, the reason they have dispersed so effectively and quickly reveals the hand of human intervention. The black rat, *Rattus rattus*, is a commensal species that has thrived alongside human civilization and readily travels in ships, wagons, and saddlebags. As we will see in the next chapter, it played a leading role in the great drama of bubonic plague. But this creature also aided in the dispersal of other diseases, like the morbilliviruses.[20]

As ever, the picture may change once more animal germs are identified and the evolutionary tree is filled in. But already this bigger story is revealing. Morbilliviruses infecting bats and rodents crossed the species barrier to infect domesticated animals, ultimately reaching cattle. Cattle were an evolutionary bridge for the ancestral form of the virus to adapt to humans. And, in a sense, we built the bridge ourselves by domesticating cattle. Wild bovids may never have been the natural host of morbilliviruses at all, making rinderpest just as much an unintended side effect of human social development as measles. In deeper evolutionary terms, both Rinderpest virus and measles virus are germs whose ancestors are parasites of small, colony-dwelling mammals. The measles virus is ultimately a descendant of rodent and bat germs, adapted to a primate that had also learned to live in the giant colonies that we call cities.

The rise of urbanism was the precondition for measles to become a specialist human disease. The latest molecular clock dating of the measles virus estimates that it diverged from an ancestor it shared with the Rinderpest virus around 600 BCE, give or take a few centuries. This evolutionary process may not have been an immediate and irreversible host switch, and the many attested outbreaks of severe disease in both humans and cattle might reflect the gradual adaptation of a pathogen that could still infect both farmers and their livestock. Eventually, the measles virus evolved to become a specialist human pathogen, and it is telling that this process unfolded in the early days of the Iron Age, at just the moment when human settlements first passed the critical population threshold required to sustain continuous transmission. The remarkable alignment tells us that ancestral measles, and other eager pathogens, were knocking at the door. Only once we built an ecosystem with enough lungs in proximity did measles become established as a permanent human pathogen—and subsequently a major burden on human health.[21]

It is also telling that the deep evolutionary background of the measles virus involves a number of pathogens infecting rodents and bats. With the rise of more complex societies in the late Holocene, humans became the evolutionary destiny for an inordinate number of experiments that originate with these small mammals. In one respect, the ecological role of bats and rodents as disease reservoirs is unsurprising. There are more than 1,200 species of bats, comprising around 20 percent of all mammalian diversity. There are nearly 2,300 species of rodents, or 40 percent of all mammal species. Together, then, three out of every five mammal species on the planet are bats or rodents. Both bats and rodents are also exceptionally numerous, far more so than their big-bodied cousins like primates or ungulates. Their importance as disease reservoirs starts with sheer numbers.[22]

The ecological importance of both bats and rodents goes beyond their abundance, though. Consider the basic biology of bats. Bats—the order Chiroptera, or "wing-hand"—are astonishing creatures. Flying

FIGURE 5.3. Montford bat cave, Philippines. Some bats live in giant colonies. Shutterstock.

nocturnal mammals, bats are as mobile as birds. They are long-lived creatures, many surviving for more than twenty or thirty years. Bats are exceptionally gregarious. In some colonies, population density may reach three thousand bats per square meter (see figure 5.3). Moreover, some bats live in roosts of up to a million individuals, and an attractive cave may host numerous different species of bat. The mobility and migratory habits of some bats also connect disparate populations. Even birds, which can have massive populations, do not have the same density as bats. And because the bat's mammalian immune system is more similar to ours, the risk of infection for humans is great.[23]

Like bats, rodents are the source for a huge number of diseases that have eventually come to infect humans. Rodents are highly social mammals, although rodent colonies reach nowhere near the size of bat colonies. Rodents are short-lived and extremely prolific. Their populations are prone to wild oscillations. Rodents and humans live in uncomfortably close ecological association. Rodents are adaptive creatures, and many species have learned to take advantage of human-altered environments. They are important agricultural pests. In many cases, rodents have evolved as part of human habitats—notably, in species such as the house mouse, the black rat, and the brown rat. Because they live on or under the ground, in burrows or nests, they are exposed to pathogens in soil and feces. In turn, because of the close quarters we share with these commensal rodents, we are exposed to rodent droppings and the microbes lurking therein. Other rodent pathogens make use of fleas, ticks, or mites as intermediaries. Unsurprisingly, rodents serve as hosts for a wide range of parasites, including viruses, bacteria, protozoa, and helminths.[24]

Bats and rodents seem implicated in the origins of many of our diseases. Mumps and, as we will see, smallpox, are important parallels to measles among viral respiratory diseases. Mumps is at least 2,400 years old, because Hippocrates, the father of Greek medicine, personally witnessed an epidemic around 400 BC. Like measles and smallpox, it was capable of causing deadly and disruptive outbreaks. The human disease pool also includes a wide range of viral respiratory diseases that are comparatively mild. The parainfluenza viruses, respiratory syncytial viruses, coronaviruses (four of which are established in human populations—now likely five, if SARS-CoV-2 joins the permanent pool), rhinoviruses, and adenoviruses all cause moderate respiratory disease. Probably countless other such viruses have come and gone, switching hosts, transiently succeeding before burning out. The notorious named viruses of history are only the most successful victors of the ceaseless Darwinian struggle to take over our cellular machinery.[25]

Viruses outnumber bacteria among our respiratory pathogens. But several bacterial afflictions rank among the true crowd diseases— notably, diphtheria and whooping cough. Diphtheria, often known as "putrid" or "malignant" sore throat, was dangerous, and as an epidemic disease it was explosive. Like mumps, diphtheria was known to classical medicine; in the Hippocratic corpus, there are unmistakable descriptions of the characteristic membrane in the throat. Of equal importance has been the bacterium that causes whooping cough, *Bordatella pertussis*. A case of whooping cough begins like an ordinary cold but progresses to a paroxysmal phase, notable for the intense dry coughs followed by powerful, desperate gasps to recover air. Whooping cough is not clearly described in written records until a series of outbreaks in Persia from the late fifteenth century. But its genome is starting to unveil its evolutionary history. A versatile ancestor that was only opportunistically a pathogen has spun off various pathogenic strains. At least twice, descendants have evolved adaptations that make them highly effective human pathogens. This is a bacterium with an eventful evolutionary history lying within the last few thousand years.[26]

The respiratory pathogens that emerged and established in human populations during the late Holocene were layered on top of the gastroenteric infections that had already taken advantage of our more sedentary lifestyles. Far from fading away or yielding in succession to a new kind of germ, intestinal pathogens continued to adapt to human societies. The great cities of classical antiquity in fact scaled up the problem of waste management. But they also undertook the first efforts to coordinate a public response, with sewers, aqueducts, and rudimentary sanitary laws. And to underscore the fact that continued human expansion provoked other evolutionary responses, we can turn to two of the most important human diseases that flourished amid the rise of large-scale civilization: tuberculosis and falciparum malaria.

Tuberculosis: The Ultimate Human Disease

Unlike the acute infections we have considered so far, TB is a respiratory disease characterized by patience. It possesses the remarkable ability to modulate the human immune responses and cause chronic infection. The burden of this disease on human health, in the past and present, is staggering. It featured prominently in the classical medical literature of China, India, and Greece, where it was known as *phthisis*, "wasting" or "consumption." It thrived throughout antiquity and the Middle Ages. In modern Europe, it was the white plague. Industrialization played directly into its hands: a medical text of 1848 called it "the destroying angel who claims a fourth of all who die." Today, there are maybe two billion humans latently infected, so more than a quarter of humanity could be carrying the pathogen. There are more than ten million new cases annually, and TB still takes 1.5 million lives each year.

TB may just be, in aggregate, the most lethal enemy our species has ever encountered.[27]

Tuberculosis takes various clinical courses. In primary tuberculosis, the infection progresses into active disease within a year or two after initial exposure. TB is first and foremost a disease of the lungs, and its chief symptom is a consuming and often bloody cough. Many cases of TB produce only latent infection, in which the bacterium persists in small numbers without causing active disease. Sometimes latent cases are subsequently reactivated years or decades after the initial infection. A host then becomes infectious, possibly distant in time and space from the environment of the initial infection.[28]

During infection with TB, bacteria can disseminate in the bloodstream and reach a variety of organs. For instance, TB is the cause of scrofula, a hard, disfiguring swelling of the lymph nodes in the neck, known as the "king's evil" from the tradition that it could be cured by the royal touch. But our lungs are the primary target, and TB is only transmitted via a droplet coughed up by one victim and inhaled by the next. Although TB has an effective dose of merely one to three individual bacteria, to establish a new infection, these bacteria must pass deep into the lungs to find the kind of immune cell they seek. The cell wall of a tuberculosis bacterium is covered with common molecular patterns that should immediately give it away to our immune system, but it wears an outer lipid layer as a cheap disguise, like a trench coat. This coat has evolved to recruit one class of macrophage cells, the workhorse of our innate immune system. This cell is the true habitat of TB.[29]

Even during the state of active disease, tuberculosis often consumed its victims without great haste. It was called "the wasting disease" for good reason. In *Nicholas Nickleby*, Charles Dickens described its lurid course with the dark romanticism that came to surround the disease in the nineteenth century. "There is a dread disease which so prepares its victim, as it were, for death . . . a dread disease in which the struggle between soul and body is so gradual, quiet, and solemn, and the result so sure, that day by day and grain by grain, the mortal part wastes and withers away . . . a disease in which life and death are so strangely blended, that death takes the glow and hue of life, and life the gaunt and grisly form of death—a disease which medicine never cured, wealth warded off, or poverty could boast exemption from—which sometimes moves in giant strides, and sometimes at a tardy sluggish pace, but, slow or quick, is ever sure and certain."[30]

We have already noted that genomic data have upended one part of the traditional story of how TB evolved, showing that human TB is ancestral to bovine TB (a pathogen that can still cause disease in humans). That is merely the beginning of one of the wildest sagas of discovery yet in the annals of pathogen genomics. Human tuberculosis is caused by bacteria belonging to the *Mycobacterium tuberculosis* complex, which is comprised of five major human-adapted lineages, two lineages known as *M. africanum* that also infect humans, and at least nine animal-adapted lineages infecting everything from cows and chimps to sea mammals like seals and dolphins. An eighth, previously unknown, human lineage (of extraordinary interest, as we will see) has just been identified. Other lineages in humans and animals surely existed in the past, while still others are probably out there waiting to be discovered.[31]

The first surprise unveiled by the evolutionary tree of all these closely related bacteria is that human-adapted strains are ancestral to all the animal strains identified so far. It suggests that *Homo sapiens* has been responsible (directly or indirectly) for introducing tuberculosis to an unsettling array of animals, wild and domestic. It has even been hypothesized that we gave TB to our cows not once but twice, in each of the two major cattle domestication events that led, respectively, to taurine and zebu cattle. We can thus probably see the wide distribution of *M. tuberculosis* in animals as a reflection of humanity's ecological versatility and planetary impact, even though all the links in the chain of TB's spread are yet to be found. TB is the ultimate *human* disease, then, in the disturbing sense that we have been unwitting agents of its global dispersal and evolutionary diversification.[32]

The second great, even befuddling, surprise to have surfaced from the study of the tuberculosis genome is the youth of the pathogen. It was formerly believed that TB had adapted to humans more than seventy thousand years ago and then migrated with our species out of

Africa. The prolonged course of the disease and latent phase of the infection made this theory perfectly plausible. Moreover, pathological lesions in ancient human skeletal remains have often been attributed to tuberculosis, and published studies have claimed to find biomolecular evidence of TB infection going back to the early Holocene. And so the disease has often been cataloged among the truly ancient scourges of humanity.[33]

The genomic evidence now compellingly demonstrates otherwise. All sampled strains of *M. tuberculosis* shared a common ancestor less than six thousand years ago, and more likely less than four thousand years ago. These estimates are bolstered by a growing body of archaeological DNA evidence, which allows these chronological measurements to be calibrated. Recently, the DNA of the bacterium was recovered from a calcified lung nodule of a mummified Swedish bishop who died in the seventeenth century. The refined molecular clock analysis now estimates that all lineages in the *M. tuberculosis* complex shared an ancestor about 3,258 years ago (within a range of likelihood that extends from 2,190 to 4,501 years ago). It is not impossible, of course, that more evidence could emerge to alter the story, and the earlier skeletal evidence for TB in human (and animal) populations remains a sticky problem. But we have to reckon with the reality that TB as we know it is a product of the late Holocene, a relatively young pathogen that emerged in the context of civilization. It is not, after all, one of our most ancient scourges.[34]

Even though TB did not disperse along with migrants out of Africa in the Pleistocene, there is still good reason to believe that Africa is the cradle of human tuberculosis. The newly discovered human lineage has only solidified the case for African origins and helped to pinpoint East Africa as the most likely region of the pathogen's emergence. Farming and pastoralism intensified in East Africa in the late Holocene, and these subsistence and demographic changes will need to be explored as the likely backdrop to the emergence of this respiratory disease. And certainly, the human networks of the Iron Age enabled tuberculosis to spread quickly in the centuries after its adaptation to the human host.[35]

The genetic diversity of TB around the globe allows us to trace in outline the otherwise lost history of its dispersal. By two thousand years ago, East Africa was connected into trade networks that reached across the Indian Ocean. Metals, slaves, ivory, spices, aromatics, salt, and glass moved between Africa and Eurasia. And deep in the lungs of merchants, migrants, soldiers, and slaves, so did *M. tuberculosis*. One lineage (known as Lineage 3) was quickly established in South Asia. Another lineage (Lineage 2) also spread east and remains prevalent in East Asia; it then diffused along with the expansion of the Han people from northern China. Lineage 4 of the bacterium evolved less than two thousand years ago, around the time of the Roman Empire. This lineage of the germ spread across Eurasia in later Roman times and, still later, European expansion carried it into Africa, the Indian Ocean, and the New World. The success of this virulent European lineage underscores the fact that larger, denser, and more interconnected human populations can favor the selection of genetic strains that are highly aggressive.[36]

The global journey of tuberculosis also presents some remarkable twists—notably, in the dissemination of the disease in the New World. Today, strains of tuberculosis dominant in the Americas are descended from strains introduced by Europeans following post-Columbian contact. This pattern seemed to conflict with the extensive skeletal evidence for pre-Columbian TB in the Americas. If TB only evolved after the Pleistocene migrations to the Americas, and if the dominant strains in the Americas today reflect post-Columbian contact, then why do so many skeletons of Americans before 1492 show the lesions characteristic of tuberculosis? Time travel has provided an unexpected answer. Three ancient TB genomes, dating to one thousand years ago, were recovered from mummies in Peru, which confirmed the presence of the disease prior to European contact and colonization. Yet the strains from Peru were most closely related to a strain that is usually found in sea mammals, like seals. It suggests that the Americans contracted TB by capturing and butchering seals. Quite how the seals contracted TB is an open question; even though humans appear to have played an instrumental role in spreading TB to animals, there are clearly parts of the story that are missing—intermediary animal or environmental reservoirs through which the bacterium has disseminated. Nonetheless, at least one strain of TB was already present in New World human populations prior to colonization. Later, Europeans brought a more virulent strain that replaced the already present lineage. The same may have occurred in the Pacific.[37]

Meanwhile, in the Old World, urbanization was an unforeseen boon to tuberculosis. The greatest limitation of this disease is that, unlike many acute respiratory infections, it is not very easily transmitted. It requires close crowding to ensure that small droplets will reach their destination in the lower lungs. As human cities grew in size and density from ancient to modern times, we were unwittingly helping the pathogen solve its hardest problem. The burden of the disease often fell on the frail bodies of children. As Malthus observed in industrial times, "There certainly seems to be something in great towns, and even in moderate towns, peculiarly unfavourable to the early stages of life: and the part of the community upon which the mortality principally falls, seems to indicate that it arises more from the closeness and foulness of the air, which may be supposed to be unfavourable to the tender lungs of children."[38]

The full burden of tuberculosis in the distant past is elusive. We know from medical texts as well as the skeletal record that the wasting disease was widespread. But the true impact of tuberculosis is hard to trace precisely because the disease was so universal, so inexorable in both time and space. It thrived on the density and squalor of towns, but the disease had no marked geographic preferences. The burden of tuberculosis was not felt in the sort of sudden, dramatic waves of mortality that fill the ancient chronicles but, rather, in the quiet, unrelenting vice grip in which it held human populations. Tuberculosis evolved to become the perfect pathogen, a methodical deceiver living inside the very cells that we expect to save us. Slow, agonizing, unaccountable loss, repeated in stupefying quantity, is the real historical legacy of tuberculosis.

Falciparum Malaria

"And truly the malaria gets into you with the bread you eat, or if you open your mouth to speak as you walk, suffocating in the dust and sun of the roads, and you feel your knees give way beneath you, or you sink discouraged on the saddle as your mule ambles along, with its head down. . . . The malaria seizes the inhabitants in the depopulated streets, and nails them in front of the doors of their houses whose plaster is all falling with the sun, and there they tremble with fever under their brown cloaks."[39]

In Giovanni Verga's nineteenth-century short story about malaria in Sicily, the disease is a haunting presence. It is everywhere, hanging in the atmosphere, poisoning human life. Malaria was always the quintessential miasmatic disease, to all appearances caused by the exhalations of the landscape. The disease was noted in one of the earliest texts of Greek medicine, *On Airs, Waters, and Places*, which described marshy and stagnant waters bringing constant fevers. People living nearby "have large and obstructed spleens, their bellies are hard, emaciated, and hot; and their shoulders, collar-bones, and faces are emaciated; for their flesh is melted down and taken up by the spleen, and hence they are slender." Malaria seemed like a curse upon the land itself.[40]

Malaria is one name for different diseases caused by protozoan parasites in the genus *Plasmodium*. All forms of the disease are transmitted by mosquitos. Vivax malaria, as we have seen, is a serious public health problem wherever it takes hold. But falciparum malaria is a monster. *P. falciparum* is one of seven members of the subgenus *Laverania*, all seven of which infect great apes. There has never been any doubt that falciparum malaria emerged in Africa, but the evolutionary age of *P. falciparum* has long been debated, and estimates have ranged from a few thousand to a few million years ago. Its closest relative is a parasite of gorillas, *P. praefalciparum*. A case has been made that *P. falciparum* had already started to separate from its gorilla-infecting ancestor in the later Pleistocene—some forty to sixty thousand years ago. For tens of thousands of years, the parasite may have retained the ability to infect gorillas. If so, it was not yet the dedicated human pathogen it was destined to become.[41]

If this view is correct, then *P. falciparum* has been making us sick since the Pleistocene, when we were hunter-gatherers. Indeed, the parasite has some genetic adaptations that might have let it survive even in low-density populations. *P. falciparum* can cause a chronic infection lasting several years. The parasite has a remarkable ability to shift the shape of its outward-facing proteins, making it hard for the body to recognize and clear the pathogen. Resistance is notoriously difficult to acquire: it is not earned quickly in a single encounter, as, say, with measles. Rather, resistance is built up, like a thick callous, over years and years of constant battle with the parasite. Moreover, one of the very tricks that make *P. falciparum* so hard for the body to clear also makes it so virulent. Inside the red blood cell, it produces a protein that makes the infected human cell latch on tenaciously to small blood vessels in our organs. The disease thus harms a range of organs, including the brain (cerebral malaria); meanwhile, the body cannot carry damaged blood cells to the spleen where they ought to be taken for elimination. *P. falciparum* gets inside us, clings on, and persists.[42]

It is plausible, therefore, that *P. falciparum* adapted to humans in our hunter-gatherer past. If so, the parasite passed through a population bottleneck around five thousand years ago. In other words, in this view, *P. falciparum* skated on the edge of extinction until, tragically, humans created the conditions for it to expand, to devote itself entirely to the infection of us. But some have doubted that a parasite so virulent could have avoided extinction without larger human populations to sustain transmission, and there is evidence that *P. falciparum* does go locally extinct where human density is too low. Genetic evidence will allow these estimates to be refined as research continues, and it may turn out that *P. falciparum* switched to humans entirely in the Holocene. Either way, its story as one of the great human pathogens is intimately connected to the social processes that unfolded during this period.[43]

The expansion of *P. falciparum* is the end result of a chain reaction driven by human ecological transformation in Africa. The spread of farming in Africa changed the evolutionary environment for mosquitos. The main vectors of malaria in Africa are *Anopheles coluzzi, Anopheles funestus, Anopheles arabiensis*, and, above all *Anopheles gambiae sensu stricto*. *A. gambiae* has the peculiar characteristic that it breeds in small, temporary pools of water. It will not lay eggs under forest cover, nor in large or moving bodies of water. It likes puddles, such as those that form at the forest's edge. And *A. gambiae* lusts for human blood. It is anthropophilic, and even when other sources of blood are on offer, it seeks out ours. In consequence, *A. gambiae* mosquitos pester humans with a diabolical vengeance and allow remarkably intense circulation of bloodborne parasites. In the most endemic regions, an individual is bitten by an infected mosquito on average 170 times per year. It would be hard to overstate the role of these vectors in creating the unique ecology of malaria in Africa.[44]

The domestication of plants and animals arose independently in Africa—and earlier than once believed. But for millennia, the spread of agriculture in Africa was slow. The forbidding physical environment and daunting disease ecology limited population growth. The appearance of iron metallurgy was critical in the large-scale expansion of agriculture. Farmers bearing iron tools cleared forest, not only increasing their numbers but also creating niches for human-feeding mosquitos. *P. falciparum* expanded in step with human population growth and the gradual ecological transformation of the continent.

The biological reason falciparum malaria is such a dangerous disease is because it attacks our red blood cells so indiscriminately. The less virulent *P. vivax*, for instance, has a strong preference for young red blood cells; it infects about 2 percent of a patient's red blood cells. By contrast, *P. falciparum* is less particular, infecting up to 80 percent of the victim's red blood cells. The disease kills 20–30 percent of those it infects and stunts the long-term development of survivors. In regions where falciparum malaria is endemic, childhood is virtually a contest to survive endless bouts of infection. To reach adulthood is to have achieved a hard-won immunological resistance. Retaining this advantage requires almost constant exposure to the disease as an adult; tragically, the immune response fades during pregnancy, meaning adult women are highly vulnerable to serious disease.[45]

The costs of living in a region with malaria are steep, and the disease has driven natural selection in the human genome. Falciparum malaria rewards human genetic variants that are otherwise disadvantageous but confer resistance against the parasite. The most noted example is sicklecell disease. The gene involved in sickle-cell disease codes for a part of the oxygen-carrying molecule hemoglobin. A person has two copies of each gene, and if a person inherits one copy of the gene carrying the

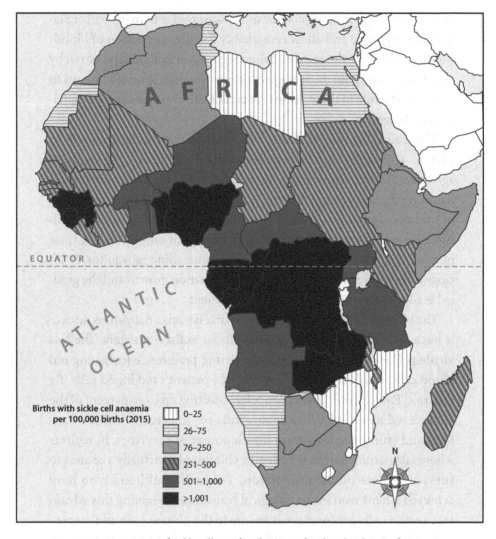

Births with sickle cell anaemia
per 100,000 births (2015)

☐	0–25
	26–75
	76–250
	251–500
	501–1,000
	>1,001

FIGURE 5.4. Maps of sickle cell trait distribution and malaria burden in Africa.

sickle-cell trait, it will provide protection against malaria mortality. But if someone inherits two copies of the gene, it misshapes the red blood cells so drastically that the carrier develops sickle-cell disease, which causes a range of health complications, including chronic anemia. In tropical Africa, more than a quarter of individuals carry one sickle-cell gene (see figure 5.4). Normally, such a harmful variant would be likely

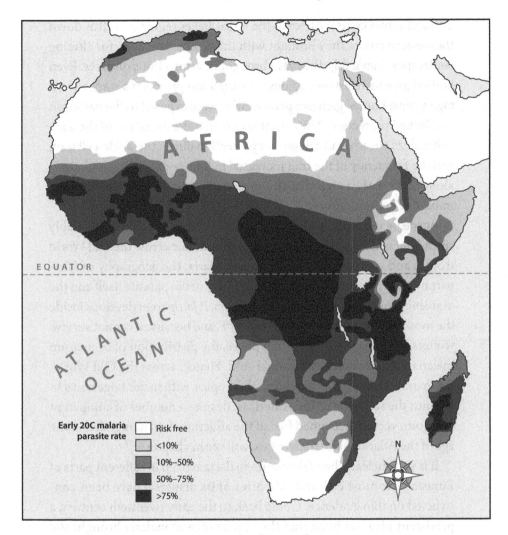

FIGURE 5.4. (*Continued*)

to decline, but the protective advantage against malaria has allowed the
sickle-cell trait to persist.[46]

The intensification of the malaria burden in Africa was implicated in
one of the most important population movements on the continent:
the Bantu expansion. Starting around 1000 BC, people speaking a
Niger-Congo language started to spread from a nucleus around modern-
day Nigeria-Cameroon. The Bantu peoples were agriculturalists who

diffused across central Africa to the Great Lakes region as well as down the western coast. They brought with them their proclivity for altering landscapes. Inevitably, they also brought new infectious diseases. Even limited genetic resistance against *P. falciparum* provided a stark advantage against hunter-gatherer peoples who were exposed to the pathogen and lacked protection. Notably, it seems that the ancestors of the agriculturalists already had a degree of protection due to the sickle-cell trait, and the frequency of the trait increased in hunter-gatherer populations along their path, a sign that the spread of agriculture broadened the impact of malarial disease.[47]

Borne by migrants, traders, and slaves, falciparum malaria inevitably spread out of Africa. The disease became endemic across the Old World tropics and subtropics. As with vivax malaria, the geography of falciparum malaria is determined by the biology of the parasite itself and the availability of competent mosquito vectors. *P. falciparum* develops inside the mosquito only between 66°F and 95°F, and because it cannot survive winters by retreating to the latent phase, the distribution of falciparum malaria is constrained by seasonal cold. Hence, across the Old World, falciparum malaria was endemic in the tropics, with major fingers reaching into the subtropics. The Americas, despite a number of competent mosquito vectors, remained free of the affliction until it migrated in the age of the Atlantic slave trade, as we will see in chapter 8.[48]

It is still unclear when falciparum malaria arrived in different parts of Eurasia. The most elaborate theories of its dispersal have been constructed on thin evidence. Going back to the early twentieth century, a persistent idea has been that the appearance of malaria brought the sunny days of classical Greece and Rome to an end. It is unclear whether falciparum malaria had reached the Mediterranean by the time of Hippocrates in the fifth century BC. This is a question that is likely to be resolved, either with archaeological DNA of the parasite itself, or by the close study of human genomes. Mediterranean populations also have extensive genetic adaptations selected because they confer some resistance to malaria (notably, the mutations that cause beta-thalassemia). As we learn more from ancient human DNA, the chronology of these recent adaptations in the human genome will become clearer.[49]

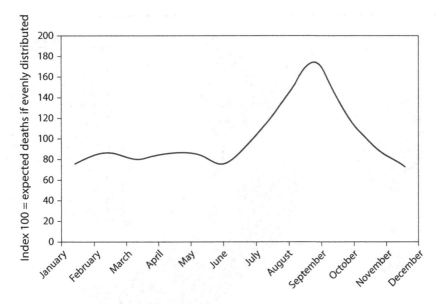

FIGURE 5.5. Seasonal mortality in ancient Rome.

The disease was vividly evident in the circum-Mediterranean by the time of the Roman Empire. Roman doctors like Galen observed a malignant intermittent fever that was unmistakably falciparum malaria. Galen thought that malaria was particularly prevalent in the capital city itself. "It is right in our sight every day, and especially in Rome. Just as other diseases are typical in other places, this evil abounds in this city." His claim finds confirmation in the seasonal patterns of death from ancient Rome, as recovered from the thousands of tombstones that survive in the catacombs (see figure 5.5). In Italy, malaria killed in the autumn, and the annual wave of death from ancient Rome is a likely signature of the disease's heavy toll.[50]

The Italian peninsula, like much of southern Europe, touches the zone of mixed infection, where falciparum and vivax can both be endemic. In fact, Italy provides a case study of a society on the fringes of falciparum malaria. In medieval and modern times, falciparum malaria was a scourge in Sardinia, Sicily, and southern Italy, reaching as far north as Rome itself and the Maremma in Tuscany (see figure 5.6). The coastal regions and lowlands were burdened by the weight of the pernicious

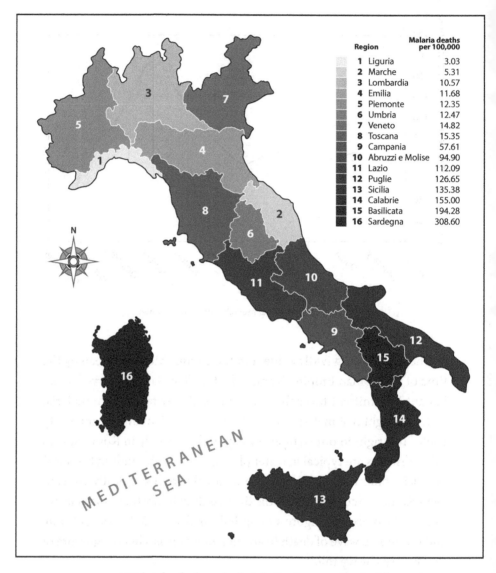

Region	Malaria deaths per 100,000
1 Liguria	3.03
2 Marche	5.31
3 Lombardia	10.57
4 Emilia	11.68
5 Piemonte	12.35
6 Umbria	12.47
7 Veneto	14.82
8 Toscana	15.35
9 Campania	57.61
10 Abruzzi e Molise	94.90
11 Lazio	112.09
12 Puglie	126.65
13 Sicilia	135.38
14 Calabrie	155.00
15 Basilicata	194.28
16 Sardegna	308.60

FIGURE 5.6. Malaria burden by region in Italy. Deaths per one hundred thousand. From official mortality data, late nineteenth century.

fevers, subject to the abundance of particular mosquito vectors. The diverging destinies of northern and southern Italy were cast in no small part by the distribution of malaria. Regions with similar environments, cultures, and institutions had dramatically different disease burdens. Where falciparum malaria took hold, it required a high-pressure demographic regime. In southern Italy, where falciparum malaria was the greatest burden, women married extremely young. As we will see in chapter 10, there is also a strong association between endemic malaria and long-run human capital formation. Italy, in short, straddled one of the most important geographical disease gradients and affords us insights into the deep historical effects of this pathogen.[51]

Falciparum malaria spread across tropical Eurasia. In India and Southeast Asia, it became a major burden on human health. The geography of the disease in China mirrors the patterns in Europe, with a stark north-south gradient in the burden of disease. In the words of one historian, "To Han Chinese from the north, all of the south looked diseased," and malaria is the major reason. As Han migrants moved south of the Nanling Mountains, they settled the northern valleys of Guangdong and Guangxi, but occupation of southern Lingnan and beyond was stalled by the disease environment. "Fear of malaria kept them from migrating elsewhere in Lingnan, even in the face of mounting population pressure in northern Guangdong." The ecological boundaries of Han power were a fundamental dynamic of Chinese imperial history, drawn in part by the distribution of the malaria parasites.[52]

Falciparum malaria was both an endemic and epidemic disease—a permanent presence in populations where it was established, but capable of rearing into large-scale outbreaks. Short-term climate variability, for instance, drove oscillations in mosquito populations that could flare into malaria epidemics. Ancient doctors like Galen noted these patterns. "When the entire year becomes wet or hot, there necessarily occurs a very great plague." In early modern times, malaria waxed and waned in Rome, intensifying every five to eight years into epidemic mortality.[53]

Malaria epidemics could be severe, especially in territories along the edges of the endemic zone. One well-documented outbreak transpired in Ethiopia in 1958. A famine had struck the year before, and then rain fell in abundance during normally dry months. An epidemic broke out and "reached into high altitude zones rarely affected by the disease and there overwhelmed a large susceptible population." The consequences were devastating. According to one observer in the field, "In each house we were able to find three or four patients who complained of subjective symptoms, such as chilling, severe headaches, sweating, pain in the back and extremities. The objective symptoms were jaundice, anemia, emaciation, high fever. After four or five relapses, the head aches and pain became unbearable for many patients, who then exhibited a muddling delirium with coma, ending in death. . . . Since they are far away from even the simplest clinic, which means no possibility of saving their lives, they are dying like bees in a smoked hive." Over three million people were infected, and conservatively, more than 150,000 lost their lives.[54]

With the diffusion of falciparum malaria across the Old World, then, one of the fundamental patterns in the global geography of infectious disease took its definitive form. Even in the Pleistocene, vector-borne diseases had created a latitudinal gradient in human health. But the most burdensome of tropical diseases followed the intensification of human ecological impact in the Holocene. The tropics became a fundamentally malarial zone. Ironically, in future centuries, as we will see, the deadly power of the disease served as a buffer against imperialism, even as it weighed on the societies that adapted to live under its terrible force.

Rome: An Iron Age Case Study

In his novel *The Plague*, a psychological study of living through a pestilence, Albert Camus (1913–60) understood something profound about the seemingly random fury of epidemic disease. In the story, the citizens of the French Algerian city of Oran live in denial of the escalating plague all around them, because they simply cannot come to terms with its appalling inhumanity. "A pestilence isn't a thing made to man's measure; therefore we tell ourselves that pestilence is a mere bogy of the mind, a bad dream that will pass away."[55]

Epidemics do not just pass away—not for those suffering them, nor for historians trying to understand them in hindsight. An *epidemic*, from the Greek roots meaning "upon the people," is an event, an outbreak, causing severe morbidity and mortality. The Centers for Disease Control and Prevention (CDC) describes an epidemic as "an increase, often sudden, in the number of cases of a disease above what is normally expected in that population in that area." Epidemics, in both their causes and consequences, are among the most complex events that a society can experience. Because they involve both human and natural factors, ecological and evolutionary forces, epidemics can seem like completely random events that inexplicably crash into the stream of history. As human societies grew in scale and complexity, so too did epidemics assume new proportions.[56]

Why do epidemics happen? The answer lies in the transmission dynamics of infectious disease. Epidemics happen when a pathogen is able to spread rapidly through a population of susceptible hosts. These conditions may arise for social reasons—when a hungry population becomes more physically frail and therefore susceptible, or when war breaks down the normal order of life. These conditions can also arise when a pathogen is introduced into a susceptible population, whether by trade or migration, or when a new microbe evolves or an old one changes its appearance so it is no longer recognized by the host's immune system. In large enough populations, contagious diseases that confer resistance (like measles) undergo epidemic oscillations, infecting children rapidly and requiring enough new susceptible hosts to be born in order to escalate again. And the climate can play a role in triggering epidemics by driving the population dynamics of reservoir hosts like rodents or vector species like mosquitos.[57]

Because epidemics involve unpredictable, nonhuman variables, there has been a temptation for historians and other students of human society to write them off as a "bad dream"—or at least to describe them as an exogenous force in human history. But that does not do justice to the human role in shaping the ecology and evolution of infectious disease. For inspiration in how we might incorporate epidemics into the fabric of human history we can look to the fourteenth-century Arab historian Ibn Khaldūn. Ibn Khaldūn was a historian who had an enviable command of what we now call economics, geography, anthropology, and political science. As a survivor of the Black Death, he knew something about epidemic disease. For Ibn Khaldūn, the basic pattern of human history was the cycle of civilizational rise and fall. And though he lacked a modern understanding of the biology of disease, he saw that epidemics were not entirely random acts of God or nature. They were a phenomenon requiring rational explanation, and they were inseparable from the cycles of expansion and decline.[58]

Ibn Khaldūn's theory of epidemics is compelling because he recognized that pestilence could be a product of a society's failure *or* its success. In other words, poverty, famine, and violence might cause disease outbreaks. But so might growth, expansion, and dynamism. In his words, epidemics could be precipitated by the "dense and abundant civilization such as exists in the later [years] of a dynasty. [Such civilization] is the result of the good government, the kindness, the safety, and the light taxation that existed at the beginning of the dynasty." A vigorous civilization with good government facilitates growth, but, paradoxically, the demographic upswing triggers lethal epidemic diseases and social disintegration. This insight is profound. Whereas a Malthusian sees epidemics as a consequence of other kinds of crisis engendered ultimately by food shortage, Ibn Khaldūn saw that epidemics might also arise because the very conditions that allow a society to flourish also increase its exposure to pathogens.[59]

Ibn Khaldūn thought he was describing a universal pattern of history, but in reality, what he offers is a model of social dynamics characteristic of agrarian empires in the Iron Age. Following the mastery of iron metallurgy, there were no breakthrough technologies, only incremental advances, for centuries. Instead, the most important innovations during this period were increases in the organizational capacity of human societies. Successful empires were not built on technological superiority so much as effective military mobilization, ideologies, political strategies, and fiscal regimes. And their vulnerability to epidemic disease was shaped by the nature and limits of agrarian-based empires.[60]

We can take the Roman Empire as a case study of an Iron Age agrarian empire and its relationship with infectious disease. It may seem unusual to place Rome in the Iron Age, because such chronological terms were developed by archaeologists precisely to describe prehistorical societies. But such divisions are arbitrary and misleading, and the Romans built an empire based on, and limited by, the Iron Age technology package. The Roman case is not just the one that I happen to know best—though it is that. The Romans are the most intimately known ancient civilization, and even though there is still much to learn, the Romans offer an irresistible chance to sketch how an Iron Age population lived and died. It also happens that their destiny intersected the arrival of an explosive new pathogen, very likely an ancestor of the smallpox virus.

For centuries the Romans were marginal players on the edge of Greek civilization who then ascended to carry out an unlikely takeover of the Mediterranean world. Rome was the beneficiary of lucky timing: the violent and fragmented interstate world of the late Hellenistic kingdoms furnished the perfect opening for a new contender. The Romans enjoyed no great technological advantages over their rivals. The key to Rome's success was the ability to conscript and mobilize military power at scale, a feature of Roman society rooted in a culture of fanatical militarism. Rome's ideology of patriotism, martial glory, and citizen sacrifice was ferociously effective.[61]

The Romans were eventually able to rein in their expansionist impulses and convert their regime of conquest into a system of stable imperial rule. But Roman power had reached the technological limits of communication and coordination by the time of the emperor Augustus (who ruled from 27 BC to AD 14). He proclaimed an age of peace and halted the massive military mobilization of the Roman citizenry. Augustus and his successors were quasi-constitutional autocrats with trappings of republicanism; the emperor controlled the senatorial class, which in turn controlled the professional army; the emperor also forged an alliance with civic elites across the empire. The Augustan regime endured for centuries.[62]

The Roman Empire stretched from the fringes of Scotland to the sands of the Sahara, from the shores of the Atlantic to the hills of eastern Syria. The Romans controlled this vast space without motorized transport or telecommunication. The population expanded in the first century and a half of the Common Era. At the height of the empire, in the middle of the second century, the population living under Roman rule may have reached 75 million, about one in four humans alive. Ancient cities burst through their old boundaries. Rome itself benefited from being the central node in the empire, and its scale testifies to the organizational capacity of the Romans—the urban populace depended on the provision of foodstuffs from North Africa and Egypt. Besides Rome, there were a handful of other true megacities, like Alexandria, Antioch, Ephesus, and Carthage. In all, there were hundreds of midsized cities and thousands of towns. The empire was an unprecedented experiment in urbanism, but it bears underscoring that the vast majority of people still lived in the countryside, in tiny villages and isolated farmsteads.[63]

Trade boomed under the Pax Romana. The signs of local and inter-regional trade, in luxuries as well as bulk and basic consumer goods, were everywhere. Moreover, long-distance trade flourished. The Red Sea corridor connected the Romans to the world of the Indian Ocean, bringing them into contact with East Africa, India, and, indirectly, China. The Romans bought silk and spices in abundance. They exported glass, red coral, wine, and coins. Goods circulated more regularly than ever before. In the AD 160s, an adventurous party of Roman traders was seized by the officials of the Chinese emperor. It was the first recorded contact between the Romans and Chinese.[64]

Peace, however, did not translate into biological well-being for the Romans. Roman progress did nothing for Roman health. In Roman Egypt, life expectancy at birth may have been in the low 20s. Roman society was simply helpless in the face of infectious disease. The poor health of the Romans is written all over their bones. The rise of Roman civilization made people shorter by an average of several centimeters. Achieved height is a complex biological phenomenon, a result of genetics, nutrition, and stress. In the Roman case, the best explanation for the short stature of the Romans is the infectious disease burden. Paradoxically, the Romans were prosperous but sick.[65]

The Roman disease environment was hazardous for the very reasons that the Roman economy thrived: towns and trade. Dense, urban environments were deadly. And the connectivity of the empire facilitated the transmission of germs. Dysentery and enteric fever—the diseases of human waste—seem to have been rife. Intestinal worms abounded. Tuberculosis was rampant. And in much of the Mediterranean heartland, malaria was a scourge. Not only vivax malaria, but the more insidious species of malaria parasite, *Plasmodium falciparum*, had become endemic in southern Europe and the Mediterranean.[66]

The Roman cycle of demographic growth peaked in the middle of the second century. The reign of the emperor Marcus Aurelius (161–80) was a subtle turning point. The challenges faced by the empire included external factors, such as the growing power of Rome's neighbors, particularly the Germans and Persians. Ecological factors also played an important role in Rome's crises, as the later second century saw global-scale climate changes that brought a favorable regime of climatic stability—known even in the scientific literature as the Roman Climate Optimum—to an end. These changes were complex and on their own might not have proven disruptive. But they coincided with violent biological shocks that severely destabilized the Roman imperial regime.[67]

Epidemic mortality was always part of the demographic fabric of the Roman Empire. The ancient sources regularly report outbreaks of disease that we cannot identify. These outbreaks were probably caused by diseases such as malaria, typhoid, and dysentery. Notably, though, over the course of several centuries, there is no evidence for severe interregional disease outbreaks. Then, in the middle of the 160s, during the reign of Marcus Aurelius, the Romans experienced a richly attested *pandemic*. A pandemic is an interregional epidemic, usually meaning an epidemic on an intercontinental scale. The term is somewhat imprecise, and despite its Greek roots, "pandemic" was not used in ancient times to describe disease events. (As we will see in chapter 11, it assumed its modern sense when it became possible to observe planetary-scale events in the nineteenth century.) Known as the Antonine Plague, the pandemic that struck under Marcus Aurelius is a landmark in the history of human disease, the earliest truly intercontinental disease outbreak that we can follow in any detail from human testimony.[68]

When William McNeill described the "confluence of the civilized disease pools" in the later Iron Age, the Antonine Plague was one of his prime examples. It was a severe mortality event quite obviously triggered by the arrival of an unfamiliar pathogen. The Romans themselves believed that the pestilence was sent by the god Apollo; the calamity supposedly started when Roman troops on campaign in Mesopotamia desecrated one of his temples. Roman legionaries returning from campaign dispersed the disease, and its destruction is attested to in all corners of the empire within a few years. The deadliness, speed, and sheer scale of the epidemic was shocking: "like some foul beast," one observer wrote, the pestilence "destroyed not a few people, but even rampaged over whole cities and destroyed them."[69]

In combination, written evidence and genomic data are starting to deepen our understanding of this biological event. The Antonine Plague struck during the career of Galen, the brilliant and prolific doctor. Galen's observations of what he called simply the "great" or "longest lasting" plague have always been at the center of efforts to identify the pathogen responsible for the Antonine Plague. He described a disease characterized by fever, a black pustular rash that rose above the skin and eventually scabbed and scarred, ulceration deep in the windpipe, and black or bloody stools. Galen also believed that the "crisis," or turning point of the disease, came around the ninth day. He described black pustules covering the entire body that then dried and fell off like scales, sometimes many days after the crisis.[70]

Galen's scattered notes on the Antonine Plague will never allow absolutely confident diagnosis. Most scholars have believed that the likeliest culprit is the smallpox virus, *Variola major*. Smallpox, as we know it from modern times, is a highly contagious respiratory disease contracted via droplets or virions shed through the skin lesions. Smallpox has a long incubation phase, seven to nineteen days, during which the victim can move the virus over distance before falling ill. The course of sickness begins with fever and malaise. Soon a rash appears on the face and body, more dense in the extremities than the trunk. The rash evolves over a long period, of about two weeks, with pox protruding from the skin. The pustular bumps eventually scab and fall off, leaving scars behind. Variations on this course of disease include an early and a late hemorrhagic form of the disease, both of which were nearly always fatal.[71]

Though Galen's descriptions of the Antonine Plague resemble smallpox, there are nagging doubts. Why, for instance, does he not describe more clearly the disfiguring scars that were such an unmistakable feature of smallpox infection? Further, why do contemporary sources claim that the disease struck both humans *and* their livestock, when the smallpox virus is specific to the human host? These are vexing questions. They would be best resolved with "smoking gun" evidence in the form of ancient pathogen DNA, recovered from the skeleton of a victim of the Antonine Plague. Smallpox is a big virus with a DNA genome that can be preserved in archaeological samples, so it is not unreasonable to hope it might be found, but thus far, paleogenomic traces of the Antonine Plague have not been retrieved.[72]

Nonetheless, the genome of the smallpox virus can still help us understand its evolutionary background. On the one hand, it has become clear that all modern strains of smallpox descend from a common ancestor that lived only four or so centuries ago. In other words, the highly virulent modern smallpox virus is not very old. This evidence, as we will see in later chapters, fits very well with the testimony of the literary evidence that a new, more deadly version of the pathogen circulated globally from around the sixteenth century. On the other hand, ancient smallpox DNA has just been recovered from northern European skeletons of the early Middle Ages. Unexpectedly, this DNA belongs to a lineage of smallpox that is now extinct, but it shows, first of all, that an ancestral version of smallpox *was* circulating—and killing people—for at least a millennium before modern smallpox took its virulent turn.

We do not even have a good way of speaking about extinct lineages of a pathogen such as this one. The team that discovered it, reasonably enough, call it "ancient smallpox." But the issues are more than semantic. We also do not know exactly what this disease would have been like, although the close resemblance to modern smallpox assures us that its biology is similar. We do not know how virulent it was, but we do know that it still contained genes that were shared by an ancestral, animal-infecting relative of all human smallpox; thus, ancient smallpox would still have infected a wider range of animal hosts. The medieval smallpox genomes also allow the molecular clock to be refined, and it can be estimated that these strains shared a common ancestor with modern smallpox around 1,700 years ago. Smallpox, as a human disease in some form, is at least that old.[73]

This new chronology for the smallpox virus opens the possibility that the Antonine Plague was an outbreak of an ancient form of smallpox. The broader family tree of the virus can also yield clues about its origins. The smallpox virus belongs to the genus *Orthopoxvirus*. The closest known relatives of human smallpox are *Camelpox virus* and *Taterapox virus*, whose only host is a rodent called the naked sole gerbil. These rodents inhabit the dry forests of the African savanna. This evolutionary tree (which could change, if new species are discovered) anchors the evolutionary background of smallpox in Africa, probably East Africa. Not only was this a vibrant region in Roman times, it was also closely connected to the busy trade routes of the Indian Ocean, Red Sea, and Persian Gulf. It may be significant that we have inscriptions speaking of a massive pestilence on the Arabian Peninsula about a decade before the Roman outbreak. All of this fits with the hypothesis that ancestral smallpox emerged in East Africa in the early first millennium and spread with trade routes and military movements into the Persian Gulf and Roman Empire, and possibly beyond.[74]

The emergence of a form of smallpox in this period also squares with the late ancient and medieval testimony regarding outbreaks of disease that often sound like smallpox. There is still much to be learned, including from the Chinese evidence. Galen's almost exact contemporary in China, Hua Tuo (about 140–208), and, a few centuries later, Tao Hongjing (456–536) describe diseases that have been thought to be smallpox. Yet, in the later medieval sources, a smallpox-like disease that was *not* especially virulent is well attested. The emergence and subsequent evolution of smallpox thus remains mysterious. Even as we have learned more, it reveals to us how much we still do not fully understand about the deep history of this important human disease.[75]

The Antonine Plague was clearly a high-mortality event, but unsurprisingly, it is a challenge to measure the demographic impact of an ancient pestilence. I have ventured a tally in the range of seven to eight million souls, but others have suggested estimates both much lower and much higher. In any case, the Antonine Plague was probably the single most lethal mortality event in human history up to that time. As populations grew in size and complexity, the potential scale of mortality shocks became larger. For the Romans, this event was an unforeseeable biological shock. It was not a Malthusian response to overpopulation: real wages were rising, right up to the outbreak of the pandemic. The disease was thus an ecological product of Rome's success, rather than its failures. Or, as Ibn Khaldūn might have put it, it was a result of their "dense and abundant civilization" and their global connections.[76]

The Roman Empire did not fold in the aftermath of the pestilence. The real effects of the plague were subtle but profound. The cycle of demographic and economic growth was halted. It became harder to recruit, and pay, the army. The tensions within the ruling classes became gradually more pronounced. The Romans' margin of advantage over their enemies was materially reduced. We cannot begin to understand the dynamics of historical change without trying to account for the powerful shocks provided by the evolution of new diseases whose emergence and transmission were, paradoxically, enabled by the very progress that human societies had achieved. The Romans were rattled by the arrival of a new disease that adapted to travel inside human airways and that emerged at a moment of intense globalization. The Romans stared down this microbial enemy and managed to survive. But as we will see in the next chapter, the arrival of another rodent disease— bubonic plague—presented insuperable challenges for one of history's most resilient agrarian empires.

History, Not Made to Human Measure

The study of health in the Roman Empire underscores the intricacy of the relationship between infectious disease and social processes. It is also a chance to remind ourselves that *health* in every period of the past was shaped by the interplay of both biological and social factors, and was not determined exclusively by the presence or absence of infectious diseases. We know that denizens of the Roman Empire experienced disease in very different ways. Town dwellers and urbanites encountered different pathogens. Latitude and altitude, gender and legal status, diet and the rhythms of labor all influenced the biological condition of the men, women, and children who lived and died inside Rome's sprawling borders. Traces of this complexity are evident in the exceptionally rich skeletal record from the Roman Empire, but usually we have only tantalizing hints of the kaleidoscopic variety of human experience. The big history of pathogen evolution often tells us more about the possibilities than the particularities—but it does, after all, give us a richer sense of the kinds of disease environments that took shape in this important chapter of the human past.[77]

The genesis of this book was the hope that a fresh, big-picture history of disease might put the pandemics that struck the Roman Empire in a deeper perspective. The search for this bigger context has strengthened the conviction that we can understand human history more profoundly if we try to understand it on multiple timescales. The Roman experience is incomprehensible without a wide-angle view of the forces of human ecological transformation and evolutionary response. Such a history does not have to overwrite our interests in the particular and the purely human. Rather, it deepens these interests and gives us a richer sense of human agency, and of its humbling limitations when confronted by the forces of nature. As the great French historian Fernand Braudel famously framed it, the gradual, sometimes imperceptible history of the environment shapes human social structures, which in turn condition the history of individuals and events. Each has their place, and the experience of Rome in the face of disease impresses on us the importance of conjuncture, of the unpredictable and particular ways that natural history and human history intersect and, sometimes violently, collide.[78]

6

The Ends of the Old World

The So-Called Middle Ages

The notion of the "Middle Ages," as medievalists will generally be the first to tell you, makes no sense. Renaissance figures like Petrarch (1304–74) originally proposed the self-aggrandizing construct of a thousand-year valley of darkness between the bright peaks of classical antiquity and themselves. From a global perspective, such a chronology is unintelligible. Even for Europe, it is, in the words of distinguished medievalist Robert Moore, "effectively useless, and, in most ways, a nuisance." Many cultures throughout world history have had a habit of looking back and idealizing classical periods. In this instance, the combination of nostalgia and hubris threatens to warp the whole way we perceive the long-term rhythms of history.[1]

We would do better to think of the millennium preceding the crossing of the Atlantic as an extension of the Iron Age, at least for the Old World. The biggest cities and empires were of the same order of magnitude as before, at least until the rise of the Mongols. Consumption habits were relatively static. The basic technological package endured, though with incremental improvements like the watermill, the stirrup, and the moldboard plow. Agrarian innovation in Asia, especially East Asia, allowed populations to surge. Gunpowder, the nautical compass, and the printing press were invented in China during this period, even though their revolutionary potential was not fully unleashed until the age of Atlantic discovery.[2]

This thousand-year interval of human history was marked by long swings of quickening demographic growth, twice interrupted by devastating ecological crises. In the sixth and the fourteenth centuries, societies across multiple continents were convulsed by a disease: the plague. The First Plague Pandemic was inaugurated by the Plague of Justinian (ca. 541–44 CE) and lasted until the middle of the eighth century. Then followed a reprieve of some six centuries, during which the plague was quiescent, and human increase was exuberant. The Second Plague Pandemic was announced by the Black Death (1346–53 CE); it lasted more than three centuries in western Europe but even longer elsewhere. (In the nineteenth century, the Third Plague Pandemic erupted, which we will treat in chapter 11.)

The geographic and chronological bounds of these plague pandemics have become fuzzier, ironically due to the very fact that we have learned more about this disease and its microbiological agent. The plague is caused by the bacterium *Yersinia pestis*. In English, the word *plague* can mean "pestilence," in the generic sense of a severe outbreak of infectious disease, or it can denote the specific epidemic disease caused by the bacterium *Y. pestis*. The most notable clinical symptom of plague is a hard purulent swelling, about the size of a golf ball, that protrudes from infected lymph nodes. These swellings are known as buboes, and thus the disease is often called the bubonic plague. The plague is a disease in a league of its own. Tuberculosis and malaria have probably, in their remorseless, steady way, killed more people. But plague was the most explosive epidemic disease in human history. It snuffed out half the population of entire continents within the space of a few years. No other pestilence really compares.

We probably know more about the deep evolutionary history of the plague bacterium than about any other ancient pathogen. Nowhere has the impact of genomic time travel been more fully felt than in the study of *Y. pestis*. In recent years, some giant questions have been definitively resolved, blank spots on the canvas colored in. At the same time, there are tantalizing hints of how much we still have to learn about the story of this singular germ and its role in our past. What we can say with certitude is this: The story of plague is a drama of animals and their ectoparasites. Humans built an ecosystem for the rapid, continental-scale transmission of animal germs. Then we were inadvertently engulfed in an outbreak of rodent disease. The plague is not a human disease, and the human body is in most instances an evolutionary graveyard for the germ—a small token of consolation for its countless victims.[3]

The history of disease in the Middle Ages is not synonymous with the history of plague, and this chapter must be considered in conjunction with our previous lines of argument on the emergence and circulation of diseases in the Iron Age. But the big swings of fortune that bookended this consequential millennium of progress in human history were decisively shaped by the plague, whose story deserves and requires our dedicated attention. The biology and ecology of the plague bacterium are fundamental to the story, and they help us to understand how human factors precipitated the natural disaster. In tracing the geographic and chronological contours of humanity's encounter with the plague, we will emphasize the importance of seeing the First and Second Plague Pandemics in the round, as centuries-long phases of human history shaped by the overbearing presence of an animal disease. The plague provided the most extreme demographic shocks in the history of social development. The consequences were both diverse and decisive.

The Biology and Ecology of *Y. pestis*

Ibn Khaldūn was seventeen years old when the Black Death struck his native Tunisia. Both of his parents were carried off by the disease. His world was thoroughly upended by the great mortality. In his summation, "Civilization both in the East and the West was visited by a destructive plague which devastated nations and caused populations to vanish. It swallowed up many of the good things of civilization and wiped them out. It overtook the dynasties at the time of their senility, when they had reached the limit of their duration. It lessened their power and curtailed their influence. It weakened their authority. Their situation approached the point of annihilation and dissolution. Civilization decreased with the decrease of mankind. Cities and buildings were laid waste, roads and way signs were obliterated, settlements and mansions became empty, dynasties and tribes grew weak. The entire inhabited world changed."[4]

The Black Death struck the Near East and Europe from about 1346–53. Because it looms so large in historical memory, it is tempting to take this fragment of the story as archetypal. The potted history of the Black Death is familiar. It starts with the hoary tale of the Mongols flinging dead bodies over the walls of Kaffa, the passage of the germ across the Black Sea and Mediterranean to Italy, and the rampage of the disease across the continent, taking out a nice round figure: a "third" of the population. All sorts of disorder and terror followed. But ultimately, the mortality was a bracing cleanse, because the peasants who survived were enriched and finally threw off the yoke of feudalism, leading to freedom, modernity, and us.[5]

It has become evident just how parochial this story really is, in large part thanks to the deluge of molecular evidence. The plague bacterium was present at the birth of paleogenomics, and *Y. pestis* research has been in the vanguard from the very inception of this new field. The history of the plague has become inconceivable except as a joint venture between the natural sciences and the humanities. Time travel and tree thinking, in combination with a greater openness to global history, teach us that the Black Death is just one part of a sprawling story.[6]

There are two features of the plague's biology that start to account for its deadliness and efficiency. First, the plague is a zoonotic disease. It naturally infects wild burrowing rodents like marmots, gerbils, jerboas, and voles. The disease can spill over into other mammal populations, including commensal rodents that live in proximity to humans. We are collateral damage. Most major human diseases *adapted* to humans from animal hosts and require sustained transmission between human hosts to survive. Plague is different. It is and ever has been a disease of rodents. In consequence, we are irrelevant to the plague's evolution—as hosts. The germ has not even the slightest incentive to moderate its virulence for humans. In that sense, the plague is a bit like rabies, a fatal animal disease that does not transmit between humans. From our self-ish perspective, plague has a kind of depraved indifference.[7]

Second, the plague is a vector-borne disease. The disease has something of the brutal efficiency of other infections adapted to spread between hosts using bloodsucking bugs as transit vehicles. The plague bacterium evolved tools that allow it to hijack ectoparasites, especially rodent fleas, as its vectors. Like many vector-borne diseases, *Y. pestis* is well adapted to survive in the environment of its temporary insect host, and then to find its way into the next mammal host. The adaptation of *Y. pestis* to its flea vectors is truly remarkable. Most notably, the plague bacteria build a biofilm—a putty-like matrix—in the alimentary canal of the flea, partly or completely blocking the ingestion of blood. The starving fleas seek blood meals ravenously, meanwhile regurgitating bacteria with each new bite. *Y. pestis* thus manipulates the flea into becoming a terrifically efficient vehicle of transmission.[8]

Most vector-borne diseases are geographically constrained by the range of their vector. Malaria, for instance, can only go where the anopheles mosquito will take it. Fleas, by contrast, thrive in warm mammalian fur. The environment of a rodent flea is rodent fur, and rodents are versatile creatures. The plague is thus a rare thing: a vector-borne disease with cosmopolitan potential. Typhus and louse-borne relapsing fever are fellow members in this exclusive club, but both of these are caused by true human pathogens, fully adapted to the human host. By contrast, the lurid disease caused by the plague bacterium is not in the least tempered by evolutionary concerns about its accidental human host.

When *Y. pestis* infects a human body, the clinical course of the ensuing disease depends on the route of infection. The bubonic course of disease typically starts with the bite of an infected flea. The bacteria enter the dermis, multiply, and blacken the local tissue. The waste disposal network that runs through our bodies, the lymphatic system, drains the bacteria to the nearest lymph node. Lymph nodes, packed with immune cells, are staggered throughout the body, and the buboes can appear in various places because the bacteria tend to migrate toward whichever lymph node is closest to the site of the flea's bite, often the groin, the neck, or the armpit. The patient starts to suffer notable symptoms within a few days—fevers, chills, malaise, and delirium. The course of disease is rapid, excruciatingly painful, and deadly. The bacteria overwhelm the body's immune defenses and sepsis ensues. Without antibiotics, case fatality rates are over 66 percent.[9]

Sometimes the flea bite instigates a course of disease known as primary septicemic plague. In such cases the bacteria enter the bloodstream directly. The immune system barely has time to mount any resistance, and sepsis progresses with astonishing speed. Even before signs of the disease are notable, victims can succumb, sometimes in less than a day. When the bacteria work their way from the lymphatic system into the lungs, they can multiply and cause what is known as secondary pneumonic plague (so called because it follows the infection via the lymphatic vessels). In this respiratory syndrome, the patient coughs, often producing a bloody sputum full of bacteria. In each of these courses of the disease the infection passes from a rodent to a human via the flea intermediary. *Y. pestis* can also transmit directly between humans via aerosol droplets expelled from the lungs. If the bacteria invade the lungs they can cause primary pneumonic plague, a course of the disease that is short and usually fatal. Inhalation of the bacteria can also cause bubonic plague if the germ enters the lymphatic system via the upper respiratory tract.[10]

The First Plague Pandemic, as we know it from human records, began in the year 541 CE when it entered the Roman Empire via a seaside town in northern Egypt. Where was the bacterium before then? That is one of many formerly intractable questions about plague that it now seems possible to answer, at least in part, with the aid of genomics. Just a decade ago, it was respectable to doubt whether the great plague pandemics of history were really even caused by *Y. pestis*. The disease managed to spread so far, so fast, that it called into question whether a vector-borne rodent germ could have been to blame. Not only have these doubts been laid to rest, but the backstory of this pathogen, before its appearance in the written record, is starting to be filled in.[11]

Both tree thinking and time travel are informative. Today the plague is enzootic (permanently established in animal populations) in rodent colonies in parts of Asia, Africa, and the United States. The genomes of these different populations of the plague bacterium can be situated in the evolutionary tree of *Y. pestis*. It is evident, as would be expected, that the plague in the United States was seeded during the Third Plague Pandemic, which disseminated globally from China in the 1890s: these are very young branches of the tree. The oldest branches of the tree, by contrast, belong to central Eurasia, along the steppe. The steppe is a sprawling ribbon of treeless grasslands stretching from the plains of Hungary to eastern Mongolia. Ancient branches of the plague belong to the steppe and the highlands that abut it, from the Caucasus Mountains west of the Caspian Sea to the Tien Shan mountains where China, Kyrgyzstan, and Kazakhstan meet. These regions are the evolutionary homeland of plague.[12]

Our knowledge of the plague has been enriched by ongoing sequencing of *Y. pestis* DNA recovered from archaeological samples. We have learned that *Y. pestis* is not terribly ancient. Its closest relative is a bacterium known as *Y. pseudotuberculosis*, a microbe that is half-hearted about being a parasite: like many bacteria, it can survive in the external environment without a mammal host. The two species diverged only around six thousand years ago, during which time *Y. pestis* acquired a suite of genetic adaptations that turned it into a highly transmissible bacterium, well suited to circulate in populations of wild rodents.[13]

Among the fauna that inhabit the steppe are a variety of rodents. One of these is the great gerbil, a big desert rat well adapted to the arid climate of central Asia. There are also about half a dozen species of marmots—plump, hibernating ground squirrels. Marmots live in underground burrows, where they spend the winter sleeping, insulated by their fatty bodies and thick fur. Some steppe rodents have a level of genetic resistance to plague, implying that they are natural hosts of the bacterium. Even so, it is an uneasy peace. Because the bacteria must be present at high levels in the blood to be reliably transmitted to the flea, *Y. pestis* possesses a range of virulence factors that seek to evade and manipulate the host's immune system. And for that reason, *Y. pestis* proves dangerous to a wide range of mammals.[14]

Plague circulates in its natural reservoirs in what is known as the sylvatic cycle. Rodent populations naturally fluctuate from year to year.

Rainfall influences the amount of grass, and therefore food, available to rodents. Predator numbers rise and fall too. The number of ectoparasites also oscillates. The plague cycle is thus naturally volatile. At times, *Y. pestis* can spill out of its reservoir hosts to infect other rodents and mammals, causing an *epizootic*, or an epidemic of animal disease. Hundreds of animals have proven susceptible to infection by *Y. pestis*, though most of these are dead-end hosts that play a limited role in sustaining outbreaks.[15]

Y. pestis emerged relatively recently, even as a rodent parasite. But one of the biggest surprises in the study of ancient DNA has been that humanity's history with this germ is much older than anyone knew. Plague has been found in human skeletons in Europe going back five thousand years, to the transition between the Neolithic and the Bronze Age (making it possible, even likely, that plague was involved in the boom-and-bust cycles and population turnovers in these earlier periods). The archaeological DNA provides snapshots of the evolutionary history of the pathogen. For instance, the very oldest plague DNA recovered still lacks some of the genes that would eventually make *Y. pestis* devastatingly effective at transmitting by flea bite. One gene, known as *ymt*, aids the bacteria in building the biofilm in the foregut of the flea. This gene was acquired during the Bronze Age, by around 2000 BC at the latest. Thus, for almost four thousand years, *Y. pestis* "has possessed all vital genetic characteristics required for flea-borne transmission of plague in rodents, humans and other mammals."[16]

This new knowledge presents new puzzles. If the bacterium was equipped with the genetic tools that made it so devastating, why did the plague *not* cause violent pandemics in the well-documented centuries leading up to the outbreak under Justinian? Were there explosive pandemics we have overlooked? The written sources do not point in that direction, but ancient DNA may eventually revise our understanding. The plain fact is that the historical record in the classical Greek and Roman periods (not to mention Persian, Indian, and Chinese civilizations) is generally informative. It is hard to imagine that a pandemic on the scale of the Justinianic Plague or Black Death happened quietly. When each of these did occur, they left a deep impression in the

FIGURE 6.1. *Rattus rattus.* The black rat is an important commensal that played
a major role in historic plague outbreaks. Etching by W. S. Howitt.
Wellcome Collection (CC BY 4.0).

documentary record: after centuries of invisibility, the plague is suddenly and vociferously attested by many independent witnesses. Moreover, both the Justinianic Plague and the Black Death mark the distinct
beginning of long periods when the plague recurred repeatedly.[17]

So why did the bubonic plague appear in AD 541 and trigger what
might have been the deadliest mortality event in the history of our species up to that point? We cannot completely answer this question in the
present state of our knowledge, and the truth is likely to be found in the
alignment of several critical factors. But one of them certainly lies in the
history of a particular rodent: the black rat, *Rattus rattus* (figure 6.1).

The black rat is a cosmopolitan rodent that evolved in the shadow of
a cosmopolitan ape. Like us, the black rat is a willing traveler; it is known
as the "ship rat" for good reason. Like us, it loves to eat big grass seeds.
Human grain production has been a feeding bonanza for these pests.
The black rat is a nifty climber. It is not terribly shy; therefore, it is willing
to live in and around—and above—human dwellings. Again for good

reason, "roof rat" and "house rat" are among its aliases. Human settlements are perfect habitats for rat nests. The black rat is a truly prolific breeder, so its populations are constrained principally by the availability of food. Humans are mobile, cosmopolitan, grass-eating, nest-building, colony-dwelling primates. Black rats have behavioral and physiological traits perfectly suited to exploit the ecological niches we create. Along with us, the black rat is among the most geographically dispersed mammals on the planet.[18]

The black rat has not always been a global species. Its success is historical and recent. The biography of the black rat can be traced with a combination of genetics and zooarchaeology (even though there is a need for more genetic work, and rat bones are not always preserved or recovered during archaeological excavations). The black rat originated in South Asia, and at least one lineage adapted to a commensal lifestyle in the Indus Valley some five thousand years ago. *R. rattus* subsequently dispersed from India to the Near East, Africa, and Europe. Trade, urbanization, farming, and grain storage fueled the spread of this rodent. It is notable that the black rat was apparently absent in much of western Eurasia and North Africa before the Iron Age. In Britain, for instance, the black rat only arrived around the time of the Roman expansion, which is hardly a coincidence. In the words of Michael McCormick, "the diffusion of the rat across Europe looks increasingly like an integral part of the Roman conquest."[19]

The plague might have remained a relatively obscure parasite of burrowing rodents, known mostly to wildlife biologists, had it not intersected the history of this commensal rodent. From this perspective, the great plague pandemics were the result of humanity's transformation of the biosphere. Just as human settlements created new waste environments, and human cities created new aggregations of human lungs, so human civilization created new rodent ecologies. The global success of the black rat is a direct effect of our own species' takeover of planet earth. The black rat has spread almost everywhere that we have. It is purely adventitious that the evolutionary adaptations that made the bacterium good at replicating its genes in rodents prepared it to become the agent of humanity's worst biological crises. Once human networks brought the plague bacterium into the web of commensal rodent colonies we had inadvertently created, the conditions were set for an unprecedented medical catastrophe.[20]

The First Pandemic

We have two detailed eyewitness accounts of the Justinianic Plague (ca. 541–44) in the eastern Mediterranean: one from a Syriac churchman named John and the other from an imperial official named Procopius. John was a Christian priest who viewed the events around him as signs of the end times. Procopius was a Greek historian who aspired to write in the educated style modeled on Thucydides; he was also a disgruntled civil servant with an ax to grind against the emperor and empress. These radically different worldviews not only frame their understanding of the plague but also tell us something about the cultural richness of this period. We can—and should—doubt our sources and question their true motives in describing events. But with entirely different outlooks and motivations, these two eyewitnesses, independently of one another, offer a remarkably coherent record of a worldshaking event.[21]

Witnesses to the Justinianic Plague unmistakably saw *the* plague. The characteristic bubonic swellings extruded from the groin, as well as the armpit, neck, and legs. John noted that a variety of animals were also afflicted, including "even rats, with swollen tumours, struck down and dying." Some victims presented the pinpoint "black blisters" on their hands. "On whomsoever these appeared, the moment they did so the end would come within just one or two hours." Vomiting blood was also considered a sign of imminent doom. There are indications of what we might take as the terrifyingly swift course of primary septicemic plague, when the bacterium multiplies immediately in the bloodstream. "As they were looking at each other and talking, they began to totter and fell either in the streets or at home, in harbours, on ships, in churches and everywhere. It might happen that a person was sitting at work at his craft, holding his tools in his hands and working, and he would totter to the side and his soul would escape."[22]

How did the plague journey from its central Asian homeland to the southern shores of the Mediterranean? Procopius reports that the disease first appeared in Pelusium, Egypt. This route of entry is suggestive: the town, located on the shores of the Mediterranean just across from the Gulf of Suez, was a hinge between the Roman Empire and the trade arriving from the Red Sea. Precisely how, and when, the plague was carried to the Red Sea region remains unknown. Perhaps it had reached Africa some time before and was now relayed north into the Roman world. Or perhaps it moved quickly and directly across the seaborne trade routes that connected the Red Sea with the Indian Ocean. The Romans were at war with Persia, which had complicated the overland passage via the silk roads. A parsimonious explanation is that the plague bacterium was a stowaway in the trade with the East, a recent arrival from across the ocean.[23]

A plague outbreak is triggered when *Y. pestis* bacteria are introduced to rodent colonies living in proximity to humans (see figure 6.2). First, the disease quickly and quietly burns through the local population of black rats, and as their numbers plunge, desperate fleas deign to drink human blood. When they do so, the bacteria start to circulate in human populations. It remains an open question how important human-to-human transmission became during the outbreaks. Humans suffering pneumonic plague may have coughed up infected droplets, and probably this route of transmission played a meaningful complementary role during the great outbreaks: certainly, the written evidence suggests as much. Human ectoparasites like fleas and lice have also been implicated in transmission, although the level of bacteria in human blood may never have been high enough to make this means of transmission very efficient. In all, the rats and their fleas seem to have been the main propellant of the disease, even through human populations.[24]

When *Y. pestis* reached the Roman Empire, it found an urbanized, interconnected society teeming with rats. The disease roared across the eastern provinces of the Roman Empire, easily the most densely populated and thriving region of the sixth-century world. It moved both by sea and over land. Procopius astutely noted that "the disease always spread out from the coasts and worked its way up into the interior." By

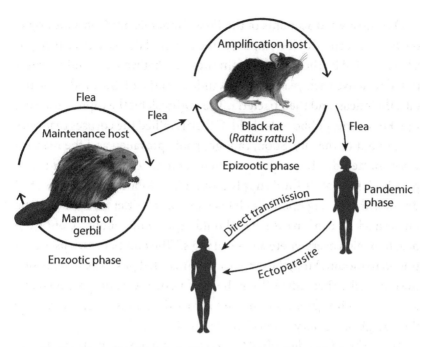

FIGURE 6.2. The plague cycle. Plague is an ecologically complex disease
involving reservoir hosts like marmots, amplification hosts like black rats,
flea vectors, and incidental human victims.

sheer luck, John was traveling across the eastern provinces as the plague
wound its way through these regions. Across "the whole of Palestine"
both villages and cities were annihilated. Syria, Mesopotamia, and Asia
Minor were struck. "We saw desolate and groaning villages and corpses
spread out on the earth, with no one to take up and bury them."[25]

When it arrived in a town, the plague "eagerly began to assault the
class of the poor, who lay in the streets." Hungry and vulnerable, the
poor may have been more biologically susceptible to the contagion, and
the squalid conditions of life for the urban poor brought them into close
quarters with rats. Ultimately, though, the plague was indiscriminate,
and for Procopius, this was the most telling feature of the pandemic.
"People differ from each other in the places that they live, the customs
that govern their lifestyle, the manner of their personality, their profes-
sions, and many other ways, but none of these factors made the slightest
difference when it came to this disease—and to this disease alone."[26]

Our most vivid accounts of the First Pandemic put Constantinople, the bustling capital of the empire, at the center of the narrative. Its population was fed by the imperial grain supplies that were carefully orchestrated to arrive each year from Alexandria. And with the food came the rats, their fleas, and their bacteria. The outbreak hit the capital in spring 542. For a time, public order held. Officials tallied the corpses that were carried out of the city. Soon, though, panic prevailed and the markets were shuttered. "The entire city then came to a standstill as if it had perished, so that its food supply stopped." "Nobody would go out of doors without a tag upon which his name was written and which hung on his neck or arm," in case they should expire while about. "Confusion began to reign everywhere and in all ways." The number of corpses continued to mount. First, the emperor commanded pits to be dug outside the city walls. These filled. Then the dead bodies were dragged on tarps, loaded onto freighters, and hauled across the straits where they were flung in giant military towers "in a tangled heap."[27]

The bishop John described this scene in the most sensational terms. The bodies of the dead were cross-hatched in layers, like "hay in a stack." To make room for the next layer, the corpses were pushed down, "trodden upon by feet and trampled like spoiled grapes. . . . The corpse which was trampled sank and was immersed in the pus of those below it." To John, the image called to mind the visions of Revelation, "the winepress of the fury of the wrath of God" that would appear as a sign of the impending last judgment.[28]

The plague's impact in Constantinople was severe. But most of the population lived outside the great cities, and the key to the plague's demographic effects lay in its ability to penetrate the countryside. The thickly settled landscapes of Egypt, Palestine, Syria, Asia Minor, and the Balkans were struck hard. In the "whole of Palestine," both town and country were struck. In Asia Minor, the survivors struggled to bring in the harvest. By 543 the plague made landfall in the western Mediterranean. It found a patchwork of war-torn societies, some of them recently reconquered under Justinian. The sources that we do have claim widespread mortality, but the evidence is more sparse than we would hope. One chronicle tells us that most of Spain was invaded by the plague. In

Italy, one chronicle mentions the first visitation of plague. In Gaul we are somewhat better informed, thanks mostly to a historian named Gregory of Tours. The plague spread far and wide, but not everywhere. Ultimately the first outbreak reached the far west, having cut a deadly swath from the uplands of central Asia to the shores of the Atlantic.[29]

The literary narratives are utterly consistent in portraying the disease as an unprecedented mortality event. But how far can we trust such testimony? Our witnesses had a limited perspective, and they all had their motives for writing history. John's history is a call for sinners to repent. Procopius had a genuine hatred for the imperial rulers. It has been noted that Procopius devotes only a couple of pages of his lengthy chronicle to the plague. Of course, the same is true of the later Byzantine writers who witnessed the Black Death, and no one doubts the severity of that event. In fact, our witnesses to the Justinianic Plague provide a strikingly coherent account. Despite differences of language, religion, geography, genre, and temperament, the contemporary witnesses, as Peter Sarris has put it, "speak with one voice in describing the plague as having had a major and sudden impact on both urban and rural communities alike." And the force of their testimony is strengthened by the fact that reports of pandemic mortality are rare in the written record and then abruptly appear en masse; the body of testimony—sudden and simultaneous, from one end of the empire to the other—only fits the shape of an exceptional pandemic.[30]

In trying to measure the scale of the disaster, the biggest unknown has always been whether the plague really managed to penetrate Europe and the western Mediterranean, and especially the countryside in these regions. There is simply a paucity of evidence, and caution is not unreasonable. Certainly, even a few years ago, when I wrote a chapter on the First Pandemic, this seemed like one of the greatest outstanding question marks. Since then, the fast-moving field of paleogenomics has continued to fill in gaps in our knowledge—and confirm the sheer reach of the biological disaster.

In 2019 a team published a study reporting the identification of the plague's DNA from newly sampled sites in western Europe. The investigators screened skeletons from twenty-two different cemeteries. At least three of these sites should *not* have yielded *Y. pestis* DNA, because the burials are dated to the fourth and fifth centuries—that is, before the First Pandemic appears in the written record. Indeed, none of those early graveyards turned up the bacterium's genome. But thirty skeletons from eight of the other sites *did* yield up the plague's DNA. This is, simply put, extraordinary, and it is worth spelling out why. Samples such as these are never an exact proxy of how prevalent the plague was. The sites were chosen because it was hoped they might produce positive results; because the DNA molecule degrades, and it is inherently hard to retrieve and sequence ancient DNA, it is a small miracle whenever it happens to be recovered. What these results do tell us, in no uncertain terms, is where and what kinds of places the plague managed to reach. Six of the sites are in southern Germany, two in Gaul, and one each in Spain and England. Most of the sites were rural. The plague victims from England, for example, belonged to a population of Anglo-Saxons living in a community with a population that totaled no more than fifty to sixty-five people. The implication is obvious: if the plague made it here, in the very far west, in the boondocks of Anglo-Saxon England, then it makes a strong case that the First Pandemic was able to spread far and wide.[31]

The paleogenomic evidence provides resounding affirmation that the ecological platform was in place for the First Pandemic to have penetrated deep into the countryside, and all the way across Europe (see figure 6.3). Still, there is much that we will never know about the First Pandemic, because the sources for this ancient period are simply so much scantier than for the Black Death. But given what we do know about the biology and ecology of the disease, the sudden ubiquity and ferocity of pandemic plague in the written record of the sixth century, along with the growing body of paleogenomic and archaeological evidence, the best comparison for the mortality event that struck in the sixth century seems to be the Black Death. This comparison is further justified by an important but underappreciated way in which the Justinianic Plague mirrors the Black Death: it inaugurated a centuries-long period during which the plague frequently recurred. To take full measure of the disease's impact in the sweep of human history requires envisioning the plague's long chronological span.[32]

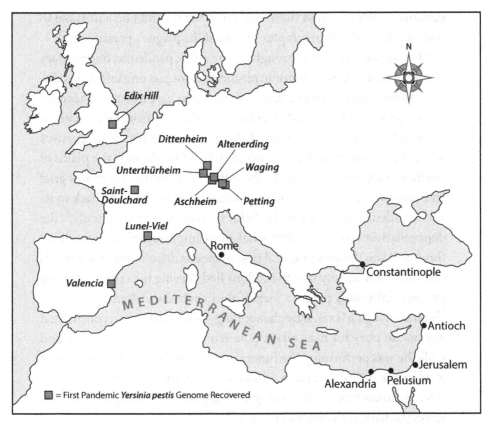

FIGURE 6.3. Map showing key locations in first plague pandemic,
including sites where *Y. pestis* DNA has been recovered.

The plague's persistence is rooted in the germ's nature as an animal
disease. When the plague spilled out of central Asia, it seeded new reservoirs, perhaps among wild rodents in the Pyrenees, Alps, Balkans, or highlands of Anatolia and Syria. The germ could thus retreat nearby and lurk
until its periodic return. Across the two centuries of the First Pandemic,
outbreaks are attested every ten to fifteen years on average, with phases of
greater and lesser intensity. We should resist calling these outbreaks
"waves" of plague, because they did not come from without and wash over
the vast territory of the Roman Empire and its successor states. Some of
the outbreaks seem local, and perhaps regional, in nature. Others do seem
like widespread episodes. There is still much to be learned about the

patterns of plague across these centuries, but it would be a mistake to underestimate the demographic effects of the plague's persistence.[33]

Our human testimony throughout the entire pandemic, fragmentary though it is, insists that bubonic plague was not just one infectious disease among others. For example, we chance to have a startling account of a secondary outbreak in Italy, ultimately drawing from an eyewitness record, that gives us a sense of what a desolating force the plague was when the disease returned around 565 CE. It tore through the plains of northern Italy from one end to the other. "Everywhere there was grief and everywhere tears. . . . You might see the world brought back to its ancient silence: no voice in the field; no whistling of shepherds." The depopulation was severe, but what most impressed those who lived through it was the shocking and instantaneous dissolution of the bonds that held their society together. "Sons fled, leaving the corpses of their parents unburied; parents forgetful of their duty abandoned their children in raging fever. If by chance long-standing affection constrained any one to bury his near relative, he remained himself unburied, and while he was performing the funeral rites he perished." Then as now, it is often the intimate trauma of loved ones dying alone or denied the solemn rituals that soothe our grief that proves most anguishing, and leaves its mark in the human record.[34]

In Gaul our most valuable testimony comes from the historian Gregory of Tours. A masterful study by Michael McCormick underscores what a sharp and sensitive observer he was. The details closest to home are most telling. When Gregory's town of Clermont, narrowly spared in the 540s, did finally meet the plague in 571, he saw it up close. The dead became so numerous that the town ran out of sarcophagi and boards for making coffins. The corpses were laid in pits, up to ten at a time. As a historian, Gregory was careful with his numbers. So it is meaningful when he tells us that "one Sunday, three hundred dead bodies were counted in the basilica of St. Peter alone." Clermont was a tiny town, deep in the heart of Gaul, home to less than a thousand souls. In the words of McCormick, Gregory's "numerical reliability argues that this number must be taken seriously and suggests that, at that one moment in this epidemic, plague killed as much as 40 percent of the population within the walls and a smaller proportion of the total population, which includes the unknown number living outside the walls." Repeated outbreaks of plague tormented Gregory's society like no other disease.[35]

There is still much to be learned about the overall shape of the First Pandemic, and the rhythms, severity, and ecology of the continuing outbreaks. We know relatively little about its severity in the middle of the seventh century, when the literary record becomes the thinnest. Did it retreat, or are the handful of hints we have signs that broader devastation continued, beyond our field of vision? By the eighth century, outbreaks seem mostly confined to the Mediterranean, but they remained ferocious. In the 740s, the disease swept across the trade routes that connected the East and West, and still retained all the inexplicable violence it had in the beginning. Whenever it did strike, the plague was by far the most fearsome disease known to our sources, for the length and breadth of the entire pandemic.[36]

How can we understand the economic and institutional reverberations of the plague? Economic historians working on the Black Death have explored the variable consequences that follow a mortality shock that suddenly eliminates a significant part of the population. One school of thought emphasizes the silver linings of living in the aftermath of plague. For those who survived, wages rose. Inequality declined as laborers unexpectedly found their bargaining power strengthened. Conversely, the plague may have been destructive even for those who lived to see the other side of it. Demographic contraction reduced the scope of market exchange and economic specialization. Towns declined, and people had fewer opportunities as laborers and consumers. These two alternatives are not strictly incompatible, and the results may have varied across regions, depending on the local severity of the epidemic and regional circumstances.[37]

In the course of the First Pandemic, we can find some evidence for both of these patterns. In western Europe, the impact of plague along with continuing political fragmentation led to economic simplification. Trade declined, and production became more local and less specialized. Towns contracted, reaching a nadir sometime in course of the seventh century. But for those who inhabited the ghostly ruins of Roman cities and abandoned villas, life was not necessarily much worse. Almost everywhere, for instance, stature increased, as people had more food (and especially meat) to eat, and deurbanization meant fewer low-level endemic infections to contend with. Inequality undoubtedly declined, as the vaulting social hierarchies of the late Roman order collapsed. In some places, it may have been a golden age for free peasants, whereas in others, new forms of serfdom and rural dependence started to take root.[38]

In the eastern Mediterranean and Near East, the plague (along with other factors like climate change) may have struck hard in its initial phases. There is, for instance, a particularly compelling new case study from the Negev highlands of the southern Levant. This region boomed in the later Roman Empire, in the fourth and fifth centuries, and exported some of the most prized wines of the period. But the region experienced profound disruption precisely in the mid-sixth century. Urban services that had operated for centuries suddenly ceased to function, and wine exports, the basis of the local economy, went into a tailspin. The plague affected not only the local population but also the distant urban consumers who had purchased the wine. It is a stunningly detailed picture of contraction and simplification.[39]

And yet, in the long view, the rebound would also prove to be most robust in the Middle East. Although the West remained fragmented, the Middle East soon became more unified than ever. The caliphs ruled from Spain and North Africa to Persia and central Asia. The Islamic heartlands of Syria and Mesopotamia once again became a center of growth, especially after the plague receded in the eighth century. Slowly but surely, the Middle East became an Islamic society, the center of a global religion stretching from the Atlantic seaboard to the Indian Ocean world. By the ninth or tenth century, the combination of reduced population and economic revitalization had raised real incomes for ordinary inhabitants of the Abbasid Caliphate. It was a "golden age."[40]

Further to the east, in the core regions of China, where the First Pandemic seems never to have reached, unbroken continuity with antiquity was the greatest. Under the Tang (618–907) and Song (960–1279) dynasties, China was indisputably the most populous and powerful polity on the planet. Here the potential of the Iron Age package was most completely realized, and ongoing intensification led to the most impressive innovations of the Middle Ages—until the monster returned once again.[41]

The Medieval Surge

Odoric of Pordenone was a Franciscan friar from the far northeastern corner of what is now Italy. Part missionary, part diplomat, he set off from Venice around 1318 on a tour that took him to the edges of the known world. The Venetians were intrepid merchants, always searching for commercial advantages against their rivals in the trade with the Far East. This commerce was ancient, but the frequency of direct contact between the ends of Eurasia was something new. Odoric followed in the footsteps of a generation or two of voyagers who had started to traverse the entire expanse of the Old World.[42]

Odoric claimed that there were "plenty" of people in Venice who could confirm his descriptions of China. Indeed, when Odoric reached Quanzhou, at the mouth of the Jin River across from Taiwan, he found not one but two houses of Franciscans in the city! Odoric's meandering itinerary to China followed much the same southern route that had, a few decades earlier, brought Marco Polo *back* on his return journey from "Cathay" (as China was known) to Venice. Odoric sailed over the Black Sea and then zigzagged across Persia, back to Baghdad, and down to the Persian Gulf. He then sailed to India before catching a junk to Sumatra. He stopped on the island of Java, where he was struck by its density of people and precious spices like cardamom and nutmeg. He worked his way to southern China, arriving in Guangzhou (Canton) and slowly winding his way via roads and canals as far north as Beijing.[43]

Almost everywhere his travels took him, Odoric was impressed by the towns he saw and the vibrant commercial networks that linked them. He reserved special wonder for what he witnessed in China. To his European eyes, it was without compare. The south of China alone had "two thousand great cities; cities I mean of such magnitude that neither Treviso nor Vicenza would be entitled to number among them."

The density he could only compare to Venice on its market days, but a city like Guangzhou he thought was three times the size of Venice. "This city has shipping so great and vast in amount that it would seem well nigh incredible. Indeed all Italy has not the amount of craft that this one city has."[44]

Odoric's breathless account of his journey provides an authentic impression of the state of world affairs in the early fourteenth century. We can make three overarching observations. First, the world was more populated than it had ever been. Second, the world was more interconnected than it had ever been. And third, both population density and commercial networks across the Old World generally intensified as one moved from west to east.

The ascendance of China is a fundamental fact of global medieval history. In the latter half of the first millennium, China lunged ahead in patterns of growth. Under the short-lived Sui dynasty (AD 581–618) and then more emphatically under the Tang (AD 618–907), China experienced robust demographic, economic, and technological progress. The Tang state was not only the most militarily dominant power on earth, asserting hegemony deep into central Asia, it also oversaw technological advances that put China in the forefront of social development for centuries. China's preeminence was vast and enduring.[45]

The basis of China's growth was the energy technology known as rice. Early Chinese civilizations had been centered in the north, in the fertile valley of the Yellow River, where millet was a dominant crop. In the Tang and then the Song Dynasty (AD 960–1279), the heartland of Chinese development shifted south. Humid, hilly, and once thickly forested, the land drained by the Yangzi had been the frontier. Now, as "rice became the central food crop of the empire," the south became the engine of China's growth. The commercialization of agriculture was facilitated by the construction of a canal network connecting the north and the south of China. The Grand Canal, a gift of the brief Sui Dynasty, transformed the economic geography of China.[46]

The digestible energy of rice was inevitably converted into more human bodies. Even in its Tang-Song efflorescence, China felt Malthusian constraints. Per capita income may never have exceeded one thousand

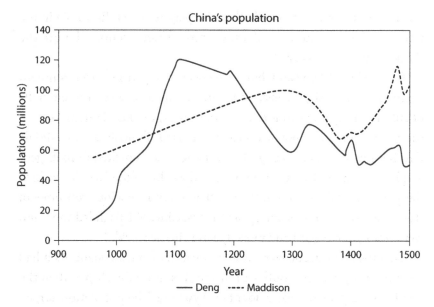

FIGURE 6.4. Population of China. (Sources: Maddison 2007a, 168; Deng 2004)

dollars in today's terms. But the population soared. China's population history is not for those who need certainty in life, but by the twelfth century, the Chinese heartlands, it is argued, were home to more than 120 million souls (see figure 6.4). One out of every four humans alive lived under the Northern Song.[47]

The English philosopher of the seventeenth century, Francis Bacon, identified three transformational inventions that had changed the world—the magnetic compass, the printing press, and gunpowder. All were created and refined by China in this period. (The Sinologist Joseph Needham added a fourth, paper, and construed them as the "Four Great Inventions.") China's navigational superiority extended to shipbuilding and was enormous. Its weaponry was far ahead of Europe's up to the end of the fifteenth century. The printing press with moveable type, along with paper (used for currency from the Song onward), were culturally transformational. In other domains—mechanized production, milling, even the use of fossil fuels—China's technical advances were equally precocious. And yet, the trajectory of China was ruptured in the thirteenth century with the arrival of Mongol conquerors. As we will see, it is an open question whether the plague struck East Asia in the midst of these tumultuous decades, more than a century before the Black Death in the West.[48]

The world of Islam was China's steady trading partner. From southern Spain to central Asia, the Islamic sphere of influence created an umbrella of cultural unity and economic integration. Agricultural intensification supported a long-term population upswing. Trade flourished as the Middle East became the fulcrum of global exchange and benefited from its geographic centrality. The relative power and wealth of the Islamic world in this period is underscored by the fact that it was a voracious consumer of slaves, including from the European fringes. Cities like Baghdad and Cairo were among the biggest and most dynamic in the world.[49]

Even though Europe was a trailer, it was far from stagnant. As it had been in antiquity, the south of Europe was more developed than the north, but expansion was evident everywhere. The population surged across the continent. Forests were cut down to make way for fields. The demographic cycles of Italy and England are particularly well known and can serve as illustrations of the long, secular swings of human population in Europe. In the Italian peninsula, there were 5.2 million souls around the year 1000 (see figure 6.5). Over the course of three centuries, the population more than doubled, reaching perhaps 12.5 million. Northern Italy was the commercial heartland of Europe, the most urbanized and prosperous region on the continent. Its leading city-states like Genoa and Venice were precocious mercantile powers with strong connections to the Near East and beyond. Italy's population and economy were dynamic right up to the eve of the catastrophe.[50]

In England at the time of the Domesday Book (the great survey commissioned by William the Conqueror in AD 1086) there were about 1.71 million people alive (see figure 6.6). The population grew thanks to progressive reclamation of arable land for farming, until almost every cultivable acre was occupied. This expansion was complemented by steady if unspectacular advances in agricultural technology. The climax of nearly five million was reached in the later thirteenth century, when Malthusian pressures stalled further progress. A major famine, exacerbated by a harrowing rinderpest epizootic that destroyed livestock

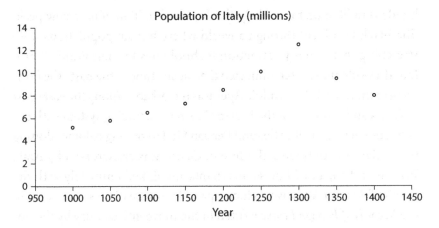

FIGURE 6.5. Population of Italy. (Sources: Pinto 1996; Pinto and Sonnino 1997;
Lo Cascio and Malanima 2005)

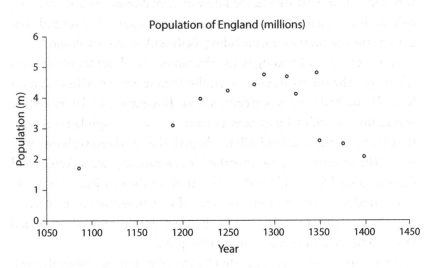

FIGURE 6.6. Population of England. (Sources: Broadberry et al. 2015; Campbell 2016)

populations, struck much of Europe, including England, in 1316–18. Living standards declined, and the population leveled off. A hesitant recovery was in swing when the plague intervened.[51]

In the year 1000, there were probably some 250 million humans on earth: roughly the level that had already been achieved at the time of the early Roman Empire. By the early fourteenth century, there were four hundred million or, more likely, five hundred million of us, a new peak. The Black Death cut through a world where human populations were stretching their energy extraction technologies to their limits. It also found a world more interconnected than at any time in the past. The flowering of trade in the late Middle Ages was remarkable. Along the east coast of Africa and throughout the Indian Ocean ran a trading system with circuits connecting the Red Sea and Persian Gulf to trading colonies dotting the Indian subcontinent. The Indian Ocean was crisscrossed by Arab, Persian, Indian, and Chinese merchants and linked ultimately with the South China Sea. We have an incomparable picture of these networks in the *Records of Foreign People* written in the thirteenth century by the nobleman Zhao Rukuo, a customs official of the Song Dynasty. He was at the center of trading circuits that ultimately connected Japan and Korea with markets in East Africa. He knew of Zanzibar as a source of ivory, gold, ambergris, and yellow sandalwood. He was aware of Egypt and even parts of the Mediterranean, including Sicily with its great volcano.[52]

Another series of trading networks ran overland, across the famous silk roads. The silk roads connected the Mediterranean with China via Syria, Persia, and the oases of central Asia. This entire circulatory system was Islamic. Mamluk Egypt was a major consumer. Baghdad was positioned to link the overland silk roads with the southern seaborne network. The commercial powers of the Mediterranean, such as Venice and Genoa, looked for beachheads in this trade in the east Mediterranean. These trading networks were ancient. They had witnessed peaks and troughs over the centuries, and by the thirteenth century they carried more commerce than at any time in the past.[53]

This world system was upended by the arrival of the Mongols, who built an empire stretching from China to the Near East. It was this Mongol corridor that had tempted the merchants of Genoa and Venice to find a way to connect their Black Sea colonies (first established as a supply for grain) with the riches of the eastern trade. But the Mongol conquests also represented one of the most violent phases in the history of Eurasia, and the chaos they brought to the steppe may have stirred the plague from its nest, and flung upon the world the greatest biological crisis in the history of our species.[54]

The Second Pandemic

In autumn of the year 1347, when the annual Nile flood had already started to turn the fields green, a plague "unlike anyone had seen since the beginning of Islam" appeared. By the following spring, it spread across the whole country, peaking toward the end of 1348. In the words of al-Maqrīzī, a historian writing a few generations later, it was a mortality without precedent, "extending to all parts of the earth, to the east as to the west, to the north as to the south." It spared nothing, taking in its deadly compass "not only the entire human race, but also the fish of the sea, the birds of the sky, and the wild beasts." The Black Death had arrived.[55]

The Arabic histories of the Black Death were not in agreement about where the plague had come from. Writing from Cairo, al-Maqrīzī thought the disease had launched from the country of the Mongols to cross the steppe; he claimed that he had sources from the "country of the Uzbeks" who asserted the catastrophe was in course by AD 1341. Ibn al-Wardi, a writer in Syria who died in the course of the pandemic, placed the origins of the Black Death in the "land of darkness," which implies the far north of inner Asia, where the plague supposedly raged for fifteen years before it arrived in the Black Sea and Near East. Writing from Andalusia, Ibn Khatimah put the beginnings of the plague on the eastern edge of the inhabited world, in China. Ibn al-Khatib, another observer of the plague, also placed the origins of the pandemic in the land of the Khitai and also the Sind (in the Indus Valley). Given the vague and contradictory testimonies of our medieval sources, modern historians have unsurprisingly been divided about the origin of the Black Death. William McNeill proposed that the Himalayas were the seedbed of a great pestilential wave which swept across the Eurasian landmass from east to west. Although it turns out he was not quite right, he was correct to insist on a wide geographic panorama. And in the meantime, genomic evidence has started to let us trace the outlines of a once invisible prehistory of the Black Death.[56]

It is now abundantly clear that *something* happened in the evolutionary history of the plague bacterium a little less than a century before the traditional beginning of the Black Death. The family tree of *Y. pestis* is

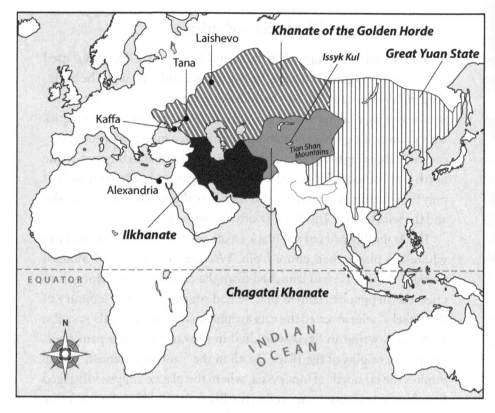

FIGURE 6.7. Mongol polities and the Black Death.

marked by a polytomy, or sudden split into multiple branches, preceding the Second Plague Pandemic. This kind of evolutionary branching could represent massive population expansion, or new evolutionary pressures, or both. One of these branches was responsible for the Black Death.[57]

The strains of *Y. pestis* that are closest to the polytomy have been recovered from the Tian Shan mountains and its foothills (see figure 6.7). This region around Lake Issyk Kul, where the autonomous Xinjiang region of China meets Kyrgyzstan and Kazakhstan, has emerged as a zone of particular interest for the evolutionary history of plague. This central-eastern region of the steppe seems the most likely source of the plague's expansion in the period leading into the Second Pandemic, but that could change with more genetic samples (especially from the

western steppe). In 2019, a plague genome from Laishevo, at the confluence of the Volga and the Kama Rivers in Russia, was published. The
bacterium that killed this individual is the closest found so far to the
great polytomy, and it is immediately ancestral to the strains that caused
the Black Death. It is a trace of the plague's movement into western
Eurasia on the eve of the Second Pandemic.[58]

The historian Monica Green, who has been a champion of integrating the genomic evidence with conventional historical archives, has
persuasively argued that the date of the polytomy should encourage us
to look earlier for the origins of the Second Pandemic, and to look beyond the western Eurasian sources. She has made a case for seeing the
Mongol expansion as the ecologically decisive fact in the dissemination
of plague. The Mongol conquests of the thirteenth century were an epochal event. Genghis Khan (ca. 1158–1227) and his successors connected
inner Asia—from central China to southern Russia, from the edges of
Siberia to the Iranian plateau—into a single zone of influence. The crux
of the Mongol expansion was the brutal yet swift takeover of the central
Asian steppe. The Mongols leveled the thriving civilizations on their
western edge, including those in Tian Shan region, the Ferghana Valley,
and Transoxania. The conquest was ecologically disruptive. The movement of giant herds, and the urgency of finding land for pasture, pushed
Mongolian pastoralists into regions where the plague was enzootic.
They also prized the meat and fur of marmots. The Mongols arrived
more than a century before the Black Death, almost coincident with the
evolutionary diversification of *Y. pestis*. It is possible that their conquest
created the ecological conditions for the evolutionary explosion of
plague and, later, the integration of the steppe that promoted the transmission of the disease.[59]

The genetic evidence underscores the fact that the Black Death must
be seen in its true geographic profile against the backdrop of the entire
Old World. This perspective is a corrective to the Eurocentric view that
begins with the supposed episode of biological warfare committed by
the Mongols at Kaffa and follows the trail of the germ through Europe.
To be sure, Europe was waylaid by the Black Death, but this is only a
narrow slice of the broader history of the pandemic.[60]

TABLE 6.1. Geography of the Black Death

World region	Affected by Black Death?
New World	Untouched by plague until Third Pandemic.
China	Highly disputed.
	Western China an ancient plague focus.
	Thirteenth-century epidemics could be connected with Black Death.
	On balance, evidence does not yet prove massive interregional mortality event.
South Asia	Probably not affected until early modern period.
Europe	Genetic and written evidence for devastating pandemic.
Middle East	Written evidence for devastating pandemic.
Sub-Saharan Africa	Some archaeological and genetic evidence of early plague.

How wide was the geographic reach of the Black Death (table 6.1)? Obviously, the New World was isolated and remained untouched by the plague until the Third Pandemic. Conversely, the evidence for Europe, central Asia, the Middle East, and North Africa is overwhelming. But what about South Asia, China, and sub-Saharan Africa? The Black Death does not seem to have reached India. The Chinese case is complicated and puzzling, and opinion has remained divided on the question of whether China was affected by the Black Death. In recent years, Robert Hymes has assembled the best case yet for the Second Pandemic in China. He draws attention to the geographical and chronological overlap between the *Y. pestis* polytomy and the Mongol takeover of China. There were certainly epidemics recorded in Chinese historical sources during the thirteenth and fourteenth centuries, and medical texts could still hold decisive clues about the identity of the pathogen. The plague may well have had a hand in massive population declines between the Song and Yuan (1279–1368) periods. But as Timothy Brook points out, the absence of really clear written evidence from China remains a stark contrast with the Middle East and Europe. In all, here is a big piece of global history where we can hope for ongoing elucidation.[61]

The question of whether the Black Death affected sub-Saharan Africa is finally receiving the attention it deserves. Of course the Islamic world of North Africa was ravaged, and the evidence that the plague crossed the Horn of Africa is compelling. But the written sources for the interior and west of the continent are not plentiful, so the issue has to be decided by the evidence of archaeology and genetics. Major settlement declines in fourteenth-century West Africa can possibly be connected with the arrival of the Black Death over the bustling Saharan caravan routes. Green has called attention to the fact that strains of *Y. pestis* enzootic in east-central Africa, in the Great Lakes region, belong to an offshoot of the lineages that erupted in the late Middle Ages. It too most likely arrived in Africa sometime in the later medieval period, via connections with the Middle East. There is more to be learned, but the balance has tilted toward the view that the Second Pandemic cut deep into the heart of Africa.[62]

The plague moved west overland, across the giant western Mongol kingdom known as the Golden Horde. Russian chronicles attest the plague by 1346, working its way through the valleys of the Don and Volga Rivers. It reached the Black Sea, where conflict between the Mongols and Italians had created a stalemate on the waters, seizing up trade. When grain started to flow again toward hungry westerners from the busy Black Sea port of Tana in summer 1347, the ships carrying food were undoubtedly crawling with rats, fleas, and germs.[63]

Black Sea shipping networks were the key to the plague's metastatic dispersal. By late summer 1347, the disease had reached Constantinople. The Byzantine emperor himself has left an eyewitness report of the pestilence: "so incurable was the evil, that neither any regularity of life, nor any bodily strength could resist it." The plague probably traveled overland across the Caucasus and moved into Persia from the north, but the seaborne routes were crucial for the diffusion of the Black Death into the Muslim world too. The disease crossed the Mediterranean and reached the port of Alexandria in 1347. Al-Maqrīzī knew that ships spread the contagion. He told of a ship that had disembarked with thirty-two merchants and nearly three hundred sailors and slaves. By the time it reached Alexandria, only forty-five of the passengers were alive, and these soon perished. In Alexandria, the Great Mosque celebrated as many seven hundred funerals on a single day. The factories and markets were shuttered.[64]

Once in Alexandria, the plague moved back eastward across the Levant. One line of transmission ran through Gaza, where the plague arrived in spring 1348. The famous traveler Ibn Battutah encountered the disease in Homs and Damascus. Al-Maqrīzī also had good information on the course of the plague in Syria. "The disease manifested itself in the following fashion. A small bud poked out from behind the ears, that festered quickly, followed by buboes in the armpits and a rapid death. One could observe the presence of a tumor that caused a severe mortality. Some time later, there was also spitting of blood and the people were terrified by the number of the dead. No one survived the spitting of blood for more than fifty hours."[65]

From Alexandria the plague moved up the Nile across Egypt. In Cairo, al-Maqrīzī's hometown, the mortality crested in late AD 1348. By January, cadavers were piled in the streets. The healthy were stationed in places of prayer to recite the funeral liturgies. Al-Maqrīzī based his daily death counts on the number of funeral prayers recited. In one two-day period, he thought there were more than 13,800 dead. He had another report of 20,000 dead in a day. According to al-Maqrīzī, Cairo was as empty as the desert.[66]

Mamluk Cairo was one of the most important cities on the globe in the fourteenth century. Thanks to the richness of the Arabic sources, it is possible to explore the demographic impact of the second pandemic in Cairo in unusual detail. Although there are inevitable uncertainties, Michael Dols estimated that the death toll of the Black Death amounted to something like two hundred thousand out of a total urban population of five to six hundred thousand. By the time al-Maqrīzī wrote, in the fifteenth century, formerly thriving quarters of the town lay in ruin. The accounts of later outbreaks in Cairo, in 1430 and 1460, are particularly rich. One study suggests mortality rates for the entire population of 46 and 40 percent, respectively, in these events. Overall, after a century of plague, the population of Egypt had decreased by half.[67]

Meanwhile, ships carried the germ to the western Mediterranean too, and by August 1347 the disease made landfall in Sicily. The Black Death leaped from there to North Africa, where Ibn Khaldūn's family was destroyed by the plague. By late 1347 the pandemic had reached mainland

Italy and southern France. The chronicles consistently repeat the same horrific accounts, not so much because these were literary tropes as because the plague's devastation was uniform. In Florence, "At every church, or at most of them, they dug wide and deep pits down to the water-table . . . and the people who were not so wealthy and died during the night, to whomever the job fell, they slung the corpses over their shoulder and cast them into the pits, or paid others a handsome price to do it. The next day as the bodies would pile up in the pit, they would throw in some dirt, and spread it around. Then more bodies would be put on top of these, and so on, layers of bodies with dirt in between, the way you use cheese to make lasagna." In the words of Petrarch, "Everywhere we see sorrow, on all sides we see terror."[68]

Public order was strained to the limit, but in regions with strong traditions of governance, the disaster called forth a heroic civic response. The well-known ordinances of the Tuscan city of Pistoia are a record of how one town reacted to the crisis. Guards were set up at the city gates to enforce a travel ban with the nearby towns of Pisa and Lucca. It was also forbidden to move any textiles between the cities for fear of contagion (indeed, not unreasonably, because infected fleas can move in cloth). Corpses were only to be transported inside wooden coffins with the planks nailed shut to contain the stench, considered a source of poisonous miasma. Other sanitary protocols—for instance, regulations on butchering—were tightened. Even in the pitch of despair, the town maintained its concern for the health of its citizens and decent respect for the victims.[69]

In Marseilles the plague arrived late in 1347 and peaked in the first half of 1348. The outbreak was severe. But thanks to the rich archives of the city, Daniel Smail has been able to recreate in minute detail the continued functioning of public order throughout the crisis. The sheer scale of mortality created plenty of business for the courts, which "far from collapsing, were actually handling more cases during the months of plague." Public officers such as notaries and judges "stuck to their posts."[70]

The plague raced northward across France in 1348. One route carried the pandemic up the Rhone Valley. A chronicle claimed that in Avignon, then home to the Papacy, half the population perished. By April it was in Lyon. That summer, it reached Paris, the largest city in western Europe. By May or June, the plague had hopped the Channel and reached England. It arrived in Dorset in the southwest. The plague established footholds along the coast, including on the east coast. By the beginning of 1349 it had penetrated into the heartland of the country. Similar events unfolded on the continent as the plague moved north and east. By the end, all of Europe was caught in the conflagration, and the big, clockwise circle that started in southern Russia was complete within three years.[71]

The impact of the Black Death has been extensively investigated. Contemporary observers offer a range of estimates, often hyperbolic. Consider a small sample of cases in which there is comparatively good documentation. Early Renaissance Florence, for instance, has left a rich archival record. The population of the town on the eve of the Black Death was probably between 100,000 and 120,000. In 1352, there were 9,955 registered households. This figure probably undercounts the poorest citizens, who were not assessed for taxes. But in all, it has been estimated that the immediate post-plague population of Florence was 37,250, for a total mortality of 55–65 percent.[72]

In England, the historical record offers a similar picture. One minutely detailed reconstruction has been drawn from the records of Glastonbury Abbey, a powerful monastery in Somerset with extensive property holdings. The court rolls of its manors list by name the men who owed a head tax to their lord on the manor. These comprise a large group of poor, landless men over the age of twelve who are known by name. Remarkably, this document notes the number of men liable on each manor for both 1348 and 1350, and also explicitly marks as "dead" those who had perished in this short space of time. The mortality during the Black Death, among these peasants in southwestern England, ranged from roughly one-third to two-thirds between manors; in aggregate, 57 percent of the men perished.[73]

These are mere examples. Almost anywhere the evidence in Europe is rich enough to form a quantitative impression, the Black Death carried off 50–60 percent of the population (see table 6.2). The historian

TABLE 6.2. Regional Mortality of Black Death
in Europe

Region	Mortality (%)
England	62.5
France	60
Italy	50–60
Languedoc/Forais	60
Piedmont	52.5
Provence	60
Savoy	60
Spain	60
Tuscany	50–60

Ole Benedictow has carefully synthesized a massive literature on the mortality of the Black Death in Europe, and the death toll is always staggeringly high.[74]

Although many a textbook still claims that the Black Death carried off a third of the continent, in reality, the best estimates are closer to half. In the words of the medievalist David Herlihy, "The more we learn of the late medieval collapse in human numbers, the more awesome it appears." In Europe alone, forty million or more might have been claimed by this bacterium. The plague is a killer in a class by itself.[75]

An Age of Plague

"Oh happy generation of our great-grandsons who will not have known these miseries and perhaps will consider our testimony as fable!" wrote Petrarch, hoping that the Black Death would come to seem like an impossibly exaggerated catastrophe. He was too optimistic. The Black Death was just the beginning, and later generations knew the misery of plague all too well.[76]

To take full measure of the plague in history is to recognize the peculiar influence of the disease over the course of centuries. The Second Pandemic spans half a millennium. In western Europe, the plague recurred up until the early eighteenth century. In North Africa and the Middle East, it recurred at least to the nineteenth century, so that it blurs into the Third Pandemic. Plague reached India by the seventeenth century and may have been in China then as well.

The Black Death looms so large that it overshadows the long reach of the pandemic. But it is a mistake to see the whole significance of the plague in terms of this singular shock. The plague was the deadliest and most dreaded disease right up to the end of its career in the Middle East, Europe, and North Africa. It did not just level the population once—it then held human numbers down, robbing generation after generation of promise and progress. In Italy, whose population history has been carefully studied, the plague was an overarching demographic fact: in phases when the plague was intense, population declined or stagnated; when it relented, population grew. And while the plague is, at least popularly, associated with "medieval" civilizations, it was truly as much a feature of early modernity as any other disease, as we will see in chapter 9.[77]

Like the Justinianic Plague, the Black Death seeded new reservoirs of plague in wild rodent populations beyond the Eurasian steppe. It cannot be excluded that some later waves of plague were reintroductions from central Asia, but the paleogenomic data push the balance in favor of regional plague persistence. Some likely hotspots have been identified. The Alps are a natural habitat for marmots. The Balkans and Anatolian highlands of eastern Turkey and northern Syria are eminently likely foci of plague. And where urban black rat populations were large enough, they might have sustained the transmission of the bacterium on a long-term basis. Any of these embers could then flare into new fires. When recurrent outbreaks did ignite, the flames spread along networks of human connection—along roads, rivers, and sea routes, between towns, from town to countryside. Plague outbreaks mirrored regional systems of trade and political integration, and, of course, plagues could follow in the trail of armies.[78]

From a European perspective, the Second Pandemic can be divided into crude phases, if we allow that there was always regional diversity. For the first century or so following the Black Death, massive and deadly outbreaks spread across the continent in waves. The *pestis secunda* or "second plague" of 1361 was a vicious relapse, sweeping up places that had been less devastated in the first visitation, like Milan. This pattern repeated itself every decade or two. There were often smaller, more local events in between. The population of Europe stagnated for a century. Then, from the fifteenth century, the plague relented, and outbreaks tended to be more regional affairs, sometimes with an urban focus. But plague was not on its way out, for in the seventeenth century, it returned with a vengeance. We will treat this pattern more fully in due course, but suffice it to say here that a proper measure of the plague's career will require attention to its later phases.[79]

Of course, none of that diminishes the fact that the initial demographic shock of the Black Death was one of the seminal events in human history. Ibn Khaldūn was right that "the entire inhabited world changed." The short-term effect of the great mortality was disequilibrium and suffering. But what about the longer-term effects? As societies started to pick up the pieces, what difference did it make that half of the population was suddenly missing?

A mortality shock is by nature a complex event, and it can be hard to untangle whether the shock merely accelerated changes that were already in course or directly altered the stream of history. Moreover, the sharp contraction of the labor supply has been interpreted in varying ways. In Egypt, for instance, the plague marked the end of a phase of dynamic expansion, rather than a stimulus to new growth. Because agriculture in the Nile Valley depended on a massive irrigation infrastructure, the plague destroyed productive capital built up over generations. The result was lower productivity and an era of stagnation.[80]

Within Europe, the effects of the negative demographic shock were uneven. A venerable hypothesis contends that in western Europe the empowerment of laborers burst the bonds of serfdom, while in eastern Europe, lords desperate for scarce labor managed to tighten the screws, reinvigorating the institutions of unfreedom that tied workers to the soil. The familiar story of the demise of feudalism can be overstated, even in western Europe, where in reality central states, gunpowder, and mercantile towns did more than *Y. pestis* to overthrow the old order. But the demographic loss seems to have triggered other changes, particularly in western Europe, with long-term consequences. People who commanded higher wages came to enjoy the goods they could buy.

They worked hard to keep their conditions from declining again, and the first stirrings of modern consumption have been traced to the post–Black Death societies. Especially with the arrival of new articles in the age of global trade, like sugar and then tobacco, this "industrious" revolution—harder work for greater consumption—was indeed a world-changing force.[81]

The demographic fallout of the Black Death also fostered capital-intensive farming, particularly in parts of northern and western Europe. Land that had been cultivated with grain in conditions of extreme population pressure was now turned over to stock-rearing. The market for processed agricultural goods expanded. Women also found it easier to participate in the labor market, whether in dairy processing or in household service. The lineaments of a new social model—with growing markets, greater levels of personal freedom, and higher levels of consumption—took shape in the aftermath of plague.[82]

The age of plague also reconfigured political incentives and military technologies. In particular, the sudden shortage of manpower incentivized the use of labor-saving devices, especially those that concentrated great violence in a few hands. In the words of James Belich, these amount to a European "expansion kit: a package of traits, transnationalisms, techniques and trajectories that encouraged long-range spread." Gunpowder and siege-craft were on the horizon, and their uptake in western Europe was more intense than anywhere else. The internal and external consequences were destined to be enormous.[83]

The history of plague is the history of fateful conjunctures. The long-term effects of the Black Death, and the Second Pandemic more generally, coincided with an age of seaborne expansion. The conjuncture of a once-in-history mortality shock with a once-in-history planetary re-alignment was fateful. Before the Black Death, the Middle East had been the geographic fulcrum of world trade, even though European ships were starting to reconnoiter in search of ways to cut out the middlemen. Soon, what had been the western periphery became the new zone of energy, bypassing the networks that linked Venice to Istanbul to Baghdad to Hangzhou. Sailors working the west coast of Africa and eventually the Atlantic turned the Old World inside out at a time when the

demographic low ebb had created a new system of incentives to concentrate power, save labor, and reward market exchange. When the Atlantic
was crossed, the Old World as it had been truly came to an end.[84]

Responses to Plague

In the history of disease, as in the history of technology, this millennium
was a continuation of the Iron Age. The established pool of fecal-oral,
respiratory, and vector-borne diseases remained a burden on human
health. Evolution continued, spinning off new strains of old diseases and
altogether novel pathogens alike. A history of infectious disease in the
Middle Ages might have zoomed in on the spread of leprosy, or the first
really clear indications of influenza pandemics. As we will explore in
later chapters, the early history of syphilis seems to lie in the late Middle
Ages, and so might also the origins of typhus. Tree thinking and time
travel are also casting light on completely hidden histories of disease.
Of the four ubiquitous human coronaviruses, all of which are cousins
of the present scourge and cause the common cold, at least one emerged
in the late Middle Ages, quietly entering the human disease pool and
adding its small increment of misery to the human condition.[85]

This period of the past also saw meaningful advances in medicine and
public health. The classic medical traditions of the Old World—the
Chinese, Indian, and Greco-Arabic—reached full flower in these centuries. The most lasting intellectual progress was in the area of diagnostics and classification, rather than therapeutics. The Persian physician
Rhazes, for instance, gave his classic differential diagnosis of measles
and smallpox in the tenth century. Still, most medical treatments were
basically futile if not actively harmful. The pharmacy was enriched by
the spread of knowledge across the Old World and the trade in botani-
cals but, unfortunately, the cumulative effects for human health were
probably negligible.[86]

More consequential progress came in the realm of public health. The
reputation of the Middle Ages for backwardness is especially apt to mis-
lead us on this front. If we define public health as concerted action by
the state to promote sanitation and hygiene, then its origins lie in the

towns of the later medieval period (at least in Europe and the Near East, and probably across much of the rest of the world). In the conventional story, public health was created by the heroic reformers of the nineteenth century in response to the vicious side effects of industrialization. There is some truth in that telling. As we will see, governments were simply much stronger by then. But the roots of public hygiene and sanitation are much deeper.[87]

Classical cities like Rome had the basic rudiments of public health, but in Europe most civic traditions were lost amid the deurbanization that followed the fall of the Roman Empire. The continuous history of European public health goes back to the town governments in the late medieval Mediterranean. Northern Italy, with the largest and most precocious cities of Europe, was also the leader in creating institutions of public health, and the region remained the pacesetter into the seventeenth century.[88]

Efforts to keep urban environments clean and habitable are as old as towns themselves. The natural aversion to the smell of feces and rotting organic matter motivated the regulation of waste disposal. The medical doctrines of Hippocrates and Galen provided a scientific rationale: putrefaction, decay, and stench polluted the atmosphere and might permeate the human body, causing disease. Urban regulations controlling butchering, waste disposal, and burial were the beginning of a new mode of preventative medicine, translated into official policy. A law from medieval Padua, for instance, forbade disposing of filth in ways that would "disturb the health of people and may bring any disease upon them." Around the same time, in late thirteenth-century London, officials were being elected at the ward level "with specific responsibility for keeping the streets free of dung and other unpleasant nuisances."[89]

The sheer ferocity of the plague also inspired more muscular collective responses to epidemic disease. Although it has rarely been noticed, the first hints of "quarantine," at least in the most elementary sense of limitations on entrance and movement, were practiced during the First Pandemic. But these measures were forgotten over the centuries and had to be invented anew. It was not so much the shock of the Black Death as the repeated bouts of epidemic mortality during the broader

Second Pandemic that taught societies how to live with the reality of plague. The practice of quarantine is first attested in Ragusa, a colony of Venice, in 1377. It spread from there, becoming throughout the western Mediterranean basin, and then beyond, the blunt instrument of plague control. Similarly, the creation of emergency health boards with powers to isolate the infected, destroy contaminated property, and restrict movement developed in the shadow of late medieval plague. These practices spread throughout Europe in the fifteenth and sixteenth centuries, part and parcel of the rise of more powerful and intrusive states, as we will see in later chapters.[90]

The broader lesson of public health in the late Middle Ages is that human progress generates negative health feedbacks, which in turn inspire adaptation and response. These early efforts to improve human health were feeble and ineffectual, judged by later standards. Only with more centralized and more intrusive states, with far greater capacity to undertake public works projects, would the riddles of densification be solved. But again, the proper perspective in which to see these experiments of the late Middle Ages is not as a contrast to triumphant modernity, but as the first lunge toward new, coordinated solutions of *Homo sapiens* to avoid early death while living in giant colonies.

PART III

Frontiers

7

Conquests and Contagions

Biological Exchanges

In a book on the history of disease, this chapter is supposed to be the one where tiny numbers of Europeans conquer the teeming populations of the New World because of the terrible and tragic fury unleashed when the germs of civilization met the virgin soil of the Americas. In the late 1960s and 1970s, scholars of pre-Columbian America started to emphasize the diffusion of Old World diseases as a component of European expansion. Historians like Alfred Crosby and William McNeill presented the Atlantic crossing as an extraordinary moment in the biological history of the planet. The shock of lethal germs when introduced to a "naïve" population "without immunity" provided a mechanism to explain the unfathomable population crash following contact. Jared Diamond's *Guns, Germs, and Steel* made European immunological advantage a crux of global history. Few academic narratives have achieved such an expansive place in the broader public consciousness.[1]

The virgin-soil hypothesis has been inordinately influential. Today, no part of this narrative stands uncontested. The evidence is ambiguous, and the issues are politically fraught. Magnifying the effects of disease had the effect of making the depopulation of the New World seem like a lamentable accident, minimizing the role of violence and deliberate exploitation. Although some clarity has been achieved by years of vigorous debate and research, there is still much that remains uncertain about the size and health of precontact populations; the relative roles of trauma, violence, and disease in the demographic disaster; and the proper place of immunity in the story. The unqualified notion that indigenous Americans "lacked immunity" to European diseases, often found in the literature, is muddled at best. Claims about the relative susceptibility of different populations to infectious disease need to be carefully reconsidered in light of modern knowledge about genetics and immunity.[2]

The virgin-soil model was created by a generation of historians and anthropologists working without the benefit of genetic evidence. Will DNA come to the rescue, relieve us of our ignorance, and settle these academic quarrels once and for all? It certainly has the potential to identify some of the pathogens carried back and forth across the Atlantic. Tree thinking can illuminate the deep and often complex histories of the microbial species crossing the ocean. Genetic evidence could provide insights into pre-Columbian populations, including their migration patterns, numbers, and genetic diversity. But the truth is that we are nearer the beginning than the end of learning what paleogenomics will teach us about the encounter between the Old World and the New. Some questions that ought to be answerable remain unresolved. There have been tantalizing hints of what is possible, and there is more undoubtedly to come.[3]

We should start by widening the frame beyond germs to envision the panorama of global biological upheavals that started in 1492. The Columbian Exchange refers to the whole ensemble of biological transfers that ensued when humans began to cross the Atlantic with regularity. Populations of *Homo sapiens* that had been out of touch for twenty thousand years were suddenly reacquainted. The ecological potential and natural resources of the New World were brought into a global circulatory system. Animals, plants, pathogens, and insects were carried across the ocean in every direction. As in all biological invasions, the results were unpredictable. Lacking natural predators or parasites, some species ran wild. Columbus brought eight pigs with him on his second voyage. They took immediately to their new surroundings and started multiplying. The feral descendants of Spanish pigs remain a prolific menace.[4]

The Columbian Exchange fundamentally redistributed human populations. Native populations were reduced when confronted with European germs, weapons, and organizational capacity. Africans were involuntarily shipped as slaves across the ocean in the biggest forced migration in the history of our species. Europeans started a process of settlement that would stretch over several centuries and reach its peak in the nineteenth century. In sum, these global displacements and migrations were comparable only to the population movements that followed the Neolithic Revolution. Their geographic sweep was even greater, and their suddenness unprecedented.[5]

The Columbian Exchange was launched by navigational accident. For centuries, Europeans had sought new routes to the riches in the east, and Christopher Columbus hoped to cut out the middlemen by sailing directly to Asia and finding what he imagined to be the bounty of the tropics. He failed to find the spices he sought, but he found something else. In the log books of his first voyage, he avidly notes signs of gold on the Taíno natives in the Caribbean. The "ravenous hunger" for gold and silver, and the brutal conscription of native populations to mining labor, was a focus of the first century of European imperialism. The Spanish and Portuguese, the dominant powers in this phase, flooded world markets with precious metals. The silver mines of Peru were linked in a global chain that connected the fortunes of the European powers in one direction to the voracious economy of China in the other.[6]

In time, plantation agriculture overtook mining as the greatest source of wealth. Old World crops like sugar and coffee took to New World soils. Brazil and then the Caribbean came to dominate world sugar production. American crops like tobacco became global commodities. As we will see, slave labor became the basis of this economy. The transition from mining to addictive tropical groceries also marked the ascendance of new powers, especially the Dutch, French, and English. The Atlantic trade became the fulcrum of power and prosperity.

When the New World had first been settled, in the Pleistocene, humans everywhere were hunter-gatherers. The domestication of animals and plants developed independently in the Americas, and the history of domestication in this hemisphere had a logic and tempo of its own. Only two birds (the turkey and a kind of duck), the guinea pig, alpaca, and llama were brought under human control. The people of the New World lacked horses, wheels, and iron metallurgy. By contrast, the Americas were blessed with some exceptionally efficient calorie-producers: corn (maize), potatoes, cassava, and sweet potatoes. These crops became the basis of complex civilizations and dense populations in the New World, especially in the American tropics, which lacked many of the ferocious pathogens that limited demographic expansion in the Old World tropics. The grains and tubers molded by generations of indigenous American farmers to suit human tastes and needs have come to feed much of the earth's population.[7]

Indeed, the ramifications of the Columbian Exchange were truly global. The adoption of corn, potatoes and cassava in Europe, Africa, and Asia had long-term demographic effects, from Ireland to China to the lands ringing the Gulf of Guinea. The diffusion of other New World crops radically altered the cuisine of the Old World. It is hard to imagine a menu without tomatoes, chili peppers, peanuts, eggplants, squash, and other American complements to the ordinary diet. The Columbian Exchange also fostered the globalization of medicine. Cinchona, a compound derived from the bark of a Peruvian tree, is an effective medicine against malaria, and it was arguably the first global drug of major medical significance. Smallpox inoculation, too, spread on global networks of knowledge from China across the steppe, from West Africa to Boston.[8]

Some of the most consequential exchanges were invisible to the naked eye. Microbes powerfully shaped human destiny in these centuries, but this is not a one-size-fits-all story of New World depopulation. We will try to trace some of the main lines of the microbial exchange over the course of the next three chapters. The history of disease in each region of the Americas depended on the interplay of four primary variables: (1) the timing, intensity, and nature of European contact; (2) the population density of native societies in the precontact period; (3) physical geography—above all, latitude and altitude—and (4) the effects of ecological transformation, especially in the creation of plantation-based societies reliant upon slave labor. Infectious diseases were indeed central to the devastation of indigenous peoples, as well as the subsequent creation of new societies in the desolation left behind. Both European and indigenous witnesses alike are insistent on that point. But the specific diseases, and the precise impacts they had, were shaped by these many factors. To capture the different configurations of these forces, we can divide the New World into epidemiological macroregions, represented in figure 7.1 (along with table 7.1).[9]

This chapter focuses on geographically indiscriminate microbes. Most of these are respiratory pathogens: smallpox, measles, influenza, mumps, scarlet fever, and diphtheria. But we should not underestimate the significance of germs that travel via the fecal-oral route. The Columbian Exchange carried diarrheal diseases, dysenteries, and enteric fevers such as typhoid and paratyphoid fever. And at least one vector-borne disease, typhus, must also rank among this number. Because it uses the human body louse as its vector, typhus, too, is geographically unconstrained, and it spread far and wide in the early modern world.

The impact of these germs after contact was rapid, in some places. The consequences were severe in the Caribbean, first of all, and soon after in the densely populated cores of Mesoamerica and South America, including the upland plateau of central Mexico and the civilizations of the Andes. The conquistadors introduced an array of pathogens evolved over millennia of farming, sedentism, and urbanization, while simultaneously imposing a traumatic new social order. Over the course of the sixteenth century, the result was one of the greatest demographic catastrophes in the history of our species. The temperate latitudes were more sparsely settled, and the influence of such pathogens was only felt from the seventeenth century, because of, and in tandem with, the intensification of settler colonialism.

The next chapter is dedicated to the role of tropical diseases, especially vector-borne diseases like malaria and yellow fever. The unification of the tropics was one of the fundamental dynamics of the Columbian Exchange. This process took longer to unfold, but its imprint has been long-lasting. The rise of malaria and yellow fever in the seventeenth

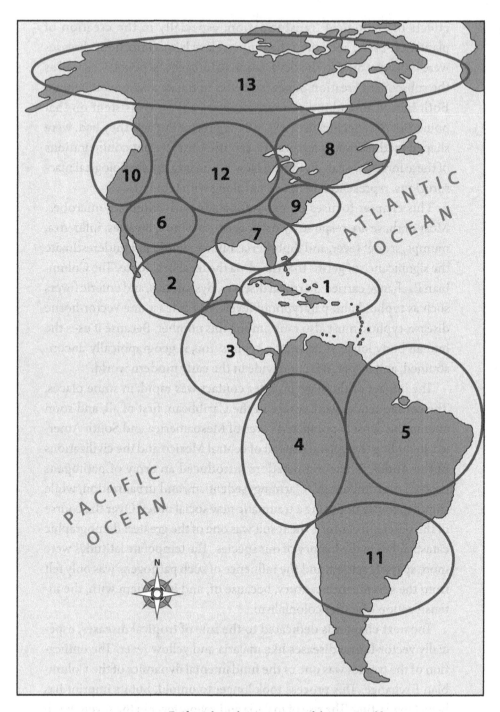

FIGURE 7.1. Epidemiological macroregions of the New World.

TABLE 7.1. Epidemiological Macroregions of the New World

Region number	Region name	Pre-Columbian density	Timing of impact	Major vector-borne diseases?
1	Caribbean	Medium	1490–1550	Yes
2	Central Mexico	High	1520–1600	No
3	Lowland Mexico/Central America	High	1520–1600	Yes
4	Andes	High	1520–1600	Yes
5	Amazon Basin	Medium	1530–1650	Yes
6	Northern Mexico/Southwest United States	Low	1590–1700	No
7	Southeast United States	Medium	1600–1700	Yes
8	Eastern Canada/New England	Low	1620–1700	No
9	Tidewater/Mid-Atlantic	Low	1620–1700	Yes
10	Pacific Coast	Medium	1700–1850	Yes
11	Temperate South America	Low	post-1600	No
12	Great Plains	Low	1700–1850	No
13	Subarctic	Low	1800–1900	No

century went hand in hand with the growth of slavery and the plantation complex. The expansion of the sugar economy created ecological niches for the mosquitos that carry deadly human diseases. The result was the imposition across the New World of a stark latitudinal gradient of health and disease, one which fundamentally shaped the relative weight of slavery and European settlement.

The final chapter of this triptych reverts our gaze back to the Old World. In Europe and Asia, the seventeenth century was an age of growth, crisis, and transformation. The globalization of calorie-rich crops from the Americas represented its own kind of energy revolution. The Columbian Exchange helped to fuel the accelerating and destabilizing growth that ultimately plunged nearly every part of the Old World into crisis. Meanwhile, psychotropic commodities like sugar, tobacco, and coffee stimulated markets. The cities of northwestern Europe ascended to primacy by virtue of their position in trade networks. What had been an impassable barrier now became the most important zone of market integration, capital investment, and specialized production in the world. A new Atlantic economy, even a new global order, took shape.

The history of disease in the Old World during these centuries was also dramatic. Famine and war created the conditions for pestilence. Institutions that brought together crowds of people—armies, jails, hospitals, and factories (mirroring the rise of plantations across the Atlantic)—created new disease ecologies. A specific early modern disease regime, dominated by smallpox, typhus, and plague, held sway. A global perspective can help us see some remarkable connections. In the sixteenth century, smallpox became worse *everywhere*—from Ming China to Mexico City. Typhus was probably not a disease that had existed from the mists of time. It was introduced to the Mediterranean in the later fifteenth century and became a new disease in Europe and the Americas simultaneously. Yellow fever became a true trans-Atlantic scourge. An outbreak in Havana could echo from Philadelphia to Seville. The reunion of the hemispheres, then, marks one of the true watersheds in the globalization of disease.

Across these chapters, a unifying theme is the inseparability of geography, biology, and power. The Columbian Exchange was not simply a collision between Old World germs and the Americas; it was the creation of a global system in which north-south gradients were as important as east-west exchanges, and in which the dynamics of slavery, settlement, and commerce were inseparable from biological exchanges. Health inequalities reinforced and amplified wealth inequalities in new and more powerful ways, even as some societies edged closer to breakaway modern growth.

European Arrival

In 1529, a German explorer named Nikolaus Federmann stayed briefly on the island of Hispaniola. It had been almost four decades since the landfall of Christopher Columbus. When Columbus had first laid eyes on the island, he was enthusiastic about its fertility and population. He recorded in his log for the day of December 6, 1492, that there must be "large settlements" because of all the giant canoes. He thought Hispaniola was "the most beautiful thing in the world," bigger than Portugal with twice the population. Columbus, of course, was a promoter, eager to aggrandize his discovery. What Federmann found, a few decades later, was desolation. "It is unnecessary to write of the nature and customs of the natives or inhabitants of this place. . . . There are not many of them left. According to reports, out of 500,000 natives or inhabitants who were in this land . . . there are not over twenty thousand living now. A large number succumbed to a disease which is called *viroles*, but some also to wars and a great many to the extreme hard labor which the Christians forced them to do in the gold mines, contrary to their ways, for they are a very delicate people who worked little."[10]

Federmann's observations bring to the surface every major challenge in understanding the biological collision between the Old World and the Americas. Are such astonishing death tolls credible? What was the relative role of infectious disease and colonial violence in the near annihilation of indigenous populations? Is it possible to identify the pathogens—such as *viroles*, usually understood to be smallpox—responsible for biological disaster? What is to be made of claims that the native peoples of the New World were particularly susceptible to European germs? The depopulation of Hispaniola is a microcosm for a whole series of dramatic and unresolved questions about the biological impact of European contact.[11]

By the late nineteenth century, imperialism and infectious disease had reduced the native populations of the Americas. Native populations declined to a fraction of their precontact numbers. It is generally agreed that native populations reached a nadir around 1900, when there were an estimated five million indigenous people remaining in the hemisphere. (Of course, these figures underscore a history of resilience and perseverance, too, in spite of the relentless impact of disease and displacement; since 1900, native populations have increased.) By the opening of the twentieth century, there were also perhaps fifty million people of European origin in the Americas. Moreover, around twelve million Africans had been imported via the slave trade, and despite the most cruel conditions, their numbers had modestly increased. Obviously, such categories simplify the realities of identity, intermarriage, and descent, but in broad strokes, the first four centuries of modern Atlantic history were characterized by these intertwined demographic forces:

the decrease of indigenous populations, the involuntary migration of Africans, and the settler colonialism of Europeans.[12]

How many natives had there been in October 1492, when Columbus first sighted land in the New World? The range of respectable opinion has been unusually wide. In the early twentieth century, the anthropologist Alfred Kroeber tried to develop a region-by-region census of indigenous peoples and argued for a total of 8.4 million at the moment of contact. His estimates were highly abstract, based on measures of carrying capacity (and plain gut feelings about the relationship between technology and population). His number stands as the lower bound of professional opinion, and over the twentieth century, the tallies started to run higher, as archaeologists found more and more evidence for complex societies and dense populations.[13]

By the 1960s, revisionist historians started to argue for vastly higher population totals. These upward adjustments had a political tint, because they were held to imply that indigenous civilizations were more "advanced." Henry Dobyns's high estimate of 112.6 million represents the upper bound in the debate. Such astronomical totals depend heavily on the belief that devastating pandemics were sparked by the earliest contacts and fanned out across the New World ahead of European observers. By the time there were estimates from European witnesses, the crash had already happened. The high-counters latched on to the idea that Native Americans were biologically susceptible to European diseases as a way of explaining the historically exceptional character of the population losses.[14]

Over the last generation, anthropologists and archaeologists have narrowed the spectrum. Specialists tend to accept that population densities were low across most of North America, with only a few million souls spread across the region that is today northern Mexico, the continental United States, and Canada. By contrast, the Aztec heartlands of central Mexico and the Andean coast of South America were far more densely settled. Even without iron technology and draught animals, the calorie-rich crops of corn, manioc, and potatoes supported a large population. Most recent estimates fall somewhere between about forty million on the low end and about sixty million on the upper end. For reference, the population of Europe in AD 1500, which had known the horse, wheel, and iron technology for thousands of years, was around forty million. Tenochtitlán may have been home to a little over two hundred thousand residents on the eve of Cortés's invasion; at this time the largest European cities were Paris and Constantinople, at roughly the same size.[15]

Human genomes potentially offer new insights into the population history of the Americas. For instance, if genetic samples from pre- and postcontact indigenous societies are available, the scope of demographic change can be inferred from changes in genetic diversity. In one population from Northern California, a genetic bottleneck in the early nineteenth century coincident with a series of smallpox epidemics points to a sudden reduction in numbers of 57 percent. Another study of South American populations found that the impact of European arrival was far more severe in lowland coastal regions than in the Andean highlands. Lowland population decline was estimated at 90 percent, in line with the worst estimates. High-altitude population numbers, by contrast, were less dramatically affected, with a reduction around 27 percent. Thus, ecological differences shaped the biological and social effects of contact. Extreme differences even at a local scale are evident in both the archival and genetic evidence, and they should remind us that the fate of New World populations writ large was anything but uniform.[16]

The classic virgin-soil hypothesis rests on three interrelated claims. (1) For biogeographic reasons, the disease pool of the Old World peoples was particularly dangerous. (2) The indigenous inhabitants of America had no experience of these diseases and suffered high mortality as a result of this immune naïveté. (3) Even with the stark advantage provided by guns and horses, there were not enough Europeans on the ground in the Americas for violence and enslavement to explain the catastrophe. After all, the pages of European, African, and Asian history are littered with episodes of conquest and expropriation that are not followed by demographic catastrophe. Europeans appeared on the shores of Africa in these centuries too, with the worst of intentions, but African populations did not dwindle by 90 percent. So, the theory goes, the best explanation for the depopulation of the New World is to be found in the microbial imbalance between the hemispheres.[17]

The first claim of the virgin-soil hypothesis is the sturdiest. The diseases of the Old World were both more numerous and more virulent than those in the Americas. Domestication in Asia and Europe had occurred earlier and was more transformational; a few thousand years is a long time for relentless evolution to conjure wicked new pathogens. Moreover, the animal ecology of the Old World favored the emergence of infectious diseases. There were more domesticated animals to act as sources of new infections and as bridges between wild animal diseases and humans. The Old World is also home to our closest relatives—the other great apes—whose immune systems are most similar to ours; their germs are ancestral to some of our worst pathogens, causing a range of diseases from malaria to (later) AIDS. The Old World was also more interconnected—with donkeys, horses, wheels, and long-distance seaborne transport—making it a relatively unified disease pool. Finally, the Old World was more urbanized, making it easier for density-dependent pathogens to become permanently endemic.[18]

What germs were shuttled across the Atlantic in the years after contact? The Columbian Exchange would have included many pathogens of the gastrointestinal tract carried in the guts and feces of the voyagers. Diseases that spread via the fecal-oral route had been adapting to human beings since the rise of sedentary societies. The Old World peoples who crossed the Atlantic would have carried many of the nondescript diarrheal diseases we met in chapter 4, as well as even more deadly forms of dysentery caused by bacteria (*Shigella*) and amoebas. They would have also ferried typhoid and paratyphoid fevers, invasive diseases caused by *Salmonella enterica*. The dangerous byproducts of humanity's unique waste environments, evolved over millennia, were one piece of the imbalanced disease exchange.[19]

The classic crowd diseases of the respiratory tract have always figured prominently in histories of the Columbian Exchange. Diseases like measles, scarlet fever, whooping cough, diphtheria, mumps, chicken pox, and rubella, not to mention a huge number of other less notorious afflictions (the common cold, respiratory syncytial virus infection, parainfluenza), are adapted to spread between human hosts through aerosols or droplets. They cause acute infection, lack nonhuman reservoirs, and tend to confer immunity on survivors, so they quickly go extinct without large, dense congregations of susceptible hosts. Most of these diseases emerged as a consequence of our urban lifestyles. They are all known or suspected to be of Old World origin.[20]

Several important diseases not mentioned so far merit brief notice. Plague, the most deadly disease in the Old World, was busy infecting humans in the early modern period, but there is no good evidence that it successfully crossed the Atlantic. We will focus on typhus in chapter 9, and propose that it was perhaps a new disease in Europe. It was carried across the Atlantic in the mid-sixteenth century and thus has a truly global career in this period. Influenza is often ranked among the European respiratory diseases imported to the New World, but its biology is unlike the classic crowd diseases. Pandemic influenza arises when strains of avian influenza successfully cross the species barrier to humans. It is thus a zoonotic disease that adapts to humans periodically, then circulates in fast-moving waves. Such waves are well attested from the sixteenth century on, and probably occurred earlier. Pandemic influenza swept across Europe in the 1550s and possibly reached the New World. It might have been the first truly global pandemic.[21]

The smallpox virus is a special case. It was imported to the New World in 1518 and was destined to become one of the most important microbes in the Columbian Exchange. But the DNA evidence has revealed to us a virus with a complex history. Smallpox started to adapt to humans a little less than two millennia ago. It may have adapted to humans in stages. Smallpox was an important childhood disease in the middle ages, but not the violent killer it soon became. New strains of smallpox emerged in the sixteenth century, and the genetic evidence now confirms the written record suggesting that the virus took a dangerous evolutionary turn in the early modern period. Where and, more precisely, when smallpox evolved into its modern form remains murky, and we would especially like to know what strains of the virus spread in the Americas.[22]

The story of syphilis is possibly even more convoluted. Syphilis is a sexually transmitted disease caused by the spiral-shaped bacterium

Treponema pallidum. Syphilis is a cruel but patient enemy. It starts as a chancre in sensitive regions and may cease its career there. Or it can diffuse and envelop the entire body in a blistering rash that seems to rot the flesh. Then it hides for an indeterminate period, sometimes years. Untreated, it will eventually progress to "tertiary" syphilis, causing slow, disseminated infection, extending to the nervous tissue. It destroys the brain, but gradually. A patient entering tertiary syphilis bobs in and out of sanity, as the victim's body sinks into paralysis. To be diagnosed with tertiary syphilis in the days before antibiotics was to be condemned to wakeful damnation. It was incurable and excruciating.[23]

Syphilis is not only a painful and deadly sickness. It is one of the major human diseases of modernity. But its origins have been controversial. Syphilis is caused by a subspecies of the bacterium known as *T. pallidum pallidum.* Other subspecies of the same bacterium cause the important skin disease yaws (subspecies *pertenue*) as well as the less prevalent diseases bejel and pinta. One long-standing theory is that syphilis was a New World disease that Columbus and his crew carried back to Europe. In support of that view, pre-Columbian skeletons from the Americas exhibit signs of treponemal disease, and an explosive European outbreak in the mid-1490s caused by the "French disease" or the "great pox" has been proposed as a virgin-soil epidemic that introduced the disease to Europe. Alternatively, textual and skeletal evidence from late medieval Europe has been alleged as proof that the disease was already there.[24]

The DNA evidence has partly resolved the controversy, but not without uncovering some plot twists. It turns out that syphilis, thanks to the recovery of its genetic remains, was indeed present in Europe before the Columbian Exchange. All strains of syphilis shared a common ancestor between the tenth and fifteenth centuries, however, so it is not an ancient disease, at least as we know it. Unexpectedly, all sampled genomes of yaws are also recent, and this disease too seems to have undergone rapid diversification in the fourteenth to sixteenth centuries. Yaws has also been found in late medieval Europe, suggesting that it may have been imported by Europeans who had started exploring the coast of West Africa. We do not yet know what strain of treponemal disease circulated in pre-Columbian America, leaving this historical mystery far from completely resolved. Native Americans might have known a now-extinct lineage, replaced by the more aggressive Old World diseases syphilis and yaws. On balance, it seems that syphilis needs to be classed as yet another affliction introduced by Europeans, even though trepo-nemal disease was not unfamiliar in the Americas.[25]

The New World was not a disease-free paradise, but its disease burden was incomparably lighter than that of the Old World. The Americas had been peopled in one or two significant migratory pulses during the late Pleistocene, starting around twenty thousand years ago. When the first settlers crossed Beringia, they left behind them the most insidious Pleis-tocene pathogens, such as vivax malaria. Most importantly, they came in the small groups characteristic of hunter-gatherers. The passage was thus a microbial cleanse, and it set New World peoples on an epidemiological trajectory of their own. But an array of pathogens lurked in wait as human populations dispersed across the New World. Dozens of identified pathogens are unique to the Americas, especially in the tropics. Most of these are the kinds of parasites that do not require large, agglomerated human populations to persist. They are zoonotic pathogens, such as viruses that survive permanently in species of birds, bats, or rodents and only sporadically transmit to humans. Some are helminths, macropara-sites that only exist in the New World. Many are vector-borne, spread by the mosquitos, sand flies, and black flies native to the hemisphere.[26]

Only a handful of these New World pathogens are a major burden on human health. One is Chagas disease, caused by a parasite that circu-lates among a wide range of vertebrate hosts, especially nesting mam-mals who are preyed upon by the only vector of Chagas disease, the kissing bug (which we met in chapter 3, sneaking in to give the sleeping Charles Darwin an unwanted smooch). Other modestly important New World pathogens include the bacterium that causes Carrion's disease, the viruses that cause Oropouche infection or Venezuelan equine en-cephalitis, the helminth that causes New World Mansonelliasis, or the protozoa that cause American leishmaniasis. Notably, the known germs of the New World are not among those that are capable of causing a major epidemic.[27]

The presence of tuberculosis in the Americas has also been long debated. The skeletal evidence indicates the presence of TB in the Americas before trans-Atlantic contact. As we have seen, this fact posed a genuine conundrum in light of the youth of the bacterial agent of TB. But the recent discovery of ancient tuberculosis DNA from Peru has offered a possible, and certainly unpredicted, resolution of the puzzle. The pre-Columbian TB was most closely related to strains found in sea mammals. The genetic evidence suggests a roundabout history in which the human disease somehow passed into animal populations and then *back* into human populations in the Americas. How—or how efficiently—these strains of the disease diffused in the New World is a major question and one that is likely to receive illumination from continued collection of evidence. TB, in some form, is now firmly established among the diseases of pre-Columbian America.[28]

The study of the New World boasts a remarkable tradition of skeletal archaeology. Bones tell stories about diet and disease and violence. The skeletal record traces profound changes in the health of the Americans in the centuries before Columbus. The transition from a hunter-gatherer lifestyle to sedentism based on the domestication of plants and animals occurred later in most of the Americas than it had in the Old World. But as in Eurasia, so in the Americas farming was harmful for human health. The bones of the New World speak to a history of stress and nutritional decline. Bioarchaeologists have traced the skeletal pathologies of farm labor, sedentism, and diets overly reliant on a narrow spectrum of carbohydrate-rich plants. In example after example, serious pathologies like osteoarthritis, anemia, and enamel growth defects became more prevalent as agriculture spread, centuries before the coming of Europeans. The stresses inflicted on indigenous societies by the transition to farming rendered them more susceptible to infectious disease when explorers and settlers from the Old World did arrive.[29]

There were probably infectious diseases circulating in the New World that are now unknown to us. Acute infections do not leave skeletal markers. It is reasonable to believe that with better evidence more diseases—especially gastroenteric infections—might be identified. Epidemics of dysentery are attested in Aztec sources, for example, in the period before Spanish conquest, and it is altogether likely that endemic indigenous diseases had evolved in the wake of agriculture. Histories of the Inca describe major epidemics in the century before Europeans stumbled onto the New World. The microbes responsible have been lost to history, unless their genomes are someday recovered.[30]

Did the lighter disease burden of the New World render Native Americans susceptible to Old World germs? Sweeping claims that indigenous peoples "lacked immunity" to European germs are misleading. In many accounts of the virgin-soil hypothesis, it is altogether unclear what immunological naïveté even means. There are at least two distinct possibilities. First, had European populations, long exposed to Old World infectious diseases, evolved greater genetic resistance to those diseases? It is plausible. There are obvious examples of pathogen-driven natural selection in the human genome. In the words of a team of geneticists, "Infectious pathogens are arguably among the strongest selective forces that act on human populations." Unsurprisingly, genes involved in immune function are highly diverse between individuals and populations, and they reveal strong indications of recent and intense selection pressure. Further, the increasing amount of ancient DNA has allowed us to observe that certain genes involved in immunity became more frequent in Old World populations over time.[31]

Several qualifications are in order, though. Often, the functional importance of genetic variants in the immune system is not completely understood, and the selective advantage they may have conferred under past conditions is just not known. In other words, we know there are genetic differences in immunity, but we do not (always) know why they exist, and how they might have helped in the past. Moreover, such differences generally conferred only incremental advantages. We should not imagine that Europeans possessed charmed genomes making them invincible against Old World diseases (a view that would be wildly incongruent with the historical record of European health history). Instead, most of these genetic variants probably do things like change the shape of a receptor ever so slightly, or enhance certain signaling pathways, that help the body respond to certain viruses or bacteria a little more efficiently. And, as we have learned just how young many of history's lethal germs really are, it has become less plausible that human populations had enough time to become truly well adapted to these pathogens. While the evidence for recent adaptation in the human genome to major infectious diseases is rapidly growing (for instance, to malaria, plague, and tuberculosis), these findings have not yet added much depth to our understanding of the Columbian Exchange. That may, of course, change in the near future.

A second possibility is that individual Europeans had been previously exposed to Old World diseases and gained acquired immunity in the form of specific B-cells and T-cells that respond quickly to reinfection. Many of the conquerors, settlers, and merchants who came from European cities would have been exposed to smallpox, measles, and other infections as children. Every adult was a survivor of at least some of these infections. Of course, it is impossible that every European would have been exposed to the entire range of pathogens, and so, again, even population-level differences in acquired immunity were a matter of degree. By contrast, entire populations of indigenous peoples were completely lacking previous exposure. These differences were transitory, but they could have factored into the early stages of contact.[32]

The case for susceptibility is thus biologically plausible when grounded on these more precise and also narrower terms. The case is bolstered by direct testimony. The Spanish regularly noted that diseases affected native populations severely (and they also noted when that was not the case). Many such testimonies come from witnesses highly sympathetic to the plight of indigenous people and critical of European expansion. Moreover, native sources also claimed that disease took a disproportionate toll and perceived disease as a force allied with white invaders. And yet, we can remain cautious about these testimonies, because early modern witnesses did not understand the biology of immunity. Susceptibility and clinical outcomes are also affected by social factors, which would have shaped perception of the effects of infectious disease.[33]

It should also be noted that the vulnerability of previously unexposed populations has been repeatedly documented in more modern times. The Plains Indians of North America from the late eighteenth century suffered egregious mortality in smallpox epidemics transmitted on long-distance networks, even without direct exposure to Europeans. The examples from the peoples of the Pacific Islands in the nineteenth century, or the Inuit populations of the later nineteenth century, or the Amazonian peoples in even more recent times, furnish tragic parallels. What these examples have in common is exceptionally high case fatality rates.[34]

What about the third leg of the virgin-soil hypothesis, the idea that Europeans were too few to have conquered the indigenous civilizations without the unwitting help of their microbial allies? In part, this question is about the politics of colonialism. If the germs did it (the story goes), then the devastation wrought by the Columbian Exchange might be represented as an accident rather than an intentional act of violence. That is an understandable concern, but this dichotomy is unnecessary. Expropriation and epidemic mortality went hand in hand. Violence and social dislocation weakened native societies, rendering them more susceptible to the ravages of infectious disease. The human trauma also depressed fertility, making it harder for societies to rebound from disastrous losses. Death by direct violence probably was a limited factor in the larger perspective of the demographic catastrophe; far deadlier was carefully organized exploitation by a technologically and organizationally more powerful society that also introduced an array of novel pathogens at the same time.[35]

The Caribbean Microcosm

In 1492, around 90 percent of everyone alive in the Americas resided in the tropics and subtropics. These core regions of Spanish conquest (and Portuguese conquest in the case of Brazil) were the first to suffer from the introduction of Old World pathogens. They were also home to the societies with the preexisting networks most favorable for the rapid transmission of contagious disease. Sustained contact with Europeans was maintained from the 1490s on Hispaniola and parts of the Caribbean, from the 1510s and 1520s in the Mexican heartlands and Central America, from the 1530s in Peru and the Andes, from the mid-sixteenth century in Brazil, and from the later sixteenth century in northern Mexico.

Consider the Caribbean as a microcosm of the forces that would engulf the New World. It was a fateful accident that Columbus first blundered onto the hemisphere by making landfall in the Caribbean. Convinced that he had navigated a new route to Asia, he and his crew met a Taíno civilization whose population was probably one million or more at the time of first contact. When Columbus returned on his second voyage late in 1493, he brought with him seventeen ships loaded with plants and animals, including sugarcane, cattle, goats, sheep, and pigs. He also, unequivocally, brought germs. The Columbian Exchange had begun.[36]

Columbus himself fell ill on the passage between the Canaries and Hispaniola, as did many of his crew and passengers. The outbreak spread to the island, where a food shortage made the situation worse. The mortality was severe, in this case for the Spanish and the Taíno alike. In the words of Gonzalo Fernandez de Oviedo, one of the important early chroniclers of Spain's New World ventures, "All through the land the Indians lay dead everywhere. The stench was great and pestiferous. The ailments that fell upon the Christians were many besides hunger. . . . The Indians who escaped went hastily inland. From this and the great humidity of this land stemmed grave and incurable diseases for those who stayed alive."[37]

The pathogen that inaugurated this new era of pestilence is impossible to identify with certainty. People fell to a highly contagious disease with a short and violent course of infection and high case fatality rates. The medical historian Francisco Guerra put forward influenza as a hypothesis, and although the flu is as good a guess as any, and better than some (like malaria and yellow fever), we have to remain circumspect about the diagnosis.[38]

The epidemic of 1493–94 was only the start. In the words of a modern historian, "Massive deaths winnowed aboriginal Hispaniola and pared its foreign settlers between 1493 and 1496." There were further epidemics in 1498, 1500, 1502, and 1507. The sources for early Spanish occupation of the Caribbean are abundantly clear that disease and violence alike took a heavy toll. One Spaniard who moved to Hispaniola in 1502 described the island as populous on his arrival. By 1520, he claimed that it was substantially depopulated, blaming "smallpox, measles, *romadizo* [most likely influenza], and other illnesses that the Spanish gave to the Indians."[39]

These first contacts were also the beginning of organized extortion. There was a bloody battle between the Spanish and the Taíno in 1495. With gunpowder, cavalry, and vicious fighting dogs on their side, the Spanish carried out a massacre. Columbus himself then instituted a system of forced labor and tribute, requiring payment in gold, cotton, or spices. Taíno men were conscripted into the hunt for gold, inaugurating a tradition of forced labor in mining that fractured native social structures, exposed the native Caribbean people to harsh working conditions, and sometimes required forced relocation that in turn triggered epidemic disease. Further military operations were conducted in 1503 and 1504. The survivors were ordered to live in towns. "It was this campaign that effectively destroyed the polities of the Taínos."[40]

There is no doubt that Hispaniola was lashed by the massive smallpox outbreak that started in 1518. There were still tens of thousands of Taíno on the island when it struck. Bartolomé de Las Casas, who was both sympathetic to the Americans and disposed to emphasize the role of Spanish violence, claimed it was brought by a man from Castile: "I do not believe that, of the enormous number of people that were once on this island that we saw with our own eyes, there were 1,000 souls who were left alive or escaped this misery." It was shortly thereafter, in the late 1520s, that the German explorer Nikolaus Federmann stopped on the island en route to South America and claimed that there were virtually no native inhabitants left.[41]

The modern-day genetics of the Caribbean reflect the large-scale loss of life, but even here, there was not complete depopulation. The Taíno contribution to modern genomes in the Caribbean is small, but it is detectible. A once large population crashed in the early sixteenth century. Within three generations, the indigenous inhabitants of the Caribbean had been reduced to a small remnant. The experience of Hispaniola was an inauspicious beginning for a new age of global connectivity, and it is hard to explain such dramatic population movements without high mortality from infectious disease. The recent conclusion of John Mc-Neill in this regard is judicious: "It is implausible to suppose that violence, reduced fertility, and starvation together could account for the reduction of populations numbering in the hundreds of thousands, perhaps the low millions, to almost zero between 1492 and 1550. Only a few thousand Spaniards settled in the Caribbean, and many of them were genteel priests or sedentary merchants, hardly men of violence. Even with steel-edged weapons, horses, and attack dogs it is far-fetched to suppose they could actually have killed more than a small proportion of Caribbean peoples, even if one accepts the lowest estimates of Caribbean indigenous population in 1492."[42]

To the Mainland

The experience of the Caribbean was an intense prelude of what was to follow. The earliest impact of European conquest and colonization on the mainland lagged by about a generation. When the Spanish did arrive in Mexico, they encountered the most developed and densely populated region of the New World. Here, as in the Andes, the demographic impact was dramatic, but less annihilating than in the Caribbean. The Spanish encountered complex empires that had already built the machinery of extraction to collect tribute from populous peasant societies (see figure 7.2). The conquerors could build on the scaffolding of Aztec and Inca structures of exploitation. We can take the epidemiological history of central Mexico as a case study, because it was both demographically the most important and also historically the most richly documented region of the Americas.

For more than two centuries, the Aztecs had dominated the sprawling plateau of central Mexico, a "great natural saucer" where the Aztecs had "transformed thousands of acres of poorly drained landed into highly productive gardens in the fourteenth and fifteenth centuries. Through canal irrigation, swamp drainage, and the cultivation of maguey and nopal plants, the Aztec economy" supported a vast population. One soldier who arrived with Hernán Cortés marveled when he

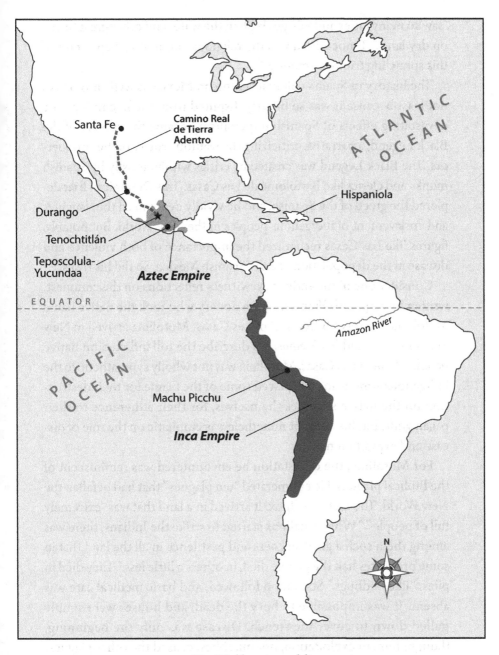

FIGURE 7.2. New World empires and disease routes.

"saw so many cities and villages built in the water and other great towns on dry land." Tenochtitlán was the religious and political epicenter of this sprawling tributary empire.[43]

The history of Spain's colonial venture in Mexico is well chronicled, not least because it was so bitterly disputed from the beginning. The devastating effects of Spanish imperialism became the subject of the Black Legend, a narrative criticizing the wanton cruelty of the conquerors. The Black Legend was created by critics within, mostly by Spanish monks and clerics like Bartolomé de Las Casas. This Dominican friar deplored the greed of the Spanish, and he vividly denounced the slaughter and enslavement of indigenous peoples in the New World. But notably, figures like Las Casas recognized the importance of both violence and disease in the depopulation of early Spanish Mexico. So did his rivals.[44]

Consider one of the earliest eyewitness reflections on the conquest, written by a Spanish Franciscan missionary who took the native name Motolinia. He was a bitter rival of Las Casas. Motolinia arrived in New Spain in 1524, and his *Memoriales* describe the toll inflicted on native peoples. Unlike Las Casas, Motolinia was not wholly sympathetic to the indigenous Americans. He placed some of the blame for their destruction on the native societies themselves, for their adherence to their pagan gods, but his account nonetheless is emphatic on the role of disease and exploitation.

For Motolinia, the devastation he encountered was reminiscent of the Biblical plagues. He enumerated "ten plagues" that had befallen the New World. The first: smallpox. It arrived in a land that was "extremely full of people." "When smallpox started to strike the Indians, there was among them such a great sickness and pestilence in all the land that in some provinces half the people died, in others a little less." They died in piles, "like bedbugs." Starvation followed, and basic medical care was absent. It was impossible to bury the dead, and houses were simply pulled down to cover the stench. Disease was only the beginning, though; human exploitation, not microbes, caused the other plagues: the violence of the initial conquest, famine, the brutality of the overseers, the extraction of tribute, the gold mines, the conscript labor used to build Mexico City, the rise of slavery to serve the gold mines, the excruciating conditions of travel to and work in the gold mines, and the civil strife caused by internal dissensions among Spanish factions. For Motolinia, biological and imperial violence worked hand in hand to accomplish violence of Biblical proportions.[45]

The arrival of the Spanish in Mexico coincided exactly with a smallpox pandemic that represents the first truly widespread disease outbreak in the New World. Even though there had been extensive trans-Atlantic movements in the generation since Columbus, the smallpox virus had not managed to cross the ocean. It took the fortuitous circumstance of a ship able to make the six- or seven-week voyage with enough susceptible passengers to sustain the chain of transmission between the hemispheres. The moment that this calamitous eventuality was realized is etched in the collective memory of both Spanish and indigenous history.[46]

The smallpox pandemic started in the Caribbean during winter 1518–19. In spring 1520, the virus jumped from the islands to the shores of Mexico. Hernán Cortés had led an unauthorized expedition with a few hundred men to the mainland, and the Governor of Cuba dispatched Pánfilo de Narváez with troops to overtake Cortés. The smallpox virus was an invisible companion among the troops of Narváez. Smallpox struck the coastal plains first and coursed inland throughout the year 1520. An eyewitness document written only months later—a letter written to Charles V—already ascribed depopulation to the ravages of the disease.[47]

Indigenous sources also describe a catastrophic mortality. One of the remarkable documents of sixteenth-century history is the massive twelve-volume compendium about the indigenous culture in Mexico assembled by Bernardino de Sahagún, who learned the Aztec language, Nahuatl. The *Florentine Codex* preserves an Aztec viewpoint. "Before the Spaniards had risen against us, first there came to be prevalent a great sickness, a plague . . . there spread over the people a great destruction of men. Some it indeed covered [with pustules]; they were spread everywhere, on one's face, on one's head, on one's breast, etc. . . . On some, each pustule was placed on them only far apart; they did not cause much suffering, neither did many of them die. And many people were harmed by them on their faces; their faces were roughened. Of some, the eyes were injured; they were blinded." The book also includes

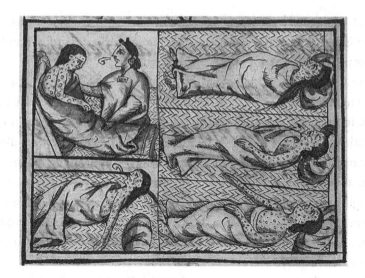

FIGURE 7.3. Pictograph of Nahua people suffering disease thought to be smallpox, from *Florentine Codex* compiled by Bernardino de Sahagún. Credit: Firenze, Biblioteca Medicea Laurenziana, Ms. Med. Palat. 220, f. 460v. Su concessione del MiC E' vietata ogni ulteriore riproduzione con qualsiasi mezzo.

pictographs (see figure 7.3), including a representation of an Aztec suffering and succumbing to smallpox. (It is a poignant note that this beautifully illustrated encyclopedia was itself made in 1576, in the midst of a later pandemic, "a fact that confers its production with special status akin to a battle waged and won by its creators against extermination and death." In Book 11, as the outbreak of 1576 raged, the illustrators ran out of pigments, and the vital, expressive colors of the pictographs in the early books of the *Codex* turned to somber monochrome.)[48]

The simultaneous appearance of the virus and the Spaniards allowed the history of disease to intersect military history at a fateful moment. The vastly outnumbered army of Cortés had initially been forced to retreat from Tenochtitlán on June 30, 1520. But when his forces returned less than a year later (along with thousands of their Tlaxcalan allies), they besieged a city that had been hollowed out by the deadly virus. Many of the native leaders had succumbed to the disease, critically weakening efforts to resist the Spanish. In the judgment of a modern historian, "The military significance of the pestilence was enormous." By the end of the year, the momentum of Cortés was unstoppable, and Spanish control of the richest part of the New World was in hand.[49]

The geography of the smallpox epidemic on the American mainland reflected native networks of communication and travel. The virus spread inexorably throughout the Aztec empire in central Mexico. There is no indication the pandemic reached northern Mexico or the present-day United States. By contrast, it did penetrate south, to the Yucatán, Guatemala, and Panama. The *Annals of the Cakchiquels*, a native Guatemalan chronicle, recorded, "Little by little heavy shadows and black night enveloped our fathers and grandfathers and also us, oh my sons! when the plague raged. The people could not in any way control the sickness. . . . Great was the stench of the dead. After our fathers and grandfathers succumbed, half of the people fled to the fields. The dogs and vultures devoured the bodies. The mortality was terrible." But further south, the evidence for the smallpox pandemic is ambiguous. If the mortality reached the Andean civilizations, it did so in advance of European contact.[50]

Witnesses in central Mexico estimated the mortality of 1520–21 at anywhere from a quarter of the population to half "in some provinces," as Motolinia put it. Without knowing the basis for these estimates, it is unwise to accept such indications at face value. It is equally unwise to dismiss such testimonies as meaningless. What we can say is that the appearance of smallpox in the New World was devastating—and worse was yet to come.[51]

Throughout the sixteenth century, central Mexico was struck repeatedly by epidemic disease. Epidemics are recorded in 1531, 1532, 1538, 1559–60, 1563–64, 1587, and 1595 (see table 7.2). There is nothing necessarily unexpected about such a pattern: periodic waves of disease rolled over the Old World in the same period. But in the Americas, three pandemics—the smallpox pandemic of 1520–21 and two later pandemics, in 1545–48 and 1576–80—seem to have been of a greater order of magnitude. In the words of sixteenth-century merchant and writer Diego Muñoz Camargo, "The first [1520] ought to be the greatest because there were more people, and the second [1545] was also very great because the land was very full [of people], and this last one [1576]

TABLE 7.2. Sixteenth-Century Epidemics in Central Mexico

Year	Likely cause	Notes
1520–21	**Smallpox**	**Pandemic**
1531	Sarampión (measles)	"Little pox" in native sources
1532	Possibly smallpox	Only native sources report
1538	Smallpox	One source reports epidemic
1545–48	**Typhoid; typhus?**	**Pandemic**
1550	Mumps?	Paperas or swelling
1559–60	Influenza?	Central American sources
1563–64	Sarampión (measles)	Only two sources
1576–80	**Typhus?**	**Pandemic**
1587	Unknown	Triggered by famine
1595	Measles, typhus, mumps?	Sarampión, tabardillo, paperas

was not as great as the first two because although many people died, many escaped with the remedies that the Spaniards and the religious people provided."[52]

The mortality of 1545–48 might have claimed fewer victims in aggregate only because the population was already drastically thinned. Proportionately, however, it was remembered as the most lethal of the biological events of the sixteenth century. Motolinia thought that 60 to 90 percent of the population died in this pandemic. The reported death tolls suggest the scope of the mortality. The remarkable Franciscan friar Juan de Torquemada estimated the dead at 800,000 across New Spain; in Tlaxcala, 150,000 died; in Cholula, 100,000; in Tlatelolco, 10,000. Muñoz Camargo held that "it ruined and depopulated the greater part of all the people in the land." Spanish and native observers alike considered the mortality of the 1540s to be distinctly severe.[53]

What pathogen, or pathogens, caused the outbreak? There is no consensus, though nearly every possibility has been compassed at some point by modern scholarship. Plague, smallpox, measles, malaria, yellow fever, dengue fever, typhus, typhoid, leptospirosis, hantavirus, and, more generically, a viral hemorrhagic fever have been accused. Typhus—a louse-borne bacterium associated with poverty, crowding, and filth—has often been forwarded as a culprit. Indeed, typhus became an important disease in the sixteenth and seventeenth centuries.

But the witnesses to the 1545–48 pandemic do not call the infection *tabardillo*, typhus, nor do they describe the splotches of darkened skin that are characteristic of typhus. A range of Spanish and native voices affirm that the most notable sign of this pandemic was hemorrhaging, from the nose most often, but also the mouth, the eyes, and the anus. The chronicle of Fray Gerónimo de Mendieta is representative: "The third great and general pestilence . . . was a violent flowing of blood, and concurrently fevers, and there was so much blood that it burst through the noses."[54]

The pandemic of the 1540s shows the frustrating limits of retrospective diagnosis: secure identification of one of the true world-historical disease events remains elusively out of reach. But it also may be a prime example of how the new science of archaeological DNA holds the potential to break the logjam of old stalemates.

Teposcolula-Yucundaa is a site in Oaxaca, southern Mexico. There, mass graves dated precisely to the middle of the sixteenth century reflect a catastrophe. Traditional burial customs broke down; the central plaza of the recently flourishing town was used as a graveyard; the young and apparently healthy were struck dead. By 1552, the site was completely abandoned, and the survivors were resettled by order of the viceroy in the nearby valley. Skeletons from Teposcolula-Yucundaa were screened for microbial DNA using high-powered tools designed to identify an enormous array of pathogens. Unexpectedly, the screening yielded evidence that the victims of the pestilence succumbed to *Salmonella enterica paratyphi C*, a bacterium that causes paratyphoid fever. The inescapable conclusion is that the germ was introduced by the Spanish and that it had a role in the pandemic.[55]

There is corroborating documentary evidence that gastroenteric diseases took a toll in the New World. In the extensive *Relaciones geográficas*, detailed questionnaires about the conditions of the provinces of New Spain completed at the behest of King Philip II, bloody diarrhea is "the most prevalent illness" reported. Its prominence argues that the sanitary conditions of sixteenth-century Mexico were ripe for the spread of dangerous fecal-oral pathogens. Of course, Teposcolula-Yucundaa is only one site, and exploration in other regions will eventually confirm

or enrich the story. Because hemorrhaging is so prominent in the contemporary descriptions, and hemorrhaging is not a primary symptom
of typhoid (or paratyphoid) fever, perhaps the event of 1545–48 was
triggered by a concatenation of diseases, among which typhoid fever
was one. Thus, the genetic evidence both illuminates and complicates
the possibilities.[56]

The pandemic of the 1540s swept across the heartlands of central
Mexico and again pushed south. All across Central America, "populous
and famous towns" were "totally destroyed." One Spanish observer
thought "God sent down such sickness upon the Indians that three out
of every four of them perished." The consequences were dire for Spanish dreams of wealth and dominion. "Because of this, all is now lost in
Mexico, and here also." The contagion ran its course down the west
coast of South America. A "general pestilence" was described in the
Kingdom of Peru in 1546, likely an extension of the pandemic that
erupted in Mexico.[57]

A third pandemic exploded in 1576 and continued for four years.
There had been a drought in 1575–76. The crops withered, and famine
followed. The mortality ignited in August 1576; it diffused across nearly
all of Mexico and Central America and flickered on and off for the next
four years. A series of letters from the archbishop of Mexico traces the
progress of the disease. Within the first two months, he claimed, it had
killed one hundred thousand people in two central dioceses. A month
later, in December 1576, it had spread further. He observed that the disease struck the native Americans hardest of all, but that it had started to
afflict mestizos, Africans, and some Spaniards. In spring 1577, as the disease abated near the capital, it continued to creep outward, to the outer
reaches of Spanish control. Writing after the event, the archbishop declared that the pandemic had killed half the population.[58]

Juan Bautista de Pomar, a descendant of native nobility, wrote the
Relación geográfica for the region of Texcoco outside Mexico City in the
1580s. He saw a landscape that had been devastated by three massive
pandemics and numerous smaller ones. "It is well known that the general pestilence that took place during the years 1576 to 1580 carried away
two persons out of three . . . and that another that took place almost

forty years ago inflicted a similar massacre, not to mention the first smallpox epidemic that took place while the Spaniards were conquering Mexico City, and that all agree caused more damage than those which came later, leaving aside many other less grave pestilences."[59]

The pandemic of 1576–80 is exceptionally well documented. The wealth of chronicles from the later sixteenth century, as well as the *Relaciones geográficas* compiled for the king, create an embarrassment of riches. Nevertheless, the identification of the biological cause has remained contested. The clues are vague and contradictory. Mendieta, the Franciscan missionary, called the disease *tabardillo*, which ordinarily meant typhus; but no other source from Mexico identified typhus explicitly as the cause of the outbreak. The indigenous sources overwhelmingly report bleeding from the nose and mouth, the ears, eyes, vagina, and anus, as well as high fever and dysentery. They called the disease by a term meaning "blood came from our noses."[60]

The epidemic raged across Central America, too, and contemporaries believed the contagion had arrived from the north. "From Mexico has entered . . . a plague of smallpox and typhus, from which have died, and die daily still, a great number of Indians, especially young children." In Nicaragua, *romadizo*—possibly influenza—struck in 1578. The demographic shock was noted by administrators whose tax collections fell short and by priests who were dismayed by the suffering. The Spanish governors and clergy were equally startled by the desolation.[61]

The population crash of Mexico in the sixteenth century is one of the most extreme demographic events attested in history. In 1519, there were perhaps eight to ten million inhabitants of what is now Mexico. By the end of the century, there were two to three million. Demographically, Mexico remained a native country, ruled over by a small Spanish elite. But 60–80 percent of the population had perished. Further south, in Central America, the impact was also profound. We gain a sense of the scope of this loss from the dean of the cathedral in Santiago de Guatemala. In the course of the outbreaks that he had witnessed, "the country has been depopulated." The loss of life was simply bewildering. "What causes the Indians to die and to diminish in number are secret judgments of God beyond the reach of man."[62]

Other Epidemiological Spheres

Let us take a brief tour through some of the other major regions of the New World during the first phases of the Columbian Exchange, tracing what is known about the timing and nature of the major disease outbreaks.

The western coast of South America was dominated by the Inca Empire, with its highland capital of Cusco. It is possible that the smallpox pandemic reached the Incas before any Europeans had actually appeared. In 1528 the Inca ruler Huayna Capac died of an infectious disease, and four years later, at the Battle of Cajamarca, Francisco Pizarro captured the Inca ruler Atahualpa. He quickly established control over the lands formerly ruled by the Incas. The conquest turned out to be a windfall for the Spanish when rich veins of silver were discovered at Potosí in what is now Bolivia. But growing numbers of Europeans also soon brought new diseases.[63]

A major epidemic was witnessed by Spanish observers in 1546. The most important early chronicler of Peru, Pedro de Cieza de León, described a "general pestilence spread throughout all of the [viceroyalty of] Peru, beginning south of Cuzco and covering all of the land; countless people died." The disease caused a headache and high fever, and it ran an acute course. It is impossible to identify. Twelve years later, smallpox and measles appeared. Epidemics—mumps, typhus, and diphtheria—continued to appear throughout the sixteenth century, adding to the misery. The silver economy, dependent on brutal mining operations and forced labor, expanded in the latter half of the century, and infectious disease followed exploitation.[64]

A concatenation of disease events from 1585 to 1591 stands as probably the most deadly of the pandemics on the continent. Smallpox and measles erupted in 1585, spreading from Cuzco northwest to Lima and then up the coast, reaching Quito by 1587. Another wave of disease, possibly typhus, spread from the north; this wave is sometimes thought to have been introduced by the expedition of Sir Francis Drake, who took Cartagena in 1586. After a slight lull, pestilence raged again in spring 1589; smallpox and measles struck Quito and headed south. In Lima, "virulent pustules broke out on the entire body that deformed the miserable sick persons to the point that they could not be recognized except by name." Then, typhus and influenza followed. The mortality became general, spreading from the coasts into the highlands, and afflicting native Americans, Africans, and Europeans alike. The viceroy wrote to Philip II in May 1589 that "everyone is ill and those who are well are very busy curing them." The impact was severe. In one district, a native chief reported that only one thousand of thirty thousand souls remained alive. In another well-documented highland community, mortality in the year 1590 alone was more than 10 percent of the population. The cluster of outbreaks in 1585–1591 was undoubtedly the climax of a deadly century for the densely populated civilizations of the Andes.[65]

In the eastern half of South America, the settlement of Brazil by Europeans introduced new diseases. At the time of contact, European explorers and settlers were thoroughly impressed by the abundance of people down the Atlantic coast and inland across Amazonia. A 1542 expedition up the river—the first by Europeans—found "numerous and very large villages ... the farther we went the more thickly populated and better did we find the land." Another observer remarked that "there are so many of them [natives] and the land is so great and they are increasing so much that if they were not continuously at war and eating one another it could not contain them." The first Portuguese governor of Brazil remarked, ominously, that "they would never lack, even if we were to cut them up in slaughterhouses."[66]

Such reports were colored by the boosterism of early settlers and explorers, but archaeology has tended to confirm the density of precontact societies in Brazil. Shortly after European arrival, the familiar sequence of epidemic disease and indiscriminate violence indeed created a kind of slaughterhouse. From the 1550s onward, the historical record is full of dire reports of epidemic disease. Missionaries and slave raiders alike were vectors for imported pathogens. In 1552 a Jesuit watched some of the earliest converts succumb near Bahia. "Almost none of these has survived and did not die. ... Our Lord wished that these people's children, who were baptized in innocence, died in the same innocence." Fevers and fluxes erupted in the fledgling settlements of Bahia, Espírito

Santo, Rio de Janeiro, and São Paulo. In Rio, a "contagious malady ran everywhere so strangely that several of us [Europeans] died of it, and an infinite number of savages."[67]

In the name of saving their bodies from slave catchers and their souls from non-Christian beliefs, countless people across Brazil were resettled in missionary villages (*aldeias*) organized by the Jesuits. In fact, across the Americas, these sorts of resettlement efforts were epidemiologically disastrous for the health and hygiene of their residents, acting as virtual death camps: "herded together in the new *aldeias*, demoralised and bewildered, these people were terribly vulnerable." In the words of a sympathetic priest, "You can imagine how one's heart was torn with pity at seeing so many children orphaned, so many women widowed, and the disease and epidemic so rife among them that it seemed like a pestilence. They were terrified and almost stunned by what was happening to them. They no longer performed their songs and dances. Everything was grief. In our *aldeia* there was nothing to be heard but weeping and groaning by the dying."[68]

The death tolls astonished contemporaries. Tens of thousands of converts perished in the first decades. According to one missionary, of some sixty thousand baptized Americans in the 1560s and 1570s, only hundreds remained by the 1580s. "If one asks about so many people they will tell you that they died. ... The number of people who have died here in Bahia in the past twenty years seems unbelievable. No one ever imagined that so many people could ever be expended, far less in so short a time."[69]

The impact of colonization in Brazil is best attested along the coast, where the written record is more abundant. There are hints that the epidemics worked their way deep into the interior, but the mortality becomes impossible to trace in any reliable way. Smallpox was certainly present, at least by the 1560s, with its usual destructive force. A range of generic fevers, hemorrhaging, dysentery, and flu-like symptoms characterized many of the epidemics. We can only hypothesize that a roster of imported respiratory and fecal-oral pathogens fell upon the traumatized societies. Before contact, there were maybe 3.5 million native people in Brazil. Today, there are only a few hundred thousand. The latter half of the sixteenth century was the most concentrated period of destruction, and it was soon followed by the massive importation of slave labor from Africa, which introduced yellow fever and malaria to the continent.[70]

Across most of North America, violent epidemics arrived a few generations later. Contacts were too ephemeral, populations too dispersed, to sustain explosive pandemics in the century after 1492. In northern Mexico, the establishment of large-scale mines in the later sixteenth century gradually brought the indigenous populations into the microbial orbit of the Spanish conquerors. The main artery of overland trade and travel, the *Camino Real de Tierra Adentro*, was extended north from Mexico City until it reached Santa Fe, New Mexico, around 1600. It carried goods, people, and, inevitably, germs. The pandemic that struck across central Mexico in 1576 is the first that definitely reached the northern parts of the country.[71]

In a vicious cycle, slave raiding and silver mining were inseparable from the introduction of new diseases, whose ravages caused labor shortages that then motivated further slaving. After the pandemic of 1576, Spaniards in Durango petitioned the king for permission to import one thousand Americans to work the mines, and slave raids penetrated farther north than ever. Again, both missionaries and slave raiders were vectors of European diseases, and Jesuit documents make it possible for the first time to track the movement of germs into what is now northern Mexico and the southwestern United States. In the 1590s, measles and smallpox—and probably other diseases like mumps and diphtheria— spread through northwestern Mexico. One priest wrote that two-thirds of the children he had baptized perished in a single event; undoubtedly, the very missionaries who sought to care for the sick and bury the dead acted as conduits for the pathogenic microbes that so devastated the indigenous population.[72]

In the first decades of the seventeenth century, European diseases inexorably crept further to the northwest, into the borderlands of the present-day United States. From 1623 to 1625, a cluster of diseases, including (probably) smallpox and typhus, broke out in the string of Jesuit missions running from the heart of Mexico to Santa Fe. But the damage was not limited to the settlements. The mortality penetrated into the backcountry, bringing death to massive numbers of people.[73]

The Columbian Exchange gathered momentum even later across the eastern seaboard of North America. Florida was crisscrossed by Juan Ponce de León on an exploratory expedition in 1513, and others followed in the next decades. Saint Augustine, the first permanent settlement, was established in 1565. It is unlikely, however, that these transient and relatively small-scale contacts were enough to engulf Florida in the pandemic events that swept across Mexico in the sixteenth century. Large-scale epidemics had to await the arrival of settlers en masse, a phenomenon that only happened a few generations later. Tragic mortality struck the region in 1613–17. One priest lamented in 1617 that over the last four years, "There have died on account of the great plagues and contagious diseases that the Indians have suffered, half of them." But after that, major outbreaks are unattested for a generation. In 1649–50, a series of epidemics began, starting with yellow fever. In 1655 smallpox struck, followed shortly by measles. Spanish governors lamented the massive loss of life. Even in a territory that lacked mining and the *encomienda* system of forced labor, depopulation was severe.[74]

Along the mid-Atlantic coast, contact and settlement grew gradually for most of the seventeenth century. Early contacts could have sparked minor outbreaks of disease. Hernando de Soto, for instance, crossed what is now South Carolina sometime around 1540, a little more than a decade after the first colonization attempts on the coast. His expedition found "large vacant towns grown up in grass that appeared as if no people had lived in them for a long time. The Indians said that two years before, there had been a pest in the land, and that the inhabitants had moved away to other towns." Even so, these early contacts were limited, and it has been doubted that they were sufficient to spark large-scale epidemics sweeping across the region.[75]

A permanent English presence in Virginia started with the foundation of the Jamestown colony in 1607, but for decades, European settlement was still thin and precarious. In the later seventeenth century, though, the tobacco economy gathered pace. In an era of quickening settlement, sweeping pandemic events can be tracked in detail. The historian Paul Kelton has reconstructed what he calls "The Great Southeastern Smallpox Epidemic" of 1696–1700—a transformational mortality event that deserves greater notoriety in the annals of biological infamy. The importation of slaves from Africa expanded dramatically in the last years of the century, and trading networks carrying slaves and rum had formed, stretching deep into the continent. This combination—European colonization in earnest, the importation of African slaves, and a trading network penetrating the native-dominated interior—built a platform for the great mortality.[76]

As settlement intensified, so did the scale of events. Kelton speculates that the virus arrived on slave ships coming from Africa to Virginia in 1696. The epidemic spread southward into the Carolinas. European settlers were hit hard too. In spring 1698 reports were sent back to England, reporting, "We have had ye Small Pox amongst us Nine or ten month, which hath been very Infectious and mortall, we have lost by the Distemper 200 or 300 Persons." The governor noted a "great mortality" among the tribes as well. A woman named Affra Coming, a settler who arrived as an indentured servant and later became a plantation owner, wrote in distress to her sister: "The whole country is full of trouble and sicknes, 'Tis the Small pox which has been mortal to all sorts of the inhabitants and especially the Indians who tis said to have swept away a whole neighboring nation, all to 5 or 6 which ran away and left their dead unburied, lying upon the ground for the vultures to devour."[77]

John Lawson, an educated English explorer with an eye for medical observation, was mapping the Carolina backcountry in the years immediately after the epidemic, and his reports follow the cumulative effects of infectious disease on the region's major indigenous groups, such as the Sewees, the native inhabitants of the Carolina coast. "These Sewees have been formerly a large Nation, though now very much decreas'd since the English hath seated their Land, and all other Nations of Indians are observ'd to partake of the same Fate, where the Europeans come, the Indians being a People very apt to catch any Distemper they are afflicted withal; the Small-Pox has destroy'd many thousands of these Natives."[78]

The devastation stretched across the southeast into the Mississippi basin. The French explorer Pierre LeMoyne d'Iberville was reconnoitering the Gulf Coast in 1699, and it is evident that his expedition moved through a landscape recently thinned and sometimes abandoned, probably due to the smallpox epidemic. Tribes in the delta that had been "formerly quite numerous" were "destroyed two years ago by diseases." The river was a conduit for the virus to surge deep into the continental interior. At the confluence of the Arkansas River, one group of French missionaries "were sensibly afflicted to see this nation once so numerous entirely destroyed by war and sickness. It is not a month since they got over the smallpox which carried off the greatest part of them. There was nothing to be seen in the village but graves."[79]

According to Kelton, smallpox reached "all but the most secluded villages tucked in the Appalachian Mountains and in the dense forests of central Mississippi." The lesson of the Great Southeastern Smallpox Epidemic is that the biological and social dimensions of the Columbian Exchange are inseparable. Trade networks constituted the platform for the disease's rapid dispersal on a continental scale. Slaving and warfare had already taken a toll on native societies and rendered them susceptible to biological catastrophe. The smallpox mortality was a moment of tremendous consequence in native history, as survivors tended to coalesce into new tribal confederations, such as the Cherokees, Creeks, and Chickasaws, that would prove enduring. Worst of all for the native populations of the southeast and interior, the Great Southeastern Smallpox Epidemic was more of a beginning than an end; it might be said to have inaugurated a new epidemiological period in the history of the region as directly contagious pathogens brought by European settlers would arrive and reverberate for the next century.[80]

European germs also arrived in Canada and the northeastern United States in the early seventeenth century. Here, the exchange of pathogens started later than in Mesoamerica, but earlier than in the mid-Atlantic. The search for a northwest passage, and the lucrative fur trade, were attractants. Missionaries, traders, and settlers quickly altered the disease landscape in Canada. One important convert to Catholicism, a Mi'kmaq Indian named Membertou (?–1611), claimed that in his youth the natives of Nova Scotia had been "as thickly planted there as the hairs upon his head." But diseases of autumn and winter—like "pleurisy, quinsy and dysentery"—had diminished their numbers. These generic symptoms—chest pain, throat inflammation, and bloody stool—suggest that an array of respiratory and gastrointestinal diseases were passed to the indigenous inhabitants by outsiders. A Jesuit source of 1616 summarized the pattern of contact and infection on Nova Scotia: "[The natives] are astonished and often complain that, since the French mingle and carry on trade with them, they are dying fast and the population is thinning out. For they assert that, before this association and intercourse, all their countries were very populous and they tell how one by one the different coasts, according as they have begun to traffic with us, have been more reduced by disease."[81]

In New England, infectious diseases undermined the strength of native societies and facilitated the seizure of land by European settlers from very early on. The sources do credibly describe significant mortality in the first days of contact, even prior to mass settlement. A pestilence swept over the coastal regions of upper New England from 1616 to 1619, centered on Massachusetts Bay. The disease was introduced by shipwrecked French sailors or English scouts. The identity of the pathogen has been extensively, and inconclusively, debated; the written descriptions we possess are bereft of diagnostic medical details, the symptoms vague and contradictory: headache, jaundice, and sores that left scars, with a seasonal peak in winter and high mortality. Typhus, typhoid, plague, yellow fever, and leptospirosis have all found their vigorous champions, but smallpox remains the likeliest culprit.[82]

The contagion followed existing links between tribes. It spared southern New England, especially the interior. Captain John Smith had explored the coast of New England in 1614 and was impressed by the density of the population. Just half a decade later, the scene was considerably altered. Thomas Dermer, an eyewitness, described "some ancient plantations, not long since populous now utterly void; in other places a remnant remaines, but not free of sicknesse. Their disease the Plague [here, simply a pestilence], for wee might perceive the sores of some that escaped, who describe the spots of such as usually die." John Smith himself noted a site where "it is certaine that there was an exceeding great plague among them; for where I have seen two or three hundred, within three yeares after remained scarce thirty."[83]

The pestilence happened to strike on the eve of the arrival of a hundred or so Pilgrims in 1620. The carnage of the recent epidemic was plain to see as they scouted this new world. "They found . . . ye people not many, being dead and abundantly wasted in ye late great mortalitie which fell in all these parts aboute three years before ye coming of ye English, wherein thousands of them dyed, they not being able to burie one another; ther sculs and bones were found in many places lying still above ground where their houses and dwellings had been; a very sad spectacle to behould." The Pilgrims saw the hand of Providence at work in such affairs, giving birth to a disturbing pattern of thought that would endure for centuries. For Smith, "God hath provided this country for our Nation, destroying the natives by the plague."[84]

The geographic scope of the early epidemics was limited, not reaching far beyond the coastal hinterland. But as settlers arrived from the 1620s, they carried Old World diseases with them and the devastation reached farther inland, up river valleys and on native trading routes. In the early 1630s, smallpox made the Atlantic crossing with English passengers, and an outbreak followed. "This epidemic was so prevalent and so destructive that nearly every contemporary writer mentions it and all Northeastern Indian groups appear to have suffered from it." Careful archaeological work on both Iroquois and Huron people attests to population crashes from the 1630s.[85]

The advent of smallpox in the north was a watershed. Large-scale outbreaks recurred every decade or so. Smallpox epidemics in Boston were recorded in 1638, 1648–49, 1666, 1675 and 1677, 1689–90, and 1702–3, 1721, 1730, 1751, 1764, and 1774, in a notorious pandemic that coincided with the American Revolution. With this series of disease events, though, we glide easily from a history of encounter with New World peoples to the shared disease regime of the Atlantic. Over the course of the seventeenth century, smallpox became one of the great killers in England and much of continental Europe, too. The history of the disease in New England mirrors contemporary patterns in the Old World. The Columbian Exchange had created a loosely integrated global disease regime.[86]

The full brunt of European disease was felt even later in the interior and west of North America. Smallpox diffused across the Great Plains from the later eighteenth century. Elizabeth Fenn has traced the forgotten western loop of the smallpox epidemic of the 1770s and 1780s; the outbreak in the backdrop of the American Revolution was an almost continent-wide event that swept across the Plains. Smallpox epidemics continued to strike into the nineteenth century, and native voices underscore the deadliness of these events and their role in white expansion. In one Kiowa legend, Uncle Saynday, a trickster who protected the Kiowa people, was roaming the prairie when he saw "a dark spot" moving toward him from the east. As Saynday approached, he saw it was a man on a horse, his face "pitted with terrible scars." The stranger announced himself as "Smallpox." "I come from far away, across the Eastern Ocean. I am one with the white men—they are my people as the Kiowas are yours. Sometimes I travel ahead of them, and sometimes I lurk behind. . . . I bring death. My breath causes children to wither like young plants in spring snow. I bring destruction. No matter how beautiful a woman is, once she has looked at me she becomes as ugly as death." The Kiowas suffered repeated encounters with smallpox throughout the nineteenth century, and the horrifying disease winnowed their numbers.[87]

Along the Pacific Coast, the sharpest impacts were felt in the early nineteenth century. As we will see in chapter 11, the epidemics on the coasts of Oregon and California belong largely to Pacific history and the story of European seaborne expansion in the great ocean. Decades before the California gold rush, new diseases arrived in the lush valleys inhabited by a rich mosaic of native societies. In the 1830s malaria reached the swarms of mosquitos that awaited en masse in the moist lowlands. The mortality was "lurid." Then came smallpox— first from Russian Alaska in 1837, then again in 1844, 1854, and 1862. Where indigenous people had been crowded into missions, the slaughter was catastrophic. And then came the crush of desperate and gold-hungry settlers, willing to finish what has been called, with due consideration, a genocide. The California gold rush in many ways completes a circle that had started when Columbus eyed the gleam of the yellow metal in the jewelry of the Taíno natives some three and a half centuries before.[88]

From Metals to Crops

For the first century and a half of the Columbian Exchange, the most valuable export of the New World was precious metal. By the middle of the seventeenth century, 181 metric tons of gold, and 17,000 metric tons of silver, had been imported to Spain from its colonial possessions. Mining was the economic basis of overseas European colonialism in its fledgling stage. But that was destined to change. The fertile soil and warm climates of the New World had too much potential. The Portuguese, in Brazil, were pioneers. They already had experience with plantation agriculture from their possessions in the eastern Atlantic—the Azores, Madeira, and São Tomé and Príncipe. By the 1550s, they started to import the plantation model to the New World. At first, Indians were enslaved and forced to labor on sugar plantations in eastern Brazil. Plantation agriculture had a long future. The enslavement of indigenous Americans proved to be limited, though. The Spanish had come to oppose the enslavement of Americans on moral grounds, and when the crowns of Spain and Portugal were united in 1580, enslaving them became (legally) off-limits. But the experiment was already faltering. Smallpox epidemics in the 1560s had decimated the gangs of enslaved indigenous Americans. The Portuguese sought other sources of labor.[89]

From the very beginning of their New World venture, the Spanish had imported enslaved persons from Africa. Africans worked as craftsmen and domestic servants; they worked in the mines; occasionally they served as soldiers. But in the latter half of the century the slave trade grew explosively with the fatal alignment of conditions: soaring market demand for addictive crops, an abundance of fertile land, a scarcity of labor, and the crystallization of racist ideologies. By the start of the seventeenth century, there were on average ten thousand enslaved Africans arriving in the New World *each year*. The next phase of the Columbian Exchange was now launched in earnest.[90]

8

The Unification of the Tropics

The Two Mayflowers

In September 1620, the *Mayflower* set sail from southern England, bound for the colony of Virginia. Just over a hundred passengers voyaged into the stormy North Atlantic. By November they had made the crossing, but badly missed their destination, making landfall on what we now know as Cape Cod. Forced to winter, they drafted the Mayflower Compact, agreeing to "covenant and combine ourselves together into a civil Body Politick." Inadequately provisioned, half of the settlers did not survive the year. But the permanent colonization of what would become New England had begun. In American lore, these wayward, hardscrabble, constitution-making settlers were the germ of a new nation.[1]

Consider the voyage of another vessel bearing the name *Mayflower*, departing from England about a generation later, in 1647. Though not the same ship that carried the Pilgrims, this *Mayflower* came from the same merchant milieu, and it was in fact owned by a trader—Samuel Vassall—who helped to establish the Massachusetts Bay Colony. Vassall's *Mayflower* was also destined to cross the Atlantic, but only after venturing first to the coast of West Africa. Goods from Europe were traded for slaves; the *Mayflower* carried 352 of them, and a smaller vessel under its command held another 113. These involuntary migrants were destined for sale in Barbados, an English possession in the first, feverish throes of its transformation into a slave-based society dedicated to the production of sugar. Nearly one in seven of the captives aboard the *Mayflower* died during the middle passage; the survivors were condemned to serve in a brutal, burgeoning plantation economy.[2]

The two *Mayflowers* symbolize different models of colonization that characterized expansion into the New World from the seventeenth century on. One was based on settler colonialism, the other, exploitation of labor in its most naked form. These two extremes were really the polar ends of a spectrum that spanned from the sugar islands of the Caribbean to the plantation worlds of rice in the Low Country and tobacco in tidewater Virginia, to the land of mostly free farmers that lay north of Maryland. A century and a half or so into Britain's New World projects, there was no question where the most valuable possessions were, in terms of value to the mother country. The most exploitative overseas possessions were also the most prized, and "the jewel in the British imperial crown in the eighteenth-century plantation colonies was undoubtedly Jamaica."[3]

Why did the colonization of the New World by the British, as well as other European states, follow such different trajectories? The answer begins in the interplay of power and ecology around the entire Atlantic basin. In the early modern period, Europeans held a global advantage in seafaring and firearms—but not medicine. Europeans could conquer maritime distance and people, but not mosquitos and microbes. Consequently, Africa was refractory to colonization, even as it was vulnerable to exploitation via the slave trade. Following the demographic losses of the sixteenth century, land was abundant and labor scarce in the Americas. What ensued was a process of trans-Atlantic movements, in which the ecology of tropical crops and infectious diseases played a role in shaping human fortunes.[4]

To understand this process, and its consequences, we must learn to see the invisible passengers on board both of the ships called *Mayflower*. Every ship was its own microcosm of people, plants, and pests. The crowded ships were cluttered with casks and vessels full of fresh water for the long voyage. (By chance, we know from court records that Samuel

Vassall's *Mayflower* was notably well provisioned, such that no one "drank salt water or his own urine because of lack of drink.") These shipboard environments were suitable habitats for mosquitos, especially a commensal species of mosquito that has evolved to thrive in our midst, *Aedes aegypti*. *A. aegypti* is the vector for a variety of dangerous viral diseases—above all, yellow fever. Vassall's *Mayflower* arrived in the New World just in time for the first major yellow fever epidemic in the Caribbean, which started in Barbados in 1647. The outbreak lasted for more than five years and transformed the face of the imperial Caribbean.[5]

Yellow fever epitomizes the way that disease ecology and social development conspired in this period. The sixteenth century had been the age of precious metals and promiscuous microbes. In the early seventeenth century, the hunt for metals still lured adventurers and colonists. As William Robertson, a Scottish historian of America, put it, these were days when "precious metals were conceived to be the peculiar and only valuable productions of the New World, when every mountain was supposed to contain a treasure, and every rivulet searched for its golden sands." In the course of time, though, the value derived from extracting precious metals was overshadowed by the rise of the plantation economy. Tropical groceries became the greater source of wealth. Sugar, known as "white gold," was pivotal. New powers—the Dutch, French, and English—vied for supremacy on the seas. And new patterns of infectious disease, contoured by the territorial limits and ecological preferences of tropical germs, took hold. This transition was not hard and fast. Communicable diseases like smallpox and typhoid continued to play a major role. But over time, the geography of tropical diseases exerted a decisive influence on the shape of New World economies and the fate of trans-Atlantic empires.[6]

The focus of this chapter is on the translocation of people, plants, and pathogens from Africa to the New World. Up to 1820, the total number of Africans brought to the New World was 8.5 million; the number of European migrants was 2.5 million. African migration was involuntary, of course, but ultimately, there were far more ships like Vassall's *Mayflower*, crossing the Atlantic as seaborne prisons, than there were ships bearing the freight of freedom-seeking settlers.[7]

This chapter makes three broad and interrelated claims.

First, infectious diseases were an integral factor in the patterns of commerce, colonization, settlement, and slavery around the Atlantic. The disease ecology of West Africa and west-central Africa shaped the entire encounter between Europeans and Africans: the array of native pathogens in tropical Africa fenced out intruders and helped to ensure that European power was concentrated in trading forts along the coasts. Gradually, as pathogens from Africa also made the middle passage, the tropics were unified. In short, this is a trans-Atlantic story.

Second, in the Old World as in the New, the endemic disease regime was structured by geographic facts. The extension of the tropical disease regime across the Atlantic is the story of a group of spatially limited human diseases: malaria, yellow fever, yaws, and hookworm, plus a supporting cast of lesser pathogens. Broadly, a strong latitudinal gradient existed, by which proximity to the equator correlated with the weight of the disease burden. But disease environments could also be eccentrically local, too, affected by altitude, soil, and regional fauna; in addition, it would be a mistake to underestimate the importance of human alteration of the physical landscape—for instance, through deforestation or the installation of sugar and rice cultivation.

Third, disease ecology shaped mortality rates and population dynamics. Even though the tropics were a daunting health hazard, the lower latitudes received far more migrants than the temperate latitudes. Yet, as Benjamin Franklin had already realized in his tract of 1751, *Observations Concerning the Increase of Mankind, Peopling of Countries, etc.*, the fecundity of the northern colonies was astounding. The contrasts with the islands, where slavery loomed so large, were stark. The historian Trevor Burnard has imagined a striking counterfactual scenario. If the settlers in what became the United States and Canada had decreased as brutally as those Europeans who migrated to the colonies of the British West Indies, there would have been only 200,000 white settlers in the thirteen colonies (instead of some 1.7 million) in the age of revolution, with only 50,000 of them thinly strewn over all of the northern colonies. By contrast, if the British migrants to the islands had thrived like the colonists on the mainland, there would have been 3 million British in the Caribbean, instead of the fewer than 50,000 that lived there by 1780.

The entire balance of colonization would have been inconceivably different. In the long run, it was obviously not just numbers that mattered, but also the social model that went hand in hand with different regimes of disease, demography, and exploitation. Where settler colonialism prevailed, more democratic norms tended to follow. Where plantation slavery dominated, extractive hierarchy and pervasive racial exclusion became the norm. In sketching the patterns of infectious disease that took shape in the Atlantic world, this chapter calls attention to the complex interrelationships between agrarian systems, demographic dynamics, social structures, and microbial ecologies.[8]

The remaking of the Americas during these centuries is a sprawling story, one that involves a huge array of actors, institutions, and ideologies. The voyages traced by the two *Mayflowers* reflect some of the vastness of that story. This chapter is premised on the belief that we can understand the human experience of these trans-Atlantic exchanges more deeply by trying to trace some of the ways that infectious disease formed the backdrop of human action. This perspective can give us a deeper sense of just how radically and rapidly humans reshaped global ecologies in the age of Atlantic sail. In the Old World, the geography of tropical disease played out gradually, over millennia, while human societies adapted to their environments. In the New World, this history was foreshortened, and it was shaped by the overriding fact of stark inequities between societies. It was against the background of those conjunctures, social and microbial, that the Americas were remade in these fateful centuries.

Disease Ecology in West Africa

In February 1722, the infamous pirate Bartholomew Roberts was killed at sea by the Royal Navy. His crewmen were taken prisoner and tried. Fifty-two of the pirates were hanged at Cape Coast, the seaside fortress that was one of the central nodes of European mercantile power in Africa for centuries. Nineteen of the crew begged for clemency, offering to serve the Royal Africa Company of England instead of facing execution. Their plea was granted. But as the historian K. G. Davies has remarked, the reprieve of serving the Royal Africa Company was only "marginally less severe" than being hanged. Twelve of the men actually

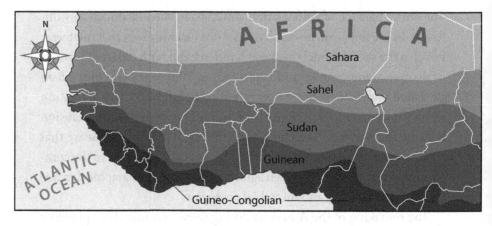

FIGURE 8.1. Ecological zones in West Africa and central Africa.

appear in records of the Royal Africa Company shortly thereafter. Seven of them died within two months of their sentence, like so many before and after them, from infectious disease. Such hasty deaths were nothing out of the ordinary for Europeans working the Africa trade.[9]

Equatorial Africa possesses one of the most complex physical ecologies on earth. The region can be imagined as a layer cake of ecological zones running east to west as the Sahara desert rapidly changes into rainforest (see figure 8.1). The sprawling Sahara receives virtually no precipitation and forms a forbidding but not impassable barrier stretching from the Atlantic to the Red Sea. To its immediate south, the harsh Sahel is a tropical steppe that is visited by the summer rains. It gives way to the tropical savanna of the Sudan, a lush carpet of grasslands sweeping across Africa. Then come the forests, nurtured by drenching seasonal rains. An important transitional zone where wet forest and grasslands intermingle—the Guinean forest-savanna mosaic—stretches from Senegal across West Africa, with a finger reaching down to the coast in the Dahomey Gap, breaking up the belt of wet forest along the Gulf of Guinea and the Congo. The true rainforests ringing the seaboard and penetrating deep into central Africa are the face of the continent to much of the Atlantic.[10]

West Africa was part of the world commercial system long before European ships arrived, and its largest states hugged the great Sahara desert. The coastal regions were the hinterlands. Built on the gold trade, states like the Mali Empire would have compared with many Eurasian powers. Fourteenth-century Arab traders and travelers were consistently impressed by the grandeur of the Malian rulers. "The king of this realm sits in his palace on a big dais . . . on a big seat made of ebony like a throne. . . . Over the dais, on all sides, are elephant tusks one beside the other. He has with him his arms, which are all of gold—sword, javelin, quiver, bow and arrows. He wears big trousers cut out of about twenty pieces which no one but he wears. About 30 slaves stand beside him, Turks and others who are bought for him in Egypt." The same source reports that the emperor could mobilize one hundred thousand troops, including ten thousand cavalry, relying on imported horses. By the sixteenth century, Mali had been eclipsed by the rival Songhay Empire, another Sahelian state fueled by the trade in gold, ivory, and salt. Cities like Gao and Timbuktu were cosmopolitan, boasting great mosques and enjoying the fruits of a caravan trade that linked Africa to Europe and Asia. These nodes of trade were already places of "global connections."[11]

In the fifteenth century, the Portuguese extended the reach of their exploratory voyages to the south, until Bartolomeu Dias rounded the Cape of Good Hope in 1488. Early expansion along the west coast of Africa was motivated by the demand for spices and gold and fired by dreams of bypassing the Ottoman behemoth that had come to loom over the eastern Mediterranean. In short, the Portuguese sought to outflank by sea what were well-worn trade routes running across the Sahara and the Mediterranean. By sailing around Africa, they opened a back door to an established network of merchants. For roughly two centuries—between the foundation of Elmina in 1482 and the chartering of the Company of Royal Adventurers Trading to Africa by the British crown in 1660—the gold trade continued to figure prominently in European ambitions in Africa. But little by little, slave trading came to dominate the economic interests of European merchants in West Africa.[12]

The impact of European contact on West African societies was not sudden, but it was ultimately profound. Coastal commerce turned the geography of Africa inside out, undermining the great empires of the

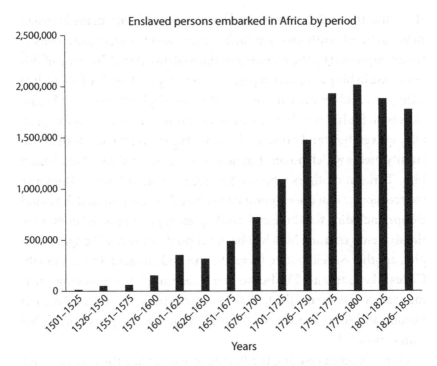

FIGURE 8.2. Growth of the slave trade from Africa to the Americas.
(Source: slavevoyages.org)

interior Sahel. The reorientation brought political fragmentation and violence in its wake. New powers arose, fueled by demand for European imports like cloth, alcohol, and, especially, iron. The mass importation of European firearms in the seventeenth century was destabilizing, and it coincided with soaring demand for slaves on New World plantations. By the middle of the seventeenth century, slaving had become the keystone of the political economy of coastal West Africa (see figure 8.2).[13]

The Arab observers of the late Middle Ages, who provided the first written records for the history of the region, had already commented upon the unhealthiness of sub-Saharan West Africa. The eleventh-century geographer al-Bakri claimed that Ghana (here referring to the medieval empire of Ghana, in modern Mauritania and Mali) was "unhealthy and not populous, and it is almost impossible to avoid falling ill there during the time their crops are ripening." He also noted that "the inhabitants have yellow complexions because they suffer from fever and splenitis." Centuries later, Ibn Khaldūn observed the effects of sleeping sickness on the Mali Empire; one ruler died of it in the late fourteenth century: "He was stricken by sleeping sickness, a disease which often afflicts the inhabitants of that region, particularly the aristocracy. The victim suffers from attacks of sleepiness at all times until he hardly wakes except for short intervals. The disease becomes chronic and the attacks are continuous until he dies."[14]

The environment that waited in coastal regions for the early Portuguese merchants and missionaries was equally unwelcoming. A group of missionaries sent to Benin in 1539 reported that the land "was very dangerous, full of illnesses, and not as profitable as had been hoped." Centuries later, Dr. James Lind (1716–94), a Scottish physician in the Royal Navy, summed up the Portuguese experience along the coast in his monumental *Essay on Diseases Incidental to Europeans in Hot Climates*: "They suffered more by sickness than by shipwrecks, though on an unknown coast, and even more than they did by their wars with the natives, and every other accident. In many places on the coast of Guinea where they were formerly settled, we can hardly trace any vestige of their posterity."[15]

Much of the early evidence for the European experience of the West African disease environment is anecdotal. In his *Essay* James Lind included the journal of a ship's surgeon on a voyage along the coast. When they reached Gambia, the English there were in good health. They sailed up the River Gambia about thirty miles into the interior and found a small outpost of Portuguese, including a governor, three friars, and fifty-one traders. "In the month of June, almost two-thirds of the white people were taken ill. Their sickness . . . approached nearest to what is called a nervous fever, as the pulse was always low. . . . It began sometimes with a vomiting, but oftener with a delirium. Its attack was commonly in the night, and the patients being then delirious, were apt to run into the open air. . . . Their skin often became yellow; bilious vomitings and stools were frequent symptoms. . . . Of 51 white men, being the companions of four ships . . . one-third died of the fever, and one-third more of the flux, and other diseases consequent upon it. . . . I believe,

TABLE 8.1. Royal Africa Company Personnel and Deaths
per Year

Period	Number of living	Number dead per year
1684–88	153	40
1689–93	152	35
1694–97	142	49
1703–7	157	34
1708–12	141	36
1717–21	125	38
1722–26	130	40
1728–32	127	35
Average	**141**	**38**

on the whole face of the earth, there is scarce to be found a more un-healthy country than this, during the rainy season."[16]

The archives of the Royal Africa Company from the later seventeenth and early eighteenth centuries reflect the mortality experience of European personnel working the Africa trade. The death rate for European arrivals in the early period has been reconstructed by Davies. Table 8.1 represents the total number of people in British service on the Gold Coast and the number who died per year.[17]

These records suggest an almost unfathomable crude death rate of 270 per 1,000. For comparison, modern societies have crude death rates below 10 per 1,000, and an ordinary premodern society might have a crude death rate of 30 per 1,000. Yet each year more than a quarter of the Europeans resident in Africa perished. Even the skeleton crews that manned European trading outposts required an annual influx to avoid surefire extinction. These levels of mortality prevailed into the nineteenth century; drawing from the richer military records of that period, Philip Curtin has reconstructed the levels of mortality faced by European troops. It is worth representing the crude death rate experienced by British and French troops in various foyers of the globe in the early nineteenth century (table 8.2).[18]

The disease ecology of sub-Saharan Africa was formative in the encounter with Europeans, right from the first Portuguese voyages of the fifteenth century. The European traders worked typically as middlemen

TABLE 8.2. All-Cause Mortality of European Troops 1817–38

Region	Country	Year	Crude death rate (deaths per one thousand)
Pacific	Tahiti	1845–49	10
	New Zealand	1846–55	9
Europe/North America	Great Britain	1830–36	15
	Northern United States	1829–38	15
Mediterranean	Algeria	1831–38	78
	Gibraltar	1818–36	21
South Asia	Bengal	1830–38	71
	Bombay	1830–38	37
Caribbean	Jamaica	1817–36	130
	Windward and Leeward Islands	1817–36	85
Sub-Saharan Africa	Senegal	1819–38	165
	Sierra Leone	1819–36	483

rather than conquerors or settlers; this was their modus operandi across most of the Old World tropics, including the Indian Ocean, until the eighteenth century. Huddled together and heavily armed, they congregated in trading fortresses like Elmina or Cape Castle. Even so, the mortality experience of Europeans in West Africa ranks as one of the most negative sustained arrangements in the annals of human demography; only a combination of ignorance, desperation, deceit, and avarice perpetually refreshed the supply of new recruits.[19]

No society can reproduce itself with a death rate such as the Europeans experienced in West Africa; of course, the experience of the Africans themselves was nowhere near so bleak. African societies had a range of cultural and genetic adaptations that protected them from the worst ravages of the disease environment. And yet, the disease burden did weigh heavily even on the societies of Africa. West and west-central Africa bear the heaviest burden of disease of any region of the globe, now as in the early modern period. The question is: Why was equatorial Africa so disproportionately burdened by infectious disease? And how might the disease environment itself have changed over the course of these centuries?

One basic dynamic at play is the fact that tropical societies were susceptible to both an array of burdensome infections that only persist in low-latitude climates *and* the increasingly dangerous pool of indiscriminate, human-to-human diseases, which must often have been introduced and reintroduced by merchants and slavers roving the coasts and river valleys of the continent. But many of these infections were not entirely novel. The cosmopolitanism of premodern West Africa, and its integration in the world system, meant that diseases like measles, smallpox, rubella, leprosy, the common cold, typhoid fever, shigellosis, and influenza were probably familiar diseases in sub-Saharan Africa even prior to European arrival. But with more frequent contact along the coast, their prevalence and intensity would only have increased.[20]

The pathogens that cause these diseases need only the human body as their environment; they can survive wherever there are humans. The tropics are also ecologically conducive to a set of major infections that require specific conditions in the external environment to be met. In some instances, as with most vector-borne diseases, the limitation to the tropics is strict; in others, the disease might exist in temperate or subtropical zones, but the equatorial climate materially intensifies the prevalence of the disease. Tropical diseases are caused by every major group of pathogens (viruses, bacteria, helminths, and protozoa). Moreover, tropical diseases are sustained by a variety of modes and media of transmission. Consider four: insects, skin, water, and soil (see table 8.3).

Among the vector-borne diseases of West Africa and west-central Africa, malaria looms largest. Here is its place of origin and the site of its most tenacious violence. The intensity of malaria in Africa is overwhelmingly due to the mosquitos that happen to inhabit the region. The world's most efficient vectors of malaria share overlapping ranges in equatorial Africa. *Anopheles coluzzi, Anopheles funestus, Anopheles arabiensis,* and *Anopheles gambiae sensu stricto* stalk human populations and impose a heavy burden of disease because they have evolved to prioritize exploiting humans (see figure 8.4). *A. funestus,* for instance, lives on the edges of swamps and bodies of water. It has a strong predilection for humans and, given its adaptation to the savanna landscapes, may be one of the oldest thieves of human blood. *A. gambiae sensu stricto* is even more versatile and more deadly, with its virtually exclusive taste for biting humans. The triad of people, mosquitos, and malaria parasites that

TABLE 8.3. Tropical Diseases and Routes of Transmission

Transmission route	Disease
Vector-borne	Falciparum malaria (protozoan)
	Sleeping sickness (protozoan)
	Yellow fever (virus)
	Dengue (virus)
	Chikungunya (virus)
	Lymphatic filariasis (helminth)
	River blindness (helminth)
	Loaisis (helminth)
Skin/contact	Yaws (bacterium)
	Buruli ulcer (bacterium)
	Impetigo (bacterium)
Water	Schistosomiasis (helminth)
	Guinea worm (helminth)
	Amoebic dysentery (protozoan)
Soil	Hookworm (helminth)
	Roundworm (helminth)
	Whipworm (helminth)

evolved in the hot, humid, and human-altered landscapes of Africa contributed enormously to the region's disease burden.[21]

Falciparum malaria is only one of the deadly sicknesses spread by insect intermediaries lurking in equatorial Africa. Sleeping sickness and its veterinary equivalent *nagana* we have met. They are transmitted by tsetse flies. There are more than twenty species of tsetse flies, which are about the size of houseflies but equipped with a long proboscis. Unlike most flies, the tsetse has the peculiar strategy of fertilizing only one egg at a time; the mother keeps the offspring inside her body through the first three larval stages and feeds it with stores of energy acquired from drinking vertebrate blood. The slow, loving parental style of the tsetse mother is thus funded by her parasitic habits. The tsetse lives only in Africa. Its lifestyle is adapted to the African climate and—in contrast to many major vectors—the tsetse has proven unable to invade other tropical regions.[22]

Tropical Africa also knows three major vector-borne diseases caused by worms: lymphatic filariasis, river blindness, and loiasis. The parasite that causes the disfiguring disease lymphatic filariasis is transmitted, like

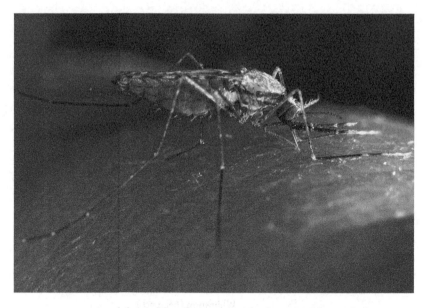

FIGURE 8.3. *Anopheles gambiae*, efficient vector of malaria. CDC/James Gathany: Public Health Image Library #18755.

malaria, by *Anopheles* mosquitos in Africa. A similar parasite, the worm *Onchocerca volvulus*, causes river blindness. Adult worms can reach up to twenty inches long, but it is the tiny larval form of the worm, living in the skin, that causes havoc, leaving disfigurement and blindness in its wake. Transmitted by the bite of *Simulium* flies, the disease is prevalent in the savanna and forest across western and central Africa. Twenty to thirty million people may be infected today, and it would have been part of the historic disease pool of Africa from the most ancient times. So, too, would have been the worm known as *Loa loa*, an incompletely understood but nonetheless widespread helminth infection in West Africa, transmitted by the bite of two kinds of deer flies.[23]

The Old World tropics suffer from a final group of vector-borne diseases caused by viruses. Yellow fever, dengue fever, and chikungunya fever are all transmitted by *Aedes* mosquitos. These mosquitos eventually invaded and colonized the New World, after voyaging as stowaways on the slave trade. These diseases have also been an important part of the endemic disease pool in Africa. As we will see, in the early modern

Atlantic, it was yellow fever—more than any other viral infection—that came to shape the disease environment.[24]

Equatorial Africa was also home to a collection of dangerous pathogens that thrived on human skin. In some cases, pathogens that cause one clinical course of disease in temperate latitudes manifest differently in the tropics. For instance, the bacterium S. *pyogenes*, cause of strep throat, is the principal agent of the widespread skin infection impetigo in the tropics. The disease known as Buruli ulcer, caused by a relative of the germs that cause tuberculosis and leprosy, is a dangerous but now rare skin disease whose means of transmission is obscure. Most of these microbes are bacteria—in effect, environmental organisms that happen to make a habitat of the human epidermis. One possible exception to the dominance of bacteria is the virus that causes hepatitis C, a disease that has dispersed globally thanks to the modern hypodermic needle. Its distant origins lie in Africa, where skin abrasions may have been an important route of infection, although its premodern epidemiology is poorly understood. Regardless, it seems to have dispersed globally in the age of the slave trade.[25]

The paradigmatic tropical skin disease is the affliction known as yaws. Yaws is caused by *Trepenoma pallidum*, a spiral-shaped bacterium that looks like the business end of a corkscrew. Closely related but distinct subspecies of the bacterium are responsible for the diseases syphilis, bejel, and pinta. Yaws and bejel are skin diseases of African origin. The subspecies of the germ that causes yaws, *Treponema pallidum pertenue*, has been found in nonhuman primates; although there is not clear evidence for ongoing transmission between humans and animals, yaws is in effect a disease we share with other primates.[26]

Yaws is highly contagious. It is spread by skin contact, often between children. The bacterium passes from the exudate of one infected person into small abrasions in the skin of the next host, often on the feet or legs. Like syphilis, the course of the disease is slow and proceeds in three stages. In the primary infection, a large lesion—known as the "mother yaw"—forms at the site of infection. It protrudes from the skin like a volcanic crater with a red ulcer at its base, but heals in a few months to form a pitted scar. Because the spiral-shaped bacterium can "swim" through tissue, the microbe disseminates, and weeks or years later, in the secondary phase, lesions or a plaque-like growth appear on other parts of the body. These scaly lesions look like raspberries, and the disease has thus been known as *framboesia tropica*. During this phase yaws attacks the bones and can cause painful swelling and malaise. A third phase of the disease can appear after years of quiescence. The resulting tissue death can be painful, disfiguring, and debilitating.[27]

The skin-dwelling bacterium that causes yaws is particular about its environmental conditions. It is sensitive both to temperature and humidity, and this human parasite is quite extraordinarily synced to the external environment. It prefers a mean annual temperature of 80°F, and annual rainfall of fifty inches. The bacterium is excited by the rainy season; it spreads preferentially in humid conditions. Europeans in the seventeenth century observed yaws and had a sense of its relationship with syphilis. The English physician Thomas Sydenham thought yaws and syphilis were the same disease: "the symptoms, the pain, and the ulcers are the same—making allowance for the difference of climate only." He also recognized the diffusion of the disease from Africa outward on slave ships. The globalization of yaws in the early modern period was a side effect of transoceanic shipping and the slave trade in particular. Today the incidence of yaws is limited to a few million cases. The bacterium is easily killed with antibiotics, and the disease is targeted for global elimination. But before massive public health campaigns by the World Health Organization in the 1950s there were fifty million cases; historically, yaws was pervasive in regions where the bacterium thrives. It is an underrated tropical disease, overshadowed by the career of its evil twin, syphilis.[28]

Tropical waters also harbored a number of parasites. The ancient disease schistosomiasis was a tropical affliction limited by the geographic distribution of its snail intermediary. Guinea worm infection (also known as dracunculiasis) was also a tropical disease that relied on watery environments. Now nearly eradicated, this disfiguring disease once afflicted millions in the Old World tropics and subtropics. The causative agent is a worm that can grow up to a yard in length inside the legs. The adult female causes blisters to form that erupt in water, discharging thousands of larvae that will be consumed by tiny freshwater crustaceans, which are then ingested in contaminated water by the human host. The larvae penetrate the human gut and then journey to the legs where they grow, mate, and spend the rest of their days. Guinea worm infection was a more serious burden in the past.[29]

Other waterborne diseases are not strictly confined to the tropics, and yet the warm and wet climate is especially amenable to their transmission. For instance, both bacillary and amoebic dysentery are today often grouped among the "tropical" diseases. But this classification reflects the confounding effects of physical geography and social development. Poverty and poor sanitation are important risk factors for such diseases, and since the tropics are relatively poor, the burden of these infections is strongly felt for social reasons. But physical geographic factors do play some role. High temperature and high humidity are conducive to the spread of these diseases, which have a strong seasonal pattern. The amoeba that causes dysentery matures more quickly and survives better at higher temperatures, for instance.[30]

Finally, the tropics are disproportionately burdened with soil-transmitted helminths. Roundworms, whipworms, and hookworms are parasites that infect human intestines, where they mate and produce eggs excreted in feces. The eggs and larvae thrive in warm, moist ground. Softer soils, often found in coastal plains or alluvial valleys, are especially hospitable to larvae. Of all soil-transmitted helminths, hookworms impose the largest burden of human disease. Humans have two species of hookworms, and their adaptation to the human host is extraordinary. The larvae invade the skin, but once inside human tissue, they must pass through a stage in the lungs, whence they will be coughed up, only to pass back down the throat and enter the intestines, where they mature and reproduce. In the intestines they rob the host's body of vital nutrients, especially iron. The whole body turns sallow, and humans suffering hookworm often experience the urge to eat clay, perhaps to replace iron. In sum, hookworm infection quietly wreaks havoc on human development, slowly stunting physiological and cognitive growth.[31]

Because of its environmental phase, the hookworm is sensitive to climatic conditions. Historically, its range extended well into the subtropics. Right up to the twentieth century, hookworm was a major infectious disease in the U.S. South, especially in lowland valleys and coasts. Its economic effects were profound, and areas that eliminated hookworm following deworming campaigns experienced large gains in educational attainment, human capital, and, ultimately, income, even controlling for other factors. It is a parasite that has weighed heavily on human health throughout the past.[32]

Finally, a note on leprosy, a respiratory disease that is concentrated in the tropics today. In part this pattern is due to the relative poverty of the lower latitudes. It may also have an environmental dimension by which transmission is facilitated in warm, humid climates, but it was historically much more widespread than its current distribution suggests. In medieval times, leprosy might have seemed more like a temperate-latitude disease than a tropical one, and it was prevalent in Europe until the sixteenth century. Although leprosy is old, it seems not to have been carried to the New World during the Pleistocene. It is certain that Old World strains were transported across the Atlantic in the age of sail, perhaps from Europe, and leprosy should be ranked among the diseases brought west during the Columbian Exchange.[33]

Geography is the substrate of disease history. But with the rise of an Atlantic economy, the part that the disease environment played in human history changed, transformed by the force of human technologies, human institutions, and human migrations, both voluntary and involuntary. With the rise of large-scale slavery and the plantation complex, the geography of health in the New World was transformed by the transfer of Old World tropical diseases to the Americas.[34]

The Transatlantic Scourge: Yellow Fever

In 1774, Edward Long published his monumental three-volume *History of Jamaica*. He was uniquely well positioned to serve as a chronicler for the wealthy English colony. Long's family had belonged to Jamaica's planter class from its inception. His great-grandfather Samuel served in the expedition that seized the island from the Spanish in 1655, and in each subsequent generation, the Longs held high office in the colonial government. Edward, born in 1734, moved easily back and forth across the Atlantic, having studied law in London before returning to the island, where he eventually served in the assembly. But in 1769 ill health forced him back to England. Ironically, this convalescent absentee planter spent the rest of his life decrying the absenteeism of white planters and championing the possibility of good health in the British West Indies.[35]

The unhealthiness of Jamaica was legendary. In the first five years of English occupation, 80 percent of the soldiers perished, mostly due to malaria and dysentery. The mortality regime of the Caribbean took a heavy toll on Europeans, who streamed to the islands nonetheless. By 1780, perhaps five hundred thousand Europeans had immigrated to the British West Indies in total. Yet the white population then stood at only a tenth that number. Even an apologist for Jamaica like Edward Long could not deny the island's notorious demographic regime, so he attributed the grim life prospects of the settlers to their own bad habits rather than the environment per se. The English in Jamaica, he claimed, were fatalistic and dissolute. Their "excessive indulgence in a promiscuous commerce on their first arrival" ensured that they were "very speedily infected" with venereal disease. Likewise the intemperate use of "ardent spirits" meant that the settlers were "in a perpetual conspiracy against their own health." "Ought the premature fate of such men, to be charged on climate?"[36]

African populations in the Caribbean also experienced a dismal demographic fate. The brutality of the plantation regime exacerbated the disease environment. Between the occupation of Jamaica by the British in 1655 and the end of the slave trade in 1807, some 800,000 enslaved people were sold to Jamaican planters. Yet, at the end of that period, there were only some 385,000 people of African descent on the island. The historian Richard Dunn has drawn a stark contrast between these Jamaican patterns and the demographic trajectory of slavery in Virginia. Over a similar period, 101,000 Africans were imported to Virginia, but the population quadrupled through natural increase, so that there were 380,000 enslaved people and 30,000 free people of African descent. That is, despite receiving less than an eighth the number of forced migrants from Africa, the population of African descent was larger in Virginia than Jamaica.[37]

Despite a perennial misinformation campaign by capital interests and imperial boosters, the health hazards of the "torrid zone" were no secret. So what lured settlers—and slave traders—to the tropics in such numbers? A big part of the answer is a tall tropical grass: sugarcane. Sugarcane has several qualities that make it one of the most transformational plants in human history. Its stalks are rich in sucrose, a sweet, energy-rich compound. Humans are primates evolved over millions of years to crave the sweetness and calories found in mother's milk and forest fruits. Our ancestors domesticated a grass whose fibers trigger a surge of dopamine in our primate brains. Sugar was not the first global commodity, but the mass commodification of sugar in the early modern period was quite unlike anything else in history. Simultaneously, the lure of profits to be made from sugar drew Europeans to the Caribbean, while craving for sugar did as much to spur modern consumerism and global trade as any other force.[38]

Sugarcane was an early domesticate, cultivated more than six thousand years ago in New Guinea. From there it was disseminated to China and India, where it hybridized with closely related wild species. The Indian version of sugar became known in the West during the classical period. The Romans knew of sugar as a medicine, and it was mostly as a medicine that sugar was known and traded through the later Middle Ages. Honey was the dominant sweetener, but it was slow and laborious to produce, and therefore scarce and dear. Though salts and spices had circulated from time immemorial, sweetness was not for sale. Life was bitter.[39]

In the later middle ages, the sugar trade started to expand. Sugar production spread into the Mediterranean. Driven by aristocratic demand, and with sugar increasingly consumed as a food rather than a drug, the sugar market was transformed in the period after the Black Death. From the fourteenth century, the Portuguese and then Spanish started to establish sugar plantations on their eastern Atlantic islands—Madeira, Porto Santo, the Canaries, and eventually São Tomé and Príncipe in the

Gulf of Guinea. Because sugarcane is intolerant of the cold, the climates were ideal. With experience in the eastern Atlantic, Europeans were interested in establishing sugar cultivation in the New World from the beginning. Fittingly, Christopher Columbus himself introduced sugar to the Americas, bringing seed cane to Hispaniola on his second voyage across the Atlantic.[40]

The Portuguese pioneered the production of sugar on a vast scale in the New World. Throughout the sixteenth century, Brazil was the dominant exporter to Europe. But over the seventeenth century, the Caribbean rose to supremacy, with the English in the vanguard. The occupation of Barbados, uninhabited when the English settled it in 1627, was a milestone. The ecological transformation of Barbados was revolutionary. Its dense tropical rainforests were felled, its land turned over to sugar planting. It stoked even bigger imperial dreams. The seizure of Jamaica in 1655, part of Cromwell's Western Design, furnished the English with what was destined to become in time their wealthiest colony.[41]

Sugar continued to reach an ever wider segment of European society. The mass market for sugar was stimulated by the expansion of the supply of cocoa, coffee, and tea, all drinks that mix well with sugar to form addictive concoctions. In the words of Thomas Dalby, governor of Jamaica in the 1690s and an ardent champion for the sugar economy, "Nor can it be imagin'd how many new ways are found dayly for Venting and Consuming usefully the products of a Sugar-Plantation." By 1700, sugar consumption in England was more than four pounds per person per year; a century later, it was twenty-four pounds per person and truly a staple, even for the poor. Sugar was not one consumer good among others. Compulsive demand for sugar brought into existence a worldwide system of production and consumption that penetrated the daily lives of ordinary men and women.[42]

Sugar, slavery, and infectious disease tended to reinforce one another. The requirements of sugar production lent themselves to gang-style slave labor. Sugar is most suitable for monoculture. Its cultivation is demanding and precise. Processing sugar was labor and capital intensive, and the plantation system that was refined over the course of the seventeenth century was a quasi-industrial operation, a hybrid of the farm and the factory. Indeed, before factories, sugar plantations were test beds for the discipline of labor, where the returns to capital could be isolated, figured, and maximized. Although the harvest was uniquely intense, sugar production lacked the seasonal lulls that left space for life and leisure in most agrarian calendars. Sugar thus offered high returns to brutality. The system of large-scale plantations took shape over the course of two or three generations in the seventeenth century, as the African slave trade ramped up and planters developed a system of violent labor management. Small producers and unfree white laborers continued to be important for decades. But the growth of the slave trade was accelerated by, and also helped to trigger, waves of death in the 1640s and 1690s that were pivotal in the expansion and crystallization of the plantation system in the West Indies.[43]

The cultivation of sugar demands ecological transformation, and New World environments were ravaged with startling speed. Forests were devoured to fuel the boilers where cane juice was refined. Native flora and fauna were wasted to create cane fields. Soils were turned over and depleted; erosion deposited silt in new-formed marshes. Weeds and invasive species, especially from Africa, filled the gaps. Rats, as ever, thrived in the interstices of the new anthropogenic environment. Native birds were decimated. Even the marine fauna were irreparably altered. This ecological havoc created a deadly environment for humans.[44]

The greatest collateral beneficiary of the special ecology of sugar might have been *Aedes aegypti* (see figure 8.5). This mosquito has been called the "most dangerous animal in the world." It is the vector of dengue, chikungunya, Zika, and, most importantly, yellow fever. *A. aegypti* is a handsome bug, jet black with silver stripes along the back of its abdomen. The females are stealthy but jittery biters, preferring to feed on human calves and ankles in the daylight hours before dusk. It is a particularly successful invasive species, following wherever its precocious primate host has taken it, so long as the climate is suitable. *A. aegypti* is a warm-weather insect, thriving when the average temperature is about 70–90° F. In the tropics, *A. aegypti* flourishes year-round. In temperate latitudes it is a summer mosquito, and in cooler climates it might be transiently introduced by ships.[45]

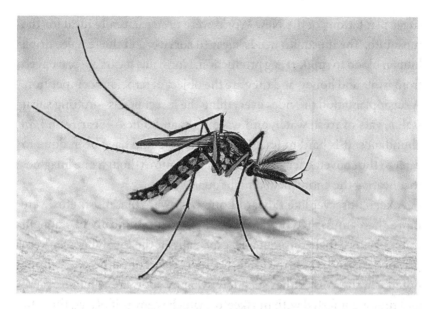

FIGURE 8.4. *Aedes aegypti*, vector of yellow fever. Shutterstock.

This bug is a curse on human expansion. It not only has a strong predilection for our blood, but it is a true commensal, fully adapted to human habitats for its breeding sites. In that sense *A. aegypti* is like the black rat or the housefly, an organism whose evolution has been driven by our tendency to redesign landscapes for our benefit. There are dozens of species of *Aedes* mosquitos on earth. Genetic evidence has helped to clarify the evolutionary history of the lineage that has hitched its wagon to the human star. Less than a thousand years ago, the ancestor of *A. aegypti* was just another mosquito, breeding in the forests of equatorial Africa, laying eggs in tree holes, drinking warm blood where it could be found. Then, around five hundred years ago, one lineage developed a partiality for human blood, and also learned to deposit eggs in the containers where humans stored water for the dry season, which provided year-round habitats. All populations of *A. aegypti* outside of Africa belong to a single, narrow lineage that evolved recently and dispersed globally starting around five hundred years ago.[46]

The sugar industry supercharged the proliferation of *A. aegypti*. Not only did the slave trade accelerate in the seventeenth century, but the sugar plantations of the New World were preternaturally ideal for the mosquito. The mosquito needs sugar to survive, and the females drink human blood to support egg production. Normally, sugars are scavenged from fruits and honey, and they are the object of ferocious competition. A sugar plantation provides everything the insect needs—rotting sugar stalks, vats of fresh water, and warm human bodies—year-round, in abundance. It is hard to imagine what more could have been done to cater to the convenience of this insidious creature (though one imagines that heating the entire planet might qualify).[47]

A keen observer like Edward Long was aware that mosquitos were more than a nuisance on Jamaica. They bred prolifically in stagnant waters, with lethal consequence, especially in the low-lying southern part of the island where the English settlers were concentrated. As Long noted, "In the West Indies such low swampy spots are still more fatal; and they are infested with muskeetos, which seem as if placed there by the hand of Providence, to assault with their stings, and drive away, every human being, who may ignorantly venture to fix his abode among them. It is most dangerous to pass the night in such places, and it is at such time that these insects collect in swarms, and make war on every daring intruder." More than a century before the mosquito was identified as the vector of deadly parasites, the relationship between mosquito prevalence and human sickness was stupendously apparent. It was a universal fact that the insects were "most numerous in the least healthful parts."[48]

The most consequential part played by *A. aegypti* was to act as the vector of yellow fever. In the words of John McNeill, "yellow fever was the most feared disease among whites in the Greater Caribbean" for two and a half centuries. Yellow fever, known also as yellow jack, yellow plague, bronze john, *vómito negro* in Spanish, bleeding fever, and, for a time, Barbados distemper, is a disease caused by an RNA virus of the genus *Flavivirus* (which simply means yellow virus). This genus includes a number of important pathogens, including several others that can infect humans, such as West Nile virus and dengue fever virus.[49]

The epidemiology of yellow fever is complex. During outbreaks, yellow fever is transmitted between humans when an *A. aegypti* mosquito takes a blood meal from an infected host and subsequently bites a susceptible host. These epidemic flare-ups are usually called the "urban cycle" of the disease. In the background, the yellow fever virus circulates among nonhuman primates, spread from host to host by a broader range of mosquito vectors. This background is known as the "sylvatic" or "jungle" cycle. Notably, many Old World monkeys can experience infection without serious harm, whereas New World monkeys suffer disease. The urban cycle is triggered when a susceptible human is caught up in the sylvatic cycle and introduces the pathogen to populations of human hosts and their domestic mosquitos. But even the wild primate hosts of the virus are not dependable reservoirs, and the secret to the success of the virus seems to be its adaptation to mosquitos. The virus can survive in the eggs of the mosquito and pass from one insect generation to the next. Yellow fever, in a sense, is a parasite of mosquitos, but it is amplified by secondary primate hosts, including, occasionally, humans. From its perspective, we are a successful side business.[50]

Like many febrile illnesses in the past, yellow fever could be confused with other infections. Yet its symptoms and course of disease were distinctive, and in the 1740s the name yellow fever came into use. Henry Warren, a doctor in Barbados, dedicated a tract to this "malignant fever" and offered a detailed clinical account of yellow fever infection. It began with "a sudden Faintness, and frequently a Giddiness too, then a Chilliness and Horror, which are immediately succeeded by an Ardent Fever, with sever darting Pains in the Head and Small of the Back." Red eyes, colored urine, a quick pulse, and dry skin followed. "Difficulty of Respiration, Sickness of the Stomach, with Reachings to vomit. . . . Soon after, all these Symptoms are aggravated with almost perpetual" retching and vomiting and extreme discomfort.[51]

The chills, fever, pain, malaise, and vomiting could be confused with symptoms of any number of diseases. But that was only the first stage, lasting a few days. Some patients recovered at that point. Others were admitted a brief respite, only to fall into a second or "toxic" phase. This phase of the disease brought on what Warren called "the universal *Yellowness* all over the surface of the Body." Jaundice was accompanied by severe pain, especially in the head, back, and limbs. Then followed the other characteristic symptom of the disease: hemorrhaging, manifest particularly in black vomit (often compared to coffee grinds in later times). This black vomit, simply blood curdled by the stomach's acid, is a highly diagnostic sign of the infection. Patients who reached this stage usually succumbed to the disease. The drama and violence of the infection fed fears of yellow fever throughout the early modern world.[52]

Although yellow fever virus has not been recovered archaeologically (and probably never will be, given that it is a small, fragile RNA virus and unlikely to be preserved for long in the external environment), modern genomes of the virus have been revelatory for untangling the evolutionary history of this species. Yellow fever as we know it is not a pathogen that has existed for an especially long time. According to the latest thinking, all circulating yellow fever virus descends from a common ancestor that lived only about one thousand years ago, probably in central Africa. The lineages split into branches that have a high degree of geographic stability (see figure 8.3). One branch is ancestral to genotypes now found in East Africa and east/central Africa, whereas another branch is ancestral to West Africa and west/central African lineages. One genotype, the west/central genotype, is focused in the region roughly corresponding to modern Nigeria, whereas another, the West African genotype, is established in West Africa, from Senegal to Ghana.[53]

The genetic evidence settles an old debate about the African or American origins of yellow fever. The greatest genetic diversity, and oldest lineages, both exist in Africa, securing it as the ancestral homeland of the virus. Moreover, molecular clock estimates suggest that the American lineages diverged from the African populations of the virus around three hundred to four hundred years ago. The genetic patterns reinforce what was already suggested by the historical record. Yellow fever was uninvited cargo aboard the slave trade, introduced across the Atlantic by ships supplying involuntary labor to the sugar plantations of the New World.[54]

The earliest history of yellow fever in the documentary record is murky. Any number of epidemics in the sixteenth century Atlantic world could have plausibly been yellow fever, and some historians have thought the pathogen made its appearance in the early days of European expansion. But the evidence is thin. There are no incontestable

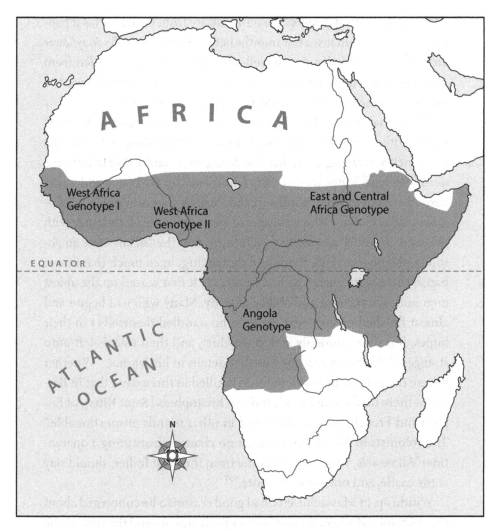

FIGURE 8.5. Geographic distribution of yellow fever virus types in Africa.
(Source: Barrett and Higgs 2007)

descriptions of the disease before the work of the Portuguese doctor
Aleixo de Abreu, who served in both Angola and Brazil. He seems to
have survived yellow fever as well as treated it, and in 1623, long since
returned to Lisbon, he authored a medical text that unmistakably ob-
serves the course of a yellow fever infection. Yellow fever lurked in the
early seventeenth-century Atlantic. And then, in 1647, it exploded.[55]

The earliest attestations of the outbreak are from Barbados (as it happens, they are dated just a few months before Samuel Vassall's *Mayflower* arrived). At least half a dozen well-attested slave voyages sailed from Africa and arrived in Barbados that year. Any of them might own the dubious distinction of having introduced the pathogen.[56]

The initial outbreak in Barbados in 1647 was explosive. Richard Ligon, author of *A True and Exact History of Barbadoes*, arrived as the pestilence was raging, such that "the living were hardly able to bury the dead." Richard Vines was an early landowner on Barbados and also a correspondent of John Winthrop, the Puritan governor of the Massachusetts Bay Colony, who was eager to foster commercial exchange with the West Indies. Vines wrote to Winthrop that the "sicknes was an absolute plague; very infectious and destroying, in so much that in our parish there were buried 20 in a weeke. . . . It first seased on the ablest men both for account and ability of body. Many who had begun and almost finished greate sugar works, who dandled themselves in their hopes, but were suddenly laid in the dust, and their estates left unto strangers." Winthrop recorded further details in his *Journal*: "Whether it were the plague, or pestilent fever, it killed in three days, that in Barbados there died six thousand, and in Christophers [Saint Kitts], of English and French, near as many, and in other islands proportionable." The colonists in Massachusetts took no chances, instituting a quarantine: "All vessels, which should come from the West Indies, should stay at the castle, and not come on shore."[57]

Winthrop, in Massachusetts, had good reason to be concerned about the epidemic. His son, Samuel, was in Barbados around the time of the outbreak; later in 1647 he was in Saint Kitts, where he barely escaped with his life. The young Winthrop, in his own words, "fell sicke of the same desease, which was so extreme then in the iland that scarce a young man scaped it. If they rubed out 3 dayes, for the most part they recovered. Myne continued ten days in such extremity that every one despaired of my health not only, but expected when I should depart to another world; but it pleased God to bless extreame bleading and command it to be a remedy to so vehement a feavor." From Saint Kitts the disease was carried to Guadeloupe aboard a vessel named *Le Boeuf*. It caused a violent pain in the head, debilitation in all the limbs, and continual vomiting that sent men to their graves in three days. Such a mortality had been "until then unknown in these islands since they were inhabited by the French."[58]

The epidemic reached the Yucatán Peninsula by summer 1648. There is a remarkable eyewitness description from a Franciscan historian, Diego López de Cogolludo, who had a sharp eye for epidemiological detail. The disease first appeared at Campeche, a port on the western coast. The victims suffered "a very severe and intense pain in the head and of all of the bones of the body, so violent that it appeared to dislocate them or to squeeze them as in a press. In a little while after the pain a most vehement fever . . . followed some vomitings as of putrefied blood and of these very few remained alive." The speed of the outbreak was overwhelming. "With such quickness and violence it came on great and little, rich and poor, that in less than eight days almost the whole city was sick at one time and many of the citizens of highest name and authority in it died." Cogolludo noted that the disease seemed to move along the coast by leaps, reaching Merida. According to Cogolludo, the disease hit the Spanish in the cities first, and only subsequently broke out in the indigenous villages. He reckoned it the greatest misfortune in the region in the entire Spanish colonial era.[59]

After ricocheting around the Greater Caribbean for a few years, the disease was mostly quiescent in the New World for decades (see table 8.4). It seems not to have established a permanent foothold during this first paroxysm of sickness. Yet the first outbreak was a premonition of what was to come. Yellow fever was a disease with explosive epidemic potential, striking the coasts and cities especially hard, following the movement of ships throughout the interconnected Atlantic world. It preyed without remorse on newcomers, taking advantage of periods of warfare that introduced susceptible European troops en masse.[60]

The preconditions for a yellow fever pandemic aligned perfectly in the 1690s, which marks the most violent episode in the history of the disease and inaugurated a new era of yellow fever in the Americas. The virus may have disembarked first in Brazil, where it is attested in the late 1680s. The Portuguese physician João Ferreira da Rosa wrote the first medical treatise dedicated to the disease, noting the extreme pain in the head, jaundice, and vomiting, all of which point to yellow fever. Brazil

TABLE 8.4. Yellow Fever Outbreaks in the Caribbean in the
Seventeenth Century

Outbreak year	Location
1647	Barbados
1648	Guadeloupe
1649	Cuba
1652	Saint Kitts
1655	Jamaica
1656	Santo Domingo
1665	Saint Lucia
1671	Jamaica
1673	San Juan
1688	Martinique
1689	San Juan
1690	Barbados, Santo Domingo
1692	Barbados
1693	Martinique
1694	Barbados
1695	Saint Domingue, Santiago de Cuba
1696	Martinique
1698	San Juan
1699	Widespread

Source: Kiple and Higgins 1992, 242.

or Africa could have been the launching pad for the career of the disease
over the next decade, what John McNeill has called the "deadly 1690s."
The disease made its debut in Jamaica in 1694. It is attested virtually everywhere there is documentation in the Caribbean. Notably, the disease
was introduced to the Atlantic seaboard of North America in this widespread outbreak, striking Charleston, Philadelphia, and Boston, where
Cotton Mather witnessed a "most pestilential Feaver" brought by a fleet
from the West Indies. "It was a Distemper, which in less than a Week's
time usually carried off my Neighbours, with very direful Symptoms, of
turning Yellow, vomiting and bleeding every way and so Dying."[61]

The deadly 1690s are part of the background for one of the most desperate failures in the history of European expansion and also an illustration of the broader dynamics of colonization and settlement: the Darien
disaster. At the time, Scotland was a poor country that had been left on
the outside looking in during the period of European mercantile growth.

Repeated harvest failures in the 1690s brought suffering and starvation. The country put its hopes on a grandiose scheme to colonize Panama and, two centuries before the canal was cut across the isthmus, control an overland connection between Atlantic and Pacific trade. Shut out of credit markets, the country had to scrounge for capital from within, and as much as one-sixth of the country's wealth was invested in the scheme. In 1698, 1,200 would-be colonists sailed for Panama, dreaming of "free" land to be grabbed from the indigenous inhabitants.[62]

The project was a debacle, and its failure was overdetermined. It failed in part because the English undermined the venture at every step. Yet many settlement attempts in the New World had persevered against long odds. The Scots had the monumentally bad fortune to launch an already perilous venture at one of the most inopportune moments. They were cut down by dysentery and malaria, and, in less than a year, the first attempt at settlement was abandoned. Fewer than three hundred survivors straggled back to Scotland. Unfortunately, a second convoy carrying another 1,300 passengers departed in 1699, unaware of the calamity unfolding across the sea. Hoping to find a colony, they arrived to "nothing but a vast howling Wilderness." The new settlers tried again, but epidemic fevers, exacerbated by the predictable Spanish assault, did them in. "Sickness and Mortality . . . was now become epidemic and raging." With the "contagious sickness raging so among us from within," they surrendered. The colony was abandoned. Ill-fated to the end, 112 of the survivors drowned in a storm off Carolina en route home. In all, about 2,000 of the 2,500 would-be tropical settlers died in the course of the venture.[63]

The Darien episode is only exceptional in its total failure. In fact it underscores how the disease environment could shape the outcome of European colonization efforts. The most dangerous climates were also the most profitable, and despite their risks they continued to draw the most migrants. Even as the health conditions in the New World worsened in the late seventeenth and early eighteenth centuries, European migrants continued to pour into the Caribbean, lured by the promise of opportunity in what was, per capita, the wealthiest region of the world. White settlers and enslaved Africans alike suffered from an increasingly severe mortality regime. Ships full of hopeful settlers continued to stream across the Atlantic, while the slave trade continued to ramp up.[64]

It became a widespread belief among people from Europe that they were more susceptible to infectious diseases like yellow fever than people from Africa. Doctors like Henry Warren were puzzled that slaves who had inferior diets and who were otherwise subjected to the brutality of the plantation system "are so little subject to this Danger." Were Africans indeed immune to yellow fever? It has been a controversial question among modern scholars. Like consideration of susceptibility to European diseases among indigenous Americans, the question of African immunity to Old World diseases should be based on careful evaluation of the evidence we have in light of our understanding of the population genetics of the immune system. In contrast to the case of genetic resistance to malaria, where the precise genes, their exact function, and their relative frequency in populations are all understood, the claims for immunity to yellow fever remain highly abstract. Still, modern investigators have argued the case for immunity to yellow fever drawing from data on a range of nineteenth-century outbreaks, such as an 1878 epidemic in New Orleans, which seem to show higher mortality rates among Europeans. The question is, why?[65]

There are several distinct possibilities, and many of them do not require genetic differences in immunity. If it is true that yellow fever affected Europeans more severely than Africans in the Greater Caribbean, then African populations in the New World could have had less exposure during the outbreaks. Yellow fever was a scourge in coastal cities, where whites disproportionately lived, so there could have been a differential impact due to the spatial distribution of populations. Edward Long thought that the English had been particularly injudicious in their occupation of the Jamaican landscape. "The English, for the convenience chiefly of their trade, and sometimes through ignorance, have generally fixed on the most unwholesome spots, for the situation of their towns in the West Indies."[66]

It is also important to distinguish between acquired and innate immunity. Acquired immunity is conferred on survivors of a disease like yellow fever. The mortality rate of new arrivals from temperate latitudes was notoriously bleak, because they lacked any previous exposure to a whole array of tropical pathogens. If people in the New World had been exposed to yellow fever in childhood, whether in West Africa or the Americas, it conferred resistance to subsequent reinfection. Worth mentioning too is the fact that infection by other flaviviruses, notably dengue fever, confers some cross-immunity, and it may have done so in the early modern period. By contrast, genetic immunity can evolve in populations that are exposed to selection pressures, like a disease, over longer periods of time. The growing evidence that yellow fever is not an ancient disease diminishes this possibility. On balance, the case for different biological susceptibility to yellow fever remains far from proven.[67]

African cultural practices could also have mitigated the risk of disease exposure. Even the prejudices of Edward Long, a thoroughgoing racist, did not blind him to the customs of the enslaved population on Jamaica. He noted in particular that the keeping of an indoor fire at night repelled mosquitos and relieved the burden of disease. These customs "may conduce as much as any thing to their enjoying health in such marshy soils, when white persons are affected by the malignant effluvia, and contract sickness; few of their huts have any other floor than the bare earth, which might possibly transmit noxious exhalations in the night, if they did not keep up a constant fire in the center of their principal room or hall; the smoak of which, though intended to disperse the muskeetos, has another good effect, the correcting the night air, and disarming it of its damp and chill, which might be prejudicial to their healths." In short, cultural adaptations, spatial distributions, and acquired immunity—rather than genetic adaptations—may be able to explain the patterns of yellow fever mortality in the New World, though the question remains open.[68]

From the 1690s onward, yellow fever was a continuous presence in the New World. It gripped port cities in the tropics and struck wherever sugar was cultivated or refined. The demography of the Caribbean was profoundly shaped by its presence. In the United States, it eventually became a perennial resident in New Orleans—but only in New Orleans, where the warm, humid climate and dense urban population allowed it to establish a base. Elsewhere it was a sporadic visitor, capable of striking with terrific force deep into the interior of the Mississippi valley and up the Atlantic seaboard. Even where it was not a major demographic factor, it haunted the dreams of settlers in the New World deep into the nineteenth century.[69]

Malaria in the New World

When the famous *Mayflower* anchored at Plymouth in 1620, the colonizing project that was launched got off to an inauspicious beginning. "It pleased God to visit us then with death daily, and with so general a disease that the living were scarce able to bury the dead and the well not in any measure sufficient to tend the sick." Over half the company died within months. And yet, the survivors endured. The death rate of that first winter proved unrepresentative, and little by little, mortality fell and then stabilized. More ships arrived. Settlers quickly came to sing the praises of the salubrious climate: "The temper of the aire of *New-England* is one speciall thing that commends this place. Experience doth manifest that there is hardly a more healthfull place to be found in the world that agreeth better with our English bodyes." A burst of immigration in the 1620s and 1630s followed, seeding one of the most demographically expansive settler societies in history.[70]

The migrants who settled colonial New England in the early seventeenth century came predominantly from the east and south of England. Clouds of economic malaise and religious discontent hung over this corner of the country. So, too, did malaria. Although we might not imagine England as a hotbed of malaria, in fact the marshes and fens of Kent, Essex, and Sussex were notorious for their "agues." The prevalence of the mosquito vector *Anopheles atroparvus* in the soggy English lowlands created an extension of the vivax malaria zone. The first settlers—at Jamestown, at Plymouth—carried *Plasmodium vivax* across the Atlantic in their blood.[71]

The story of malaria in the New World is a massive one, with a cast that includes mosquitos, pathogens, crops, and migrants both voluntary and involuntary. It is a story about the interplay of fixed features—the stark realities of geography and climate—and dynamic social responses, usually driven by humans with only incomplete understanding of the forces at work. Yet the patterns of malaria in the Americas were a great subsurface force shaping the destiny of colonial societies. In the *longue durée*, malarial fevers persistently, pervasively shaped the course of social development in the New World.[72]

Let us take the protagonists in this order: mosquitos, malaria parasites, crops, and human hosts, focusing on the colonies that became the United States as a detailed case study. The genus *Anopheles* we have already met many times in the Old World. Of the seventy or so species that can transmit one or more of the malaria parasites, only a few dozen are especially efficient vectors. In fact, a handful of *Anopheles* mosquitos account for the preponderance of the human suffering caused by malaria, both now and in the past. Among these is an American mosquito with four blotchy marks on its wings, *A. quadrimaculatus* ("four spot").[73]

The ecological contrasts with the yellow fever vector are revealing. *Aedes aegypti* had to migrate across the Atlantic Ocean before the disease could follow. *A. aegypti* has evolved a strong preference for human blood, and it has adapted to lay eggs in human-created environments like water casks. Hence, by the age of sail, *A. aegypti* was able to survive the long passage from Africa as a passenger on the slave trade. In contrast, *Anopheles* species could not survive the long voyage. (The potential of African species of *Anopheles* to colonize the New World was demonstrated in the 1930s, when *A. gambiae* made a sudden and terrifying appearance in Brazil. It was quickly recognized and eliminated.) Unfortunately for humans, *Anopheles* did not have to make the leap to the New World in order for malaria to become established. Competent vectors were already present, and the geography of malaria in the Americas is a distorted reflection of its patterns in the Old World.[74]

A. quadrimaculatus is really a complex of closely related species that thrive from the Gulf of Mexico to southern Canada, from the Atlantic shores to the Mississippi valley. It is an ugly, brown mosquito with a delicate bite that can go unnoticed. It has no distinct predilection for human blood, and it flourished long before people settled the continent. *A. quadrimaculatus* is a creature of the wetlands. The female, who lays hundreds of eggs at a time and a few thousand in her lifetime, sets them afloat in shallow fresh water with green vegetation. Swamps, of course,

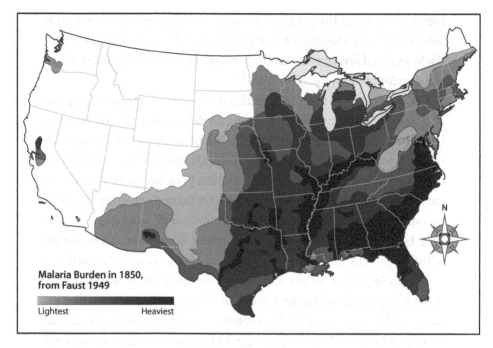

Malaria Burden in 1850,
from Faust 1949

Lightest   Heaviest

N

FIGURE 8.6. Distribution of malaria in the United States, circa 1850 (after Sloane 1949).

but also ponds and sluggish streams, creeks, and sloughs are perfect habitat. Warmer temperatures dramatically accelerate the developmental cycle of the mosquito. The mosquito is most abundant in the southeast.[75]

A. *quadrimaculatus* is an efficient vector for both vivax and falciparum malaria. It allowed both diseases to establish in colonial America. But the geographical inequities were immense. Because A. *quadrimaculatus* proliferated in warm and wet conditions, it was more abundant in southern climates, and within any particular region, it was concentrated along coasts and rivers, in lowlands and marshes (see figure 8.6). The biology of the Plasmodium parasites also influenced the geography of malaria in the Americas. *P. vivax* was the more versatile species, able to hibernate in the liver of its human host as mosquito populations crashed during the cold months; it was simply less finicky about external temperature, more tolerant of temperate conditions. *P. falciparum*, by contrast, cannot survive low temperatures and multiplies faster in warm environments. It is a tropical parasite that ranges into the subtropics, but not beyond.[76]

Consequently, vivax malaria could be present almost everywhere in the colonies, whereas falciparum was only meaningfully present as far north as Chesapeake Bay. Vivax would have been repeatedly introduced by European traders and settlers coming from the malarial regions of the Old World. Oliver Wendell Holmes Sr., the poet and physician, published a brilliant dissertation on the role of "intermittent fevers" in colonial New England. He rightly deduced that in the first century of European settlement, these fevers "prevailed but to a very limited extent." He well understood the greater prevalence of the disease in marshy and riverine landscapes. Some years were more deadly than others. The diary of a Harvard student recorded a bad year in 1683, for instance, in which a friend "died at Salem of ye Feaver at [a] time [when] many were visited with ye feaver and ague which was very mortal."[77]

As is often the case with vivax malaria, sickness was more common than death. In Boston, in 1690, it was observed that "Epidemical Fevers and Agues grow very common, in some parts of the Country, whereof, tho' many dye not, yet they are sorely unfitted for their imployments." Yet even the limited prevalence of vivax in New England was apparently not enduring. Despite continued population growth in the eighteenth century, the burden of malaria in New England seems to have waned for reasons that are not well understood. "The northern boundary of malaria shifted in the eighteenth century, leaving New England entirely free of the disease after roughly the mid-century mark."[78]

Colonies farther south were not so fortunate. The Mason-Dixon Line traces an important contour in the medical geography of the Americas. A study of Yale graduates in the eighteenth century, for instance, reveals the dramatic differences in survivorship experienced by northerners and southerners, with the inhabitants of New England enjoying the best life prospects of all (see table 8.5).[79]

Right up to the twentieth century, malaria was a pernicious presence in the American South. Vivax was almost universal in the coastal lowlands, whereas falciparum was a devastating presence in the foci where it took hold. In the vast tidewater region stretching from Maryland to North Carolina, malaria arrived early and shaped the course of settlement from the start. "Agues" are documented from the very beginning

TABLE 8.5. Additional Life Expectancy at Thirty, Yale Graduates 1701–1805, by Region of Residence

Region	Number of years lived beyond 30 (mean)	Number of graduates
Connecticut	34.2	1,357
Massachusetts	36.9	312
Other New England	38.6	136
New York	32.7	297
Middle Colonies[a]	32.7	64
Southern Colonies[b]	19.9	71

[a]Middle Colonies: Pennsylvania, Delaware, New Jersey.
[b]Southern Colonies: Maryland, Virginia, North Carolina, South Carolina, Georgia, Florida, Alabama, Mississippi, Louisiana.

of the Jamestown settlement and may have contributed to the abysmal demographic experience of the colony in its infancy. Between 1607 and 1624, 6,454 of the 7,549 settlers perished. Later, an observer noted that "the air is exceeding unwholesome, insomuch as one of three scarcely liveth the first year at this time." Still, he claimed, it used to be worse, with eleven of twelve dying due to the swamps, standing waters, and marshes.[80]

The same fertile soils that gave birth to the tobacco economy were apt to create a malarial ecology. The soft, sandy plains carrying the runoff of the Piedmont into the Atlantic Ocean were a mosquito's paradise, and inevitably a hot zone of malaria. In 1823, an experienced Virginia doctor named Alexander Somervail described the "medical topography" of the Rappahannock valley, tracing in vivid detail the soft, level banks of the river and the sprawling, "miry" marshes that lay on either side. Everywhere the river was fed by creeks, "having banks and marshes exactly like the river." Over the decades the trees had been cut out. The "intermitting fever was universal," rising up every spring and lasting right until the "frost and stormy north winds drove all away" in the winter. "Few indeed escaped some of these fevers."[81]

This tidewater region was a zone of mixed infection, with both vivax and falciparum in circulation. Falciparum may have been more erratic, spiking in years when the climate favored mosquito breeding. For example, one eighteenth-century doctor in Maryland had been abroad but returned in the midst of a sickly year. "I should have known the time had been unhealthy . . . by only observing the washed countenances of the people standing att their doors and looking out att their windows, for they looked like so many staring ghosts." Colonial medical terminology is rarely precise, and yet it has been possible to follow the almost immediate arrival of vivax on the Atlantic seaboard and the subsequent appearance of falciparum later in the seventeenth century. The intensification of the tobacco economy, and the rising number of Africans brought in chains to the mid-Atlantic, introduced falciparum from about the 1670s. The solidification of a slave-based society and the hardening of the new disease regime went hand in hand.[82]

Whereas there remains doubt about the role of heritable immunity in the case of yellow fever, it is not so with malaria. The Europeans who settled the New World lacked innate immunity to the disease. Hence, a violent "seasoning"—a bout of malaria—awaited for virtually all arrivals in the south. Sickness was a rite of passage in adjusting to the unfamiliar climate. West Africans, by contrast, were largely protected against vivax malaria, carrying the Duffy-negative trait that had become fixed in the Pleistocene. Moreover, the sickle-cell trait conferred some advantages against falciparum malaria, but these were far more limited, and on the whole the population of African descent in the south remained vulnerable to this form of malaria. Unfortunately for the victims of malaria, African and European alike, acquired immunity is partial and temporary. Infection by vivax seems to leave survivors protected, but only for a few years. Falciparum can confer resistance, but it takes frequent exposure for the resistance to build up and continuous infection for it to last.[83]

The symbiosis of disease and exploitation was pronounced in the Carolina Low Country. Ecologically and culturally, South Carolina was an extension of the Greater Caribbean. Many of the early settlers came from Barbados, and Carolina's economy depended on exports of foodstuffs and firewood to the West Indies. Permanent European settlement was established from 1670s, and the first days brimmed with hopefulness. "The Heavens shine upon this famous Country the soveraign Ray of health: and has blest it with a serene Air, and a lofty Skie, that defends it from noxious Infection." But the optimism soon faded, and a reputation for unhealthiness spread. In Boston, 1687, "Two young men have just arrived from Carolina, who give some account of the country. In the first place, they say, they have never before seen so miserable a country, nor an atmosphere so unhealthy. Fevers prevail all the year, from which those who are attacked seldom recover; and if some escape, their complexion becomes tawny. . . . They bring us also tidings that before their departure a ship had arrived from London, with one hundred and thirty persons on board, including the crew, of whom one hundred and fifteen died as soon as they landed, all from malignant fevers."[84]

Carolina had to compete with other New World frontiers for free colonists, and many arrivals in Carolina quickly changed their minds. "White Carolinians of all stations continued to remove themselves to other English colonies." A saying had made its way across Europe: "They who want to die quickly, go to Carolina." The colony was increasingly populated by servants and enslaved persons who had no choice. The large-scale importation of slaves from the 1680s ensured the introduction of falciparum malaria. Charlestown itself was a notorious focus of disease, "the great charnel house of the country." In the swamps turned over to the cultivation of rice, which quickly became the staple export of the Carolina economy, malaria was now a menace unparalleled anywhere in North America. As a German visitor famously described it, "Carolina is in the spring a paradise, in the summer a hell and in the autumn a hospital."[85]

The colonial period of history in North America was dominated by the cities of the Atlantic seaboard and their immediate agrarian hinterlands, lying in the wide plains behind the coast. These regions were conducive to the transmission of malaria, and the disease left an irreversible imprint on the patterns of early American history. But further inland both the physical geography and the patterns of disease changed. Even in the south, the hilly interior was poorer but healthier, less hospitable for mosquitos and plantations alike. As settlement moved deeper inland, patterns of disease changed, and on the other side of the mountains lay new disease ecologies still. Malaria came to exert a dominant force in the Deep South, where the fields turned over to cotton and sugar in the lower Mississippi valley offered a humid, sweltering atmosphere for the disease.[86]

And in the sprawling upper Mississippi basin, from the Ohio River valley to the Great Lakes and the Great Plains, vivax malaria was an integral part of the frontier dynamic. Before railways, settlement fanned out along the rivers, and settlers carried vivax in their blood to awaiting four-spotted mosquitos. Although this fact has largely dissolved from the national memory, malaria was "*the* American disease and, while the older states already had emerged from its worst vexations, its hotbed was what up to the 1850's was still called 'the West'; the valley of the Mississippi and its tributaries."[87]

Malaria left its mark on the pioneers who ventured across the continent. A memoir from the 1830s records a scene from Iowa, where "on the river bank, sat a girl and a lad—most pitiable looking objects, uncared for, hollow eyed, sallow faced. They had crawled out into the warm sun with chattering teeth to see the boat pass. . . . If you've never seen that kind of sickness I reckon you must be a Yankee. That's the ague. I'm feared you will see plenty of it if you stay long in these parts. They call it here the swamp devil." Charles Dickens journeyed from Cincinnati to St. Louis in 1841 and found the undrained interior dreadful: "a breeding-place of fever, ague, and death . . . a dismal swamp, on which half built houses rot away . . . a hot bed of disease, an ugly sepulchre, a grave uncheered by any gleam of promise, a place without one single quality, in earth or air or water, to commend it." These impressions were not ungrounded. In the Civil War, Union army recruits from malarial counties were on average 1.1 inches shorter than their peers who grew up in areas free from the disease. But population growth, the triumph of road and rail, and, above all, landscape drainage caused the disease to recede from the interior, its imprint mostly forgotten today.[88]

We have explored the story of malaria in the colonies that became the United States in some detail because it is an important chapter in the human past but also because it illustrates the dynamics of malaria in the New World. Yet it is only a piece of the even broader story of malaria in the Americas. Throughout Mexico and Central America, the Caribbean and South America, even California and the Pacific Coast, new patterns of malarial disease were established in the centuries following European arrival. The same factors—mosquito ecology, landscape

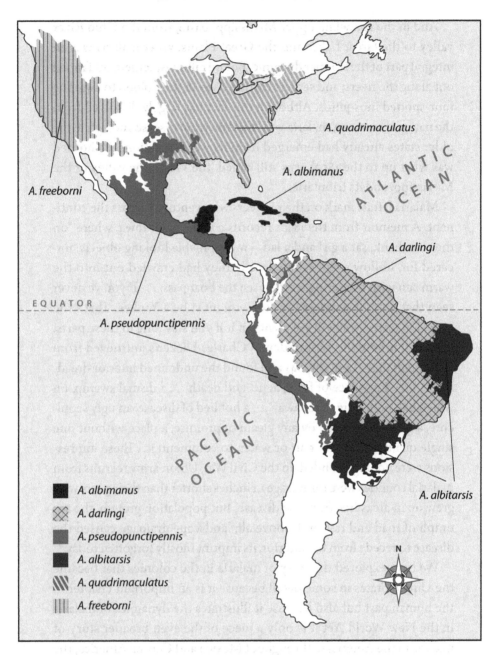

FIGURE 8.7. Distribution of important mosquito vectors of malaria in the Americas
(data from Malaria Atlas Project).

transformation, and human migration—decided the patterns of malaria prevalence, in all their kaleidoscopic complexity.[89]

The presence of competent mosquito vectors was a prerequisite (see figure 8.7). A. albimanus was abundant in Mexico, the Caribbean, and the northern coasts of South America. Able to mature in fresh or brackish waters, its importance as a vector was blunted by its preference for nonhuman blood. More important was A. pseudopunctipennis, whose range stretched from Texas to Argentina. Because A. pseudopunctipennis can survive at relatively high altitudes, it was the crucial vector in the Andes. A. aquasalis was common in the Caribbean and coastal South America, but it also prefers nonhuman blood. A. darlingi was the most deadly vector of malaria in the New World. With a taste for human blood, it haunted the river basins of the Americas and parts of the Caribbean. In Central America and South America east of the Andes, it predominated as a vector. In the giant Amazonian basin, where deforestation only opened new environments for the insect, A. darlingi cast a long shadow over human health.[90]

Although yellow fever was more dramatic, malaria was more persistent. The Spanish would have carried vivax malaria in their bodies from the early days of exploration and conquest. Malaria probably played a complementary role in the devastation wrought on indigenous peoples from the sixteenth century onward. And matters only got worse with time. As the slave trade ramped up, falciparum malaria followed. Lowland Mexico and Central America quickly became hot zones of infection, as did much of Brazil and the Caribbean. Wherever falciparum malaria became endemic, it was a stark demographic fact.

Repercussions in the Old World

The transplantation of tropical crops and pathogens to the New World was one of the crucial dimensions of the Columbian Exchange. It established sharp geographical gradients of health in the western hemisphere, mirroring those of the Old World, but in the context of violent colonialism, plantation economics, and a burgeoning capitalist network stretching across the Atlantic. Yellow fever and malaria were the most dramatic exemplars of this trans-Atlantic disease exchange, but the role of hookworm, yaws, schistosomiasis, and other tropical diseases should not be forgotten. The mortality regimes that took shape influenced patterns of demography and settlement across the New World.

We can mention in brief one important coda to the story of power and disease in the Americas. Over the course of the eighteenth century, the number of settlers and enslaved persons in the New World grew, and so did their political aspirations. The disease ecology of the Americas proved to be a significant ally of freedom fighters during the age of revolution that unfolded in the last decades of the 1700s. The colonial rebellions and slave revolts coincided with a wave of yellow fever, most intensely in the 1790s, helping to loosen the grip of Old World powers. The toll of disease among susceptible European troops was astonishing, especially during the liberation of Saint-Domingue, now Haiti. In the words of John McNeill, given that malaria and yellow fever had played such a role in making "African labor especially attractive to Caribbean and Brazilian planters" and caused "untold misery for millions of Africans over centuries, it is altogether fitting that these two infections should have helped world history's largest slave revolt succeed." The loss of Saint-Domingue deprived the French of their most valuable colonial possession, and the cost sheet of American imperialism convinced Napoleon to sell Louisiana to the fledgling United States for pennies an acre.[91]

A full accounting of the Columbian Exchange, though, must also look back across the Atlantic, and trace the impact of American colonization on the Old World. The migration of disease to the Old World was limited, but other channels of feedback reverberated. New staples like potatoes and maize fed rapid population growth, while new consumer goods like sugar, coffee, and tobacco fueled market expansion and the rise of a merchant elite with political clout. When Vassall's *Mayflower* set sail in 1647, it left behind an Old World engulfed in crisis almost from one end to another. Civil wars raged from England to China. The European continent was staggering from decades of conflict in the Thirty Years' War. In the midst of these crises, power decisively shifted toward Atlantic-facing Europe, and the lineaments of a more familiar modern order, in which health and wealth became reinforcing, started to take shape.

9

Of Lice and Men

Disease and Global Crisis?

The Thirty Years' War (1618–48) was a tragic episode, scarring the landscapes of central Europe in what is often considered the first truly modern war. Equally cruel for soldiers and civilians, it was, proportionally, the deadliest conflict in European history. One of the most memorable works of art to come from the tragedy is a semiautobiographical novel named after the main character, *Simplicius Simplicissimus*. The hero is a naïve but irrepressible observer of the war's unaccountable brutality. In one scene, Simplicius comes to find himself plunged into a gory battle—against the lice that have roosted under his armor.[1]

> The lice were tormenting me so dreadfully, I worried they were making a home for themselves under my skin. . . . Oh, they're a plague! One day, feeling I couldn't bear the torment any longer, while some of the troopers were feeding the horses, some sleeping, and some on watch, I went off a little way under a tree to wage war on my enemy. Pulling off the cuirass (I know: most folk don one when going into battle), I launched such an attack of squashing and squeezing, in minutes my twin swords (i.e. thumbnails) dripped with blood and dead bodies (empty skins, I should say) lay at my feet. Those I didn't kill I left to die slowly, crawling around beneath the tree. Every time I think

of that encounter I itch all over and I'm back under that tree, battling away. I shouldn't be fighting my fellow creatures, I kept thinking, particularly not such faithful servants, who wouldn't desert their master on the gallows or as he was being broken on the wheel and on whom, given their huge numbers, I'd often slept in comfort outdoors on the hard ground. (Grimmelshausen 2018)

This delousing scene is a picaresque comment on the inhumanity of a conflict that slaughtered its human participants like so many bugs. The Thirty Years' War was many things at once: a humanitarian catastrophe, a religious struggle, a constitutional crisis, a European civil war, and the crux of the "military revolution." The war was also, from another point of view, a bonanza for lice, fleas, rodents, and all manner of vermin that thrive on human misery.[2]

This chapter tries to keep our focus on the part played by such tiny yet prolific agents of human suffering. The death tolls from the Thirty Years' War make a *prima facie* case for doing so. In the words of Peter Wilson, it was a war where "disease proved more potent that muskets, swords and cannon." Over the course of the prolonged conflict, some 450,000 troops lost their lives on the field of battle. Three times as many succumbed to infectious disease. For civilians, the ravages of disease and hunger were far more fearsome than direct violence. Typhus and plague, carried by lice and fleas, respectively, were the gravest threats. The demographic shock was compounded by a sharp decline in fertility. The overall impact was uneven, but across broad stretches of central Europe, the population declined by a third to a half. It took a century for human numbers to recover in the heart of the continent. The Thirty Years' War has been called "the greatest man-made disaster to befall Europe prior to the Napoleonic Wars." We might equally imagine it as a prolonged epidemiological crisis triggered by human conflict.[3]

The Thirty Years' War is a compelling example, because even in this struggle where military engagement was truly central, with the highest battlefield casualties of any early modern conflict, disease was still the primary—indeed, the overwhelmingly primary—cause of death.

Disease was not a mere byproduct of war; rather, war was the ecological context for disease. The displacement and disorder of warfare created a dangerous disease ecology. In the long seventeenth century, the disease ecology of human conflict became particularly hellish.[4]

From a global perspective, the Thirty Years' War was just one episode in the broader pattern that some historians call the "general crisis of the seventeenth century." War, famine, and plague seemed universal across the Old World. The perception of general crisis was shared by people living at the time. In the words of a sermon delivered before the English Parliament in the 1640s, these "days are days of shaking . . . and this shaking is universal." Historians have endlessly debated whether it makes sense to define the entire period as one of crisis, or whether such calamities are simply what passes most of the time for plain history. But, in fact, the period does stand out as exceptionally troubled, which is of central relevance for the history of disease. War was one manifestation of a thoroughgoing crisis that shaped the disease regime in the early modern period. To understand the history of infectious disease in Europe and Asia during the early modern centuries is to treat seriously the ecology of crisis: Why was the seventeenth century so turbulent, and what did it mean for human health?[5]

Across most of Eurasia, the period between the crossing of the Atlantic and the eve of the Industrial Revolution (ca. 1500–1750) was an age of growth punctuated by severe convulsions: a long cycle of demographic and economic expansion, repeatedly interrupted by staggering crises (see figure 9.1). In vivid contrast to the trajectory of the New World, Europe and Asia experienced a phase of headlong growth throughout the sixteenth century. People multiplied. Wars, famine, and pestilence were limited in their scope—at least, relative to what followed. There was still room to grow in the gap left by the Black Death and recurrent outbreaks of plague. But from the 1580s or 1590s, limits started to impose themselves. Resources were stretched thin. For instance, the worst famines since the early 1300s struck in the 1580s and 1590s across wide stretches of both Europe and Asia. But this was only a prelude of worse to come. In the seventeenth century, the apocalyptic horsemen of war, famine, and pestilence were let out of the stable. How

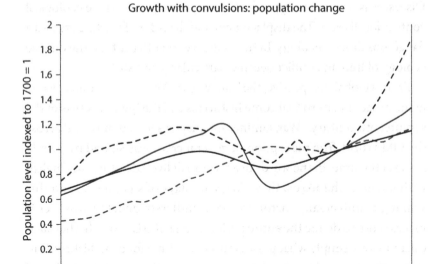

FIGURE 9.1. Population growth with convulsions.

can this synchronicity be explained? There are at least three possibilities, and they are not mutually exclusive.[6]

The first is climate change. The climate is arguably the only forcing mechanism big enough to coordinate the destiny of such various human societies on a global scale. The Little Ice Age was a cold and unstable period centered on the seventeenth century, one of the most distinct phases of climate history in the entire Holocene epoch. The cooling is usually thought to have been brought on by decreased solar output or volcanic eruptions. One additional hypothesis is that the depopulation of the New World following European contact triggered massive reforestation in the Americas. The regrowth of forests, in turn, acted as a carbon sink, pulling carbon out of the atmosphere and cooling the planet. Although more of a provocative possibility than accepted consensus, the idea remains intriguing: Old World diseases devastated New World populations, and the expanding woodlands cooled the climate, triggering crisis across Eurasia. Whatever its causes, though, the Little Ice Age contributed to harvest failure, epidemic mortality, and widespread violence, particularly in the 1580s/1590s, 1640s, and 1690s.[7]

A second possibility is overpopulation, what Malthus called the "positive check." Malthusian doctrine holds that premodern populations could grow faster than their food supplies. Demographic increase thus meant declining well-being, and eventually famine, plague, or war. Indeed, population growth in the sixteenth century seems to have put pressure on resources, so that when the climate became less favorable for agrarian production, societies were unable to feed themselves adequately. In more elaborate versions of this model, population growth led not only to widespread hunger and misery, but also to more intense strife and competition among elites. Power struggles, civil war, and class conflict should thus be seen as manifestations of subsurface movements of population. The age of crisis, then, was the ineluctable penalty for overexuberant demographic growth.[8]

A third possibility is that the crises of the period should be seen as the consequence of infectious disease, of simply random evolutionary outcomes that rocked human societies. In the words of economic historian Jan de Vries, "Mortality rates rose significantly during the seventeenth century. . . . Epidemiological factors, substantially exogenous to the socioeconomic systems of the time, appear to have dominated mortality and, hence, the overall course of population change. Thus, rather than a crisis provoked by endogenous processes, unique to the technologies, institutions, and reproductive practices of particular societies, the seventeenth-century demographic crisis appears to have had a proximate cause that was exogenous—infectious-disease vectors possessing a history of their own, and before which societies stood powerless."[9]

One goal of this chapter is to bring these approaches a little closer together. Climatic instability and population pressure prepared the ground for crisis, and infectious diseases were a terrific force across the Old World in the seventeenth century. But we should not treat the biology of disease like a kind of ghost in the machine, beyond all explanation. All too often, epidemics are treated as "exogenous" or "autonomous" factors, coming and going inexplicably. As we have seen throughout the human past, on long enough timescales pathogens respond to the ecological conditions with which they are presented. To understand the convulsive seventeenth century, we have to ask what diseases were at work, what ecological conditions summoned them forth, and how societies responded to their disease environments. This approach makes it easier to see the lines of connection between human agency and biological factors in the early modern world.[10]

The epidemics of the seventeenth century were a response to four distinctive ecological factors: (1) population pressure and food shortage, (2) urbanization, (3) the birth of modern institutions like jails and hospitals, and (4) the military revolution that increased the frequency and scale of armed conflict. The first part of the chapter surveys these changes in the background of the early modern world. The chapter then turns to three specific diseases: typhus, plague, and smallpox. This unholy trinity, which came to overlay the entire range of diarrheal and respiratory diseases that had accumulated over the millennia, created the distinctive disease regime of early modern Eurasia. The disease environment created by the conjunction of these three pathogens is often imagined as the ancien régime of health and disease, ultimately overcome by triumphant modernity. In reality, the conjunction of these three pathogens was a product of the structural features of the early modern world.

Plague remained the biggest killer. Plague has an unshakable reputation as a medieval disease, but it was just as much a player in the early modern period. The seventeenth century must be reckoned among the great ages of plague. At the same time, a more virulent strain of smallpox emerged in the early modern period and wreaked havoc on human populations across the planet. And typhus was perhaps the purest reflection of early modern disease ecologies. Typhus was a corollary to other kinds of misery. In the judgment of August Hirsch, "The *history of typhus* is written in those dark pages of the world's story which tell of the grievous visitations of mankind by war, famine, and misery of every kind. In every age, as far back as the historical inquirer can follow the disease at all, typhus is met with in association with the saddest misfortunes of the populace." But typhus should not be treated as the punctuation mark duly appearing at the end of each disaster. The ecology of this louse-borne disease merits more patient elucidation. Typhus flourished amid density, poverty, and filth. Famine, war, and urban squalor all promoted the transmission of typhus. And typhus was a disease almost peculiar to the kinds of modern institutions that took shape in this period: camps, jails, hospitals, and eventually factories and tenements.[11]

The patterns of similarity across the Old World say something about the unity of the epidemiological regime across Europe and Asia. The seventeenth century was also a period when the patterns of modern growth first become faintly visible. Yet here careful qualifications are in order. The "rise of Europe" has been considered from every conceivable angle. In this period, Europe's ascendance was hardly evident in the geopolitical order of the Old World, at least by traditional measures like population, territory, and aggregate war-making ability. The windfall of New World conquests had put massive surfaces in the nominal grip of European powers, and Europe's maritime prowess was unmatched. But the giant, territorial empires of the Ottomans, Safavids, Mughals, and Qing remained titanic powers on land and demographically the weightiest polities on earth. From a global perspective, the world was dominated by great sprawling empires on land. And European powers were not preeminent among them.

The deeper changes whose earliest stirrings may lie in this period cannot be measured in square miles or men-at-arms, but in new patterns of growth, and the configurations of science, statecraft, and social development that would ultimately prove transformational. Economic historians know this period as the age of the Little Divergence, when northwestern Europe started to achieve sustained per capita income growth despite population increase for the first time in human history. The following chapter will explore the relationship between wealth and health in the "Great Escape" from the Malthusian trap, but some of the lineaments of that story become perceptible in this chapter. The general crisis of the seventeenth century propelled the centralization of European states and vigorous expansions in governmental capacity—inadvertently making possible more robust public health interventions.

The escalating health challenges faced by early modern societies were a byproduct of global modernization. We will repeatedly find that these challenges, sometimes arising at opposite ends of the Old World, have a surprising amount in common. Similarly, the most effective responses to infectious disease in this period were geographically diffuse. The Chinese discovered inoculation, the first really important medical intervention against infectious disease. Japan had the most advanced urban sanitation in the world. The finest hospitals anywhere might have been in Baghdad or Damascus. But systemic control of infectious disease remained out of reach, everywhere, and only in the eighteenth century did science and statecraft truly catalyze transformational change.

The Ecology of Early Modernity

The sixteenth century was a demographic golden age across the Old World. The Black Death and repeated bouts of plague had held populations low for a century and a half. In England, where historical demography is uniquely well studied, the population "remained prostrate" until about 1500. The same was true of Italy and much of the continent. In Asia, the demographic downturn started earlier, with the violent disruptions of Mongol expansion (and possibly also the first thrust of plague). The recovery too may have started sooner, but even so, the sixteenth century was a time of roaring growth. In the Ottoman heartlands, there was vigorous expansion. The tempo of demographic increase in Mughal India is obscure, and may have started later than elsewhere. In Ming China the population doubled in less than two centuries, from around 80 million in 1400 to 160 million in the mid-sixteenth century, stalling by the 1580s.[12]

Why was there such robust demographic increase, across such a wide area? There is not a fully satisfying answer. The plague had brought a long cycle of stagnation. It eventually drove up real wages, and after some delay, higher wages stimulated demographic growth. There was room to multiply and food to eat. Trade and economic specialization expanded. This growth was organic growth, in the sense that it was achieved without modern machines or fossil energy. Gradually, human capital became more important. In Europe, literacy rates started a permanent ascent. Although it might not have been obvious at the time, the formula of simultaneous population growth, commercial expansion, and increasing human capital would plant the seeds of escape from the Malthusian trap of poverty and early death.[13]

Mortality crises were less frequent and less severe between the late fifteenth and the late sixteenth century. Plague lurked and continued to be the most dangerous disease, but its impact was far less than it had been or would become again in the seventeenth century. There was a widespread and severe mortality event in the later 1550s in parts of Europe, probably caused by a combination of influenza and typhus. But typhus, as we will see, was still perhaps a relatively new disease, radiating out of southern Europe only from the early sixteenth century.[14]

Eventually, inevitably, demographic growth crunched the food supply, as population densities increased and farmers were pushed onto less productive land. There are signs of pressure in Europe from the 1550s onward. And from around 1590 there were more serious challenges. A sequence of abrupt climate changes seems to have been the trigger. Parts of Europe felt dire famines, first in the south and then in the north. The Ottoman Empire faced a series of violent rebellions. In China the troubles started slightly earlier, from the 1580s, but were nearly synchronous.[15]

These challenges inaugurated a long period during which pressure on the food supply was a constant theme. The seventeenth century "clearly stands out as the period during which food security across the [European] continent became a truly critical issue." Famines rocked India and China in this period, too. Food shortage caused starvation and death. But it also drove innovation and creative social response. Early social welfare systems—like the system of public relief created by England's Poor Law—were born. Northern Europe came to rely more heavily on Baltic grain. Southern Europe eventually took up maize cultivation, as did China. The dispersal of the potato started to be felt; the nutritious tuber was turned into more human bodies worldwide. In the words of William McNeill, the Thirty Years' War was "remembered afterward with special horror largely because it was the last war fought in northern Europe before potatoes became widespread enough to cushion the human cost" and prevent outright rural starvation.[16]

The proportion of the population living in towns grew. Of course, the pace of preindustrial urbanization was still limited: for perspective, as late as 1800, only 2 percent of humans on the planet lived in a town with a population larger than one hundred thousand. But in the period leading into the Industrial Revolution, there was steady urban growth across most of Europe and Asia. In 1500, 5.6 percent of the European population lived in towns of ten thousand or more. By 1700, 9.2 percent did. What mattered even more is *where* urban growth happened. Italy, already relatively urbanized, stayed at the same overall level across this entire period. Towns ravaged by the Thirty Years' War and cycles of pestilence struggled to maintain their populations. Instead, growth came disproportionately in commercial towns, especially those facing the Atlantic and North Sea. In the British Isles, the percent of the population living in a town nearly quintupled between 1500 and 1700. The whole weight of urban Europe shifted decisively toward the north and west—one of the most consequential geopolitical changes of the period.[17]

Also consequential was the spectacular success of the very largest cities in Europe. The hundreds of small towns across the continent failed to expand in aggregate. Instead, growth was concentrated in the top twenty or so cities, the big ports, capitals, and financial and proto-industrial centers: Amsterdam, Antwerp, Brussels, Danzig, Dublin, Hamburg, Ghent, Leiden, Lisbon, Livorno, London, Lyon, Madrid, Marseilles, Middleburg, Nantes, Paris, Rome, Rotterdam, Rouen, and The Hague. By the middle of the seventeenth century, they were home to a quarter of the total urban population of the continent.[18]

The cities of the Near East and Asia had always been the biggest in the world, and they continued to represent the vanguard of urbanization through the seventeenth century. In Japan, for instance, the growth of Edo (Tokyo) was explosive. It went from a small provincial stronghold in 1400 to a city of one million by shortly after 1700—possibly the largest city in the world. In China, the Ming period (1368–1644) saw a steady revival of towns following the disruptions of the previous period.

Nanjing was probably the biggest city in the world in the fifteenth century. It was eventually outpaced by Beijing, which doubled in size by 1600. Cairo, Istanbul, and Isfahan remained among the biggest cities on the planet. Over the course of the seventeenth century, they continued to grow. In 1650, it was not obvious that London was poised to become the colossus of the world's leading economy or a major center of culture; a century later, when Samuel Johnson declared with pride that whoever is tired of London is tired of life, the city's destiny was apparent.[19]

Across Eurasia, urbanization increased death rates. Towns were always and everywhere less salubrious than the countryside. Large cities were powerful demographic sinks, requiring a constant influx of migrants. The rise of London shaped the entire demographic history of England. The pull of the capital was irresistible, but lethal. Not all cities need have been equally deadly. Japan's urban surge, for instance, developed in step with innovations in the water supply and waste disposal; a rollicking trade in "night soil" (feces to be used as fertilizer) helped keep the streets clean and fields nourished. But at least in Europe, the urban century of 1650–1750 was unusually deadly. Plague, typhus, and smallpox made cities as dangerous as they had ever been. We must be aware of these powerful cross-currents. The increasing weight of urbanism disguises modest but meaningful improvements. In towns, people learned by degrees to control and eventually to prevent diseases. By the late eighteenth century, London not only became the biggest city in the world; it may also have been the first big town to experience natural increase, its birth rates exceeding its death rates.[20]

As towns grew, so did the number, size, and formality of institutions of all kinds. Crowds, queues, dormitories, and other experiences of human density are such a normal part of our lives that it is easy to forget such aggregations are a historical development, and one that was accomplished by deadly trial and error. There were medieval precedents, to be sure. But familiar modern institutions such as hospitals and asylums, jails and prisons, workhouses and factories took shape in the early modern period. Hospitals, for example, have deep roots in the medieval period. In the late medieval Near East, quite elaborate medical hospitals

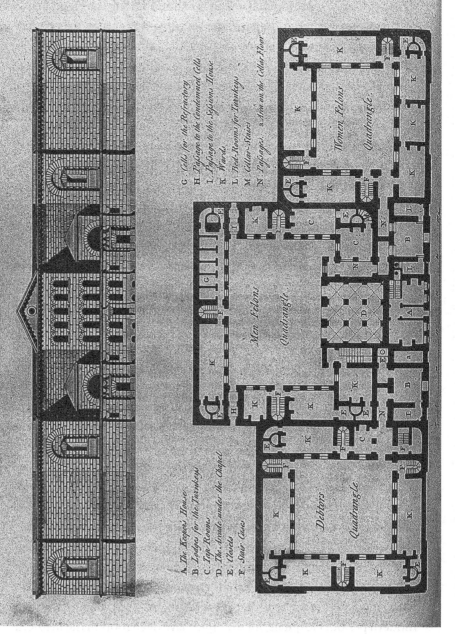

NEWGATE.

Plate 20.

A. The Keeper's House.
B. Lodges for the Turnkeys.
C. Tap-Rooms.
D. The Arcade under the Chapel.
E. Closets.
F. Stair-Cases.

G. Cells for the Refractory.
H. Passage to the Condemned Cells.
I. Passage to the Sessions House.
K. Wards.
L. Bed-Rooms for Turnkeys.
M. Cellar-Stairs.
N. Passage: a Area on the Cellar Floor.

Women Felons Quadrangle.

Men Felons Quadrangle.

Debtors Quadrangle.

developed. In the early modern period, such institutions proliferated, and their purposes became more differentiated. Across Europe, orphanages, poorhouses, military hospitals, and lying-in hospitals arose, while the medical focus of general hospitals was sharpened. Typhus was known as "hospital fever" because it preyed on the density of bodies, especially those of the poor. One of the crucial innovations in the 1700s was the development of the fever hospital, an institution that isolated patients with typhus or other fevers.[21]

The rise of the prison epitomizes these social transformations. Medieval towns had known incarceration on a smaller scale, often in quasi-feudal and religious forms, but from the sixteenth century "imprisonment and other forms of bondage grew increasingly popular in several European countries." The system of justice was increasingly secularized. In the south of Europe, as well as North Africa and the Ottoman Empire, condemnation to naval service on the giant galleys was a common form of detention, whereas in northern Europe penal workhouses and then specialized prisons came to predominate. Northern Europe led the world in the development of carceral institutions (see figure 9.2). Prisons were established in London (1555) and throughout England, Amsterdam (1596) and other Dutch towns, and Copenhagen (1605). The rise of the prison went hand in hand with urban growth, the spread of bourgeois cultures, and the secularization of justice.[22]

The history of typhus is intertwined with the rise of these new penal institutions. Before typhus was recognized as a single disease, "gaol [jail] fever" was one of its most notorious manifestations. The so-called black assizes that struck England regularly (for instance, in 1521, at Cambridge) may reflect the penetration of typhus into northern Europe from the Mediterranean. Assizes were periodic circuit courts, and thus suspected criminals (usually poor) were forced to endure lengthy detentions in dismal conditions waiting for the courts to arrive. Disease outbreaks during these detentions drew attention because they spilled over into the general population, killing wealthier judges, juries, and officers in ghastly epidemics. The notorious black assize of Oxford in 1577 was an outbreak that killed hundreds, including a high-ranking judge. One of the defendants, "a saucy foul-mouthed bookseller," uttered a curse that was blamed for the deaths, but typhus is a more plausible culprit.[23]

Prisoners in early modern England suffered deplorable conditions, almost perfectly calculated to promote the spread of typhus. Damp, dirty, and deprived, "the wretched inmates huddled together for warmth upon heaps of filthy rags or bundles of rotten straw reeking with foul exhalations, and fetid with all manner of indescribable nastiness." Density was the basic problem. "The immediate parent of gaol fever was the disgraceful and almost indiscriminate overcrowding of the gaols." In the 1770s, one of the great early social reformers, John Howard, captured public and parliamentary attention with his reports on the conditions of prisons in England and Wales, based on personal inspection in every county. For Howard, the ravages of gaol fever were synonymous with the inhumanity of the prison system. As he pointed out, more people died of gaol fever than execution. Unfortunately, this impossibly decent man contracted typhus while inspecting Russian hospitals in Ukraine, and he perished of the disease.[24]

Early modern societies were not carceral societies by contemporary standards, and the absolute number of those behind bars was limited. But the way that typhus haunted prisons illuminates the importance of the disease in societies that were learning to aggregate human bodies on a new scale. The ability of states to concentrate masses of people like never before reached its purest expression in military affairs. War looms over the early modern period. The sixteenth and seventeenth centuries were objectively belligerent. The nature, frequency, and scale of conflict changed, most dramatically in Europe. In 1955 Michael Roberts sketched the outlines of what he characterized as the "military revolution," a series of interrelated transformations that unfolded from about 1560 to 1660. He put technological change in the foreground, as the refinement of gunpowder weaponry displaced feudal forms of warfare. The introduction of the musket in the 1550s was a watershed. The size of armies grew, in some cases tenfold between 1500 and 1700. Strategies became more intricate and the impact on civilian society more profound. These changes deeply affected the disease environment from one end of Eurasia to the other.[25]

The two centuries from 1500 to 1700 were marked by conflict. The frequency, duration, and magnitude of war increased in Europe. In the early phase, from about 1494 to 1559, Italy was the proving grounds for new-style military engagements—and new diseases. Charles VIII of France invaded Italy in 1494 with an army of eighteen thousand men and a massive siege train. Allegedly, the French soldiers spread "the great pox" (often thought to have been syphilis) across Europe; it was probably not a totally new disease, but troop movements (and troop habits) accelerated its transmission. It is unsurprising that the first convincing reports of typhus also appear at just this moment—in 1491 in Granada, where the combined forces of Ferdinand and Isabella amounted to an extraordinary sixty thousand troops. Two generations later, the emperor Charles V commanded armies of 150,000 soldiers. In the seventeenth century, the size of the biggest European forces grew again, doubling within a few generations, as the balance of power and main theaters of conflict also shifted to the center and north of Europe. By the early eighteenth century, there were 1.3 million troops simultaneously deployed on the continent.[26]

These changes were mirrored across Eurasia. The Ottoman armies of the later fifteenth and early sixteenth centuries were superior in size and technological sophistication to the European forces they met, and this imbalance motivated Europeans to innovate and field larger armies too, especially in the Habsburg territories. The tempo of warfare in East Asia was also remarkably similar. The period 1550–1683 has been called "the most warlike in East Asia's history," with the Ming-Qing transition representing the eastern equivalent to the Thirty Years' War: a devastating period of engrossing conflict. (One consequential difference, however, was the long period of relative peace that followed in Qing-dominated East Asia, while Europe remained bloody, competitive, and terrifyingly innovative in military affairs.)[27]

Warfare is worse than bad for public health. It is often catastrophic. Conflict disrupts the production and distribution of food, as marauding troops destroy, steal, or requisition crops. Ensuing food crises spark famine and pestilence. War brought trauma and severe stress in its train. War also meant density, especially as armies got larger: some armies in the field ranked among the largest cities of the time. The army camp was

a place of dubious hygiene. Sieges also disrupted what forms of sanitation existed. Armies on the march were vehicles for germs, vectors, and
vermin. In short, war destroyed already fragile forms of order, subsistence, and cleanliness. Human conflicts always have a way of giving
reign to microparasites.[28]

Typhus: Microbe of Misery

In 1862 the British doctor Charles Murchison, author of a magisterial
Victorian treatise on fevers, remarked in a footnote that "a complete
history of typhus would be the history of Europe for the last three and
a half centuries." The same could probably be said for much of the early
modern world.[29]

Typhus is caused by the organism *Rickettsia prowazekii*, which belongs to a highly successful genus of bacteria. The rickettsia are tiny,
spherical bacteria that have adapted to live in arthropods like ticks, fleas,
and lice. Because many of these bugs learned to eat the blood of vertebrate hosts, a number of rickettsia have evolved the clever ability to infect vertebrates, especially mammals whose furry skin is a paradise for
bloodsuckers. In the vertebrate's body, the bacteria must replicate inside
the host cell (i.e., they are intracellular parasites—bacteria that are a
little like viruses in their small size and their need to invade host cells).
The rickettsia have a strong preference for the cells that line the inside
of blood vessels, which is important for understanding the diseases they
cause.[30]

The crucial adaptation of *R. prowazekii*, what has made it the cause
of such an audaciously prolific and nasty disease, is that it figured out
how to take advantage of the human body louse. Lice are wingless parasitic insects that exploit mammals and birds, nesting in feathers and hair
(see figure 9.3). Nature has been overly generous in furnishing humans
with two species of lice. Crab lice, whose natural habitat is human pubic
hair, are most closely related to a louse that infests gorillas. The other
species, *Pediculus humanus*, is closely related to the lice of chimpanzees.
Further, this second species of the human louse has two subtypes, each
of which has adapted to specific ecological niches: one the human head,

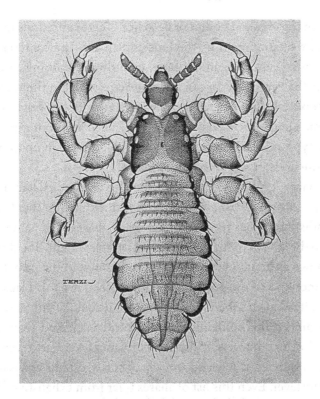

FIGURE 9.3. The human body louse, *Pediculus humanus
humanus*. Drawing by A.J.E. Terzi, circa 1919.
Wellcome Collection (CC BY 4.0).

the other the human body. The body louse is a particularly resilient
creature. It lays eggs in clothing and can survive for days apart from a
host. It gorges on human blood, taking five or so meals a day. The body
louse is thus a potentially efficient vector for pathogens. Fortunately,
only a handful of diseases—typhus, trench fever, relapsing fever—have
found a way into this specialized niche.[31]

The body louse eats human blood, but typhus bacteria are actually
not transmitted by the sucking parts of the louse. Instead, louse droppings are the lynchpin of the invasion strategy. Lice defecate where they
take meals. The tiny typhus bacteria are rife in the waste matter of the
louse, and they can survive for as long as one hundred days in this environment. Humans are infected when bacteria in the feces—or, for that

matter, in the crushed bodies of dead lice—enter abrasions in the skin, caused by scratching or by the louse bite itself. The bacteria can also enter across a mucous membrane, including the lining of the eyes. Because the typhus germ can become aerosolized in the fecal dust of lice, people who are not necessarily infested with lice might catch the infection. Hence, medical personnel have been at risk of exposure. But mostly, typhus is transmitted when the bacteria-laden poop of the ectoparasite finds its way into human skin.[32]

The name "typhus fever" only came into use in the later eighteenth century. Because the disease was both historically prevalent and clinically indistinct, it has traveled under many aliases. The name "typhus" refers to the stupor or foggy-headedness of the patient. The disease was also known as brain fever or head fever; because of the rash it was also sometimes known as spotted fever or petechial fever or black fever. In Spanish it is called *tabardillo*, "the colored cloak." Typhus was sometimes simply called epidemic fever or putrid fever. And given its predilection for close quarters, it also went by camp fever, gaol fever, hospital fever, and ship fever. A friend and ally of chaos, typhus was also known as famine fever. Even this list of aliases is far from exhaustive.[33]

A typhus infection launches with a ten- to fourteen-day incubation period, followed by a few days of malaise. Typhus causes a headache that can be extreme for a week or so, followed by neurological signs, including confusion. The face assumes a dull appearance, becoming "oppressed, vacant and bewildered." The profound stupor turns into a violent delirium, or, in some cases, seizures or coma. The disease is also frequently accompanied by a rash of irregular spots that erupt slightly and have a mottled appearance. The spots begin on the trunk and creep outward toward the extremities. In fact, the brain and the skin are suffering from the same underlying tendency of the bacterium to infect and destroy cells in the lining of the capillaries. Because the pathogen infects blood vessels, almost anything can go wrong; thus, typhus has a wide variety of clinical manifestations, including pulmonary complications, shock, gangrene, and tissue necrosis. The breath of typhus patients is often fetid, and constipation is not rare. Before antibiotics, the case fatality rate was high, up to 50 percent. The bacterium persists asymptomatically for years in some survivors, causing sudden relapse in times of stress or immune suppression.[34]

Because of its protean nature, typhus could be confused with a number of other diseases. Relapsing fever is also a louse-borne infection with a similar presentation; it often became epidemic at the same time as typhus. Murine typhus, too, although less fatal, was hard to distinguish from epidemic typhus in individual cases. As its name suggests, "typhoid fever" was easily confused with typhus, and the two were not reliably distinguished until the nineteenth century. Typhus could be misdiagnosed as any number of diseases, including measles, that presented with fever and discoloration of the skin. It was even conflated with bubonic plague, which it could resemble, minus the bubo; typhus often appeared amid plague outbreaks in the early modern period, further complicating differential diagnosis.[35]

Because typhus is hard to identify in older records, its origins remain obscure. The genetic evidence has not been illuminating so far. *R. prowazekii* probably evolved from an ancestor resembling the germ of murine typhus, capable of infecting rodents and humans alike. It is notable that an animal reservoir of typhus exists in eastern North America, where flying squirrels are a stable host of the pathogen; even now, every so often, an Appalachian hiker sleeping in a cabin with squirrel nests contracts the disease. If human typhus evolved first as a disease of North American rodents, it raises the possibility that typhus was a New World germ imported to Europe. As a team of geneticists observed, "It is tempting to speculate that typhus was born in the chance meeting of an American rickettsia and a Spanish louse."[36]

By contrast, typhus may have been brought to the Americas along with so many other diseases, and the greatest likelihood is that the disease is of Old World origins. There is indirect evidence for outbreaks of typhus in Europe by the second half of the fifteenth century. The historian of medicine Ann Carmichael has identified what seems like an outbreak of typhus in Milan in 1477, during a time of terrible famine. Contemporaries described a deadly disease characterized by severe headache and a purplish rash with pinpricks. Milan had the most advanced system of mortality surveillance in the world, and the number

Timeline of Typhus

Pre-1450	1450–1550	1550–1750	1750–1918
Obscure origins	Early diffusion	Heyday of typhus	Twilight of typhus
Evolved from rodent Rickettsial pathogen	Appears first in Italy, Spain, spreads to central Europe, northern Europe	Thrives in conditions of famine, war, institutions, urbanization	Endemic urban disease, with spectacular outbreaks in Napoleonic Wars and WWI
		Major epidemic disease	Increasingly a disease of poverty

FIGURE 9.4. Timeline of typhus (sometimes known as epidemic typhus, caused by *Rickettsia prowazekii*).

of deaths in 1477 and 1478 attributed to continuous fever, acute fever, choleric fever, "measles," and "alienation" jumped. All of these could be typhus, and this epidemic should probably count as the earliest attested typhus outbreak in Europe—fifteen years before the voyage of Columbus, thus excluding the possibility of American origins.[37]

Typhus may not be an ancient affliction (see figure 9.4). A Spanish doctor (writing several generations after the fact) thought that the disease had appeared in the 1490s, during the siege of Granada by the armies of Ferdinand and Isabella. Typhus became more visible in Italian and Spanish sources of the sixteenth century, and it was regarded as a new disease by medical authorities. Unambiguous evidence arrives in 1505, in the context of the Italian Wars that pitted the great powers of Europe against each other. A diarist in Venice, who lived through the epidemic there, claimed the disease was diffused throughout all of Italy in 1505 and reached his city by spring 1506. Victims suffered fever, severe pain in the head, delirium, and a blotchy rash—as exact a description of typhus as might be hoped for. The diarist noted that the disease was one unknown to Galen and Avicenna—which is to say that it was something new indeed.[38]

The outbreak of 1505 in Italy also figures in the remarkable work *On Contagion and Contagious Diseases* by the Italian physician Fracastoro. He believed that Italy had been struck in 1505 and 1528 by a pestilential

fever that "had not been previously known there in our time." His clinical notes unmistakably describe a typhus epidemic: "The head became
heavy, the senses dulled, and in the majority of cases, after the fourth or
seventh day, the mind would wander." The disease was "stupefying."
About the fourth or seventh day, "red, or often purplish-red spots broke
out on the arms, back and chest, looking like flea-bites, though they
were often larger and in the shape of lentils." The "tongue became foul."
Fracastoro claimed that the disease was familiar in Cyprus and the
neighboring islands. In general, the appearance of the disease in the
eastern Mediterranean in the fifteenth century might raise the suspicion
that the germ was introduced by the expansionist Ottoman Empire,
which took Constantinople in 1453, surged west in the following decades under Mehmed II, and abortively invaded Italy in 1480. But this
is a question that requires further investigation.[39]

Genomic evidence, hopefully, may resolve important questions
about the evolutionary history of typhus. There is no doubt that the
disease, if it was not already present, became established across Europe
in the sixteenth century and was a primary ingredient in the mix of early
modern afflictions. It was also clearly present in the New World in the
second half of the same century, probably imported there from Europe
as invisible cargo on Spanish ships. Typhus was both endemic and epidemic, which is to say that it was a constant fixture in the background,
capable of violent flare-ups when circumstances proved conducive to
its transmission. Three factors above all promoted its spread: squalor,
density, and crisis. Wherever these prevailed, typhus followed. It was a
disease of the poor, the crowded, and the desperate.[40]

The London Bills of Mortality, one of our best sources for early modern cause-of-death data, indirectly highlight the role of typhus as both
an endemic and epidemic disease. The Bills of Mortality counted the
number of Londoners who died of "fever" each year, which was normally 10–20 percent of all deaths in the later seventeenth and eighteenth
centuries (see figure 9.5). Deaths from fever might encompass any number of minor diseases, but typhus and typhoid have plausibly enough
been thought to represent the leading causes within this category. In the
nineteenth century, typhus was recognized as a distinct disease and was

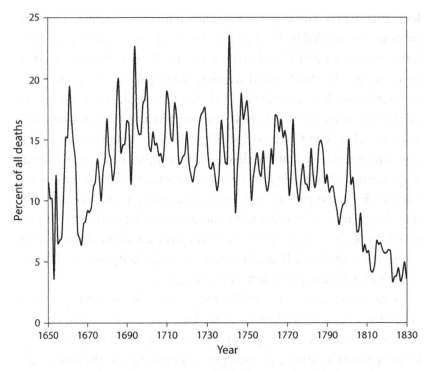

FIGURE 9.5. "Fevers" as a percentage of all deaths in London Bills of Mortality.

endemic in London, though it declined rapidly from the later 1870s thanks to public health efforts. But for centuries, typhus was a permanent health problem for the urban poor.[41]

Typhus was *the* great attendant of warfare in the early modern period. We do an injustice to history if we assume it was always so. The advent of the pathogen, combined with the scaling up of conflict, aligned in ways that made typhus a particularly important feature of these centuries. The army camp and the besieged city were the two great scenes of typhus outbreaks. The Italian Wars of the sixteenth century prefigured the kind of conflict that would spread over Europe; so too did the Ottoman-Habsburg wars of the period, where typhus became known as the *morbus hungaricus* and was associated with Hungarian armies. During the Thirty Years' War, typhus was second only to plague in its deadly work, and typhus dominated the first decade of the conflict.

Soldiers like Simplicius, infested with lice, were both victims and vectors of the disease. With the war raging on the continent, typhus also crossed the channel and caused an outbreak in the 1620s. The English poet John Donne caught the spotted fever in 1623, and the resulting *Devotions upon Emergent Occasions*—which gave us "no man is an island" and "never send to know for whom the bell tolls; it tolls for thee"—forms one of the most beautiful meditations on sickness ever written. The disease had a long future in Europe. Typhus haunted the Napoleonic Wars and remained a potent factor in military fortunes right through World War II.[42]

Famine also brought typhus in its tracks. Typhus frequently escalated to epidemic proportions in the midst of hunger and dearth. In the lean 1690s and 1740s, periods of extreme cold and famine across Europe, typhus was especially active. (The troubles of the 1690s triggered the famines in Scotland that helped to motivate the ill-fated Darien expedition, and much of France felt hunger following food scarcity.) In 1698 there was crop failure all over England, and the "spotted fever" soon followed. The early 1740s were a particularly straitened time across northern Europe. A series of anomalously cold years brought forth one of the last continent-wide subsistence crises. Typhus was epidemic across England, and for the last time the disease presumably accounted for more than a fifth of all deaths in London. It was perhaps the final reflex of the Malthusian "positive check" in England, which had already weakened considerably by this time.[43]

In Ireland, by contrast, the Great Famine in the 1840s was a devastating subsistence crisis. As we will see in chapter 11, the potato blight that caused the famine was a modern ecological crisis brought on by a global agricultural pest. But the Great Famine harkened back to the food shortages of the early modern period. It was unusual to have such an unmitigated episode of hunger and epidemic disease transpire so late in western Europe. What the famine makes excruciatingly clear is that during a severe food crisis, most death comes not from hunger itself but from infectious diseases that prey on the desperate. In the words of one eyewitness from Cork, "The scenes that presented themselves were such as no tongue or pen can convey the slightest idea of. In the first [home], six famished and ghastly skeletons, to all appearance dead, were huddled in a corner on some filthy straw, their sole covering what seemed a ragged horse-cloth and their wretched legs hanging about, naked above the knees. I approached in horror, and found by a low moaning they were alive, they were in fever—four children, a woman, and what had once been a man . . . in a few minutes I was surrounded by at least 200 of such phantoms, such frightful spectres as no words can describe. By far the greater number were delirious either from famine or from fever." In all, an estimated one million people perished, about one-eighth of the Irish population.[44]

By the nineteenth century, though, such episodes were becoming rare in Europe. The typhus epidemics of the 1740s were a turning point in England. They stimulated tremendous medical attention. Observers started to connect the dots between various manifestations of the fever. The common identity of jail fever, ship fever, hospital fever, and camp fever was recognized. Treatments started to change, as some doctors argued against the bloodletting of typhus patients. Fever hospitals were born, which not only protected other patients from typhus but also made it possible to provide supportive care to sufferers of the disease. Military medicine played a major role in describing the nature of the disease and advocating for good hygiene and sanitation to prevent it. A doctor who had served in the army recognized in 1780 that the poor in London suffered a form of the disease too. "Though the fever in the confined habitations of the poor does not rise to the same degree of violence as in jails and hospitals, yet the destruction of the human species occasioned by it must be much greater, from its being so widely spread among a class of people whose number bears a large proportion to that of the whole of the inhabitants."[45]

Typhus was thus not only a quintessential early modern disease; its prevention and treatment also helped to provoke some of the most enlightened medical science of the eighteenth century. To the extent that the ability to mobilize and concentrate masses of humans was an integral part of the transition to modernity, learning to mitigate the dangers of typhus played some small role in helping to make us modern.[46]

Plague Resurgent

William Lilly rose from humble origins to become the most eminent English astrologer of the seventeenth century. He was in his early twenties and newly arrived in London as a servant, when he lived through what his autobiography describes as the "greatest plague" there ever was in London. It was 1625. His master left the metropolis, taking his money and plate with him, leaving Lilly and one other servant to watch the house and execute the master's parish obligations, such as dispensing weekly alms. As the plague started to ramp up, Lilly did what anyone might do under the circumstances: he tells us he bought a bass viol and started taking lessons. He also spent his time bowling in the Lincoln's Inn Fields, with his friends Wat the Cobler and Dick the Blacksmith. In the face of the plague, Lilly was unruffled.[47]

The city itself was eerily quiet. "The most able people of the whole city and suburbs were out of town; if any remained, it were such as were engaged by parish offices to remain . . . the woeful calamity of that year was grievous, people dying in the open fields and in the open streets." The plague wiped out the priests in his parish (excepting one tough old priest "given to drink" and only able to preach "one quarter of an hour at a time," who came through fine). By August, "very few people had thoughts of surviving the contagion." Lilly's remarks are only a little exaggerated. The plague of 1625 was in fact one of the worst in London's history. Of a total population of around 206,000, 41,312 Londoners died, 26,350 of them of plague (according to the Bills of Mortality). The death toll amounted to 20 percent of the entire population of the metropolis. That was more than six times the normal annual mortality in the city. It is jarring to observe how a city could lose one-fifth of its residents in a single fatal year and yet, at the same time, life simply had to go on, music lessons and all.[48]

Although there is not a single name for it (like the Black Death), this wave of plague swept across Europe with gratuitous violence. The epidemic was first visible in the Low Countries by 1622, England and central Germany in 1625, southern France and Switzerland by 1628. In 1629, it crossed the Alps. The plague of 1629–30 in northern Italy was immortalized in Alessandro Manzoni's historical romance *The Betrothed*, virtually the national novel of Italy. In Milan, it had been a good half century since the last visitation of plague. Bad harvests and ongoing warfare—a satellite conflict of the Thirty Years' War known as the War of Mantuan Succession—had created misery and migration. Milan was ruled by a Spanish governor who downplayed the risk of the epidemic. The city was slow to declare a quarantine and inept in its enforcement. By late spring, a full-blown medical emergency was underway. The *lazaretto*—a kind of isolation hospital—became a pitiful scene, with sixteen thousand victims crowded together, desperate for food and care. It became impossible to bury all the dead with traditional solemnity, and corpses were heaved into giant pits outside the city.[49]

This plague was in reality just as devastating as Manzoni portrayed it. The disease took the lives of some 60,000 of Milan's 130,000 inhabitants. Proportionally, the death toll in Milan was more than twice what it was in London. But that only begins to account for the differences. In England the mortality was concentrated in London. Overall, the outbreak was barely a blip in the demographic history of England. In Italy, by contrast, Verona, Padua, and Mantua lost more than half of their populations. Venice and Bologna lost a third. Most importantly, the plague became pervasive in the countryside. Across northern Italy, with a population of 4 million (roughly the size of England), a total of 1,100,000 were carried to their graves. It was the worst mortality since the Black Death.[50]

The course of the seventeenth century in Europe is epitomized in these contrasts. It is the English experience, where the damage of the plague was minimal, that is peculiar. Between the 1620s and 1650s, continental Europe suffered from spells of bubonic plague worse than any since the Black Death. Moreover, the Thirty Years' War obscures the nature and extent of the plague in this century. Somehow, the medical catastrophe has hidden itself behind the military and political drama of the period. And that is only in Europe. More clearly than ever before, the plague was a factor across the Old World. In Mughal India, it erupted. In the waning hours of Ming China, it struck. For decades historians have debated whether to imagine this period as one of "global crisis," an all-encompassing stew of political, military, and natural disasters. Perhaps that construction makes it harder to recognize the demographic rupture in its midst. As in the fourteenth century, the plague was preceded, accompanied, and followed by other kinds of disaster, and yet it stands out as the focal point. In many ways, the hinge of the seventeenth century was this second Black Death.[51]

Throughout this period, plague and war were conjoined twins. The Italians believed that German mercenaries had carried the contagion with them across the Alps. Deaths from plague were almost accounted as collateral damage of war. This intimate association creates a genuine conceptual problem. The outbreaks of plague were an effect of other kinds of crisis, insofar as their incidence and magnitude were inseparable from the misery and dislocation engendered by famine and conflict. But the scale of death that was accomplished by the plague was all out of proportion to the troubles that provoked the epidemics. The course of events was swayed by the unpredictable severity and extreme variation of plague mortality.

The molecular evidence has helped to clarify an important question about the Second Plague Pandemic. The Black Death of the fourteenth century seeded local reservoirs of plague that persisted for centuries. Most outbreaks were thus probably amplifications spreading from foci in the west. The precise locations of these regional foci are unknown. Probably Syria, Anatolia, and the Balkans were part of an interconnected Mediterranean circuit. A compelling case has also been made for the Alps as a plague reservoir; the Alpine marmots that flourish there—distant cousins of the steppe rodents that are the plague's natural reservoir—may well have been a suitable host for the bacterium. A North Sea plague circuit also operated, and its reservoir remains unknown. It is not unreasonable to hope that more archaeological DNA samples will further clarify this picture, but for centuries, plague had taken hold as a domestic threat, simmering in nearby rodent populations.[52]

The viciousness of seventeenth-century plague was felt across the Old World. In China, the plague was present at the violent death of the Ming Dynasty. Torrential rains in 1640 brought floods, which were reversed in the following year by drought and a devastating plague of locusts. The drought continued for two more years and famine followed on its heels. The starvation was pitiful. In 1643 "there was a great epidemic. For several thousand *li* north and south, northwards to beyond the frontier and southwards to across the Yellow River, out of every ten households there was scarcely one that escaped." In 1644 the bubonic plague raged. One provincial gazetteer records that "In the autumn there was a great epidemic. The victims first developed a hard lump below the armpits or between the thighs or else coughed thin blood and died before they had time to take medicine. Even friends and relations did not dare to ask after the sick or come with their condolences. There were whole families wiped out with none to bury them." There is also unequivocal evidence for the spread of smallpox in the midst of this crisis. The Ming-Qing transition was a multifaceted medical and dynastic crisis.[53]

Plague also struck India. It is still uncertain whether the Black Death had reached India in the fourteenth century. The same uncertainty clouds epidemics in India through the sixteenth century. A famine struck in 1589–90 and was accompanied by great mortality, but it is impossible to assign responsibility to bubonic plague, and here too typhus and other pathogens may just as well have been to blame. From the 1610s, however, doubts are unnecessary. In 1615 the Mughal emperor, Jahangir, described "a great pestilence that appeared in some places in Hindustan" spreading in an arc from west to east, stretching from Punjab to Delhi, where it "desolated" the surrounding countryside. "This disease had never shown itself in this country. Physicians and learned men were questioned as to its cause. Some said that it came because there had been drought for two years in succession and little rain fell; others said it was on account of the corruption of the air which occurred through the drought and scarcity. Some attributed it to other causes." In Agra, "daily about 100 people, more or less, were dying of it. Under the armpits, or in the groin, or below the throat, buboes formed, and they died." He even observed the mass dying of rodents that preceded the human epidemic.[54]

Remarkably enough, an English diplomat named Thomas Roe was a witness both to the plague in India under Jahangir as well as a catastrophic outbreak a few years later in the Ottoman Empire. The correspondence of Roe, on assignment in Istanbul, chronicles the course of the deadly outbreak. His meticulous dispatches from summer 1625 are all the more poignant in that London was suffering a grievous plague epidemic simultaneously. By July, the mortality had risen to such a height that the mufti ordered prayers and processions, "which ceremonye is never used, untill the mortalitye exceed 1000 a day; which is easely knowne by the burials, that are all made without the walls." By the end of the month, "the sickness rageth as if it would dispeople the citty, and the villages adiacent." By the fall he estimated that "the great contagion, that hath carried away in this citty, and the suburbs, neare 200,000 people." The great Ottoman traveler Evliya Çelebi noted that the sultan "took a count of all the deaths during the worst of the plague and found that some 70,000 had perished in a week." Although plague was part of the general background of the disease environment in Istanbul and the Ottoman Empire, the limited sources give the sense that this was a distinctly severe outbreak.[55]

In Europe the course of the plague in the seventeenth century can be followed in more detail than in previous times, thanks to the abundance of surviving parish registers that offer pointillist detail on baptisms, burials, and marriages in village churches across western Europe. There is no doubting the overall pattern. The outbreaks were more infrequent than at any time since the fourteenth century. They were also more severe, with the notable exception of the British Isles and the Low Countries. The wealthy and populous heartlands of Europe were afflicted by two separate cycles of bubonic plague during the Thirty Years' War. The first struck in the middle of the 1620s. It simultaneously spread inward from the coastal regions, up the Rhine, and from the east, to coalesce in central Europe in 1625–26. Over the course of two years, "the greater part of Germany had been blanketed with outbreaks." Around half of all communities experienced a mortality spike five times the normal level. Something like 15 percent of the population perished.[56]

And yet, this epidemic was only an intense version of the familiar plague crisis. The cycle that followed in the 1630s was something else besides, a truly harrowing chapter in the history of European plague.

Not coincidentally, perhaps, the year 1630 marked the advent of the Swedes under Gustavus Adolphus and the most gruesome phase of the entire Thirty Years' War. From 1632, plague started to spread from Bohemia, tracking troop movements closely. Then it diffused throughout the Rhine valley and into southern Germany, before crossing into France and the Low Countries. The epidemic reached virtually all corners of human settlement, and its mortality toll was grim. According to a historian who has studied the parish records closely, "In terms of the percentage of the population estimated to have died in an area, loss of 10–15 percent of the inhabitants would be considered a severe regional crisis in earlier cycles, but in the period 1632–39, estimated losses of 40 percent were commonly approached or exceeded." Across wide parts of central Europe, population levels did not recover until the middle of the eighteenth century.[57]

Why did the war trigger such an exceptionally deadly pandemic? There is no completely satisfying answer. Troop movements aided and abetted the transmission of disease. The violence of war had left civilians susceptible. War brought hunger, which brought desperate migration and crowding. Other diseases too—above all, typhus, and to some extent probably relapsing fever, dysentery, and typhoid—exacerbated the medical crisis. Typhus often preceded and accompanied the plague outbreaks, and its ubiquity in the seventeenth century might be an underestimated factor in the ferocity of the epidemics in this period. The conditions of war made it hard to maintain order, hygiene, and sanitation. Rodents, fleas, and lice all flourished in the shadow of human misery.

The case of Italy in the seventeenth century demonstrates that neat explanations still lie out of reach. The outbreak of 1629–30 was horrific in northern Italy, and though the War of Mantuan Succession was in the background, and may have contributed to the arrival of the epidemic, the Italian peninsula was spared the kind of total war that ravaged central Europe. Northern Italy was home to a leading global economy, and its traditions of civic governance were as longstanding and sophisticated as those anywhere. Despite foreign domination, local governments functioned. To add to the puzzle, southern Italy was largely spared this outbreak, but a generation later, in the 1650s, it suffered a devastating plague epidemic to match that of the north. The classic demographic studies recognize the sheer magnitude of this outbreak in Italian history, and the economic historian Guido Alfani's recent work from parish sources confirms the pervasiveness and devastating toll of the plague.[58]

Plague, that most ecologically complex disease, is a riddle. Often, the best advice for trying to understand its mysterious ways is to follow the rodents, but there is no satisfying reason why the rodents, or insect vectors, of Italy proved particularly effective in spreading the plague. Some have trotted out the usual answer of last resort: perhaps a more virulent strain emerged. For now, the scope of the catastrophe defies complete understanding.

If the recrudescence of the plague in the seventeenth century is a puzzle, so is its disappearance thereafter. Let us defer for a moment consideration of the possible causes and simply describe the pattern. In the last third of the seventeenth century, plague ceased to afflict most of western Europe. An outbreak erupted in Marseilles in 1720 and represented the last spasm of the disease in this part of the continent. But the plague did not recede from the eastern Mediterranean, from Russia, or from Iran, all of which suffered calamitous outbreaks in the late eighteenth century. As we will see, in some sense, the Second Plague Pandemic never completely ended in the Middle East. All of which makes the fact that it vanished from western Europe, after rearing its head with such tremendous violence, even more enigmatic. Whatever alignment of circumstances allowed its cessation in the west, the end of the Second Plague Pandemic in Europe marks the passing of a biological era.[59]

Smallpox: Global Symmetries

In 1643, when Hong Taiji, the founding member of the Qing Dynasty (1636–1912), died, the elaborate funeral ceremonies held in his honor segregated the members of the imperial family into two groups: those who had had smallpox and those who had not. Terror of smallpox consumed the Manchu conquerors of China, and with good reason. The disease was always a wild card in the relations between the peoples of the far north, where smallpox was not established, and China, where it was endemic. The conquest of China required the Manchus to develop a sophisticated system of smallpox surveillance and containment, first applied to the army, then more generally. During the campaigns of conquest, military operations were suspended or redirected when smallpox stood in the path of the army.[60]

The disease was a "constant nightmare" for the ruling family. Hong Taiji was succeeded by his five-year-old son, the Shunzhi emperor (who ruled from 1643 to 1661). He was obsessed with avoiding smallpox. Not only was he a child upon assuming power, but he was also the first Manchu emperor to reside inside China. His palace included a *biduosuo*, a "shelter for keeping smallpox at bay," to which he frequently resorted. He fled Beijing when smallpox was epidemic and shunned public exposure when the disease was raging. In the interest of dynastic continuity, he promulgated a law that imperial rule could only pass to an heir who had already survived smallpox. (His son, the Kangxi emperor, was chosen in part because of this qualification.) All of these precautions did nothing for the Shunzhi emperor himself, who contracted smallpox and died at the age of 22.[61]

Contemporaneously, on the other end of Eurasia, smallpox was a specter over the British ruling house, the Stuarts (1603–1714). In no small part, the family's rule passed to the House of Hanover due to the indiscriminate violence of the disease. Henry, Duke of Gloucester, died of smallpox in 1661 at age twenty-one; it took Princess Mary in 1660 at age twenty-nine; Queen Anne survived it in 1677, but she had already lost a young brother and later her husband and two daughters to the disease, and possibly also her son, William, Duke of Gloucester, who died in 1700 at age eleven, bringing hopes of Stuart succession to an end. Her sister, Queen Mary II (daughter of James II and wife of William III of Orange), fell sick of the disease just before Christmas in 1694, at the age of thirty-two. Macaulay's melodramatic narrative of her demise is famous.[62]

> [A physician named] Radcliffe, who, with coarse manners and little book learning, had raised himself to the first practice in London

chiefly by his rare skill in diagnostics, uttered the more alarming words, smallpox. That disease, over which science has since achieved a succession of glorious and beneficent victories, was then the most terrible of all the ministers of death. . . . The smallpox was always present, filling the churchyard with corpses, tormenting with constant fear all whom it had not yet stricken, leaving on those whose lives it spared the hideous traces of its power, turning the babe into a changeling at which the mother shuddered, and making the eyes and cheeks of the betrothed maiden objects of horror to the lover. Towards the end of the year 1694 this pestilence was more than usually severe. At length the infection spread to the palace, and reached the young and blooming queen. She received the intimation of her danger with true greatness of soul. She gave orders that every lady of her bedchamber, every maid of honour, nay, every menial servant who had not had the smallpox should instantly leave Kensington House. She locked herself up during a short time in her closet, burned some papers, arranged others, and calmly awaited her fate.

William attended her bedside "night and day." By the end her face and trunk were covered with pustules, and she was vomiting blood. Mary took the sacrament and twice tried but failed to summon the strength "to take a last farewell of him whom she had loved so truly and entirely." In the small hours of December 28 her agony ended.[63]

The parallels between the Manchus and the Stuarts underscore the global dimensions of this disease. Recall, too, that the 1690s also witnessed the Great Southeastern Smallpox Epidemic across the future United States. Yet the history and geography of smallpox remain imperfectly understood. As we have already seen, the emergence of smallpox might be responsible for some of the pandemics of the early first millennium in Rome and East Asia. Throughout the Middle Ages, a smallpox-like disease was familiar across the Old World, but it was not always the deadly presence it later became. For example, in the tenth century, the doctor Rhazes considered smallpox infection to be a universal affliction, but not an acutely dangerous one. This reputation held all the way up to the sixteenth century. Fracastoro, in the same book that first clearly identified typhus, still thought of *variola* as a "salutary" disease that especially attacked children.[64]

Historians have often invoked autonomous changes in the virulence of pathogens when all other explanations fail. In this instance, however, the case is overwhelming. In one of the gems of medical historiography, Ann Carmichael and Arthur Silverstein confirmed, largely from Italian and English evidence, the longstanding suspicion that smallpox in early modern Europe transformed from an inconspicuous resident of the disease pool to a violent killer. The strain of the virus that had caused a benign, childhood disease across much of the Old World was replaced by a far more deadly variant, seemingly in the course of the sixteenth century. By the early seventeenth century, smallpox was installed alongside plague and typhus as a leading cause of early death, one of the quintessential pathogens of the early modern period.[65]

The molecular and written evidence concur that a virulent form of smallpox became a global menace in the early modern period. Where, exactly, did this more deadly version of the germ come from? Did the trade networks connecting Europe, Africa, and the New World stir evolutionary change? Were the New World outbreaks of the early sixteenth century, with the virus suddenly introduced to the dense low-latitude civilizations of the Americas, a chance for new strains to emerge? Or should we look, rather, to the thickening populations of Eurasia? At present, we do not know. One attractive possibility is that modern smallpox emerged in East Asia, but the evidence is only circumstantial. China had the world's largest population and its biggest cities throughout the late Middle Ages. And the amount of evidence for smallpox in China from the Northern Song period (907–1127) dwarfs the record from anywhere else. Smallpox was a ubiquitous pediatric disease known as the "gate of life or death." As in the West, the disease took an explosive turn later, and large-scale outbreaks became more frequent starting in the sixteenth century. One effort to make a comprehensive list of smallpox epidemics in China found only a handful prior to the 1520s and a basically continuous series of outbreaks thereafter.[66]

The history of inoculation throws a sidelight onto the global diffusion of smallpox. Inoculation (also known as variolation) is the practice of deliberately infecting a person with pathological matter from an infected person in order to induce a mild disease that hopefully leaves the inoculated patient with lasting resistance. Inoculation was the predecessor of vaccination and ranks as one of the first great medical innovations in human history. Joseph Needham held that Chinese physicians had developed inoculation as early as the eleventh century; in his view, it was closely guarded as a sort of trade secret for centuries. However, more critical review of the evidence has exposed the flimsy basis of this story and redated the origins of inoculation in China: "at least from the sixteenth century onwards, the Chinese adopted variolation. This technique was initially applied in the south of China and later gradually introduced to the north of China, Russia, Japan and Korea." It is tempting to think that inoculation is a response that reflects the intensification of smallpox in this period. Both modern smallpox and inoculation may have arisen in later Ming times (but see also chapter 10).[67]

The virulent modern strains of the smallpox virus quickly took advantage of global trade networks. Smallpox was behind the deadly outbreaks in the New World at least by 1519. Major epidemics are attested in Africa from the late sixteenth century. In Asia, too, smallpox epidemics flared in the sixteenth century. China was devastated in the 1580s and the 1640s. In Europe, deadly epidemics are attested from the sixteenth century, and in the seventeenth and eighteenth centuries smallpox came to occupy a leading place in the mortality regime. The force of a smallpox epidemic was terrifying, and when the disease did not kill, gruesome scars remained as a permanent reminder of infection. (The hard-luck Simplicius Simplicissimus survived smallpox, but he was left unrecognizable and unable to ply a living as a gigolo in consequence of his pitted face.) In the eighteenth century, smallpox was the single most threatening infectious disease in Europe. Plague receded. Typhus lurked. But smallpox raged.[68]

Smallpox single-handedly distorted the history of health and mortality in the eighteenth century. As we will see in the next chapter, its rise to dominance conceals the early progress that was otherwise underway. It became endemic in growing urban areas, and recurred repeatedly in the countryside. For town dwellers, it became a childhood disease, a rite of passage. For migrants who moved to the city, smallpox often provided a deadly welcome. When the disease reached populations where no one had been previously exposed to the infection, its effects were shocking. An epidemic on Iceland that started in 1707 carried off almost a quarter of the entire population.[69]

To appreciate the place of smallpox in history is to recognize its particular role in shaping the disease pool of the early modern world. The history of smallpox in this period is truly global. And like the other great scourges of early modernity, the imposing dangers of smallpox called forth ingenious responses—in this case, inoculation.

Divergence, Disease, and State Capacity

The period between about 1550 and 1750 was the scene of the Little Divergence. Everywhere, at the beginning of this period, agrarian economies had much in common. By most measures—per capita income, urbanization—it is difficult to distinguish the most technically advanced economic regions of Asia and Europe. And within Europe, Italy seemed the most likely site of transformational growth. In the mid-sixteenth century, the role that England and the Low Countries would come to play was far from self-evident. Yet by the time King William sat watching his wife die convulsively of smallpox, at the end of the seventeenth century, the ground had decisively shifted.[70]

There is little doubt that the mortality shocks of the seventeenth century were destructive. Although the long-term effects of the Black Death are debated, in this case the regions that suffered most found that their development was stalled at a momentous juncture of human history. The crisis wrecked accumulated capital, destabilized markets, and disrupted urbanization. Within Europe, for instance, Italy was hard hit by pestilence and entered a profound slump. By contrast, the Atlantic-facing regions of northwestern Europe were less devastated by the mortality shocks, and they were soon ascendant. Their rise was much more than a mere geographic relocation of economic energy. When population growth resumed here in the later seventeenth century, the Malthusian cycle was weakened and eventually broken. Real wage levels were maintained or even increased, despite demographic expansion. It is one of the enduring ironies in the history of social thought that Malthus was most emphatically wrong about his own society, where long-term intensive growth had begun.[71]

The modern regime of growth started to take shape. The next chapter tells that story. Health, human capital, and the control of infectious disease had an important part to play. But we can detect the first stirrings of the Great Escape in the confrontation between modernizing societies and the unholy trinity of smallpox, plague, and typhus. Consider, in particular, the waning of the bubonic plague in the West. Its disappearance, as we have noted, is an enduring puzzle, variously attributed to natural or human causes. The ongoing evolution of the pathogen Y. pestis has been suggested, but so far the ancient DNA evidence does not support the idea that genetic changes can explain the end of the pandemic. Another classic explanation is that the black rat (which shamelessly colonizes human habitats) was displaced by the bigger, meaner, but more reclusive brown rat. And, more obscurely, changes in the populations of rodent reservoirs like marmots or jerboas could have played a role. The fact that the First Plague Pandemic petered out in the mid-eighth century without strong human intervention adds to the plausibility of a purely natural explanation. In this view, western European societies were simply lucky that the plague disappeared at a pivotal moment.[72]

Conversely, human factors may have played a part. The plague did not just disappear on its own—it was disappeared, by human design. Better construction and the use of brick instead of timber created microenvironments less hospitable to rodent infestation. It has also been argued that the rise of arsenic mining and the creation of a rat-poison industry helped bring rodent populations under control. But by far the most persuasive explanations center on the institution of quarantine. Quarantine was a late-medieval invention, but from the mid-seventeenth century, its enforcement was more vigorous (see figure 9.6). Information about infection in foreign ports became more widespread and more reliable. Furthermore, the creation of a giant overland *cordon sanitaire* by the Austrians in the eighteenth century surely helped to insulate

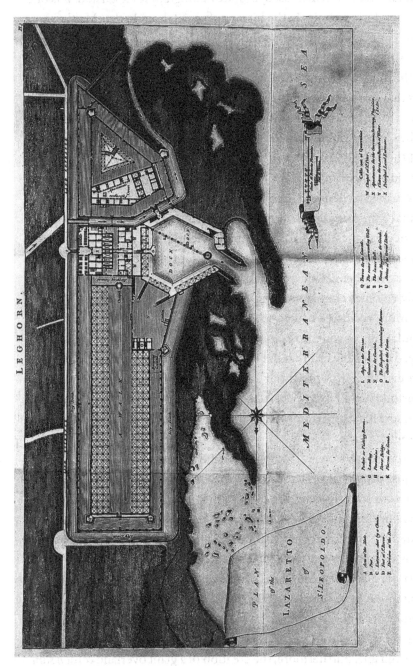

FIGURE 9.6. Lazaretto at Livorno, Italy (Leghorn). Such quarantine facilities were instrumental in disrupting transmission of the plague. Wellcome Collection (CC BY 4.0).

all of Europe. A militarized strip stretching a thousand miles from the Adriatic to the mountains of Transylvania, this heavily patrolled zone was a systematic buffer against one of the major routes of bacterial transmission.[73]

The end of the plague in western Europe resists tidy explanation, but perhaps the most decisive change was in the nature and power of the state. The general crisis helped to generate more powerful, more centralized states. In the well-known formulation of Charles Tilly, "War made the state, and the state made war." In 1500, there were 127 sovereign states in Europe. By 1800, there were only 75. A semifeudal world of overlapping, hierarchical sovereignties was slowly replaced by an order organized around clearly demarcated territorial nation-states. The eruption of plague in Marseilles is instructive. On a local level, it was an egregious failure of the quarantine system, and it was recognized as such. But energetic action from Paris confined the disaster to a small region in the south, and this containment might be reckoned a victory for vigorous centralized statecraft. The British government, despite vociferous, self-serving lobbying from merchants, enforced quarantine and managed to keep the plague out, as it did on numerous occasions in the eighteenth century. In all, though there have been (and remain) thoughtful skeptics, the judgments of the historian Paul Slack remain convincing: though never perfectly effective, human interventions to control plague made the difference, and increasingly so.[74]

The troubles of the seventeenth century might thus be seen as a particularly consequential instance of the dialectic between social progress, unintended biological feedbacks, and subsequent human adaptation. The scaling up of famine and war created epidemiological disaster, which in turn proved conducive to more centralized solutions. The general crisis of the seventeenth century was not the last spasm of the old regime but, rather, the beginning of a new, violent, and ongoing phase of global combat between humanity and its microbial enemies.

PART IV

Fossils

10

The Wealth and Health of Nations

The Great Escape

Up to around 1700, life on earth was short and full of sorrow. Most everyone except for members of a narrow elite was poor. Across the planet, annual per capita incomes ranged from about $500 to $1,000 in today's terms. Life expectancy was below thirty years, maybe a little higher in some places, and lower in the tropics and in towns. Most people died of infectious disease. Income and life expectancy might oscillate, but these were fluctuations rather than sustained trends. In the first edition of his essay on population, Malthus claimed, "With regard to the duration of human life, there does not appear to have existed from the earliest ages of the world to the present moment the smallest permanent symptom or indication of increasing prolongation." Similarly, the human lot might transiently improve when a new technology was invented, or when a pestilence reduced the population, but inexorably, demographic growth would swallow up the gains and return the poor to "severe distress."[1]

For most of our history as a species, this regime of stagnation prevailed. But over the course of the last three centuries, much of humanity has escaped from the doom of poverty and early death. The economist Angus Deaton has fittingly called this achievement "the Great Escape." Continuous technological advance has vastly increased human productivity and per capita incomes. Infectious diseases have been brought under control. Wealth and long life replaced poverty and premature death, first in England, then in western Europe and its settler offshoots, and ultimately over most of the planet. We can agree with the health economists David Bloom and David Canning: "It is difficult to conceive of a more remarkable global human achievement over the past two centuries than the greater-than-doubling of life expectancy."[2]

How the Great Escape happened is perhaps the most profound question of human history. As the economist Robert Lucas famously said, once you start thinking about the mystery of economic growth, it is hard to think about anything else. The puzzle involves at a bare minimum three inseparable questions. Why did the transition to a regime of growth happen? Why did it happen when and where it happened? And what is the relationship between economic growth and the mortality decline?[3]

This chapter, and the two that follow, synthesize and contribute to an already ample literature by exploring the last of these three questions: the relationship between wealth and health in modern history. Wealth and health are strongly associated almost any way we look at them—over time, within societies, or across countries. Over time: societies became wealthier and healthier during roughly the same time period. Within societies: richer people live longer, poorer people die sooner. Across countries: richer countries are healthier countries. This correlation is not just striking; it is one of the most robust in the social sciences (figure 10.1).[4]

But as any freshman economics major could tell you, correlation is not causation, and there are several conceivable explanations for the association between wealth and health. A first possibility is that higher incomes cause better health: to get healthy, a society should get rich. A second possibility is that the causal arrow runs in precisely the opposite direction: improvements in health result in economic growth. In this view, to get rich, a society should get healthy. There is also a third possibility: that some other factor or factors can account for both gains in life expectancy and economic growth. And of course, none of these explanations is mutually exclusive. The right answer involves a combination of all three.[5]

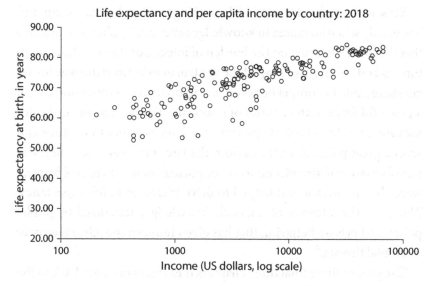

FIGURE 10.1. The Great Correlation: national life expectancy and per capita incomes, 2018. (Source: World Bank)

We will explore each of these channels in due course. All of them mattered for the Great Escape. Economic growth indeed contributed to gains in life expectancy. The reverse is also true, and the control of infectious disease proved instrumental for economic growth. But ultimately, the most powerful factors are those that have simultaneously driven increases in economic output as well as improvements in human health: namely, knowledge of the natural world and powerful states that coordinate human action. Science and statecraft are the keys to the Great Escape. Over the last three centuries, humans have learned how to control infectious disease and how to exploit natural resources with ever more efficient and powerful technologies. In the words of the economist David Weil, "The contemporaneous advance of income and health in the leading countries over the last several centuries (after millennia of stagnation) is explained largely by changes in knowledge. More specifically, productive knowledge and health knowledge advanced together, driven by the underlying advance of science and the spirit of experimentation born of the Enlightenment."[6]

Yet science in the abstract can do nothing to affect human health, and it was only when advances in knowledge influenced policy and practice that they had a bearing on the burden of infectious disease. Thus, institutions and culture also shaped the control of infectious disease. Stronger states, able to compel behavior and to provision public goods, were a powerful force in the control of infectious disease. The public health movement, which took shape from the later eighteenth century and scored great political victories from the later nineteenth century, was transformational. Broader efforts to popularize new concepts of hygiene were also important and helped to drive increases in life expectancy. Thus, it is the advance of scientific knowledge, actualized by public policy and private behavior, that has given humans the advantage over microbial threats.[7]

The goal of these final three chapters is to trace this story back to the eighteenth century. This chapter is focused on western Europe, and Britain in particular, where the Great Escape started. But the goal of these chapters, collectively, is to bring a global perspective to bear on the theme of modernization. This approach has several advantages. It will highlight the pervasive influence of geography on the origins and course of both economic development and changes in health. In addition, it will help us to see that progress in the control of infectious disease started earlier than often assumed. The early stages of the mortality decline need to be part of the story in order to appreciate that negative health feedbacks have been a constant feature of modern growth. In other words, modern growth has only made the challenge of controlling infectious disease even greater. Urbanization, demographic expansion, modern transportation technologies, and intensified pressure on natural resources have made the ecology of infectious disease progressively *more* dangerous for humans. Humanity's adaptations thus had to outrun challenges that were simultaneously gathering steam. As we will see in the next chapter, these cross-currents are important for understanding the Great Escape in global terms. Progress, to put it mildly, has not been smooth, frictionless, or equally distributed.

We can summarize the progress achieved in western Europe and its colonial offshoots between about 1670 and 1820 as the *early* health transition. In 1971, professor of public health Abdel Omran proposed the framework of an "epidemiological transition" to explain the decline of mortality, and although his model has its limitations, he was prescient in emphasizing this early phase as the "age of receding pandemics." The early health transition was that and more. We should underscore four consequential changes that characterize the early health transition: the stabilization of epidemic mortality, modest but meaningful gains in life expectancy, changes in the causes of death and age structure of mortality, and the entrenchment of class-based differences in health. By the end of this period, the control of infectious disease remained highly incomplete. And yet truly systemic progress had been made, and we cannot understand the complex feedbacks that ensued without understanding these prior developments.[8]

The main driver behind the early health transition was the progress of scientific knowledge, translated into practice and policy. Even though germ theory and robust public health policies still lay in the future, we should not pass over the advances of Enlightenment medicine. A new empiricist mindset, and a more intense focus on preventative medicine, carried material consequences for public health. Enlightenment approaches to health worked—sort of. At the same time, European states (and their colonial offshoots) continued to consolidate, and their capacity to execute policies continued to expand. We will take two figures as symbols of the changes that unfolded in this early period: Samuel Pepys and John Pringle. Both men served as president of the Royal Society of London for Improving Natural Knowledge, Pepys from 1684 to 1686 and Pringle from 1772 to 1778. Although separated by less than a century, they embodied different attitudes to hygiene and health, and they help us measure the distance traveled in this consequential phase of the transition to modernity.[9]

Growth and Health: Causes and Connections

The Industrial Revolution is, in the most elemental sense, a historical event that started in eighteenth-century Britain. It was characterized by the invention of machines that transformed production in core industries. First the textile, mining, and metal industries were revolutionized by the mechanization of processes that had relied on handcraft and human or animal power. Machines like the steam engine and spinning jenny symbolize the combination of ingenuity and practical application that define the Industrial Revolution. From the perspective of deep history, what made the Industrial Revolution so transformational was the development of machines that harnessed the potential of fossil fuels—first coal, later hydrocarbons—to augment or replace humanity's dependence on living phytomass as a source of energy. In the words of John McNeill, "the adoption of fossil fuels made us modern." Since the onset of industrialization, human energy use has increased one hundredfold.[10]

The Industrial Revolution marks the transition from stagnation to modern growth. In the regime of stagnation, real wages were held near the subsistence level in the long run. "In the long run" is an important qualification—one that Malthus had already noted. Whenever trade expanded, or technologies improved, or populations sharply fell, people could enjoy periods of relief from misery. These periods, sometimes called cycles of efflorescence, could last for decades or even centuries. Cycles of efflorescence recurred throughout human history, but they never led to sustained or breakaway growth that materially improved the lot of the average person. Technical improvements were slow, and thus the end result was more people, not more per capita output. In the regime of growth, by contrast, there is long-run intensive growth. The level of output not only increases in aggregate, but also per capita. Thus, sustained increases in real wages are possible. Even though population continued to rise during and after the Industrial Revolution, the level of productivity has continued to rise even faster, and human well-being has vastly improved.[11]

The contrast between western Europe and China is illustrative, not because China was somehow fundamentally backward and incapable of growth but precisely because China was consistently one of the most technologically dynamic regions throughout the history of our species. Yet China remained locked in the Malthusian trap during the eighteenth and nineteenth centuries. New technologies (most importantly, the adoption of American crops like maize and potatoes) produced more people but not more per capita wealth. The population of China nearly tripled between 1500 and 1900, but incomes remained at the subsistence level, close to $600 per person per year in modern terms. The increased output in the agricultural sector "failed to free the Chinese economy from the stranglehold of Malthusian forces" and "underscores the sharp contrast between Europe and China in their diverging growth trajectories."[12]

How did societies spring loose from the trap that had held fast for millennia? A first cause of economic growth was already described by Adam Smith in *An Inquiry into the Nature and Causes of the Wealth of Nations* (1776). For Smith, the basic cause of growth was to be found in the miracle of trade. Market exchange facilitates specialization, division of labor, and efficient resource allocation. As he observed in the late eighteenth century, the factory system, dependent upon the division of labor, had increased productivity and thus output per capita. This kind of growth is known as Smithian growth. Smithian growth was important during cycles of efflorescence in premodern times. The Romans, for example, enjoyed meaningful economic growth largely because of trade. But the Romans, like all other preindustrial societies, failed to break free from the Malthusian trap. Even at the height of the Roman efflorescence, annual per capita incomes were less than $1,000 in today's terms. As for most of premodern history, the middle class was tiny, and the road to riches was through violent appropriation or extracting rents.[13]

A second proximate cause of economic growth is technical innovation. Modern growth is technology led. In preindustrial times, technological advance was relatively sluggish and limited. Therefore, prosperity was modest and transient, and it was inevitably consumed by population growth. But the steam engine and spinning jenny were the beginning of a tidal wave of innovation that has still not stopped: what the Austrian-American economist Joseph Schumpeter famously called "the perennial gale of creative destruction." In the Schumpeterian vision, growth is driven by technological and organizational innovations that enhance productivity. This kind of growth is the growth of the inventor, the engineer, and the entrepreneur. It is the disruptive innovation of the railway, the automobile, and the airplane. Over the past three centuries, technical innovation has continued to improve the material condition of humanity.[14]

If trade and technology are the most important direct causes of economic growth, there are also intermediate factors that shape the efficiency of markets and the pace of technological innovation. Development economists (and economic historians) are often interested in these intermediate factors because they help to account for differences in performance between countries. Effective institutions—things like the protection of private property rights, efficient enforcement of contracts, and limits on arbitrary government authority—are a potent factor in fostering growth. So is human capital. Healthy and educated people are on average more productive and more skilled. They are also more inventive—more capable of scientific discovery and technical innovation. Science has been instrumental in generating and sustaining modern growth. Knowledge of the natural world, and the application of that knowledge by engineers and entrepreneurs, has been responsible for the technical innovations that have massively increased human productivity. Thus, cultural or institutional factors that promote scientific discovery and its application for productivity-enhancing ends contribute to economic growth.[15]

Why, then, did modern growth begin in England? This is an old question that has been reinvigorated thanks to the stimulus provided by scholars who have argued that parts of China were as economically developed as western Europe until almost 1800. On this view, European leadership was both late and highly contingent upon such fortuitous geographical factors as the coal deposits of England and easy access to the raw materials of North America. Yet the revisionist challenge has also led to more rigorous demonstrations that the transition to growth was not so sudden or accidental. The takeoff to modern growth required a lengthy ramp-up, what the economic historian Jan Luiten van Zanden has called "the long road to the Industrial Revolution."[16]

By 1700, real wages were higher and human capital more developed in western Europe than anywhere else. In England, a number of geographic, institutional, and cultural factors aligned to allow a cycle of efflorescence to become a more permanent shift to the regime of growth. The Atlantic economy stimulated a sophisticated market in goods and services. Merchants enjoyed unusual political clout. The power of the crown was limited, and property rights were secure. England had high levels of human capital and a skilled labor force. Most importantly, it had a "culture of growth" that channeled scientific discovery toward useful ends, like engines and labor-saving machines. For instance, the Royal Society of London for Improving Natural Knowledge was founded in 1660; emblematically, the society's charter called for it to advance "the sciences of natural things and of useful arts" by trusting only "the authority of experiments."[17]

By the late seventeenth century, England's workers were already enjoying relatively high wages. Wages were high not because labor was particularly scarce but, rather, because England's workers were productive. They were relatively healthy (by premodern standards) and highly skilled. High wages (that is, a high cost of labor) created a strong incentive to find mechanical alternatives to replace or amplify human labor, and England's coal beds provided the fuel. The fact that the British sat atop a great "carboniferous crescent . . . stretching from Silesia to the Scottish lowlands" was serendipitous but hardly determinative; there is a lot of coal in the world, and England had long since learned to import raw materials and manufactures efficiently when needed. The concatenation of human capital, a culture of useful knowledge, favorable institutions, and fossil energy lit the spark of transformation. Across the eighteenth century, per capita output grew even as the population expanded (see figure 10.2). In the nineteenth century, after a brief lull, growth was even more pronounced, thanks to a wave of innovations we will consider in the next chapter, known as the Second Industrial Revolution.[18]

But the advent of modern economic growth is only half of the Great Escape. The freedom from infectious disease is its equally important counterpart. Over the past three centuries, humanity has left behind a world of pestilence and premature death, and we have come to expect stability and long life. Before the modern decline in mortality, most people died of infectious disease, so the revolutionary rise in life expectancy is

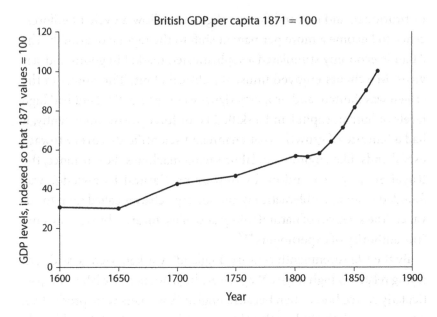

FIGURE 10.2. Leading the way in the Great Enrichment: British GDP per capita. (Source: Broadberry, Custodis, and Gupta 2015)

largely (but not completely) synonymous with the control of infectious disease. In other words, the decline in mortality was characterized by profound changes in the main causes of death, from diseases caused by microorganisms to diseases like cancer, heart disease, diabetes, neuro-degenerative conditions, and other organ diseases.[19]

The secular decline in mortality happened almost precisely when and where the transition to modern growth first occurred: in Britain, western Europe, and European settler societies around the globe. It might seem intuitive, then, that improvements in health were a byproduct of economic growth, and this view has had illustrious champions, including the medical historian Thomas McKeown. McKeown made his case by contending that medical interventions were ineffective during the period of the mortality decline. Antibiotics and vaccines (other than the smallpox vaccine) were brought into use *after* the major gains in life expectancy had already been accomplished. Whatever explanation was left must, therefore, be true. He argued that economic development improved nutrition, thus enhancing the body's ability to resist infection.

Indeed, nutritional deficiency is often important in clinical outcomes during infection. Measles, for instance, is a dangerous disease, but far more so when it infects a child whose body is already stressed. Deprivation and disease go hand in hand; ergo, the freedom from deprivation spelled freedom from disease.[20]

Nutrition is only one of the channels through which economic growth can influence health outcomes. Economic growth funds investments in health infrastructure: wealthier societies can build massive and expensive water treatment facilities, for example. Higher incomes allow people to live in better, and less crowded, housing. As we will see, all of these channels played a part in the control of infectious disease. And yet, despite its intuitive appeal, the link between economic growth and improved health has proven to be relatively weak, and certainly not the predominant factor in the strong correlation between wealth and health. Maybe the most powerful demonstration of this was offered by the demographer Samuel Preston. Studying the dramatic gains in life expectancy around the world in the twentieth century, he showed that the structural relationship between income and life expectancy had changed radically. Over time, it became possible to achieve higher life expectancy at lower levels of income, and in his estimate, only about one-third of the increase in life expectancy could be explained by improvements in income. Something else—namely, medical knowledge and health policy—had to explain why people stopped dying of infectious disease prematurely and attained longer life.[21]

As we will see in chapter 12, Preston was concerned with the global decline of mortality in the twentieth century, but the lessons apply to the deeper past as well. Consider that consistent class differences in health outcomes only appeared in the eighteenth century. Before modern times, people who did enjoy higher incomes did not necessarily live longer lives. Roman emperors—who ate lavishly and lived in luxuriant palaces—died on the same schedule as their humblest subjects. A British aristocrat up to the end of the seventeenth century had no greater prospects for long life than the average bloke. But by 1800, stark class gradients in mortality had emerged. Something had changed that allowed the educated upper classes to convert their social advantage to biological advantage. Namely, the rich increasingly had access to new ideas and new technologies that prolonged their lives.[22]

What about causal mechanisms running in the other direction, from health to wealth? There are several channels through which good health contributes to economic growth. Healthier individuals are on average more productive workers. They attain higher levels of human capital, in part because the burden of disease during childhood shapes physiological and cognitive development, and in part because people who have the privilege of living in a state of good health also seek and achieve higher levels of education. Where life is short and uncertain, it is hard to plan for the long term and invest years of unproductivity acquiring knowledge and skills. By the same logic, reductions in the disease burden increase savings and decrease risky behavior.[23]

Health also shapes fertility. Where mortality is high due to the burden of infectious disease, fertility is also high to offset the inevitable loss of children. Lower fertility not only improves the health of children but also allows more parental investment in a small number of offspring. Further, lower fertility is associated with later marriage for women, female empowerment, and greater market participation. Areas of northern Europe, where malaria and other vector-borne diseases were largely absent, may have had lower levels of fertility for centuries. As far back as can be measured, the societies of northwestern Europe practiced what is known as the European Marriage Pattern, in which women marry relatively late. Women from southern Europe married earlier, and women in South Asia and East Asia earlier still. As the eminent demographer E. A. Wrigley argued, "The European marriage system is a 'luxury' that populations through much of the traditional world may have been unable to afford. Where endemic diseases were many and fatal, where epidemic diseases were frequent and devastating, where food supplies were subject to violent and unpredictable fluctuations, or where some combination of these dangers prevailed, early and universal marriages may have been mandatory" because death rates were so high.[24]

Although the effects of health on economic development have been carefully studied in the context of the past century, it is plausible that

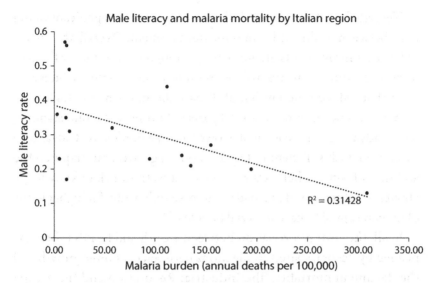

FIGURE 10.3. Regional malaria burden and literacy rates (in 1821), Italy.
(Malaria burden: compiled by author from late nineteenth-century official data;
literacy: see Ciccarelli and Weisdorf 2018.)

these mechanisms acted to give western Europe a head start in earlier times. Even before the onset of modern growth, European societies, especially in the northwest, enjoyed lower mortality rates. The same is probably true of Japan. As dire as the premodern disease environment was in comparison to that of our own times, life expectancies may already have been in the low thirties, which is high by premodern global standards. Longer life expectancy created a lower-pressure demographic system (i.e., with lower fertility, later marriage, and/or more flexibility in the female age at first marriage). These patterns are evident in, for example, the geography of development within Italy in modern times (see figure 10.3). The territorial boundary of falciparum malaria, as we have seen, cut across the peninsula, creating steep natural gradients in the disease burden. These health inequities created different patterns of marriage and disparate rates of human capital formation. Even prior to industrialization, literacy rates were much higher in the north than the south, suggesting that deep geographical features shaped the course of development in Italy.[25]

Nevertheless, it has proven difficult to demonstrate significant causal links between health and economic development. Overall, the effects of health improvements are not strong enough to account for the patterns of growth. There are striking examples where dramatic interventions that reduced the burden of disease did not generate higher incomes or economic growth. And if parts of Europe had a long-standing health advantage in the form of a lower disease burden, that advantage was not in itself sufficient to trigger modern growth, but required the addition of some other factors. Conceivably, the stock of knowledge about the natural world first had to increase sufficiently for higher levels of human capital to have material benefits.[26]

In all, the strong correlation between wealth and health is best explained by deeper, shared connections between economic growth and the decline in mortality. The Industrial Revolution and the escape from premature death have the same root causes, which are the progress of human understanding of the natural world and the application of that knowledge. The clearest evidence for this link undoubtedly comes from the twentieth century, when major discoveries like antibiotics and DDT diffused quickly, with sudden and synchronous effects across societies at very different levels of economic development. But again, the pattern is much older, and it goes back to the eighteenth century, to the Enlightenment.[27]

Knowledge in the abstract, however, is not enough. Ideas are free to copy, and they travel at the speed of thought. So what stopped progress in the control of infectious disease from being even more synchronous? Why were there such stark differences in health, both within and between countries? In part it was because wealth does influence health outcomes. In part it was because of geography and underlying natural differences in disease ecology. But it was also because institutions and culture shape the application of scientific knowledge. Improvements in life expectancy are generated not by ideas alone but by ideas that are put into action, especially by capable governments that care about the health of their citizens, and by cultures that translate scientific advances into behavioral adaptations. And, as we will see in chapter 11, imperialism also shaped the course of modernization; colonization deprived

societies of autonomy over their own citizens during a particularly turbulent and transformational moment. State capacity, power, and culture
are thus part of the story, and advances in knowledge had to be translated into action in order for the effects to be fully felt.

There is still much to be learned about the relationship between politics, institutions, and health in the past. But what is clear is that public
institutions have been profoundly important in advancing human
health. The control of infectious disease, by its very nature, requires
collective and coordinated action. To put it in economic terms, markets
that distribute goods via private consumption choices are genuinely bad
at providing solutions to the control of infectious disease: pervasive
factors include information failures (Will I get sick?), externalities (If I
dump my waste in the gutter, or go to the store with a cough, my neigh-
bor is the one who might catch a disease.), and public goods problems
(Who pays for the big water treatment facility?). Societies that were
good at solving collective action problems were thus most effective in
controlling infectious disease. The question then becomes why modernizing states were successful in doing so, and why some were more
successful than others.[28]

Part of the answer is simple: because states became more powerful
in modern times. By any measure, state capacity increased dramatically
between 1700 and 1900. States became more centralized, more able to
tax their populations, more able to force compliance with a broader set
of rules, and so on, to a greater degree than ever before. In fact, public
health was a driving force in the growth of the modern state, requiring
and justifying more intrusive interventions. Effective states had to do
two very different kinds of things: (1) ensure compliance with costly
and inconvenient rules (quarantine, compulsory vaccination, notification, labor and food safety laws, etc.) and (2) provide public goods (like
basic welfare, education, health care, and, most directly, infrastructure
like water treatment). Those states that were effective on both of these
fronts improved the health of their populations.[29]

The control of infectious disease was not only the achievement of
states, however. Culture and civil society could foster new attitudes and
behavioral changes that helped to curb the transmission of germs.

Mediating institutions of civil society have also helped to improve human health, especially during the progressivist high tide of the public health movement. Think, for instance, of the role of the Boy Scouts in fostering the spread of window screens and fly swatters to control insect vectors. Here, too, there is still much to be learned, but we can postulate that high levels of education, respect for science and empiricism, and democratic or communitarian values that promote sacrifice for the common good were all at times conducive to beneficial adaptations.

In the conventional story, the control of infectious disease was accomplished in the course of two or three generations beginning around 1870, first in western Europe and its settler societies. Rapid industrialization galvanized the public health movement. Germ theory provided a scientific basis for new interventions to control disease. And the formation of modern states with sufficient regulatory power allowed the implementation of effective public health measures.[30]

There is obviously much that is true in this account. Sustained improvements in life expectancy can be dated to about the 1870s, and the successes of the public health movement were indeed a watershed. But we only see a slice of the whole story if we start in the later nineteenth century, cutting off the centuries-long interplay among technological progress, negative feedbacks, and subsequent adaptation. The rise of cities in the later Middle Ages had already stimulated early forms of public health, and the severity of plague provoked stricter modes of quarantine and isolation. It is true that up to around 1700, human societies had little to show for their efforts in terms of average life expectancy. But in the eighteenth century, that started to change.

The early health transition was achieved with medical science that now appears obsolete, yet many of the recommendations of medical science were salutary. The historian James Riley has called this body of thought "environmental medicine." It was in many ways built on a more expansive version of older humoral doctrines, overlaid with an empiricist spirit. Preventative medicine increasingly promoted a war on filth, on dirty water, on bugs, on marshes, on closed and crowded spaces. These campaigns brought real benefits. There is thus an important intellectual continuity between Enlightenment medicine and the broader public health movement of the nineteenth century.[31]

This longer perspective helps us see the powerful negative health feedbacks generated by industrialization and the rise of global capitalism. For several decades in the mid-nineteenth century, progress stalled, even in western Europe where early gains had been achieved. As we will see in the next chapter, the emergence of new diseases, and the recrudescence of old ones, proved devastating around the globe. To understand the interplay of health, wealth, and power in the formation of the modern world, we need to see this story in full planetary perspective. The narrative is not one of unbroken progress, but one of countervailing pressures between the negative health feedbacks of growth and humanity's rapidly expanding but highly unequal capacities to control the threats to our health.

The Early Health Transition

Samuel Pepys (rhymes with *beeps*) was a Londoner, a graduate of Cambridge, a member of Parliament, and a high-ranking administrator of the Admiralty (figure 10.4). He survived the Great Plague of London in 1665. Pepys moved in the highest intellectual circles, and from 1684 to 1686 he was president of the Royal Society. During his tenure as president, the society published Isaac Newton's *Principia*, whose title page thus carries Pepys's imprint. But his name is immortal for other reasons: namely, from 1660 to 1669, Pepys kept what amounts perhaps to the most unfiltered diary in the history of the English language.[32]

The diary of Samuel Pepys is an entrée to the experience of daily life in late seventeenth-century London. There is an ample modern literature on the conditions of life in premodern cities. Sometimes these accounts indulge a lopsided focus on the dirty and disgusting circumstances that our ancestors endured. We should not imagine that our forebears were indifferent to living in filth. In fact their frustrated efforts and unfulfilled desires testify all the more poignantly to the magnitude of the challenges they faced. Despite earnest efforts to practice rudimentary hygiene, the technical and organizational capacities of premodern

Painted by John Hayls.   Etched by C.O. Murray

FIGURE 10.4. Samuel Pepys in an engraving for the 1825 edition
of his book, from a painting by G. Kneller. Pepys authored the
most unfiltered diary in the English language, perhaps ever.

cities were often overwhelmed by the challenges of maintaining public
health. Pepys's diary is a valuable text in this regard, because it is neither
normative nor polemical. With all the usual caveats about a sample size
of one, we can take his intimate diary as a snapshot of how a reasonably
affluent and highly intelligent Englishman lived just *before* the early
health transition.[33]

Pepys' government job entitled him to a handsome dwelling on
Seething Lane, near the Tower of London in the oldest part of the city.
Before the Great Fire (1666), London was still a town of wood and
earth, of cobbled streets that sloped inward to drain runoff. There were

few houses with piped water, and fewer still with plumbing to carry off waste. Chamber pots were the norm. One night Pepys came home to find "my wife and maid Ashwell had between them spilt the pot of piss and turd upon the floor and stool and God knows what, and were mighty merry washing of it clean. I took no notice." He once walked into his own house and stumbled upon Lady Sandwich in the middle of a necessary act, but Pepys handled it with grace. "I perceive by my dear Lady's blushing that in my dining-room she was doing something upon the pott; which I also was ashamed of and so fell to some discourse."[34]

Food quality standards were lax. The freshness of meat was judged by whether its smell could be cooked away. Despite the sequelae, Pepys could not resist oysters, which are mentioned more than seventy times in his diaries. "While I was at dinner with my wife I was sick, and was forced to vomitt up my oysters again, and then I was well." Pepys would cut into his fish to find it crawling with worms. Predictably, his intestines would revolt. When Pepys retreated from London during the plague, he awoke one night "mightily troubled with a looseness . . . and feeling for a chamber pott, there was none. . . . I was forced in this strange house to rise and shit in the Chimny twice; and so to bed and was very well again."[35]

Waste was usually emptied into cellar vaults, through a chute leading to the basement. In the world of Pepys you knew your neighbors and their stink intimately. Pepys went to work on his roof one evening but was driven back indoors by "Sir W. Pen's emptying of a shitten pot in their house of office close by; which doth trouble me, for fear it do hereafter annoy me." The subterranean cellars were at least partly shared between houses or apartments, and Pepys frequently had issues with the other residents of Seething Lane on account of their excreta. "This morning one came to me to advise with me where to make me a window into my cellar in lieu of one that Sir W. Batten had stopped up; and going down into my cellar to look, I put my foot into a great heap of turds, by which I find that Mr. Turners house of office is full and comes into my cellar, which doth trouble me." Excrement was valuable as "night soil," and crews regularly came to clean out the cellars. After a dinner one evening, Pepys returned "home, where my house of office was emptying, and I find they will do it with much more cleanness then I expected. I went up and down among them a good while."[36]

Samuel Pepys had a limited discipline of personal hygiene. In the words of Peter Razzell, "There is no evidence that Pepys ever took a bath, although he did occasionally wash his hands and face in cold and warm water." Filth, phlegm, and fluids were irregularly removed from the body and clothes. One night in bed "my head began to turne, and I to vomitt, and if ever I was foxed it was now—which I cannot say yet, because I fell asleep and sleep till morning—only, when I waked I found myself wet with my spewing." Pepys, not renowned for his chastity, reports a sexual encounter with the housekeeper of the Earl of Sandwich. "I went up to her and played and talked with her and, God forgive me, did feel her; which I am much ashamed of, but I did no more, though I had so much a mind to it that I spent in my breeches. After I had talked an hour or two with her, I went and gave Mr. Hunt a short visit." Walking home, Pepys met a friend who took him on an unscheduled visit to, of all places, Somerset House, a royal residence, where Pepys duly saw the entire royal family in the presence chamber.[37]

Fleas and lice were a frequent nuisance. Sometimes Pepys became irritated by his body lice. "I have itched mightily these six or seven days; and when all came to all she [his wife] finds that I am louzy, having found in my head and body above twenty lice, little and great; which I wonder at, being more then I have had I believe almost these 20 years." Another time he had been "this day or two mightily troubled with an iching all over my body, which I took to be a louse or two that might bite me—I find this afternoon that all my body is inflamed and my face in a sad redness and swelling and pimpled; so that I was, before we had done walking, not only sick but ashamed of myself to see myself so changed in my countenance."[38]

Head lice were a menace. Pepys used powder liberally and often shaved his head. Because aggressive haircuts were the best means of delousing, wigs were much in fashion, but Pepys even had trouble with lice in his wigs. "Thence to Westminster to my barbers, to have my periwigg he lately made me cleansed of its nits; which vexed me cruelly, that he should put such a thing into my hands." (One of Pepys' wigs was bought during the Great Plague, but Pepys only wore it after a suitable delay: "It is a wonder what will be the fashion after the plague is done as to periwiggs, for nobody will dare to buy any haire for fear of the infection—that it had been cut off of the heads of people dead of the plague.")[39]

Such was life in later seventeenth-century London. Pepys is extraordinary for his candor, but his personal regime was not eccentric, and his diary helps us envision the disease ecology of a European city on the brink of momentous change. The early health transition was a series of interrelated changes in the infectious disease environment that unfolded between about 1670 and 1820, particularly from about 1750 on. The changes progressed with local variations across western Europe and its settler offshoots, in step with the early phases of both the European Enlightenment and modern economic growth.[40]

Four features above all define the early health transition. First, mortality stabilized—that is, there was a radical decline in the interannual volatility of the death rate, what Omran called "the age of receding pandemics." Second, infectious disease mortality also declined, and life expectancy improved, albeit modestly. Third, there were structural changes in the cause of death and the age structure of mortality; background diseases came to play a bigger role, and infectious disease mortality was even further concentrated among children: disease was pediatricized. Fourth, a strict class gradient in mortality emerged, as elites came to enjoy longer lifespans than ordinary people. More rigidly and more consistently than before, health inequities started to mirror social inequities.

The Stabilization of Mortality

Repeated mortality shocks were a hallmark of the early modern period, but from around 1750, the magnitude of these crises declined. What had once been sharp peaks became small oscillations (and eventually, an all but flat line). In England, where the mortality shocks had not been so violent to begin with, the break is evident (see figure 10.5). If a severe mortality crisis is defined as one in which the death rate was 30 percent above

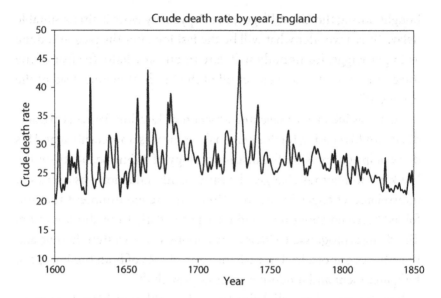

FIGURE 10.5. Crude death rate by year, England. (Source: Wrigley and Schofield 1981)

the trend, there were eleven crises between 1541 and 1750—and none afterward. The pattern was mirrored across western Europe: "In general, the 18th century is a period lacking in grave mortality crises."[41]

The recession of bubonic plague helped check the incidence of severe mortality shock. Samuel Pepys could not have known that he was living through the last plague of London in 1665. Plague disappeared from western Europe in the last third of the seventeenth century, as we have seen, probably to be reckoned one of the first clear achievements of public health. The outbreak in southern France in the early 1720s, as well as explosive epidemics in the Ottoman Empire and Russia, underscore the fact that bubonic plague could easily have flared into a wider problem again.[42]

The trend of dampening mortality crises went beyond the control of the plague to include other diseases like typhus. Famine and extreme food shortages became more infrequent, and the great wars mostly played out overseas (until Napoleon, anyway, and then for a century thereafter). The cholera epidemics of the nineteenth century were a rude reminder of the power of epidemic mortality, particularly in parts

FIGURE 10.6. Life expectancy at birth, England. (Source: Wrigley and Schofield 1981)

of southern and eastern Europe, and a virulent strain of influenza in 1918–19 caused a last mortality spike. However, even these unfortunate events would have scarcely appeared as blips in an earlier time.[43]

Improvements in Life Expectancy

Malthus was wrong that history had never seen improvements in human longevity. In parts of western Europe, there were sustained improvements in life expectancy at birth between about 1750 and 1820. In Sweden—a rural and poor country—longevity improved almost continuously from 1750 on. In England—an urbanized and rich country—life expectancy at birth had actually declined between about 1600 and the 1730s (see figure 10.6), when a steady ascent began (so, in fairness to Malthus, life expectancy in his own day had just about returned to the all-time premodern peak). The pattern in France was very similar. These gains stalled in the mid-nineteenth century, before rapidly accelerating thereafter.[44]

The increase in life expectancy accomplished between about 1750 and 1820 is more impressive even than it first appears. It was an immutable law of premodern history that death rates were higher in cities than in the countryside. Towns were demographic sinks, due to urban disease ecologies. Water-, air-, and vector-borne diseases alike benefited from human density, and migrants attracted to the food and economic opportunity of the city were immunologically unprepared for their new environments. The urban mortality penalty was stark in England. All else equal, mortality *should* have continued to increase dramatically in the eighteenth century, given the increase in urban populations. In the late seventeenth century, less than one in five inhabitants of England and Wales lived in a town of more than 2,500 souls. In the space of just over a century, the proportion doubled, as industrialization pulled migrants into the cities. Clearly, if improvements were to be made despite the increasing density of human populations, it would require adaptation and ingenuity.[45]

The story of London is revealing. Around 1800, London became the first European city since ancient Rome to surpass one million residents. The metropolis had been, for centuries, a death trap and a brake on the population growth of the entire country. Even in the eighteenth century it remained grievously unhealthy; yet, despite its expansion, the city passed an important milestone toward the very end of the 1700s. For the first time in its history, births exceeded deaths, and the metropolis enjoyed natural increase. The early health transition progressed straight into the teeth of headlong urbanization.[46]

Changes in Causes of Death and Age Structure of Mortality

The early health transition witnessed complex structural shifts in the causes of death and the age structure of mortality. Even as infectious diseases remained dominant, the nature of the diseases responsible for mortality subtly changed. Of course, the overriding influence of smallpox mortality distorts almost all features of eighteenth-century demography. Smallpox was the greatest killer of the era, and it also summoned forth the most remarkable biomedical advances of the period. The savagery of this singular virus masks some of the progress made during the early health transition.[47]

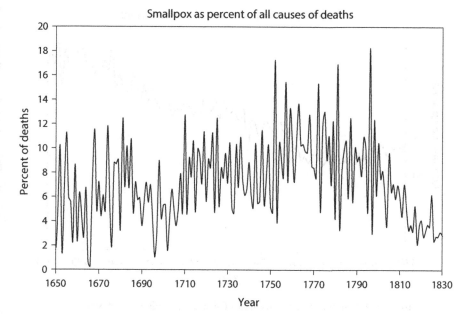

FIGURE 10.7. Smallpox as percentage of all deaths, London Bills of Mortality.

In London, smallpox accounted for about 5 percent of all burials in the years around 1700 (see figure 10.7). By the second half of the eighteenth century, it was responsible for proportionately twice as many deaths. Smallpox accounted for 10–15 percent of all mortality in eighteenth-century Europe; a physician in Geneva claimed at midcentury that less than 5 percent of adults who died had never contracted the disease. In Japan, it was a dreadful burden, in one region claiming 20 percent of all children. Smallpox typically fell hardest on the young, putting small children in their graves, although survivors were left with lifelong resistance. There are intriguing geographic patterns in the age structure of smallpox mortality in England. In the north (as in most of Europe), smallpox was a disease of childhood. However, in the south and in London, young adults were disproportionately killed by smallpox. It has been argued that widespread inoculation and aggressive isolation of the sick to control outbreaks did partly work, especially in the London hinterland. Thus, some children avoided exposure in their early

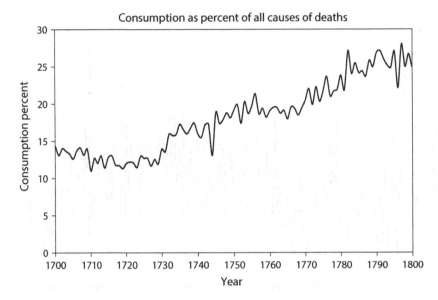

FIGURE 10.8. Consumption as percentage of all deaths, London Bills of Mortality.

years, but when they moved to the metropolis as young adults, their susceptible immune systems were exposed to the disease.[48]

With the control of plague and eventually smallpox, the role of other endemic respiratory and gastroenteric diseases in the background became more evident. Typhus, which had been an indiscriminate epidemic disease, became more obviously a disease of poverty. No disease benefited more from the early phases of industrialization than tuberculosis. By the first half of the eighteenth century, "consumption" was already blamed for 14 percent of all deaths in London (see figure 10.8). By the end of the century, a quarter of all burials in London were ascribed to consumption. Partly, people now simply survived long enough to succumb to what was always a serious disease; paradoxically, the "catchment area" of tuberculosis was expanded by the prolongation of life achieved by the control over other diseases. Furthermore, the disease ecology of industrializing towns fostered the kind of crowding and squalor in which the tuberculosis bacterium thrived. Deplorable housing conditions and brutal factory labor created deadly congestion. The eighteenth century created a kind of tubercular society.[49]

The indistinct welter of diarrheal and respiratory diseases did much of the killing. Measles, whooping cough, diphtheria, dysentery, typhoid fever, and scarlet fever asserted themselves. The infectious disease burden fell more directly on children. In general, neonatal health mirrored patterns of adult mortality, suggesting that the first days of life were highly dependent on maternal well-being. Infant mortality improved in the later eighteenth century. But children suffered in the throes of industrialization, especially in the early nineteenth century, when urbanization was rapid and housing and labor systems remained largely unregulated.[50]

One important disease that lets us trace the ways social and evolutionary change conspired in this period is scarlet fever. Scarlet fever was not a completely new disease, and genomic evidence has yet to fully elucidate its history. But the biology of the pathogen can help us understand why it fell so hard upon modernizing societies, and especially upon children. Scarlet fever is caused by the ubiquitous bacterial pathogen *Streptococcus pyogenes*, the agent of strep throat. A case of scarlet fever announces itself with fever, aches, and a painful sore throat. A day or two later, the tokens of real danger appear in the form of a systemic rash. The rash starts on the trunk and spreads outward to the extremities, covering the body with tiny red papules that feel like sandpaper. The cheeks are flushed, except for a ghostly white ring that remains around the mouth. The rash endures for about a week, as the immune system rallies against the invasion. With antibiotic treatment, scarlet fever can be tamed, but in the preantibiotic era, scarlet fever became at times a deadly epidemic disease. In 1865, the *Lancet* called it "the deadliest of fevers . . . sparing neither the young nor the old, but chiefly infecting the very young, and not unfrequently sweeping off the whole of the children of a family."[51]

Scarlet fever captured greater attention from the late seventeenth century on. The great English doctor Thomas Sydenham included a chapter on scarlet fever in a work of 1675, noting it as a disease that disproportionately affected children. Throughout the eighteenth century, scarlet fever was capable of causing outbreaks, but the disease was not necessarily a death sentence. A provincial doctor chronicled an epidemic that occurred in the small town of Chesham in Buckinghamshire in 1788.

He made astute clinical observations about the disease, whose outstanding feature he regarded as the violent sore throat. The rash turned the skin dry and very red ("which redness some have compared with propriety to the colour of a boiled lobster"), until it fell off in branny scales. It was highly contagious. While there were fatalities, these were the exception rather than the norm: "This disease carried off but few patients, considering the great number who were affected with it."[52]

In the nineteenth century, though, scarlet fever suddenly became a more serious threat, especially for children. The mortality statistics kept by the British government follow the transformation of scarlet fever into one of the most nightmarish diseases of the industrial age. As the English historian of disease Charles Creighton noted, "The enormous number of deaths from scarlatina during some thirty or forty years in the middle of the 19th century will appear in history as one of the most remarkable things in our epidemiology." The early industrial city allowed the disease to become one of the classic endemic diseases of childhood. At the same time, the dramatic increases in mortality from scarlet fever surely had a biological dimension. *S. pyogenes* is a highly diverse bacterial species, and scarlet fever is caused by strains that carry a gene for making a deadly toxin. It is likely that a more virulent strain circulated in the nineteenth century. Children of all classes were swept up. Henry Adams, scion of America's most eminent political family, barely survived scarlet fever in Boston in 1841. Three of Charles Darwin's daughters fell sick of the disease a few years later; one of them, his beloved Anne, recovered but succumbed shortly thereafter to what was probably tuberculosis. The wave of scarlet fever deaths at the peak of industrial growth was an unlucky conjuncture of social and biological change.[53]

The early health transition stabilized a U-shaped mortality pattern, in which the burden of disease fell most heavily and most consistently on the very young and very old. In part this was because pathogens like plague and then smallpox receded, and typhus became an endemic disease of poverty rather than an epidemic disease. As adult mortality from infectious disease was brought partly under control, the burden on children and the elderly, which had always been there, became more visible. We can also imagine, though, that with rapid urbanization and the rise of industrial labor regimes, the entire suite of endemic infectious diseases stabilized in many cities at the same time, making childhood a true gauntlet. The challenges of pediatric infectious disease were enormous, and they were only overcome amid the rapid changes brought by the health transition of the later nineteenth century.

Class Gradients in Mortality

In the 1820s, the French intellectual Louis-René Villermé set out to answer definitively the question of whether the rich lived longer than the poor. Villermé had served as an army surgeon for ten years under Napoleon and then earned his doctorate in medicine. He had the means to set up as an independent intellectual in Paris, and he devoted himself to the study of population health. To test whether social status influenced mortality, Villermé did something on the cutting edge of social thought: he used statistics. Drawing from new sources of public data, he conducted an ingenious analysis of mortality in Paris. He looked at mortality rates in every district (*arrondissement*) of the city, and then explored a range of variables for each district in search of associations with the mortality rate. One clearly stuck out: a poverty index that he had created for each district. The parts of Paris with the highest proportion of poor households also suffered the highest death rates (see figure 10.9).[54]

These results might seem unsurprising to us. Today, people who enjoy higher socioeconomic status also enjoy longer and healthier lives thanks to greater access to medical care, lifestyle differences, and lower physiological stress, among other things. But in the past, social inequities did not necessarily translate into health inequities. The relationship between social status and health outcomes is a product of history. When and how did wealth come to entail greater health?

It is hard to say. The evidence is contradictory. The issue is complicated first and foremost by the urban mortality penalty. Even though by 1800 improvements in urban health had been achieved, the countryside was still far more salubrious than the city. In 1811, people in urban England had life expectancies ten years shorter than those of their rural counterparts; half a century later, the gap was seven years; in 1911, it was

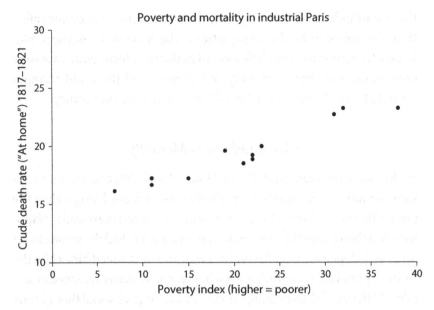

FIGURE 10.9. Mortality and poverty in industrial Paris. Louis-René Villermé constructed a poverty index and showed a strong association with mortality rates.

reduced to three. Because elites tended to live in towns, their health was concomitantly endangered. Moreover, correlations between status and health are sensitive to how "elites" are defined, especially given the changing nature of social relations in a period that fostered the rapid rise of a middle class. Nevertheless, behind the noise, there are signals of an epochal shift in the history of health inequality, as for the first time social and biological status came to mirror one another consistently.[55]

In 1967, the social scientist Aaron Antonovsky proposed that class differences in life expectancy could be divided into three periods. During the first, which lasted until about 1650, there were not class gradients in mortality. From about 1650 to about 1850, the class gap widened, and in the period since, it has narrowed. The schema remains useful. Before the early health transition, when infectious disease was effectively uncontrollable, high social status had a negligible, variable, and at times even inverse relationship to health status. The early health transition then created health inequities, as elites were able to convert social advantage to longer life. Later, the more sweeping transition of the late 1800s dispersed the benefits of scientific and economic progress more widely, narrowing the gap in life expectancy but never completely closing it.[56]

Most of the early evidence for elite life expectancy comes from the top echelons of society. Infectious disease was not a respecter of persons. The Roman emperors, for example, had poor lifespan prospects due to the hazardous disease environment of the ancient Mediterranean. A thorough study of European nobility since AD 1000 found that life expectancy fluctuated, suffering in times of war and plague. It was not unusual for aristocrats to experience *higher* mortality than average people, especially people who lived in the countryside. A famous study of the British peerage shows that its members suffered higher-than-average mortality rates until the eighteenth century.[57]

But there must often have been times when higher social status improved the prospects of survival. Even in premodern times, the affluent fared better during periods of crisis. Malthusian theory predicts that the "positive check" will affect the destitute, whose conditions fall below the minimum level required for subsistence. The great famines of early modern history no doubt carried off the poor in disproportionate numbers. In the London plagues of the seventeenth century, the poorest parishes in the metropolis suffered higher mortality than the wealthier, central parishes. A careful study of the population of Geneva, going back to 1625, shows that there were already gaps between the well-to-do and the poor, and that the lower classes benefited from a general increase in life expectancy during the eighteenth century. In some contexts, therefore, social advantage surely led to longer lifespans even before the early health transition.[58]

What happened between about 1750 and 1850, then, was the formation of persistent social cleavages in health. Elite and bourgeois life expectancy rose, while the poor struggled to climb at the same pace. The British royal family, a small sample, turned a corner after 1700, with much greater chances of survival from the eighteenth century on. But they were ahead of the curve. Adult survivorship among elites only surpassed that of the lower classes around the middle of the century, and even then the pattern is clouded until the early nineteenth century. Other data sets corroborate that over the course of the eighteenth century, even middling elites—merchants and professionals—were able to achieve lower infant and child mortality rates than the working classes.[59]

Early public health reformers started to explore the complex links between health inequities and social inequities. The German physician Johann Peter Frank published the first volume of his monumental *Complete System of Medical Policy* in 1779. It was a landmark in "the history of thought on the social relations of health and disease." When Frank lectured in 1790 on "the people's misery" as the "mother of diseases," he observed the multifaceted connections between class and the experience of disease: "Every social group has its own type of health and diseases, determined by the mode of living. They are different for the courtiers and noblemen, for the soldiers and scholars. The artisans have various diseases peculiar to them, some of which have been specially investigated by physicians. The diseases caused by the poverty of the people and by the lack of all goods of life, however, are so exceedingly numerous that in a brief address they can be discussed only in outline."[60]

By the early nineteenth century, the resulting gap was visible to the naked eye. The first wave of industrialization was brutal for the working poor. As de Tocqueville observed of 1830s Manchester, "From this foul drain the greatest stream of human industry flows out to fertilize the whole world. From this filthy sewer pure gold flows. Here humanity attains its most complete development and its most brutish; here civilization works its miracles, and here civilized man is turned back almost into a savage." This was the stark inequity that inspired sanitary reformers like Edwin Chadwick, whose *Report on the Sanitary Condition of the Labouring Population of Great Britain* appeared in 1842, with consequences that we will follow in chapter 12. In sum, in the words of historian Peter Razzell, "Poverty became more important in shaping mortality in the nineteenth century through its association with disease environment. With the development of large cities and industrial areas, social classes became increasingly geographically segregated, leading to an association of poverty with 'the slum.'"[61]

Villermé was right: industrialization had left the poor more susceptible to infectious disease and early death than their bourgeois counterparts. There is a silver lining, though, in that these inequities galvanized the public health movement and created the political energy for reform. From Frank to Villermé to Chadwick, the political energy of health reform took shape in different guises across western Europe and the United States. The shorter and unhealthier lives of the poor seemed an affront to justice and a problem that could be remedied. Villermé's methods—using statistical investigation to understand the range of influences on health outcomes—pointed toward the future. Villermé's career reminds us that the golden age of public health reform has its roots in the preceding generations, in the ideas and methods of the Enlightenment and in the negative feedbacks of industrial growth.[62]

Medicine Enlightened

In 1772, Sir John Pringle (figure 10.10) was elected as the president of the Royal Society, an office he held for six years. Pringle was a Scotsman and a quintessential product of the Enlightenment (a man with doubts about the Trinity, an overfondness for Voltaire, and a wide and enviable circle of friends, including Benjamin Franklin, Adam Smith, and David Hume). He studied classics at Saint Andrews. Like many intellectuals with an interest in medicine, his horizons were broad, and he trained at Edinburgh, Leiden, and Paris, before settling back in Edinburgh. Pringle assumed a teaching post but kept a medical practice on the side, and in 1742 one of his patrons brought him into service as a physician for the British Army. For six years Pringle served in the field, shuttling between Britain and Holland, and what he learned changed his life—and, more generally, the course of medical knowledge and practice in Europe.[63]

In 1746, back home between campaigns, Pringle observed outbreaks of "jail fever" and "hospital fever." The outbreaks (which we recognize as typhus) followed troop movements but spilled over into civilian populations. It was evident to him that crowded, poorly ventilated conditions were conducive to the transmission of this fever, but also that the fever could be carried to a new place by those already sick. The disease was both contagious and preventable. After his service ended, Pringle settled in London to write up his observations. There, he

FIGURE 10.10. Sir John Pringle (1707–82), father of military medicine
and president of the Royal Society from 1772 to 1778. Stipple engraving
by W. H. Mote after Sir J. Reynolds, 1774. Wellcome Collection
(CC BY 4.0).

witnessed an alarming outbreak of typhus at Newgate Prison. In 1750
Pringle published *Observations on the Nature and Cure of Hospital and
Jayl-Fevers*, arguing that hospital fever, jail fever, camp fever, and ship
fever were the same disease. More radically, he argued that outbreaks
might be prevented by improving sanitary conditions. The same year,
he published *Experiments on Septic and Antiseptic Substances*, a pioneering exploration that coined the very term *antiseptic*. Three years later he
brought out his *Observations on the Diseases of the Army*, a landmark of
military medicine, with implications that went far beyond its primary
field. A star was born.[64]

The ascendance of Pringle to the presidency of the Royal Society is a measure of how much had changed since the times of Pepys, in the realm of something so elusive and indefinite as attitudes toward public and private hygiene. Pringle was obsessed with clean and sanitary environments, with washed clothing and good ventilation. More importantly, Pringle's attitudes were not a matter of personal idiosyncrasy; they were connected to science, empirical science turned prescriptive. Pringle stood in the vanguard of the "medical Enlightenment" of the eighteenth century. The underrated medical Enlightenment deserves to be accorded a part in the improvements achieved during the early health transition.[65]

We can attribute the early gains in life expectancy to several interrelated causes. In the background, nascent economic growth enhanced nutrition and underwrote improvements in physical infrastructure. As we have already seen, stronger, more centralized states used quarantine, isolation, and the *cordon sanitaire* to protect their populations from plague. Beyond that, however, European societies (in addition to American ones) benefited from the globalization of medical knowledge. Most consequentially of all, preventative medicine was translated into both public policy and private habit. Inspired by empiricist science that worked without a complete understanding of the underlying mechanisms, the crusade in favor of sanitation, personal hygiene, lavation, laundering, ventilation, isolation, insect extermination, and landscape drainage materially improved the control of infectious disease.

In the eighteenth century, human health benefited from the globalization of medical interventions and ideas. The European pharmacy had already been broadened by the imperial ventures of preceding centuries. Unfortunately, relatively few pharmacologically active compounds derived from plants are effective against microparasites. Many remedies—such as the New World plant guaiacum, used for syphilis—could have had little more than a palliative or placebo effect, if even that; still others—such as tartar emetic, a drug used since ancient times—were harmful. Some drugs—like the mercury treatments for syphilis—were partly effective, yet toxic for the human host too. Others—like ipecacuanha root (an emetic) or sarsaparilla (with some antibacterial properties)—were effective but only of very limited medical value. A modest salutary effect may have been obtained from some remedies, like cabbage bark or sabadilla, used as an antihelminth, or *Cassia fistula*, an Indian plant taken to the Caribbean and used globally as a purgative. In China, the medicinal value of sweet wormwood (*Artemisia annua*) had been recognized for centuries, and it was used as an antimalarial in Asia. And in the early modern period, there was one addition to the global pharmacy that did bring unqualified benefits for human health: cinchona bark, the first miracle drug.[66]

Cinchona bark is derived from trees that are native to the wet montane forests of the tropical Andes. The bark is rich in quinine and other alkaloids; these compounds disrupt the metabolism of the *Plasmodium* parasites that cause malaria. The bark is a wonder drug against one of the great enemies of the human species. Credit for its discovery belongs to indigenous healers in the Andes, who brought the medicinal properties of the bark to the attention of Spanish authorities and Jesuit missionaries. Although the tree-derived drug was probably witnessed by Europeans as early as the 1570s, it was not until the 1630s that the bark was first imported to Europe. The use of Peruvian bark radiated outward from Seville and Rome in the second half of the seventeenth century, but its efficacy was controversial, and its association with Catholicism slowed its uptake in Protestant Europe. Some medical authorities resisted it on the grounds that it did not square with the prevailing humoral paradigm. However, the tide turned in the decades around 1700. Cinchona steadily gained legitimacy, and its popularity soared. It was the source of a lucrative trade for the Spanish, and by the 1770s there were already anxieties about the scarcity of the Andean trees that yielded the bark.[67]

Even more revolutionary were smallpox inoculation and its successor, vaccination. The origins of inoculation probably lie in sixteenth-century China, where it was first definitely attested in the *Dou Zhen Xin Fa* by Wan Quan. Following the establishment of Manchu rule, the Qing state widely promoted smallpox inoculation. The Chinese practiced inoculation by a method known as nasal insufflation, in which the dust of dried smallpox scabs was blown into the nose. The Kangxi

Emperor (r. 1661–1722), whose face bore the pits of smallpox scars, was an energetic proponent of inoculation. He systematically explored the most effective methods of variolation and, consequentially, in the later seventeenth century, he instituted the first mass inoculations in history, mandating variolation for millions of his subjects.[68]

These mass inoculations brought knowledge of inoculation to nomadic tribes on the steppe, and it may have been across the steppe that the practice spread in the late seventeenth century. The practice was common among the Circassians, a people who inhabited the northern Caucasus and were in close contact with steppe groups. Europeans became aware of smallpox inoculation by around 1700. An employee of the British East India Company described it in a letter of that year, and over the next two decades, the number of reports multiplied. The Royal Society was informed of the efficacy of this practice, but resistance prevailed—after all, infecting oneself or one's patients with the purulent material of a deadly disease is not intuitive as prevention. Even as smallpox continued to take its toll, Europeans were slow to adopt inoculation.[69]

In the 1720s that changed, both in England and its North American colonies. Remarkably, in Boston, the Puritan minister Cotton Mather learned of inoculation from an enslaved West African named Onesimus, who came into his possession in 1707. It is impossible to know whether inoculation had developed independently in West Africa or whether it had been transmitted from somewhere in Asia or Europe and adopted; the former seems perhaps more likely. Mather, who was struck by the inaction of the Royal Society, vowed to use inoculation if smallpox reappeared in Massachusetts, which it did in 1721. With great success (and against ferocious resistance), he helped to orchestrate mass inoculation of Bostonians, using the techniques learned from Onesimus. As in England, the practice would remain controversial for decades, despite outstanding evidence for its efficacy.[70]

In England the impetus for smallpox inoculation came from Lady Mary Wortley Montagu, the wife of the ambassador to the Ottomans. She was a paragon of the British Enlightenment. Her brother had died of smallpox in 1713, and two years later, at the age of 26, she survived the disease. Reputed to have been a great beauty, she was left scarred by the infection. Stationed in Istanbul, she witnessed smallpox inoculation around 1717 among Greek Christians who had learned the practice from the Circassians. (It is a common misconception, going back to Lady Mary's friend Voltaire, that inoculation was widely practiced by the Ottoman Turks.) She reported on it in her letters home. In 1718 Lady Mary had her young son inoculated, against her husband's will. Three years later she was in London again, and she had her daughter inoculated. She preached the value of inoculation to Princess Caroline, who had two young daughters. In 1721, the king allowed six volunteers— prisoners in Newgate awaiting the death penalty—to undergo the procedure in exchange for a reprieve. Its success was followed by another test of its safety on children, enlisting a group of orphans who safely underwent inoculation. Then the royal children were variolated.[71]

The practice of inoculation spread slowly in England, as in the rest of Europe. The Royal Society instituted a reporting system in order to retrieve data about the safety and efficacy of smallpox inoculation. The evidence was overwhelming. Still, there was obstinate resistance, especially in religious quarters, and pious scruples retarded the spread of the practice for several decades. A turning point came midcentury. Inoculation had proven successful throughout the Americas, and reports filtered back across the Atlantic. The Smallpox and Inoculation Hospital was founded in London in 1745. Cheaper and simpler methods were popularized, most notably by the entrepreneurial Sutton family. By the 1760s inoculation was practiced on a scale that noticeably affected patterns of smallpox mortality across Britain. Importantly, England became an "epicentre" for the diffusion of inoculation across the rest of Europe. By 1776, a Parisian study estimated that two hundred thousand people were inoculated in England that year, compared to fifteen thousand in France; this number, if perhaps exaggerated, reflects the success of British inoculation.[72]

Vaccination was an improvement on inoculation—a revolutionary one. By the 1790s, the belief that exposure to cowpox conferred immunity to smallpox was widespread. The idea of using cowpox infection to protect against smallpox was in the air, but it was the physician-scientist Edward Jenner who demonstrated its safety and efficacy. Jenner

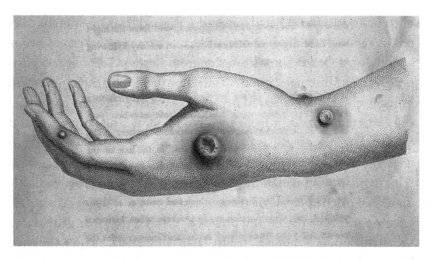

FIGURE 10.11. The hand of Sarah Nelmes with cowpox, from Jenner's 1798 *Inquiry*.
Wellcome Collection (CC BY 4.0).

understood that humanity's relationship with animals had exposed us
to the diseases of our companions. "The deviation of Man from the state
in which he was originally placed by Nature seems to have proved to
him a prolific source of Diseases. . . . He has familiarized himself with a
great number of animals, which may not originally have been intended
for associates." Jenner also believed that this proximity to animals could
be the source of salvation, and in 1796 he used the pustular material from
an infected dairyworker's hand to vaccinate an eight-year-old old boy
(figure 10.11). Two years later, he published his findings. Smallpox still
killed 10 percent of all Britons in 1800. Within half a century, it was responsible for 1 percent of all deaths. By 1900 it was gone from Britain.[73]

Jenner announced his results in 1798, the very year that Malthus
brought out his pessimistic essay on the human condition. Almost immediately, Jenner foresaw the possibility of "extirpating from the earth
a disease which is every hour devouring its victims." The spread of vaccination in the nineteenth century and beyond was a truly global triumph. Against the backdrop of the Napoleonic Wars, vaccination disseminated through networks of medical knowledge that transcended
national boundaries. Not just knowledge, but starter kits of the

miraculous vaccine radiated outward. "The early transmission of cow-pox was almost literally diasporic, with cotton threads soaked in cowpox lymph dispatched in some profusion from England." To relay vaccina-tion over long distances, chains of infection had to be maintained, often by using children or enslaved persons as human conveyors of the vac-cine. Vaccination was propelled west, throughout the Portuguese and Spanish Empires as well as the fledgling United States. By 1806, Presi-dent Thomas Jefferson thanked Jenner for erasing this scourge "from the calendar of human affliction." Vaccination rippled eastward too. Though it reached Japan via the thinnest of threads, the uptake of vac-cination was remarkable and proved a "catalyst for Japan's rapid and successful modernization a century later." Ultimately, by 1977, the virus became the first, and still only, human pathogen driven completely to extinction, fulfilling Jenner's visionary optimism.[74]

Cinchona bark and immunization against smallpox were important tools added to the health-care regime during the early health transition. But they were admittedly one-offs, involving considerable good fortune. Despite efforts to extend the application of Jennerian vaccination to other diseases, it was not until Louis Pasteur's work in the later nine-teenth century that new vaccines were developed, and other drugs of major medical importance were not identified until Paul Ehrlich's discovery of Salvarsan (see chapter 12). Yet in the eighteenth century, more systemic progress was already being achieved by preventative medicine. We can summarize the nature of these intellectual changes under several headings.[75]

First, in the words of historian of medicine Margaret DeLacy, conta-gionism caught on. The idea of contagion had existed along the fringes of medical thought since antiquity (not to mention its place in folk un-derstandings of disease). But from the late seventeenth century, the idea that disease was transmitted by contact gained momentum, and so too did the possibility that invisible agents—microbes—might be the mechanism of transmission. Pringle, for instance, was on the cusp of germ theory, but his high standards as a scientist prevented him from drawing conclusions. "Of what nature is this infection? In the former editions of this work, I considered the spreading of the distemper as owing to putrid exhalations from the humours of those who first fall ill of it." He had since read new ideas about contagion caused by microscopic beings, and he declared that "it seems reasonable to suspend all hypotheses, till that matter is further inquired into." His beliefs were not isolated or idiosyncratic. According to DeLacy, "Earlier works on contagion had fallen in small dispersed flurries; now they were melding into a movement much larger than the work of a single person."[76]

Second, medical thought came to focus on the environment as a source of disease in the broadest terms. James Riley has explored this new "environmental" medicine that could draw on ancient traditions of thought about pollution and filth. There is a continuity between the ancient paradigms going back to Galen, and running through medieval medicine, but the old humoral theory was constrictive. Heat, cold, and moisture might act on the body and cause disease, but now, there was a "boundless search for associations between the human organism and its environment." Medicine turned a keen eye on ways to *prevent* disease by altering habitats and environments, and this preventative dimension became a more forceful and broad-ranging program. Although public health—encompassing everything from quarantine to public sanitary laws—had existed for centuries, the scope and force of eighteenth-century environmental medicine was novel.[77]

Third, medical ideas entered the burgeoning "public sphere." In this period, as literacy spread, newspapers proliferated, and public spaces like coffee houses sprouted up, the market for medical ideas was enlarged. Medical writing was conveyed in the plain style, written in a nontechnical vernacular that was more widely accessible and more easily applied. It is telling that Benjamin Franklin, for instance, immediately published Pringle's study of jail fever in the *Pennsylvania Gazette*: it was a matter of general interest. Public lectures, professional societies, and medical journals accelerated the dissemination of knowledge. A medical society was formed abortively in Massachusetts from the 1730s and permanently from the 1780s. Moreover, population health became the object of statecraft; since the late seventeenth century, the "political arithmetic" of John Graunt and William Petty brought statistics to bear on population dynamics, to the end of promoting policy that would enhance the nation's power. The arena where these connections were most obviously and easily applied was the military. It is no coincidence that so many of the finest medical minds of the age were associated with the military: Pringle, of course, but also others like James Lind, who was to the Navy what Pringle was to the Army, or John Hunter, who perceived that the fevers of the urban poor were the same as jail fever and hospital fever.[78]

Fourth, medical science in the eighteenth century was empiricist in spirit. Knowledge was to be gained by experience and proved by experimentation. Pringle, naturally, revered Francis Bacon. The effort to gather data on the effects of smallpox inoculation is a testament to the empiricist spirit. It is unsurprising that, at the end of the century, Jenner would argue for the efficacy of vaccination by appealing to experimental outcomes rather than dogma; it is simply notable that his tract is almost nothing *but* a string of case studies. Jails, ships, and hospitals became testing grounds for new ideas and new methods. James Lind used a sort of clinical trial to test his cure for scurvy. On an even larger stage, he was appointed the physician in chief at the Royal Naval Hospital at Haslar from 1758 to 1774, making it a test bed for his ideas about sanitary practice and the control of fevers. As DeLacy put it, "His example did more to buttress his arguments than any amount of theorizing: his most important treatise by far was Haslar itself." Haslar was not alone. Hospitals became more closely linked with universities and their faculty, especially in Scotland, and hospital practice "decisively changed the character, content, and direction of medicine" during the Enlightenment.[79]

Medicine in the eighteenth century lacked the political clout that the public health movement would gain a century later. But it did influence policy and practice, and it planted the seeds for later progress. The urban environment was slowly rebuilt with superior infrastructure. Streets were widened and paved. Timber walls and earthen floors were replaced with brick and tile. Piped water became far more common. As an observer remarked in the early eighteenth century, "there is not a street in London, but . . . [that] Waters run through it in Pipes, conveyed under Ground: And from those Pipes there is scarce a House, whose Rent is 15 or 20 pounds per Annum But hath the Convenience of Water brought into it, by small Leaden Pipes laid into the great ones." In England, a series of Improvement Acts from the 1760s drove progress in urban sanitary infrastructure. Drains were built that carried off effluvia, and even though adequate sewers and water treatment lay in the future, the days of chamber pots and cesspits were starting to recede.[80]

Water technology took early strides, too. The search for pure water is as old as our species. Machines to filter water are ancient, and basic mechanisms such as sand filtration were effective but usually uneconomical at scale. Over the course of the eighteenth century, Enlightenment science and industrial engineering sought new mechanisms and methods to secure safe supplies of drinking water. In midcentury France the first book on water purification was published and the first patent for water filtration issued. Progress was slow, but toward the end of the century, the virtues of charcoal filters were discovered and promoted. In London, more than half of the water supply companies simply served raw water from the Thames in the early nineteenth century, but expectations were rising, and industry competed to provide cleaner water more efficiently.[81]

The quest for potable water was matched by a new obsession with fresh air and a campaign against stench. In parallel with bulky and expensive water filters, the eighteenth century saw the development of unwieldy ventilators. A man named Stephen Hales presented ideas to the Royal Society in 1741, proposing a device that was a kind of giant bellows to circulate air through tight quarters. Prisons, ships, and hospitals were the first to adopt mechanical ventilation, and physicians like Pringle and Lind were champions of fresh air as a key to human health. The period also witnessed the first experiments in chemical disinfection, although the purpose was usually to alter smells in an effort to cleanse the air or counteract putrefaction. Similarly, crude insecticides came onto the market. These early and halting experiments presaged a future in which humans would chemically alter our living environments on a massive scale.[82]

Norms of personal hygiene also started to change, little by little. By and large, the development of modern hygienic routines and disinfected personal environments belongs to the later nineteenth century, but early advances in the eighteenth century foretold progress to come.

Soap became a common consumer good. Linen and then cotton clothing replaced woolens, to the chagrin of the human body louse. Among
the virtues of cotton is that it can be easily washed, and industrial textile
production meant that people had more clothing than before. James
Lind was obsessed by the idea that disease was transmitted through
dirty clothes, and on his ships and in his hospital new disciplines of
laundry were rigorously enforced.[83]

In the eighteenth century, landscapes were altered on a large scale.
Primeval swamps were drained and turned over to arable farming. It is
easy to forget that much of Europe was quasi-malarial until modern
times. The vivax parasite was common even in pockets of northern
Europe. The dangers of soggy, low-lying landscapes had long been recognized and attributed to the mysterious "exhalations" of the swamp. In
the eighteenth century, though, passivity gave way to campaigns of
transformation, matched by the wherewithal for success.[84]

In England, the marshy lowlands of the south and east were notorious for the "ague," the intermittent fever caused by vivax malaria, as the
historian Mary Dobson has powerfully shown. The county of Kent was
one of the most affected in the country. In 1700, Kent parishes lying in
the marshes had death rates equivalent to the most unhealthy regions
on earth. By 1800, these disadvantages had been almost completely
erased, thanks to drainage of the marshes. As a local antiquarian writing
in 1799 observed of one malarial parish along the coast, "It has till of late
been considered as an unhealthy one, owing partly to the damps arising
from the salt marshes on the southwest side of the street, and partly to
the general badness of the water thereabouts, though these objections
have been since in a great measure remedied, for a few years ago the
marshes were drained, and thrown into arable land." The improvements
in health in these forgotten marginal lands within Europe were not
inconsequential.[85]

These changes, driven by the medical Enlightenment, were all of a
piece. By the early nineteenth century, their effects were evident to the
careful observer. As one London physician remarked, "The same spirit
of improvement, which has constructed our sewers, and widened our
streets, and removed the nuisances with which they abounded, and

dispersed the inhabitants over a larger surface, and taught them to love airy apartments and frequent changes of linen; has spread itself likewise into the country, where it has drained the marshes, cultivated the wastes, enclosed the commons, enlarged the farmhouses, and embellished the cottages." The contrast with the past was striking: "Any body, who will be at pains to compare the condition of London, and of all great towns in England during the seventeenth century, with their actual [current] state, and note the corresponding changes which have taken place in diseases, can hardly fail to consider cleanliness and ventilation as the principal agents in producing this reform."[86]

Global Repercussions

From 1772 to 1775, during Pringle's tenure as president of the Royal Society, Captain James Cook carried out his second voyage of exploration across the Pacific. The first voyage (1768–71) had seen his crew in good health for much of the journey, until a third of them were lost to disease following a stop in Batavia, the Dutch capital in the East Indies. These kinds of voyages had always been deadly. In the early eighteenth century, a Dutch mathematician named Nicolaas Struyck gathered data on eighty-four voyages between the Dutch Republic and the Dutch East Indies, voyages that traversed many of the same waters that Cook would sail. On the outbound voyages, passengers died at a rate of twenty-three per thousand, per month, meaning more than a quarter of the passengers might perish in a year; on the return voyage, 10 percent a year died. Long-distance sail through the tropics was an existential gamble.[87]

Before setting out on his second voyage, Cook systematically investigated ways to reduce mortality among his men. He implemented a new hygienic regimen informed by Enlightenment medicine. (It was a small world: Cook offered a young Edward Jenner the post of naturalist on the second voyage, but thankfully the future discoverer of vaccination declined and returned to his native Gloucestershire.) Cook's ship became a floating public-health experiment and a microcosm of the early health transition: ventilation, filtration, rigorous cleaning, regular laundry, and assiduous avoidance of marshy coasts. On his return, Cook duly reported his methods and results to Pringle, who published them under the imprimatur of the Royal Society, closing the loop on this experiment. Cook's second voyage was far more successful, measured by the survivorship of his crew: after three years and eighteen days at sea roving throughout the tropics, out of a crew of 118 men only 1 had died.

The indigenous peoples met by Cook on his voyage did not fare so well. Their fate was a harbinger of worse to come, as the progress of globalization accelerated. The nineteenth century brought new health challenges everywhere, in Europe and across the rest of the planet. The negative feedbacks of economic growth threatened to overwhelm the fragile progress of the early health transition. We need to follow these cross currents in the history of disease. They underscore that further scientific advance, and the translation of knowledge into policy and practice, were needed to secure control over a dynamic and increasingly threatening disease environment. But above all, in the nineteenth century, the biological shocks of modernization were felt worldwide at a moment when the capacity of different societies to respond was quickly diverging.[88]

11

Disease and Global Divergence

Successes and Failures in the Wonderful Century

In 1801, when he finished his term as president of the United States, John Adams magnanimously left his incoming rival Thomas Jefferson seven horses in the White House stables. Means of travel and communication had changed little since the days of Caesar (fittingly, the name of one of Adams's favorite horses). A century later, Adams's great-grandson Henry stood in Paris at the world's fair, the 1900 Paris Exposition, mesmerized by an electrical turbine, the "dynamo." Although he himself felt out of place in it, Henry lived in an age of steamships and trains, telegraphs and light bulbs. In the world of John Adams, medicine meant bloodletting and surgery that was little more than a gory gamble. Henry Adams, who narrowly survived the scarlet fever wave as a boy, lived to see anesthesia and antisepsis, the triumph of germ theory and the age of vaccines and pharmaceuticals.[1]

The nineteenth century is the crux of modernity. In 1899 Alfred Russel Wallace, the codiscoverer of evolution with Darwin, published *The Wonderful Century*, a reflection on the dazzling progress of the last hundred years, as well as a clear-eyed reckoning with its shortcomings and unfinished business. He concluded that "not only is our century superior to any that have gone before it, but that it may be best compared with the whole preceding historical period. It must therefore be held to constitute a new era of human progress." Yet, he soberly admitted, "this is only one side of the shield. Along with these marvellous Successes—perhaps in consequence of them—there have been equally striking Failures, some intellectual, but for the most part moral and social."[2]

Wallace counted thirteen innovations of the highest order: railways, steamships, telegraphs, telephones, matches, gas lights, electric lights, photographs, phonographs, X-rays, spectrum analysis to study the stars, anesthetics, and antiseptics. Set against this, he identified militarism, exploitation and humanitarian catastrophe in the colonies, the "plunder of the earth," the diseases and "insect enemies" that followed environmental degradation, and the squalor of the working class. The last was for Wallace an unforgiveable stain on the wonderful century: "the condition of the bulk of our workers, the shortness of their lives, the mortality among their children, and the awful condition of misery and vice under which millions are forced to live in the slums of all our great cities." Setting aside some lapses of judgment (Wallace championed phrenology and railed against vaccination), his balance sheet is remarkably broad-minded and perceptive.[3]

This is a chapter that is sometimes missing from big histories of both health and of economic growth, which either gloss over the setbacks of the nineteenth century or start after progress had resumed. In part this tendency is driven by a lack of good health data, especially globally, before the late nineteenth century. The most valiant effort to locate early sources of data was undertaken by James Riley, and it is evident from his findings that the statistical record for morbidity and mortality is hard to take back much further than 1900 for most of the world. But lack of data is not the only issue. There has also been a habit of treating infectious disease as a static and monolithic problem to be overcome, which ignores the negative consequences of growth and excludes the possibility that health conditions may actually have worsened.

We will try to work around some of these very real challenges. One way is to highlight the emergence of the most severe new disease in this period, cholera, whose radically different impacts around the globe are one proxy for the diverging patterns of health in the nineteenth century. Another is to bring plant and animal health into the discussion as a way of tracing some of the obviously negative ecological impacts of global-ization. Finally, we can look closely at the case of India. Although obviously no country is representative of the entire developing world, there are reasonably good data for India from the 1880s. India bore the full brunt of the great pandemics of cholera, plague, and influenza. Old scourges like malaria became an even greater problem not despite but *because* of modernization. In consequence, life expectancy in India stagnated at best and probably declined.

The history of disease deserves to figure prominently in both the successes and failures of the nineteenth century. The paradox of progress is a common pattern in the human past: the material forces that enable population growth and human connectivity also create new ecologies of infectious disease and stimulate the emergence of new pathogens. This pattern played out on a grander scale than ever before. In the nineteenth-century context, there was a new twist: some human societies were gaining the ability to control infectious disease. This imbalance played out in fateful ways in a rapidly changing world. Germs have often worked to amplify, undermine, and shape differences between human societies. But now, for the first time, the relative ability to mitigate the impact of infectious disease became a major feature of global power dynamics.[4]

The global history of infectious disease in the nineteenth century is more than a story of successes and failures. It is about the counterintuitive and causal relationships between homogenization and divergence. The nineteenth century was a time of global homogenization in countless ways: Western dress, French culinary habits, German systems of ordering knowledge, Greenwich Mean Time, and much else besides. Fashions and ideas circulated faster than ever. So, too, did pathogens—pathogens of humans and, as we will see, of plants and animals as well. It is telling that the very word "pandemic," in the sense of a global-scale outbreak of infectious disease, came into currency over the course of the nineteenth century. Not only were such events more likely to happen than ever before; human observers could also perceive and talk about and respond to them in ways that were impossible prior to modern communication and transport.[5]

The flip side of homogenization was divergence. What economic historians call "the Great Divergence" refers to the dramatic gaps that arose between the West and the "rest" in this period. Divergence is often measured in terms of power or money. By the time of World War I, Europe and its offshoots had commandeered most of the land surface of the planet. Meanwhile, differences in standards of living also widened. Ordinary laborers in western Europe and the United States came to enjoy per capita incomes ten times greater than those of their counterparts elsewhere. Although the issue has received far less attention, these gaps are paralleled in the history of health and infectious disease. Global divergence in life expectancy peaked in the early twentieth century before starting to converge again.[6]

We should emphasize that, even in the most economically and scientifically developed societies, the "wonderful century" did not bring unbroken progress, and the triumphs of modern medicine hardly seemed foreordained. For a time, urbanization, industrialization, and globalization outran advances in science and public health. By the 1860s, improvements in life expectancy had actually stalled or regressed in much of western Europe. In Britain, the pacesetter of industrial transformation, the achievements of the previous decades appeared tenuous, and science seemed impotent in the face of nature's whims. In 1865, with a gruesome cattle plague raging and a global cholera outbreak knocking at the door, one English churchman crowed that disease had humbled modernity: "All the medical men, all the learned men and philosophers, and all the practical men, and all the farmers, are puzzling and perplexing themselves about it, yet they cannot find out the cause of it. . . . It baffles their skill!"[7]

With hindsight, we know that he was wrong. Cattle plague was quickly controlled in Britain, while the cholera pandemic sweeping the planet was kept out. But in many places the confrontation with an ever more integrated global disease pool proved overwhelming. In the late nineteenth century, cholera killed tens of millions in British India. The cattle plague brought fresh misery to Africa. In short, the divergence in incomes and power was inseparable from the diverging experience of infectious disease around the globe.

The Global Context of Modernization

In 1798, when Malthus published the first edition of his essay, there were a billion people on the planet, give or take. By 1900, there were 1.6 billion humans alive. And while stagnation ruled over vast parts of the earth, industrial societies had started to make the Great Escape from hunger and premature death. Industrialization brought massive productivity increases and per capita economic growth in western Europe, the United States, and Japan. Elsewhere, per capita income remained low. In the early nineteenth century, the gap in per capita income between western Europe and the United States, on the one hand, and the rest of the world, on the other, was maybe two to one or three to one. In 1820, annual per capita income in China—one of the most advanced regions of the global economy outside Europe and its offshoots—was $624 in modern terms. In France, it was $1,442. By 1900, China had moved only a little ($840 per person, per year), and most of the tropical world still endured incomes near the subsistence level (Peru at $604, Brazil at $606, Indonesia at $1,076). Incomes in France had reached $4,214 per capita, Germany $4,596, and the United Kingdom $5,608. Although precision is specious, the overall pattern is clear enough. A yawning gap had opened.[8]

Modern growth had started with the application of coal-fired steam power to machines in mining and textile production. In the nineteenth century, the range of applications widened, as manufacturing and eventually transportation were transformed by fossil energy. Both technical innovation and the use of fossil fuels expanded to become systemic. The geographic scope of the industrializing world simultaneously grew. Although England was the early leader, other western European countries and the United States rapidly followed in the early nineteenth century.[9]

Innovation was reinforced by expanding markets and the rise of mass education. Schooling became compulsory in the industrialized world, and the public provision of education was enlarged, providing a massive boost to human capital. Basic scientific discovery accelerated, and knowledge of the natural world in turn created innovation and wealth.

By the 1880s, these changes catalyzed what is known as the Second Industrial Revolution, a great burst of new innovations driven by big steel, electricity, hydrocarbons, the internal combustion engine, and industrial chemistry. This new generation of technical marvels, put on display in Paris in 1900, is what so impressed Henry Adams as a rupture with all of previous human history.[10]

The innovations of the nineteenth century would have amounted to little without the energy to fuel them. In 1800, 70 percent of mechanical energy used globally came from human muscle. Power was thus fundamentally constrained by the physical limits of the human body. With industrialization, it became possible to convert fossilized solar energy to mechanical power. Already by 1800, steam engines could achieve 20 kilowatts of power. Over the course of the next century, that capacity increased thirtyfold, and engines became relentlessly more efficient. World production of coal exploded. The possibilities of petroleum were discovered in the 1850s, and from the 1880s oil gained practical importance with the development of the internal combustion engine. By 1900, mineral energy had passed biomass energy as a source for global energy use.[11]

From the very beginnings of industrialization, anxieties about resource exhaustion coexisted with blustery promises of infinite growth. Humans had been pushing remorselessly against limits for centuries—felling forests, hunting and fishing to extinction, strip-mining the earth, depleting soils, and expanding frontiers. In the 1780s, British mining engineers were already worried about "peak coal." But breakaway growth in the nineteenth century inspired new visions of cornucopian plenty: limitless growth, the substitutability of scarce resources, the power of human ingenuity to overcome ecological constraints. The great world's fairs of the age were an expression of this confidence and helped to cement it in the public mind. But this exuberant optimism should not obscure the fact that modern growth was, and still is, predicated on the use of finite resources—what Wallace evocatively called "the plunder of the earth."[12]

Over the course of the nineteenth century, behind machine-driven growth, the weight of global population shifted to the west. The Asian share of global population fell from two-thirds to a little over half, while

TABLE 11.1. Annual Growth Rates by Period and Region

	1500–1820	1820–70	1870–1913
Western Europe	0.26	0.69	0.77
Russia	0.37	0.97	1.33
United States	0.5	2.83	2.08
Latin America	0.07	1.26	1.63
India	0.2	0.38	0.43
Japan	0.22	0.21	0.95
China	0.41	−0.12	0.47

Europe, Russia, and the Americas grew from about a fifth to a third. Growth rates in the United States were stupendous, thanks to frontier expansion and mass-scale immigration, but even in western Europe, growth rates doubled or tripled, which makes the per capita income growth even more remarkable (see table 11.1).[13]

Population expansion in Europe and the United States was achieved, in part, by avoiding major cataclysms; the century between the Napoleonic Wars and World War I was a period of relative internal peace in Europe. Food production, complemented by food importation, kept up with demographic increase, in defiance of persistent Malthusian concerns. The exception that proves the rule is the Great Famine in Ireland, which was "*the* disaster of the century in Europe." Otherwise, such unmitigated humanitarian catastrophes were conspicuously absent. Cholera, as we will see, threatened to spiral into a calamity, but by tremendous exertions of effort it was mostly kept under control in Europe and the United States.[14]

By contrast, nearly everywhere outside of Europe and its settler offshoots experienced crises of enormous magnitude in the course of the century. The most dramatic instance is China, whose population actually contracted in the mid-nineteenth century. The eighteenth century had been prosperous and remarkably stable under Qing rule. But this stability was interrupted from around 1850 by a sequence of revolts and famines. The death tolls from these crises are staggering. Numbers can be taken with a grain of salt, but the Taiping Rebellion (1850–64)—an anti-Manchu uprising, with millenarian elements—may have claimed thirty million lives in the fertile southeastern provinces and in much of the Yangzi valley. The Nian Rebellion (1851–68) was a peasant revolt in the north that also brought devastation. The Chinese empire threatened to come unbundled with Muslim revolts in both the northwest and southwest (the Dungan and Panthay Rebellions) seeking liberation from the Qing state. And in the 1870s and 1890s, terrific famines swept the country. The Great North China Famine of the late 1870s put some ten million victims in their graves.[15]

The Chinese disasters of the nineteenth century were a dynastic crisis of the Qing. They were simultaneously crises of Chinese imperialism, with tensions flaring in quasi-autonomous frontier regions. It is also necessary to see these upheavals as Malthusian-ecological crises. China's population had grown from 150 million to 300 million between 1700 and 1800, and then by another 150 million over the next fifty years. Potatoes and other New World crops fed this expansion, but there was no transition to sustained technology-led growth. Demographic pressures set the stage for mass-scale violence. Changes in the global order exacerbated problems. Even as European power expanded globally, China was never colonized. Instead, western powers demanded access to trade. The British, in particular, coveted tea, and wished to pay for it with opium produced by their Indian colonies. Objections by the Chinese state were forcefully overridden in the two Opium Wars (1839–42 and 1856–60). These conflicts made apparent the military chasm that had opened up between East and West, embarrassed the Qing rulers, and worsened the problem of narcotics addiction.[16]

India's population history sits somewhere between the Chinese and European examples, and here colonialism was a primary factor. India achieved slow and modest demographic growth, despite a series of major famines in the late eighteenth and late nineteenth century. These were humanitarian catastrophes on the biggest scale, with tens of millions perishing. The famines in India were front of mind for Wallace as an indictment of modern progress. Moreover, as we will see, the globalization of infectious disease hit India especially hard.[17]

In Australia and much of the Pacific, the demographic trajectory of the nineteenth century was in some ways a replay of the Columbian

Exchange. Contact with relatively remote islands introduced novel pathogens to native populations. The indigenous inhabitants of Tahiti, Fiji, and New Caledonia suffered severe demographic losses. The story of Hawai'i is illustrative and well documented. When Captain Cook arrived in 1778, he ended a long period of isolation. The islands were home to more than half a million people. Westerners introduced syphilis and gonorrhea, and in the following years came typhoid, dysentery, whooping cough, measles, and smallpox. The tragedy played out in miniature in 1824, when a royal delegation from the island including King Kamehameha II and Queen Kamamalu traveled to London on a whaler to seek a British alliance; they were received with polite fascination in England, but within a month measles struck the royal party. Both the king and queen died. The lopsided disease exchange meant that within a century of European contact, the indigenous population of Hawai'i declined by more than 90 percent.[18]

Africa's population history in the nineteenth century remains obscure. The decline of the slave trade, first in West Africa and then in the eastern half of the continent, might have cleared the path to new growth. But it seems that there was stasis. By 1900, the continent was home to around 150 million people, not far above what it had been a century before. The burden of infectious disease kept mortality rates high. And the already hazardous disease ecology only became worse as the continent was more deeply integrated into global trading networks. The introduction of cholera was lethal, and old germs, like smallpox, were repeatedly reintroduced to the continent. The "scramble for Africa," the sudden onset of direct colonization, brought new forms of exploitation and violence. Among the worst effects of modern globalization was the introduction of unfamiliar veterinary diseases, the rinderpest virus above all. The decades immediately following colonization were an "epidemiological disaster for Africa." In all, "the stasis and even decline in African populations of the nineteenth century suggest that a combination of global conditions and domestic crises were constraining Africa in this era of imperialism and industrialization."[19]

Globally, besides the sheer multiplication of human numbers, there were also profound transformations in the spatial ordering of human

populations. Virtually everywhere on earth, human populations became simultaneously more dense, more mobile, and more interconnected. These changes were pushed by industrialization and new technologies of transportation and communication, but they also
transcended purely material stimuli. The rise of the modern city is a
phenomenon in its own right, and one with many consequences for
human disease.[20]

Cities grew larger, and in industrializing societies the proportion of
the population living in a town increased dramatically, particularly from
about the 1870s. Transportation systems enabled urban growth and
linked towns into networks of production, distribution, and finance. It
was the golden age of the port city, and railroads gave rise to the "junc-
tion." Growth was most spectacular at the intersection of industrialization, frontier expansion, and transportation hubs. Chicago embodied
these changes in exaggerated form: a city of thirty thousand at midcentury, it was home to 1.1 million residents only four decades later.[21]

Cross-currents of health and disease coursed underneath the rise of
the modern city. As we saw, the timeless role of cities as demographic
sinks started to change in the eighteenth century, behind the early
health transition. In some European towns, birth rates surpassed death
rates, allowing natural increase. However, in 1800, there was still an
urban penalty, and the countryside remained far healthier than the city.
In the early stages of urbanization, national-level life expectancies actually declined as the weight of populations shifted toward the city. But in
the latter half of the century, improvements accelerated in the developed world. By the early twentieth century, urban populations were
healthier than their rural counterparts, a pattern that endures.[22]

Urbanization represented a kind of internal mobility. But long-
distance migration was also a form of mobility accentuated by changes
in the nineteenth century. In the words of the historian Jürgen Osterhammel, "No other epoch in history was an age of long-distance migration on such a massive scale." In the century before World War I, more
than eighty million people migrated from one country to another. There
were three main flows. The first was the "settler revolution," the push of
populations into conquered regions, mainly in temperate climates. This

FIGURE 11.1. Age of Steam, Nanterre, France. Engraving by Charles Rauch.
In the nineteenth century, steamships and railroads started to replace horse-,
wind-, and human-powered transportation. Wellcome Collection (CC BY 4.0).

was mostly an Anglo phenomenon in Canada, the United States, and
Australia, but it had analogues in Russia and China. The second was the
transition from the slave trade to contract labor. Indian and Chinese
"coolies" were pulled by the millions into the tropics and the American
west. The third was the magnetic attraction of the United States for European migrants. Novel in their scale, these migrations continued many
of the processes set in motion in previous centuries, including the long
tragedy of indigenous dispossession. The swashbuckling "land runs" of
Oklahoma, for instance, carved up remaining pieces of Indian Territory
for settlement at the end of the century.[23]

Human movement was driven in part by the revolution in transportation (see figure 11.1). In *The Wonderful Century*, Wallace put transportation technologies at the head of his list of life-changing innovations. The
steamship and the railroad were arguably the most transformational
technologies of the century. Before the nineteenth century, the most

advanced modes of transportation depended on wind power or horses. Both imposed considerable constraints on the volume and speed of movement that had changed little over the millennia. Napoleon's army deployed to Egypt in 1798 no faster than a Roman army could have; two decades later, when the *Savannah* became the first steamship to cross the Atlantic, there were worries it would be dispatched to Saint Helena, the remote island where Napoleon had been exiled, to bring him to Europe.[24]

The impact of the steamship was first felt along rivers and canals, and soon ocean voyages were possible. In 1828, the governor-general of India arrived in Calcutta by steamship to great fanfare. Steamers were outfitted with heavy artillery, and the spectacular defeat of China in the Opium Wars was decided by gunboats. The opening of the Suez Canal in 1869 knocked four thousand miles off the voyage from Europe to Asia. Steamships grew in size, number, and fuel efficiency, and by century's end, nearly all steamships in service were made of steel. The railroad accomplished an analogous revolution on land. The 1840s "were a time of railroad fever in the Western world." The golden spike joining the eastern and western rail networks of the United States was hammered in 1869, and transcontinental networks connected most of the Old World; by 1910, "with only one short interruption to switch gauges, people could travel by train all the way from Lisbon to Beijing." Rail construction was integral to colonial projects, most notably in India, where it was vastly more efficient than riverine transport. Railroads allowed humans to impose transportation grids that effaced natural constraints and obstacles. Tellingly, railroad schedules also played an important role in the standardization of time.[25]

The transport revolution quickened the pace of global trade and altered its character. Before the nineteenth century, most long-distance trade carried high-value commodities, usually goods that could not be produced or supplied locally, such as tropical groceries. But as freight costs plunged, it became economical to ship bulk goods. Basic foodstuffs came to occupy a much larger share of trade. The British Empire promoted free trade, and in real terms of value, global trade increased tenfold between 1840 and the eve of World War I. Prices were increasingly coordinated by global markets, and capital flowed from centers of finance to investments worldwide. Very often, this meant that capital from Europe secured ownership over raw materials or natural resources vital to production, like minerals or plantation goods, as supply chains became more complex. The growth of trade also marks a point of inflection in the history of disease. Trade surpassed war as the greater force in the transmission of contagious disease. More often than not, the outbreaks of the nineteenth century came in peace.[26]

Fuel-powered transportation was a watershed. It forever broke what the historian Braudel called the "tyranny of distance." Not since the domestication of the horse had there been innovations in the means of transport with such radical implications for the transmission of disease. The triumph of steamships and railroads marked a new epoch in the long history of globalization, one that was only left behind by the rise of jet travel in the late twentieth century.

The Age of Pandemics

The globalization of disease in the nineteenth century gave the word *pandemic* its current meaning. Despite its Greek roots (meaning "all" and "the people"), *pandemic* only came into usage as a medical term in the early modern period. For centuries, it was synonymous with *epidemic*, and meant simply a disease outbreak. In the 1828 edition of Noah Webster's dictionary, for example, a pandemic is still defined as an epidemic. Over the course of the century, the word *pandemic* came to be reserved for epidemics of interregional scope, for planetary waves of infectious disease. The evolution of the word reflected both reality and perception. Diseases like cholera and influenza rippled out across the earth in widening circles with startling speed. Scientific and political interest in global public health was increasing. Mass media and telecommunications made it easier to track global-scale disease events in real time.[27]

The transformations of the nineteenth century created a global disease ecology. The density, mobility, and connectivity of human populations played to the advantage of our parasites. Cholera was the quintessential emerging disease of the nineteenth century. It could both travel

BLUE STAGE OF THE SPASMODIC CHOLERA.
Sketch of a Girl who died of Cholera, in Sunderland, November, 1831.

FIGURE 11.2. Cholera in Sunderland, England, in *The Lancet*, 1831.
Wellcome Collection (CC BY 4.0).

quickly and take hold tenaciously. But long-familiar epidemic threats like yellow fever, influenza, and bubonic plague circulated farther and faster than ever before on global networks. And endemic diseases such as malaria also cast a pall over modern growth. Although less spectacular, these ancient scourges were destructive of human life and became more important than ever in the modern age. Genomic evidence is now enriching our understanding of the "homogenization" of human diseases that were already globally dispersed. Traces of European expansion are reflected in the spread of more virulent lineages of TB, for instance, which "'swamped' pre-existing local indigenous strains."[28]

Let us consider cholera as an exemplar of new ecologies of disease and disparate social responses. It is hardly original to treat cholera as the germ of the century and a symbol of its paradoxes. Cholera, a bacterial disease transmitted via fecal contamination of water, was not the most deadly affliction of the nineteenth century. But it was the most feared, at least in the West, where its appearance threatened the tenuous control over epidemic mortality that had so recently been won (see figure 11.2).

In the words of historian Christopher Hamlin, cholera "grew up in conjunction with Enlightenment liberalism, nationalism, imperialism, and the rise of global biomedical science. It was most problematic— as opposed to causing the greatest mortality—in precisely the places where these darlings thrived." Western societies managed to bring the threat of cholera under control, yet globally, the cholera pandemics of the nineteenth century carried tens of millions into their graves.[29]

Cholera is a disease caused by a comma-shaped bacterium, *Vibrio cholera*. The word *cholera* had been used as a medical term to describe gastroenteritis for centuries (reflecting its roots in ancient humoral theory: *choler* is the word for yellow bile). In the nineteenth century, the name was lent to describe a new disease that exploded into a series of global pandemics. The first cholera pandemic is conventionally dated to an outbreak that erupted in 1817. Successive waves of disease seemed to emanate from South Asia, and the new disease was sometimes called "Asiatic cholera" to distinguish it from more benign diarrhea and vomiting. Some medical writers even started referring to *cholera nostra*, or *our* cholera, to specify the generic diarrheal disease of old. The new cholera was something altogether more dangerous.[30]

There have been seven global pandemics of cholera since 1817. In reality, we should imagine these pandemics as pulses of disease diffusion, followed by long-lasting establishment of the bacterium in many regions. Tree thinking and time travel have confirmed that all of these pandemics were caused by a single lineage sharing a common ancestor only a few hundred years ago. Thus, it was only recently that the cholera bacterium acquired the necessary adaptions allowing it to be an effective human pathogen. Crucially, *V. cholera* evolved the ability to know from chemical cues when it is in the human gut. When it senses that it is in this environment, it activates virulence genes that not only make us very sick but also guarantee the massive expulsion of watery diarrhea that supports its transmission in human populations.[31]

The chain of evolutionary events that led to modern human-adapted *V. cholera* probably happened in the Ganges Delta (see figure 11.3). The Ganges Delta is the world's largest delta, today home to more than one

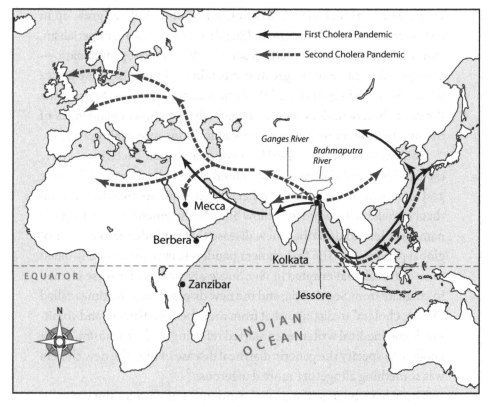

FIGURE 11.3. Cholera helped create the modern understanding of "pandemics" as planetary-scale disease events.

hundred million people. It has the climate and landscape to concentrate human beings in an ecosystem where *V. cholera* is rife. The Ganges River is sacred in Hinduism. Over the centuries, as people drank its slightly saline water, or bathed in its cool stream, they ingested the bacteria, and those bacteria that had the genetic makeup to multiply explosively in the human body and eject prolifically into the water supply were an evolutionary success. The Ganges Delta would prove to be the epicenter of the global pandemics and a stable reservoir between pandemics. It is likely the evolutionary birthplace of the pathogen.[32]

The outstanding feature of infection with pathogenic *V. cholera* is the loss of fluids. The bacterium enters the body via the mouth in contaminated food or water. The incubation period ranges from a few hours to a few days. Some patients suffer a mild disease, with modest amounts

TABLE 11.2. Chronology of Seven Global Cholera
Pandemics

First	1817–24
Second	1829–51
Third	1852–59
Fourth	1860–75
Fifth	1881–95
Sixth	1899–1923
Seventh	1960–present

of loose stool. Most, however, experience a fast and furious battle in the bowels. The first symptoms are vomiting and watery diarrhea. There is no mistaking the "truly amazing copiousness of these evacuations." The diarrhea continues even after the bowels are empty, ejecting a clear fluid often called "rice-water stool." As the tissues under the skin are drained of fluid, the skin loses turgidity. The patient turns bluish, and the body appears sunken. The loss of salt and water is so sudden and severe that many patients die within a day.[33]

Cholera might not have been entirely new in the nineteenth century. It is possible that the bacterium had occasionally diffused before the start of the modern pandemic era. The molecular clock analysis does suggest that pathogenic cholera has been adapting to humans for a few hundred years. A series of outbreaks attested in India from the 1760s is especially likely to have been the prelude to the first pandemic. But the outbreak of 1817 marked the beginning of a new era in the history of the disease, both in perception and reality (see table 11.2).[34]

By August 1817, following unusually heavy rains, an outbreak was in progress near Jessore, a town in the Ganges Delta. Jessore is about fifty miles from Calcutta (modern Kolkata), the capital of British India, where escalating mortality startled the imperial authorities. Over the next three years, the disease affected most of India. It spread outward overland through South Asia. It also moved by sea, curling to the east, where it reached Indonesia, China, and Japan, as well as to the west, sprawling over the Middle East. The first pandemic touched the edges of eastern Europe but failed to penetrate farther. Similarly, it reached the coast of East Africa but spared the interior.[35]

The arrival of global cholera was a conjuncture of natural and human history. A bacterium that normally clings to crustacean shells had learned to invade the human gut. But this was not sufficient to spark the global health disasters that ensued from 1817. Colonialism and capitalism were necessary for that. Calcutta in particular was in the throes of rapid urbanization. The Ganges Delta sat at the nexus of British commerce in the east and was a global hub. Following the victory over Napoleon in 1815, the British Empire was ascendant, and its active promotion of international trade, now amplified by new transportation technologies, created the great expansion of global commerce that lies behind the cholera pandemics.[36]

The second (1829–51) and third (1852–59) pandemics were vast in their geographic reach. They were by far the deadliest outbreaks in Europe and the United States. In the industrial world, the cholera pandemics struck along class lines, devastating the slums where the working poor were concentrated. Because the cholera bacterium spreads via the fecal-oral route, it thrives on squalor. But the overlap between the risk of contracting the disease and social stratification was always imperfect: at any time, the germ might find its way through runoff or soil to the drinking water of the affluent. Cholera was thus quickly entangled with concern for, and fear of, the poor. Consequently, the cholera epidemics in Europe helped to galvanize the public health movement and strengthen its calls for sanitary reform, even as the nature of the disease and the value of quarantine were hotly debated for decades.[37]

Over the course of the nineteenth century, the differences *between* societies in the ability to withstand cholera became sharpened. In Europe and the United States, the fourth (1860–75), fifth (1881–95), and sixth (1899–1923) pandemics were either kept out or quickly contained. Where cholera did strike, it was a scandalous exception, as in Hamburg in 1892. But globally, cholera continued its devastating career.[38]

The patterns of global divergence in the course of the cholera pandemics can be starkly illustrated by the course of the fourth pandemic on the island of Zanzibar in 1869. Zanzibar is an archipelago of small islands off the coast of Tanzania. It offers ready access to interior Africa and has been a node for exchange since ancient times. It was a global meeting place, where Indian and Arab traders rubbed shoulders with Africans and Europeans. Zanzibar was the most important entrepôt in the eastern slave trade, a fact that made it of special interest to the British, whose gunships patrolled the coasts trying to suppress the trade. The islands also boast some of the finest clove plantations anywhere in the world. In the 1860s Zanzibar was controlled by the sultan of Oman, whose sovereignty was underwritten by British naval power. The gathering forces of globalization were refracted through this busy hub.[39]

We can follow the course of the outbreak on Zanzibar in unusual detail through the eyes of Dr. James Christie. Christie was a Scotsman educated at Glasgow, and from 1865 to 1874 he served as the personal physician to His Highness the sultan of Zanzibar. Christie was a sharp-eyed observer with a sensitive understanding of the Zanzibari milieu. Christie's studies of the outbreak, first in a series of reports published in the medical journal *The Lancet*, then more expansively as a book, *Cholera Epidemics in East Africa*, are a vivid chronicle of the deadly disease. The themes that Christie explored were of urgent interest, not least because the Suez Canal had been opened in 1869, the very year the outbreak reached Zanzibar. Europe had drawn closer to the Indian Ocean than ever before.[40]

The fourth pandemic had arrived in Mecca by 1865. Pilgrimages had become major conduits for global disease transmission, and from Mecca, the outbreak crossed the Red Sea and arrived at the great trading center of Berbera on the Somali coast. Berbera was "one of the oldest trading localities in the world," where caravans from interior Africa met to exchange with merchants on the coast. Cholera diffused inland along the arteries of Africa, infecting the Masai country dominated by powerful tribes of herders. The mortality was "appalling." Christie believed that the disease had spread overland and then curled back to the shores of East Africa. From there, in December 1869, the disease jumped to the island.[41]

The city of Zanzibar lacked sanitary infrastructure. "There are no sewers for carrying off the water from the place, and all the filth and rubbish of the town is swept to the beach by the street torrents." Cesspits were ubiquitous, plumbed into the soft, sandy soil. "The latrinae, which are in connection with every house . . . are merely shallow pits or wells, and the contents are not discharged by sewers to the sea-beach. . . . The fluid contents percolate the porous soil, and gradually find their way to the adjacent shore. When the latrinae become blocked up with the accumulations of a generation or two, as the case may be, they are either closed up and new ones excavated, or the slimy, semi-solid contents, are baled out on the public streets, and left to find their way by the nearest slope towards the sea-beach." The town was crawling with vermin. "Countless myriads of ants and beetles, millions of rats, and armies of wild dogs, aid in removing the garbage of the town and suburbs." The stench of the beach was also legendary.[42]

Christie understood that the water supply was essential to the epidemiology of cholera. He also recognized that ethnic segregation on the island, accentuated by social and cultural differences, shaped the course of the outbreak. The epidemic first ravaged the poor quarter of the town, and there were reports of slaves "suddenly ill at their work . . . staggering home to die." Early in December, as the fast of Ramadan began, the outbreak spread. Christie treated his first case, an enslaved girl. He described "a peculiar coldness . . . a cold clamminess of death, which, when once felt, can never be forgotten." His patient suffered intense thirst, and her pulse weakened. "The skin of the fingers, toes, hands, and feet became shrivelled; the features pinched; the eyes sunken, and glaring; and the entire aspect of the countenance changed." Like many cholera victims, she sank toward death with lucidity. Her "intellectual faculties were clear to the last."[43]

As the contagion spread, a gloom fell over the city. Yet no one tried to flee, and Christie was struck by the charity that everyone showed to members of their own community. At first bodies were at least wrapped in mats and dragged with a pole to the outskirts of town, where they were put in shallow graves. But gradually all customs were overwhelmed. "At last, tired of scooping out even the shallow graves, they began to expose the dead on the sea-beach, and to throw them over the bridge into the sea." Christie noted that the spread of the epidemic to the plantations was erratic, because only some of the outlying villages became infected by laborers who came into the city. Christie was also keenly interested in the variable fate of ships in the harbor, which often drew their water from the unsanitary wells along the shore. Several American ships called during the pandemic, but the two that hurried off were spared any deaths. In all, the mortality was both severe and lopsided. Nineteen Europeans and Americans died on ships. But not one of the resident westerners, all of whom had access to clean water, fell to the disease. The Hindu population, too, was spared. But the mass of destitute men, women, and children on the island, who did not have access to clean water, were unable to escape. By the end, Christie estimated that twelve to fifteen thousand residents of the city had died, out of a population of eighty to one hundred thousand. On the entire island, with a population of three hundred to four hundred thousand, some twenty-five to thirty thousand perished.[44]

What happened on Zanzibar is thus a microcosm of the nineteenth century. The 1860s were a turning point in the global history of cholera. Thereafter, the germ was almost entirely absent from western Europe and its offshoots. By contrast, it continued to produce grisly death tolls in regions where it found poor and crowded populations. In India, where there are some official records from which mortality totals have been reconstructed, cholera claimed an estimated fifteen million lives between 1817 and 1865; between then and 1947, it carried off, conservatively, another twenty-three million people. Cholera launched as a disease of globalization, and it subsequently became a disease of poverty and underdevelopment, intertwined with the patterns of global divergence during a decisive phase of transformation. It remains a devastating disease today, amid the ongoing seventh pandemic.[45]

Cholera was only the most dramatic example of a parasite that cunningly took advantage of the age of steamships and railroads. Yellow fever, influenza, and plague quite evidently belong on the list too. The vector-borne viral disease yellow fever had diffused from West Africa in the age of the slave trade. Although the tropics were the permanent homeland of yellow fever, summer shipping had long provided a means for the disease to make deadly seasonal forays farther north. The Atlantic coast of North America was struck repeatedly from the 1690s on. Steamships only extended its range. Outbreaks reached the Mediterranean and southern Europe sporadically in the early nineteenth century. Quarantine regulations were enforced to keep yellow fever off European shores. Aside from bubonic plague, the disease was the most important target of quarantine efforts until cholera took its place.[46]

For a time, from the 1820s to 1840s, it seemed that yellow fever had been corralled in its natural habitats. It was absent from Europe for a generation. But then, from the middle of the century, there was a "massive surge" of yellow fever. The long-feared potential of the disease to spread via steamship became a reality. The disease struck along the coasts of South America, Europe, and North America. In 1857, five thousand people died in an outbreak in Lisbon, and the disease appeared in French ports. In 1865 the disease arrived in Wales, where it docked along with a ship that had sailed from Cuba. The power of steamships to disperse the disease was evident inland as well. Yellow fever spread repeatedly up the Mississippi River. One of the worst outbreaks occurred in 1878, reaching Memphis, Tennessee, and killing at least twenty thousand people in total. It was against the backdrop of yellow fever's continued ravages that, in 1881, the Cuban physician Carlos Finlay presented his hypothesis that the disease was transmitted by mosquitos—a milestone on the path to systematic control of vector-borne disease.[47]

There are parallels in the history of influenza, except that unlike yellow fever, the flu is caused by a respiratory virus unbound by the limits of its insect vector. Its pandemic potential only continued to escalate into the twentieth century, such that the period from the late nineteenth century to present marks a distinct phase in the history of the infection. Influenza is a severe respiratory disease caused by several species of virus, the most important of which is *influenza A*. The virus has a segmented genome, made up of eight separate links of RNA. These segments can easily be reassorted—a kind of genetic mix and match—when different strains of the virus infect the same cell. The flu is a virus of birds but can also infect mammals, like humans and pigs. The planet's billions of wild waterfowl form a natural reservoir for *influenza A*. Human influenza is a kind of long-lasting crossover event, in which a parasite of avian origin circulates in populations of an abundant global primate.[48]

The early history of influenza is obscure, but from the sixteenth century, large-scale waves of acute respiratory disease are attested every twenty or thirty years. With a few exceptions, these historic waves of pandemic influenza appear to have been relatively mild. The spread of influenza had always been limited by the speed of transportation. In the pandemic of 1781–82, it was noted by one observer that the disease spread exactly as fast as a horse could travel. The impact of steamships and railroads was not immediate. There was a surprising lull in the history of influenza in the middle of the nineteenth century. But in 1889, the virus returned with a vengeance. The beginning of the pandemic was heralded in central Asia in spring 1889, and after a few quiet months it spread rapidly in the fall. As a historian of the outbreak has noted, "This explosive spread was doubtlessly made possible by the extensive railroad network that connected Lisbon and London to Vienna and Moscow. Indeed, for the first time in history, virtually all contemporary observers linked influenza diffusion to transportation networks." This outbreak was truly global and recurred in many places in three successive years. It was moderately severe, with case fatality rates around 0.1–0.2 percent. Known as the "Russian flu" at the time, the collective experience of a global mortality event in the age of telegraphs made "pandemic" a household word.[49]

Unfortunately, the pandemic of 1889–92 was a portent of worse to come. The pandemic of 1918–19 was the ultimate manifestation of a disease event in the age of steamships and railroads. It was in absolute terms one of the single most deadly events in global history, claiming the lives of maybe fifty million victims. (Proportionately, though, its impact on global mortality was far less than that of the Black Death or post-Columbian epidemics, because human numbers were so much greater by 1918.) It infected perhaps one in three persons alive, making it probably the single most coordinated rapid attack by a parasite in the history of the planet.[50]

The genetic material of the 1918–19 influenza virus has been recovered (from tissues preserved in formaldehyde, rather than archaeological material). The pandemic was caused by an H1N1 strain of avian origins. Why it was so pathogenic remains partly mysterious, but this strain seems to have activated secondary bacterial infection, leading to pneumonia in severe cases. The virus struck the young and healthy unusually hard. The exact geographic source of the great influenza remains equally obscure. In early fall 1918, it was suddenly "everywhere at once," suggesting that the virus had been disseminating for months before it became apparent that a mortality crisis was already in progress. The pandemic crested in the winter and then returned a year later. The global impact was staggering, but uneven. In the United States, there were 548,000 deaths, about 0.5 percent of the population. In India, the precise mortality is disputed, but the best estimate is around fourteen million deaths, about 5 percent of the total population.[51]

The lingering impact of the 1918–19 pandemic is as remarkable as its explosive beginnings. We are still living through it. The virus that swept the globe in 1918 became a "founder virus," and it has fittingly been called the "mother of all pandemics." Every subsequent epidemic of *influenza A*, including the seasonal influenza outbreaks, has been caused by a descendant of the virus that caused the 1918–19 pandemic. This crossover event from birds to humans was thus exceptionally successful. And the threat of future genetic reassortments that spin off novel influenza strains, replaying the events of 1918–19, remains one of the most dangerous lurking threats to human health.[52]

The only disease that rivaled cholera and influenza for explosiveness in this period was the bubonic plague. In the preantibiotic era, this bacterial infection made one last campaign to become a world-shaking disease. The Second Plague Pandemic that started with the Black Death in the fourteenth century had never really ended. Outbreaks of the disease petered out in western Europe, but plague epidemics in eastern Europe and the Ottoman Empire continued through the eighteenth century and even beyond. What is traditionally known as the Third Plague Pandemic overlaps the Second Pandemic, chronologically and spatially. And the genetic evidence has revealed an even closer association between the two historic pandemics. The strain of plague that caused the Third Plague Pandemic actually descends from a lineage that had arisen during the Black Death. The Third Plague Pandemic is, genetically, an extension of the late medieval outbreak.[53]

The beginning of the Third Plague Pandemic is dated by convention to 1894, when the outbreak reached Guangzhou (Canton) and British-controlled Hong Kong. This chronology obscures the Chinese back-story of the pandemic, however, which has been traced by the historian Carol Benedict. Plague epidemics had been simmering since the 1770s in the southwestern province of Yunnan. In the later eighteenth century, demographic and economic growth brought humans into greater contact with local rodent reservoirs of the plague throughout the western part of the province. Trading networks helped the plague to strike farther to the east, inching closer to the populous coastal regions. The plague became a major problem during the conflicts between the Han Chinese center and the Muslim periphery; for most of the period between 1856 and 1873, Yunnan was the scene of a bloody civil war. The demographic toll was heavy: the registered population dropped from 7.5 million to 3 million, with famine, violence, and plague combining to account for the heavy losses.[54]

The arrival of plague in Guangzhou and Hong Kong in 1894 was the end point of plague's overland expansion stretching back more than a century. It was also a fateful new beginning. Guangzhou, perched on the mouth of the Pearl River, was under Qing control and home to more than two million residents. In the course of the outbreak, as many as one hundred thousand residents of the city perished. Eighty miles away was the British-ruled island of Hong Kong, a "commercial colossus." Half of China's imports passed through the entrepôt. Its slums were deplorable, and its medical infrastructure meager. At least six thousand residents died in summer 1894 from the plague.[55]

The plague outbreak in Hong Kong set off alarms worldwide, and it was soon the occasion for a scientific milestone. As news of the epidemic spread, the Japanese government dispatched a team of researchers led by Kitasato Shibasaburō, a bacteriologist who had trained in Robert Koch's lab in Berlin (figure 11.4). Three days after the arrival of the Japanese team, Alexandre Yersin, an acolyte of Louis Pasteur serving in the French colonial health service in Saigon, also slipped into Hong Kong. The race to identify the microbial cause of the disease was fiercely competitive. Priority is still murky: Shibasaburō seems to have looked

FIGURE 11.4. Photograph of Kitasato Shibasaburō,
who raced to discover the plague bacterium in Hong Kong.
Wellcome Collection (CC BY 4.0).

at the bacterium first and beat Yersin to publication. But the French
scientist was only days behind, and his descriptions are regarded as superior. Yersin also emphasized the importance of rats in the plague
cycle. Fairly or not, he is immortalized in the nomenclature of the species, *Yersinia pestis.*[56]

Once the plague-infested rodents reached this hub of global commerce, the plague spread farther than ever before, riding in the hulls of giant steamships bound for every port in the world. The global effort to disrupt the spread of the plague was unprecedented in its scale and coordination. Quarantine and fumigation were at the heart of a massive scheme to prevent the plague from becoming a replay of the Black Death. The plague reached San Francisco and ultimately seeded rodent populations in the western United States (where it still lurks in prairie dog colonies), but only a few hundred Americans ultimately perished. Similarly, despite wild fears in Europe, the Third Plague Pandemic was demographically negligible there, claiming only seven thousand or so victims. The plague reached East Africa, where it is still enzootic in places like Madagascar. But its direst effects were felt in Asia. It killed millions in China. And the most affected region during the Third Plague Pandemic was India. Conservatively, plague claimed twelve million victims in India during the course of the pandemic.[57]

It is easy to think of epidemic diseases like cholera, yellow fever, influenza, and plague as relics of a premodern past. In reality, each of these diseases seized the opportunities presented by motorized transport to become thoroughly modern diseases. Only in those few societies that had undergone the early health transition, and learned to control the wild oscillations of epidemic disease early on, could the mortality crises of modernity seem like something from another epoch. Indeed, the success of containment efforts in protecting industrializing societies from the new threats of the period might be ranked among the more underappreciated accomplishments of the wonderful century. Unfortunately, the benefits were not universally shared.

Globalizing Plant Disease

In summer 1889, Paris played host to the Universal Exposition—the tenth such convention since the first world's fair in London in 1851. In conjunction with the exposition of 1889, France also hosted the first International Congress of Agriculture, which gathered 1,400 experts and officials from around the globe to discuss the state of the industry.

Like the exposition, the congress was a venue for the exchange of ideas and innovations, with a touch of nationalist showmanship. But the congress was tinged by urgent misgivings about globalization. The French minister presiding at the congress, a fervent protectionist, opened the proceedings by decrying market integration, which had been "disastrous for the old nations," whose tired soils struggled to compete with the virgin fields of America and Russia. To make matters worse, global integration had also brought pests, blights, and rots to the farms of the world.[58]

The homogenization of human disease pools has exact parallels in the diseases of plants and animals. This phenomenon merits a brief detour in a history of infectious disease. The topic has been relatively neglected; though some of its individual pieces have received attention, the bigger picture has hardly ever been sketched, despite its importance and the obvious parallels with human health. The history of plant disease also illustrates the role of science, ingenuity, and public action in countering the dangers posed by new diseases. Yet there is not even a word that describes a spatially widespread outbreak of plant disease, such as *pandemic* for humans and *panzootic* for animals. Nonetheless, rapid, widespread outbreaks of plant disease have been an important part of humanity's efforts to feed itself.[59]

Plant diseases have plagued farmers since the dawn of agriculture. Parasitism of plants is a pervasive part of nature. But from the moment humans started the bioengineering project of farming—selecting particular species, manipulating desired genetic traits, reducing natural diversity—we have incentivized parasites to adapt to our favored breeds. Humanity's scheme to harvest energy from a few preferred species allows plant pathogens to thrive for a simple reason: the "environmental and genetic uniformity of the agricultural ecosystem." Modernity has supercharged the kind of ecological transformation that is conducive to the evolution of plant pathogens. Previously intricate patchworks of interdependent species have been slashed and burned, replaced with dense, monotonous rows of human-preferred energy producers. Industrialization accelerated the process, as did global trade that allowed specialization and further manipulation of genetic lines.[60]

The U.S. delegate to the International Congress of Agriculture in 1889 was Charles V. Riley, who organized the American exhibition in Paris. Riley was a key figure at a key moment. A native Londoner who immigrated to Illinois, he established the applied study of plant pests in the United States. He rose to prominence as the head of the Grasshopper Commission, an entity that he convinced the congress to create in response to a plague of grasshoppers that threatened American farming in the 1870s. He was the perfect person to represent the Americans in Paris; indeed, if you like French wine, you should count Riley a hero. He played a leading role in recognizing that certain American vine stocks could resist the *Phylloxera* aphid, a tiny sap-sucking insect that had come to threaten European vineyards (see figure 11.5). The insect is native to North America, and the importation of American vines in the 1850s or early 1860s inadvertently carried the pest to Europe. "Once steamships began plying the trade routes, the bug could survive the trip, alight in Europe, and, soon enough, find a marvelously undefended environment."[61]

The Great French Wine Blight threatened to wipe out millennia of viticultural craft. The *Phylloxera* pest spread with terrifying speed, and it struck farmers as a kind of "tuberculosis for grapes," causing the plants to weaken, rot, and die. The cause was identified, and cures were desperately sought as the pest ravaged vineyards across France. A third of France's grapes were ruined, and fear of losing the entire industry gripped the nation before a suitable solution was found. Although there were some advocates for chemical treatment, Riley and others—called the "Americanists"—promoted the solution of grafting European *vinifera* onto resistant rootstocks imported from across the Atlantic. The latter solution prevailed and worked splendidly. Riley was awarded the Legion of Honor by the French government just a few years after the congress.[62]

The Great French Wine Blight is famous enough in viticultural lore, but its larger context is not. The reason the French were importing the American vines that brought the pest in the first place was, in fact, to counter another introduced pathogen: powdery mildew. And then the success of the American rootstocks in providing resistance to *Phylloxera*

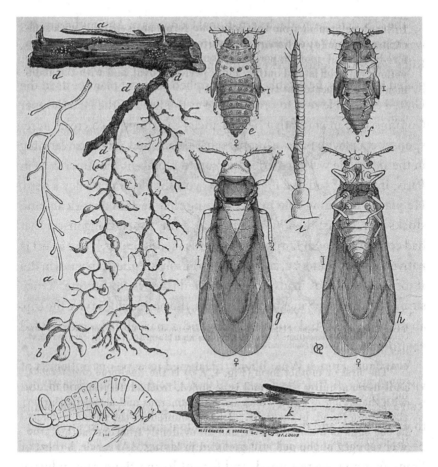

FIGURE 11.5. *Phylloxera,* cause of the Great French Wine Blight that threatened French vineyards. From *Popular Science,* 1874.

had an unwelcome sequel: it allowed downy mildew, yet another plant disease, to cross the Atlantic and establish in the vineyards of Europe. Every solution seemed to entail a new problem, and the succession of unintended biological consequences in the global wine industry is a parable for the endless evolutionary game between parasites and hosts, now fought out under human control.

The nineteenth century was the golden age for plant pests. The most spectacular and tragic example is the potato blight, also known as the late blight. Potatoes were an introduction from the New World, native to the Andes. Hardy, nutritious, and with a high yield per acre, potatoes became fundamental to Eurasian diets in the eighteenth century. Potatoes could be cultivated on marginal ground, in small plots, without animal traction, so they were a staple for the poor. In Ireland, almost a third of the arable acreage was given over to the potato—more than anywhere else in Europe. The daily consumption of potatoes per capita in Ireland amounted to two thousand calories. The ecological shock of the potato blight thus hit Ireland hardest. There had been omens in the decades leading into the crisis of the 1840s. Diseases had imperiled European potato harvests since the late eighteenth century. A viral disease known as potato curl, and a fungal infection known as dry rot, had struck in the 1830s. But these were nothing compared to the arrival of *Phytophthora infestans* in 1845.[63]

P. infestans is an oomycete, a fungus-like parasitic organism. *P. infestans* turns the outside of the tuber splotchy and turns the inside into a fetid mush. Some contemporaries called it the "potato cholera." It is native to South America, and by the early 1840s (possibly via Mexico) *P. infestans* had arrived on the eastern seaboard of the United States. It was first noticed around New York and Philadelphia and radiated outward over the next few years, reaching Canada and the Great Lakes. In 1845, it crossed the Atlantic, and in June of that year made its European debut in Belgium. Paleogenomic evidence has demonstrated that the American outbreak and the European outbreak were caused by the same lineage. The disease damaged the harvest in winter 1845 across swaths of western Europe. But in 1846, a full-on subsistence crisis unraveled when the potato harvest was almost completely lost. There was an 88 percent harvest reduction in Ireland, coincident with a terrible year for wheat, rye, and oats.[64]

The failed harvests were widespread across Europe, and the poor suffered in many regions, but only in Ireland did a famine follow. Ireland was not only uniquely dependent on the potato to feed its population but also uniquely reliant on a single varietal of potato, the lumper, that proved exceptionally susceptible to *P. infestans*. The Irish famine can be seen as a colonial crisis too, because an inept response from London, coinciding with a sharp turn toward free-market liberalism, failed to alleviate the hunger. Over a million people were sent to their graves in the shadow of the richest region on the planet. It was an ecological catastrophe produced by the conjunction of local agrarian circumstances and global disease networks—exacerbated by political failure.[65]

Like the potato blight of the 1840s, a number of plant diseases have threatened staple crops in modern times. As late as 1943, the Great Bengal Famine, caused by the fungal disease known as brown spot, led to widespread starvation and up to three million deaths. The westward expansion of the United States, as farms were cut into the Mississippi valley and Great Plains, created a new heartland for plant disease. Wild prairies, where new flowers bloomed by the week amid the tall native grass, were suddenly replaced with monotonous, rectilinear fields of grain. Rapid ecological homogenization, warm summers, and a high degree of market integration formed a deadly combination. Throughout the nineteenth century, American farmers faced dire outbreaks of cereal rusts and cereal smuts, fungal diseases that regularly damaged harvests. At times 20–30 percent of the harvest failed, and entire regions were temporarily forced to abandon wheat production rather than risk the ravages of rust. And where farming did prove resilient, it was due to savvy agricultural science that helped farmers stay a half step ahead of their microbial enemies. The federal government erected an infrastructure for agricultural (and veterinary) science early on, and precocious American agroscience is an underrated storyline in the global emergence of germ theory and the biochemical control of infectious disease.[66]

The nineteenth century also saw a great expansion of plantation agriculture. Plantation monoculture was imposed on once wondrously diverse tropical ecosystems. The swollen shoot and witches' broom of cocoa, the leaf blight of rubber, the mosaic disease of sugarcane, and a whole host of citrus fruit and banana diseases thwarted the hopes of capitalist enterprise. A paradigmatic example is the coffee leaf rust. The Industrial Revolution went hand in hand with an expansion of consumer demand for coffee, and suitable environments for growing the bean were sought worldwide by European capital interests. Wallace refers to this disease in his *Wonderful Century* as the quintessential example of how "the desire to get rich as quickly as possible has often defeated the planter's hopes."[67]

Bushes of the genus *Coffea* grow across equatorial Africa, but the species *Coffea arabica* produces especially rich and delicious beans. It was native to the highland forests of western Ethiopia but transplanted to Yemen long ago. As demand for coffee exploded, seeds from Yemen were used to establish coffee plantations throughout the tropics. The global coffee market was fed by production from South Asia and the East Indies, where small and medium farms lost ground to giant, mono-cultural plantations producing coffee with gangs of laborers. In Sri Lanka, "the virgin forests were entirely removed, producing unnatural conditions." The novelist Anthony Trollope commented on a visit that "the lovely sloping forests are going, and the very regular but ugly coffee plantations are taking their place."[68]

In 1869 a farmer on Sri Lanka noticed discoloration of his bushes. The British botanist stationed on the island was notified, and he in turn sent specimens to London. Coffee rust is caused by a fungus, *Hemileia vastatrix*. Like coffee, *H. vastatrix* is native to Ethiopia, but in a natural ecosystem its spread is constrained by climate controls. For centuries the Yemeni coffee industry had been spared because it is too hot and arid for the fungus. But the coffee plantations of South Asia were like an unguarded treasure left open to the parasite. Production of coffee plunged, and the remaining smallholders watched their already parlous condition ruined. The disease went global, and it remains a threat still. In the space of fifteen years in the late nineteenth century it reordered the global coffee economy. In the words of the historian Stuart McCook, who has written a close study of the episode, the coffee rust was "a product of conquest, of empire, of liberalism, of steamships, and of migrations."[69]

The plant diseases of the nineteenth century ruined small farmers and dashed the hopes of capitalists worldwide (see table 11.3). But they also inspired scientific research that would eventually deepen human control of planetary ecosystems. An array of regulatory measures, like quarantines and inspections, were mobilized, complemented by traditional biological approaches to disease control like selecting and breeding resistant

TABLE 11.3. Major Plant Diseases

Fungal	Viral	Insect	Other
Banana wilt	Barley yellow dwarf	Coffee bearer borer	Potato late blight
Brown spot of rice	Citrus tristeza	Cotton boll weevil	Root knot
Cereal rusts	Plum pox	Japanese beetle	Soybean cyst nematode
Cereal smuts	Potato curl or leafroll	Nutmeg canker beetle	Sugar beet cyst nematode
Chesnut blight	Sugar beet yellows		Wine blight (*Phylloxera*,
Coffee leaf rust	Sugarcane mosaic		aphid)
Downy mildew of grapes	Swollen shoot of cocoa		
Downy mildew of tobacco	Tobacco mosaic virus		
Dutch elm disease	Tomato spotted wilt virus		
Ergot of rye/wheat	Tomato yellow leaf curl		
Frosty pod rot of cacao			
Leaf blight of rubber			
Pine stem rusts			
Potato dry rot			
Powdery mildew of grapes			
Scab of wheat			
Sigatoka leaf spot of banana			
Southern corn leaf blight			
Witches' broom of cacao			

See also Agrios 2005.

strains. By the late nineteenth century, chemical interventions were increasingly used. Fungicides and insecticides were perfected and commercialized. It is telling that biological and chemical mechanisms of disease control were a dominant topic at the Paris Congress in 1889. As the economic historians Alan Olmstead and Paul Rhode have pointed out, agricultural progress in the nineteenth century was as dependent on biological science as mechanical innovation. Humanity's effort to feed itself requires the disinfection of the environment for our preferred species of plants. The same can be said of our favored animals.[70]

Global Animal Disease

In 1799, George Washington asked the U.S. consul in Tunis to acquire ten sheep from the Bey of Tunis. Washington was eager to promote the agricultural development of the young republic. "I know of no pursuit in which more real and important service can be rendered to any country, than by improving its agriculture, its breed of useful animals, and other branches of an husbandman's cares." English breeds of sheep struggled in America, so ten Tunisian sheep were shipped across the Atlantic. Only two—charmingly named Caramelli and Selina—survived the crossing. They were put in the care of a federal judge and friend of Washington, Richard Peters of Pennsylvania. He bred them prolifically, and Tunisian sheep became a sensational success and national favorite. John Adams loved them, and during the presidency of Thomas Jefferson they were known to graze on the White House lawn.[71]

Fifty years later, pigs started dying. From the 1850s, an infectious disease that contemporaries dubbed "hog cholera" became an explosive problem in America, and then globally. (There is also a bacterial disease known as fowl cholera, to go along with human, potato, and hog cholera, all of which are extremely unrelated.) Hog cholera is a highly lethal viral disease that causes fever, diarrhea, skin lesions, and a range of other symptoms in pigs. From 1856 to 1858, in the reconstruction of Alan Olmstead and Paul Rhode, "the disease swept across the Midwest and Northeast, often killing the entire population of infected herds." The disease was established across the continent, and then worldwide. Before it was brought under control, hog cholera was easily the most deadly disease of pigs in the world, and a constant threat to the pork industry.[72]

Hog cholera, properly known as classical swine fever, is one of the nineteenth century's many panzootics—emerging veterinary diseases that diffused swiftly and forcefully in the age of globalization. The genome of hog cholera has recently revealed its hidden evolutionary history. The family tree of classic swine fever virus shows that its closest known relative is, in fact, the Tunisian sheep virus. Classic swine fever virus evolved from Tunisian sheep virus following a host switch that happened in the late eighteenth century. Hog cholera was first described in the United States, and it seems likely that it was created by the great American experiment in adapting species from around the world to the agricultural possibilities of the continent. President Washington is, alas, indirectly to blame for this lamentable biological accident.[73]

The animal diseases of the nineteenth century mirror the dynamics of plant diseases. Natural ecosystems were replaced with landscapes of extreme genetic homogeneity. Domestic animal populations soared. Local farming gave way to agroindustry and long-distance shipping. Like plant disease outbreaks, the epizootics of the nineteenth century are illustrative of global patterns, and at times they sharply influenced the course of human history. But there is a crucial difference. With the rarest of exceptions, humans are not vulnerable to plant pathogens. By contrast, animal diseases are often dangerous to humans, and vice versa. Microbes that solve the riddles of the mammalian immune system pose a threat to cross the species barrier to us. Modernization, even though it has moved most of humanity out of the farmyard and into the city, has paradoxically drawn human and animal health closer together.

Livestock plagues are as old as recorded history. Even in classical antiquity, the integration of the steppe into the economic systems of Eurasia had already created a superhighway for animal germs across the giant continental landmass. At times, virulent animal plagues swept across herds on a massive scale. The rinderpest epizootic of the fourteenth century was a notorious catastrophe. Less is known about livestock disease outside of Europe in the earlier period, but rinderpest certainly was a problem from one end of Eurasia to another for centuries. In the calamitous seventeenth century, the disease wiped out entire herds in East Asia.[74]

A comprehensive history of animal disease in the modern world is yet to be written, and we can do no more than pull on a few threads. The modern era of animal disease launched in Europe in the eighteenth century, in the first phases of economic growth, preceding the transport innovations of steam and rail. Driven by urbanization and expanding markets, the agricultural sector saw continuous advances in specialization and growth in economies of scale. Nutritional habits also changed, as the members of the growing middle class incorporated meat into their regular diet. The interregional cattle trade grew rapidly, as western European wealth fueled specialized cattle rearing in eastern Europe. Hundreds of thousands of animals per year were moving from the Hungarian plain to the markets in the west. As the historian Karl Appuhn put it, "The eighteenth-century increase in the consumption of animal protein could not have happened without access to vast numbers of animals raised on central European grasslands."[75]

Market integration had ecological consequences, most notably transcontinental waves of rinderpest. Rinderpest is maybe the most destructive livestock disease in the annals of human farming; tellingly, it stands with smallpox as one of only two pathogens completely eradicated by human intervention. Rinderpest is caused by a virus whose closest known relative is the measles virus. This cattle disease has existed for thousands of years. For centuries, Europeans believed that it came from central Asia, and they were probably not wrong. Some breeds of steppe cattle are highly resistant to the disease, in contrast to the cattle of Europe, which are hopelessly susceptible to infection and suffer case fatality rates as high as 90 percent. As market integration drew western Europe into closer contact with the herds of the steppe, rinderpest inevitably followed.[76]

In 1709, a destructive panzootic diffused from east to west. Then, from 1745, the disease spread again over the entire continent, killing an estimated three million cattle. It ricocheted around the continent for the next few generations, and "Rinderpest was never absent from some part of Europe." Control measures like quarantine, inspection, and the culling of sick herds were refined. As with plant diseases, humanity's ecological dominance carried negative feedbacks for animal health, which in turn inspired scientific advance and governmental response. But the growth of commercial agriculture, and the transport revolution, outstripped the control measures, as the volume, velocity, and spatial reach of the cattle trade expanded in the nineteenth century. Again in the 1860s, western Europe found itself engulfed in a rinderpest panzootic.[77]

In England, this outbreak of cattle plague prompted Queen Victoria to authorize a prayer of confession and petition seeking divine intervention to stave off a disease reminiscent of an Old Testament scourge. The outbreak in England was traced back to cattle imported from Russia via the Baltic ports. From London the pestilence radiated outward across the farmyards of rural England. The government response was fragmented and disorganized. It took two years to bring the outbreak under control; by then three to four hundred thousand head of cattle—almost 10 percent of the national herd—had been lost. The destruction on the continent was equally vast. And yet, this outbreak was the beginning of the end . . . in Europe. Superior control measures, especially in Russia, brought rinderpest to heel in Europe in the last decades of the nineteenth century. The advent of refrigeration also reduced the need to import live cattle across national lines by making it possible to ship meat.[78]

Tragically, just as rinderpest was being brought under control in Europe, it was unloosed upon much of the Old World. The disease was already familiar in India, but modernization—principally in the form of market integration, population growth, and railways—opened a new chapter in the history of the disease from the 1860s. Huge epizootics struck the subcontinent. Although fatality rates may have been lower among Indian cattle more familiar with the virus, the disease undermined an already impoverished peasantry at a time of population increase, rapid transformation, famine, and human disease.[79]

Later in the century, rinderpest reached Africa. No animal plague was more consequential. Africa's massive herds of wild ungulates were also susceptible to the disease. The outbreak lasted from 1889 to 1898, overlapping the most intense phase of European imperialism. The virus was introduced via Ethiopia. The outbreak spread into the Sudan and south into the Great Lakes region. An Englishman in the employ of Cecil Rhodes, Alfred Sharpe, reported what he witnessed in 1892 in Zambia. "Here enormous quantities of game have died. . . . At the time of my passing up through these swamps the plague was at its height. Dead and dying beasts were all around. The first day I counted over forty dead pookoo within half a mile of my camp. Subsequently, on my return down the river, I saw scarcely any live game near the mouth, but the whole country was scattered with dead bodies." In 1896 the plague crossed the Zambezi River and entered South Africa, where it reached all the way to the cape before working its way north along the Atlantic coast.[80]

The African rinderpest panzootic was devastating, and the veterinary mortality coincided with the dislocations brought on by sudden colonization. Swaths of Africa lost up to 90 percent of their cattle. It ruined the subsistence base of herding groups like the Masai across the eastern part of the continent. In farming regions, animal traction was fundamental, and the loss was economically calamitous. Hides were a main source of clothing, dung was a main source of fuel and fertilizer, and ox-drawn carts were a major means of transportation across the east and south of the continent. Cattle were a form of money and a store of wealth, and they were integral to exchanges in the marriage market. A French missionary recorded a mournful dirge of those stricken:

No more cattle, no more milk, what shall we eat?
No more cattle, no more fuel, what shall we use for making fire?
No more cattle, no more skin clothes, what shall we wear?
No more cattle, no more marriages, how shall we marry?
No more cattle, no more ploughing, what shall we eat and where
   shall we get money?[81]

The ecological shock reverberated for generations. The amazing long-range ecological dynamics of rinderpest in the Serengeti are the text-book model of pathogen-driven ecosystem control: the rise and fall of herbivores has affected predator populations, the advance and retreat of grasslands, and the frequency of fires—in short, the entire ecosystem. Food webs spanning from microbial parasite to apex predator have been linked in oscillatory dynamics, distantly perturbed by humanity's role in globalizing animal disease.[82]

Livestock diseases in the nineteenth century affected every species of farm animal. They moved breathtakingly fast and befuddled control efforts. The speed and spatial reach of these events is epitomized by the avian-equine influenza that struck Canada and the United States in 1872–73. In late September 1872, horses in Toronto started falling ill, showing respiratory symptoms. Toronto was quickly a "vast hospital for diseased horses." The equine influenza caused debilitating sickness, though fatality rates were low. By October 20, New York was struck, and two days later reports of horse disease are recorded in Massachusetts. The disease spread south to New Orleans, as well as west, reaching Wisconsin by early November and Missouri by December. In the eastern United States, the progression of the disease maps onto the railway network. The panzootic was manifestly transmitted from town to town by trains. However, as the scourge spread west, across the Great Plains and beyond, it is equally apparent that the flu spread on hoof. Following two major lines of westward expansion, one in the north and another in the south, it moved from horse to horse across the prairies and mountains until, the following spring, it reached the Pacific Coast.[83]

Before the triumph of the automobile, cities still depended utterly on horses, and urbanization had massively increased horse populations in the United States. The horse flu brought urban life to a sudden halt across the continent. From England, Charles Dickens wrote a detached summary of the outbreak. "The real inconveniences to the public, impediments to traffic, and interferences with business of all kinds, were not only annoying but productive of heavy pecuniary losses. The American cities have no underground railways, nor do they use the steam railways over ground, as we do, to relieve the street traffic, and connect suburban homes with city offices and workshops. Carts and drays for goods and merchandise, omnibuses and tram ways for passengers, are their sole means of conveyance, and, for these, horses are indispensable. At the height of the epidemic all the horses were practically useless, and business was at a standstill." America was horse country, halted in its tracks by this virus.[84]

As modern economic growth liberated ever greater numbers of humans from barebones subsistence, one of the first desires to be sated was the lust for meat. The creation of giant middle classes fueled the rise of the global beef industry, one of the most ecologically demanding systems of production on the planet. The increase in the number of beef cattle in the nineteenth century was astonishing. By 1900, there were four hundred million cows on planet Earth. As beef became synonymous with American prosperity, and as vast tracts of the interior were given over to cattle ranching, disease inevitably followed. The United States managed to keep rinderpest out, but other infections like bovine pleuropneumonia and foot-and-mouth disease posed serious threats to the industry. The most gruesome was a tick-borne disease known as Texas fever. The southern longhorn breeds were resistant to the infection, but they carried it north on cattle drives bound for railheads that

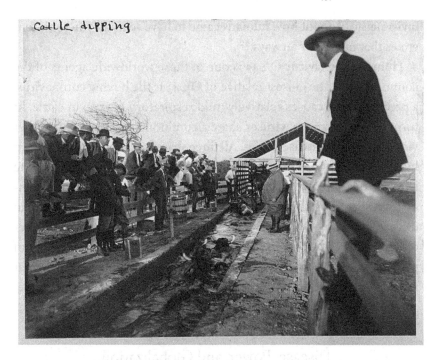

Cattle dipping

FIGURE 11.6. President Taft watches cattle dipping in 1909. To disrupt transmission of tick-borne Texas fever, Oklahomans required cattle arriving from Texas to be submerged in crude oil. Frederick S. Barde Collection, Oklahoma Historical Society.

would connect them to the stockyards and slaughterhouses of Chicago. The cows of the Midwest were susceptible to the disease, and regional politics became bitter (see figure 11.6).[85]

Industrial-scale agriculture creates evolutionary breeding grounds for pathogens. Where large mammals are crammed together by the thousands, pathogens can experiment and potentially cross to humans. Consider something as simple as the common cold, caused by an array of respiratory viruses including rhinoviruses, adenoviruses, and coronaviruses. Four (now five) of the coronaviruses are endemic to humans and virtually ubiquitous. You have almost certainly been infected with coronaviruses at some point in your life. They are relatively avirulent, and more of a nuisance than a threat, a virtual rite of passage for membership in human society. But their genomes unveil an otherwise invisible story about how humans came to have so many microbial enemies that infect our airways.[86]

Human coronavirus OC43 is one of these worldwide agents of the common cold. The closest relative of OC43 is the bovine coronavirus, a pathogen that causes relatively mild respiratory disease in cattle. In turn, these two coronaviruses share a common ancestor with another virus that causes disease in pigs. All three shared an ancestor around two hundred years ago, when the branch that includes human and bovine coronavirus split apart. The human coronavirus diverged from the ancestor it shared with the cattle virus sometime around 1890. The human disease caused by OC43 is not an ancient affliction; it joined the roster of human illnesses only in the midst of humanity's great reordering of planetary biota to slake our hunger for beef. The modern global meat industry gave us the common cold—or at least one of its most widespread agents.[87]

Disease, Power, and Globalization

Spring, 1885: As one international conference adjourned in Berlin, another convened in Rome. The Berlin Conference was the most decisive moment in the "scramble for Africa," the process by which the European powers partitioned a continent to delineate imperial territories. Meanwhile, in Rome, the sixth International Sanitary Conference met to discuss how the threat of contagious disease, above all cholera, could be safely met in an increasingly connected world. Although the Berlin Conference is remembered as an infamous moment in the history of colonialism while the Rome conference is celebrated as a precursor to modern global public health, the two meetings have more in common than it might first appear. Both conferences were European-dominated attempts to solve the problems presented by a new global order through negotiation among nation-states.

The two decades between the middle of the 1860s and 1880s were decisive in making this new order. Three interrelated processes coalesced with gathering speed in these pivotal years. The first was a turning of the tide in the control of infectious disease in industrializing societies. We will consider this momentous transition in the next chapter, but the permanent increase in life expectancy in places like western Europe dates to this moment. There is no single explanation for such a profound change, but at last sanitary reform, germ theory, and the hygiene revolution gave human societies control over infectious disease.

In tandem with these internal improvements and the confidence they engendered, two more international dynamics played out in these decades, symbolized by the conferences of 1885: the "globalization" of public health and the advent of high European imperialism. In describing the globalization of public health in the middle of the nineteenth century, we should neither diminish the precedents for international cooperation that had come before, nor overstate the aims of the scientists and diplomats who gathered with limited goals and scant formal power to achieve them. But both the cultural and institutional frameworks to envision global public health were irreversibly altered.

Italian city-states had entered cooperative agreements concerning plague and quarantine from at least the seventeenth century. In the eighteenth century, port cities from France and Italy to the Ottoman Empire collaborated on surveillance and control policies. These were limited efforts to coordinate and standardize quarantine policies. A major breakthrough came in the 1830s, when the pasha of Egypt, Muhammad Ali, asked the foreign consuls of Egypt to establish a consular commission of health to regularize quarantine in Egyptian ports and build a lazaretto (a detention station for those infected or suspected of infection), all in the name of containing cholera and plague. Tunisia followed suit. The ultimate purpose of these efforts was to ensure the unobstructed flow of trade through the Mediterranean. The consular commissions were the germ of new international cooperation on matters of health. They spurred visions of even broader collaboration. As early as the 1830s, the French were calling for an international conference to negotiate fair standards of quarantine in the Mediterranean. But inertia and diplomatic tensions stalled progress until the 1850s.[88]

The first International Sanitary Conference was at last held in Paris, in 1851. Ten conferences would follow over the course of the next fifty years. The immediate impetus was cholera; indeed, until the recrudescence of plague in the 1890s, cholera was the pressing concern behind the International Sanitary Conferences. In no small measure, international cooperation on matters of public health was propelled into a new age because of European dread of this fecal-oral pathogen.[89]

The larger context of the International Sanitary Conferences was both technological and cultural. New technologies of transportation and communication had brought the world into closer contact, with all the exhilaration and foreboding that such proximity entailed. One of the delegates at the first conference captured this sensibility: "Today, as steam power has made communication so swift, as thoughts, associated to electricity, travel the immensity of space in a moment, as, in a word, man attempts to nullify time and space," new approaches to the control of disease were urgently needed. The danger of distant disease in an interconnected world was palpable. He went on, "The Asiatic cholera, profiting, like man, from the modern discoveries, makes its incursions much easier than fifty years ago, and it spreads afar with all the rapidity of steamships and railways."[90]

The more subtle context for these International Sanitary Conferences was the growing spirit of internationalism itself. Fittingly, the very year that the first International Sanitary Conference took place in Paris, the Great Exhibition in London inaugurated the tradition of world's fairs (the 1900 Paris Exposition visited by Henry Adams was the thirteenth). Beyond these famous gatherings, the nineteenth century saw an "explosion" of international events of all types. In one comprehensive tally, there were 24 international meetings in the first half of the century and almost 1,400 in the second half. These congresses promoted cooperation on everything from agriculture to postal service, and led to the standardization of weights and measures (in 1875), time zones (1884), and the classification of disease (from 1893). The ordering of medical knowledge took on broader dimensions. Europeans had been interested in tropical disease since the beginning of colonization, but knowledge about global health was projected onto a global frame in the nineteenth century. The first global map of diseases was made in 1827. The field of "medical geography" sought to gather information systematically about the prevalence of disease in all parts of the world. Global health could now be envisioned in planetary perspective.[91]

The kind of internationalism embodied in the sanitary conferences, paradoxically, worked to strengthen the power of the nation-state. The greater volume and ease of movement across borders in the nineteenth century generated a sharper definition of those very borders. The aim of global sanitary cooperation was to create what has been called, in a brilliant metaphor, "semipermeable membranes." The world would be made safe for globalization because stronger nation-states could control what passed across borders, on what terms. There was expansion in the administrative technologies that grew out of quarantine: visas, bills of health, sanitary passports, and other forms of state control over citizens, merchants, pilgrims, migrants, and other travelers. The vision of globalization that resulted was not a borderless world inhabited by a common human race, but a world of nation-states and citizens where colonialism and commerce could proceed safely, which meant on Europe's terms.[92]

It is easy enough to insist on the limited aims and even more limited practical achievements of the sanitary conferences. Controlling the menace of "Oriental" diseases was hardly a humanitarian vision. The international conferences were patently Eurocentric, especially in the beginning. Few of the conventions were ratified until later in the century. The British were truculent, resistant to any infringement on their power at home or in the colonies. But from the beginning, the conception was novel. Countries sent both diplomats and medical scientists. By the 1880s representation had broadened, with delegations from the United States, South America, India, Japan, and eastern Europe joining the traditional western European and Turkish members. The conferences helped to foster international scientific networks, and they brought the British to the table. In sum, the International Sanitary Conferences, for all their limitations, form an important chapter in the emergence of global public health.

In these same decades, European geopolitical advantage became overwhelming. Combined with the expansion of global trade and fierce but sublimated interstate rivalry in Europe, the age of "high European imperialism" took shape. In 1800, Europeans already occupied or commanded 35 percent of the earth's land surface; on the eve of World War I, the figure had risen to 84 percent. A "first age of imperialism" from the

1760s saw the British establish control over much of India and the French establish an empire in North Africa. In addition to these overseas imperial ventures, contiguous land-based expansion by Russia and later the United States and Canada must also count as a form of imperial expansion. From the 1880s, an even more explosive phase of imperialism, the classic or high European imperialism, unfolded. The "scramble for Africa" saw a handful of European powers carve up the continent in the space of a decade. In parallel, the British also expanded their influence in Asia by occupying Burma, while the French seized Indochina to keep pace.[93]

The importance of disease in the dynamics of power was nothing new, but its role started to change. For two centuries after Columbus's Atlantic crossing, microbes had amplified European power over indigenous societies. The unification of the tropics created stark gradients of infectious disease in the New World that ultimately loosened the grip of European states over some of their possessions. In the long run, European settlement was most prolific in the healthier temperate climates. New regions like Australia, New Zealand, South Africa, and Argentina increasingly became home to self-reproducing settler societies.[94]

The heavy disease burden of the Old World tropics had made the equatorial zone into the proverbial "white man's grave." Diseases imposed almost unimaginably heavy costs on explorers, merchants, missionaries, and armies until the mid-nineteenth century. Around 1800, the death rates of European troops stationed in Africa were stunningly high. The historian Philip Curtin has carefully reconstructed the dangers faced by Europeans who ventured to equatorial regions. Annual mortality of 50 percent or more was not unusual. But gradually, military medicine became a major source of European power and weakened the invisible force field of infectious disease that had protected African and Asian societies against hostile takeover. The prospects of troops deployed in tropical climates improved. Military medicine, in general, was a field of steady advances between 1750 and 1850. The earliest gains were achieved by hygiene and clean water; then a sort of "magic bullet" was found in the form of quinine.[95]

Quinine is the active alkaloid compound of cinchona bark; in 1820, French chemists extracted it, allowing the drug to be manufactured in refined form. Quinine was immediately effective as a treatment for vivax malaria: if taken at the onset of symptoms, it aided in the patient's recovery. But it took time for the drug's potential against falciparum malaria to be recognized. Small dosages of quinine taken after an infection has started are insufficient. The idea of using high-dosage quinine as a prophylactic was not immediately obvious. It took good fortune and then careful experimentation before the medical virtues of prophylactic quinine were recognized and accepted. A highly publicized expedition up the Niger River in 1854 used prophylactic quinine to great success. Thereafter, death rates among Europeans in the tropics fell precipitously. The miraculous effect of quinine, however, can be overstated. Africa would not have been opened without advances in the use of *actual* bullets: the breech-loading rifle and the Maxim gun concentrated European power in these same years. In tandem, life-giving medicine and death-dealing machine guns opened the interior of Africa to European exploitation.[96]

The Berlin Conference defined the borders of European control in Africa. It drew geometric lines to create artificial territories where once patchworks of societies had lived in uneasy equilibrium with their dangerous disease environments. The rinderpest panzootic was only the most spectacular health catastrophe that followed European colonization. European takeover was motivated in part by commercial ambitions—a desire for minerals, rubber, palm oil, and other tropical crops. The extraction that followed—requiring roads and railways, urbanization and deforestation—disrupted what delicate balances did exist. The integration of the continent into global markets meant exposure to all the world's pathogens, with virtually no modern infrastructure to mitigate the risks, in addition to a worsening of tropical diseases. Predictably, the results were grim. To note just one example, the influenza of 1918–19 has been called "probably the greatest short-term demographic disaster in the history" of sub-Saharan Africa. In the earliest colonial documents, the mortality rates recorded are abysmal, reflecting a health situation created when the natural disease environment of Africa was suddenly and brutally incorporated into the global network of human diseases. In the words of the historian Emmanuel Akyeampong: "the divergence between knowledge and power was an important paradox of this period: Africans who had enough knowledge about their environment and knew how to manage it to keep endemic diseases at a low level were politically disempowered, and Europeans who now had political power lacked knowledge of the African environment."[97]

Global Divergence

"The world is quite vast," says one of the characters of Jules Verne's *Around the World in Eighty Days*, published in 1872. "It used to be," replies the protagonist, Phileas Fogg. Transportation technologies had made the world smaller, both for humans and for the microbes that exploit our success. Paradoxically, the ecological feedbacks of technological advance caused increases in life expectancy to stall in the mid-nineteenth century, even in western Europe. But as we will see in the next chapter, advances then resumed, and now moved faster than ever. Not only that, but they rippled outward; good health went global, as people all over the world exuberantly seized the opportunity to improve their lives. But the earlier onset of progress in western societies coincided with catastrophe in much of the world. In consequence, global divergences in health may have reached their maxima in the early twentieth century.

The lack of good data obscures the overall global trends, but we should not exclude the possibility that in large parts of the world, life expectancy stagnated or even declined in the "wonderful century." Certainly that seems to have been the pattern in India, where the British colonial administration started taking censuses in the 1870s and tracking vital rates. By the time estimates are possible, from the 1870s, life expectancy at birth was a dismal twenty-four to twenty-five years. Then it fell, reaching a nadir in the 1890s in the low twenties, which is about the lowest that life expectancy could have been for any sustained period of time in India's history. It languished there for another generation, and sustained improvements did not begin until the 1920s.[98]

The British believed that their administration conferred the blessings of civilization on their colonial subjects. On leaving office after eight years as governor-general of India in 1856, Lord Dalhousie claimed with pride that he had introduced "three great engines of social improvement" to India: the railway, the electric telegraph, and uniform postage. But it was precisely these technologies of integration and modernization that also exacerbated the disease burden. India was cholera's birthplace as well as the region most affected by it. The Third Plague Pandemic was a global event that hit India hardest. And the influenza of 1918–19 claimed more victims in India than anywhere else. Worse still, modernization made endemic diseases like tuberculosis, smallpox, and especially malaria a greater problem.[99]

The Indian intellectual and civil servant Romesh Dutt witnessed firsthand the paradoxes of development across India. He believed that colonization had led to simplification in the Indian economy, while British taxation contributed to food shortage. On top of that, the ecological transformation of the subcontinent was deadly. He was serving as a magistrate in West Bengal in 1890 when he saw how diseases like malaria had taken hold. The region of Burdwan once had a reputation for being "healthy and flourishing." "How changed the district is now, with its malaria fever! The fever has spread north and south, east and west, over both banks of the Hughli River, and over the whole of West Bengal. It is a national calamity which affects and enfeebles twenty millions of the people." In the name of progress, the course of the Ganges was altered and the small channels and watercourses that once flowed had turned into stagnant pools and rice fields. Mosquitos multiplied. "Villages all over the district were desolated." From the mid-nineteenth century, malaria killed around two million people per year in India. By one estimate, "malaria accounted for between a quarter and a third of all deaths in India during 1821–71." In the later period, between 1890 and 1920, malaria probably took twenty million lives in India, and debilitated many tens of millions more.[100]

The negative feedbacks of global modernization were severe. The wrenching passage to modernity has had lingering effects on patterns of development, its imprint far from vanished today. And this chapter between two periods of progress reminds us that the rapid successes soon to follow have been achieved by containing ecological pressures that continue to build in the era of human domination.

12

The Disinfected Planet

Visions of Long Life

In 1879 Jules Verne published a science-fiction novel, *The Begum's Millions*. In the story, two rival heirs—a French doctor and a German chemist—fall into a fortune left by a long-lost relative. They each use their share of the inheritance to build model cities far in the American West. The contrasts are not subtle. The German establishes "Steel-City," a nightmarish industrial town dedicated to the manufacture of destructive weapons. The doctor, by contrast, founds a city (called "France-ville") premised from top to bottom on scientific principles of hygiene. In France-ville, public spaces and private habits were minutely regulated to promote healthy living. "To clean, clean ceaselessly, to destroy as soon as they are formed those miasmas which constantly emanate from a human collective, such is the primary job of the central government." Citizens were indoctrinated from childhood "with such a rigorous sense of cleanliness that they consider a spot on their simple clothes as a dishonor." Hygiene was a public imperative and private duty. In exchange for uncompromising vigilance, the residents of France-ville enjoyed the blessings of long life.[1]

Verne's story is a fable of modern science. It envisions a future in which human ingenuity is used to destroy or to preserve life. In the novel's happy ending, Steel-City destroys itself. But there is something unsettling about France-ville, too. Life is consumed in the crusade against disease and death. Such visions were in the air when Verne wrote. He cribbed the sanitary rules of France-ville almost verbatim from a contemporary British reformer named Benjamin Ward Richardson. In a speech delivered in 1876, Richardson imagined a utopia that he called Hygeia, the City of Health. For Richardson, there was nothing inherently fictional about this future. "The details of the city exist. They have been worked out by those pioneers of sanitary science." In the coming years, he hoped the "desires and aspirations" of the hygienic reformers would become the lived reality of the mass of humanity.[2]

Today many of us live in a version of Hygeia, the City of Health. Around 1870, even in the most rapidly developing nations, infectious disease still filled the graveyards. Then, human societies brought infectious disease under control. Toward the end of the nineteenth century, in the United States and Britain, a great threshold was crossed for the first time in the history of our species: noninfectious causes of death—cancer, cardiovascular disorders, and other chronic and degenerative diseases—accounted for a greater portion of total mortality than did infectious diseases. By 1915, an American social reformer could observe that "a generation ago we could only vainly mourn" the deaths of children from disease. "To-day we know that every dying child accuses the community. For knowledge is available for keeping alive and well so nearly all, that we may justly be said to sin in the light of the new day when we let any die." By midcentury, dying of infectious disease had become anomalous, virtually scandalous, in the developed world.[3]

The control of infectious disease is one of the unambiguously great accomplishments of our species. It has prevented immeasurable bodily pain and allowed billions of humans the chance to reach their full potential. It has relieved countless parents from the anguish of burying their children. It has remade our basic assumptions about life and death. Scholars have found plenty of candidates for what "made us modern" (railroads, telephones, science, Shakespeare), but the control of our microbial adversaries is as compelling as any of them. The mastery of microbes is so elemental and so intimately bound up with the other features of modernity—economic growth, mass education, the empowerment of women—that it is hard to imagine a counterfactual path to the modern world in which we lack a basic level of control over our germs. Modernity and pestilence are mutually exclusive. The COVID-19 pandemic, with death rates that pale in comparison to those of historic plagues, underscores their incompatibility.

We now live in such artificial, plastic environments that it might seem to make the ecological and evolutionary terms that have guided our story irrelevant. Yet to grasp the history of infectious disease, we need more than ever to understand our recent success through the lens of ecology and evolution. Modern human expansion is unnatural in its scale. Global population in 1900 was 1.6 billion; in 2020, humans numbered 7.8 billion. The reason for such vertiginous increase is that human ingenuity has relaxed the constraints, such as energy availability and parasitism, that regulate animal populations in nature. Until the recent past, these limits acted to hold our own numbers in check. But global food production has managed to keep pace with human multiplication, thanks to the mechanization of agriculture, the biocontrol of pests, and the synthesis of nitrogen fertilizer. And the primary and proximate reason the human population has ballooned is the control of infectious disease. Human beings have multiplied deliriously not because they "suddenly started breeding like rabbits: it is just that they stopped dying like flies."[4]

Verne's visionary novel does not foresee that improvements in health will result in unconstrained human expansion. And there is something else missing in his picture of the future. Although it was published in 1879, there is no trace of "germ theory" in its pages. That is unsurprising. Sanitary reformers were often motivated by faulty ideas about diseases, imagining that disease was caused by filth or environmental pollution. In their vision, the threat of disease might be extinguished, with a kind of finality, if only sanitation and hygiene could be truly achieved. Germ theory is necessary to understand why this is not so. Infectious disease is caused by invisible agents with their own aims, and they adapt even as we seek to control and eliminate them. In short, germs evolve, and human mastery is always therefore incomplete.

This final chapter has three parts. The first explores the health transition in the societies that pioneered the escape from infectious disease.

Through a succession of overlapping and mutually reinforcing innovations, humans have learned to make the environments we inhabit unsafe for microbes that cause us harm. The second part traces the globalization of long life and its demographic fallout. Mortality declines eventually trigger fertility declines, but only after a lapse of time during which human numbers soar. Thus, the rapid development and diffusion of disease-control technologies helped to provoke what is known as the Great Acceleration, the startling intensification of human impact on the planet from the middle of the twentieth century. Our indelible impact has led many earth scientists and others to propose that we now live in the Anthropocene, a geological epoch defined by humanity's pervasive imprint on the planet. The Anthropocene has a microbiological dimension too, as microbes respond and adapt to the human-dominated Earth.[5]

Throughout, we try to call attention to the continuous emergence of novel threats to human health, from polio to influenza to AIDS. The third part of the chapter is dedicated to the challenge of such emerging infectious diseases today. As human control of the environment has expanded, Darwinian evolution has continued, or even accelerated. The evolution of new pathogens is not an anomaly but rather the strictest obedience to the laws of nature. COVID-19 was the evolutionary product of the ecological conditions we have created—our numbers, density, and connectivity, especially in the age of jet travel. The ongoing pandemic has been a jarring reminder that humanity's control over nature is necessarily incomplete and unstable. We urgently need to learn from the experience of this pandemic to ready ourselves for the inevitable next one.

Roads to Disease Control

In Verne's fictional city of health, France-ville, it was boasted that the crude mortality rate had been reduced to 12.5 per 1,000. Such a low level of mortality was indeed futuristic, only attained in England in the 1920s and in France in the 1950s. For most of premodern history, a normal crude death rate was around 30 per 1,000. Today, developed countries experience a death rate of around 8–10 per 1,000. In 1870, the crude death rate in England was still around 23 per 1,000; in France it was 28 per 1,000. Yet change was just around the corner.[6]

In premodern societies, death rates were high, due above all to infectious disease. Although cause-of-death records from the nineteenth century are imperfect, they offer insights into the structure of mortality. In England, tuberculosis was the leading killer. Other respiratory diseases figured next, along with dysentery. Typhoid was a major problem, and so were other generic diarrheal diseases. Besides tuberculosis, the other named respiratory diseases were prominent: scarlet fever, diphtheria, whooping cough, and measles. In the United States, national cause-of-death statistics only go back to 1900, but the situation mirrored that in England. Tuberculosis was the most deadly pathogen by far, followed by other respiratory and diarrheal diseases such as typhoid, diphtheria, measles, whooping cough, and scarlet fever. Syphilis was also a major disease and a ticket to an early death.[7]

These were the diseases that reigned in countries that had experienced modern economic growth earliest and already managed to control plague, malaria, typhus (partly), and smallpox (mostly) by the later nineteenth century. Across the globe, the mix of diseases varied according to geographic factors, social conditions, and cultural practices. Hence, the path to good health was characterized by local particularities. Plague, cholera, and smallpox remained formidable challenges. In the lower latitudes, the burden of tropical diseases remained heavy. Above all, malaria was overbearing.[8]

The 1870s mark a point of departure when mortality from infectious disease started a sustained decline in precocious societies like Britain, France, Germany, and the United States. Over the course of two or three generations, death by microbe became rarer and rarer, and what had once been unavoidable became a "sin in the light of the new day." The revolution was subsequently widened to encompass other societies, and good health went global. The convergence of life expectancies over the twentieth century is a triumph, though it also remains incomplete.

Although there have been vigorous efforts to decide how much credit to assign to various factors like economic growth, public health reform, and biomedical advances, from a global perspective there was no one formula for the control of infectious disease. In the first place, the composition of the disease pool varied regionally. Moreover, the technologies that have allowed humanity to control infectious disease are numerous and complementary, and they were rapidly refined over the course of a few transformational generations. At a high level, we should note that economic growth was helpful for the reduction of the disease burden but never sufficient by itself. Public health reforms were most important in the first societies to undergo the health transition, whereas interventions like vaccines, pharmaceuticals, and insecticides became more effective over time. Advances in science drove all of these innovations, even before the breakthroughs of germ theory, which supercharged efforts already in course to control the threat of infectious disease.

The public health movement arose in response to the challenges of modernization. With industrialization and urbanization at full tilt in western Europe and the United States, the sanitary reformers coalesced as a political force. Figures like Johann Peter Frank and Louis-René Villermé were in the vanguard of efforts to alleviate sickness and suffering for the population as a whole. In response to outbreaks of typhus and cholera, Edwin Chadwick led his official inquiry into the "chief removable circumstances affecting the health of the poorer classes of the population" and published his landmark *Report* in 1842. Whereas many early public health thinkers, such as the German Rudolf Virchow, argued that poverty caused disease, Chadwick emphasized that disease was also a primary cause of poverty. As he put it, "fever precedes the destitution, not the destitution the disease." Chadwick's report focuses on squalid, stuffy, and overcrowded housing in the slums, contamination of water supplies, close and filthy streets, stifling factories. He was also concerned with "vices" such as prostitution and alcoholism. For Chadwick, the moral deficiency of the poor was inextricable from their sanitary and social conditions: depravity, destitution, and disease were a tangled knot.[9]

The crowning achievement for Chadwick and his allies was the passage of the Public Health Act in 1848 by Parliament, which created local boards of health to supervise the sanitary conditions of towns. It was the beginning of a new age of intervention in the name of health. Parallel sanitary reform movements were mobilized across western Europe and the United States, drawing inspiration and sharing ideas across national boundaries. It is one of history's ironies that the sanitary reformers based their progressive public health politics on scientific principles that were already becoming obsolete. The sanitarians were mostly committed to the miasma theory of disease. In this view, filth, pollution, and putrefaction are the agents of sickness. Chadwick's investigations found that preventable disease was rampant among the laboring classes because of "atmospheric impurities produced by decomposing animal and vegetable substances, by damp and filth, and close and overcrowded dwellings." The sanitarian view is summed up in his pithy slogan: all stench is disease.[10]

Even as changes were being legislated in its name, miasma theory lost its dominant position. The miasmatist view had been challenged from the eighteenth century by "contagionists" who believed that disease was transmitted from one infected person (or infected article, like a piece of clothing or agricultural product) to another. Throughout the nineteenth century, a number of compromise positions emerged. Doctors could admit that some diseases—like smallpox and measles—were evidently contagious, while others—like fever—were caused by environmental conditions. Moreover, what we might call early epidemiology built a compelling case for contagionism. Oliver Wendell Holmes Sr. and then the Hungarian doctor Ignaz Semmelweis proved that childbed fever (puerperal sepsis) was contagious and preventable. In the 1850s, John Snow traced a cholera outbreak to a particular pump in one London neighborhood. Though a little later, James Christie's study of cholera in Zanzibar was in this same spirit. Even before the triumph of "germ theory," then, the idea that diseases were contagious was on the advance.[11]

The world may be more deeply indebted to miasma theory than to any other flawed idea in history. The energy necessary to launch the public health movement was organized around the sanitary campaign against filth, squalor, and poverty. Put simply, miasma theory, when translated into action, worked to improve human health. Smell is, after all, not the worst indication of potential disease: your nose warns you that water is dangerous to drink if it reeks of feces. Clean air and clean water are the building blocks of good health.

Germ theory is the radical idea that disease is caused when the body is invaded by microorganisms invisible to the naked eye. Germ theory gathered a widening circle of adherents in the middle decades of the nineteenth century, and its most triumphant breakthroughs were achieved in the 1860s and 1870s. Above all, the French chemist Louis Pasteur helped germ theory gain respectability through a method based on control experimentation. In the late 1850s, Pasteur studied fermentation in the alcohol industry and showed that it was caused by microorganisms; he also recognized that microbes caused beer, wine, and milk to spoil. He devised a method, pasteurization, to prevent these "diseases." He also disproved the age-old theory of spontaneous generation, showing that boiling liquid would kill the microorganisms and prevent them from growing, unless they were introduced again from the outside. He went on to discover in the 1870s that attenuated pathogens could provide immunity to disease. Pasteur thus turned the isolated invention of Edward Jenner's smallpox vaccine into a science that could be methodically carried forward for other diseases. Fittingly, it was Pasteur who named the principle *vaccination* in Jenner's honor (since *vacca*, the Latin word for "cow," was the root of the name for the cowpox material Jenner used to immunize patients).[12]

Pasteur's ideas won adherents internationally. In England Joseph Lister applied germ theory to surgery, using antisepsis to prevent infection. Most importantly, in the 1870s, the German country doctor turned laboratory scientist Robert Koch built on Pasteur's discoveries (even though he quickly became an unfriendly rival). Koch's contributions were nearly as revolutionary. He developed techniques to culture bacteria in the lab, and he also used advanced microscopes to see bacteria. In 1876 Koch isolated the bacterium that causes anthrax and explained its ability to form spores, connecting a specific microbe to a specific disease. In 1882, he discovered the bacterial cause of tuberculosis, the disease that more than any other haunted western Europe. It was a sensational victory for the advocates of germ theory. Koch's work as a scientist also underscores something distinctive about this intellectual revolution: for the first time, a scientific paradigm was born in the artificial environment we know as the laboratory.[13]

The "golden age of bacteriology" was now launched, and discoveries came at a furious clip. Even so, consensus hardly turned overnight. There was resistance, confusion, and compromise within the scientific community. Clinical physicians changed their mind slowly. But in deeper perspective, this revolution was achieved with remarkable swiftness. As of 1870, a small avant-garde of researchers believed that familiar diseases were caused by invisible living agents. By 1900, for a scientist or medical professional to believe anything else was becoming ignorant or downright mulish.[14]

One of the most consequential extensions of germ theory was the discovery that insects could serve as vectors for deadly microbes. In fact, as a collective intellectual epiphany, the idea that biting bugs could transmit germs was nearly as remarkable as germ theory itself. The discovery of disease vectors was achieved stepwise in the last decades of the nineteenth century. In the late 1870s, Patrick Manson, the Scottish physician we met in chapter 3, published his findings that mosquitos served as intermediate hosts for the tiny worms (microfilaria) that cause lymphatic filariasis. In the coming decades, the idea was extended to unlock the riddle of major diseases like malaria, yellow fever, typhus, and plague.[15]

Germ theory would suggest new ways to prevent and control infectious disease. But crucially, it did not mean the sanitarian political agenda had to be scuttled. Germ theory explained, more accurately than miasma theory did, why exactly filth and excrement were able to cause disease. The new science could be incorporated into the old campaigns "to clean, to clean ceaselessly." The discovery of germs boosted progress that was already well underway. So how did humans come to control infectious disease and more than double the length of the average human lifespan? We learned to control environments at all scales—from the proteins of our immune system to entire landscapes—in order to disadvantage the microbes that cause us harm. We can summarize the main mechanisms under four headings: (1) public health reform; (2) the hygiene revolution; (3) chemical control of pathogens and vectors; and (4) improved biomedical interventions, including patient care, pharmaceuticals, and vaccines. We will explore each of these, but it is also important to recognize that economic growth allowed and re-inforced gains in human well-being throughout, and it enabled states to fund both interventions against disease and improvements in welfare.

Public Health Reform

Effective public health reform required states to enact and enforce poli-cies along two axes: compulsion and provision. On one front, states had to have the means of surveillance and punishment to carry out intrusive intervention and regulation—for instance, mandatory vaccination and notification, food safety and labor laws, and building and zoning re-quirements. At the same time, states had to provision public goods like waste disposal and water treatment, and more broadly health care, edu-cation, and social welfare.[16]

The control of infectious disease thus went hand in hand with the growth of government. The scope of state power expanded rapidly in the late nineteenth century. People came to tolerate the government taking a more active role in the prevention and treatment of infectious disease—they even expected it. Naturally, countries took different paths to public health reform. In general, the pursuit of public health drove calls for greater centralization and more bureaucratic rationalization focused on health outcomes. But local institutions remained important vehicles for health policy. In Britain, the rise of public health was part of the nineteenth-century "revolution in government," in which a state "with a minimal central government" in 1800 was transformed into "a model bureaucratic state, a land of inspectors and clerks." In the United States, the residual power of the states over health and welfare meant that robust reform happened beneath the national level. Boards of health proliferated: there were around two dozen in the United States in 1850, and four decades later there were more than 225. Other coun-tries took similar paths, conditioned by their constitutional particulari-ties, in growing numbers.[17]

While the compulsory powers of the state helped to disrupt the transmission of disease, the provision of public goods has been the most consequential form of statecraft. Massive public works projects helped to prolong human life. For instance, the investments in public water systems were "among the largest, and might even have been *the* largest, public investments in American history" and they had "a larger impact on human mortality than any other public health initiative." The campaign to build better sewers, expensive water filtration systems, and sturdier and better-ventilated housing, gathered steam in the early twentieth century. This remarkable progress was now disproportionately achieved in urban areas. Since the birth of the city, living in the country had been healthier than living in town. Now, for the first time in history, urban residents in the most highly developed economies had greater lifespan prospects than did their rural counterparts.[18]

The Hygiene Revolution

The sanitary reformers had long urged the importance of domestic cleanliness. But in the decades around 1900, the hygienics of everyday life were transformed by an active campaign to disinfect the person and the household environment. The principles of germ theory were preached beyond scientific and medical circles. The historian Nancy Tomes has framed this message as the "gospel of germs," and indeed it bore some resemblance to a missionary religion, teaching a belief in the invisible and calling for wholesale transformation of private discipline. In France hygienism became "a secular religion." The German medical historian Alfons Labisch aptly described the hygiene revolution as the rise of *Homo hygenicus*, likening it to the evolution of a new being. We are a species whose personal habits and domestic spaces are committed to the project of disinfection.[19]

The home was transformed into the aseptic ecological niche that we recognize today. White china toilets came into widespread popularity. Cold, easily scrubbed tile surfaces came to dominate bathrooms. Bodily hygiene became more punctilious and reliant on chemicals. Beards went out of fashion, and ladies turned away from skirts with hems touching the ground. Spitting was forcefully driven out of style, turned into an act of uncouth barbarity. The twentieth century also witnessed radical changes in food safety, particularly in the processing of

The Fatal Housefly

"Swat Him!" Is the Seasonable Slogan—For This Multitudinous Pest Is as Serious a Menace to Our Soldiers as German Bullets, and as Deadly a Blight on the Whole Community as Poison Gas.

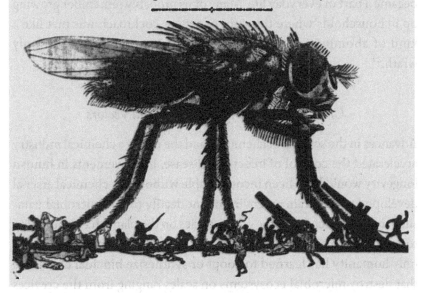

FIGURE 12.1. The War on the Housefly, from the *Pittsburgh Press*, June 2, 1918.

meat and milk, and soon saw the spread of refrigeration. Ideas about everyday hygienics became intertwined with gendered space and family roles: the burden of maintaining and enforcing good household hygiene fell heavily upon women. Despite rapid and continuous innovations, there was "always more work for mother," because "increases in knowledge on the causes and transmission mechanisms of infectious diseases persuaded women that household members' health depended on the amount of housework carried out."[20]

Insects that had once seemed a mere nuisance were now seen as vehicles with deadly payloads (see figure 12.1). Bugs had to be systematically destroyed and screened out of the human environment. The window screen was patented in the late nineteenth century and quickly became a fixture in home construction. The domestic fly, recognized as a carrier of germs such as the typhoid bacterium, was targeted with especial vigor. In the United States, a public relations campaign demonizing the fly went on for years. Around the same time, that ultimate device of household insect control—the flyswatter—was invented and became a part of everyday life. Many of us probably remember growing up in households where the sight of a fly or cockroach was met like a kind of abomination, and the swatter was an instrument of holy wrath.[21]

Chemical Control of Pathogens and Vectors

Advances in the science of chemistry and the rise of a chemical industry accelerated the control of infectious disease. Improvements in human longevity would have been inconceivable without the chemical arsenal developed to maintain an environment deadly to our microbial parasites and their vectors. Some other species on the planet have the ability to produce or manipulate chemical compounds to their advantage, but only humanity has learned to coopt or synthesize biocidal chemicals that destroy microbial ecosystems on scales ranging from the crevices of our bodies to entire landscapes. We have coated our bodies and misted the earth with a thin glaze of disinfectants.[22]

The roots of chemical disinfection are deep. The authors of the Homeric poems knew of sulfuric fumes as a disinfecting agent, and practitioners of ancient Indian medicine used sulfur gas in medical procedures. Sulfur fumigation was used to combat the plague. Copper, mercury, and alkaline sodas were important in the array of early chemical disinfectants, whose smells and observable effects made them popular long before the chemistry was actually understood.[23]

As knowledge of basic chemistry expanded, new elements and compounds were added to the human toolkit. Chlorine was isolated in the 1770s and became popular; by the 1840s its use was introduced to hospitals. Phenol, an organic compound derived from tar, was discovered in the 1830s and became a first-line disinfectant. In the Second Industrial Revolution of the late nineteenth century, a chemical industry developed that was capable of synthesizing and mass producing chemical products for ordinary consumers. From the 1870s onward, there was intense scientific interest in trying to bring more rigor to the use of disinfectants. In the 1880s the American Public Health Association commissioned a "committee on disinfectants" because "many of the agents which have been found useful as deodorisers, or as antiseptics, are entirely without value for the destruction of disease germs." Germ theory explained why disinfection worked—by killing microbes—and it is no accident that Koch's lab played a leading role in testing the efficacy of supposed disinfectants on various bacteria.[24]

The use of chlorine is the paradigmatic example of how chemical disinfection came to serve the project of disease control (and it further underscores the role of states in public health). Sewers and water filtration had already achieved significant progress by the later nineteenth century, but these methods were imperfect, and ongoing urbanization challenged the ability of civil engineers to maintain pure, safe drinking water by mechanical methods alone. Dysentery was still a major health problem in the developed world, and typhoid remained one of the great adversaries that had not been brought to heel—until chlorination.

The most important reason we can drink a glass of water today and not feel even a hint of dread is because it has been treated with chlorine. The French pharmacologist Antoine Germain Labarraque discovered the disinfecting properties of calcium hypochlorite in the 1820s. Chlorine ascended to the front ranks of humanity's preferred agents of disinfection. The decisive turn came in the United States at the turn of the century, when mass scale filtration systems were installed in New Jersey and Illinois. The chlorination of drinking water virtually eliminated the danger of typhoid (figure 12.2). In the 1910s, municipalities across the country adopted chlorination. With almost unbelievable speed, typhoid fever disappeared as a danger in the developed world.[25]

Biocidal chemicals were also turned against insect vectors. Insecticides had an extensive history, but as long as the active compounds had to be extracted from botanical sources their use was limited. It was cumbersome and prohibitively expensive to mass produce early insecticides based on compounds like pyrethrum, which was derived from

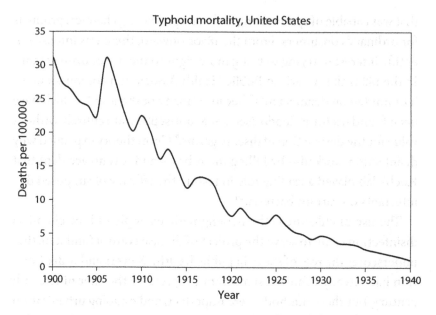

FIGURE 12.2. Typhoid deaths per one hundred thousand, United States.
(Source: Linder and Grove 1947)

ground-up chrysanthemum petals. But synthetic chemistry and a burgeoning chemical industry soon brought to market an array of bug-killing chemicals. Chemical science, capitalism, and visions of mass-scale "extermination" merged.[26]

The historian Edmund Russell has shown how the use of insecticides was ideologically and technologically inseparable from warfare in the twentieth century. "War created a powerful motive and rationale for a huge leap in the scale on which people controlled insects." The contest between humans and bugs was promoted as a "total war," a struggle for "mastery of the planet." Both the actual chemicals and the technologies used to disperse them were developed in the context of military conflict. One class of potent insecticides was, quite literally, a byproduct of the science that created more lethal explosives (TNT) and weaponized gas (mustard gas) during World War I. From about the 1920s, the ability to synthesize complex organic compounds proved a breakthrough, allowing humanity to mimic the destructive inventiveness of eons of natural evolution. (In a strange way, then, the two rival cities of Verne's imaginary future came together in the science of war and vector control.)[27]

The most important insecticide was discovered by a chemist at a Swiss dye company in the 1930s: dichlorodiphenyltrichloroethane, or DDT. The application of DDT was not immediate, but World War II made DDT a star when its potential was first realized as a way to control louse-borne typhus. The United States assumed global leadership in the research and application of DDT, which for a time proved to be a miraculous weapon against mosquitos. Following the war, DDT and the machinery used to spray it were recommissioned for civilian purposes. From the late 1940s to the 1960s, DDT was the single most powerful tool of malaria eradication, and a major prop in the broader geopolitical strategy of the United States. The allure of DDT as a solution provided a new venue for old debates about whether the control of infectious disease was best addressed as a technical problem or a more deeply rooted social problem. Many malariologists from the beginning had been wary of approaching the challenge of malaria apart from broader questions of poverty and equity. The toxic effects of DDT also eventually forestalled wider application, and of course inspired Rachel Carson's *Silent Spring*.[28]

Improved Biomedical Interventions

Patient care, pharmaceuticals, and vaccines all played a role in reducing mortality from infectious disease. It is easy to point out the lateness of antibiotics and most vaccines. The great gains in life expectancy were accomplished *before* these interventions made a major impact—at least in pioneering societies. But the importance of biomedicine should not be underestimated. It has helped to complete humanity's control over many infectious diseases in developed societies, to extend health improvements globally at a rapid pace, and to safeguard our protections in the face of constantly emerging threats.

Improvements in patient care played some part in the mortality decline. Pediatric medicine, in particular, saw advances from the mid-nineteenth century. In England, figures like Charles West promoted the care of children as its own field. In 1851, West founded the Hospital for Sick Children in London; the model took hold, and children's hospitals proliferated. West's efforts extended beyond hospital care to promote healthy practices in the home. He published *The Mother's Manual of Children's Diseases*, a text aimed at a wide audience by trying to avoid "all technical detail." The book was meant to provide "such an account of the diseases of infancy and childhood, as might be of use and comfort to the intelligent mother."[29]

Primary care aided the steady decline of respiratory diseases like whooping cough, diphtheria, measles, and tuberculosis. The decline of tuberculosis is central to the control of infectious disease in general. It has been called the "heart of the puzzle." The decline of tuberculosis did not begin until the 1880s in England, and it took three generations to corral the disease. Rising living standards meant that people had stronger physiological resistance to the disease, and prosperity played a role through improving housing: congested urban tenements are a perfect breeding ground for tuberculosis. The broader hygienic revolution—cleanliness and disinfection—helped to reduce transmission of the disease. Moreover, coinfection is an important factor in tuberculosis mortality. The control of smallpox, typhus, and other diseases had knock-on effects in the control of tuberculosis.[30]

TB became the target of a deliberate public campaign by the medical establishment, and the approach to tuberculosis treatment was radically changed. In the mid-nineteenth century, sufferers of tuberculosis were kept at home, in closed, dark rooms, attended by a family caretaker day and night. The campaign against tuberculosis promoted good ventilation; it discouraged close nursing and the practice of sleeping with patients. Isolation of tuberculosis patients spread, and sanatoria came into vogue. Undoubtedly these measures diminished the spread of the disease. Germ theory extended and reinforced such changes, helping to convince both doctors and the public that tuberculosis was a communicable, and therefore preventable, disease, rather than a heritable one. The ability to imagine its microbial cause further energized other fronts, like the battle against spitting. Bacteria-ridden milk was also a major source of infection caused by the related germ *Mycobacterium bovis*.

Improvements in safety standards, pasteurization, and bottling made significant headway against the disease at least by the 1920s.[31]

Even after the burden of tuberculosis had been reduced, vaccines and antibiotics helped to seal the victory and to export it globally. Germ theory spawned attempts to find a medical solution for tuberculosis, and in the 1890s, Koch himself raised hopes that tuberculin would cure the dreaded disease. This idea, however, only yielded disappointment. Instead it was the patient work of scientists affiliated with Pasteur Institutes who developed a vaccine. Albert Calmette and Camille Guérin worked for two decades to attenuate the pathogen causing bovine tuberculosis into a safe and effective vaccine. The BCG (bacillus Calmette–Guérin) vaccine debuted in the 1920s but only became broadly used from the 1940s. Although it is not completely effective, it is an important tool in controlling tuberculosis and was especially important in reducing the incidence of the disease in regions where it remained prevalent.[32]

One last innovation in twentieth-century patient care must be mentioned, simple in its ingredients but monumental in its life-saving effects: oral rehydration therapy (ORT). In the 1950s, Hemendra Nath Chatterjee demonstrated the benefits of adding salt and sugar to water administered to patients suffering vomiting or severe diarrhea. A cheap, noninvasive, and highly effective means of fluid replacement, ORT dramatically improves the patient's chances against a huge array of dangerous diseases, not least of which is cholera. Its popularization has saved countless lives.[33]

Antibiotics have played a major role in the control of bacteria and the consolidation of human mastery over infectious disease. The term *antibiotic* was coined as early as the 1880s by the French scientist Jean Paul Vuillemin, who recognized that a toxin secreted by a common bacterium (*Pseudomonas aeruginosa*) was deadly to other microbes—but too toxic to be useful. The German medical researcher Paul Ehrlich turned the search for chemical interventions into a systematic science. He recognized that it might be possible to find compounds that would target the parasite while sparing the host—he called these compounds *Zauberkugeln*, "magic bullets." Ehrlich set up a modern pharmaceutical lab to hunt for magic bullets. His team eventually found one: compound #606, arsphenamine, trade name Salvarsan, an effective cure for syphilis.[34]

The drug Salvarsan might have opened a new era in chemical therapeutics, but it proved to be an isolated success. Knowledge of organic
chemistry was too limited, and scientific interest focused on vaccines
and serum therapies. Ehrlich had quipped that drug discovery required
the four Gs: *Geld* (money), *Geduld* (patience), *Geschick* (ingenuity),
and *Glück* (luck). It was not until the 1930s that the four Gs really started
to align. The big breakthrough was a spinoff from a German dye manu-
facturer that routinely tested its products for biological effects. In 1932,
a red dye known as prontosil was synthesized and found to have antibiotic effects in live animals. In 1935, the active compound, sulfanilamide,
was isolated and then synthesized. Sulfa drugs were the first mass-scale
cure for bacterial infection brought to market.[35]

The 1940s were the miracle decade for antibiotics. While Alexander
Fleming made his fortuitous observation about the effects of the peni-
cillium mold on staph bacteria in 1928, nothing useful came of the discovery until penicillin was isolated and tested in 1940. Penicillin and its
derivatives, which stop gram-positive bacteria from building their cell
walls, are still among the most powerful and widely used antibiotic
drugs. Other antibiotics were quickly identified. In 1943, streptomycin,
highly effective against gram-negative bacteria, was discovered. In 1947,
chloramphenicol became the first broad-spectrum antibiotic as well as
the first that could be manufactured completely from raw materials. And
in the next year, the first of the tetracycline drugs—another broad-
spectrum antibiotic, easy to administer orally—was discovered. Massive, often indiscriminate use of tetracyclines took off immediately.[36]

In the developed world, the demographic impact of antibiotics was
modest, simply because most bacterial diseases had already been
brought under control. But antibiotics helped complete the victory over
tuberculosis and diminish the threat of alarming infections like menin-
gitis. Antibiotics delivered us from the long period of human history
when the simplest wound was a mortal threat. And most importantly
of all from a demographic perspective, antibiotics arrived in time to
assist with speedy mortality reductions in the developing world.

Finally, vaccines have been and remain instrumental in clinching victory over some of the otherwise most intractable infectious diseases,

TABLE 12.1. Timeline of Major Vaccines

	Attenuated (live)	Inactivated (dead)	Subunit/Toxoids
Eighteenth century	Smallpox		
Nineteenth century	Rabies	Typhoid	
	Cholera		
	Plague		
Pre–World War II	TB	Pertussis	Diphtheria
	Yellow fever	Influenza	Tetanus
	Rickettsia		
	Influenza		
Post–World War II	Polio (Sabin)	Polio (Salk)	Pneumococcus
	Measles	Hepatitis A	Meningococcus
	Mumps	Hepatitis B	
	Rubella	Haemophilus influenzae	
	Adenovirus	Rotavirus	
	VZV (chickenpox)	HPV	
	VZV (shingles)	VZV (shingles)	

especially viral diseases (see table 12.1). The adoption of Jennerian vaccination was a watershed, and smallpox mortality rapidly fell. But progress skidded off the tracks in the middle of the nineteenth century, mostly because compulsory vaccination rules were not matched by adequate enforcement. In England, this backsliding resulted in an epidemic in 1870–72 that killed more than forty-four thousand people, but the disaster also inspired more robust measures to ensure universal vaccination. "Stamping out" the disease became the object of public policy. Vaccination, isolation of smallpox patients, and compulsory notification made that goal a reality. By 1900 endemic smallpox was gone in England.[37]

Jenner's discovery of a smallpox vaccine was a stroke of genius and a stroke of luck. Germ theory gave vaccine development a scientific foundation—and moved it into the laboratory. Pasteur experimented with methods to attenuate pathogens to make them safe for use as vaccines. His initial discoveries focused on veterinary diseases like "fowl cholera." Pasteur aged the bacteria that cause the disease at room temperature and then inoculated healthy chickens with the germs. The attenuated vaccine conferred resistance. His lab went on to explore other methods, such as serial passage through various hosts, to make microbes less deadly. Pasteur and his associates soon developed vaccines for anthrax and rabies. In the 1890s, vaccines for typhoid, plague, and cholera appeared, with one for whooping cough close behind.[38]

Early vaccines were not always highly effective, and immunization programs were often weak or spotty. Moreover, organized resistance to compulsory vaccination has been a force from the beginning. It was not always limited to the fringe. Alfred Russell Wallace, codiscoverer of evolution with Darwin, interrupts his survey of modernity's glorious achievements in *The Wonderful Century* with a tirade against vaccination. The antivax movement has waxed and waned ever since, and it remains even today a potent obstacle to disease control and threat to our collective well-being.[39]

Even though vaccines were not the instrument of humanity's initial victories, they stand at the center of our dominance over microbial parasites. We can measure the contribution of vaccines in three ways:

- Vaccines have reduced morbidity and often sealed the final victory over major diseases.
- Vaccines helped to globalize good health much more rapidly than would otherwise have been possible.
- Vaccines enable humanity to maintain control against new or escalating threats, especially as world population has grown.

Consider the measles virus. Before a vaccine was introduced in the early 1960s, mortality from the disease had been reduced to tolerable levels in the developed world, at least by the standards of the time. Measles is a severe disease, but outcomes are highly sensitive to the host's underlying health. In stable, well-nourished societies with adequate supportive care, case fatality rates had fallen below 0.2 percent. Nevertheless, the highly contagious disease was virtually unstoppable. Measles infection was an unavoidable trial of childhood. There were conservatively still half a million cases a year in the United States, resulting in five hundred or more annual deaths.[40]

A vaccine was strenuously pursued. By 1954 the virus had been isolated in the laboratory, and human trials using an attenuated strain began in 1959. Because the measles virus is so stable, the isolate used to develop this vaccine—named the Edmonston strain after a thirteen-year-old patient from whose blood the virus was extracted—has remained highly effective right up to the present. The vaccine was licensed in the United States in 1963, and measles infections fell instantaneously. A disease that once caused a million cases a year in the United States was reduced to an annual incidence of fewer than one hundred.[41]

Globally, the measles vaccine was a factor in the mortality decline. In the early 1980s, 2.5 million children died annually from measles. By 2000, vaccination programs had reduced that number to about 700,000 globally, and by 2018, mortality had been reduced again to 140,000 deaths. Smallpox is, of course, the signal example of a vaccine used to reduce mortality globally on an accelerated timescale. In the 1950s, there were still upwards of fifty million cases of smallpox per year. Technical advances—from a heat-stable, freeze-dried vaccine to the bifurcated needle—improved vaccine delivery, and these were matched by unprecedented international efforts, starting in the 1950s, to attack smallpox in the Americas, and then globally. With Cold War politics in the background, an audacious plan for global eradication was launched in the late 1960s (the campaign has been described as "a humanitarian mission driven by political calculations"). In 1977, the last naturally acquired infection occurred.[42]

Vaccines continue to protect us against new diseases, which have perpetually threatened to reverse gains that have been achieved. The history of the polio virus is highly instructive. Poliomyelitis is a viral disease caused by strains of *Enterovirus C*. There are three circulating strains of wild poliovirus, the most virulent of which is known as Type I. Poliovirus is transmitted via the fecal-oral route, and we are its only known reservoir. A human infected with polio may be asymptomatic or experience mild gastroenteritis that resolves naturally. But the virus may also disseminate to the central nervous system, and poliovirus has a dangerous proclivity to cause destruction of cells in the spinal cord. Notoriously, polio infection can leave survivors paralyzed. The disease is fatal in a minority of cases that involve the brain stem or cause respiratory paralysis.[43]

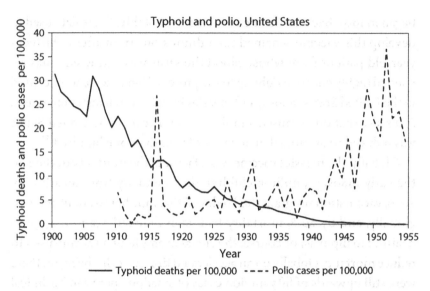

FIGURE 12.3. Changing patterns of typhoid and polio, deaths and cases per one hundred thousand, United States.

There is no evidence that polio is an ancient disease, although it is not impossible that extinct lineages of a related virus existed in the past. The genomic evidence suggests that all human enteroviruses circulating on the planet today evolved only in the last millennium. Premodern doctors could well have missed its clinical subtleties in times when childhood disease was pervasive, but the first convincing clinical descriptions of polio are from the later eighteenth century. As it happens, the earliest case of polio on record may be that of the Scottish novelist Sir Walter Scott, who was born in 1771 and suffered a fever when he was eighteen months old that paralyzed his right leg. From the 1830s, clusters of infantile paralysis were sporadically noted. But it was not until the 1860s that epidemics were observed, first in Scandinavia. The earliest epidemic in the United States was in summer 1894, in Vermont. With 132 cases, it was a large outbreak by the standards of the time, but nothing in light of what was to come.[44]

Polio epidemics first appeared in places where fecal-oral disease might seem least likely: among prosperous, northerly, and often rural populations. As the hygiene revolution spread, so did polio (figure 12.3). Jumps

in polio cases almost invariably followed improvements in the water supply and reductions in water-borne bacterial diseases. In the United States,
for example, as typhoid fever fell, polio escalated. The first widespread
epidemic of polio—making the previous outbreaks look tiny by
comparison—hit in summer 1916, just a few years after mass chlorination
had put most fecal-oral diseases on the path to extinction in the country.
Moreover, polio sought out the seemingly healthiest and wealthiest segments of society. The poor were relatively protected, although hardly
immune. And another important clue lay in the fact that the disease was
more apparent and more dangerous the older the patient. Rates of paralysis and death were higher for adolescents and adults who contracted
the virus. Most famously, the blue-blooded Franklin D. Roosevelt was
diagnosed with the disease in 1921, at the age of thirty-nine.[45]

The epidemiology of polio was thus puzzling. Global investigations
revealed that people in underdeveloped countries had acquired antibodies to polio by a very young age. In East Asia and the tropics, most people
were exposed as infants or young children, but severe disease was rare
before improvements in public health. What this pattern suggests is that
poliovirus, or enteroviruses more broadly, commonly infect the human
gut in infancy, when a baby still has the benefit of maternal antibodies.
Exposure provoked a protective and lasting immune response without
causing severe disease. By disinfecting the environment—and by filter-
ing and treating water in particular—we reduced early exposure to such
invaders, postponing the confrontation until later in childhood, when
the encounter is far more dangerous. It is also possible that the highly
virulent Type I became more prevalent globally at the same time. What
had been a mild, almost universally endemic visitor to the infant gut
became a nightmarish epidemic disease.[46]

The rise of polio was a public health crisis. Up to the early 1950s, the
incidence of polio continued to escalate. Not least of all because it
struck children and left them cruelly paralyzed, the specter of polio was
terrifying. The dread inspired by polio is also a measure of the progress
achieved in controlling infectious disease. Whereas once childhood had
been a succession of dangers, the threat of polio was now intolerable.
The fight against polio instantly became a cause célèbre for medical

science; polio research was funded by big philanthropy, and it stimulated new forms of mass fundraising, notably the March of Dimes.[47]

The race for a vaccine stumbled in the 1930s, when an unsafe prototype was brought to trial with tragic results. In the 1950s, however, a better understanding of the virus and its genetic diversity allowed effective vaccines to be developed. In 1953, to enormous fanfare, Jonas Salk of the University of Pittsburgh announced a vaccine using inactivated (dead) poliovirus. It was widely administered in the United States from 1955 and brought the epidemic to a halt. Just a few years later, his rival Albert Sabin presented an attenuated (live) virus vaccine that could be administered orally. This oral polio vaccine became the predominant tool in the global fight against the disease. Polio has now been cornered into just three countries, and global elimination is conceivable in the near future.[48]

In sum, the burden of infectious disease has been reduced by a series of progressive and overlapping innovations, reinforced by broader gains in economic growth and human welfare. Like the immune system itself, humanity's control over infectious disease relies on a multilayered network of barriers, generic chemical controls, and specific interventions such as vaccines. In a sense, we have extended the features of our immune system outward, into the environments we inhabit, by building screens and seals, deploying biocidal chemicals, and priming our immune systems against specific invaders. Consider just one beautiful illustration of these connections. Our innate immune cells use hypochlorous acid to kill bacteria. The chlorination of our drinking water is an industrial-scale application of a chemical mechanism used by our own cells. But the vertebrate immune system evolved over hundreds of millions of years, whereas our wholesale effort to disinfect the earth for our benefit has unfolded over a few human generations, a mere split second on planetary timescales.[49]

The Globalization of Health

In 1956 the American demographer Kingsley Davis published a paper called "The Amazing Decline of Mortality in Underdeveloped Areas." Kingsley was an influential academic whose work on global population shaped international policy. He wrote at a time when it was becoming evident that massive improvements in health were possible even without equivalent progress in the economic realm. "The truth is that these areas [i.e., low-income societies] do not need to become economically developed to reduce their death rates drastically." There were some spectacular examples that underscored his point. During the 1940s, the mortality rate in Puerto Rico fell by 46 percent. In Taiwan it fell by 43 percent; in Jamaica by 23 percent. In Sri Lanka, where DDT was used to suppress the mosquito vectors of malaria, the crude mortality rate fell by 34 percent—in one year. As Kingsley noted, "this was no fluke, because the death rate continued to fall." Gains that had once taken decades to achieve might now be compressed into a few years.[50]

At the cost of simplification, we can bunch the countries experiencing the health transition in the twentieth century into three groups. The first followers were those countries where sustained mortality decline started around 1900, just on the heels of the pioneers; health often preceded economic development; sanitation and hygiene played a leading role; and major gains were still to be achieved midcentury. Then, the global majority experienced headlong transition later, centered on the period from the 1940s to the 1970s; because the full kit of biomedical interventions and insecticides was now available, this transition was the largest and fastest mortality decline in human history—amazing indeed. A third group of countries still had life expectancies in the thirties or forties by 1970. Largely though not exclusively in Africa, these countries were located in regions with the heaviest burden of infectious disease, especially falciparum malaria. Mosquito abundance, insecticide resistance, AIDS, and poverty have made progress slower and more grinding.[51]

There was no single logic determining which countries joined the first followers. It helped to be northerly, like Japan and Korea, but places like Costa Rica and Jamaica managed to defy the geographic odds. Japan, as a temperate-latitude island, enjoyed a naturally favorable geography, and the nation's culture reinforced sanitary and hygienic programs. Life expectancy was already in the thirties during the Tokugawa Period (1603–1868). The Meiji Restoration of 1868 launched a modernization project that deliberately emulated aspects of western culture, including medical science and industrialization. In 1870 the government formally adopted German medicine as its model and hired professors from Germany, who came to dominate the medical establishment in Japan. Smallpox vaccination was officially adopted in the 1870s. At least by the 1890s, the health transition was underway in Japan, and by the start of World War II, life expectancy was in the high forties, even though incomes remained modest. Progress resumed after the war, and economic growth took off. Japan invested heavily in health and education, and by the end of the century it had achieved the longest life expectancy in the world.[52]

Korea is an interesting parallel, because it too launched into the health transition early, and it did so as a colonial society under Japanese rule. The health transition started around 1910, largely due to economic and social reforms imposed by Japan. These reforms included smallpox vaccination, quarantine, sanitary policy, and the expansion of medical care. In 1910 life expectancy was only around 23.5 years, but by 1942 it had reached 44.9. The country remained poor, and the midcentury conflicts interrupted progress. But from 1953, improvements resumed quickly (in South Korea), as mortality from infectious disease declined for two decades. South Korea became one of the healthiest and most educated populations on the planet, and prosperity followed.[53]

There is some uncertainty about when life expectancy started to increase in Costa Rica, but it was probably in the 1890s. The country attained independence in the 1820s, and in the later nineteenth century an export-based plantation economy—largely financed and controlled by foreign capital—grew up around coffee and bananas. The United Fruit Company, an American corporation that came to own vast properties, sponsored campaigns against hookworm and malaria, extended by the Rockefeller Foundation's programs to include diarrheal disease. The "targeted" campaign against specific diseases became an important approach in the early twentieth century. Progress was slow at first but gathered pace from the 1920s. Insecticides like Paris Green were sprayed to combat malaria, and the school system was used as a conduit to teach health and hygiene. The Costa Rican state reinforced social development with investment in public health and welfare programs. The heavy artillery of antibiotics and DDT arrived midcentury, and gains continued apace through the 1970s.[54]

Jamaica is a unique case. In this former British colony once dominated by the plantation system, mortality had been very high, with malaria, yellow fever, and diarrheal disease taking a heavy toll. But the colony experienced a form of the early health transition, thanks to drainage, quarantine, cinchona bark, sanitation, and hygiene. White mortality declined from the mid-eighteenth century, in parallel with western Europe. Among the enslaved population, mortality improved later, and the institution of slavery was abolished by 1838. Across the nineteenth century, life expectancy hovered in the high thirties. The island enjoyed greater autonomy from Britain in the 1890s. Gains were achieved against yellow fever and malaria, and progress accelerated in the 1920s. The Rockefeller Foundation was one catalyst, seeking to eliminate hookworm and carrying out wider health promotion campaigns. These broad-based efforts were remarkably successful in spreading knowledge about infectious disease and empowering Jamaicans to take ownership in the public health movement, as well as in building durable local infrastructure to maintain public health advances. Improvements in life expectancy stretched from the 1920s to the 1970s.[55]

These first followers were slightly ahead of the global curve. From the 1920s, the number of countries entering the health transition climbed rapidly, with the era of greatest improvement concentrated in the middle decades of the twentieth century. The global majority came to enjoy long life as humanity's control over its parasites was extended worldwide. Let us look briefly at how infectious diseases were brought under control in two small countries (Ghana and Sri Lanka) and then the world's two most populous countries (India and China).

Ghana (known as Gold Coast prior to independence in 1957) sits on the Gulf of Guinea in West Africa. The coastal south of Ghana is equatorial forest, whereas the north is an arid savanna. The country bears the full burden of tropical diseases, including malaria, schistosomiasis, tropical ulcers, sleeping sickness, yellow fever, and yaws. A long history of trading ensured that the cosmopolitan diseases were either permanently present or repeatedly introduced. A burst of development around 1900 only made the disease environment more perilous: roads and railways expanded, forest was cleared (this was especially conducive to malaria), and headlong urbanization proceeded. Accra, the capital, was home to 18,000 people in 1900, 135,000 half a century later, and 2.5 million today.[56]

Ghana was a British colony; as in most European colonies, a medical department had been established by the imperial government. However, the mission of the medical administration was to make the colony safe for Europeans. Racist ideas bred fatalism about the poor health of colonial populations. Public health was beyond the scope of official concern, except insofar as the general sanitary and hygienic conditions of the territory infringed on the well-being of whites. Gradually, paternalistic attitudes fostered broader interest in the population, allowing limited if insufficient improvements. In 1908, a committee assessing Britain's imperial medical administration in Africa baldly stated, "The idea that the officers of the West Africa Medical Service are appointed only to look after Government officers should be discouraged. It is a part of the duty of a medical officer to increase the progress of sanitation amongst natives dwelling in his district." Missionaries and private companies (with different motives) also helped to promote the diffusion of medical science.[57]

In Ghana, the imperial medical administration expanded from the 1910s. Clinics and dispensaries were opened across the country, inadequate in proportion to the population but broader than had existed before. A new health branch promoted sanitation, hygiene, vector control, and vaccination. Life expectancy in the 1920s, the earliest that any estimates can be made, was still in the twenties. But progress over the next few decades was rapid. Sleeping sickness and yaws were targeted. Antibiotics reduced mortality rates from respiratory infections. Vaccination was carried out more widely. Modest economic development alleviated the most grievous poverty. Malaria remained intractable, although therapeutics blunted the mortality rate. Mortality declined rapidly in the 1930s and 1940s. By midcentury, life expectancy in Ghana was forty-one years, the highest in sub-Saharan Africa. Progress broadened in the postcolonial period, and life expectancy is now sixty-four years.[58]

The experience of Sri Lanka (known as Ceylon during the colonial period) is also illustrative. The island was a British colony, and sustained increases in life expectancy began in the 1920s. The Rockefeller Foundation's campaign against hookworm had positive spillover effects in promoting better sanitation. Public-sector investments by the local government helped to build a robust social welfare system, providing education and health care broadly across the population. A malaria outbreak in 1934–35 interrupted this early progress, but in the space of about a decade after World War II, Sri Lanka achieved maybe the most rapid sustained improvement in population health in the history of our species. The heavy weaponry of human disease control—DDT, antibiotics, vaccines—was deployed in full force. The rapid gains were followed by five decades of steady progress. The case of Sri Lanka involves both "magic bullets" and broad investment in social welfare.[59]

The demographic history of India recapitulates these themes on a grander scale. As late as 1920, life expectancy in India was only around twenty. Malaria, cholera, plague, and influenza had kept mortality rates high. The crude death rate hovered around forty per one thousand. Mortality then declined gradually before independence (in 1947). Thereafter, gains in life expectancy were truly impressive. Broader access to health care, economic development, and improvements in sanitation (e.g., sewage, piped water) reduced the prevalence of infectious disease. The National Malaria Control Programme was established in 1953 and proved radically successful. By 1965 malaria was basically eliminated as a cause of death, but DDT-resistant mosquitos evolved, and soon the disease was in resurgence. Vaccination programs reduced the incidence of smallpox. Cholera was targeted and has declined. TB programs met with limited success. But by the early 1970s life expectancy was above fifty; today life expectancy has surpassed seventy years.[60]

China arrived at similar results by a different route. Around 1930, life expectancy in China was between twenty-five and thirty-five years. Diarrheal disease, tuberculosis, and other respiratory infections were rife. Malaria was endemic in the south, and schistosomiasis was a major burden in rice-producing regions. Under Mao, who seized power in 1949, China experienced rapid modernization in the arena of public health,

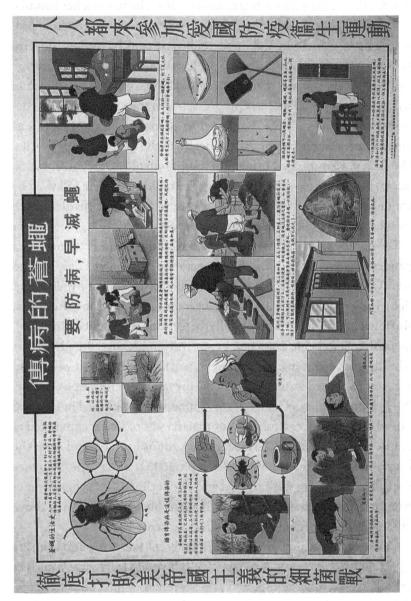

FIGURE 12.4. Poster from China's Four Pests Campaign. National Library of Medicine, Bethesda, Maryland.

despite the horrific famine of 1959–61. The government carried out mass vaccination, and in 1952 it launched the Patriotic Hygiene Campaign to control infectious disease, build sanitary infrastructure, and implement vector eradication (see figure 12.4). These efforts were accompanied by health education and expansion of health-care provision as well as medical training. In the space of a few decades, China was transformed from a stagnant peasant society with life expectancy near the bottom of the international rankings into a modern nation with life expectancy near seventy years.[61]

These cases illustrate common themes in the patterns of midcentury development. The first is an enduring tension in global health between, on the one hand, "magic bullets" or targeted technical or biomedical interventions to control specific diseases and, on the other, broader development programs. This tension runs throughout the entire history of public health. It was there in the beginning, in European debates over whether disease caused poverty, or poverty caused disease. It has been a constant question for governments, philanthropies, and global governance organizations operating on finite budgets: whether to invest in projects that reduce morbidity and mortality, or in reforms that focus more holistically on equity and human development. The two can be complementary, but visions compete for resources and influence.[62]

In the course of this longstanding tension, the 1940s were the pivot of a structural change in which the control of infectious disease became possible at unprecedentedly low cost. Scientific and medical advances enabled underdeveloped societies living on near-subsistence wages to achieve life expectancies that were previously impossible. To put it crudely, before vaccines, antibiotics, and insecticides, it was impossible to have a society with per capita income of less than $1,000 and life expectancy above fifty years. But health without wealth—or, rather, the control of infectious disease absent economic development—became progressively more attainable. The allure of low-cost interventions had greater appeal than ever before.[63]

Not coincidentally, the miraculous midcentury progress took place against the background of decolonization and the Cold War. Progress preceded the end of imperialism and also helped to hasten its demise.

Social development raised expectations and political engagement. Newly sovereign nations, like India, were then able to expand and sustain progress, often on a broader scale. But international support remained critical, and the geopolitics of the Cold War loomed large over international health efforts from the 1950s to 1970s. America was the world's supplier and promoter of DDT, and malaria eradication was a focus throughout the 1950s and early 1960s, when advances against the disease stalled. The campaign to eradicate smallpox was born of uneasy cooperation between the Soviet Union and United States, inseparable from jostling between the West and Communism to earn goodwill in the so-called Third World.[64]

The flip side of rapid progress, from the earliest health transition to the present, has been unprecedented population expansion. The passage that all modernizing societies have undergone from a high-mortality, high-fertility regime to a low-mortality, low-fertility regime is known as the demographic transition. It is part and parcel of modernization—no society has modernized without passing through this biological and social transformation. Despite the variety of human cultures, and variations in the timing and mechanisms, the demographic transition has virtually always happened in the same sequence: mortality falls, then total population grows for a time, then fertility falls. The decline in mortality can be seen as the proximate cause of explosive population growth and the remote cause of fertility decline. Mortality decline was achieved more slowly in the early movers, and more abruptly in societies that started the transition later. Population growth was therefore even more rapid in late starters. But every modernizing society has contributed to the dramatic expansion of human numbers.[65]

As the global majority experienced mortality decline, anxieties regarding overpopulation only intensified; these anxieties formed the explicit background of the academic scholarship on the demographic transition represented by Kingsley Davis's study. Tellingly, the full title of his article refers to "the population specter." Population control—often tainted by racist and eugenic assumptions—became entwined with global development and health initiatives. A whole range of intrusive and sometimes involuntary measures were enacted, requiring sterilization and fertility limitation, such as the "one child" policy introduced in China in 1979. Some of these programs may have hastened the fertility decline. But ultimately the mortality decline has reliably triggered a fertility decline with a two- or three-generation lag, and in most of the countries that experienced midcentury improvements the demographic transition is now starting to reach its equilibrium.[66]

By the 1960s and 1970s, a number of countries still seriously lagged behind in the control of infectious disease. There are several common ingredients. One is persistent conflict, civil war, or kleptocracy—often a legacy of colonialism and artificially drawn state boundaries—which have hindered economic growth, social development, and adoption of public health measures. Another is geography, because most of these nations are in the Old World tropics and bear the heaviest natural burden of infectious disease. Malaria and diarrheal diseases, which proved most obstinate in poor and rural areas, have remained overarching factors. Not all mosquito vectors are created equal, and malaria programs proved insufficient in regions with the species of *Anopheles* that are most adapted to bite humans. The environmental side effects of DDT made it less appealing from the late 1960s, and mosquitos have evolved resistance to insecticides as fast as new ones can be brought to use. In the context of these challenges, the tensions between broader development programs and technical interventions flared anew.[67]

The single greatest reason for the slow pace of gains among the trailing countries, though, is the evolutionary misfortune of HIV and the conditions that allowed it to become a catastrophe. The AIDS pandemic was *the* global health calamity of the late twentieth century. Its emergence was enabled by the forces that brought the modern world into being. Most AIDS cases are caused by the HIV-1 virus, a pathogen whose history has been elucidated in detail from the study of its genome. HIV is closely related to a group of viruses known as simian immunodeficiency viruses that are widespread in Old World primates. Most of these viruses infect monkeys, but at some point a few centuries ago one of the viruses crossed the species barrier and established a durable presence in our closest relative, the chimpanzee. From chimpanzees and monkeys alike the virus has repeatedly jumped to *Homo sapiens*.[68]

The viruses that cause AIDS are retroviruses of the genus *Lentivirus* (the aptly named "slow" viruses). The key to the pathogen's success in humans is insidious stealth. The virus is transmitted from a sick patient in blood or sexual fluids. The initial infection can produce an indistinct sickness, followed by a period during which the virus circulates in the body at high concentrations. The sufferer is especially infectious during this period, but then the virus is quiescent, and after a period of years, will slowly wear down the body's immune system. HIV prefers to hide and replicate in cells of the host's immune system. Hence, sufferers of acquired immunodeficiency syndrome struggle to fight other infections and are susceptible to ordinarily harmless microbes. The long course of an HIV infection has been instrumental to the global diffusion of AIDS.[69]

One of the true revelations of the genomic evidence is that the viruses that cause the disease have repeatedly crossed the species barrier between primates and humans. HIV-1 has jumped from chimpanzees to humans a minimum of four times. HIV-2 has jumped at least eight times from monkeys to humans in West Africa. These are just the cross-species events that have left a trace. It surely means that such transmission events were common in the past too. But for centuries, these jumps were evolutionary dead ends. What changed was us.[70]

Tree thinking is instrumental in retracing the origins of HIV. Indeed, the study of HIV was one of the first applications of the use of genomes as a way to explore the history of a major disease. Sleuthing in colonial archives has taken the history of AIDS back to the mid-twentieth century, but genomic evidence can take its history back even where all written evidence disappears. A specimen of the viral genome has been recovered from a human blood sample dating as far back as 1959. Such early samples have been decisive in refining the evolutionary history of the pathogen.[71]

Sometime around 1920 or a little before, in Belgium-occupied Congo, a hunter likely killed a chimpanzee. He became infected with its blood-borne pathogens while butchering the meat. This exchange might have ended like any of history's forgotten evolutionary experiments, simmering for a few years before running out of hosts in a remote village. For years, the chain of transmission must have hung on a thread. But change was afoot in central Africa in the middle of the century. Roads and railways fostered development. The virus journeyed in the blood of rural migrants down the Congo River to Kinshasa (colonial Leopoldville) or Brazzaville, cities in the throes of rapid urbanization. Here, it found a much larger population of susceptible hosts.[72]

Two fortuitous factors aligned to accelerate the transmission of the virus: sex and medicine. Midcentury Kinshasa and Brazzaville were characterized by gross imbalances in the sex ratio. Adult men were dragooned into corvée labor by colonial authorities. At times they outnumbered adult women by as much as four to one. The sex industry boomed. Then, in the 1950s, decolonization propelled rapid influxes of migration. Nearly as important for the silent spread of the virus in the midcentury period was the reuse of medical needles. Underfunded campaigns against sleeping sickness, yaws, and syphilis engendered the reuse of hypodermic needles on an unimaginable scale.[73]

Sometime around 1970, the virus crossed the Atlantic and, unbeknownst to anyone, established an endemic focus in Haiti. From there it reached the United States, where it spread first through sex between men. The commercial plasma and blood trade, as well as intravenous drug use, were also modes of diffusion. AIDS was first clearly recognized in the early 1980s, far from its place of origin. In 1981, a cluster of patients, all otherwise healthy men in California, contracted a rare form of pneumonia. CDC officials observed the unusual pattern, and the scope of the crisis was soon revealed. Prejudice against gays led not only to stigmatization but also a stumbling public health response. The western public shamefully failed to come to grips with the nature of the infectious disease. As of 2018, at least 770,000 people had died of AIDS in the United States, and another 1.2 million are presently infected. Meanwhile, in Africa, AIDS had quietly diffused from its central African birthplace to the rest of the continent.[74]

AIDS is a global humanitarian crisis that has fallen hardest on sub-Saharan Africa. The virus originated there and had a head start, disseminating in populations before any response was possible. Moreover, the pandemic took hold in a region of the world that already suffered the heaviest burden of infectious disease, where centuries of slavery and violent colonialism had exacted a heavy toll, and where the health transition was least advanced. As impressive advances in therapeutics have made it possible to manage HIV infection, the delivery of these high-priced interventions has been sluggish and incomplete in poor countries. The demographic results have been dire. Life expectancies decreased, even in some of the most economically developed sub-Saharan countries like Ghana and South Africa. This single disease managed to bend history in the wrong direction for a period of about three decades, across the better part of a continent.[75]

In the early twenty-first century, dedicated efforts have helped to bring the crisis under partial control. The reduction in the prevalence and mortality from AIDS has allowed life expectancies to rise again. Programs aimed at malaria and diarrheal disease have also made an impact, as have vaccination efforts. So too have campaigns to bring attention, and funding, to neglected tropical diseases, a group of infections that cumulatively take a heavy toll but which have often lacked dedicated attention from countries in temperate climates. Since 2000, life expectancy in sub-Saharan Africa as a whole has climbed from about fifty to sixty years, while infant mortality has halved. The progress can be celebrated while recognizing that remaining gaps are both an affront to humanity and a lingering peril for global health.[76]

Over the past generation, the fight against infectious disease has been shaped by structural shifts in the framework of the post–Cold War world. Notably, a system of "international health" gave way to the regime of "global health" in which nonstate actors, notably philanthropies, play a massive role in funding projects, measuring progress, and setting priorities. Simultaneously, the power and budget of the World Health Organization remains anemic relative to its vision and purpose. Critics of this order point to the lack of accountability inherent in a system where private actors loom so large. Defenders underline the value of entrepreneurial approaches, and they point to the measurable progress that has undoubtedly been achieved. Meanwhile, the old tension between holistic social welfare and targeted technical intervention persists. The United Nations' Millennium Development Goals (affirmed in 2000) and subsequent Sustainable Development Goals (affirmed in 2015) represent a collaborative "blueprint" in which the control of infectious disease is part of a more encompassing vision of equity and human well-being. Whether that blueprint can succeed—within the structures of endless growth that it presumes and the consequent environmental effects that are hard to control or predict—is the open question. Forebodingly, perhaps, progress toward each of the development goals has already been gravely interrupted by a pandemic that "has quickly become the worst human and economic crisis in a lifetime."[77]

Microbial Darwinism in the Anthropocene

In 1991, in response to the rise of HIV and a range of other novel threats to human health, the Institute of Medicine commissioned an expert panel whose charge was to assess the future of infectious disease. The panel's report, published the following year as *Emerging Infections: Microbial Threats to Health in the United States*, was a broadside against "complacency." One of its cochairs, the Nobel Prize–winning microbiologist Joshua Lederberg, was a pioneering expert in microbial evolution. He knew better than anyone that nature does not stand still, and he had been sounding the alarm for years. "In the context of infectious diseases, there is nowhere in the world from which we are remote and no one from whom we are disconnected." The arsenal of magic bullets had given humans the upper hand, but this advantage was unstable. "Because of the evolutionary potential of many microbes," the panel warned, "the use of these weapons may inadvertently contribute to the selection of certain mutations, adaptations, and migrations that enable pathogens to proliferate or nonpathogens to acquire virulence."[78]

The institute's report gave "emerging infectious diseases" a place in both scientific and public consciousness. This clarion call still echoes. Complacency and alarm have coexisted in an uneasy mix for the past generation. Sometimes our anxiety has been rational, leading to smarter investments in disease surveillance, global public health, international development, and basic science. Anxiety also manifests itself in collective fascination with new diseases, in sensationalist journalism, in lurid fiction and films, even in zombie apocalypses. Prophets in the line of Lederberg have continuously forewarned us that new diseases were one of the most fundamental risks we face as a species. And now, the COVID-19 pandemic makes it all too evident that their alarms were both prescient and unheeded. We were, in short, complacent.[79]

For the lawyers, the COVID-19 pandemic was *force majeure*, an act of God. For scholars who study the past or present of infectious disease, the pandemic was a perfectly inevitable disaster. No one could have known that a novel coronavirus would jump from animals to humans in central China late in 2019 and instigate a global pandemic. Yet it was bound to happen that some new pathogen would emerge and evade our collective defense systems. It was a reasonable likelihood that the culprit would be a highly contagious RNA virus of zoonotic origins spread via the respiratory route. In short, a destabilizing pandemic was inescapable, its contours predictable, its details essentially random.

The COVID-19 pandemic is part of a deep pattern, a pattern described by the interplay of ecology and evolution. The combination of predictability and unpredictability, of structure and chance, of pattern and contingency, lies in the very nature of infectious disease. New diseases emerge at the meeting point between long-term ecological changes and constant but essentially random evolutionary processes. Humans have uniquely sped-up ecological timescales, experiencing dizzying population growth and unparalleled resource usage. Humanity's ecological supremacy is unnatural—or, perhaps more accurately, a force of nature itself. What we think of as a medical triumph—the control of infectious disease—is from a planetary perspective a truly novel, systemic breakdown of an ecological buffer. And, as ever, our parasites respond to the ecological circumstances we present them.

In 2000, the atmospheric scientist Paul Crutzen and biologist Eugene Stoermer proposed that we are living in a new geological epoch, the successor to the hospitable Holocene. This new epoch, they offered, should be called the Anthropocene, in recognition of humanity's overarching influence on the earth's natural systems. The idea has caught on, and even as it is still being debated by the geologists who formally control the labeling of planetary epochs, the Anthropocene has become an indispensable concept for thinking about the relationship between humanity and the environment. It recognizes the sheer dizzying novelty of the current experiment in human supremacy. And although climate change is often considered the preeminent environmental problem of the Anthropocene, humanity's influence on planetary biota is as important as, and inseparable from, our influence on the physical climate. This influence extends to microorganisms, which now must learn to live on a human-dominated planet.[80]

In the Anthropocene, humans have become "the dominant animal." Organisms either adapt to the human-dominated planet, or they go extinct. *Homo sapiens* now fundamentally drives patterns of evolution across the biosphere, directly and indirectly. We favor some species intentionally (cows, chickens, pigs), others unintentionally (squirrels, pigeons). We harm some species deliberately (cockroaches, bedbugs), others inadvertently (polar bears, black rhinos, and, well, thousands of other animals). Pathogens are a special case; we harm them intentionally but benefit them inadvertently because our own biological success is an opportunity for organisms that can exploit us as sources of energy, nutrients, and cellular machinery.[81]

The evolution of pathogens is the basic reason we can never entirely escape the risk of global pandemics. Evolution is the source of new diseases and new strains of old diseases. New diseases emerge when microorganisms that infect animals cross the species barrier and adapt the ability to transmit between humans. New strains of old diseases evolve in response to selective pressures that we place upon them. Antibiotic resistance, for example, is a form of evolutionary response to our ample use of a select number of chemical weapons against bacteria. Similarly, microbes have strong incentive to change their outward appearance in order to escape from our vaccines. On basic Darwinian principles, those strains that adapt the ability to survive and reproduce in such an environment will pass on their genes to future generations—to our peril.[82]

Over the past few generations, infectious diseases have emerged faster than ever. Anything that affects either the *exposure* to potential pathogens or the *transmission dynamics* of infectious disease will bear strongly on the Darwinian pressures and opportunities for disease-causing microbes. Our exposure to the threat of new diseases has never been greater, simply because of our numbers. There are now nearly eight billion of us, and by midcentury there will be more than ten billion of us. Moreover, the knock-on effects of demographic increase also widen our exposure to potential pathogens. Human land use continues to expand, and the human-animal interface is dominated by our need to feed ourselves and, in particular, the unslakable global demand for meat. Industrial farming, and especially meat production, creates evolutionary environments where new germs adapt and emerge. Chickens are now the most numerous bird on the planet; there are more than twenty-three billion of them. The hundreds of millions of cows and pigs brought together in unnatural aggregations are also an evolutionary stewpot of new germs. To make matters more perilous, the overuse of antibiotics in farm animals, largely to promote weight gain, supercharges the evolution of antibiotic resistance.[83]

The way we live also shapes the transmission dynamics of infectious disease, in turn providing the context for the evolutionary prospects of our germs. Today we live more densely than at any time in the past. A number of cities have populations above twenty million. The population of Tokyo is about double the number of humans that existed on the planet at the beginning of the Holocene epoch. Moreover, we are more interconnected and interdependent than ever before. The jet airplane is a transportation technology of fundamental epidemiological significance, on par with the horse, the steamship, and the railroad. Since the mid-twentieth century, international travel has grown continuously. It has become possible to travel between virtually any two points on the planet during the incubation phase of any infection, no matter how rapid its course. The 1968 influenza, which claimed more than one million victims globally, might be said to mark the first pandemic of the jet age. For directly transmitted diseases—especially acute respiratory infections—distance has effectively disappeared; at the same time, older border-based health controls have fallen into desuetude. Biosecurity policy and international cooperation have not caught up to the new reality.[84]

There are also environmental and human wild cards that will shape the future of infectious disease. Climate change is one. As greenhouse gas emissions heat the planet, the biological repercussions are unpredictable. Warming is likely to expand the territorial range of vector species. Mosquitos that transmit malaria, dengue fever, chikungunya fever, yellow fever, Zika fever, and so on may find that they can thrive at higher latitudes and higher elevations for more of the year, with consequences for human health. Similarly, regional changes in patterns of precipitation are likely to alter the breeding habitats of mosquitos and thus affect the geography of infectious disease. And the vicious cycle of climate crisis, subsistence migration, and violent conflict remains a multifaceted threat to health that may be no easier to contain in the future than it has been throughout our past. Finally, if continuing demographic and economic growth pushes the earth system beyond sustainable boundaries in the Anthropocene, then the dream of limitless global development will fail, and future convergence in living standards and life expectancy will be unlikely.[85]

A final wild card is biological warfare. The intentional weaponization of biological agents is within humanity's technical capacity. In principle, existing or potential pathogens could be genetically manipulated in the laboratory to be made more deadly or more contagious. Although the deployment of biological weapons is a violation of international law and moral norms, the ability of global institutions to enforce these legal and ethical standards is highly limited. Only a few states have traditionally had the wherewithal and infrastructure for advanced programs of research, but the democratization of knowledge means that a growing number of states have or will become players in biological research that is either directly or indirectly relevant to the weaponization of disease. Moreover, the potential for nonstate actors to develop or deploy biological weapons will only continue to increase. When it comes to infectious disease, we might prove to be our own worst enemy.[86]

The COVID-19 pandemic did not appear out of the blue. The virus responsible stands in a continuous line of emerging threats, and it follows an unbroken series of near misses. These near misses even include other coronaviruses, such as those that cause Middle East Respiratory

Syndrome and the first SARS. We have also escaped brushes with new, highly pathogenic strains of influenza, which still stand as a grave threat. The Ebola virus has repeatedly spilled into human populations. More quietly, a number of vector-borne diseases have evolved or expanded their range, such as the West Nile virus that reached North America in 1999 via jet travel, or the Zika virus that suddenly mutated and became far more widespread in humans. We should also not neglect the subtle dangers of chronic infections, such as the bacterial infection Lyme disease, whose slow, quiet damage in leafy suburbia has exacted a heavy toll in recent decades.[87]

Historians tend to make poor journalists and even worse futurists. It is too soon to take stock of the COVID-19 pandemic in the round, or to know what its ultimate legacy will be. But it is clear that this virus created what David Morens and Anthony Fauci have called a "perfect storm." The virus possesses a set of insidious biological features that make it highly transmissible and difficult to control. With hindsight, we will need to sort out the chain of preventable, human failures that let it become overwhelming. The lack of transparency, especially in the first days, the bumbling global health response, and the unconscionable failures of leadership will share part of the blame. So will deeper, structural faults, such as the gradual withering of public health infrastructure and the profound inequalities that have manifested in such disproportionate impacts. Thus far, it seems that countries with a high degree of social trust, a willingness to sacrifice for the public good, and a respect for science have been most able to comply with effective interventions. The worldwide mobilization of scientific resources to meet the challenge of COVID is truly marvelous, and the rapid development of new vaccines (and new vaccine platforms) is the latest chapter in the long dialectic of disease evolution and human ingenuity. But the present predicament underscores the stark limits of technical solutions on their own, and the evolutionary contest between the virus and our vaccines will play out in unpredictable fashion, inevitably on a global stage. There will be a time for a detached retrospective analysis, but already the virus has reminded us that the fundamentals of biology and the politics of health remain as entangled as ever.[88]

It is also too early to know whether the COVID-19 pandemic is a painful lesson on our path to even greater control over microbial threats or the harbinger of a new period in which our freedom from infectious disease becomes increasingly less secure. The unsettling truth about the current pandemic is that it could be much worse. Diseases with higher case fatality rates, like Ebola or the first SARS, have so far proven less effective at transmitting, or more susceptible to our interventions. Even though SARS-CoV-2 emerged in just the manner we were warned was most predictable, it has still managed to buckle our systems of response. While it is disquieting to consider, the long history of disease counsels us to expect the unexpected. The worst threat may be the one we cannot see coming.[89]

The closing words of William McNeill's *Plagues and Peoples* remain as true today as they were when he wrote them four and a half decades ago. "Infectious disease which antedated the emergence of humankind will last as long as humanity itself, and will surely remain, as it has been hitherto, one of the fundamental parameters and determinants of human history." Human mastery over nature may wax and wane, as the unprecedented experiment in planetary dominance plays out, its destiny uncertain. Paradoxically, we are in some ways more fragile than our ancestors, precisely because our societies depend on a level of security against infectious disease that may be unrealistic. Even though our tools of control are vastly more powerful than in the past, we still have much to learn from the experience of those who lived and died before us. It is urgent that we do so. Our salvation in the long term is unlikely to be technical, or at least not purely so. The future of health is, as ever, a question of values and cooperation. In short, it remains a matter of both chance *and* choice, and the role of history is to help us see our choices a little more clearly, by seeing ourselves a little more clearly: as one species, ingenious and vulnerable, whose health is intimately dependent on each other and on the planet we share with our invisible companions.

ACKNOWLEDGMENTS

I STARTED WRITING THIS BOOK in 2017, just as I finished a book on the role of pandemic disease (and other environmental factors) in Roman history. Fascinated by the significance of microbes in the human past, I was also convinced that the deep patterns of history might help us understand the ongoing risks of infectious disease. I could never have imagined that I would come to finish the book under the cloud of a new pandemic.

Writing a book about the history of disease in the midst of COVID-19 has been both challenging and surreal, and it would not have been possible without the strong support of friends, family, and colleagues. I am deeply grateful for all the support provided by my alma mater and my home, the University of Oklahoma, in so many different forms. I had the opportunity to present drafts of various chapters in the History of Science Colloquium, in the Humanities Forum, and at the College of Public Health. I received valuable feedback from colleagues (and helpful references from Miriam Gross and Kathleen Brosnan). In trying to write an interdisciplinary book such as this one, I have benefited from conversation with colleagues in countless departments across the university. Because I cannot adequately keep track of these debts, I ask my OU colleagues to accept my heartfelt thanks for all their guidance, support, and stimulating dialogue. I also express my gratitude to the wonderful team members in University Libraries. Throughout the pandemic they have displayed extraordinary commitment, and this book would not have been possible without them. I thank Karen Rupp-Serrano, Doni Fox, JoAnn Palmeri, and especially Alexis Beaman and the Interlibrary Loan team for their tireless efforts.

The team at Princeton University Press has once again helped me, at every stage, turn an idea into a book. Matt Rohal, James Schneider, and Rob Tempio are fun to work with, as well as outstanding partners in publishing. I am grateful for their support and for their love of the craft. I have been luckier than I deserve in having some wonderful assistants while writing this book. Michele Angel drew the maps throughout. Matthew Wennemann provided outstanding help in crafting the bibliography. I am grateful to Annie Doyle for her instrumental work in developing the human pathogens checklist. Finally, I am thankful to Taylor Jipp, who meticulously edited the manuscript in its final phases, helping enormously to bring it into form. Thank you all.

The anonymous readers for the Press provided valuable feedback, and I especially thank Joel Mokyr for including this book in the Princeton Economic History of the Western World series. It is an honor to contribute to such a distinguished collection. My friend Chris May read every line of the book with a physician's eye and made countless improvements. Thank you to Daniel Sargent for bracing suggestions that made the arguments much stronger and clearer, to David Wrobel for incisive comments on several chapters, and to Scott Johnson for thoughtful suggestions on the whole manuscript. Given my admiration for his work (and knowing his obvious love of history), I reached out to David Morens of the National Institute of Allergy and Infectious Diseases. While battling a pandemic, he was kind enough to read parts of a manuscript from a total stranger and to make extremely helpful suggestions. Finally, in the course of things, the identity of one of the readers for the Press became known to me. John McNeill's comments on this manuscript were so exceptionally generous—above and beyond what any reader could expect—that I cannot adequately express my gratitude. His scholarship and leadership in the field have helped to make this kind of history possible, and this book is much better because of his extensive feedback.

Finally, and most importantly of all, I send my gratitude and love to my pandemic pod. Sylvie, August, Blaise, and Max were the only people in the world who wanted "daddy's book" to be done more than I did, and they made writing it worthwhile. Michelle is my everything. Thank you, and I love you.

Checklist of Major Identified Species
of Human Pathogens

See chapter 1 for a discussion of the composition and limits of the checklist, including criteria for terms such as "major," "identified species," and "human pathogen."

Pathogen	Taxon	Zoonotic?	Vector-borne?	Geography
Aeromonas hydrophila	Bacteria	Zoonotic/ environmental	No	Cosmopolitan
Atopobium vaginae	Bacteria	Human	No	Cosmopolitan
Bacillus anthracis	Bacteria	Zoonotic/ environmental	No	Cosmopolitan
Bartonella quintana	Bacteria	Zoonotic	Yes	Cosmopolitan
Bordetella pertussis	Bacteria	Human	No	Cosmopolitan
Borrelia afzelii	Bacteria	Zoonotic	Yes	Europe
Borrelia bavariensis	Bacteria	Zoonotic	Yes	Asia and Europe
Borrelia burgdorferi	Bacteria	Zoonotic	Yes	Cosmopolitan
Borrelia crocidurae	Bacteria	Zoonotic	Yes	Africa, Near East
Borrelia duttonii	Bacteria	Human	Yes	Africa, Europe
Borrelia garinii	Bacteria	Zoonotic	Yes	Europe
Borrelia recurrentis	Bacteria	Human	Yes	Cosmopolitan
Brucella abortus	Bacteria	Zoonotic	No	Cosmopolitan, primarily tropics
Brucella melitensis	Bacteria	Zoonotic	No	Cosmopolitan, primarily tropics
Burkholderia pseudomallei	Bacteria	Zoonotic/ environmental	No	Southeast Asia, tropics
Campylobacter coli	Bacteria	Zoonotic	No	Cosmopolitan
Campylobacter jejuni	Bacteria	Zoonotic	No	Cosmopolitan
Chlamydia pneumoniae	Bacteria	Human	No	Cosmopolitan
Chlamydia trachomatis	Bacteria	Human	No	Cosmopolitan
Clostridioides difficile	Bacteria	Human	No	Cosmopolitan

Continued on next page

(*continued*)

Pathogen	Taxon	Zoonotic?	Vector-borne?	Geography
Clostridium perfringens	Bacteria	Zoonotic/environmental	No	Cosmopolitan
Clostridium tetani	Bacteria	Environmental	No	Cosmopolitan
Corynebacterium diphtheriae	Bacteria	Human	No	Cosmopolitan
Corynebacterium minutissimum	Bacteria	Human	No	Cosmopolitan
Coxiella burnetii	Bacteria	Zoonotic	No	Cosmopolitan
Enterococcus faecium	Bacteria	Human	No	Cosmopolitan
Escherichia coli	Bacteria	Human	No	Cosmopolitan
Gardnerella vaginalis	Bacteria	Human	No	Cosmopolitan
Haemophilus ducreyi	Bacteria	Human	No	Cosmopolitan, primarily tropics
Haemophilus influenzae	Bacteria	Human	No	Cosmopolitan
Klebsiella aerogenes	Bacteria	Human	No	Cosmopolitan
Klebsiella granulomatis	Bacteria	Human	No	Cosmopolitan
Klebsiella pneumoniae	Bacteria	Human	No	Cosmopolitan
Leptospira interrogans	Bacteria	Zoonotic	No	Cosmopolitan
Leptotrichia spp.	Bacteria	Human	No	Cosmopolitan
Megasphaera phylotype 2	Bacteria	Human	No	Cosmopolitan
Mobiluncus curtisii	Bacteria	Human	No	Cosmopolitan
Mobiluncus mulieris	Bacteria	Human	No	Cosmopolitan
Moraxella catarrhalis	Bacteria	Human	No	Cosmopolitan
Mycobacterium bovis	Bacteria	Zoonotic	No	Cosmopolitan
Mycobacterium leprae	Bacteria	Human	No	Cosmopolitan
Mycobacterium lepromatosis	Bacteria	Human (though see text)	No	Mexico, Caribbean
Mycobacterium tuberculosis	Bacteria	Human	No	Cosmopolitan
Mycobacterium ulcerans	Bacteria	Environmental	Yes	Tropical
Mycoplasma hominis	Bacteria	Human	No	Cosmopolitan
Mycoplasma pneumoniae	Bacteria	Human	No	Cosmopolitan
Neisseria gonorrhoeae	Bacteria	Human	No	Cosmopolitan
Neisseria meningitidis	Bacteria	Human	No	Cosmopolitan
Orientia (formerly Rickettsia) tsutsugamushi	Bacteria	Zoonotic	Yes	Asia, Pacific
Peptoniphilus lacrimalis	Bacteria	Human	No	Cosmopolitan
Prevotella spp.	Bacteria	Human	No	Cosmopolitan
Pseudomonas aeruginosa	Bacteria	Human	No	Cosmopolitan
Rickettsia africae	Bacteria	Zoonotic	Yes	Tropical/subtropical, mainly Africa
Rickettsia conorii	Bacteria	Zoonotic	Yes	Old World
Rickettsia prowazekii	Bacteria	Zoonotic	Yes	Cosmopolitan
Rickettsia rickettsii	Bacteria	Zoonotic	Yes	Americas
Rickettsia typhi	Bacteria	Zoonotic	Yes	Cosmopolitan
Salmonella enterica	Bacteria	Human	No	Cosmopolitan

Pathogen	Taxon	Zoonotic?	Vector-borne?	Geography
Sneathia amnii	Bacteria	Human	No	Cosmopolitan
Sneathia sanguinegens	Bacteria	Human	No	Cosmopolitan
Staphylococcus aureus	Bacteria	Human	No	Cosmopolitan
Streptococcus agalactiae	Bacteria	Human	No	Cosmopolitan
Streptococcus mutans	Bacteria	Human	No	Cosmopolitan
Streptococcus pneumoniae	Bacteria	Human	No	Cosmopolitan
Streptococcus pyogenes	Bacteria	Human	No	Cosmopolitan
Treponema carateum	Bacteria	Human	No	New World tropics, subtropics
Treponema pallidum	Bacteria	Human	No	Africa, Asia
Vibrio cholerae	Bacteria	Environmental	No	Cosmopolitan
Vibrio parahaemolyticus	Bacteria	Zoonotic/ environmental	No	Cosmopolitan, especially Asia
Vibrio vulnificus	Bacteria	Zoonotic/ environmental	No	Cosmopolitan
Yersinia enterocolitica	Bacteria	Zoonotic	No	Cosmopolitan
Yersinia pestis	Bacteria	Zoonotic	Yes	Cosmopolitan
Yersinia pseudotuberculosis	Bacteria	Zoonotic	No	Cosmopolitan
Aspergillus flavus	Fungi	Environmental	No	Cosmopolitan
Aspergillus fumigatus	Fungi	Environmental	No	Cosmopolitan
Aspergillus niger	Fungi	Environmental	No	Cosmopolitan
Aspergillus terreus	Fungi	Environmental	No	Cosmopolitan
Candida albicans	Fungi	Human	No	Cosmopolitan
Candida glabrata	Fungi	Human	No	Cosmopolitan
Cryptococcus neoformans	Fungi	Environmental	No	Cosmopolitan
Ancylostoma braziliense	Helminth	Zoonotic	No	Cosmopolitan, mainly tropical/ subtropical
Ancylostoma ceylonicum	Helminth	Zoonotic	No	Australia, Asia
Ancylostoma duodenale	Helminth	Zoonotic	No	Cosmopolitan
Ascaris lumbricoides	Helminth	Zoonotic	No	Cosmopolitan
Brugia malayi	Helminth	Zoonotic	Yes	Tropical/subtropical East Asia and Pacific
Brugia timori	Helminth	Human	Yes	Indonesia
Clonorchis (Opisthorchis) sinensis	Helminth	Zoonotic	No	Asia, Pacific
Dibothriocephalus latus (Diphyllobothrium latum)	Helminth	Zoonotic	No	Cosmopolitan
Dracunculus medinensis	Helminth	Zoonotic	No	Tropical
Echinococcus canadensis	Helminth	Zoonotic	No	Cosmopolitan
Echinococcus granulosus	Helminth	Zoonotic	No	Cosmopolitan
Echinococcus multilocularis	Helminth	Zoonotic	No	Cosmopolitan
Echinostoma cinetorchis	Helminth	Zoonotic	No	Asia

Continued on next page

(*continued*)

Pathogen	Taxon	Zoonotic?	Vector-borne?	Geography
Enterobius vermicularis	Helminth	Human	No	Cosmopolitan
Fasciola gigantica	Helminth	Zoonotic	No	Cosmopolitan
Fasciola hepatica	Helminth	Zoonotic	No	Cosmopolitan
Fasciolopsis buski	Helminth	Zoonotic	No	East Asia
Heterophyes heterophyes	Helminth	Zoonotic	No	Old World
Hymenolepis (Rodentolepis) nana	Helminth	Zoonotic	No	Cosmopolitan
Isthmiophora (Echinostoma) hortense	Helminth	Zoonotic	No	Cosmopolitan
Loa loa	Helminth	Human	Yes	Africa
Mansonella ozzardi	Helminth	Human	Yes	Americas
Mansonella perstans	Helminth	Human	Yes	Africa/Americas
Mansonella streptocerca	Helminth	Human	Yes	Africa
Metagonimus yokogawai	Helminth	Zoonotic	No	Europe, Asia, Africa
Necator americanus	Helminth	Zoonotic	No	Cosmopolitan
Oesophagostomum bifurcum	Helminth	Zoonotic	No	South America, Africa, Asia
Opisthorchis felineus	Helminth	Zoonotic	No	Cosmopolitan, mostly Asia
Opisthorchis viverrini	Helminth	Zoonotic	No	Cosmopolitan, mostly Asia
Paragonimus westermani	Helminth	Zoonotic	No	Asia, Pacific
Prosthodendrium molenkampi	Helminth	Zoonotic	No	Old World
Schistosoma guineensis	Helminth	Zoonotic	No	Africa, South Asia
Schistosoma haematobium	Helminth	Zoonotic	No	Africa, South Asia
Schistosoma intercalatum	Helminth	Zoonotic	No	Africa
Schistosoma japonicum	Helminth	Zoonotic	No	Southeast Asia, Pacific
Schistosoma mansoni	Helminth	Human	No	Mostly Africa and South America
Schistosoma mattheei	Helminth	Zoonotic	No	South Africa
Schistosoma mekongi	Helminth	Zoonotic	No	Southeast Asia
Strongyloides stercoralis	Helminth	Zoonotic	No	Cosmopolitan
Taenia asiatica	Helminth	Zoonotic	No	Cosmopolitan
Taenia saginata	Helminth	Zoonotic	No	Cosmopolitan
Taenia solium	Helminth	Zoonotic	No	Cosmopolitan
Toxocara canis	Helminth	Zoonotic	No	Cosmopolitan
Toxoplasma gondii	Helminth	Zoonotic	No	Cosmopolitan
Trichinella spiralis	Helminth	Zoonotic	No	Cosmopolitan
Trichuris trichiura	Helminth	Human	No	Cosmopolitan
Wuchereria bancrofti	Helminth	Human	Yes	Tropical
Blastocystis hominis	Protozoa	Human	No	Cosmopolitan

Pathogen	Taxon	Zoonotic?	Vector-borne?	Geography
Cryptosporidium hominis	Protozoa	Zoonotic	No	Cosmopolitan
Cryptosporidium parvum	Protozoa	Zoonotic	No	Cosmopolitan
Entamoeba histolytica	Protozoa	Human	No	Cosmopolitan
Giardia lamblia	Protozoa	Zoonotic	No	Cosmopolitan
Leishmania braziliensis	Protozoa	Zoonotic	Yes	South America
Leishmania donovani	Protozoa	Zoonotic	Yes	Old World
Leishmania guyanensis	Protozoa	Zoonotic	Yes	South America
Leishmania major	Protozoa	Zoonotic	Yes	Old World
Leishmania mexicana	Protozoa	Zoonotic	Yes	South America
Leishmania panamensis	Protozoa	Zoonotic	Yes	Central America
Leishmania tropica	Protozoa	Zoonotic	Yes	Africa, Europe
Plasmodium falciparum	Protozoa	Human	Yes	Tropical
Plasmodium knowlesi	Protozoa	Zoonotic	Yes	Southeast Asia, Pacific
Plasmodium malariae	Protozoa	Human	Yes	Tropical
Plasmodium ovale	Protozoa	Human	Yes	Africa
Plasmodium vivax	Protozoa	Human	Yes	Tropical, subtropical
Trichomonas vaginalis	Protozoa	Human	No	Cosmopolitan
Trypanosoma brucei gambiense	Protozoa	Zoonotic	Yes	Africa
Trypanosoma brucei rhodesiense	Protozoa	Zoonotic	Yes	Africa
Trypanosoma cruzi	Protozoa	Zoonotic	Yes	Americas
Alphapapillomavirus 1	Virus	Human	No	Cosmopolitan
Alphapapillomavirus 10	Virus	Human	No	Cosmopolitan
Alphapapillomavirus 11	Virus	Human	No	Cosmopolitan
Alphapapillomavirus 13	Virus	Human	No	Cosmopolitan
Alphapapillomavirus 14	Virus	Human	No	Cosmopolitan
Alphapapillomavirus 3	Virus	Human	No	Cosmopolitan
Alphapapillomavirus 4	Virus	Human	No	Cosmopolitan
Alphapapillomavirus 5	Virus	Human	No	Cosmopolitan
Alphapapillomavirus 6	Virus	Human	No	Cosmopolitan
Alphapapillomavirus 7	Virus	Human	No	Cosmopolitan
Alphapapillomavirus 8	Virus	Human	No	Cosmopolitan
Alphapapillomavirus 9	Virus	Human	No	Cosmopolitan
Astrovirus	Virus	Human	No	Cosmopolitan
Cache Valley orthobunyavirus	Virus	Zoonotic	Yes	North America
Chikungunya virus	Virus	Zoonotic	Yes	Cosmopolitan, mainly tropical, subtropical
Dengue virus	Virus	Zoonotic	Yes	Cosmopolitan
Enterovirus A	Virus	Human	No	Cosmopolitan
Enterovirus B	Virus	Human	No	Cosmopolitan
Enterovirus C	Virus	Human	No	Cosmopolitan
Hepatitis A virus	Virus	Human	No	Cosmopolitan
Hepatitis B virus	Virus	Human	No	Cosmopolitan

Continued on next page

(*continued*)

Pathogen	Taxon	Zoonotic?	Vector-borne?	Geography
Hepatitis C virus	Virus	Human	No	Cosmopolitan
Hepatitis D virus	Virus	Human	No	Cosmopolitan
Hepatitis E virus	Virus	Zoonotic	No	Cosmopolitan
Human adenovirus a	Virus	Human	No	Cosmopolitan
Human adenovirus b	Virus	Human	No	Cosmopolitan
Human adenovirus c	Virus	Human	No	Cosmopolitan
Human adenovirus d	Virus	Human	No	Cosmopolitan
Human adenovirus e	Virus	Human	No	Cosmopolitan
Human adenovirus f	Virus	Human	No	Cosmopolitan
Human alphaherpesvirus 1 (herpes simplex virus 1) (HHV-1)	Virus	Human	No	Cosmopolitan
Human alphaherpesvirus 2 (herpes simplex virus 2) (HHV-2)	Virus	Human	No	Cosmopolitan
Human alphaherpesvirus 3 (varicella zoster virus) (HHV-3)	Virus	Human	No	Cosmopolitan
Human betaherpesvirus 5 (human cytomegalovirus) (HHV-5)	Virus	Human	No	Cosmopolitan
Human betaherpesvirus 6A (HHV-6A)	Virus	Human	No	Cosmopolitan
Human betaherpesvirus 6B (HHV-6B)	Virus	Human	No	Cosmopolitan
Human betaherpesvirus 7 (HHV-7)	Virus	Human	No	Cosmopolitan
Human coronavirus 229E	Virus	Human	No	Cosmopolitan
Human coronavirus HKU1	Virus	Human	No	Cosmopolitan
Human coronavirus NL63	Virus	Human	No	Cosmopolitan
Human coronavirus OC43	Virus	Human	No	Cosmopolitan
Human coronavirus SARS-CoV-2	Virus	Human	No	Cosmopolitan
Human gammaherpesvirus 4 (Epstein-Barr virus) (HHV-4)	Virus	Human	No	Cosmopolitan
Human gammaherpesvirus 8 (Kaposi's sarcoma-associated herpesvirus) (HHV-8)	Virus	Human	No	Cosmopolitan
Human immunodeficiency virus 1	Virus	Human	No	Cosmopolitan
Human immunodeficiency virus 2	Virus	Human	No	Cosmopolitan

Pathogen	Taxon	Zoonotic?	Vector-borne?	Geography
Human metapneumovirus A1	Virus	Human	No	Cosmopolitan
Human metapneumovirus A2	Virus	Human	No	Cosmopolitan
Human metapneumovirus B1	Virus	Human	No	Cosmopolitan
Human metapneumovirus B2	Virus	Human	No	Cosmopolitan
Human orthopneumovirus	Virus	Human	No	Cosmopolitan
Human orthorubulavirus 2	Virus	Human	No	Cosmopolitan
Human orthorubulavirus 4	Virus	Human	No	Cosmopolitan
Human parechovirus A	Virus	Human	No	Cosmopolitan
Human pegivirus	Virus	Human	No	Cosmopolitan
Human respirovirus 1	Virus	Human	No	Cosmopolitan
Human respirovirus 3	Virus	Human	No	Cosmopolitan
Human T-lymphotropic virus 1	Virus	Human	No	Cosmopolitan
Human T-lymphotropic virus 2	Virus	Human	No	Cosmopolitan
Influenza virus A	Virus	Zoonotic	No	Cosmopolitan
Influenza virus B	Virus	Human	No	Cosmopolitan
Influenza virus C	Virus	Zoonotic	No	Cosmopolitan
Japanese encephalitis virus	Virus	Zoonotic	Yes	Cosmopolitan
Lassa mammarenavirus	Virus	Zoonotic	No	Africa
Measles morbillivirus	Virus	Human	No	Cosmopolitan
Molluscum contagiosum virus	Virus	Human	No	Cosmopolitan
Mumps orthorubulavirus	Virus	Human	No	Cosmopolitan
Norwalk virus	Virus	Zoonotic	No	Cosmopolitan
Onyong-nyong virus	Virus	Zoonotic	Yes	Africa
Oropouche orthobunyavirus	Virus	Zoonotic	Yes	South America
Primate erythroparvovirus 1	Virus	Human	No	Cosmopolitan
Rabies lyssavirus	Virus	Zoonotic	No	Cosmopolitan
Rhinovirus A	Virus	Human	No	Cosmopolitan
Rhinovirus B	Virus	Human	No	Cosmopolitan
Rhinovirus C	Virus	Human	No	Cosmopolitan
Ross River virus	Virus	Zoonotic	Yes	Australia, Pacific
Rotavirus A	Virus	Zoonotic	No	Cosmopolitan
Rubella virus	Virus	Human	No	Cosmopolitan
Tick-borne encephalitis virus (European)	Virus	Zoonotic	Yes	Europe
Tick-borne encephalitis virus (Far Eastern)	Virus	Zoonotic	Yes	Asia
Tick-borne encephalitis virus (Siberian)	Virus	Zoonotic	Yes	Asia
Variola virus	Virus	Human	No	Cosmopolitan
Venezuelan equine encephalitis virus	Virus	Zoonotic	Yes	Americas
Yellow fever virus	Virus	Zoonotic	Yes	Cosmopolitan
Zika virus	Virus	Zoonotic	Yes	Tropical, subtropical

NOTES

Introduction

1. The hygienic revolution that brought these modern routines into being is explored in chapter 12. See Tomes 1998, Ward 2019, and, for a popular account, Ashenburg 2007. For the bacteria count, the numbers are based on Sender, Fuchs, and Milo 2016. See Urban et al. 2016 for the armpit microbiome, describing the mechanisms of hygienic products and effects on the species diversity of the microbes living on human skin.

2. For premodern life expectancies, which were quite variable, see chapters 3 (hunter-gatherers) and 10 and 11 (late preindustrial figures).

3. It is worth observing that the division between infectious and noninfectious causes of disease is useful but imperfect. Some chronic and organ diseases and types of cancer are caused by infectious agents; for example, stomach cancer is usually caused by the bacterium *H. pylori* (see, generally, Mercer 2018). Conversely, outcomes in infection are shaped by underlying health conditions, including chronic disease (consider, for instance, the influence of metabolic disease on mortality rates in COVID-19 cases).

4. The major exception, of course, is that now chimpanzees are sporadically exposed to human germs, with effects that are often devastating. See chapter 2 for chimpanzee health, and chapters 2 and 3 for human evolution.

5. For chimpanzee numbers, see Strindberg et al. 2018; see Pepin 2011 for a million in the past. Similarly, the shared ancestors between humans and chimpanzees likely had population sizes on the same order of magnitude (Schrago 2014).

6. On the geographical ecology of infectious disease, see Guernier, Hochberg, and Guégan 2004; Bonds, Dobson, and Keenan 2012; and Cashdan 2014.

7. For the definitions, see CDC 2012, 172. The word *pandemic* only came into widespread use to mean an interregional epidemic in the nineteenth century. See Morens, Folkers, and Fauci 2009 and chapter 11. It is worth observing that despite their technical aura, the words *epidemic*, *endemic*, and *pandemic* are rough and ready terms, without precise quantitative dimensions, used pragmatically in the study of disease. For the similarity of the parasite burden in different chimpanzee populations, see, for example, Gillespie et al. 2010.

8. Such a history might be confronted with charges of biological determinism or reductionism. At times, historians are uneasy allotting agency to natural factors. Hopefully the book builds a compelling case that human history is enriched by understanding its material context, which includes microbial pathogens. Let us point out a few introductory reasons why blanket charges of determinism impoverish the way we can understand human history. First, to allege

that causal frameworks limited to human factors are somehow innocent of determinism is fallacious. There is just as much risk that human-only history attributes too much agency to humans and creates a false dualism in which humans are separate from nature. Second, charges of determinism are particularly senseless in the case of infectious disease, because humans shape the ecological conditions that affect pathogen evolution; unlike volcanoes and earthquakes, which truly strike from without, infectious diseases are partly phenomena of our own making. See the compelling remarks of McNeill 2010, 1–11, on balancing the agency of humans and microbes in history by paraphrasing Marx: "People made their own history but they did not make it as they pleased because ecology would not let them." Along the same lines, see Brooke 2014, 1–13. Finally, one of the goals of the book is to historicize human agency in the face of challenge from infectious disease. The growing ability of societies to control diseases is a major feature of modern history and inseparable from questions of changes in governmentality and state capacity, processes that I try to place in a broader perspective. These same arguments are relevant to questions of geographic determinism. I emphasize throughout the book that physical geography shapes disease ecology, which is abundantly obvious. However, one of the main themes of the book is the *changing* ways that these ecologies have shaped human demography, institutions, and so forth throughout our past, and the different ways that humans have shaped and responded to the environment.

9. There is a resemblance here to the project of "big history" (e.g., Christian 2011 and Spier 2010) in the use of long timescales and the effort to situate the human story within nature. Yet this book devotes proportionally more attention to the human chapters of the earth's history. It is deeply indebted to the idea of "deep history," which erases the arbitrary distinction between prehistory and history (e.g., Smail 2008). For the Roman pandemics, see Harper 2017.

10. On the theme of globalization and the history of disease specifically, see Green 2017, drawing from new genomic data and the classic statement of Ladurie 1973.

11. For an attempt to characterize globalization on these timescales, see Therborn 2000; Osterhammel 2005 is in the same spirit but only goes back a millennium or so; also see Sachs 2020.

12. See Deaton 2013, 23–56, for a discussion of the value and limits of different ways to measure changes in well-being. The essays in Adams 2016 offer a range of critical perspectives on the challenges of measurement in the context of health. It would be otiose to declare all the things that this book is *not*, but I can make a small exception to note that this book is not a history of medicine. Although it could not have been written without the rich body of scholarship produced by historians of medicine, the focus throughout these pages must remain on the interplay of infectious disease and human social development, with only occasional glimpses of important related questions in the history of medical thought and practice.

13. Deaton 2013.

14. Probably every historian has a book that they cherish and secretly wish they had written. I am hardly original in confessing that, for me, that book is McNeill's *Plagues and Peoples* (1976). McNeill was a pioneer of global history who saw human history in ecological terms. His book captures the dynamism of infectious disease as a force in human history, a force partly of our own making. It is a masterpiece. We of course have far more scholarship to work with today, and, above all, we have new kinds of evidence like genomes that were unavailable in 1976. Since

then, big histories of particular diseases have been written by historians (Webb 2009 on malaria and Webb 2019 on diarrheal disease are shining examples, and chapter 6 explores the especially valuable body of literature on the plague), and there are a handful of notable general histories of disease by historians, though with something of a European emphasis (Hays 1998; Kiple 1999; Snowden 2019). For the most part, big histories of disease have been written by geographers, anthropologists, microbiologists, or nonacademics (McKeown 1988; Karlen 1995; Diamond 1997; Oldstone 1998; Greenblatt and Spigelman 2003; Crawford 2007; Callahan 2007; Crawford 2009; Barrett and Armelagos 2013; Shah 2016; McMichael 2017; Kenny 2021). For a classic statement of the problems of retrospective diagnosis, see Arrizabalaga 2002. P. D. Mitchell 2011 and A. J. Larner 2019 provide more recent overviews. For doubts about plague and the resolution by DNA, see chapter 6.

15. Reuter, Spacek, and Snyder 2015 addresses high-throughput sequencing technologies. One proxy measure for the expansion of data could be measured by the number of bases in GenBank, which doubles every eighteen months ("GenBank and WGS Statistics," National Center for Biotechnology Information, US National Library of Medicine, https://www.ncbi .nlm.nih.gov/genbank/statistics/).

16. Helpful overviews of paleogenomics, including the coined phrase *genetic time travel*, are found in Krause and Pääbo 2016. Also see Achtman 2016; Hofman and Warinner 2019; all of the essays in Lindqvist and Rajora 2019 but especially Marciniak and Poinar 2018; Spyrou et al. 2019a; and Duchêne et al. 2020. For tree thinking in general, see Baum and Smith 2013. See chapter 1 for a more detailed overview.

17. Wilson 1999.

Chapter 1

1. Darwin 2017, 543–44.

2. See chapter 12 for the emergence and reception of germ theory or the "bacteriological revolution," which involved a wide range of ideas and actors leading up to Pasteur and Koch, and took several decades to become established as a consensus. On Pasteur, see Geison 1995. On Koch, see Brock 1988 and Gradmann 2009.

3. Though other chapters will present some of the tongue-twisting names of our parasites, this chapter presents by far the most technical language of any in the book, which I have sought to soften as responsibly as possible with the aim of exploring the wondrous biology of our germs in an accessible manner.

4. Dobzhansky 1973.

5. Achtman and Wagner 2008 provide an overview of the impact of genomics on microbial taxonomy.

6. Yong 2016 provides a beautiful synthesis of new thinking about microbial diversity. See Gilbert et al. 2018 on the human microbiome. These questions are trickier than they might first appear because words like *pathogen, parasite,* and *germ* are not taxonomical terms, and they are not used consistently across fields like microbiology, medicine, and ecology.

7. The Oxford English Dictionary reports the first use of the word *pathogen* as late as 1880. Viruses were only discovered at the end of the nineteenth century (tobacco mosaic virus was

filtered in the 1890s) and only in the twentieth century could "pathogen" be used to describe a disease-causing organism from any of these taxa. For thoughts on what makes a pathogen, see Balloux and van Dorp 2017.

8. Authoritative treatments use the word *parasite* in different ways. Ashford and Crewe 2003 provides the classic checklist of human parasites, meant to include protozoa, helminths, and insects. Schmid-Hempel 2013 uses the word *parasite* in the encompassing fashion employed here.

9. Wilson 2014, 180. Parasites (except viruses) must acquire both energy and required elements. We would do well not to underestimate the twenty-five elements required for life as a limiting factor on genetic success; free iron, for instance, is a critical and scarce biological resource, and hosts and parasites tussle over it. See Kaspari and Powers 2016 on the elements required for life. See Nairz and Weiss 2020 for a recent overview of "nutritional immunity."

10. See Taylor, Latham, and Woolhouse 2001 for the oft-cited number of 1,415. Again, this number is relatively meaningless and more a reflection of the state of genome sequencing at the turn of the millennium than any intrinsic facts about the biology or ecology of human disease. See Wardeh et al. 2015 for the more up-to-date list. Other important contributions to this literature include Guernier, Hochberg, and Guégan 2004; Wolfe, Dunavan, and Diamond 2007; Smith et al. 2007; Jones et al. 2008; Dunn et al. 2010; Smith and Guegan 2010; Kuris 2012; and Murray et al. 2015. The number from GIDEON (https://www.gideononline.com) was current as of early 2020, and it grows continuously.

11. Wardeh et al. 2015 lists sixty-four species, whereas Taylor, Latham, and Woolhouse 2001 reports twenty-eight.

12. The procedure for determining this list was to build as comprehensive a catalog of human diseases caused by infectious agents as possible. To do this, I created a list of all pathogens that have infected humans, using data from the studies of Taylor and Wardeh, the GIDEON database (a remarkably comprehensive resource), and historical lists such as that in Kiple 1993. Then, I identified the agents of each disease that are recognized as species (following the International Committee on Taxonomy of Viruses for viruses, the *International Journal of Systematic and Evolutionary Microbiology* for bacteria, Species Fungorum for fungi, and Ashford and Crewe 2003 for helminths). I excluded from the "major" pathogens any which had never had a recorded mortality episode in excess of fifty thousand, or annual prevalence of greater than five million (regardless of clinical outcome), according to a literature review. Although this threshold is inevitably arbitrary (as well as surely vulnerable to sampling bias), it is a step forward from the previous lists that make no discrimination on the importance of disease and thus report numbers that are meaningless other than as an artefact of sampling.

13. For leprosy in wild animals, see the following: Avanzi et al. 2016 for squirrels; Truman 2005 for armadillos; and Honap et al. 2018 for primates.

14. Helminth is not technically a taxonomic category, but most treatments of human disease group all pathogenic worms of various taxa under this catch-all category, a convenient practice that I follow here. For fungal threats to human health, Olsen et al. 2011 provides a thorough overview. The most common prion disease is Creutzfeldt-Jakob disease (CJD), which occurs sporadically and is not transmissible under normal conditions. On prion disease generally, see Colby and Prusiner 2011; Chen and Dong 2016; and Sigurdson, Bartz, and Glatzel 2019.

15. See Zimmer 2015 for a readable account of the biology of viruses. See Crawford 2009 on viruses in human history. Also see Strauss and Strauss 2008; Shors 2013; and Cordingley 2017. The Medawars' famous quip has been quoted in a variety of forms, with loose support. I find these exact words as quoted at Medawar and Medawar 1983, 275, but would not claim this as the original use of the phrase.

16. For the estimate of forty thousand (which is lower than other recent estimates), see Carlson et al. 2019.

17. Crawford 2009.

18. See Locey and Lennon 2016 for high estimates of microbial diversity. See, however, Louca et al. 2019 for much lower estimates. I follow modern taxonomies in classifying the genus *Rickettsia* among bacteria. Rickettsial species are agents of important diseases, like typhus. The *Rickettsia* are tiny, spherical bacteria, virus-like in their size and in the fact that they enter host cells. Many older accounts treat the *Rickettsia* apart from bacteria.

19. Sender, Fuchs, and Milo 2016. See Gilbert et al. 2018 on the human microbiome. See Abt and Pamer 2014 for commensals and immunity.

20. TB is considered in more detail in chapter 5. Plague figures prominently in chapters 6 and 9.

21. See chapter 2 for more on chimpanzee parasites.

22. On leishmaniasis, see Hotez 2013, 133–40. On sleeping sickness, see Brun et al. 2010 and Büscher et al. 2017. On malaria, see chapter 3 for vivax malaria and chapter 5 for falciparum malaria, and Packard 2007 and Webb 2009 for invaluable historical overviews. See Sharp, Plenderleith, and Hahn 2020 for an overview of the evolutionary background. Three species of malaria parasites (*P. malariae, P. ovale wallikeri,* and *P. ovale curtisi*) are human-adapted but cause a much lower burden of disease.

23. See Ashford and Crewe 2003 for a catalog. For the burden of helminth disease, see Hotez 2013, 17–96; and Bruschi 2014.

24. See Browne 1995, vol. 1, for the voyage and Darwin's background. See Weiner 1994; Grant and Grant 1996; and Donohue 2011 on the evolution of finches. Relentless evolution is described by Thompson 2013.

25. Duffy, Shackelton, and Holmes 2008; Sanjuán et al. 2010; Flint et al. 2015, 2:319. In general, RNA polymerases in RNA viruses lack proofreading capabilities.

26. On rhinoviruses, see Cordey et al. 2010 and Lewis-Rogers, Seger, and Adler 2017. On quasispecies, see Domingo and Perales 2019.

27. Raccianello 2012. See Weaver et al. 2016 on viral evolution generally.

28. See Juhas 2015 for a review of horizontal gene transfer mechanisms in human pathogens.

29. Sompayrac 2016 provides a wonderfully readable summary of human immunology. Carver 2017 and Klenerman 2017 are also helpful guides.

30. Elias 2007 discusses the skin as an immune barrier. Turner 2009; France and Turner 2017; Smith et al. 2020.

31. Sompayrac 2016, 13–26.

32. Flajnik 2018 provides a recent review of the origins of adaptive immunity.

33. Sompayrac 2016, 42–71.

34. In general, see Karlsson, Kwiatkowski, and Sabeti 2014; Casanova and Abel 2018; and Quintana-Murci 2019. On malaria, see chapters 3 and 5; on familial Mediterranean fever, see Park et al. 2020. For tuberculosis (and "pathogen-imposed selective pressures"), see Kerner et al. 2021.

35. These five routes are all instances of horizontal transmission. Vertical transmission—from parents to progeny—is also important in nature, but only in a handful of human diseases, such as AIDS.

36. Chapter 3 offers a general overview of vector-borne disease, which is then a prominent theme throughout the rest of the book.

37. Alizon et al. 2009; Schmid-Hempel 2013, 312–53; Alizon and Michalakis 2015; Alizon and Méthot 2018. It is important to highlight that there is not a strong empirical foundation for claims about the relative virulence of pathogens between host species, which is difficult to measure for a variety of reasons. So this claim is merely impressionistic, but it is logically sound in terms of epidemiology and disease ecology, and it seems overwhelmingly likely to me. We will explore the nuances of this claim throughout the book, with a look at chimpanzee disease in chapter 2. It might be safest to say that acute, virulent diseases with a narrow host range are rare in nature.

38. For the older view, see Burnet and White 1972. For changing views in the late twentieth century, see Anderson and May 1991; Ewald 1994; and Frank 1996. For more on smallpox, see chapter 5.

39. Alizon and Michalakis 2015.

40. See Wasik and Murphy 2012 for a history of rabies.

41. On *vivax*, see White 2011; on herpesvirus, see Arvin et al. 2007; and on microworms, see chapter 3 on lymphatic filariasis.

42. Ewald 1991.

43. See Fiers et al. 1976, specifically on *Escherichia* virus MS2, a virus that infects the bacterium *E. coli*. See Reuter, Spacek, and Snyder 2015 on high-throughput sequencing technologies.

44. Gould 1988, 24. On chimps and humans, see Muller et al. 2017.

45. Molecular clock methods have been used since the 1960s (Zuckerkandl and Pauling 1965). The accumulation of genetic data, more sophisticated evolutionary models, and more powerful computational methods have allowed important refinements (Ho et al. 2005; Yang and Rannala 2012). See Young and Gillung 2020 for a moderately technical overview of big-data phylogenetics and its models and methods.

46. See Membrebe et al. 2019 for an up-to-date perspective on molecular clocks models and methods. The work of Duchêne et al. 2020 is also useful. To give two relevant examples, the divergence between measles and the closely related rinderpest virus moved back by over a millennium, thanks to an earlier sample (recovered from an early twentieth-century museum specimen of a human lung) and more sophisticated evolutionary models (Düx et al. 2020). Similarly, the estimated origin of *Variola major*, the smallpox virus, has shifted in recent years, with Mühlemann et al. 2020 describing the latest.

47. For applications of phylogenetics by historians, see, for example, Green 2014 and 2020. For the Columbian Exchange specifically, see McNeill (forthcoming). Harper 2020 synthesizes some of the early applications by historians.

48. On TB, see Brosch et al. 2002 and Comas et al. 2013. See chapter 5. For a review of *anthroponosis*, or reverse zoonosis, the transmission of diseases from humans to animals, see Messenger, Barnes, and Gray 2014. Most discussion of anthroponosis focuses on recent evolutionary history, and I am not aware of a comprehensive study of the diseases that have established in animal populations after establishing in human populations.

49. See Krause and Pääbo 2016; Hofman and Warinner 2019; Lindqvist and Rajora 2019, (especially) Marciniak and Poinar 2018; Spyrou et al. 2019a; and Duchêne et al. 2020. For the first whole pathogen genome, see Bos et al. 2011. See Reich 2018, xvi, on whole-genome analysis.

50. On the photo album concept, see Smith and Gilbert 2019. On plague DNA, see Haensch et al. 2010; Bos et al. 2011; and Wagner et al. 2014. See chapter 6 for the ongoing work on *Y. pestis* that has further enriched our understanding of this pathogen. On New World paratyphoid, see Vågene et al. 2018. See chapter 7.

51. See Austin et al. 2019 on some of the important ethical dimensions of studying ancient biomolecules. "It is essential . . ." comes from McCormick 2021, 44.

52. The passage from Darwin is found in chapter 17 of *The Voyage of the Beagle* (Darwin 1959).

53. Gould 1996, 14.

Chapter 2

1. See Boesch and Boesch-Achermann 2000.

2. Formenty et al. 2003; Leendertz et al. 2006; Patrono and Leendertz 2019.

3. Formenty et al. 2003; Leendertz et al. 2006; Köndgen et al. 2008. For more on RSV, see Shi et al. 2017.

4. Leendertz et al. 2006; Grützmacher et al. 2018. Similarly, in Uganda in 2013, a lethal disease outbreak among chimps was caused by *Human rhinovirus C*, the common cold (Scully et al. 2018). In 2016, an outbreak was caused by *Human coronavirus OC43*, another cause of the common cold (Patrono et al. 2018).

5. See below on the Global Mammal Parasite Database, and also the insightful overview of Calvignac-Spencer et al. 2012.

6. In fairness to chimpanzees, coprophagy is most often practiced when edible seed remains can be extracted from their feces. See Sarabian, Ngoubangoye, and MacIntosh 2017.

7. Schmid-Hempel 2013 is one of the best summaries of the evolutionary ecology of parasites. Poulin and Morand 2000; Morand 2000; Thomas, Renaud, and Guégan 2005; Poulin 2007; Lindenfors et al. 2007; Han, Kramer, and Drake 2016; Schmid-Hempel 2017.

8. Nunn et al. 2003; Kamiya et al. 2014; Schmid-Hempel 2017.

9. Nunn et al. 2012. On promiscuity, see Wlasiuk and Nachman 2010.

10. Côté and Poulin 1995; Altizer et al. 2003; Capitanio 2012. On group structure, see Griffin and Nunn 2012 and Nunn et al. 2015.

11. Rifkin, Nunn, and Garamszegi 2012.

12. On the latitudinal species gradient, see Jablonski et al. 2017. On primates, see especially Nunn et al. 2005. On parasites more generally, see Guernier, Hochberg, and Guégan 2004; Bonds, Dobson, and Keenan 2012; Cashdan 2014; and Stephens et al. 2016.

13. Cooper and Nunn 2013. On primates and parasites more generally, see Huffman and Chapman 2009; Gillespie et al. 2010; and Brinkworth and Pechenkina 2013. The database is accessible at https://parasites.nunn-lab.org.

14. For instance, of the approximately thirty-four unique viral species associated with the genus *Pan* in the database, at least a third of them are manifestly human viruses (*Betacoronavirus 1*, *Enterovirus C*/polio, adenoviruses A–E, *Metapneumovirus*, RSV, parainfluenza virus, etc.). See also Calvignac-Spencer et al. 2012.

15. Pedersen et al. 2005; Cooper, Kamilar, and Nunn 2012.

16. Nunn and Altizer 2006, 255. See also the observations of Calvignac-Spencer et al. 2012: "Most microorganisms identified in wild great apes appear to be enzootic (that is, they persistently infect wild great ape populations), and are not known to be associated with acute disease. . . . One may argue that this is simply because of a lack of surveillance in wild ape populations; however, habituated communities of wild great apes are distributed across each species range, and some of these communities have been under continuous observation for decades, so massive die-offs would not have gone unnoticed. A more likely explanation is that great ape demography (i.e., low-density, fragmented populations) is not compatible with the sustained circulation of such acute disease-causing pathogens. Known acute diseases in wild great apes originated either from other species (Ebola), the environment (anthrax), or humans (respiratory diseases)."

17. For this metastudy, see Gurven and Gomes 2017. See also Hill 2001; Wood 2017; and Muller and Wrangham 2018.

18. For estimates of gorilla and chimpanzee populations, see Strindberg et al. 2018.

19. Lee 1987; Murdoch 1994; Turchin 2003; Sibly 2005; Turchin 2009.

20. On chimpanzee diets, see Hohmann 2009; Phillips and Lancelotti 2014; and Wood and Gilby 2017.

21. See chapter 3 for insights from human hunter-gatherer demography along these lines.

22. Frazer 1930, 123–24.

23. Frazer 1930, 226.

24. Crosby 2006. See also Goudsblom 1992 and 2015.

25. Wrangham 2009; Burton 2009; Wrangham 2017.

26. "If they still lived . . ." quoted from Wrangham 2009, 2.

27. There is controversy over whether the first representative of *Homo*, *Homo habilis*, should truly be included in the genus *Homo*. *Homo habilis* had a modestly larger brain than the australopithecines, at about 600 cm^3, but this species was still rather small, still adapted to climbing, and still in possession of a mouth and digestive toolkit that were ape-like. On hunting, see Wood and Gilby 2017. For possible very early archaeological evidence for fire, see Hlubik et al. 2017.

28. Wrangham 2009; Antón and Snodgrass 2012.

29. Carmody 2017.

30. The "expensive tissue" hypothesis was proposed by Aiello and Wheeler 1995. Snodgrass, Leonard, and Robertson 2009. For critical views, see Navarrete, van Schaik, and Isler 2011 and Cornélio et al. 2016.

31. On species monopoly, see Goudsblom 2015, 185, and Goudsblom 1992. Archaeologists have found a remarkable demonstration of our ancestors' newfound power at a site in South

Africa known as the Sterkfontein caves. For millennia, big cats used the cave as a den to munch on their prey, as evidenced by australopithecine bones. Sometime after, following the mastery of fire, *Homo* not only evicted the cats but took control of the cave as their new home (Reynolds, Clarke, and Kuman 2007).

32. Wrangham 2009; Wood and Gilby 2017.

33. Lordkipanidze et al. 2005; Haeusler et al. 2013; Schiess et al. 2014. See Spikins et al. 2019 for medical care among Neanderthals.

34. Fleagle et al. 2010; Carotenuto et al. 2016; Détroit et al. 2019.

35. Wertheim et al. 2014; Underdown, Kumar, and Houldcroft 2017; Forni et al. 2020.

36. Braun et al. 2010; Archer et al. 2014.

37. On fishing generally in human history, see Fagan 2017, 21–26. On hominins, see Stewart 1994.

38. See Jamieson 2016 for the general biology of the disease. See Hotez 2013, 41–55, for a concise overview. The burden of the disease is disputed: see King 2015, arguing that the methods employed by the *Global Burden of Disease* underestimate the true burden of schistosomiasis. On Bilharz, see Bergquist, Kloos, and Adugna 2016, 16. For a history of the disease more generally in the context of tropical medicine, see Farley 1991.

39. Bergquist, Kloos, and Adugna 2016, 16.

40. Colley et al. 2014.

41. Madsen 2016.

42. Webster, Southgate, and Littlewood 2006; Standley et al. 2012.

43. Colley et al. 2014.

44. See Bergquist, Kloos, and Adugna 2016 for a broad overview of the parasite's history.

45. Morgan et al. 2005; Webster, Southgate, and Littlewood 2006; Attwood et al. 2007; Attwood, Fatih, and Upatham 2008; Lawton et al. 2011; Standley et al. 2012.

46. See Desprès et al. 1992 for the suggestion of a link with hominin evolution. See Morgan et al. 2005 for molecular clock estimates putting the origins of *S. mansoni* at 300,000–430,000 years ago. See Crellen et al. 2016 for a split between *S. mansoni* and *S. rodhaini* around 126,500 years ago.

47. Mouahid et al. 2012.

48. On eradication in China, see Gross 2015.

49. See Morris 2010 and 2013 for the data underlying his framework. The chimpanzee data are from Pontzer et al. 2016. See also Pontzer 2017. The gazelle analogy is meant loosely, because herd size and energy intake vary by species, season, and so forth, but a herd of Thomson's gazelles (about one hundred animals) consuming an average of 10 megajoules or about 2,400 kilocalories each per day (see Wilmhurst, Fryxell, and Colucci 1999) represents about the same level of consumption as a modern American.

Chapter 3

1. The "worst mistake" quote comes from Diamond 1987. The "history's biggest fraud" quote is from Harari 2014, 77. In part these claims can be traced to the influence of Marshall Sahlins (e.g., Sahlins 1972), whose work helped to broaden appreciation for hunter-gatherer societies and

allows more critical considerations of the Neolithic revolution or evolutionary models of human social history in general (also discussed in the next chapter).

2. See Trueba and Dunthorn 2012 and Houldcroft and Underdown 2016 for rare efforts to emphasize the importance of this deeper past. There is probably a kind of implicit Eurocentrism (or at least a latitudinal bias) in the relative neglect of vector-borne diseases in studies of deep history.

3. Tallavaara, Eronen, and Luoto 2018 shows that in tropical/subtropical regions, parasite burden rather than energy availability played a relatively greater role in regulating population density.

4. See Mounier and Lahr 2019 for a recent summary.

5. See Stringer 2016 on the emergence of *Homo sapiens*. On interbreeding, see Sankararaman et al. 2012; Sankararaman et al. 2014; Pääbo 2015; Fu et al. 2016; Kuhlwilm et al. 2016; and Rogers et al. 2020. On brains, see Neubauer, Hublin, and Gunz 2018. See Pimenoff, Mendes de Oliveira, and Bravo 2017 for a plausible reconstruction of the evolutionary history of human papilloma-virus 16.

6. The extinction of the Neanderthals is at present dated to fifty to thirty-five thousand years ago (Timmermann 2020). The braided stream analogy was proposed by Xinzhi Wu (e.g., Athreya and Wu 2017).

7. López, van Dorp, and Hellenthal 2015; Groucutt et al. 2015; Tierney, deMenocal, and Zander 2017; Groucutt et al. 2018; Hershkovitz et al. 2018.

8. See Gamble 1993 and Oppenheimer 2004 for classic accounts of dispersal written prior to the avalanche of modern genomic data. See Nielsen et al. 2017 and Reich 2018 for the state of the question and use of genomic data to fill in gaps in our knowledge about the timing and itinerary of human migrations. On savannahstan, see Dennell 2003 and 2010. On the mangrove highway, see Erlandson and Braje 2015. See Gruhn 2020 for a discussion of recent work that has suggested these earlier dates for the peopling of the Americas.

9. On projectiles, see Sisk and Shea 2011; O'Driscoll and Thompson 2018; and Sano et al. 2019. The date of human seafaring is debated. See Cherry and Leppard 2015 and Howitt-Marshall and Runnels 2016. On pottery, see Huysecom et al. 2009.

10. Diamond 1997.

11. Morris 2010, 80.

12. The "only inhabitants" quote comes from Ross 1819, 123–4. "They live . . ." comes from Cook 1894. For an ethnographic summary, see Gilberg 1984.

13. Gilberg 1984; Peary 1898a, b. Seals were the mainstay of subsistence. But they also hunted walruses, whales, narwhals, caribou, fox, hares, musk-oxen, and even polar bears—with traps, spears, and knives made only from stones and animal parts such as ivory, bones, and skins.

14. Cook 1894; Gilberg 1984, 586.

15. Ross 1819; Peary 1898a. See especially Gilberg 1976. For the effects of these postcontact diseases among the Nunamiut of northern Alaska, see Gubser 1965, 53.

16. On the origins and significance of these disciplinary divisions, see Smail 2005 and 2008.

17. There is an extensive anthropological literature on how representative or not modern foragers are and what methods are appropriate for comparisons. For overviews, see Binford 2001; Marlowe 2005; Panter-Brick, Layton, and Rowley-Conwy 2001; and Johnson 2014. It is

perhaps especially difficult to know what life was like for hunter-gatherers in the temperate latitudes of the Old World—not coincidentally, the region of most intense social development in later times.

18. Tanaka 1980.

19. Tanaka 1980.

20. Silberbauer 1965; Tanaka 1980. For San groups living in less arid regions, malaria was present (Singer 1960).

21. Early and Headland 1998.

22. Early and Headland 1998.

23. Early and Headland 1998, 102.

24. See especially Gurven and Kaplan 2007.

25. See table 3.1 on hunter-gatherer life expectancies.

26. On population densities, see Hassan 1981; Binford 2001; and Marlowe 2005. The metastudy is Gurven and Gomes 2017.

27. Early and Headland 1998, 102. Besides the Agta, there are estimates of cause-specific mortality for several other hunter-gatherer groups from the twentieth century. Among the Hadza, a carefully studied society inhabiting the savanna in eastern Africa, crowd diseases like smallpox and measles have been sporadically present, but "most deaths under Hadza conditions arise from 'coughs and colds' and diarrhea"—symptoms ascribable to acute infectious diseases (Blurton Jones 2016). Among the precontact Hiwi, hunter-gatherers in the savannas of Venezuela, infectious diseases were the leading cause of death for nearly every age group and the dominant cause for most age classes (see Hill, Hurtado, and Walker 2007). Among infants (younger than one year), infectious diseases accounted for 29 percent of male deaths and 25 percent of female deaths, exceeded only by infanticide of females as a cause of mortality. For children between 1 and 9 years of age, infectious diseases accounted for 59 percent and 73 percent of deaths among boys and girls, respectively. In early adulthood (10–39 years), those figures were 55 and 29 percent of deaths, respectively, whereas in late adulthood (older than 39 years) infectious diseases caused 43 percent of deaths in men and 88 percent in women. Among the Dobe !Kung, a San people who live in the north of the Kalahari, infectious diseases were the main cause of death. Tuberculosis was perhaps the leading killer. Sexually transmitted diseases were common. Respiratory and gastroenteric diseases were frequently deadly. Malaria was widespread; notably, the Dobe region has more standing water than the central Kalahari. Overall, "it is likely that 70–80% of deaths to the !Kung are due to these infectious and parasitic causes" (Howell 1979). Among the Ache people of eastern Paraguay, infectious diseases were a prominent cause of mortality, but here, violence was the leading cause of death in each age class, making the Ache exceptional among closely studied hunter-gatherer populations (Hill and Hurtado 1996). Finally, among the Inughuit in the mid-twentieth century, infectious diseases accounted for 61 percent of deaths with a known cause, and the impressions gathered from the earlier reports of Peary and his team are consistent with that pattern (Gilberg 1976). The influence of contact was clearly of overwhelming significance, because tuberculosis was prominent. It is impossible to recover any truly reliable profile of mortality by cause for any arctic population before contact with agricultural or industrial societies.

28. Trueba and Dunthorn 2012; Houldcroft and Underdown 2016.

29. On the hookworm distribution and burden, see Hotez 2005; Loukas et al. 2016; and Bartsch et al. 2016. On the whipworm burden, see Else et al. 2020. On whipworm phylogeny, see Hawash et al. 2016. On hookworm phylogeny, see Monteiro et al. 2019. Roundworm infection in humans is caused by *Ascaris lumbricoides*, which probably emerged in the Holocene (Nejsum et al. 2017), but because it is closely related to a pig worm, and hybridizes with it, the evolutionary history of this parasite is still being elucidated (Easton et al. 2020).

30. Hotez 2013, 17–40.

31. For herpesviruses generally, see Houldcroft 2019. For VZV, see Pontremoli et al. 2020. The authors are cautious to note that all sampled strains share a recent common ancestor, which does not exclude the idea that ancestral forms once existed. In general, it would not be surprising if VZV were shown to be older. The same is true of the other chronic infectious diseases discussed in this paragraph—hence the caution in definitively assigning these to the Holocene. On TB, see chapter 5. On syphilis and yaws, see chapters 7 and 8.

32. For a similar view, see Blurton Jones 2016. The pervasiveness of host-switching and relentlessness of evolution means that ancestral humans in the deep past would have had pathogens that are no longer visible to us. Because tree thinking only allows us to make inferences based on pathogens whose descendants still exist (or can be recovered from archaeological samples, which only go back a few thousand years), we cannot observe ancestral pathogens that have gone extinct. We can only make ecological inferences about them. For example, given the number of times that *Plasmodia* pathogens have crossed to humans in more recent times, such events could have happened in the past. If ancestral hominins or early humans had other species of human-adapted malaria parasites (which seems not unlikely) we cannot detect them now if their genetic descendants are not alive.

33. Though older, Cloudsley-Thompson 1977 and Busvine 1980 remain outstanding overviews of the biology of vector-borne disease. Monath 1988, on viruses, is also helpful.

34. Ellis 1921, 67. See Spielman and D'Antonio 2001 for a wonderful overview of the natural history of mosquitos and the "as a larva" quote at xviii. In August 2020, there were 3,578 recognized species of mosquitos (Harbach 2013; Mosquito Taxonomic Inventory, http://mosquito -taxonomic-inventory.info/, accessed August 26, 2020).

35. Spielman and D'Antonio 2001, 9–10.

36. Spielman and D'Antonio 2001.

37. For this diversity, see Marshall 2012, 120–25.

38. Masters and McMillan 2001. On host preference, see Takken and Verhulst 2012. On mechanisms, see Wolff and Riffell 2018.

39. "Cumulatively the deadliest . . ." is quoted from Webb 2009, 1. "It is a tolerant . . ." is quoted from Hackett 1937, xi. Histories of malaria are found in Hackett 1937; Harrison 1978; Bruce-Chwatt and Zulueta 1980; Sallares 2002; Carter and Mendis 2002; Packard 2007; Shah 2010; and Webb 2014.

40. The "can make you" quote comes from Geisel 2005, 15–16. For the phylogeny of human *Plasmodia*, see below. On *P. vivax* generally, see Price, Baird, and Hay 2012.

41. Raina 1991.

42. Galinski, Meyer, and Barnwell 2013, 5.

43. N. J. White 2011.

44. Karunaweera et al. 1992, 2003; Cowman et al. 2017.

45. "It seems remarkable . . ." is from Marshall 2012, 63. On anopheles and the diversity of malaria, see Manguin 2008. "Everything about . . ." comes from Hackett 1937. See especially Ohm et al. 2018 for the environmental determinants of vector and parasite biology.

46. See Hay et al. 2010; Sinka et al. 2010, 2012; and Dalrymple, Mappin, and Gething 2015 on efforts to map the malaria burden. For Europe, see Bruce-Chwatt and Zulueta 1980. On Malaysia, see Sandosham 1970 and Alias et al. 2014.

47. Lysenko and Semashko 1968; Bruce-Chwatt and Zulueta 1980. For one particularly rich study of malaria in Europe, Dobson 1997 focused on southeast England. See Swellengrebel and Buck 1938 for the Netherlands. For the late period and eradication in Italy, see Snowden 1999, 2006. See Knottnerus 2002 for the North Sea region. For malaria in the early medieval period in Europe, see Newfield 2017.

48. "A benign . . ." comes from Battle et al. 2012, 2; see this source generally on the burden of vivax malaria. Poespoprodjo et al. 2009; Baird 2013; Howes et al. 2016; Battle et al. 2019. For a sense of what a strong force vivax malaria was in the pockets of England where it took hold, see Dobson 1997.

49. Howes et al. 2013; Sepúlveda et al. 2017. On Haldane's "malaria hypothesis," see Weatherall 2004.

50. McManus et al. 2017.

51. See Cutbush and Mollison 1950 for the discovery of the blood group. See Miller et al. 1976 for the initial discovery of the mechanism of resistance.

52. See Howes et al. 2011 on the global distribution of the Duffy blood group. See McManus et al. 2017 on the strength of the signal for natural selection in this genomic region.

53. An Asian origin for *P. vivax* was the dominant view for a time (Escalante et al. 2005; Hayakawa et al. 2008; Carlton, Das, and Escalante 2013). But in the last five years or so, the tide has turned toward an African origin (Prugnolle et al. 2013; Liu et al. 2014; Loy et al. 2017, 2018; Arisue et al. 2019). On *P. vivax* in Africa, see Twohig et al. 2019. Gilabert et al. 2018 offers cautions.

54. McManus et al. 2017. See also Loy et al. 2018.

55. On Manson, see, in general, Haynes 2001. "British hunting squire" comes from Chernin 1983. "Superlatively dirty" is from Manson's own 1871 report on the medical conditions in Amoy, available in Hughes 1872, 51.

56. Manson 1883, 10.

57. Chernin 1983; Haynes 2001, 51–55.

58. See Hotez 2013, 57–66, for an overview. Sasa 1976 is an older account, but one of the only monograph-length treatments. Lindsay and Thomas 2000; Ottesen 2006; Cromwell et al. 2020.

59. Ottesen 2006.

60. Hotez 2013, 57–66.

61. Kumari et al. 2005.

62. See Laurence 1970, with Pires at 355.

63. Small, Tisch, and Zimmerman 2014; Small et al. 2019.

64. Ford 1971; Brun et al. 2010; Brun and Blum 2012. On the history of the disease, see Cox 2004 and Steverding 2008.

65. Balmer et al. 2011; Sistrom et al. 2014.

66. See Spinage 2012, 821–913, for the history and veterinary aspects of the disease. Also see Nash 1969 and Ford 1971 (145 for ecological equilibrium). Gifford-Gonzalez 2000 explores nagana along with other veterinary diseases. See Brown 2008 for the debt of modern science to African knowledge of the tsetse fly and efforts to control animal disease. The "greatest curse" quote is from Johnston 1894. On rigorous empirical testing, see Alsan 2015; also Mitchell 2018a for a valuable overview, encompassing other animal diseases. But see Chritz et al. 2015 for evidence that at least some regions presumed to be afflicted by tsetse flies in the past (and thus recalcitrant to herding) were perhaps amenable to pastoralism. On low population density as a theme, see Iliffe 2017.

67. Rassi, Rassi, and Marin-Neto 2010; Hotez 2013, 127–33. See Darwin 2001, 315, with the editor's notes on whether or not Darwin might have acquired trypanosomiasis from the encounter, which is not impossible. See Stanaway and Roth 2015 on the global burden.

68. See Alvar et al. 2012; Karimkhani et al. 2017 (on cutaneous leishmaniasis); Gradoni and Bruschi 2018; and Wamai et al. 2020 (on visceral leishmaniasis).

69. Because they are based on so little actual evidence, estimates of human population at the beginning of the Holocene have varied widely, from as low as one million to as high as twenty million. See HYDE 3.1 (the History Database of the Global Environment; Klein Goldewijk et al. 2011), which favors an estimate of two million, which is probably too low. Livi Bacci 2012, 24–25, favors six million.

70. See, especially, Blurton Jones 2016; Bettinger 2016; Zahid, Robinson, and Kelly 2016.

71. See Braje and Erlandson 2013 on ecosystem transformation by early humans. See Goldberg, Mychajliw, and Hadly 2016 for "boom and bust" in prehistoric South America.

72. Gat 2000a, b. See Allen et al. 2016 for a recent contribution to the anthropological literature. For the application of Malthusianism to the study of conflict in later history, see Goldstone 1991 and Turchin and Nefedov 2011. The relative role of human predation and climate change in Pleistocene megafaunal extinctions has been intensely debated; for a recent overview and state of the question, see MacPhee 2019.

73. On nutrition and disease, see Livi Bacci 1990. See Turchin 2003, 128–31, on microparasitism as a regulatory mechanism in natural populations.

74. Blurton Jones 2016, 209.

75. Tallavaara, Eronen, and Luoto 2018.

Chapter 4

1. Black 1788. On the wider context of numerical methods in the eighteenth century, see Tröhler 2011.

2. Harris 1693.

3. See Harper 2017, 74, on Marcus Aurelius and Faustina.

4. The initial work appeared in World Bank 1993; Murray 1994; and Murray and Lopez 1996. The surveillance was continued under the auspices of the World Health Organization in the early 1990s and published in a series of world health reports. Updates were made (with funding from the Bill and Melinda Gates Foundation) in 2010, 2013, 2015, 2016, and 2017, with the work

carried on at the Institute for Health Metrics and Evaluation at the University of Washington. See Murray and Lopez 1996, 26. For a critical history of the project, see Mahajan 2019.

5. See Smil 2015 on agriculture and energy in the big picture. See Boivin et al. 2016 for a brilliant overview of human impacts on biodiversity.

6. See Webb 2019 for a wonderful recent overview, hands-down the best treatment of intestinal disease in human history. See Cockburn 1967 and 1971 for older accounts of human disease.

7. Belfer-Cohen, Schepartz, and Arensburg 1991; Smith 1991; Banning, Rahimi, and Siggers 1994; Akkermans 2003; Goring-Morris and Belfer-Cohen 2010.

8. Mithen 2003. Barker 2006 is a compelling exploration of the much-debated question of why foragers took up farming. See Boserup 1965 and 1981 on the dynamics of intensification from a more theoretical perspective.

9. Childe 1936. For revisions to the basic proposition, see below.

10. On agriculture and energy, see Crosby 2006 and Smil 2015 and 2017.

11. Cowan and Watson 1992; Bellwood 2005; Zohary, Hopf, and Weiss 2012. The essays in Barker and Goucher 2015 provide a wide-ranging set of introductions to domestication with a global perspective. See Kantar et al. 2017 for a review of how genomics has contributed to a more complex picture of the process of plant domestication. And see Denham et al. 2020 for an up-to-date overview.

12. See table 4.1 for references to plant domestications.

13. The "foremost prerequisite" quote comes from Jensen 2014. In general, see MacHugh, Larson, and Orlando 2017.

14. To be more precise, Childe belonged to a generation of neo-evolutionists responding to the challenges laid down by Franz Boas and others (Sanderson 1990, 75–82). Worster 2017, 6.

15. Both sedentism and social stratification were exhibited in hunter-gatherer societies (see Bar-Yosef 2001 for sedentary foragers, Kelly 2013; Binford 2001, and Hamilton et al. 2007 for complex social structures). Similarly, domestication did not lead to absolute sedentism in all cases (e.g., nomads have moveable camps, and swidden farmers often move from year to year).

16. Cohen, Armelagos, and Larsen 1984; Swedlund and Armelagos 1990; Larsen 2006; Cohen and Crane-Kramer 2007; Pinhasi and Stock 2011; Larsen et al. 2018; Larsen 2019. For TB, see Roberts and Buikstra 2003.

17. The *Nature* article is Wolfe, Dunavan, and Diamond 2007. Cohen 1989 is a thorough statement of the traditional narrative. McNeill 1976; Diamond 1997; Barrett et al. 1998; Weiss 2001; Barrett and Armelagos 2013; Harper and Armelagos 2013.

18. McNeill 1976; Crosby 1996; Diamond 1997.

19. The question of human domestication is often taken quite literally (Wilson 1988; Hodder 1990; Leach 2003; Scott 2017).

20. "Our foraging ancestors . . ." comes from Worster 2017, 6. Webb 2019 is another rare effort to capture historically this grand transition in human ecological history.

21. Byers, Guerrant, and Farr 2001.

22. Webb 2019, 2.

23. Moore et al. 2000.

24. Moore et al. 2000, 268.

25. The "unprecedented gathering" quote comes from Scott 2017, 103; this source also contains a wonderfully evocative account of how human sedentarism created the ecological conditions for commensal species. O'Connor 2014 is a comprehensive study of human commensals.

26. Goring-Morris and Belfer-Cohen 2010. See Pawłowska 2014 for one effort to imagine the smells of a Neolithic town.

27. On *Musca*, see Marshall 2012, 397–99. Hewitt 1914; Scott and Littig 1962; Junqueira et al. 2016; Panagiotakopulu and Buckland 2017, 2018.

28. Scott et al. 2014; Haseyama et al. 2015; Panagiotakopulu and Buckland 2017, 2018; Sackton, Lazzaro, and Clark 2017.

29. Busvine 1980, 191–211.

30. Busvine 1980, 191–211.

31. "It is common knowledge . . ." comes from Greenberg 1971, 134. The "most deadly" quote is from Marshall 2012, 398. Greenberg 1965; Sasaki, Kobayashi, and Agui 2000; Rahuma et al. 2005; Farag et al. 2013. Cloudsley-Thompson 1977, 124–45.

32. Greenberg 1971, 2:15; Cloudsley-Thompson 1977, 124–45.

33. See also chapter 12 for the context of these efforts.

34. Rush 1818.

35. Rush 1818, 215.

36. Rush 1818, 215–16.

37. Rush 1818, 216.

38. Levine et al. 2012; results published in Kotloff et al. 2013.

39. Quigley 2013. See Quigley 2017 for overviews.

40. Martella et al. 2010; Gautam et al. 2015; Dóró et al. 2015; Bányai and Pitzer 2016; Li et al. 2016.

41. Keusch 2009. See Trofa et al. 1999 on Kiyoshi Shiga. Whereas amoebas such as *Entamoeba histolytica* cause amoebic dysentery, shigella bacteria are the most important bacterial agents of dysentery.

42. Keusch 2009; Khalil et al. 2018.

43. The four traditional species are *Shigella flexneri*, *S. sonnei*, *S. boydii*, and *S. dysenteriae*. Escobar-Páramo et al. 2003; Yang et al. 2007; Hazen et al. 2016.

44. Croxen et al. 2013.

45. Croxen et al. 2013; The et al. 2016; Levine and Levine 1991; Farag et al. 2013.

46. Pringle 1764. On Pringle and eighteenth-century medicine, see chapter 10.

47. Holt et al. 2012; Croxen et al. 2013; Connor et al. 2015; Sahl et al. 2015; The et al. 2016. The "Neolithic revolution" quote is from Mira, Pushker and Rodríguez-Valera 2006.

48. *Entamoeba histolytica*, the causative agent of amoebic dysentery, is also a specialist in humans, and at least eight different species can infect humans. The genus *Entamoeba* is widespread in nature, and various primates, ungulates, rodents, reptiles, birds, and amphibians are known to act as hosts. It is not clear how or when the human specialists evolved. It is possible that species of *Entamoeba* have passed back and forth between humans and domesticated animals numerous times. The story is similar with *Campylobacter*, a genus of bacteria that still today moves back and forth between humans and animals, especially our domesticated animals. On

Entamoeba histolytica, see Le Bailly and Bouchet 2006 (especially for the Neolithic period); Weedall and Hall 2011; Weedall et al. 2012; Samie, ElBakri, and AbuOdeh 2012; Nozaki and Bhattacharya 2015; Das and Ganguly 2014; and Le Bailly, Maicher, and Dufour 2016. On *Campylobacter,* see Gripp et al. 2011; Iraola et al. 2014; Sheppard and Maiden 2015; and Iraola et al. 2017.

49. Jackson 1835, 230. This case history is described in the memoirs of James Jackson, a young American doctor who studied with Pierre Louis.

50. Jackson 1835, 238.

51. See Louis 1829 for his own seminal study of typhoid. See Adler and Mara 2016, 56–57, on Louis.

52. See Hamlin 2015, 167–205, on the differentiation of typhus and typhoid in the nineteenth century. Adler and Mara 2016 provides a general history of the disease. On typhus, which perhaps arrived in Europe in the later fifteenth century, see chapter 9.

53. See Moorhead 2002 for a brief appreciation of Budd. See Steere-Williams 2020 for a rich study that puts Budd in context of early epidemiology.

54. The "a population" quote is from Budd 1873, 1. "No one can know . . ." comes from Budd 1873, 2. "Having been . . ." is quoted from Budd 1873, 3.

55. See Steere-Williams 2020 for the broader context.

56. The "great bulk" quote comes from Budd 1873, 10–11.

57. The "privies, pigstyes" quote comes from Budd 1873, 11.

58. "The contagious element . . ." is quoted from Budd 1873, 39–40.

59. Holt et al. 2008.

60. Parry 2006; Coburn, Grassl, and Finlay 2007.

61. Gal-Mor et al. 2014; Hiyoshi et al. 2018.

62. Parry 2006; Gal-Mor et al. 2014.

63. Parry 2006; Gal-Mor et al. 2014.

64. Parry 2006. Much like *Shigella* species, the strains of *S. enterica* dedicated to humans have acquired a few crucial molecular tools and muted many of their other genes to focus on their narrower niche. The five strains of the bacterium that cause enteric fever and invasive disease evolved independently from the broader background of *S. enterica* (Hiyoshi et al. 2018).

65. Kidgell et al. 2002; Roumagnac et al. 2006; Yap and Thong 2017.

66. Liu et al. 2009; Zhou et al. 2018; Key et al. 2020. On the New World, see Vågene et al. 2018 and chapter 7.

67. Hirsch 1883, 617.

68. Parry 2006; Wain et al. 2015.

69. For the decline of typhoid, see chapter 12. McGuire 2013, focused on America, is a compelling account. Wain et al. 2015. "The members . . ." is quoted from Budd 1873, 183.

70. Bocquet-Appel and Bar-Yosef 2008. See Gage and DeWitte 2009 for a cautious view.

71. Bocquet-Appel 2011.

72. Shennan et al. 2013; Downey, Haas, and Shennan 2016. See Torfing 2015 for a dissent.

73. Reich 2018 provides an overview of the genetics. See Shennan 2018 more broadly.

74. Allentoft et al. 2015; Lazaridis et al. 2016; Skoglund et al. 2017; Lipson et al. 2017, 2018; Mathieson et al. 2018.

Chapter 5

1. See Wylie 1987 on the islands. The episode was recorded in Danish by Peter Panum in 1847, and I use Hatcher's translation (Panum 1940).

2. Panum 1940, 29.

3. See Rosen 1993, 260–61, for Panum's place in the history of medical thought.

4. See Tahara et al. 2016 on immunity to measles.

5. Laksono et al. 2016.

6. Cliff, Haggett, and Smallman-Raynor 1993.

7. In McNeill's words, beginning in the first century, "travel across the breadth of the Old World from China and India to the Mediterranean became regularly organized on a routine basis." Therefore, "conditions for the diffusion of infections among the separate civilizations of the Old World altered profoundly. The possibility of homogenization of those infections, whose most critical limit was defined by the number of new human hosts available day in and day out, opened up" (McNeill 1976, 124).

8. The term "crowd disease" is an epidemiological one, not a medical one. It seems to have been brought into widespread usage by Major Greenwood (1937), a British epidemiologist who helped formalize the use of statistics in the analysis of infectious disease.

9. See Hanks and Linduff 2009 for a recent overview. On the origins of metallurgy, see Roberts, Thornton, and Pigott 2009; Roberts 2011; Roberts and Radivojević 2015; and Radivojević and Roberts 2020. It is worth reminding ourselves that until the advent of radiocarbon dating in the mid-twentieth century, absolute chronologies were murky at best. See Renfrew 2008 on concepts of prehistory and the importance of radiocarbon dating. The compression of disease history in the Neolithic and later Bronze and Iron Ages is probably to some extent a distant echo of the lack of good chronologies in the mid-twentieth century.

10. Donkeys: see, above all, Mitchell 2018b for domestication and a vigorous appraisal of their significance. Horses: see Anthony 2007. The understanding of horse domestication is being clarified by genomics (Gaunitz et al. 2018; Fages et al. 2019, 2020; Frantz et al. 2020). On the camel, see Burger and Palmieri 2014 and Fitak et al. 2015 and 2020.

11. See Woolf 2020 for a recent account of the rise of urbanism. On city sizes, see Morris et al. 2013; Inoue et al. 2015; and Reba, Reitsma, and Seito 2016. These works draw from Chandler 1987 and Modelski 2003.

12. On urban populations, see the studies cited in the previous note.

13. Taagepera 1978a, b, and 1979 are fundamental, enhanced by Scheidel 2019.

14. The "unique position" quote comes from Iliffe 2017, 4. The "allowed Africans" quote is from Iliffe 2017, 34. The language and idea of microbial unification is indebted to Ladurie 1973, though focused on a later period.

15. On silk roads, see Frankopan 2016. On monsoons, see Casson 1989. On the Sahara, see Mattingly 2003.

16. On respiratory diseases in general, see Mandell et al. 2006, Nichols et al. 2008, and Jartti et al. 2012. See Roberts 1986, 114, for the tennis court fact.

17. Most human leprosy is caused by the bacterium *Mycobacterium leprae*, but just over a decade ago, a second, related bacterial agent of the disease, *Mycobacterium lepromatosis*, was

discovered. The divergence between these two species lies millions of years in the past. *M. leprae* may be one of our very old diseases, but it became far more prevalent in the Iron Age. In Europe, for instance, it was not found before the Roman Empire and then it became prevalent in late antiquity. Moreover, the continuing discovery of animal hosts, especially nonhuman primates, is calling into question to what extent this is a human disease. Schuenemann et al. 2013; Han and Silva 2014; Donoghue et al. 2015, 2018; Schuenemann et al. 2018b; Honap et al. 2018.

18. On land use, see Klein Goldewijk et al. 2017.

19. See chapter 11 for Rinderpest virus in modern times and McVety 2018 for the elimination campaigns. See Düx et al. 2020 for the evolutionary history of the measles virus.

20. Ghawar et al. 2017.

21. Düx et al. 2020. Previous studies (with less complex evolutionary models) had suggested a more recent date (Furuse, Suzuki, and Oshitani 2010). In modern times, with otherwise healthy populations and good nursing, the fatality rate of measles is relatively low, which can give the misleading impression that measles is a mild pediatric disease. In premodern, under-nourished populations in which coinfections were common measles was, and is, deadly. Measles also struck previously unexposed populations hard. Examples from the history of the Pacific are particularly well chronicled. In 1875, for instance, measles was introduced on Fiji, and the epidemic carried 30,000 of the 140,000 islanders to their graves. See Moss 2017 on the modern burden of disease, and Wolfson et al. 2009 on modern variety in case fatality rates. See Cliff, Haggett, and Smallman-Raynor 1993 for the historical epidemiology of measles. On Fiji, see Cliff and Haggett 1985 and Morens 1998. For parallels, see Ray 1976 on interior Canada, Boyd 1994 on the Pacific Northwest, and Galois 1996 on indigenous British Columbia.

22. On rodents, see Dobson 2005; Calisher et al. 2006; Turmelle and Olival 2009; Drexler et al. 2012; Luis et al. 2013; Brook and Dobson 2015; Plowright et al. 2015; Hayman 2016; Olival et al. 2016; Wang and Anderson 2019; Carlson et al. 2019; and Han et al. 2015. On bats, see Kunz and Fenton 2003.

23. O'Shea and Bogan 2003; Kunz and Fenton 2003; Klimpel and Mehlhorn 2014; Tuttle 2015.

24. Hendrickson 1983; Bordes, Blumstein, and Morand 2007; Meerburg, Singleton, and Kijlstra 2009; Singla et al. 2008; Krebs 2013; Han et al. 2015.

25. Mumps is a member of the genus *Rubulavirus*, a number of species of which have been identified in bats. (Two other species of human pathogens, *Parainfluenzavirus 2* and *4*, also belong to the genus.) See Drexler et al. 2012. See Jin et al. 2015 on the genomics of mumps virus. On Hippocrates, see Grmek 1989. For the history of mumps, see Kim-Farley 1993.

26. It is worth noting that some bacterial infections caused by common microbes like *Streptococcus pneumoniae* are a deadly complication of viral respiratory infections (Dickson, Erb-Downward, and Huffnagle 2014; Lee, Gordon, and Foxman 2016). There are more than one hundred species of *Corynebacterium*. At least three of them are pathogenic, and two of them have zoonotic reservoirs and infect humans sporadically. Only *C. diphtheriae* is specific to humans. Nutall and Graham-Smith 1908 is a gold mine of information about the history and pathology of diphtheria. Bolt et al. 2010; Trost et al. 2012; Bernard 2012; Sangal and Hoskisson 2016; Oliveira et al. 2017. Carmichael 1993, on the history of the disease, rightly points out that the study of diphtheria's past has been largely confined to its role in the emergence of

bacteriology. See Duffy 1953, 113–29, on outbreaks in colonial America. Regarding whooping cough, there are two deep lineages of the human-specialist bacterium that diverge around two thousand years ago. One of these branches has expanded rapidly in the last five hundred years, perfectly consistent with the written evidence for whooping cough from 1500 onward. The bacterium that causes whooping cough is a specialist human parasite. It evolved from a recent ancestor of *Bordatella bronchiseptia*. For the (fascinating) evolutionary background and genomics, see Parkhill et al. 2003; Bart et al. 2014; Diavatopoulos et al. 2005; Belcher and Preston 2015; Aslanabadi et al. 2015; Linz et al. 2016; Taylor-Mulneix et al. 2017; Soumana, Linz, and Harvill 2017; and Dewan and Harvill 2019.

27. For general historical accounts of TB, see Dubos and Dubos 1952; Bryder 1988; Barnes 1995; Murphy and Blank 2012; and Bynum 2012. The current status is available in the World Health Organization's annual *Global Tuberculosis Report*. The "destroying angel" quote comes from Yeoman 1848, 1.

28. Cosma, Sherman, and Ramakrishnan 2003; Zondervan et al. 2018.

29. Gupta et al. 2012; Cambier et al. 2014; Cambier, Falkow, and Ramakrishnan 2014.

30. Dickens 1865, 129.

31. On phylogeny, see Pepperell et al. 2013; Luo et al. 2015; Stucki et al. 2016; O'Neill et al. 2019; and Brynildsrud et al. 2018. On the new sister lineage, see Ngabonziza et al. 2020.

32. Brites et al. 2018.

33. See Roberts 2015 for a review of previous scholarship.

34. For older estimates see, for example, Comas et al. 2013 and Chisholm et al. 2016. Pepperell et al. 2013; Bos et al. 2014; Kay et al. 2015. On the Swedish bishop, see Sabin et al. 2020.

35. On the African origins, see Wirth et al. 2008; Hershberg et al. 2008; Comas et al. 2013; and Ngabonziza et al. 2020.

36. Stucki et al. 2016; O'Neill et al. 2019; Sabin et al. 2020.

37. Bos et al. 2014. Even these investigators are skeptical that sea mammals contracted TB directly from humans. For the Pacific, see McDonald et al. 2020.

38. Malthus 2018 (1803 edition), 245. On TB in industrial Britain, see Hardy 1993, 211–66.

39. Verga 1928 (translated by D. H. Lawrence), originally 1883. Verga's novella belongs to a particular moment when malaria entered Italian consciousness as a distinctly national disease (Snowden 2006, 7–8).

40. Adams 1849 (*On Airs, Waters, and Places*, chapter 7).

41. Carter and Mendis 2002; Webb 2009. This interpretation follows Otto et al. 2018. See also Loy et al. 2017; Sundararaman et al. 2016; Silva et al. 2015; Liu et al. 2014; and Volkman et al. 2001.

42. On the chronic infection, see Ashley and White 2014. On attachment to small vasculature, see Miller et al. 2002 and Otto et al. 2019. On immunity, see Doolan, Dobaño, and Baird 2009 and Long and Zavala 2017. On antigenic variation, see Recker et al. 2011. For a good summary of all of these mechanisms, see Rénia and Goh 2016.

43. See Sharp, Plenderleith, and Hahn 2020 for the recent origin. The evidence of human adaptation can also be brought to bear on the question (Laval et al. 2019). The epidemiology of falciparum malaria is especially complex and there is no consensus on the population threshold of humans or mosquitos required to sustain transmission. The issue has been debated since the 1930s. See McKenzie et al. 2001 and McKenzie and Bossert 2005.

44. Carter and Mendis 2002; Hume, Lyons, and Day 2003; Webb 2014.

45. On the preferential entry of *P. vivax* to young red blood cells (known as reticulocytes), see Chan et al. 2020. On immunity, see Doolan, Dobaño, and Baird 2009 and Long and Zavala 2017. On fatality, see Carter and Mendis 2002.

46. Livingstone 1958; Piel et al. 2010; Laval et al. 2019.

47. Webb 2014. See Laval et al. 2019 on the acquisition of the sickle-cell mutation by hunter-gatherers during the past six thousand years. On migrations in general, Pakendorf et al. 2011 provides an overview, and on the overall complexity of the Bantu dispersal, interactions with hunter-gatherer peoples, and subsistence changes, see Crowther et al. 2018.

48. Ohm et al. 2018. *P. falciparum* has also adapted to different anopheline mosquito vectors in different regions (Molina-Cruz et al. 2016).

49. On the migration of *P. falciparum*, see Coluzzi 1999. Gelabert et al. 2017 did not find evidence for natural selection on the human genome in ancient European samples, but most of their samples are from northern Europe. The key will be to explore genetic change across time in data sets like those in Antonio et al. 2019 and Marcus et al. 2020. On thalassemia, see Silvestroni and Bianco 1975; Marinucci 1982; Angastiniotis and Modell 1998; Flint et al. 1998; Modell and Darlison 2008; Cao and Galanello 2010.

50. For malaria and Rome, including Galen, see Sallares 2002. Harper 2017, 84–88. See Viganó et al. 2017 for a case of beta-thalassemia in Roman Sardinia. See Marciniak et al. 2016 for ancient DNA evidence.

51. On medieval times, see Newfield 2017. On development, see Bonelli 1966; Corti 1984; and Percoco 2013.

52. "To Han Chinese . . ." quoted from Marks 2012, 128. See also Elvin 2004. On fear of malaria, see Marks 1998, 74. See Bello 2005 on the importance of malaria in Chinese history. On India, see Das et al. 2012.

53. Sallares 2002, 229.

54. Fontaine, Najjar, and Prince 1961.

55. Camus 1948.

56. CDC 2012, 72.

57. See Anderson and May 1991 for the classic modern synthesis of the dynamics of infectious disease. On evolution, see Mukherjee 2017. On climate, see McMichael 2017 and Gage et al. 2008.

58. I have used the second edition of the translation of the *Muqaddimah* by Rosenthal (Ibn Khaldūn 1967). For general appreciations of Ibn Khaldūn, see Baali 1988 and Talbi 2012. See Turchin 2018 for an application of his thought.

59. Ibn Khaldūn 1967, 2:136–37 (*Muqaddimah*, 3.49).

60. For the dynamics of premodern empires, see especially the essays in Morris and Scheidel 2009 and Scheidel 2015.

61. See Scheidel 2019 for a brilliant account of Rome's rise in global and geographic perspective, with Scheidel 2014. See Harris 1985, on Roman militarism. See Eckstein 2006 on the interstate context.

62. See Whittaker 1994 on the limits of Roman power. See Hopkins 2018 on how Roman power worked. On provincial relations, see Woolf 1998; Ando 2000; Mattingly 2006; and Noreña 2011.

63. See Hanson 2016 for an overview of Roman urbanism. Population estimates have been much debated going back to Beloch 1886. Brunt 1987; Lo Cascio 1994, 2009; Frier 2000; Launaro 2011; De Ligt 2012; Hin 2013.

64. The extent of trade has been debated. In general, there has been a growing appreciation of the extent of private trade in the Roman Empire, including long-distance trade. On the trade across Roman frontiers, see Raschke 1978; Casson 1989; De Romanis and Tchernia 1997; Mattingly 2003; Cappers 2006; Tomber 2008; McLaughlin 2010; Cherian 2011; Sidebotham 2011; Tomber 2012; Seland 2014; and Purcell 2016.

65. See Harper 2017 synthesizing bioarchaeological work up to that point. See especially Giannecchini and Moggi-Cecchi 2008. Jongman, Jacobs, and Klein Goldewijk 2019 is currently the most comprehensive study of Roman bone length and Roman health, coming to the same conclusions as Harper 2017: the Romans were rich but sick and the efflorescence of the Roman economy coincided with a deterioration in biological well-being.

66. Scheidel 2001; Sallares 2002; Harper 2017, 65–91.

67. Birley 1987; Kulikowski 2016. For the broader ecological crisis, both focused on Egypt, see Blouin 2014 and Elliott 2016.

68. See especially the list of attested epidemics (Harper 2017, 89). For the basic literature on the Antonine Plague, see Gilliam 1961; Littman and Littman 1973; Duncan-Jones 1996 (especially important in renewing interest in the topic); Scheidel 2002; Bagnall 2002; Marcone 2002; Zelener 2003; Greenberg 2003; Jones 2005b and 2006; Bruun 2007; Gourevitch 2009; the essays in Lo Cascio 2012; Harper 2017; Duncan-Jones 2018; and Flemming 2019. The epigraphic evidence (which is quite remarkable) continues to accumulate (Thonemann forthcoming).

69. See Harper 2017, 99–100, on these sources.

70. Flemming 2019 is a remarkable and sensitive analysis of Galen's response to the pestilence, with healthy skepticism toward the retrospective diagnosis of smallpox.

71. Littman and Littman 1973 has been influential. See Gourevitch 2009. The essays in Lo Cascio 2012 treat the diagnosis as virtual fact. See Harper 2017. See Flemming 2019 for well-reasoned doubts.

72. See Mühlemann et al. 2020 on "Viking" smallpox. See Duggan et al. 2016 on the recovery of seventeenth-century smallpox. Pajer et al. 2017.

73. Mühlemann et al. 2020. Both Aelius Aristides and Herodian observed animal deaths. Although such reports can be taken with a grain of salt, the possibility that ancient smallpox infected a wider range of hosts is an important response to previous objections that the Antonine Plague could not have been smallpox on these grounds (e.g., Flemming 2019, 233).

74. See Harper 2017 for this interpretation. See Babkin and Babkina 2015 on the phylogeny of orthopoxviruses.

75. For the Chinese evidence, see Needham 2000, 6:125. In the second century, Hua Tuo described a disease in which "the low fever patients will have red herpes, and the high fever patients will have black herpes. Twenty percent of patients with red herpes will die, while patients with black herpes have no chance to survive." Tao Hongjing describes "seasonal epidemic eruptions which attack the head, face and trunk. In a short time they spread all over the body. They look like fiery [red] boils, all containing a white fluid. The pustules arise all together, and later dry up about the same time. If they are not treated immediately, many of the more severely

afflicted patients will die in a few days. Those who recover are left with purplish or blackish scars, the colour of which takes years to fade." I am grateful for this knowledge, which was shared by my Chinese colleague Xiao Rong at Shenzhen University. Other traces of late antique medieval smallpox: An outbreak of smallpox in upper Mesopotamia was clearly described around AD 500. In Indian medical texts, smallpox was certainly known by the sixth or seventh century. Evidence of smallpox in Japan is almost equally ancient (Farris 1985). In India, the *Aṣṭāṅgahṛdayasaṃhitā*, written by Vagbhata in the sixth or seventh century, describes masūrikā as a deadly disease characterized by a rash with "coral globules." Most important of all, the *Madhava nidanam*, written by Madhava-kara in the early eighth century, devotes a chapter to masūrikā, displaying knowledge of smallpox as well as other diseases apparently including measles and chickenpox. See Gupta 1987. Around AD 900, the brilliant Persian physician Rhazes wrote about acute pustular diseases he called *al-judari* and *al-hasbah*. See Flemming 2019, 236–40, for a reading of this crucial text. It is also notable that Rhazes knew the work of Aaron of Alexandria, a medical writer of the early seventh century, to whom he attributes writings on the diseases that in the text of Rhazes are considered measles and smallpox. There are also references to smallpox-like disease in early medieval European sources that have received little attention so far, such as the *Life of St. Eligius*.

76. See Harper 2017, 108–15, for the estimate and previous literature.

77. For some of the remarkable work in Roman bioarchaeology, which is especially rich in England and Italy, see Manzi 1999; Bonfiglioli, Brasili, and Belcastro 2003; Prowse et al. 2004; Cucina et al. 2006; Prowse et al. 2007 and 2008; Peck 2009; Killgrove 2010; Gowland and Garnsey 2010; Redfern and DeWitte 2011a and b; Killgrove 2014; Redfern et al. 2015; Prowse 2016.

78. Braudel 1966.

Chapter 6

1. Moore 2016. For a brief statement on why the Middle Ages make no sense for the Islamic world, see Bauer 2020.

2. The idea of the "global Middle Ages" is an object of intense and stimulating discussion at the moment. For reflections, see Holmes and Standen 2018 and the essays they introduce, as well as Frankopan 2019. Historians of disease and medicine have helped to foster this perspective. See Green 2014. On China in this period, see Kuhn 2009. See Morris 2010 for a compelling comparative assessment of social development in the East and West.

3. See below for the large and constantly expanding paleogenomic literature.

4. Ibn Khaldūn 1967, 1:64.

5. The single best one-volume overview of the Black Death in Europe, written before the aDNA revolution, is Benedictow 2004. For the Near East, Dols 1977 remains the fundamental survey. See Tuchman 1978 for a version along the older lines.

6. As early as 1998 (Drancourt et al.) and 2000 (Raoult et al.), it was claimed that archaeological DNA of *Y. pestis* had been recovered and identified. However, the validity of the techniques and replicability were subject to question (Gilbert et al. 2004). Technical breakthroughs—high-throughput genome sequencing, techniques for capturing targeted DNA, and analytical methods to discriminate between ancient and modern (contaminant)

molecules—have definitively allowed the identification of archaeological pathogen DNA, with *Y. pestis* playing the key role. Bos et al. 2011; Schuenemann et al. 2011; Wagner et al. 2014; Rasmussen et al. 2015; Feldman et al. 2016; Valtueña et al. 2017; Spyrou et al. 2018; Rascovan et al. 2019; Keller et al. 2019; Spyrou et al. 2019b.

7. For general overviews of the plague's biology, see Stenseth et al. 2008; Slack 2012; Yang and Anisimov 2016; Demeure et al. 2019; and Vallès 2020. On natural hosts, see Dubyanskiy and Yeszhanov 2016 and Gage and Kosoy 2005.

8. Hinnebusch, Chouikha, and Sun 2016; Hinnebusch, Jarrett, and Bland 2017.

9. Du and Wang 2016; Demeure et al. 2109. In the early twentieth-century United States, the case fatality rate prior to antibiotics was 66 percent (Kugeler et al. 2015), and it is extremely likely that historic case fatality rates (especially in crisis conditions) were much higher. Even with treatment, case fatality rates have still been about 15–20 percent (Nelson et al. 2020).

10. Pechous et al. 2016; Nikiforov et al. 2016.

11. On doubts, see Twigg 1984; Cohn 2002; and Duncan and Scott 2004.

12. Morelli et al. 2010; Cui et al. 2013; Eroshenko et al. 2017.

13. Rasmussen et al. 2015; McNally et al. 2016; Valtueña et al. 2017; Spyrou et al. 2018; Rascovan et al. 2019.

14. For recent overviews, see Dubyanskiy and Yeszhanov 2016 and Kotti and Zhilzova 2020. On marmots in general, see Armitage 2014. On gerbils, see Wilschut et al. 2015; Suntsov 2017.

15. Gage and Kosoy 2005; Dubyanskiy and Yeszhanov 2016.

16. Rasmussen et al. 2015; Valtueña et al. 2017; Spyrou et al. 2018; Rascovan et al. 2019. On *ymt*, see Sun et al. 2014. See Spyrou et al. 2018 on the acquisition of *ymt*.

17. Mulhall 2019 shows that bubonic plague was not completely unknown to Roman doctors, who were aware that what sound like regional outbreaks had occurred in the past.

18. See Shiels et al. 2014 for an overview of the biology of *Rattus rattus*. See Sullivan 2004 for a general account of rats.

19. For the origins and dispersal of *Rattus rattus*, see Audoin-Rouzeau and Vigne 1994; McCormick 2003; Ruffino and Vidal 2010; Aplin et al. 2011; Colangelo et al. 2015; Baig et al. 2019; and Puckett, Orton, and Munshi-South 2020. For *Rattus rattus* as far west as Morocco in the first century BCE, see Oueslati et al. 2020. Rielly 2010, focused on Britain, is especially revealing of the temporal dynamics of *Rattus rattus* at the western end of Eurasia, and one can hope for more detailed work in the near future.

20. Emphasizing the role of black rats in the great plague pandemics, see McCormick 2003; Audoin-Rouzeau 2003. Benedictow 2004 and 2016 provide strong statements on behalf of the classic rat model. There have always been contrary views and criticisms, most recently Walløe 2008, Hufthammer and Walløe 2013, and Dean et al. 2018. The chronology of the black rat's expansion broadly fits with an ecological explanation for the plague pandemics. But even if the black rat did play a primary role, it is worth underscoring that pandemics of bubonic plague were perhaps the most ecologically complex disease events in the history of the planet. A range of wild and domestic animals, including camels, might have played at least a peripheral role as amplifiers, and various ectoparasites may have helped spread the contagion as additional vectors. More than 300 species of mammals and about 280 species of fleas have been observed to be infected with plague (Dubyanskiy and Yeszhanov 2016). See Hinnebusch, Jarrett, and Bland

2017 on the biology of transmission (and note that they take human fleas as one of their examples of an *inefficient* vector).

21. Harper 2017, 220–21. On Procopius as a source, see Kaldellis 2004 and Cameron 1985, 42–43. On John, see especially Morony 2007; Kaldellis 2007; van Ginkel 1995; and Harvey 1990. For the full written record, see Stathakopoulos 2004, 277–94.

22. See Procopius, *Wars* (in Kaldellis 2014): symptoms at 2.22.15–17 and blisters at 2.22.30. The "even rats" quote is from John in Witakowski 1996, 87. "On whomsoever . . ." is quoted from John in Witakowski 1996, 88. "As they were looking . . ." is quoted from John in Witakowski 1996, 88.

23. The Roman sources believed the plague came from the south, and the Persians only got the disease after the Romans (which counts as a serious argument against overland travel via the silk roads). Green 2018 and Sarris 2020 suggest the possibility of an earlier dispersal and establishment in Africa, which seems to me not impossible, though in Harper 2017, I provide the background for recent importation from the east. As Green points out, the genetic distance between the specimens from the First Pandemic and the main lineage of *Y. pestis* allows the possibility that there was enough time for a lineage to have reached Africa and focalized there before moving into the Roman Empire. Yet "Kush" and "Ethiopia" were extremely vague geographic concepts at the time, and the late antique sources cannot bear the critical weight of meaning that the plague was focalized in Africa and then imported north, so it is entirely an inference. The reports would look exactly the same if the plague had come across the Indian Ocean recently, then hit the Himyarite Kingdom and Axumite Kingdom before moving to Pelusium. The central Asia region that seems (based on the samples we have, see Eroshenko et al. 2017 and Damgaard et al. 2018) to have been home to branches of *Y. pestis* immediately ancestral to the branches that caused the Justinianic Plague was under the control of a group known as the Hephthalite Huns (Enoki 1959; Skaff 1998; Kurbanov 2013; Potts 2018). It is unknown what involvement they may have had in commercial circuits, though more might be learned. On Pelusium, see Tsiamis, Poulakou-Rebelakou, and Petridou 2009.

24. Benedictow 2004 provides a clear overview. For pneumonic plague and human-to-human transmission, see, e.g., Borsch and Sabraa 2016. For the view that human ectoparasites were important, see Drancourt, Houhamdi, and Raoult 2006, but above (note 20) for critiques.

25. Procopius, *Wars* (in Kaldellis 2014) at 2.22.9. John is quoted from Witakowski 1996, 80.

26. "Eagerly . . ." is quoted from John in Michael the Syrian, *Chron.* 235–36. Procopius, *Wars* (in Kaldellis 2014) 2.22.4.

27. For the grain system as an ecological platform for disease, see McCormick 1998. Justinian, Edict 7. "The entire city . . ." is quoted from John in Witakowski 1996, 88. "Nobody would go . . ." is quoted from John in Witakowski 1996, 93. "Confusion began . . ." is quoted in Procopius, *Wars* (in Kaldellis 2014) 2.23.3. The "tangled heap" quote is from Procopius, *Wars* (in Kaldellis 2014) 2.23.10.

28. From John in Witakowski 1996, 96: an allusion to the Biblical *Revelation* (14:19 and 19:15).

29. Harper 2017, 220–35. On Palestine and Asia Minor, see John of Ephesus in Witakowski 1996, 77 and 80. The impact in Palestine is corroborated by one of the few epigraphical series that has been sufficiently studied in a critical assessment (Benovitz 2014). For an incisive study

of Gregory as a witness to the plague, see McCormick 2021. For the West overall, see Little 2007b. For the Atlantic, see Keller et al. 2019.

30. Sarris 2020. Doubts about the extent of the Justinianic Plague were reasonably laid out in Durliat 1989, which in particular emphasizes the lack of evidence for the West (the author did not really doubt the impact in the cities of the East). More recently, radically minimizing views have been expressed, for example in Mordechai et al. 2019, which goes so far as to suggest the pandemic was "inconsequential." The radical minimalist view requires an implausibly negative assessment of the entire written record, in addition to reading the paleogenomic data more narrowly than is defensible. In response, see Meier 2020 and Sarris 2020. See McCormick 2021 for a knowledgeable statement of what the DNA evidence means, and for a compelling demonstration that close, critical reading of the written record makes it clear how consequential the arrival of the plague appeared at the time. There is still scope for debate about the impact of the First Pandemic, to be sure, but in the wake of rebuttals like McCormick 2021 the reasonable range of debate cannot extend to the possibility that the plague was inconsequential. Or, in the words of Bresson 2020 (not entirely in agreement with the larger impacts that I have argued are possible), "The minimalist view of the First Pandemic must certainly be rejected." The new evidence that has accumulated in the last few years (genomic: Keller et al. 2019; indirect archaeological impact: Fuks et al. 2020 and Bar-Oz et al. 2019) has also resoundingly vindicated the long-standing view that the plague was demographically consequential. Broader treatments include Biraben and Le Goff 1969; Allen 1979; Conrad 1981; Sarris 2002; Meier 2003; Stathakopoulos 2004; Meier 2005; Horden 2005; Little 2007a; Meier 2016; and McCormick 2015 and 2016.

31. Keller et al. 2019. For Edix Hill (and the other sites more generally), see the supplementary material of Keller et al. 2019.

32. See Conrad 1981, still the only comprehensive study of the Near Eastern dimensions of the plague. Stathakopoulos 2004; Harper 2017, 235–45. See McCormick 2021 for sixth-century Gaul. It should go without saying that we do not assume that the First Pandemic was exactly the same as the Second in every regard. Rather, given the strong similarities in the written and paleogenomic record and the broadly similar social and ecological conditions of preindustrial societies in western Eurasia and North Africa in the early and late Middle Ages, the Second Pandemic offers the only sensible material for comparative analysis.

33. See below for the important recent work on persistence in the Second Plague Pandemic.

34. The Italian source is Paul the Deacon, *History of the Lombards* (Foulke 1907) at 2.4. Paul's source for this episode was in turn Secundus of Trent, a contemporary of the outbreak. This outbreak should be dated to circa 565 CE.

35. See McCormick 2021, 78, and his translation of Gregory's *History of the Franks*, 4.31.

36. See Stathakopoulos 2004, 379–85, on the outbreak of the 740s.

37. I have found Jedwab, Johnson, and Koyama 2020 a valuable framing of these issues and synthesis of previous literature.

38. On stature, see chapter 5. Jongman, Jacobs, and Klein Goldewijk 2019. On trade, see McCormick 2001. On forms of unfreedom (which still included slavery), see Rio 2020.

39. Fuks et al. 2020; Bar-Oz et al. 2019.

40. The later seventh or eighth century was the bottom of a downward swing, out of which Europe and the Near East would begin a long ascent. See Lo Cascio and Malanima 2005 for the

long-run Italian population. See Pamuk and Shatzmiller 2014 for the Near East. See Tannous 2018 for the gradual Islamicization of the Near East in these centuries.

41. On Chinese growth generally, see Kuhn 2009 and Lewis 2009a and b. For the possibility that plague did reach China see Twitchett 1979, and for eastern central Asia more generally see Schamiloglu 2016.

42. A text of Odoric's account (the *Relatio de mirabilibus Orientalium tatarorum*) is available in a critical edition (Marchisio 2016) and an English translation (Yule 1866, 1:43–162). See Abu-Lughod 1989, 29, on the context of these lines of connectivity.

43. Yule 1866, section 28.

44. Yule 1866, section 28, 104. "This city . . ." quoted from Odoric in Yule 1866, section 29, 106.

45. See Abu-Lughod 1989, 316–51, on China's place in the late medieval world system. See Morris 2010 on measuring this development in global perspective.

46. The "rice became" quote is from Lewis 2009b, 21. China's agrarian revolution was multifaceted, and rice production was enhanced in various ways, including by the introduction of new rice strains, especially Champa rice from Vietnam, which allowed multiple cropping. Elvin 1973, 136.

47. On the Chinese population, see Maddison 2007a, 168. See also Deng 2004. On per capita income, see Broadberry, Guan, and Li 2018.

48. Kuhn 2009. On gunpowder, see Andrade 2016.

49. Cook 2015. On Baghdad, see Abu-Lughod 1989, 189–93.

50. Pinto 1996; Pinto and Sonnino 1997. See Lo Cascio and Malanima 2005, which puts the population in AD 1000 higher (at ten million). I use the estimates of Pinto because it is highly unlikely that the population of Roman Italy reached the extreme maxima of fifteen to sixteen million.

51. Broadberry et al. 2015; Campbell 2016.

52. These figures follow Livi Bacci 2012. See HYDE 3.1 (Klein Goldewijk et al. 2011) for a tremendously helpful aggregation of existing estimates, some higher, some lower than those in Livi Bacci. There is more agreement about the long-term secular movements than the absolute values, which rely on a large number of assumptions. If anything, I contend that Livi Bacci's estimates are somewhat conservative. For global commercial connections, see McNeill and McNeill 2003, 116–54; Findlay and O'Rourke 2007, 87–110; and Smith 2015. See the English translation of Hirth and Rockhill 1911.

53. In general, see Frankopan 2016.

54. See Abu-Lughod 1989, 141–45, on the northern route. See Di Cosmo 2010 for the role of Italians in the Black Sea emporia. See Jackson 2014, 290–328, for a balanced account, reminding us that this route was relatively ephemeral and not always "peaceful." See Kuroda 2009 on the first silver century.

55. The passage of al-Maqrīzī's *Kitāb al-sulūk* is available (in French) in Wiet 1962, which I have used here. On al-Maqrīzī see Alazzam, Alazzam, and Al-Mazyid 2013.

56. On al-Maqrīzī, see Wiet 1962, 368. On Ibn al-Wardi, see Dols 1977, 51–52. On Ibn Khatimah, see Dinānah 1927. On Ibn al-Khatib, see Müller 1863. McNeill 1976, 169–70.

57. Cui et al. 2013; Morelli et al. 2010.

58. Cui et al. 2013. On Tian Shan, see Eroshenko et al. 2017. The Tian Shan plague focus lies at an important juncture between the Mongolian heartlands and the central steppe. It has been

known since the 1950s that a series of gravestones carved by Nestorian Christians in this region suggested a severe epidemic in 1338–39. Ten of the inscriptions even mention a "pestilence." Recently, Philip Slavin has restudied these documents carefully and confirmed that the mortality appears extraordinary, in line with the kind of devastation caused by the bubonic plague. It is not certain that *Y. pestis* caused the epidemic, but if it did this raises the intriguing possibility that the pandemic explosion of the Black Death was here in the years before its appearance in the west (Slavin 2019). This was first noted by Pollitzer 1954. On the importance of marmot hosts in this region, see Sariyeva et al. 2019. On Laishevo, see Spyrou et al. 2019b.

59. Green 2020. For first-hand attestation of the consumption of marmots, see the account of Friar William of Rubruck (Van Ruysbroeck 2009).

60. See the essays in Green 2015.

61. Hymes 2014. Hymes credits the Chinese scholar Cao Shuji for his studies dating from the 1990s on the Chinese source material; unfortunately these are not available to scholars limited to European languages. Cao argues for a Mongolian origin of the plague. For the contra perspective, see Buell 2012 and Sussman 2011. Brook 2019, 63–70, is open-minded on the question but skeptical. On India, the Arab traveler Ibn Battutah mentioned an epidemic at the time, but it was probably not bubonic plague. Arab and European chroniclers vaguely assert that the pandemic swept through India, but local sources from the Delhi Sultanate do not corroborate these claims (Sussman 2011).

62. Chouin 2018; Gallagher and Dueppen 2018; Green 2018.

63. See Barker 2021 for a remarkable study on the appearance of the plague in the Black Sea and its early diffusion, emphasizing the limits of Gabriele de' Mussi as a source and the importance of the grain trade.

64. On the Byzantine emperor, see Bartsocas 1966. On Alexandria, see Wiet 1962. See also Borsch 2005, 1.

65. Wiet 1962; Dols 1977.

66. Wiet 1962; Dols 1977.

67. Cairo: Abu-Lughod 1989, 212–16. Overall: Borsch 2005, 15; Borsch and Sabraa 2016.

68. See the standard collection of written accounts in Horrox 1994. For the best comprehensive survey of the Black Death in Europe, see Benedictow 2004. The Florentine source is the chronicler Marchionne di Coppo Stefani, in *Rerum Italicarum Scriptores*, 30.1: 231. See Henderson 1992, 145. Petrarch, *Epistolae familiares* (Bernardo 2005) 8.7.

69. See Geltner 2020 on the background of these ordinances.

70. Smail 1996, 19–20.

71. On England, see Ziegler 1969, 90–209, and Shrewsbury 1970. On London, see Sloane 2013.

72. Benedictow 2004, 291. See also Carmichael 1986. It is often hard to know how much population decline can be equated with mortality per se, because migration or changes in the reach of the state or patterns of property ownership can also affect counts. Often, we have information on the number of households, but not the number of individuals. And any sample raises questions of representativeness. Different social groups could have had different exposure to the plague and different mortality experience.

73. Thompson 1997; Ecclestone 1999.

74. Benedictow 2004, 383, table 38. According to Campbell 2016, 14, by the 1380s, there had been a net decline in the European population of 50 percent; also p. 310, with figures of 40–45 percent for the first wave in England. According to Green 2014, 9, "The Black Death killed an estimated 40% to 60% of all people in Europe, the Middle East, and North Africa when it first struck there in the mid-fourteenth century." DeWitte 2014, 101. See Jedwab, Johnson, and Koyama 2020, 48, for more variable estimates, essentially dependent on Christakos et al. 2005, which in turn depends on an older generation of scholarship (and contains some egregious errors). Spot-checking suggests that most of the numbers in Christakos et al. 2005 need to be revised upward in light of more recent and thorough scholarship.

75. "The more we learn . . ." is quoted from Herlihy 1997, 17.

76. Petrarch, *Epistolae familiares* (Bernardo 2005) 8.7.

77. For Italy, see especially Del Panta 1980.

78. On black rats and the maintenance of plague, see Keeling and Gilligan 2000a and b. On Anatolia (and the eastern Mediteranean more generally), see Varlik 2015. On the Balkans, see Eckert 2000. On the Alps, see Carmichael 2014. On paleogenomic evidence for persistence, see Bos et al. 2016; Seifert et al. 2016; and Spyrou et al. 2019b. Conversely, for the argument that plague was reintroduced, see Schmid et al. 2015 and Namouchi et al. 2018.

79. Biraben 1975. See Hatcher 1977 and Slack 1985 for England, Alfani 2013b for Italy, and chapter 9 for further literature on the seventeenth century.

80. On Egypt, see Borsch 2005. Even in parts of western Europe such as Spain the plague was damaging (Álvarez-Nogal and Prados de la Escosura 2013).

81. On England, see Campbell 2016. More generally, see Pamuk 2007.

82. On factor substitution and capital investment, see Herlihy 1997, 49. On pastoralism and female labor-market participation, see Voigtländer and Voth 2013a and b.

83. See Belich 2016 on the expansion of Europe. See Mitterauer 2010 for the argument that many of these trends pre-existed the Black Death; see also Chaney 2018.

84. Darwin 2007.

85. On coronavirus, see Forni et al. 2017.

86. On the flourishing of Islamic medicine, see Pormann and Savage-Smith 2010. See chapter 10 for more on premodern pharmaceuticals.

87. Rawcliffe 2013; Geltner 2019b for positive assessments of medieval public health.

88. On Rome, see Wazer 2017.

89. On Padua, see Pittarello et al. 2017, 446, with Geltner 2019b, 48. On London, see Rawcliffe 2013, 27.

90. For the First Pandemic, see McCormick 2021, 92. For late medieval quarantine, see Cipolla 1981.

Chapter 7

1. For a fuller discussion of indigenous numbers, see below, but the upward revisions started with Cook and Borah 1960 and Borah and Cook 1963, and then especially Dobyns 1966 and 1983. See Crosby 1967, and then, more expansively, Crosby 1972. McNeill 1976; Diamond 1997; Mann 2005, 2011.

2. For important critiques and assessments of the virgin-soil model, see Jones 2003; Kelton 2007; McMillen 2008; the essays in Cameron, Kelton, and Swedlund 2015; and Archer 2016.

3. The biggest impact of genomics so far has been to refine our understanding of the peopling of the New World (Mendes et al. 2020). The most important paleogenomic discovery of a pathogen so far is probably the identification of *S. enterica* in a mass grave from sixteenth-century Mexico, on which see below. It is worth underscoring again that RNA viruses preserve poorly and cannot be identified by traditional aDNA methods, so diseases like influenza and measles will remain invisible (unless paleoproteomics can identify their traces by other means). The absence of smallpox (a double-stranded DNA virus that has been recovered from even older Old World contexts) and typhus (a bacterial disease) is somewhat notable, although negative findings in archaeogenetics are not to be overinterpreted. Among the obvious questions that ought to be solvable are the origins of syphilis (there has been progress: see Giffin et al. 2020 and Majander et al. 2020 for the latest) and typhus (see below and chapter 9).

4. Crosby 1972 is classic. See Bentley, Subrahmanyam, and Wiesner-Hanks 2015 for recent essays on these themes.

5. See Livi Bacci 2008 for a summary of the population movements.

6. The "ravenous hunger" quote comes from Peter Martyr (Arber 1885, 199). On Columbus, see Gómez 2008. On gold, see, for example, Dunn and Kelly 1989, 299. On global circulation, see Wallerstein 1974, 1:329–30, and Findlay and O'Rourke 2007, 143–226.

7. On domestication, see Stahl 2008. On American crops feeding much of the world, see Nunn and Qian 2010.

8. Nunn and Qian 2010, 2011. See McNeill 1999 on the potato. For more on cinchona and smallpox inoculation, see chapter 10.

9. Alchon 2003 follows a similar geographic organization.

10. Federmann 1859, 9–10. The "large settlements" quote comes from Dunn and Kelly 1989, 207. The "most beautiful thing" quote is from Dunn and Kelly 1989, 217.

11. The literature is massive and involves multiple interrelated issues, including indigenous numbers in 1492, the relative role of germs and other factors, and the question of whether to frame the encounter as a genocide. For balanced overviews, Alchon 2003, Newson 2006, and Livi Bacci 2008 are eminently helpful. On the role of disease, see Ramenofsky 1987; Cook and Lovell 1991; Verano and Ubelaker 1992; and Cook 1998. On the discourse of genocide, see Madley 2015 and Edwards and Kelton 2020. Further literature is cited throughout this chapter and the following.

12. Livi Bacci 2008. See Thornton 1987 on native populations in the United States, and pp. 91–133 on the nadir; also see Thornton 1997. See Klein 2010 on the slave trade.

13. Kroeber 1934, 1939. For the method, see Kroeber 1934, 13, where he takes an estimate of the carrying capacity of Mexico, only to claim that he would "prefer to reduce the figure by three-fourths or more," based on things like the kinds of agricultural technology available.

14. See, for example, Dobyns 1983, 8–10.

15. See especially Alchon 2003; see Livi Bacci 2008 for broad-ranging and balanced overviews. Thornton 1987; Ramenofsky 1987; Denevan 1992; Henige 1998. See Ubelaker 1992 for North America. Estimates of the population of Peru have ranged from two to thirty-two million but the totals were probably between six and thirteen million (Verano 1992, 16). For the

Caribbean, see Higman 2011, 49–51, "conservatively" two million. On Paris/Constantinople, see Chandler 1987. On Tenochtitlán, see Smith 2005 and Ossa, Smith, and Lobo 2017.

16. On California, see Lindo et al. 2016. On Andean populations, see Lindo et al. 2018. For an overview, see Bolnick et al. 2016.

17. McNeill 1976, chapter 5, remains the best short statement of the classic virgin-soil hypothesis.

18. Diamond 1997.

19. Webb 2019. Also chapter 4.

20. See Wolfe, Dunavan, and Diamond 2007 on the Old World origins.

21. Plague is sometimes alleged to have crossed the ocean (e.g., Alchon 2003, 95), but not on firm evidence. Europeans were intimately familiar with plague, and the lack of buboes in all the sources for the Americas is striking. On influenza, see McBryde 1940; Pyle and Patterson 1984; Pyle 1986; Patterson 1986; and Morens and Taubenberger 2010a.

22. On smallpox, see Mühlemann et al. 2020 and Duggan et al. 2016. See chapter 9.

23. Arrizabalaga 1993. On tertiary syphilis in the nineteenth century, see Pearce 2012. Tertiary syphilis was such a terrible and incurable condition that Julius Wagner-Jauregg was awarded a Nobel Prize for Medicine in 1927 for having developed malaria therapy, in which patients were intentionally infected with malaria to induce fevers that might destroy the syphilis bacterium. Soon rendered unnecessary by antibiotics, malaria therapy also played an important role in the recognition of population differences in malaria susceptibility.

24. On the history of syphilis, see Quétel 1990. On the disease in Renaissance Europe, see Tognotti 2009 and Arrizabalaga, Henderson, and French 2014. On possible pre-Columbian skeletal evidence in Europe, see, for example, Lopez et al. 2017. Drake and Oxenham 2013 offers a summary of the extensive literature on treponemal disease in pre-Columbian America.

25. Arora et al. 2016; Schuenemann et al. 2018a. See Giffin et al. 2020 and Majander et al. 2020 for the latest.

26. See Raghavan 2015 on the peopling of the New World from a genomic perspective. See Drake and Oxenham 2013 on the migration and disease. I am not aware of a comprehensive catalog of the various minor diseases unique to the New World, but the GIDEON database provides an extensive number of such pathogens—for example, Junin virus, Lechiguana virus, Machupo mammarenavirus, Bermejo virus, Sabia virus, Anajatuba virus, various leishmaniases, Bussuquara virus, Ilheus virus, Candiru phlebovirus, *Inermicapsifer cubensis, Paragonimus mexicanus, Gnathostoma binucleatum*, various rickettsial diseases, *Paragonimus kellicotti*, various orthobunyaviruses, Colorado tick coltivirus, various hantaviruses, Monongahela virus, New York-1 virus, Heartland bandavirus, St. Louis encephalitis virus, helminths in the genus *Echinococcus*, various vesiculoviruses, Cardiovirus A, Rocio virus, various *Borrelia* bacteria, *Monnsonella ozzardi*, Venezuelan equine encephalitis virus, eastern equine encephalitis virus, Group C viral fever viruses, Mayaro virus, and western equine encephalitis virus.

27. On these diseases, see chapter 2.

28. Stone et al. 2009; Bos et al. 2014.

29. Martin and Osterholtz 2015. On disease stress in precontact Andes, see Verano 1992, 21. See Buikstra 1992 on maize and disease in the continental interior. See Larsen et al. 1992 on the American southeast.

30. On pre-Columbian diseases in Inca history, see Bell 2019, 30, citing Guaman Poma, a Quecha (indigenous Peruvian) nobleman, who described the military exploits of Pachacuti (the probable builder of Machu Picchu): "The defeat of Chile was made possible by the ravages of plague, which lasted for ten years. Disease and famine, even more than force of arms, brought about the downfall of the Chileans." On North America, see Milner 1992.

31. Jones 2003, 705–6, catalogs a number of these overgeneralized claims. For the immune system, see chapter 1. See Quintana-Murci 2019 for an overview. Barreiro et al. 2009; Pickrell et al. 2009; Casals et al. 2011; Fumagalli et al. 2011; Chapman and Hill 2012; Daub et al. 2013; Casanova, Abel, and Quintana-Murci 2013; Nédélec et al. 2016; Field et al. 2016. On infectious pathogens, see Karlsson, Kwiatkowski, and Sabeti 2014.

32. See McNeill forthcoming for a concise statement of this argument.

33. See below for examples ranging from sixteenth-century sources from Mexico to examples drawn from the central Plains (Kiowa) in the United States in the nineteenth century.

34. See McNeill forthcoming for a number of these examples. On the Plains Indians, see Sundstrom 1997 and Fenn 2001. On the Pacific, see Archer 2018 for an especially important recent study of Hawaii. See Cliff and Haggett 1985, especially for the measles epidemic on Fiji. On the Inuit, see Kleivan 1966 and Gilberg 1976. On the Amazon, see Walker, Sattenspiel, and Hill 2015.

35. Livi Bacci 2008 rightly emphasizes the importance of fertility in addition to mortality.

36. McNeill forthcoming; Guerra 1988.

37. "All through the land . . ." is translated in Guerra 1988, 312–13.

38. See Guerra 1988; McNeill forthcoming is disposed toward the same conclusions. Pestilence—sometimes thought to be syphilis, sometimes bubonic plague—raged in Italy in 1493, but it is hard to draw any connections. Corradi 1865–94, 1:345–49.

39. "Massive deaths . . ." quoted from Cook 1998, 37; on further epidemics, see Cook 1998, 58. The Spaniard who arrived in 1502 was named Hernando de Gorjon, and his testimony given in 1520 is preserved in volume 1 of Pacheco et al. 1864, 428–29.

40. "It was this campaign . . ." quoted in Higman 2011, 72; also see Higman 2011, 64–80.

41. Las Casas 1876, 23.

42. On genomes, see Moreno-Estrada et al. 2013 and Schroeder et al. 2018. Cook 1993; McNeill forthcoming.

43. The "great natural saucer" quote comes from Carrasco 2012, 42–43. In general, see Townsend 2019.

44. On Las Casas and the origins of the Black Legend, see Greer, Mignolo, and Quilligan 2007. Las Casas's *Very Short Account* was widely translated and became the basis of the Black Legend.

45. Foster 1950. See Livi Bacci 2008, 25–28. Writing a decade or so after the fact, Motolinia noted that the traces of the pestilence were still visible on the faces of the people, which were "full of holes." The disease was called "the great leprosy" in the native language (Motolinia was fluent in Nahuatl, the indigenous tongue of central Mexico) because the victims were covered from head to toe with pockmarks. Then, in 1531, eleven years after the smallpox epidemic, Mexico was struck by an outbreak of *sarampión*, the traditional Spanish word for measles. The native peoples called this the year of the "little leprosy"; the damage was severe, though not as catastrophic as the smallpox pandemic.

46. Cook 1998, 60–72; Alchon 2003, 63–68.

47. The earliest source for the event dates to January 1519, in a letter from two friars: "It has pleased Our Lord to bestow a pestilence of smallpox among the said Indians, and it does not cease. From it have died and continued to die to the present almost a third of the said Indians. And Your Highness must know that all that is possible has been done, and continues to be done, to cure them." See Cook 1998, 60, and Alchon 2003, 63.

48. These passages come from Sahagún's *Florentine Codex* (Anderson and Dibble 2012, 12.29). On its production, see Kerpel 2014.

49. On the military significance, see McCaa 1995, 411.

50. Alchon 2003, 66. See Newson 1991, 88–90, on the possibility of the pandemic in South America.

51. See Motolinia 1970 and McCaa 1995, 399.

52. For overviews, see Prem 1991 and McCaa 1995. On Muñoz Camargo, see McCaa 1995, 428.

53. Prem 1991, 31–34. See Cook 1998, 102, for the death tolls.

54. For Mendieta (this passage from *Historia Eclesiástica Indiana* 4.36), see Jay 1997. Some (Acuña-Soto et al. 2002) have been tempted to attribute the pandemic of 1545–48 to a viral hemorrhagic fever. The rodent-borne viruses that can cause hemorrhagic fever in humans, however, are not known to have been as lethal, or as propulsive, as the germ that carried off millions of victims in the mid-sixteenth century.

55. Vågene et al. 2018. See Warinner et al. 2012 on the site itself.

56. The "most prevalent" claim is from the supplementary material of Vågene et al. 2018, 22. It is not immediately evident how the typhoid bacterium could have caused such a widespread pandemic on its own. In early modern Europe, typhoid epidemics occurred when the germ was introduced into new regions with poor sanitation. Continent-wide pandemics of typhoid killing massive proportions of the population, however, are otherwise unknown.

57. Lovell 1991, 71. On Peru, see Newson 1991, 94–95.

58. Prem 1991, 38–42; Cook 1998, 120–23.

59. This is translated in Livi Bacci 2008, 137.

60. Prem 1991, 38: "If one chose to measure the importance of an event based on the number of authors who wrote about it, then the epidemic of 1576–80, without doubt, would be among the most significant in the history of colonial Mexico." One *Relación geográfica* describes the symptoms in detail. "It is the nature of this illness that it causes great pain at the 'mouth of the stomach' and is accompanied by a high fever in all parts of the body. Death sets in after six or seven days. . . . the sick who survive this time become healthy. At the same time, there are cases of relapse with deadly consequences. No medicinal plant is effective against this disease" (Prem 1991, 39–40).

61. Cook 1998, 120–33.

62. Cook 1998, 122–23. On population numbers, see McCaa 1997, 253, for a helpful table of various estimates. I am taking the range of middle-counters, though there are plenty of minimalists and maximalists.

63. Cook 1981; Newson 1991, 1995; Cook 1998, 72–83, 92–94; Alchon 2003, 75–79.

64. Cook 1998, 132; Alchon 2003, 75; Cieza de León 1998.

65. Cook 1998, 124–32. On smallpox, see Cook 1998, 124. On typhus, see Cook 1998, 126. On Drake, see Cook 1998, 125–26: the captain's fleet was devastated by infectious disease on their venture of 1585–86, including something that caused a "rash of small spots," which *could* be typhus, later known as ship fever. They took Cartagena in early 1586 and then returned to England with a fraction of the original force. "Virulent pustules broke . . ." is quoted in Dobyns 1963, 507, translating the Jesuit provincial in Lima. For the original text, see Toribio Polo 1913, 55–56. On the viceroy, see Dobyns 1963, 505. The one thousand of thirty thousand souls figure comes from Alchon 2002, 42. The 10 percent figure comes from Evans 1991.

66. See Hemming 1978, 139, for these first impressions.

67. On the archaeology, see Rebellato, Woods, and Neves 2009 and Stenborg 2016. "Almost none . . ." is quoted in Hemming 1978, 140. The "contagious malady" quote comes from Alchon 2003, 86.

68. The "herded together" quote comes from Hemming 1978, 144. "You can imagine . . ." is quoted in Alchon 2003, 113.

69. "If one asks . . ." is quoted in Hemming 1978, 144.

70. Hemming 2006, 13.

71. See Reff 1991 for the fundamental study.

72. Reff 1991.

73. For the possibility of earlier outbreaks, see Stodder and Martin 1992. On smallpox and typhus, see Reff 1991. Liebmann et al. 2016 argues from archaeological and dendrochronological evidence for a late but dramatic population decline in New Mexico.

74. Larsen et al. 1992.

75. On Soto, see Ranjel 1922, 1:66. Alchon 2003, 93.

76. Kelton 2007, 143–59.

77. "We have had . . ." is quoted in Salley 1916, 103. Kelton 2007, 146. "The whole country . . ." is quoted in Spruill 1936, 213.

78. Lawson 1967 (originally published in 1709), 17.

79. Kelton 2007, 147–49.

80. Kelton 2007, 157.

81. The Membertou quote comes from Thwaites 1898, 1:176. The Jesuit quote comes from Thwaites 1898, 3:103. Alchon 2003, 96; Carlson, Armelagos, and Magennis 1992, 147–48. French observers like Cartier and Champlain noted fevers and sicknesses among the indigenous Americans, but there are no firm grounds to ascribe these illnesses to novel pathogens or widespread pandemics.

82. See Marr and Cathey 2010 for a medical perspective. Bratton 1988; Booss 2019.

83. Dermer's quote comes from Tiffany 1900, 161. Smith's quote comes from Cook 1976, 31. In general, see Cook 1973 and Snow and Lanphear 1988.

84. Alchon 2003, 98. "They found . . ." is from Bradford's *Of Plymouth Plantation*, 1651 (Bradford 1952). Smith's quote is from *Advertisements for the Unexperienced Planters*, 1631, 3. For the development and function of these narratives of providence, see Silva 2011, especially chapter 1.

85. "This epidemic was . . ." quoted from Snow and Lanphear 1988, 23. On the archaeology, see Warrick 2008 and 2010, and Jones and DeWitte 2012.

86. Duffy 1953; Fenn 2001.

87. Isenberg 2020, 53–62 and 113–121; Fenn 2001. The Kiowa myth can be found in Marriott and Rachlin 1968. In the story, Saynday was able to save the Kiowa by diverting Smallpox toward the Pawnee, the inveterate enemies of the Kiowa, tempting the disease with tales of their big villages along the river. But the Kiowa were struck with smallpox about every fifteen years in the nineteenth century (Sundstrom 1997).

88. The use of "lurid" comes from Cook 1955. Generally, see Igler 2004 and 2013 and Madley 2016.

89. For the gold and silver figures, see Livi Bacci 2008, 68. On Brazil, see Klein 2010, 28–29.

90. See Klein 2010, 216, for the figures.

Chapter 8

1. See Philbrick 2006, from a crowded field.

2. The second *Mayflower* was not the same ship: it was about twice as large, and the name was common. There are rather extensive archival records of this 1647 voyage courtesy of a ribald legal dispute. On Vassall, see Andrews 1991, 59–61, and Brenner 2003, 135–37. For the information about the slaves on board, see https://www.slavevoyages.org/voyages/6HZWm3Dl.

3. The "jewel" quote comes from Burnard 2015, 157.

4. Curtin 1993; Coehlo and McGuire 1999; McGuire and Coehlo 2011. See Sharman 2019, emphasizing the stark technological limits of European powers in the early modern period.

5. The "drank salt water" quote comes from Coldham 1984, 46. On the transformational impact of this epidemic, see Kiple and Higgins 1992.

6. Robertson 1817, 189–90.

7. For numbers, see Keeling 2013 and Horn and Morgan 2005.

8. See Franklin 1751, discussed in Aldridge 1949, Hodgson 1991, and Houston 2003. Burnard 1999, 72. See also Burnard 1996. See Grob 2002, 59–69, on the demographic gradients. See Kiple 1984 and 1987 for earlier studies. On the role of mortality rates in shaping long-run institutional development in colonial contexts, see Acemoglu, Johnson, and Robinson 2001 for a seminal study that has engendered extensive debate. Settler mortality rates are such a powerful indicator of institutional choice that Acemoglu, Johnson, and Robinson 2001 used them as the best in-strumental variable to measure institutional differences in the deep past. Notably, much of the debate has focused not on *whether* the disease burden shaped long-run development, but rather *how*—that is, the relative weight to assign various channels (i.e., institutional choices made by imperial powers, or the burden of disease more directly). The issues are discussed critically in Sachs 2012. In my view, one thing that has been missing from some of this discussion is the role of mortality in early public investments in, for example, education. By 1775, Massachusetts had perhaps the highest rate of literacy in the world, whereas observers decried the lack of similar investments in the British West Indies (e.g., Long 1774, 2:258). On literacy rates in colonial United States, see Lockridge 1974; Soltow 1981; Grubb 1990; Monaghan 2005; and Crayen and Baten 2010. See Go and Lindert 2007 and 2010 on the connections between democracy and educational investments.

9. Davies 1975.

10. Webb 2006; Spinage 2012.

11. "The king . . ." is quoted from Ibn Fadl Allah al-Umari in Hopkins and Levtzion 1981, 265–66. The "global connections" quote comes from Green 2019, 47. More generally, see Iliffe 2017, 73–102, Fauvelle 2018, and Gomez 2018.

12. On Portuguese exploration and imperialism, see Newitt 2005, Disney 2009, and Subrahmanyam 2012. See Klein 2010 on the slave trade.

13. Green 2019. On the slave trade and numbers, see Klein 2010.

14. On al-Bakri, see Levtzion and Spaulding 2003, 17. On Ibn Khaldūn, see Akyeampong 2006.

15. On the missionaries, see Blake 1942, 79. Lind 1771, 3. For the formation of medical ideas about the tropics in this period, see Cagle 2018.

16. Lind 1771, 69–70.

17. Davies 1975.

18. Curtin 1964, 1989, and 1998. See Feinberg 1974 for Dutch records suggesting a mortality rate of 20 percent in West Africa during the eighteenth century.

19. Davies 1975.

20. Akyeampong 2006, 191.

21. Carter and Mendis 2002; Webb 2014.

22. See chapter 3. Ford 1971; Brun et al. 2010; Brun and Blum 2012. On the history of the disease, see Cox 2004 and Steverding 2008.

23. See, in general, Hotez 2013, as well as chapter 3.

24. On yellow fever, see below. On dengue, see Bhatt et al. 2013, Stanaway et al. 2016, and Wilder-Smith and Byass 2016. On chikungunya, see Paixão, Teixeira, and Rodrigues 2018.

25. Lupi et al. 2006; Lupi and Tyring 2003. On hepatitis C, see Tibbs 1997; Markov et al. 2009 and 2012; Rose et al. 2013; Iles et al. 2014; and Pybus and Thézé 2016.

26. See chapter 7. Arora et al. 2016; Schuenemann 2018b; Giffin et al. 2020; Majander et al. 2020.

27. Mitjà, Asiedu, and Mabey 2013.

28. Hill 1953; Kazadi 2014. On Sydenham, see Latham 1850, 2:33.

29. Muller 1971; Ruiz-Tiben and Hopkins 2006; Iriemenam et al. 2008; Sankara et al. 2016.

30. For the present-day global epidemiology of amebiasis, see Ximénez et al. 2009 and Samie, ElBakri, AbuOdeh 2012.

31. On hookworm, see Hotez et al. 2006, Loukas et al. 2016, and Bartsch et al. 2016. On whipworm and roundworm, see Else et al. 2020.

32. Bleakley 2007.

33. Stone et al. 2009; Han and Silva 2014. See Schuenemann et al. 2013, noting the similarity between strains in American armadillos and European medieval strains, indicating its transmission across the Atlantic in the age of sail.

34. See Green 2019 for a recent overview of the negative impacts on West Africa.

35. Long 1774. On Long, see Burnard 2015, 163–64.

36. On the English conquest of Jamaica, see McNeill 2010, 97–104. On immigration, see Burnard 1996. The "excessive indulgence" quote comes from Long 1774, 2:535.

37. Dunn 1977, 2014.

38. Mintz 1985 is a classic exposition from an anthropological point of view. Smith 2015, though derivative, is a concise overview. See Higman 2000 for a balanced review of the "sugar revolution" as a concept.

39. On the origins of sugar, see Grivet et al. 2004 and Denham 2011 and 2013.

40. Mintz 1985, 23–32.

41. See Curtin 1990 on the emergence and formation of the plantation context broadly. For Barbados, see Dunn 1972 and Gragg 2003. On the Western Design, see Lay 2020.

42. Dalby 1690, 17. See De Vries 2008 and Hersh and Voth 2009 for sugar consumption in Europe.

43. See Burnard 2015, emphasizing the refinement of techniques of violent domination. Dunn 1972; Sheridan 1974; Menard 2006.

44. Watts 1987 is the classic study. See McNeill 2010 and forthcoming for the disease ecology.

45. The "most dangerous" quote comes from Powell 2016. More generally, see Spielman and D'Antonio 2001; Powell 2018; and Powell, Gloria-Soria, and Kotsakiozi 2018.

46. Brown et al. 2013; Crawford et al. 2017; Powell 2018; Powell, Gloria-Soria, and Kotsakiozi 2018; Kotsakiozi et al. 2018.

47. Goodyear 1978; McNeill 2010, forthcoming.

48. Long 1774, 2:506.

49. The "most feared" quote comes from McNeill 2010, 33. McNeill 2010 is the best guide to the history and significance of yellow fever in the colonial Caribbean, and McNeill forthcoming summarizes the latest work. Carter 1931 has a wealth of detail. Other important treatments include Patterson 1992; Humphreys 1992; Harrison 2012; Willoughby 2017; and Barcia 2020.

50. Barrett and Higgs 2007; Vainio and Cutts 1998.

51. The "sudden Faintness" quote comes from Warren 1741, 9–10. On Warren and his context, see especially Seth 2018, 74–77.

52. The "universal *Yellowness*" quote is from Warren 1741, 10. Vainio and Cutts 1998; Monath 2001.

53. Bryant, Holmes, and Barrett 2007; Beck et al. 2013; Chippaux and Chippaux 2018. The phylogeny of the yellow fever virus might provide even further historical specificity into the transoceanic itinerary of this pathogen. The New World specimens of the virus that have been sampled (all from South America, mostly from Brazil) are most closely related to the West African genotype. Today, this lineage of the virus dominates from Senegal to Ghana. Precisely this region of Africa was dominated by Dutch slave traders and, from the 1640s, English interlopers like Samuel Vassall who had recently started to wedge their way into the lucrative Guinea trade. The exchange of slaves from precisely this region of Africa to Barbados exploded in the 1640s, and the first definite pandemic of the disease erupted in the later years of that decade.

54. Bryant, Holmes, and Barrett 2007; Cathey and Marr 2014; Li and Yang 2017.

55. This is to agree with the chronology proposed by McNeill 2010 (and reiterated in McNeill forthcoming), against the view sometimes expressed that yellow fever crossed earlier. Although it is not implausible, the two important considerations are that yellow fever became a huge force in the New World from the mid-seventeenth century, and that European-led ecological changes allowed it to play that role. See Abreu 1623; for work on Abreu, see Guerra 1968.

56. See Gragg 1995 on the beginnings of the slave trade to Barbados. For the outbreak of the 1640s, see Kiple and Higgins 1992 and McNeill 2010.

57. Ligon 1673, 21. He noted that "ten men" died for every woman. Vines's writing may be found in *Winthrop Papers* 5 (MHS 1947), 219–20. Also see Gragg 2003, 166, and Winthrop 1908 (originally published in 1647), 329. Letters also reached merchants in Scotland, claiming that six thousand died on Barbados alone.

58. The "fell sicke" quote is found in *Winthrop Papers* 8 (MHS 1882), 238. On Samuel Winthrop, see Gragg 1993. For the perspective of a French observer, see Du Tertre 1667.

59. Cogolludo 1868.

60. See McNeill 2010 and forthcoming for a compelling emphasis on troop arrivals.

61. On the 1690s outbreak, see McNeill 2010, 144–49. On Rosa, see Baer 1949 and Dos Anjos 2016. Mather 1708, 166–67.

62. Prebble 1968; Hidalgo 2001; Gallup-Diaz 2005; McNeill 2010, 105–23.

63. McNeill 2010, 121.

64. See Burnard 1996 on the lure of the Caribbean.

65. Warren 1741, 13–14. On the question of race and immunity to yellow fever, see Pritchett 1995; Kiple 2001; Watts 2001; Espinosa 2014; Blake and Garcia-Blanco 2014; Olivarius 2016; and Richardson 2019. On Warren and his intellectual context, see the insightful study Seth 2018.

66. Long 1774, 2:508.

67. See especially McNeill 2010, 44–46, for a balanced review of the question of acquired immunity.

68. Long 1774, 2:510.

69. Patterson 1992.

70. "It pleased God . . ." is quoted from Bradford 1952 (originally published in 1651), 95. "The temper . . ." is quoted from Higginson 1908 (originally published in 1630).

71. Kukla 1986; Dobson 1989. See Dobson 1997 on malaria in England. See Fischer 1991, 13–206, on the migration more generally.

72. For malaria in the New World, Webb 2009, 66–91, is the best concise overview. Grob 2002 is valuable for the United States but not focused on malaria specifically. For regional studies, see below.

73. Carpenter and LaCasse 1974; Manguin 2008, 282.

74. Carpenter and LaCasse 1974; Krzywinski and Besansky 2003; Manguin 2008. See Parmakelis et al. 2008 on the episode in Brazil.

75. Carpenter and LaCasse 1974.

76. Carpenter and LaCasse 1974. On temperature and falciparum, see Waite et al. 2019.

77. Holmes 1838. For the Harvard diary, see Duffy 1953, 207.

78. The "Epidemical Fevers" quote is from Duffy 1953, 207. Duffy 1953, 213, discusses the shifting boundary. Cook 1889; Quinn 1926.

79. Unfortunately, the place of malaria in the history of the middle colonies, including New York, remains rather obscure. For the Yale analysis, see Hacker 1997.

80. The "air is exceeding" quote comes from Gardyner 1651, 99. See Dobson 1989, 269, for mortality figures, and Grob 2002, 51–53, generally.

81. Somervail 1823. Rutman and Rutman 1976; Smith 1978; Earle 1979.

82. For the Maryland doctor, see Kupperman 1984, 26. Kulikoff 1986; Dunn 2014.

83. Curtin 1994; Doolan, Dobaño, and Baird 2009.

84. "The Heavens shine . . ." is quoted from Wood 1975, 63. "Two young men . . ." is quoted from Wood 1975, 67. In addition to Wood 1975, see Waring 1964; Merrens 1969; Merrens and Terry 1984; Dubisch 1985; Coclanis 1989; and McCandless 2011.

85. "White Carolinians . . ." is quoted from Wood 1975, 68. The "they who want" quote is from Merrens 1969, 18. The "great charnel house" quote is from Wood 1975, 67. "Carolina is in the spring . . ." is quoted from Schoepf 1911, 2:172. For an early medical survey, see Chalmers 1776.

86. See the geography of malaria in the early twentieth century, Maxcy 1923.

87. Ackerknecht 1945, 16. Drake 1850 is a remarkable survey of malaria in the interior in the nineteenth century. Grob 2002, 127–33.

88. The "on the river bank" quote comes from Ackerknecht 1945, 5. The "breeding-place of fever" quote comes from Patterson 2009, 114–15. Dickens 1911, 170. On Union soldier height, see Hong 2007.

89. See Webb 2009 for the Americas in general, and McNeill 2010 for the Caribbean.

90. Manguin 2008.

91. See McNeill 2010, 264, which carefully works out the hypothesis of disease's role in the geopolitical dynamics of the later eighteenth century. See also Smith 2013.

Chapter 9

1. See Otto 2003, for critical and historical essays on the author of *Simplicius Simplicissimus*, Hans Jacob Christoffel von Grimmelshausen (ca. 1621–76).

2. For general overviews of the conflict, see Burkhardt 1992; Parker 1997; Asch 1997; Arndt 2009; and Wilson 2011.

3. The "disease proved" quote is from Wilson 2011, 790. The "greatest man-made" quote is from Clodfelter 2017, 36. Raudzens 1997; Outram 2001, 2002. Lammert 1890 is an indispensable reference.

4. Smallman-Raynor and Cliff 2004. Prinzing 1916 still has valuable material.

5. The "days of shaking" quote is from Jeremiah Whitaker, Εἰρηνοποιός, *Christ the Settlement of Unsettled Times* (republished as Whitaker 2007). Debates about the validity of a "general crisis" go back to the 1950s (Hobsbawm 1954; Trevor-Roper 1959). The essays in Parker and Smith 1997 and Benedict and Gutmann 2005 showcase the range of issues and perspectives. See De Vries 2009 for a survey of the relevant economic literature. Parker 2013 is the most authoritative proponent of the concept, emphasizing in particular the role of climate instability. For the concept applied to China, see Adshead 1973.

6. The population figures are derived from Broadberry et al. 2015 (England); Lo Cascio and Malanima 2005 (Italy); Maddison 2007a (China); and Pfister and Fertig 2010 (Germany).

7. Parker 2013. See S. White 2011 for a particularly compelling study of the climate background to political and socioeconomic turbulence in the Ottoman Empire, and Degroot 2018 for Dutch responses to the Little Ice Age. Blom 2019. See Koch et al. 2019 for the latest contribution to the literature on the reforestation hypothesis, and Dull et al. 2010 for an earlier statement.

The New World population estimates of Koch et al. are probably unrealistically high, and this argument in general is tied to the view (Ruddiman 2003) that anthropogenic climate forcing precedes the Industrial Revolution, which is not a consensus view. In all, solar and volcanic forcing remain the most accepted factors.

8. See especially the essays in Alfani and Ó Gráda 2017 on famine in this period; most of them follow a line of interpretation that seeks to integrate population dynamics with climate history. For the more elaborate version of Malthusian theory, see Goldstone 1991 and Turchin and Nefedov 2011.

9. De Vries 2009, 160.

10. The tradition of construing epidemic mortality as "exogenous" or "autonomous" is rooted in Malthusian theory. In strict Malthusian terms, an epidemic is "endogenous" if it is determined by changes in the level of the real wage, which is a function of the population level. One of the most consistent findings of economic/demographic studies of premodern times is that mortality moves independently of the wage level (usually, at least). Yet, the thrust of this chapter is that we should not leave the issue there. Even if a pestilence is not explicable within the Malthusian framework, it is not necessarily beyond structural explanation. I thus object to lumping together premodern climate change and epidemic disease as "exogenous" factors on the same terms (see my exchange with Brooke 2014, Harper 2016), because solar forcing and volcanism are truly exogenous to all human systems. In the same spirit, see Gutmann 1980, 4: "The great catastrophes of early modern Europe took place when war, harvest failure, and epidemic disease came all at once." Also see Landers 1993.

11. "The *history of typhus* . . ." is quoted from Hirsch 1883, 545. Hirsch was a pioneering medical geographer and historian. See Flinn 1981, 53, for an instance of treating epidemics as a sort of epiphenomenon to other kinds of crisis.

12. The "remained prostrate" quote comes from Hatcher 2003, 93. On the Ottomans, see S. White 2011, 52: "Ottoman numbers soared in the classical age, and agriculture in the core Mediterranean provinces expanded to the limits of arable land." On China's population, see Maddison 2007a. See Brook 2010 for the dynamism of the Ming before the crises that started in the late sixteenth century. On Mughal India, see Dyson 2018, 57.

13. Hatcher 1977. On wages, see Broadberry et al. 2015 for England. Allen 2001. On literacy, see Cipolla 1969 and Houston 2014.

14. On the outbreak of the late 1550s, see Slack 1985, 23, 71; and Cipolla 1981, 7.

15. Alfani and Ó Gráda 2017 is the most comprehensive survey of subsistence crises in Europe. See Alfani 2010 2013b for Italy. On subsistence-related crises in England in 1587 and 1597, see Slack 1985, 117; Appleby 1978; and Walter and Schofield 1989. On the Ottomans, see S. White 2011. On China, see Brook 2019.

16. The "clearly stands out" quote is from Alfani and Ó Gráda 2017, 8. On India, see Dyson 2018, 57–58. On China, see Brook 2020. On the Poor Law, see Slack 1988. The "remembered afterward" quote is from McNeill 1999, 72.

17. De Vries 1984; Hohenberg and Lees 1985; Friedrichs 1995; Cowan 1998; Clark 2009. For the shift, see especially De Vries 2009, with Acemoglu, Johnson, and Robinson 2005.

18. De Vries 1984.

19. See Chandler 1987 and Modelski 2003 for city sizes. For eighteenth-century London, see Schwartz 1983.

20. Wrigley 1967; Wrigley and Schofield 1981, 166–74; Landers 1993. On Japan, see Hanley 1987.

21. For surveys that include medieval developments, see Imbert and Mollat 1982; Orme and Webster 1995; Watson 2006; and Scheutz et al. 2008. On medieval Islamic precedents, see Pormann and Savage-Smith 2010, 96–101. For the early modern hospital, see Arrizabalaga, Cunningham, and Grell 1999; Henderson 2006; and Lindemann 2013, 107–11.

22. The "imprisonment and other forms" quote is from Spierenburg 1995, 58. In general, see Foucault 1975 and Spierenburg 2007.

23. On the "gaol fevers," see Slack 1985, 70. The remembrance of the "saucy" fellow is from a plaque in the Old County Hall of Oxfordshire. A thorough investigation of the diffusion of typhus is still lacking, but see below.

24. The "wretched inmates" and "immediate parent" quotes are from Griffiths 1884, 1:433. Howard 1777.

25. See Roberts 1956, a thesis refined, expanded, and vigorously supported by Parker 1996. Rogers 2018 helpfully brings together many of the important statements. For a variety of views, see Black 1991; Tallett 1992; Black 1999 and 2011; and Hammer 2017.

26. This information follows Parker 1996. On syphilis, see chapter 7—why reports of the new disease proliferated from the 1490s is an open question.

27. On the Ottoman military, see Murphey 1999 and Streusand 2010. See McNeill 1989: "Until about 1600, therefore, the Ottoman army remained technically and in every other way in the very forefront of military proficiency." On China, see Andrade 2016, 4.

28. Smallman-Raynor and Cliff 2004. Prinzing 1916 is a trove of information, focused on this period. Gutmann 1980, 164–65.

29. Murchison 1884, 26. The history of typhus is perhaps the most neglected of any major human disease. Maybe the insightful yet incomparably zany study by Zinsser (1935) has deterred others from entering the field. The story of typhus is also dauntingly vast, and because it was perceived within the generic category of "fever," retrospective diagnosis is enormously challenging. We can do no more than offer some preliminary thoughts here, but the thrust of my argument is that we need to take seriously typhus as a particularly *early modern* disease. See Cowan 2016 for a rare historical account.

30. Drevets, Leenen, and Greenfield 2004, 334–36; Darby et al. 2007; Merhej and Raoult 2011; Parola et al. 2013; Thomas 2016; Diop, Raoult, and Fournier 2018. The closest relative of the species that causes typhus is known (confusingly enough) as *Rickettsia typhi*. *R. typhi* is adapted to rodents and their fleas, so when it gets into humans, *R. typhi* causes the disease known as murine typhus. (To avoid conflating the two different diseases, the louse-borne disease caused by *R. prowazekii* is sometimes called "epidemic typhus.") Murine typhus is an important disease, though it is not as severe or deadly as typhus. It is a zoonosis: humans are only incidental hosts. But because of the close association between humans and rats, murine typhus has been a prevalent disease wherever humans live in squalor and poverty. On murine typhus, see Azad 1990.

31. On human lice, a good recent overview is Amanzougaghene et al. 2020. Boutellis, Abi-Rached, and Raoult 2014.

32. Raoult et al. 2004.

33. The word was first used to mean a kind of fever in 1759 (Smith 1981, 122). On its various historical appellations, Murchison 1884, 23–26, gives scores of examples.

34. The "oppressed" quote is from Murchison 1884, 129. In general, see Andersson and Andersson 2000; Bechah et al. 2008; and Angelakis, Bechah, and Raoult 2016.

35. Smith 1980, 1981. On relapsing fever, see Cutler 2010.

36. "It is tempting . . ." quoted from Raoult et al. 2004. See also Nguyen-Hieu et al. 2010 for an analysis of eighteenth-century DNA. On genomics, see Bishop-Lilly et al. 2013 and Murray et al. 2016. On flying squirrels, see Sonenshine et al. 1978.

37. Carmichael 1998. Usually, studies will cite Zinsser (who in turn was mining Hirsch) who points to several medieval chronicles that indicate outbreaks of a febrile disease with a rash. Not only are these sources few and far between, they are an exceedingly uncertain basis for retrospective diagnosis. Any number of diseases could have been responsible. The evidence becomes much more compelling from the late fifteenth century. The fact that Fracastoro (discussed in the text of the chapter), among others, felt it was a new disease, but previously known in Cyprus, points to Asian origins; although such exotic origins for infectious disease were a common trope, and we should be wary of reproducing Orientalist notions of eastern origins for a disease, the observation about its familiarity in Cyprus is a notable detail that is not obviously aligned with conventional accusations of Ottoman or eastern origins for disease.

38. The Spanish doctor's account is available in De Toro 1564, 26–27, and De Villalba 1802, 1:112–14. On Italy, see Corradi 1865–94, 2:8–14. The diarist is Girolamo Priuli (Priuli 1938) in April 1506, at p. 414.

39. See Fracastoro 1930 for the translation. See Nutton 1990 for his ideas of contagion.

40. On the New World, see Guerra 1999 and Carrillo-Esper et al. 2018. On sixteenth-century Spanish medical sources, see Vázquez-Espinosa, Laganá, and Vazquez 2020.

41. See Murchison 1884, 31. Mercer 2014, 77–81. On the decline of typhus, see Hardy 1988.

42. On typhus in the English Civil War, see Slack 1985, 123. On the Italian Wars, see Alfani 2013b, 13–18. On *morbus hungaricus*, see Györy 1901 and Schmitz-Cliever 1954. For a vivid account of typhus among Napoleon's troops, see Talty 2009.

43. On the 1698 crop failures, see Murchison 1884, 31. On the 1740s, see Post 1984.

44. The classic medical study of the famine is MacArthur 1956. "The scenes . . ." is quoted from Farrell 2006, 79. Ó Gráda 1995; Mokyr and Ó Gráda 2002; Ó Gráda, Vanhaute, and Paping 2007. For the failure of the potato harvest that triggered the famine, see chapter 11.

45. Smith 1981; Risse 1985. "Though the fever . . ." is quoted from Creighton 1891–94, 2:15. On the importance of military medicine, and figures like John Pringle and James Lind, see chapter 10.

46. For reasons that are utterly unclear, typhus was rare in the United States compared to Europe: Humphreys 2006. See Grob 2002, 113–14, for a few instances of its presence.

47. Lilly and Ashmole 1774. See Slack 1985, 20.

48. Slack 1985, 151. On the Bills in this period, see Robertson 1996.

49. On the itinerary of this outbreak in northern Europe, see Eckert 1996, 132–46. On Milan, the vivid fictional account in Manzoni 1924 (originally published in 1840–42) is worth reading and based on Ripamonti 1841 (originally published in 1640), by a Milanese historian who lived through the event.

50. For the Italian death tolls, see Cipolla 1981 and especially Alfani 2013a. On plague in England, see Slack 1985, 151.

51. The history of plague in the seventeenth century lacks a unified treatment, although there are a growing number of excellent regionally focused studies. For early modern plague, see the collection of sources in Bell 2019. Biraben 1975, 1:192–230, 386–87. For northern Europe, see Eckert 1996. For England, see Slack 1985. For Italy, see Cipolla 1978, Fusco 2007 and 2009, and Alfani 2013a. For Spain, see Pérez Moreda 1980. For India and China, see below.

52. On Ottoman reservoirs, see Varlik 2015. On the Alps, see Carmichael 2014. On the North Sea, see Eckert 1996. On molecular evidence, see Spyrou et al. 2019b. Of course our knowledge is dependent on the DNA samples that have been recovered and sequenced, and it is not impossible that the plague could have been reimported from central Asian reservoirs at times, too, although this mechanism is now unnecessary (as well as not directly in evidence).

53. All quotes are from Dunstan 1975, which remains essential for scholars without the ability to read Chinese sources or scholarship. Brook 2020 supports the presence of *Y. pestis* in the crisis of the Ming-Qing transition, citing the work of Cao Shuji.

54. On Jahangir, see Bell 2019, 40–41. Plague returned to India with a terrible outbreak in 1687–90 (Bell 2019, 27). Khan 2013; Dyson 2018, 59.

55. The history of plague in the Ottoman world has been well served by scholars in recent years. As in so many parts of the Old World, the 1590s were a turning point in environmental and demographic history; grave famine beset the Ottoman Empire and disease inevitably followed, yet diagnosis is uncertain. That is not the case with the devastating epidemics that struck in the mid-1620s. See Varlik 2015 for plague in the sixteenth-century Ottoman Empire, noting that "plague outbreaks gradually became more frequent and more widespread in Ottoman cities" (5). S. White 2011, 269, considers the outbreaks of the early 1620s, the early 1660s, and the late 1770s as plainly "the most serious" in the Ottoman period. White 2010; Bulmus 2012; Ayalon 2015. Roe 1740, 420, 427, 444. On Çelebi, see S. White 2011, 269.

56. Plague relented during the sixteenth century, before intensifying again, but the timing was not uniform. The so-called San Carlo plague of 1575–77 in northern Italy was severe. Maybe the Spanish plagues of 1599 could be considered a harbinger of the new epoch at hand. Some 10 percent of the entire population was lost in the devastation. Then again came a lull, and with it the false sense of security that allowed places like Milan to be caught off guard when the unwelcome visitor returned. On the decline of plague in England from 1479, see Slack 1985, 16. See Biraben 1975 for what is still the most comprehensive record of the Second Plague Pandemic. For examples of intense sixteenth-century plague, see Naphy 2002 (in the western Alps, in the 1570s). On the San Carlo plague, see Alfani 2013b. On Spain, see Pérez Moreda 1980. Great use has been made of these sources by Alfani 2013a, Slack 1985, and Eckert 1996. The "greater part" quote is from Eckert 1996, 135, and the mortality spike is discussed at 144.

57. Eckert 1996, 150, for the mortality totals, and Pfister and Fertig 2010, for long-term population context.

58. On the traditions of civic governance and public health, see Cipolla 1978. Alfani 2013a.

59. Biraben 1975. The decline in England has been closely studied (Slack 1985, 199–337). For France, see Ermus 2015 and 2016. On the eastern Mediterranean, see Varlik 2020. On Russia, see Alexander 2003. On Iran, see Shahraki, Carniel, and Mostafavi 2016.

60. Serruys 1980; Chang 1996, 171–72; Chang 2002; Brook 2010, 250.

61. Chang 1996, 174.

62. See Holmes 2003 for a dedicated study of the medical history of the Stuarts. Macaulay 1856, 4:369.

63. Macaulay 1856, 4:370.

64. On the Southeastern Smallpox Epidemic, see Kelton 2007, 143–59. For the earlier outbreaks, see chapter 5.

65. Carmichael and Silverstein 1987.

66. See Chang 1996, 31, and the list on 24. By the eleventh century, there was already some testimony to its severity. A doctor of the Northern Song period, Pang Anshi (1042–99?), wrote, "In recent times, there was not a single year without this disease (smallpox). In serious cases, five or six out of ten died. Although it was caused by poisonous *qi* inside the body, physicians should also be held responsible for more than half of the deaths."

67. Chang 1996, 151. Needham 2000, 6.6:116–49, still provides an invaluable discussion.

68. On the New World, see chapter 7. On Africa, see Spinage 2012, 1246, and Alden and Miller 1987, 198. On China, see Dunstan 1975, Chang 1996 and 2002, and Brook 2010 and 2020.

69. On Iceland, see Hays 2005, 131–34. See Marshall 1832 for London, with Davenport, Schwarz, and Boulton 2011. See Sköld 1996 for a close study of smallpox in eighteenth-century Sweden.

70. Allen 2001 put the idea of a Little Divergence on empirical grounding and has generated further research and debate about the data for wages. For recent contributions to the discussion, see Stephenson 2018; Allen 2019; Rota and Weisdorf 2020; and López Losa and Piquero Zarauz 2020.

71. See especially Alfani 2013a and Alfani and Percoco 2019 for statements of this position, which are further supported by new wage data in Rota and Weisdorf 2020.

72. Appleby 1980 surveys these theories and argues that rodents progressively developed immunity to plague, a hypothesis that has not convinced the field. The brown-rat replacement theory developed in the mid-twentieth century (Loosjes 1956) is still often mooted (e.g., Monecke, Monecke, and Monecke 2009; Spyrou et al. 2016) but strong empirical support is lacking.

73. Slack 1981 is nuanced and still convincing. On arsenic, see Konkola 1992. For the Austrian *cordon sanitaire*, see Rothenberg 1973 from an ample literature.

74. Tilly 1975. For the number of states, see Jedwab, Johnson, and Koyama 2020. On the Marseilles plague, see Ermus 2015 and 2016. For British measures in this episode, see Booker 2007, 85–121.

Chapter 10

1. For a vivid portrait of the Malthusian regime, see Clark 2007. Ashraf and Galor 2011. The "duration of human life" quote comes from Malthus 1798, chapter 9. The "severe distress" quote is from Malthus 1798, chapter 2. As we will see, Malthus was wrong about both real wages and life expectancy in his own society.

2. Deaton 2013. On life expectancy, see Riley 2001. On living standards, see Floud et al. 2011. "It is difficult to conceive . . ." is quoted from Bloom and Canning 2007.

3. Lucas 1988.

4. Weil 2014.

5. Bloom and Canning 2000; Weil 2014, 2015.

6. Weil 2015, 113. Easterlin 1995, 1996; Deaton 2013.

7. See Troesken 2015 for a rich summary of these themes.

8. Omran 1971. The essays in Schofield, Reher, and Bideau 1991 are especially valuable. For a recent reflection on the Omran thesis and its subsequent influence, see Mercer 2018. Also see Shaw-Taylor 2020 on the importance of this longer view.

9. In writing these last three chapters, I have found the difficulties of working between disciplines more challenging than anywhere else. It will be obvious that the architecture and argument draw from scholars working in economic history. For instance, the contributions of Easterlin (1999), Weil (2014), and Deaton (2013) frame the presentation of the modern period as presented here. (Although I suggest that these contributions, quite focused on the need to persuade us that science rather than economic growth per se accounts for improvements in health, tend still to underplay the role of institutions.) The parallel body of scholarship produced by historians of medicine and public health is rich and helpful, but these two literatures are not usually in dialogue and are generally asking different questions. Because economic historians are trying to explain change, they prefer to identify factors cleanly and seek common patterns (and they tend to focus on natural experiments that allow specific causal mechanisms to be isolated). Very often, the motivation of historians of medicine is nearly the opposite—that is, to emphasize particularity. Consider, for instance, one of the monuments in the historiography of public health, Baldwin 1999, which is a comparative study of public responses to health challenges in nineteenth-century western Europe, as richly particular as a study can be. Or see Crook 2016, 7, in which a historian summarizes the achievements of historical scholarship in the study of public health, noting the "absence of any overarching modernizing trajectory" and "the constitutive importance of national and local peculiarities," while praising the tendency of historians to pile "variation upon variation, complexity upon complexity, at all levels, at all moments." Historians may bristle at the claims of economists that there was any such thing as "Enlightenment medicine," "public health," or "germ theory." (In part because historians of science and medicine have taught us that things like "germ theory" reflect truly complex phenomena.) Yet we need to explain why changes happened, especially improvements in the control of disease, which is the kind of question that calls for causal frameworks. Ultimately, I think we lose sight of the real nature of change if we only focus on the particularities. After all, within two or three generations, most western societies adopted public sewage and water treatment, compulsory notification and vaccination, chemical disinfectants, antibiotics, and the like, so that focusing on the differences alone is to miss the forest for the trees. In any case the modest aim in these final chapters is to draw insights from both literatures.

10. See Allen 2009 for a general overview. McNeill 2015, 53.

11. Goldstone 2002.

12. Chen and Kung 2016. For a critique of this view, however, see Lavely and Wong 1998.

13. Aghion and Howitt 2008 provides an overview of growth theories. See Temin 2012 on Roman growth.

14. C. I. Jones 2005; Vries 2013.

15. On institutions, see North and Thomas 1973; Acemoglu, Johnson, and Robinson 2001; and Acemoglu and Robinson 2012. On human capital, see Easterlin 1981; Lucas 1988; Glaeser et al. 2004; and Goldin 2016.

16. Pomeranz 2000. See Parthasarathi 2011 for India. Van Zanden 2009.

17. On income, see Broadberry and Gupta 2006; Broadberry 2013; and Broadberry, Custodis, and Gupta 2015. On human capital, see A'Hearn, Baten, and Crayen 2009. On Atlantic merchants, see Acemoglu, Johnson, and Robinson 2005. On the culture of growth, see Mokyr 1990 and 2017. There is increasing interest in high-end intellectual elites and innovators, or what is known as "upper tail human capital" (Squicciarini and Voigtländer 2015).

18. On high wages, see Allen 2009. On highly skilled workers, see Kelly, Mokyr, and Ó Gráda 2014. The "carboniferous crescent" quote comes from McNeill 2015, 54. For GDP data, see Broadberry, Custodis, and Gupta 2015.

19. Mercer 1990; Armstrong, Conn, and Pinner 1999; Mercer 2014. Of course subsequent gains from the mid-twentieth century have also occurred due to, for instance, declines in tobacco use, improvements in cardiovascular medicine, and expanded delivery of primary care, but these lie outside the scope of this study.

20. McKeown, Brown, and Record 1972; McKeown 1976. See Harris 2004 for a qualified defense of McKeown. On the relationship between income and nutrition, see Floud et al. 2011. On the causal influence of income on health, see Acemoglu and Johnson 2007.

21. On health infrastructure, see Chapman 2019. Preston 1975, 1976. See also Szreter 1988 and 2002 for important reflections on the McKeown thesis, and Szreter 2005 for a compelling statement of the importance of health policy.

22. See below for the emergence of class gradients.

23. Gallup and Sachs 2001; Bloom, Canning, and Graham 2003; Weil 2007; Lorentzen, McMillan, and Wacziarg 2008; Aghion, Howitt, and Murtin 2010; Beach et al. 2016. On physiological/cognitive development and health, see Eppig, Fincher, and Thornhill 2010; Daniele and Ostuni 2013; and Madsen 2016. On infection and educational outcomes, see Almond 2006 for a brilliant study of long-term effects of in utero exposure to the 1918–19 influenza; also see Bleakley 2007 and 2010, Cutler et al. 2010, and Lucas 2010.

24. On the European marriage pattern, see Hajnal 1965 and 1982. Foreman-Peck 2011; Foreman-Peck and Zhou 2018. Wrigley 1988. As a source of economic growth in deeper time, see van Zanden, Carmichael, and de Moor 2019. For a critique, see Dennison and Ogilvie 2014. Although it has been debated whether the European Marriage Pattern took shape before or after the Black Death, on balance the evidence favors a very early date. See Edwards and Ogilvie 2018.

25. On Italy, see Felice 2007 and Ciccarelli and Weisdorf 2018. On longevity and early human capital advantages, see Boucekkine, de la Croix, and Licandro 2004 and Boucekkine, de la Croix, and Peeters 2007a and 2007b. The regional malaria data I have compiled using a six-year average of deaths from "malarial fevers and swamp wasting" during the years 1887–92, along with the regional populations from the 1881 census. Pretransitional life expectancies are exceedingly difficult to estimate. See Riley 2005b for one enterprising attempt. It should be remarked that Tokugawa Japan also experienced low mortality rates and relatively long life expectancy through a combination of strict isolation, urban sanitation, and, perhaps, cultural values that conduced to hygiene (according to Hanley, these were derived from Shinto concepts of pollution). See Jannetta 1987 and Hanley 1987. These favorable mortality conditions may help to explain the rapid course of modernization in Japan.

26. Weil 2014, 2015.

27. Cutler, Deaton, and Lleras-Muney 2006; Soares 2007; Deaton 2013.

28. See Easterlin 1996 and 1999 on market failures and health.

29. To make matters more complicated, these two categories of state action could be in direct tension. The concentration of power might be good for compelling obedience but bad for investing in big infrastructure projects or distributing public goods equitably (Troesken 2015).

30. Easterlin 1996.

31. Riley 1987. Thus John Pringle, and reformers of later decades like John Howard. Félix Vicq d'Azyr, Johann Peter Frank, A. J. B. Parent-Duchâtelet, and Louis-René Villermé, can be said to stand in a line of continuity. See Coleman 1982 and La Berge 1992 for classic treatments.

32. For Pepys as a way to understand hygienic conditions, see Razzell 2007, 157–68, which has inspired the passage here. See Tomalin 2002 for a general biography.

33. For balanced overviews, see, generally, Corfield 1982; Friedrichs 1995; Cowan 1998; and Clark 2009, 109–219.

34. I have used the complete edition of the diary edited by Latham and Matthews (1971). The "my wife" quote is dated May 25, 1663. "I perceive . . ." is dated April 21, 1664.

35. "While I was at dinner . . ." is dated March 23, 1662. The "mightily troubled" quote is dated September 28, 1665.

36. "Sir W. Pen's . . ." is dated April 30, 1666. "This morning . . ." is dated October 20, 1660. The "home" quote is dated July 28, 1663.

37. Razzell 2007, 162. The "my head" quote is dated April 23, 1661. "I went up . . ." is dated September 7, 1662.

38. "I have itched . . ." is dated January 23, 1669. The "this day" quote is dated February 8, 1663.

39. "Thence to Westminster . . ." is dated July 18, 1664. The "it is a wonder" quote is dated September 3, 1665.

40. England was in the vanguard, and the uniquely valuable insights on causes of death furnished by the London Bills of Mortality mean that the English experience has been reconstructed in the most detail.

41. On the crude death rate, see Wrigley and Schofield 1981. In general, see Del Panta and Livi Bacci 1977, 420. See Schofield and Reher 1991, 3, noting some exceptions too. Perrenoud 1991.

42. For Ottoman plagues in the eighteenth century, especially the late 1770s and 1780s, see Panzac 1985, 58–68. For Russia, especially the horrifying outbreak in Moscow in 1771, see Alexander 2003.

43. On famines, see Appleby 1978 and Alfani and Ó Gráda 2017. For the 1918 influenza, see chapter 11.

44. Malthus 1798, chapter 9. On France, see Blayo 1975 for the increases and Bourdelais and Demonet 1996 for the mid-nineteenth-century stagnation. Similarly, for Belgium, see Neven 1997. Wrigley and Schofield 1981; Riley 2001, 33–34. Similarly, for the United States, see Grob 2002, 96–179 and Troesken 2015, 27, observing that the crude death rate in New York increased from about 25 to 35 per 1,000 between 1800 and 1860, as the "existing township approach to public health was overwhelmed" by precisely the sort of negative feedbacks proposed here.

45. Davenport 2020.

46. Landers 1987, 1993; Woods 2003.

47. On eighteenth century smallpox, see Davenport, Schwarz, and Boulton 2011 and Davenport, Boulton, and Schwarz 2016.

48. Marshall 1832. Davenport, Schwarz, and Boulton 2011. On the Geneva physician, see Bennett 2020, 15. On Japan, see Jannetta 1987, 19.

49. Marshall 1832. Schofield and Reher 1991, 12. For the social history of tuberculosis in western Europe, there is a rich literature, notably Bryder 1988, the sources collected by Rosenkrantz 1994, and Barnes 1995. Its rise was paralleled in the United States (Grob 2002, 110).

50. Riley 2001, 16–17; Razzell 2007, 128; Mercer 2014; Davenport 2015, 2017.

51. When a strep throat infection is untreated, it is also liable to cause serious complications such as rheumatic fever, a potentially fatal autoimmune disease that often damages heart tissue and sometimes the brain. About 3 percent of untreated cases of *S. pyogenes* infection will develop rheumatic fever, so in a society without antibiotics it could have been a common complication. Further, a minority of cases of rheumatic fever will progress to the disorder known as Sydenham's chorea, characterized by involuntary jerking motions that resemble dancing, sometimes years after the initial infection (Martino et al. 2005; Vale and Cardoso 2015). Sydenham did not connect scarlet fever with the syndrome—Sydenham's chorea—that bears his name, but the coincidence is telling. Sydenham offered the first clinical account of the dancing disease in 1686, noting that it struck children from around the age of ten. The fact that we have an accurate description of this peculiar syndrome is a testament to Sydenham's genius, but also to the greater visibility and perhaps prevalence of such a childhood disease. See Hardy 1993b for a brief historical overview. There is not a monographic history of scarlet fever. For its seeming absence in antiquity, see Grmek 1989, 337. See Corradi 1865–94, 1:1064, on an epidemic in 1583 that was likely scarlet fever. Creighton 1891–94, 2:678–747, has a great deal of historical information. Hirsch 1883, 1: 71–96; Rolleston 1928. See Duffy 1953, 129–37, for colonial America.

52. Creighton 1891–94, 2:680. Rumsey 1789.

53. For the basic biology of *S. pyogenes*, Ferretti, Stevens, and Fischetti 2017 is comprehensive. Bessen 2009; Bessen et al. 2015. On the evolution of *S. pyogenes* generally, see Wilkening and Federle 2017 and Sitkiewicz 2018. Wong and Yuen 2012; Nasser et al. 2014; You et al. 2018; Wong and Yuen 2018. Davenport 2020. For its historical rise, see Creighton 1891–94, 2:726. Hardy 1993b, 56–79; Duncan, Scott, and Duncan 2000. On Henry Adams, see Adams 1918, 5. On Darwin's daughters, see Browne 1995, 1:498–503, and Keynes 2001.

54. Villermé 1830. See La Berge 1992, 59–75.

55. Woods and Williams 1995; Clouston et al. 2016. On the urban mortality penalty, see Kearns 1988, 223. In the United States, the urban mortality penalty became an advantage in the early twentieth century (Haines 2001). See Reher 2001 for Spain. Bengtsson and van Poppel 2011 reports ambiguous findings regarding the relationship between health inequality and industrialization, and Bengtsson, Dribe, and Helgertz 2020 finds health inequality emerging in Sweden only in the mid-twentieth century.

56. Antonovsky 1967.

57. Cummins 2017. On the British peerage, see Hollingsworth 1977. On the Roman emperors, see Scheidel 1999.

58. Plague came to affect the poor disproportionately at least by the seventeenth century (Slack 1985, 143; Cummins, Kelly, and Ó Gráda 2016). On Geneva, see Perrenoud 1975. Riley 2001, 140–41.

59. On the royal family, see Razzell 2007, 91, and David, Johansson, and Pozzi 2010. More generally, see Woods and Williams 1995.

60. The "history of thought" quote is from Rosen 1974, 120. Frank's 1790 lecture comes from Sigerist 1941.

61. De Tocqueville 1958 (originally published in 1835), 107–8. On poverty, see Razzell 2007, 122.

62. On the French origins of public health, see La Berge 1992.

63. Singer 1949, 1950; Selwyn 1966; Weidenhammer 2016.

64. Pringle 1750, 1753.

65. See Cunningham and French 1990 in general. See Porter 1995 for a brief overview of medicine in England, emphasizing its limits in society. For Pringle's place, see especially DeLacy 2017, 55–66.

66. For the global circulation of these pharmaceuticals, see Howard 1994 and Chakrabarti 2010. Johansson 2010.

67. Jarcho 1993; Crawford 2014, 2016.

68. Chang 1996. See the background for these developments in chapter 9.

69. Razzell 2003; Boylston 2012b; Grant 2019; Eriksen 2020.

70. On the episode and the possibility of African origins (though inconclusive), see Herbert 1975. Wisecup 2011. For the debates more generally, see Silva 2011, 142–79.

71. On Lady Mary, see Miller 1981. See especially Grant 2019 on the Circassian background.

72. Davenport, Boulton, and Schwarz 2016. On the Suttons, see Boylston 2012a. On the role of the Americas, see Bennett 2020, 23.

73. See Mercer 1990 for the mortality rates. See Bennett 2020 for Jenner in global context.

74. The vision of extirpating smallpox appeared in the 1800 edition (Jenner 1800, 41–42). See Bennett 2020: Jefferson on p. 7 and "early transmission" on pp. 142–43. On Spain, see Mark and Rigau-Pérez 2009. On Japan, see Jannetta 2007, 2.

75. On Enlightenment medicine generally, see the essays in Cunningham and French 1990.

76. Pringle 1764, 264–65. DeLacy 2017, 77.

77. Riley 1987. For medieval antecedents, see Rawcliffe and Weeda 2019 and Geltner 2019b.

78. On the public sphere, see DeLacy 2017, 65. On military medicine, see Geltner 2019a, Chakrabarti 2010 (emphasizing the global context), and Hudson 2007. For political arithmetic, see Rusnock 2008. On Massachusetts, see Blake 1959, 47.

79. "His example . . ." is quoted from DeLacy 2017, 73. For the "decisively changed" quote (and the role of hospitals generally), see Risse 1986, 279. The same patterns prevailed across the Channel, in some cases earlier than in Britain. See La Berge 1992, 11, for the Enlightenment approach to health, with its "emphasis on progress, rational reform, education, natural law, orderliness, empiricism, and humanitarianism."

80. Razzell 2007, 122, 169. On piped water, see Razzell 2007, 169. See generally Corfield 1982.

81. Baker and Taras 1981, 30.

82. Riley 1987, 100, 134.

83. Buer 1926. See Styles 2007, however, for a balanced view on the shift to cotton. "Most of the above improvements were the result of a cultural shift in attitude towards better hygiene, cleanliness and more effective medical treatment. Many environmental improvements were the results of local improvement acts, whereas others—such as the drainage of land—were introduced for mainly economic reasons. Contemporaries became increasingly aware of the

importance of these measures for the health of both themselves and their children, although some of the improvements resulted from cultural changes in architectural fashion and personal taste" (Razzell 2007, 121).

84. Dobson 1980, 1997.

85. See especially Riley 1986 on drainage and its intellectual context.

86. Heberden 1813.

87. Riley 1981. See the remarkable compilation of data in Haines and Shlomowitz 1998, which concludes (46) that there was a "percolation of experimental sanitary ideas and practices emerging from some institutions and naval ships in the last quarter of the eighteenth century and widely practised in later decades."

88. See Igler 2013 for the background of these voyages and, with Igler 2004, a guide to wider debates about contact, disease, and depopulation.

Chapter 11

1. A Feb. 20, 1801, letter from Adams to Jefferson is quoted in Oberg 2006, 23–24. On his experience with scarlet fever, see Adams 1918, chapter 1.

2. Wallace 1899, vii.

3. Wallace 1899, 340–41.

4. Headrick 1981; Watts 1997. One could also follow these themes through the rich literature on colonization and medicine (e.g., Arnold 1993; Harrison 1994).

5. These uniformities are a major theme of Bayly 2004, 1: "As world events became more interconnected and interdependent, so forms of human action adjusted to each other and came to resemble each other around the world." For the word *pandemic*, see below.

6. For quantification of imperial scales, see Etemad 2007. On the Great Divergence in living standards, see Bolt et al. 2018; Broadberry, Guan, and Li 2018; Broadberry et al. 2015; Maddison 2007b; Clark 2007; Broadberry and Gupta 2006; and Broadberry, Custodis, and Gupta 2015. On life expectancy, see below.

7. Close 1865, 17.

8. For population figures, I follow the synthesis presented in HYDE 3.1 (Klein Goldewijk et al. 2011). On the Great Escape, see Fogel 2004 and Deaton 2013. See the Maddison database (Bolt et al. 2018) for income figures.

9. Allen 2009.

10. See Gordon 2016 for an American-focused account. Easterlin 1996; Mokyr 1999; Smil 2005.

11. McNeill 2000; Smil 2017.

12. See Jonsson 2014 on cornucopianism. For the early modern exhaustion of resources, see Richards 2003 and Brooke and Otter 2016.

13. For this summary, and the data in table 1, see Osterhammel 2014, 121.

14. The "disaster of the century" quote comes from Osterhammel 2014, 124.

15. Rowe 2009. See Davis 2001 on the famines.

16. For the crises generally, see Rowe 2009, 165–74. For the demographic context, see Yi et al. 2016; Chen and Kung 2016; Baten et al. 2010; and Maddison 2007a. See Lee and Feng 2009 for an interpretation of Chinese demographic growth critical of Malthus.

17. On India and disease, see below. On the famines, see Roy 2000, 277–78, and Dyson 2018, 103–5, 134–40.

18. For Hawai'i, see especially Archer 2018. See more generally McArthur 1967; Cliff and Haggett 1985; Cliff, Haggett, and Smallman-Raynor 1993; Morens 1998; Igler 2004 and 2013; and La Croix 2019. On the journey of the king and queen, see Shulman, Shulman, and Sims 2009.

19. On Africa's demography in the big picture, see Iliffe 2017. For population figures and stasis, see Manning 2010, 266. On the epidemiological disaster, see Ransford 1983. See also Aky-eampong 2006, 195–201.

20. Hohenberg and Lees 1985; Lenger 2012; Osterhammel 2014, 241–321.

21. Clark 2009. On Chicago, see Cronon 1991.

22. See Melosi 2008 for a perspective from America. See chapter 12.

23. "No other epoch . . ." is quoted from Osterhammel 2014, 154. McKeown 2004. On the settler revolution, see Belich 2009. On contract labor (focused on the United States), see Cohen 1995. For the background to the land runs, see Debo 1940.

24. Headrick 1981.

25. Bagwell 1988. The "railroad fever" quite comes from Headrick 1981, 181. The "one short interruption" quote comes from Osterhammel 2014, 717.

26. Findlay and O'Rourke 2007, 365–428. On trade and disease, see especially Harrison 2012.

27. See Morens, Folkers, and Fauci 2009 on the rise of the term in the late nineteenth century. Webster's 1828 dictionary defined pandemic as "incident to a whole people; epidemic; as a pandemic disease." See also Honigsbaum 2014; McMillen 2016.

28. The "swamped" quote comes from Green and Jones 2020, 35.

29. Hamlin 2009, 4. Historians of medicine and historians of society have found cholera a rich topic. From a vast literature, see Pollitzer 1954; McGrew 1960; Briggs 1961; Rosenberg 1962; McGrew 1965; Morris 1976; Durey 1979; Delaporte 1986; Bourdelais and Raulot 1987; Evans 1987 and 1988; Snowden 1995; MacPherson 1998; Echenberg 2011; and Harrison 2020.

30. Barua and Greenough 1992, 2–7; Hamlin 2009, 19–20. Classic overviews of cholera are found in Pollitzer 1954; Barua and Greenough 1992; and Wachsmuth, Blake, and Olsvik 1994.

31. *V. cholera* is an old and widespread environmental bacterium. Its natural home is the brackish water of tidal estuaries, where rivers meet the ocean. *V. cholera* is an exceptionally diverse species, with more than two hundred different types (or serogroups). Many of these are free-living aquatic bacteria, or they are adapted to live on the surface of marine creatures like copepods, tiny crustaceans that are ubiquitous in the ocean waters. Wherever you are on the planet, *V. cholerae* lurks in an estuary near you. A few of these strains of *V. cholerae* will cause sickness in humans if ingested, in essence a kind of food poisoning. But these are dead-end infections and not the cause of the historic cholera pandemics. Human cholera is the story of how one lineage of an omnipresent aquatic bacterium adapted to the strange environment of our gut. For the genetic evidence, see Devault et al. 2014; Boucher, Orata, and Alam 2015; Azarian et al. 2016; Boucher 2016; and Islam, Alam, and Boucher 2017. The convention of dividing the outbreaks of the nineteenth century into discrete "pandemics" has some grounding in reality but is based on limited perusal of the global evidence; the lack of total agreement on the dating of the pandemics reflects the ambiguity of the evidence, and, given that cholera could establish locally and persist, it is likely that some of the successive waves overlapped, so that the convention of discrete waves understates the complexity of the disease's history.

32. Boucher, Orata, and Alam 2015.

33. The "truly amazing" quote comes from Pollitzer 1954, 607. See Rabbani and Greenough 1992.

34. MacNamara 1876, 28–45; Pollitzer 1959; Barua 1992, 2–7.

35. Pollitzer 1954, 17–21.

36. On colonial Calcutta, see Bhattacharyya 2018. See Harrison 2015 on commerce and disease.

37. Pollitzer 1954, 21–31; Barua 1992, 8–12.

38. The cholera outbreak in Hamburg has been the object of a masterful study (Evans 1987).

39. On Zanzibar, see Gray 1962.

40. Christie 1876. See Echenberg 2011, 52–64, for an appreciative assessment of Christie and his work.

41. When cholera reached Zanzibar in December, it was not the first time the disease had struck the island, but memory of the earlier pandemics was already hazy. Christie could not find solid evidence that the first cholera pandemic, which started in 1817, had reached the island, but he believed that it likely had. Similarly, details of the second pandemic in the 1830s were "exceedingly scant." After two decades of reprieve, cholera returned in 1858. This, the third pandemic of cholera, was firmly attested in Zanzibar. Cholera arrived on the Somali coast with the first appearance of the *dhows*, the traditional sailing vessels of the Indian Ocean. Then it crept inexorably down the coast. The British adventurer Richard Burton was just south of Zanzibar when it arrived, and he recorded its destructiveness. Christie also had access to the papers of the British consul in Zanzibar at the time, who estimated seven to eight thousand deaths in the main city, and twenty thousand for the island as a whole. Christie suspected that these figures were, if anything, an underestimate.

42. The explorer David Livingstone claimed the island could be smelled from two miles away and proposed it be renamed Stinkibar. The Zanzibar city quotes are from Christie 1876, 271.

43. The "suddenly ill" quote is from Christie 1876, 367. "The skin . . ." is quoted from Christie 1876, 378–79. The "intellectual faculties" quote is from Christie 1876, 379.

44. Christie 1876, 385. "At last . . ." is quoted from Christie 1876, 387. For the death tolls, see Christie 1876, 419.

45. On these contrasts, see Arnold 1993 and Watts 1997. See also Harrison 2020 for thoughts on the mortality estimates in the early outbreaks. On the origins of the seventh pandemic, see Hu et al. 2016. *V. cholerae* still causes about three million infections and about one hundred thousand deaths per year (Ali et al. 2015).

46. On North America, see Patterson 1992. On Europe, see Harrison 2012.

47. The "massive surge" quote is from Harrison 2012, 107. On the 1878 outbreak, see Patterson 1992, 859.

48. Webster et al. 1992; Baigent and McCauley 2003; Nelson and Holmes 2007; Rambaut et al. 2008; Taylor 2014.

49. For an influenza wave in the fourteenth century, see Bauch 2020. Patterson 1986; Pyle 1986; Beveridge 1991; Potter 2001; Honigsbaum 2014; Saunders-Hastings and Krewski 2016; Hill, Tildesley, and House 2017; Alibrandi 2018. On spreading at the speed of a horse, see Pyle 1986, 28. "This explosive spread . . ." is quoted from Pyle 1986, 31. Valleron et al. 2010.

50. Crosby 2003; Barry 2004; Taubenberger and Morens 2018.

51. On the genetic material, see Taubenberger et al. 1997 and 2005 and Nelson and Worobey 2018. For the death tolls, see Patterson and Pyle 1991; Johnson and Mueller 2002; and Spreeuwenberg, Kroneman, and Paget 2018. The "everywhere at once" quote is from Taubenberger and Morens 2019, 4. In general, see Morens and Fauci 2007. On India, see Chandra, Kuljanin, and Wray 2012.

52. Morens and Taubenberger 2018.

53. On the continuity of the second pandemic, see Panzac 1985; Bell 2019, 53–57; Varlik 2020. On Russia, where terrible outbreaks struck in the eighteenth century, see Alexander 2003. On genomics, see Wagner et al. 2014 and Spyrou et al. 2016.

54. This paragraph draws from Benedict 1996, an important history of plague in nineteenth century China.

55. The "colossus" quote comes from Echenberg 2007, 15; see this source also on the third pandemic more generally.

56. For Yersin's work, see Echenberg 2007, 32–38, and Velmet 2020, 24–31.

57. Arnold 1993; Harrison 1994; Echenberg 2002; Bramanti et al. 2019; Velmet 2020. On the death figures, see Klein 1973, Arnold 1993, and Echenberg 2007, 5.

58. Nützenadel 2008.

59. Olmstead and Rhode 2008, which focuses on the economics of American agriculture in the nineteenth century, offers one of the richest overviews of the importance of the topic. McCook 2006 and 2019, focused on coffee leaf rust, cover all of the main issues. Agrios 2005 is a helpful overview of plant disease. Cook 1913 has much information about tropical plant diseases. See Beinart and Middleton 2004 for thoughts on historicizing plant transfers.

60. Stukenbrock and McDonald 2008.

61. On Riley, see Sorensen et al. 2008 and 2019. "Once steamships . . ." is quoted from Gale 2011, 4.

62. Gale 2011; Simpson 2011, 36–37.

63. See especially Ó Gráda, Vanhaute, and Paping 2007. See McNeill 2000 for the place of the potato in world history.

64. On genomics, see Yoshida et al. 2013, Martin et al. 2015, and Saville et al. 2016. Bourke 1964.

65. Bourke 1964; Vanhaute, Paping, and Ó Gráda 2006.

66. See Olmstead and Rhode 2008, especially 41: "Wheat farmers were cursed by the Red Queen's dictum: they had to run hard just to stay in one place."

67. Wallace 1899, 373.

68. The "virgin forests" quote comes from Wallace 1899, 373. On Trollope, see McCook 2019, 38.

69. McCook 2019, 8.

70. See Riley 1889 for the American exhibit. Harrison 2012, 232–46. On fungicides, see Morton and Staub 2008. Overall, see the essays in Brown and Gilfoyle 2010 and the two monographs of Olmstead and Rhode (2008 and 2015) for the scientific and policy responses that followed.

71. Brier 2013.

72. Agricultural Research Service 1962. See Olmstead and Rhode 2015, 138–55, on hog cholera.

73. On the genomics, see Rios et al. 2017.

74. Spinage 2003 is the most compendious treatment of cattle plague. See Newfield 2012, 2013, and 2015 for early medieval cattle plagues. See Newfield 2009, as well as Slavin 2012, for the fourteenth-century panzootic. See McVety 2018 for the twentieth-century history of cattle plague. See Scott 1990 for a medical perspective.

75. Appuhn 2010, 278.

76. On resistance, see Roeder, Mariner, and Kock 2013. On the divergence from the shared ancestor with measles virus, see Düx et al. 2020.

77. The "never absent" quote is from Spinage 2003, 103. Harrison 2012, 212–24. Van Roosbroeck and Sundberg 2017. On eighteenth-century responses, see La Berge 1992, 17.

78. On Queen Victoria, see Spinage 2003, 389–90, and Robinson 2009.

79. Spinage 2003, 447–71.

80. Mack 1970; Phoofolo 1993; Spinage 2003, 497–681.

81. Phoofolo 1993, 118.

82. Plowright 1982; Dobson 2009.

83. Kheraj 2018, for railway transmission in the east. See Andrews 2021 for its spread in the west (and also on the nature and effects of the outbreak more generally).

84. Dickens 1873, 105. Although it was less sensational at the time, a massive outbreak of disease among birds, including domesticated chickens as well as wild waterfowl, was coincident with the equine influenza. The interplay between avian reservoirs of influenza virus and industrial poultry farming has been, and remains, one of the gravest threats to human well-being. The possibility has been mooted that the horse flu of 1872–73 was related to highly pathogenic avian influenza, given the extraordinary overlap between the bird outbreak and the equine influenza (Morens and Taubenberger 2010a and b).

85. On Texas fever, see Olmstead and Rhode 2015, 94–114, and Specht 2019, 145–52 (which is a compelling treatment more generally of the interplay between the rise of global capitalism and the ecology of beef production, with insights into the ecology of disease). For cattle numbers, see HYDE 3.1 (Klein Goldewijk et al. 2011); Skaggs 1986; Rimas and Fraser 2008; and Specht 2019; including on the ecological transformations required by large-scale capitalist beef production.

86. Forni et al. 2017; Decaro et al. 2020.

87. On the bovine coronavirus, see Saif 2010. On OC43, see Vijgen et al. 2005 and 2006.

88. Harrison 2012, 50–78, is the best account of these early efforts at coordination. See Panzac 1985, 456–92, on the importance of Ottoman involvement and enlistment of European help from the 1830s.

89. Howard-Jones 1975 is the fullest treatment of the International Sanitary Conferences, focused on the scientific/medical aspects. Barkhuus 1943; Bynum 1993; Huber 2006.

90. Huber 2006, 455.

91. Huber 2006. On the map of global disease, see Brömer 2000. See Valenčius 2000 on the rise of medical geography. Tworek 2019, focused on the twentieth century, draws out the connections between communications and global health.

92. Bashford 2004. On semipermeable membranes, see Huber 2006. For the continuation of these themes seen through the lens of twentieth-century Israel, see Seidelman 2020.

93. For these figures, see Headrick 1981. See also Etemad 2007 for more detailed reconstructions. See Osterhammel 2014, 59–60, on the "first" age of European imperialism. See Porter 1994 for a survey of high imperialism.

94. For the large-scale dynamics of power and disease, see Headrick 1981 and Watts 1997. For settler colonialism, see Bayly 1989 and Belich 2009.

95. Curtin 1989, 1998; Etemad 2007, 11–24.

96. Headrick 1981, 58–79, is the classic account of quinine as a "tool of empire." Etemad 2007, 31–36, is a balanced update, concluding that "quinine was a decisive innovation for the Europeans of West Africa."

97. On the partition of Africa, see Wesseling 1996. Akyeampong 2006, 196. On influenza, see Patterson and Pyle 1983.

98. Davis 1951; Das Gupta 1971; Visaria and Visaria 1982; Bhat 1989.

99. On malaria, see Klein 1973. On smallpox, see Banthia and Dyson 1999.

100. On Dutt, see Gupta 1911, 88. Klein 1973; Dyson 2018, 108; Klein 2001.

Chapter 12

1. I have used Stanford Luce's 2005 translation (Verne 2005). As with several of Verne's novels, the original version of the story was by Paschal Grousset, who sold a draft to the editor Pierre-Jules Hetzel, who then commissioned Verne to rewrite it.

2. Richardson 1876. On Richardson, see Otter 2008, 62–63, and Crook 2016, 1–4.

3. The "generation ago" quote comes from Kelley 1915. On the dominance of infectious disease as cause of death, even in some of the world's healthiest places like New England, see Noymer and Jarosz 2008. Mooney 2007 has noninfectious causes of death in a slight majority by the mid-nineteenth century, but uses restrictive definitions of infectious disease. On the mortality decline, see Preston 1976; Bengtsson, Fridlizius, and Ohlsson 1984; Mercer 1990; Schofield, Reher, and Bideau 1991; Chesnais 1992; Riley 2001; Fogel 2004; Bengtsson et al. 2004; Bourdelais 2006; Dyson 2010; Deaton 2013; and Mercer 2014.

4. I found the "suddenly started breeding" reference in Russell 2001, 7, ultimately from Lean, Hinrichsen, and Markham 1990.

5. On the Anthropocene concept, see below. For the microbiology of the Anthropocene, see Gillings and Paulsen 2014 and Hirschfeld 2020.

6. Mitchell 1998a; B. Mitchell 2011.

7. See B. Mitchell 2011 for the raw data for England/Wales; see Carter 2006, volume 1, for the United States. Mercer 1990; Hardy 1993a; Woods and Shelton 1997; Mercer 2014.

8. Although there are not good global cause-of-death data before the late twentieth century, James Riley has meticulously gathered different national data sets. Riley 2005a offers a wealth of information, and B. Mitchell 1998a and b, 2007, and 2011 collate data helpfully.

9. See Chadwick 1965 (originally published in 1842), 210. Hamlin 1998 persuasively argues that Chadwick's narrow focus on filth actually served to limit the attention on poverty as a cause of disease. Pickstone 1992.

10. Chadwick 1965, 422. Coleman 1982; Duffy 1990; La Berge 1992; Rosen 1993; Porter 1999; Barnes 2006; M. Brown 2008. See Latour 1993 for a classic account of transition from miasma to germ theory in France.

11. See Susser and Stein 2009, 73–97, on mid-nineteenth-century epidemiology. Steere-Williams 2020. In Britain, at least, miasmatist theory proved harmonious with laissez faire ideology. Free trade, social reform, and public health went hand in hand. By contrast, contagionism

appealed to conservatives and landed interests. The classic study is Ackerknecht 1948. See DeLacy 2017 on the growth of contagionism in the eighteenth century. See Baldwin 1999 for the political valence of medical ideas about disease in nineteenth-century Europe more broadly. See Barnes 2014, especially on the importance of infected articles.

12. On Pasteur, see Dubos 1951 and Geison 1995. See Worboys 2007 in general.

13. See Pennington 1995 on Lister. See Brock 1988 for an appreciative biography of Koch. See Gradmann 2009 on Koch and laboratory science.

14. See Romano 1997 and Worboys 2000 on the uptake of and resistance to germ theory.

15. Haynes 2001. In 1880, the French army doctor Alphonse Laveran, working in Algeria, discovered the protozoan that caused malaria. A British doctor (and erstwhile poet) in the employ of the Indian Medical Service named Ronald Ross is the discoverer of the mosquito-malaria cycle. Almost simultaneously (priority is controversial and long disputed), the Italian Giovanni Battista Grassi also described the mosquito vector.

16. On housing acts, see Wohl 1977, 73–108.

17. See Hamlin 2011 for a brief summary. Szreter 1988; Duffy 1990; Rosen 1993; Porter 1999; Szreter 2005; Melosi 2008; Mooney 2015; Crook 2016. See below for global dimensions.

18. The "among the largest" quote comes from Troesken 2015. "If any one approach dominated the public health movement, it was statism, the notion that it was the responsibility of the state to provide for public health through administrative, legislative, and institutional means" (La Berge 1992, xii). On Britain, see Hamlin 2011, 417.

19. Labisch 1992; Tomes 1998; Mooney 2015. On France, see La Berge 1992, 41.

20. Tomes 1998. The "always more work" quote comes from Mokyr 2000.

21. On the flyswatter, see Soppelsa and Rodgers 2019.

22. Overall, a comprehensive survey of chemical disinfection is yet to be written, although we can be thankful for important work on major parts of the story. Russell 2001, on chemical vector control starting in World War I, has a wealth of insight and information. Although focused on the use of sulfur for ship-borne fumigation, Engelmann and Lynteris 2020 is likewise indispensable. I am in agreement with Whyte 2015: "Despite disinfection's key role in public health policy, it has thus far not received significant investigation or historiographical attending."

23. Knaysi 1930; Hugo 1991; Blancou 1995; Engelmann and Lynteris 2020.

24. Bartholow 1867; American Public Health Association 1885; Krönig and Paul 1897. See Schlich 2012 on the relationship between medical practice and laboratory bacteriology in Germany.

25. Alcock 1827 and Scott 1828 (a translation of Labarraque) brought these discoveries to the attention of the English scientific community. On chlorination, see Alvord et al. 1917, Melosi 2008, and McGuire 2013.

26. The toxic arsenical compound marketed as Paris Green was widely used as an agricultural insecticide from the 1860s. In general, see Russell 2001.

27. Russell 2001. On organic chemistry, see Steen 2014.

28. Dunlap 1981; Kinkela 2011.

29. See Hardy 1993a, especially 24–25.

30. See Hardy 1993a for the "heart of the puzzle" (211) and "one of the best overall treatments" (211–16). See McKeown, Brown, and Record 1972 and McKeown 1976 for living

standards. The discussion is very old, including Newsholme 1910 and Greenwood 1937. Wilson 1990; Vynnycky and Fine 1999; Woods 2000; Lipsitch and Sousa 2002; Davenport 2013; Mercer 2014; Anderson et al. 2017.

31. Wilson 2005. On milk, see Atkins 1992 and 1999.

32. Gheorgiu 2011.

33. Chatterjee 1953.

34. Gensini, Conti, and Lippi 2007; Williams 2009; Kirsch and Ogas 2016.

35. Lesch 2007.

36. Greenwood 2008; Silver 2011; Lewis 2013; Leisner 2020.

37. Fenner 1989; Hardy 1993a, 110–50; Glynn and Glynn 1994; Hopkins 2002.

38. Although Jenner's discovery was long without equal, it was not completely isolated. Experiments with measles inoculation were tried from the late eighteenth century. I have found the chapters in Plotkin 2011 immensely useful, and see Kinch 2018 for a history of vaccines.

39. On the history of antivaccination, see Grignolio 2018. See also Porter 1999, 129–30, on nineteenth-century Britain.

40. Hinman et al. 1983. Globally, see Shanks et al. 2014.

41. Baker 2011.

42. On measles, see Stein et al. 2003, Dabbagh et al. 2018, and Patel et al. 2019. On smallpox, see Fenner et al. 1989. For the political context, see Manela 2010 and 2015.

43. Paul 1971.

44. Paul 1971; De Jesus 2007. See Jiang et al. 2007 for the genetic evidence.

45. Nathanson and Martin 1979; Nathanson and Kew 2010. See Dauer 1938 on the epidemiology of polio in the United States. The appearance of outbreaks in Sweden in the second half of the nineteenth century coincided too with expansion of public health measures such as the Public Health Act of 1874 (see Porter 1999, 98–99, though connections are not drawn with polio).

46. On global epidemiology, see Sabin 1949. On the possible importance of other enteroviruses, see Voroshilova 1989. See Nathanson and Martin 1979 and Nathanson and Kew 2010 for the hygiene hypothesis.

47. Oshinsky 2006.

48. Oshinsky 2006. See Roberts 2020, on the current status of the elimination program (which has hit setbacks over the past year or so).

49. Klebanoff 2005.

50. Davis 1956. See Packard 2016, 181–86, for the intellectual context.

51. The remarkable work of James Riley is a guide, one of the most sustained efforts to describe the decline in mortality from a truly global perspective. Riley 2001, 2005a and d, 2008.

52. Riley 2008, 55–61. On the adoption of German medicine, see Bowers 1979.

53. Riley 2008, 61–64.

54. See Riley 2008, 79–86. On the Rockefeller Foundation, see Farley 2004 and Palmer 2010.

55. Riley 2005c.

56. Patterson 1981.

57. Scott 1965; Patterson 1981; Engmann 1986. Compare Beck 1970 for East Africa. More generally, see Akyeampong 2006 for the changes in broader perspective in West Africa.

58. Patterson 1981.

59. Riley 2008, 65–74.

60. Caldwell, Reddy, and Caldwell 1988; Visaria and Visaria 1995; Dyson 2018.

61. Coale 1984; Caldwell 1986; Banister 1987. See Gross 2015 on the schistosomiasis campaign, emphasizing grassroots efforts.

62. Packard 2016.

63. See especially Preston and Nelson 1974; Preston 1975, 1976, and 1980; Caldwell 1986.

64. On polio, see Oshinsky 2006, 251. On DDT, see Kinkela 2011. On the geopolitics of smallpox, see Manela 2010 and 2015.

65. I follow Dyson 2010, a recent and authoritative overview, for the case that the mortality decline is the "remote" trigger of fertility decline, even if the mechanisms leading to fertility decline are various (that is, whether it is driven by exogenous desires for a surviving number of children, the cost of raising a child, declining need for private old age support, or contraceptive technologies). See Guinnane 2011 for a helpful survey of the issues, not entirely in agreement with this view. See Chesnais 1992 for a classic, data-rich survey.

66. Connelly 2008.

67. Development economists debate to what extent malaria impedes development directly—that is, through the channel of human health (Gallup and Sachs 2001; Sachs 2020)—or indirectly—that is, through the historical legacy of institutional development mediated by disease environments (Acemoglu, Johnson, and Robinson 2001; Acemoglu and Robinson 2012). On mosquitos' resistance (including resistance to other classes of insecticides, too, such as pyrethroids), see Hemingway and Ranson 2000; Hemingway, Field, and Vontas 2002; Hemingway et al. 2004; and Coleman et al. 2017.

68. Sharp and Hahn 2008; Pepin 2011; Faria et al. 2014.

69. Sepkowitz 2001; Whiteside 2008.

70. Pepin 2011.

71. Gao et al. 1999; Sharp and Hahn 2011; Pepin 2011.

72. Pepin 2011.

73. Pepin 2011.

74. Pepin 2011. See CDC 2021 for mortality and infection estimates in the United States.

75. Barnett and Whiteside 2006; Engel 2006; Iliffe 2006; Timberg and Halperin 2013.

76. See Hotez et al. 2006 and 2020 for the origins and development of the concept of neglected tropical diseases in the early 2000s.

77. Generally for these developments, see Clinton and Sridhar 2017; for their deeper historical context, see Packard 2016. For critical assessments, see McGoey 2015 and Mahajan 2019. For more positive assessments, see Reubi 2018 and Moran and Stevenson 2013. The "has quickly become" quote is from United Nations 2020.

78. Lederberg, Shope, and Oaks 1992.

79. Prophets (for the sake of example) include Garrett 1994; Quammen 2012; Wolfe 2013; and Osterholm and Olshaker 2017. For pandemics and cultural manifestations of fear such as zombie apocalypses, see for example Dehority 2020; Khan and Huremović 2019; Verran and Reyes 2018; and Lynteris 2016.

80. Crutzen and Stoermer 2000. See Zalasiewicz et al. 2019 for an overview and history of the concept, which had been used before Crutzen made it prominent. For one of the few efforts to think comprehensively about the microbiology of the Anthropocene, see Gillings and Paulsen 2014.

81. Human population growth and resource usage in the twentieth century have been construed as "the great acceleration" in McNeill and Engelke 2016. The "dominant animal" quote is from Ehrlich and Ehrlich 2009.

82. Lederberg, Shope, and Oaks 1992. On antibiotic resistance as evolution, see Salmond and Welch 2008 and Davies and Davies 2010.

83. For population projections, see Bongaarts 2009; Lutz and KC 2010; and Lutz, Butz, and KC 2017. See Otter 2013 on global meat production. See McKenna 2017 on the dangers of antibiotics in agriculture.

84. On urban population, see United Nations 2018.

85. McMichael 2017. See Hirschfeld 2020 on conflict in the Anthropocene.

86. Price-Smith 2009; Casadevall 2012; Jansen et al. 2014.

87. Morens and Fauci 2020.

88. Morens and Fauci 2020; Jones et al. 2008.

89. See Osterholm and Olshaker 2017, written before COVID-19, but prescient.

REFERENCES

Abreu, A. D. 1623. *Tratado de las Siete Enfermedades*. Lisbon.

Abt, M. C., and E. Pamer. 2014. "Commensal Bacteria Mediated Defenses against Pathogens." *Current Opinion in Immunology* 29: 16–22.

Abu-Lughod, J. L. 1989. *Before European Hegemony: The World System A.D. 1250–1350*. Oxford.

Acemoglu, D., and S. Johnson. 2007. "Disease and Development: The Effect of Life Expectancy on Economic Growth." *Journal of Political Economy* 115: 925–85.

Acemoglu, D., S. Johnson, and J. A. Robinson. 2001. "The Colonial Origins of Comparative Development: An Empirical Investigation." *American Economic Review* 91: 1369–401.

———. 2005. "The Rise of Europe: Atlantic Trade, Institutional Change, and Economic Growth." *American Economic Review* 95: 546–79.

Acemoglu, D., and J. A. Robinson. 2012. *Why Nations Fail: The Origins of Power, Prosperity and Poverty*. New York.

Achtman, M. 2016. "How Old Are Bacterial Pathogens?" *Proceedings of the Royal Society B* 283: 20160990.

Achtman, M., and M. Wagner. 2008. "Microbial Diversity and the Genetic Nature of Microbial Species." *Nature Reviews Microbiology* 6: 431–40.

Ackerknecht, E. H. 1945. *Malaria in the Upper Mississippi Valley, 1760–1900*. Baltimore.

———. 1948. "Anticontagionism between 1821 and 1867." *Bulletin of the History of Medicine* 22: 562–93.

Acuña-Soto, R., et al. 2002. "Megadrought and Megadeath in 16th Century Mexico." *Emerging Infectious Diseases* 8: 360–62.

Adams, F. 1849. *The Genuine Work of Hippocrates*. London.

Adams, H. 1918. *The Education of Henry Adams: An Autobiography*. Boston.

Adams, V., ed. 2016. *Metrics: What Counts in Global Health*. Durham.

Adler, R., and E. Mara. 2016. *Typhoid Fever: A History*. Jefferson.

Adshead, S. 1973. "The Seventeenth Century General Crisis in China." *Asian Profile* 2: 271–80.

Aghion, P., and P. Howitt. 2008. *The Economics of Growth*. Cambridge.

Aghion, P., P. Howitt, and F. Murtin. 2010. "The Relationship between Health and Growth: When Lucas Meets Nelson-Phelps." National Bureau of Economic Research working paper 15813. Cambridge.

Agricultural Research Service. 1962. *History of Hog Cholera Research in the United States Department of Agriculture 1884–1960*. Washington, DC.

Agrios, G. N. 2005. *Plant Pathology*. Burlington.

A'Hearn, B., J. Baten, and D. Crayen. 2009. "Quantitative Literacy: Age Heaping and the History of Human Capital." *Journal of Economic History* 69: 783–808.

Aiello, L. C., and P. Wheeler. 1995. "The Expensive-Tissue Hypothesis: The Brain and the Digestive System in Human and Primate Evolution." *Current Anthropology* 36: 199–221.

Akkermans, P. 2003. *The Archaeology of Syria: From Complex Hunter-Gatherers to Early Urban Societies (c. 16,000–300 BC)*. Cambridge.

Akyeampong, E. K. 2006. "Disease in West African History." In *Themes in West Africa's History*, edited by E. K. Akyeampong, 186–207. Athens.

Alazzam, I. M., S. M. Alazzam, and K. M. Al-Mazyid. 2013. "Plagues, Epidemics and Their Social and Economic Impact on the Egyptian Society during the Mameluke Period (648 Hegira/1250 AD –923 Hegira/1517 AD)." *Asian Culture and History* 5: 87.

Alchon, S. A. 2002. *Native Society and Disease in Colonial Ecuador*. Cambridge.

———. 2003. *A Pest in the Land: New World Epidemics in a Global Perspective*. Albuquerque.

Alcock, T. 1827. *An Essay on the Use of Chlorurets of Oxide of Sodium and of Lime as Powerful Disinfecting Agents*. London.

Alden, D., and J. C. Miller. 1987. "Out of Africa: The Slave Trade and the Transmission of Smallpox to Brazil, 1560–1831." *Journal of Interdisciplinary History* 18: 195–224.

Aldridge, A. O. 1949. "Franklin as Demographer." *Journal of Economic History* 9: 25–44.

Alexander, J. 2003. *Bubonic Plague in Early Modern Russia: Public Health and Urban Disaster*. Oxford.

Alfani, G. 2010. "Climate, Population and Famine in Northern Italy: General Tendencies and Malthusian Crisis, ca. 1450–1800." *Annales de démographie historique* 2: 23–53.

———. 2013a. *Calamities and the Economy in Renaissance Italy: The Grand Tour of the Horsemen of the Apocalypse*. Basingstoke.

———. 2013b. "Plague in Seventeenth-Century Europe and the Decline of Italy: An Epidemiological Hypothesis." *European Review of Economic History* 17: 408–30.

Alfani, G., and C. Ó Gráda, eds. 2017. *Famine in European History*. Cambridge.

Alfani, G., and M. Percoco. 2019. "Plague and Long-Term Development: The Lasting Effects of the 1629–30 Epidemic on the Italian Cities." *Economic History Review* 72: 1175–1201.

Ali, M., et al. 2015. "Updated Global Burden of Cholera in Endemic Countries." *PLoS Neglected Tropical Diseases* 9: e0003832.

Alias, H., et al. 2014. "Spatial Distribution of Malaria in Peninsular Malaysia from 2000 to 2009." *Parasites & Vectors* 7: 186.

Alibrandi, R. 2018. "When Early Modern Europe Caught the Flu. A Scientific Account of Pandemic Influenza in Sixteenth Century Sicily." *Medicina historica* 2: 19–26.

Alizon, S., and P.-O. Méthot. 2018. "Reconciling Pasteur and Darwin to Control Infectious Diseases." *PLoS Biology* 16: e2003815.

Alizon, S., and Y. Michalakis. 2015. "Adaptive Virulence Evolution: The Good Old Fitness-Based Approach." *Trends in Ecology and Evolution* 30: 248–54.

Alizon, S., et al. 2009. "Virulence Evolution and the Trade-Off Hypothesis: History, Current State of Affairs and the Future." *Journal of Evolutionary Biology* 22: 245–59.

Allen, M. W., et al. 2016. "Resource Scarcity Drives Lethal Aggression among Prehistoric Hunter-Gatherers in Central California." *Proceedings of the National Academy of Sciences* 113: 12120–25.

Allen, P. 1979. "The 'Justinianic' Plague." *Byzantion* 49: 5–20.

Allen, R. 2001. "The Great Divergence in European Wages and Prices from the Middle Ages to the First World War." *Explorations in Economic History* 38: 411–47.

Allen, R. C. 2009. *The British Industrial Revolution in Global Perspective.* Cambridge.

———. 2019. "Real Wages Once More: A Response to Judy Stephenson." *Economic History Review* 72: 738–54.

Allentoft, M. E., et al. 2015. "Population Genomics of Bronze Age Eurasia." *Nature* 522: 167–72.

Almond, D. 2006. "Is the 1918 Influenza Pandemic Over? Long-Term Effects of In Utero Influenza Exposure in the Post-1940 U.S. Population." *Journal of Political Economy* 114: 672–712.

Alsan, M. 2015. "The Effect of the Tsetse Fly on African Development." *American Economic Review* 105: 382–410.

Altizer, S., et al. 2003. "Social Organization and Parasite Risk in Mammals: Integrating Theory and Empirical Studies." *Annual Review of Ecology, Evolution, and Systematics* 34: 517–47.

Alvar, J., et al. 2012. "Leishmaniasis Worldwide and Global Estimates of Its Incidence." *PLoS One* 7: 35671.

Álvarez-Nogal, C., and L. Prados de la Escosura. 2013. "The Rise and Fall of Spain." *Economic History Review* 66: 1–37.

Alvord, J., et al. 1917. "Recent Progress and Tendencies in Municipal Water Supply in the United States." *Journal of the American Water Works Association* 4: 278–99.

Amanzougaghene, N., et al. 2020. "Where Are We with Human Lice? A Review of the Current State of Knowledge." *Frontiers in Cellular and Infection Microbiology* 9: 474.

American Public Health Association. 1885. *Disinfection and Disinfectants: Preliminary Report Made by the Committee on Disinfectants.* Baltimore.

Anderson, A., and C. E. Dibble, trans. 2012. *Florentine Codex: General History of the Things of New Spain.* Salt Lake City.

Anderson, D. M., et al. 2017. "Was the First Public Health Campaign Successful? The Tuberculosis Movement and Its Effect on Mortality." National Bureau of Economic Research working paper 23219.

Anderson, R. M., and R. M. May. 1991. *Infectious Diseases of Humans: Dynamics and Control.* Oxford.

Andersson, J. O., and S. G. E. Andersson. 2000. "A Century of Typhus, Lice and Rickettsia." *Research in Microbiology* 151: 143–50.

Ando, C. 2000. *Imperial Ideology and Provincial Loyalty in the Roman Empire.* Berkeley.

Andrade, T. 2016. *The Gunpowder Age: China, Military Innovation, and the Rise of the West in World History.* Princeton.

Andrews, K. R. 1991. *Ships, Money and Politics: Seafaring and Naval Enterprise in the Reign of Charles I.* Cambridge.

Andrews, T. 2021. "Influenza's Progress: The Great Epizootic Flu of 1872–1873 in the North American West." *Utah Historical Quarterly* 89: 4–30.

Angastiniotis, M., and B. Modell. 1998. "Global Epidemiology of Hemoglobin Disorders." *Annals of the New York Academy of Sciences* 850: 251–69.

Angelakis, E., Y. Bechah, and D. Raoult. 2016. "The History of Epidemic Typhus." In M. Drancourt and D. Raoult, eds. *Paleomicrobiology of Humans.* Washington, DC: 81–92.

Anthony, D. W. 2007. *The Horse, the Wheel, and Language: How Bronze-Age Riders from the Eurasian Steppes Shaped the Modern World*. Princeton.

Antón, S. C., and J. J. Snodgrass. 2012. "Origins and Evolution of Genus Homo: New Perspectives." *Current Anthropology* 53 (S6): S479–96.

Antonio, M. L., et al. 2019. "Ancient Rome: A Genetic Crossroads of Europe and the Mediterranean." *Science* 366: 708–14.

Antonovsky, A. 1967. "Social Class, Life Expectancy and Overall Mortality." *Milbank Memorial Fund Quarterly* 45: 31–73.

Aplin, K. P., et al. 2011. "Multiple Geographic Origins of Commensalism and Complex Dispersal History of Black Rats." *PLoS One* 6: e26357.

Appleby, A. B. 1978. *Famine in Tudor and Stuart England*. Stanford.

———. 1980. "The Disappearance of Plague: A Continuing Puzzle." *Economic History Review* 33: 161–73.

Appuhn, K. 2010. "Ecologies of Beef: Eighteenth-Century Epizootics and the Environmental History of Early Modern Europe." *Environmental History* 15: 268–87.

Arber, E. 1885. *The First Three English Books on America: [?1511]–1555 AD*. Birmingham.

Archer, S. 2016. "Colonialism and Other Afflictions: Rethinking Native American Health History." *History Compass* 14: 511–21.

———. 2018. *Sharks upon the Land: Colonialism, Indigenous Health, and Culture in Hawai'i, 1778–1855*. New York.

Archer, W., et al. 2014. "Early Pleistocene Aquatic Resource Use in the Turkana Basin." *Journal of Human Evolution* 77: 74–87.

Arisue, N., et al. 2019. "Apicoplast Phylogeny Reveals the Position of *Plasmodium vivax* Basal to the Asian Primate Malaria Parasite Clade." *Scientific Reports* 9: 7274.

Armitage, K. B. 2014. *Marmot Biology: Sociality, Individual Fitness and Population Dynamics*. Cambridge.

Armstrong, G. L., L. A. Conn, and R. W. Pinner. 1999. "Trends in Infectious Disease Mortality in the United States during the 20th Century." *Journal of the American Medical Association* 281: 61–66.

Arndt, J. 2009. *Der Dreissigjährige Krieg 1618–1648*. Stuttgart.

Arnold, D. 1993. *Colonizing the Body: State Medicine and Epidemic Disease in Nineteenth-Century India*. Berkeley.

Arora, N., et al. 2016. "Origin of Modern Syphilis and Emergence of a Contemporary Pandemic Cluster." *Nature Microbiology* 2: 1–6.

Arrizabalaga, J. 1993. "L'émergence du mal francese à Ferrare à la fin du XVe siècle à partir de chroniques locales de l'époque." *Maladies, Médecines et Sociétés. Approches historiques pour le present* 2: 36–46.

———. 2002. "Problematizing Retrospective Diagnosis in the History of Disease." *Asclepio* 54: 51–70.

Arrizabalaga, J., A. Cunningham, and O. P. Grell. 1999. *Health Care and Poor Relief in Counter-Reformation Europe*. London.

Arrizabalaga, J., J. Henderson, and R. K. French. 2014. *The Great Pox: The French Disease in Renaissance Europe*. New Haven.

Arvin, A., et al., eds. 2007. *Human Herpesviruses: Biology, Therapy, and Immunoprophylaxis.* Cambridge.

Asch, R. 1997. *The Thirty Years War: The Holy Roman Empire and Europe, 1618–1648.* Basingstoke.

Ashenburg, K. 2007. *The Dirt on Clean: An Unsanitized History.* New York.

Ashford, R., and W. Crewe. 2003. *Parasites of Homo Sapiens: An Annotated Checklist of the Protozoa, Helminths and Arthropods for Which We Are Home.* 2nd ed. Baton Rouge.

Ashley, E. A., and N. J. White. 2014. "The Duration of *Plasmodium falciparum* Infections." *Malaria Journal* 13: 500.

Ashraf, Q., and O. Galor. 2011. "Dynamics and Stagnation in the Malthusian Epoch." *American Economic Review* 101: 2003–41.

Aslanabadi, A., et al. 2015. "Emergence of Whooping Cough: Notes from Three Early Epidemics in Persia." *Lancet Infectious Diseases* 15: 1480–84.

Athreya, S., and X. Wu. 2017. "A Multivariate Assessment of the Dali Hominin Cranium from China: Morphological Affinities and Implications for Pleistocene Evolution in East Asia." *American Journal of Physical Anthropology* 164: 679–701.

Atkins, P. J. 1992. "White Poison? The Social Consequences of Milk Consumption, 1850–1930." *Social History of Medicine* 5: 207–27.

———. 1999. "Milk Consumption and Tuberculosis in Britain, 1850–1950." In *Order and Disorder: The Health Implications of Eating and Drinking in the Nineteenth and Twentieth Centuries,* edited by A. Fenton, 83–95. Edinburgh.

Attwood, S. W., F. A. Fatih, and E. S. Upatham. 2008. "DNA-Sequence Variation among Schistosoma Mekongi Populations and Related Taxa; Phylogeography and the Current Distribution of Asian Schistosomiasis." *PLoS Neglected Tropical Diseases* 2: 200.

Attwood, S. W., et al. 2007. "A DNA Sequence-Based Study of the Schistosoma Indicum (Trematoda: Digenea) Group: Population Phylogeny, Taxonomy and Historical Biogeography." *Parasitology* 134: 2009–20.

Audoin-Rouzeau, F. 2003. *Les chemins de la peste: le rat, la puce et l'homme.* Rennes.

Audoin-Rouzeau, F., and J.-D. Vigne. 1994. "La colonisation de l'Europe par le rat noir (*Rattus rattus*)." *Revue de paléobiologie* 13: 125–45.

Austin, R., et al. 2019. "To Curate the Molecular Past, Museums Need a Carefully Considered Set of Best Practices." *Proceedings of the National Academy of Sciences* 116: 1471–74.

Avanzi, C., et al. 2016. "Red Squirrels in the British Isles Are Infected with Leprosy Bacilli." *Science* 354: 744–47.

Ayalon, Y. 2015. *Natural Disasters in the Ottoman Empire: Plague, Famine, and Other Misfortunes.* New York.

Azad, A. F. 1990. "Epidemiology of Murine Typhus." *Annual Review of Entomology* 35: 553–69.

Azarian, T., et al. 2016. "Non-toxigenic Environmental Vibrio Cholerae O1 Strain from Haiti Provides Evidence of Pre-pandemic Cholera in Hispaniola." *Scientific Reports* 6: 36115.

Baali, F. 1988. *Society, State, and Urbanism: Ibn Khaldun's Sociological Thought.* Albany.

Babkin, I., and I. Babkina. 2015. "The Origin of the Variola Virus." *Viruses* 7: 1100–12.

Baer, K. A. 1949. "The First Description of Yellow Fever: Joam Ferreyra Da Rosa's 'Trattado Unico Da Constituiçam Pestilencial de Pernambuco.'" *Bulletin of the History of Medicine* 23: 48–56.

Bagnall, R. 2002. "The Effects of Plague: Model and Evidence." *Journal of Roman Archaeology* 15: 114–20.

Bagwell, P. S. 1988. *The Transport Revolution*. 2nd ed. London.

Baig, M., et al. 2019. "Phylogeography of the Black Rat *Rattus rattus* in India and the Implications for Its Dispersal History in Eurasia." *Biological Invasions* 21: 417–33.

Baigent, S. J., and J. W. McCauley. 2003. "Influenza Type A in Humans, Mammals and Birds: Determinants of Virus Virulence, Host-Range and Interspecies Transmission." *Bioessays* 25: 657–71.

Baird, J. K. 2013. "Evidence and Implications of Mortality Associated with Acute *Plasmodium vivax* Malaria." *Clinical Microbiology Reviews* 26: 36–57.

Baker, B., et al. 2020. "Advancing the Understanding of Treponemal Disease in the Past and Present." *American Journal of Physical Anthropology* 171: 5–41.

Baker, J. P. 2011. "The First Measles Vaccine." *Pediatrics* 128: 435–37.

Baker, M. N., and M. J. Taras. 1981. *The Quest for Pure Water: The History of Water Purification from the Earliest Records to the Twentieth Century*. Denver.

Baldwin, P. 1999. *Contagion and the State in Europe, 1830–1930*. Cambridge.

Balloux, F., and L. van Dorp. 2017. "What Are Pathogens, and What Have They Done to and for Us?" *BMC Biology* 15: 91.

Balmer, O., et al. 2011. "Phylogeography and Taxonomy of Trypanosoma Brucei." *PLoS Neglected Tropical Diseases* 5: e961.

Banister, J. 1987. "A Brief History of China's Population." In *The Population of Modern China*, edited by D. L. Poston and D. Yaukey, 51–57. Boston.

Banning, E., D. Rahimi, and J. Siggers. 1994. "The Late Neolithic of the Southern Levant: Hiatus, Settlement Shift or Observer Bias? The Perspective from Wadi Ziqlab." *Paléorient* 20: 151–64.

Banthia, J., and T. Dyson. 1999. "Smallpox in Nineteenth-Century India." *Population and Development Review* 25: 649–80.

Bányai, K., and V. E. Pitzer. 2016. "Molecular Epidemiology and Evolution of Rotaviruses." In *Viral Gastroenteritis*, edited by L. Svensson, 179–99. Cambridge.

Barcia, M. 2020. *The Yellow Demon of Fever: Fighting Disease in the Nineteenth-Century Transatlantic Slave Trade*. New Haven.

Barker, G. 2006. *The Agricultural Revolution in Prehistory: Why Did Foragers Become Farmers?* Oxford.

Barker, G., and C. Goucher, eds. 2015. *A World with Agriculture, 12,000 BCE–500 CE*. Vol. 2 of *The Cambridge World History*. Cambridge.

Barker, H. 2021. "Laying the Corpses to Rest: Grain, Embargoes, and *Yersinia pestis* in the Black Sea, 1346–48." *Speculum* 96: 97–126.

Barkhuus, A. 1943. "The Sanitary Conferences." *Ciba Symposia* 5: 1563–79.

Barnes, D. S. 1995. *The Making of a Social Disease: Tuberculosis in Nineteenth-Century France*. Berkeley.

———. 2006. *The Great Stink of Paris and the Nineteenth-Century Struggle against Filth and Germs*. Baltimore.

———. 2014. "Cargo, 'Infection,' and the Logic of Quarantine in the Nineteenth Century." *Bulletin of the History of Medicine* 88: 75–101.

Barnett, T., and A. Whiteside. 2006. *AIDS in the Twenty-First Century: Disease and Globalization.* 2nd ed. Basingstoke.

Bar-Oz, G., et al. 2019. "Ancient Trash Mounds Unravel Urban Collapse a Century before the End of Byzantine Hegemony in the Southern Levant." *Proceedings of the National Academy of Sciences of the United States of America* 116: 8239–48.

Barreiro, L. B., et al. 2009. "Evolutionary Dynamics of Human Toll-Like Receptors and Their Different Contributions to Host Defense." *PLoS Genetics* 5: 1000562.

Barrett, A. D. T., and S. Higgs. 2007. "Yellow Fever: A Disease That Has Yet to Be Conquered." *Annual Review of Entomology* 52: 209–29.

Barrett, R., and G. Armelagos. 2013. *An Unnatural History of Emerging Infections.* Oxford.

Barrett, R., et al. 1998. "Emerging and Re-emerging Infectious Diseases: The Third Epidemiologic Transition." *Annual Review of Anthropology* 27: 247–71.

Barry, J. M. 2004. *The Great Influenza: The Epic Story of the Deadliest Plague in History.* New York.

Bart, M. J., et al. 2014. "Global Population Structure and Evolution of *Bordetella pertussis* and Their Relationship with Vaccination." *MBio* 5: e01074-14.

Bartholow, R. 1867. *The Principles and Practice of Disinfection.* Cincinnati.

Bartsch, S. M., et al. 2016. "The Global Economic and Health Burden of Human Hookworm Infection." *PLoS Neglected Tropical Diseases* 10: e0004922.

Bartsocas, C. 1966. "Two Fourteenth Century Greek Descriptions of the 'Black Death.'" *Journal of the History of Medicine and Allied Sciences* 21: 394–400.

Barua, D. 1992. "History of Cholera." In *Cholera*, edited by D. Barua and W. B. Greenough, 1–36. Boston.

Barua, D., and W. B. Greenough, eds. 1992. *Cholera.* Boston.

Bar-Yosef, O. 2001. "From Sedentary Foragers to Village Hierarchies: The Emergence of Social Institutions." *Proceedings of the British Academy* 110: 1–38.

Bashford, A. 2004. *Imperial Hygiene: A Critical History of Colonialism, Nationalism and Public Health.* Basingstoke.

Baten, J., et al. 2010. "Evolution of Living Standards and Human Capital in China in the 18–20th Centuries: Evidences from Real Wages, Age Heaping, and Anthropometrics." *Explorations in Economic History* 47: 347–59.

Battle, K. E., et al. 2012. "The Global Public Health Significance of *Plasmodium vivax*." *Advances in Parasitology* 80: 1–111.

———. 2019. "Mapping the Global Endemicity and Clinical Burden of *Plasmodium vivax*, 2000–17: A Spatial and Temporal Modelling Study." *Lancet* 394: 332–43.

Bauch, M. 2020. "'Just the Flu' in 1323? The Case Study of a Highly Contagious Epidemic with Low Mortality and Its Possible Origins in Late Medieval Europe." *Journal for the History of the Environment and Society* 5: 53–63.

Bauer, T. 2020. *Warum es kein islamisches Mittelalter gab: Das Erbe der Antike und der Orient.* Munich.

Baum, D. A., and S. D. Smith. 2013. *Tree Thinking: An Introduction to Phylogenetic Biology.* Greenwood Village.

Bayly, C. A. 1989. *Imperial Meridian: The British Empire and the World, 1780–1830.* London.

———. 2004. *The Birth of the Modern World, 1750–1914: Global Connections and Comparisons.* Malden.

Beach, B., et al. 2016. "Typhoid Fever, Water Quality, and Human Capital Formation." *Journal of Economic History* 76: 41–75.

Bechah, Y., et al. 2008. "Epidemic Typhus." *Lancet Infectious Diseases* 8: 417–26.

Beck, A. 1970. *A History of the British Medical Administration of East Africa, 1900–1950.* Cambridge.

Beck, A., et al. 2013. "Phylogeographic Reconstruction of African Yellow Fever Virus Isolates Indicates Recent Simultaneous Dispersal into East and West Africa." *PLoS Neglected Tropical Diseases* 7: 1910.

Beinart, W., and K. Middleton. 2004. "Plant Transfers in Historical Perspective: A Review Article." *Environment and History* 10: 3–29.

Belcher, T., and A. Preston. 2015. "*Bordetella pertussis* Evolution in the (Functional) Genomics Era." *FEMS Pathogens and Disease* 73: ftv064.

Belfer-Cohen, A., L. A. Schepartz, and B. Arensburg. 1991. "New Biological Data for the Natufian Populations in Israel." In *The Natufian Culture in the Levant*, edited by O. Bar-Yosef and F. Valla, 411–24. Ann Arbor.

Belich, J. 2009. *Replenishing the Earth: The Settler Revolution and the Rise of the Angloworld.* Oxford.

———. 2016. "The Black Death and the Spread of Europe." In *The Prospect of Global History*, edited by J. Belich et al., 93–107. Oxford.

Bell, D. P. 2019. *Plague in the Early Modern World: A Documentary History*. Milton.

Bello, D. A. 2005. "To Go Where No Han Could Go for Long." *Modern China* 31: 283–317.

Bellwood, P. S. 2005. *The First Farmers: The Origins of Agricultural Societies.* Malden.

Beloch, J. 1886. *Die Bevölkerung der griechisch-römischen Welt.* Leipzig.

Benedict, C. 1996. *Bubonic Plague in Nineteenth Century China.* Stanford.

Benedict, P., and M. Gutmann, eds. 2005. *Early Modern Europe: From Crisis to Stability.* Newark.

Benedictow, O. J. 2004. *The Black Death, 1346–1353: The Complete History.* Woodbridge.

———. 2016. *The Black Death and Later Plague Epidemics in the Scandinavian Countries.* Warsaw.

Bengtsson, T., M. Dribe, and J. Helgertz. 2020. "When Did the Health Gradient Emerge? Social Class and Adult Mortality in Southern Sweden, 1813–2015." *Demography* 57: 953–77.

Bengtsson, T., G. Fridlizius, and R. Ohlsson, eds. 1984. *Pre-industrial Population Change: The Mortality Decline and Short-Term Population Movements.* Stockholm.

Bengtsson, T., and F. van Poppel. 2011. "Socioeconomic Inequalities in Death from Past to Present: An Introduction." *Explorations in Economic History* 48: 343–56.

Bengtsson, T., et al., eds. 2004. *Life under Pressure: Mortality and Living Standards in Europe and Asia, 1700–1900.* Cambridge.

Bennett, M. 2020. *War against Smallpox: Edward Jenner and the Global Spread of Vaccination.* Cambridge.

Benovitz, N. 2014. "The Justinianic Plague: Evidence from Dated Greek Epitaphs of Byzantine Palestine and Arabia." *Journal of Roman Archaeology* 27: 487–98.

Bentley, J., S. Subrahmanyam, and M. Wiesner-Hanks. 2015. *The Construction of a Global World, 1400–1800 CE.* 2 parts. Vol. 6 of *The Cambridge World History.* Cambridge.

Bergquist, R., H. Kloos, and A. Adugna. 2016. "Schistosomiasis: Paleopathological Perspectives and Historical Notes." In *Schistosoma: Biology, Pathology and Control*, edited by B. Jamieson, 9–33. Boca Raton.

Bernard, K. 2012. "The Genus *Corynebacterium* and Other Medically Relevant Coryneform-Like Bacteria." *Journal of Clinical Microbiology* 50: 3152–58.

Bernardo, A. 2005. *Letters on Familiar Matters*. New York.

Besnard, G., et al. 2013. "The Complex History of the Olive Tree: From Late Quaternary Diversification of Mediterranean Lineages to Primary Domestication in the Northern Levant." *Proceedings of the Royal Society B: Biological Sciences* 280: 20122833.

Bessen, D. E. 2009. "Population Biology of the Human Restricted Pathogen, *Streptococcus pyogenes*." *Infection, Genetics and Evolution* 9: 581–93.

Bessen, D. E., et al. 2015. "Molecular Epidemiology and Genomics of Group A *Streptococcus*." *Infection, Genetics and Evolution* 33: 393–418.

Bettinger, R. 2016. "Prehistoric Hunter-Gatherer Population Growth Rates Rival Those of Agriculturalists." *Proceedings of the National Academy of Sciences* 113: 812–14.

Beveridge, W. I. B. 1991. "The Chronicle of Influenza Epidemics." *History and Philosophy of the Life Sciences* 13: 223–34.

Bhat, P. N. M. 1989. "Mortality and Fertility in India, 1881–1961: A Reassessment." In *India's Historical Demography: Studies in Famine, Disease and Society*, edited by T. Dyson, 73–118. London.

Bhatt, S., et al. 2013. "The Global Distribution and Burden of Dengue." *Nature* 496: 504–7.

Bhattacharyya, D. 2018. *Empire and Ecology in the Bengal Delta: The Making of Calcutta*. Cambridge.

Binford, L. R. 2001. *Constructing Frames of Reference: An Analytical Method for Archaeological Theory Building Using Hunter-Gatherer and Environmental Data Sets*. Berkeley.

Biraben, J. N. 1975. *Les hommes et la peste en France et dans les pays européens et méditerranéens*. Paris.

Biraben, J.-N., and J. Le Goff. 1969. "La Peste dans le Haut Moyen Age." *Annales. Histoire, Sciences Sociales* 24: 1484–1510.

Birley, A. 1987. *Marcus Aurelius: A Biography*. New Haven.

Bishop-Lilly, K. A., et al. 2013. "Genome Sequencing of Four Strains of Rickettsia Prowazekii, the Causative Agent of Epidemic Typhus, Including One Flying Squirrel Isolate." *Genome Announcements* 1: e00399–13.

Black, J. 1991. *A Military Revolution?: Military Change and European Society 1550–1800*. Atlantic Highlands.

———. 1999. *War in the Early Modern World*. Boulder.

———. 2011. *War in European History, 1660–1792: The Essential Bibliography*. Dulle.

Black, W. 1788. *A Comparative View of the Mortality of the Human Species, at All Ages: And of the Diseases and Casualties by Which They Are Destroyed or Annoyed*. London.

Blake, J. B. 1959. *Public Health in the Town of Boston, 1630–1822*. Cambridge.

Blake, J. W. 1942. *Europeans in West Africa: 1450–1560*. London.

Blake, L., and M. Garcia-Blanco. 2014. "Human Genetic Variation and Yellow Fever Mortality during 19th Century US Epidemics." *MBio* 5: e01253-14.

Blancou, J. 1995. "History of Disinfection from Early Times until the End of the 18th Century." *Revue scientifique et technique* 14: 21–39.

Blayo, Y. 1975. "La Mortalité en France de 1740 a 1829." *Population* 30: 123–42.

Bleakley, H. 2007. "Disease and Development: Evidence from the American South." *Journal of the European Economic Association* 1: 376–86.

———. 2010. "Malaria Eradication in the Americas: A Retrospective Analysis of Childhood Exposure." *American Economic Journal: Applied Economics* 2: 1–45.

Blom, P. 2019. *Nature's Mutiny: How the Little Ice Age of the Long Seventeenth Century Transformed the West and Shaped the Present.* New York.

Bloom, D., and D. Canning. 2000. "The Health and Wealth of Nations." *Science* 287: 1207–9.

———. 2007. "Mortality Traps and the Dynamics of Health Transitions." *Proceedings of the National Academy of Sciences* 104: 16044–49.

Bloom, D., D. Canning, and B. Graham. 2003. "Longevity and Life Cycle Savings." *Scandinavian Journal of Economics* 105: 319–38.

Blouin, K. 2014. *Triangular Landscapes: Environment, Society, and the State in the Nile Delta under Roman Rule.* Oxford.

Blurton Jones, N. G. 2016. *Demography and Evolutionary Ecology of Hadza Hunter-Gatherers.* Cambridge.

Bocquet-Appel, J.-P. 2011. "When the World's Population Took Off: The Springboard of the Neolithic Demographic Transition." *Science* 333: 560–61.

Bocquet-Appel, J.-P., and O. Bar-Yosef, eds. 2008. *The Neolithic Demographic Transition and Its Consequences.* Dordrecht.

Boesch, C., and H. Boesch-Achermann. 2000. *The Chimpanzees of the Taï Forest: Behavioural Ecology and Evolution.* Oxford.

Boivin, N., et al. 2016. "Ecological Consequences of Human Niche Construction: Examining Long-Term Anthropogenic Shaping of Global Species Distributions." *Proceedings of the National Academy of Sciences* 113: 6388–96.

Bolnick, D. A., et al. 2016. "Native American Genomics and Population Histories." *Annual Review of Anthropology* 45: 319–40.

Bolt, F., et al. 2010. "Multilocus Sequence Typing Identifies Evidence for Recombination and Two Distinct Lineages of *Corynebacterium diphtheriae*." *Journal of Clinical Microbiology* 48: 4177–85.

Bolt, J., et al. 2018. "Maddison Project Database 2018." Groningen Growth and Development Centre, University of Groningen. https://www.rug.nl/ggdc/historicaldevelopment/maddison/releases/maddison-project-database-2018.

Bonds, M., A. Dobson, and D. Keenan. 2012. "Disease Ecology, Biodiversity, and the Latitudinal Gradient in Income." *PLoS Biology* 12: e1001456.

Bonelli, F. 1966. "La malaria nella storia demografica ed economica d'Italia: primi lineament di una ricerca." *Studi storici* 7: 659–87.

Bonfiglioli, B., P. Brasili, and M. G. Belcastro. 2003. "Dento-Alveolar Lesions and Nutritional Habits of a Roman Imperial Age Population (1st–4th c. AD): Quadrella (Molise, Italy)." *Homo* 54: 36–56.

Bongaarts, J. 2009. "Human Population Growth and the Demographic Transition." *Philosophical Transactions of the Royal Society B: Biological Sciences* 364: 2985–90.

Booker, J. 2007. *Maritime Quarantine: The British Experience, c. 1650–1900*. London.

Booss, J. 2019. "Survival of the Pilgrims: A Reevaluation of the Lethal Epidemic among the Wampanoag." *Historical Journal of Massachusetts* 47: 108–33.

Borah, W., and S. F. Cook. 1963. *The Aboriginal Population of Central Mexico on the Eve of the Spanish Conquest*. Berkeley.

Bordes, F., D. T. Blumstein, and S. Morand. 2007. "Rodent Sociality and Parasite Diversity." *Biology Letters* 3: 692–94.

Borsch, S. 2005. *The Black Death in Egypt and England: A Comparative Study*. Austin.

Borsch, S., and T. Sabraa. 2016. "Plague Mortality in Late Medieval Cairo: Quantifying the Plague Outbreaks of 833/1430 and 864/1460." *Mamlūk Studies Review* 19: 115–48.

Bos, K. I., et al. 2011. "A Draft Genome of *Yersinia pestis* from Victims of the Black Death." *Nature* 478: 506–10.

———. 2014. "Pre-Columbian Mycobacterial Genomes Reveal Seals as a Source of New World Human Tuberculosis." *Nature* 514: 494–97.

———. 2016. "Eighteenth Century *Yersinia pestis* Genomes Reveal the Long-Term Persistence of an Historical Plague Focus." *Elife* 5: e12994.

Boserup, E. 1965. *The Conditions of Agricultural Growth: The Economics of Agrarian Change under Population Pressure*. London.

———. 1981. *Population and Technological Change: A Study of Long-Term Trends*. Chicago.

Boucekkine, R., D. de la Croix, and O. Licandro. 2004. "Early Mortality Declines at the Dawn of Modern Growth." *Scandinavian Journal of Economics* 105: 401–18.

Boucekkine, R., D. de la Croix, and D. Peeters. 2007a. "Disentangling the Demographic Determinants of the English Take-Off: 1530–1860." CORE discussion paper no. 2007/33.

———. 2007b. "Early Literacy Achievements, Population Density, and the Transition to Modern Growth." *Journal of the European Economic Association* 5: 183–226.

Boucher, Y. 2016. "Sustained Local Diversity of *Vibrio cholerae* 01 Biotypes in a Previously Cholera-Free Country." *MBio* 7: e00570–16.

Boucher, Y., F. Orata, and M. Alam. 2015. "The Out-of-the-Delta Hypothesis: Dense Human Populations in Low-Lying River Deltas Served as Agents for the Evolution of a Deadly Pathogen." *Frontiers in Microbiology* 6: 1120.

Bourdelais, P. 2006. *Epidemics Laid Low: A History of What Happened in Rich Countries*. Translated by B. K. Holland. Baltimore.

Bourdelais, P., and M. Demonet. 1996. "The Evolution of Mortality in an Industrial Town: Le Creusot in the Nineteenth Century." *History of the Family* 1: 183–204.

Bourdelais, P., and J.-Y. Raulot. 1987. *Une peur bleue: histoire du choléra en France 1832–1854*. Paris.

Bourke, P. M. A. 1964. "Emergence of Potato Blight, 1843–46." *Nature* 203: 805–8.

Boutellis, A., L. Abi-Rached, and D. Raoult. 2014. "The Origin and Distribution of Human Lice in the World." *Infection, Genetics, and Evolution* 23: 209–17.

Bowers, J. Z. 1979. "The Adoption of German Medicine in Japan: The Decision and the Beginning." *Bulletin of the History of Medicine* 53: 57–80.

Boyd, R. 1994. "The Pacific Northwest Measles of Epidemic of 1847–1848." *Oregon Historical Quarterly* 95: 6–47.

Boylston, A. 2012a. "Daniel Sutton, a Forgotten 18th Century Clinician Scientist." *Journal of the Royal Society of Medicine* 105: 85–87.

————. 2012b. "The Origins of Inoculation." *Journal of the Royal Society of Medicine* 105: 309–13.

Bradford, W. 1952. *Of Plymouth Plantation, 1620–1647*. New Brunswick. First published 1651.

Braje, T. J., and J. M. Erlandson. 2013. "Human Acceleration of Animal and Plant Extinctions: A Late Pleistocene, Holocene, and Anthropocene Continuum." *Anthropocene* 4: 14–23.

Bramanti, B., et al. 2019. "The Third Plague Pandemic in Europe." *Proceedings of the Royal Society B* 286: 20182429.

Bratton, T. 1988. "The Identity of the New England Indian Epidemic of 1616–19." *Bulletin of the History of Medicine* 62: 351–83.

Braudel, F. 1966. *La Méditerranée et le monde méditerranéen à l'époque de Philippe II*. 2nd ed. Paris.

Braun, D. R., et al. 2010. "Early Hominin Diet Included Diverse Terrestrial and Aquatic Animals 1.95 Ma in East Turkana, Kenya." *Proceedings of the National Academy of Sciences* 107: 10002–7.

Brenner, R. 2003. *Merchants and Revolution: Commercial Change, Political Conflict, and London's Overseas Traders, 1550–1653*. Princeton.

Bresson, A. 2020. "Fates of Rome." *Journal of Roman Studies* 110: 233–46.

Brier, C. E. 2013. "Tending Our Vines: From the Correspondence and Writings of Richard Peters and John Jay." *Pennsylvania History* 80: 85–111.

Briggs, A. 1961. *Cholera and Society in the Nineteenth Century*. Oxford.

Brinkworth, J. F., and K. Pechenkina, eds. 2013. *Primates, Pathogens, and Evolution*. New York.

Brite, E. B., and J. M. Marston. 2013. "Environmental Change, Agricultural Innovation, and the Spread of Cotton Agriculture in the Old World." *Journal of Anthropological Archaeology* 32: 39–53.

Brites, D., et al. 2018. "A New Phylogenetic Framework for the Animal-Adapted *Mycobacterium tuberculosis* Complex." *Frontiers in Microbiology* 9: 2820.

Broadberry, S. 2013. "Accounting for the Great Divergence." Economic history working paper 184/2013. London School of Political Science.

Broadberry, S., J. Custodis, and B. Gupta. 2015. "India and the Great Divergence: An Anglo-Indian Comparison of GDP per Capita, 1600–1871." *Explorations in Economic History* 55: 58–75.

Broadberry, S., H. Guan, and D. Li. 2018. "China, Europe and the Great Divergence: A Study in Historical National Accounting, 980–1850." *Journal of Economic History* 78: 955–1000.

Broadberry, S., and B. Gupta. 2006. "The Early Modern Great Divergence: Wages, Prices and Economic Development in Europe and Asia, 1500–1800." *Economic History Review* 59: 2–31.

Broadberry, S., et al. 2015. *British Economic Growth, 1270–1870*. New York.

Brock, T. D. 1988. *Robert Koch: A Life in Medicine and Bacteriology*. Madison.

Brömer, R. 2000. "The First Global Map of the Distribution of Human Diseases: Friedrich Schnurrer's 'Charte über die Geographische Ausbreitung der Krankheiten' (1827)." *Medical History* 44: 176–85.

Brook, C. E., and A. P. Dobson. 2015. "Bats as 'Special' Reservoirs for Emerging Zoonotic Pathogens." *Trends in Microbiology* 23: 172–80.

Brook, T. 2010. *The Troubled Empire: China in the Yuan and Ming Dynasties*. Cambridge.

————. 2019. *The Great State: China and the World*. London.

————. 2020. "Comparative Pandemics: The Tudor-Stuart and Wanli-Chongzhen Years of Pestilence, 1567–1666." *Journal of Global History* 15: 363–79.

Brooke, J. 2014. *Climate Change and the Course of Global History: A Rough Journey*. Cambridge.

Brooke, J., and C. Otter. 2016. "Concluding Remarks: The Organic Anthropocene." *Eighteenth-Century Studies* 49: 281–302.

Brosch, R., et al. 2002. "A New Evolutionary Scenario for the *Mycobacterium tuberculosis* Complex." *Proceedings of the National Academy of Sciences* 99: 3684–89.

Brown, J. E., et al. 2013. "Human Impacts Have Shaped Historical and Recent Evolution in *Aedes aegypti*, the Dengue and Yellow Fever Mosquito." *Evolution* 68: 514–25.

Brown, K. 2008. "From Ubombo to Mkhuzi: Disease, Colonial Science, and the Control of Nagana (Livestock Trypanosomosis) in Zululand, South Africa, c. 1894–1953." *Journal of the History of Medicine and Allied Sciences* 63: 285–322.

Brown, K., and D. Gilfoyle, eds. 2010. *Healing the Herds: Disease, Livestock Economies, and the Globalization of Veterinary Medicine*. Athens.

Brown, M. 2008. "From Foetid Air to Filth: The Cultural Transformation of British Epidemiological Thought, ca. 1780–1848." *Bulletin of the History of Medicine* 82: 515–44.

Brown, T. A., et al. 2009. "The Complex Origins of Domesticated Crops in the Fertile Crescent." *Trends in Ecology & Evolution* 24: 103–9.

Browne, E. J. 1995. *Charles Darwin: A Biography*. London.

Bruce-Chwatt, L. J., and J. de Zulueta. 1980. *The Rise and Fall of Malaria in Europe: A Historico-Epidemiological Study*. Oxford.

Brun, R., and J. Blum. 2012. "Human African Trypanosomiasis." *Infectious Disease Clinics* 26: 261–73.

Brun, R., et al. 2010. "Human African Trypanosomiasis." *Lancet* 375: 148–59.

Brunt, P. A. 1987. *Italian Manpower, 225 BC–AD 14*. Oxford.

Bruschi, F., ed. 2014. *Helminth Infections and Their Impact on Global Public Health*. Vienna.

Bruun, C. 2007. "The Antonine Plague and the 'Third-Century Crisis.'" In *Crises and the Roman Empire: Proceedings of the Seventh Workshop of the International Network Impact of Empire, Nijmegen, June 20–24, 2006*, edited by O. Hekster, G. de Kleijn, and D. Slootjes, 201–18. Leiden.

Bryant, J. E., E. C. Holmes, and A. D. T. Barrett. 2007. "Out of Africa: A Molecular Perspective on the Introduction of Yellow Fever Virus into the Americas." *PLoS Pathogens* 3: e75.

Bryder, L. 1988. *Below the Magic Mountain: A Social History of Tuberculosis in Twentieth-Century Britain*. Oxford.

Brynildsrud, O. B., et al. 2018. "Global Expansion of *Mycobacterium tuberculosis* Lineage 4 Shaped by Colonial Migration and Local Adaptation." *Science Advances* 4: 5869.

Budd, W. 1873. *Typhoid Fever: Its Nature, Mode of Spreading, and Prevention*. London.

Buell, P. 2012. "Qubilai and the Rats." *Sudhoffs Archiv* 96: 127–44.

Buer, M. C. 1926. *Health, Wealth and Population in the Early Days of the Industrial Revolution*. London.

Buikstra, J. 1992. "Diet and Disease in Late Prehistory." In *Disease and Demography in the Americas*, edited by J. Verano and D. Ubelaker, 87–101. Washington, DC.

Bulmus, B. 2012. *Plague, Quarantines and Geopolitics in the Ottoman Empire*. Edinburgh.

Burger, P., and N. Palmieri. 2014. "Estimating the Population Mutation Rate from a *de novo* Assembled Bactrian Camel Genome and Cross-Species Comparison with Dromedary ESTs." *Journal of Heredity* 105: 839–46.

Burkhardt, J. 1992. *Der Dreissigjährige Krieg*. Frankfurt am Main.

Burnard, T. 1996. "European Migration to Jamaica, 1655–1780." *William and Mary Quarterly* 53: 769–96.

———. 1999. "'The Countrie Continues Sicklie': White Mortality in Jamaica, 1655–1780." *Society for the Social History of Medicine* 12: 45–72.

———. 2015. *Planters, Merchants, and Slaves: Plantation Societies in British America, 1650–1820*. Chicago.

Burnet, F. M., and D. O. White. 1972. *Natural History of Infectious Disease*. 4th ed. Cambridge.

Burton, F. 2009. *Fire: The Spark That Ignited Human Evolution*. Albuquerque.

Büscher, P., et al. 2017. "Human African Trypanosomiasis." *Lancet* 390: 2397–409.

Busvine, J. R. 1980. *Insects and Hygiene: The Biology and Control of Insect Pests of Medical and Domestic Importance*. 3rd ed. Boston.

Byers, K., R. Guerrant, and B. Farr. 2001. "Fecal-Oral Transmission." In *Epidemiologic Methods for the Study of Infectious Diseases*, edited by J. Thomas and D. Weber, 228–48. Oxford.

Bynum, H. 2012. *Spitting Blood: The History of Tuberculosis*. Oxford.

Bynum, W. F. 1993. "Policing Hearts of Darkness: Aspects of the International Sanitary Conferences." *History and Philosophy of the Life Sciences* 15: 421–34.

Cagle, H. 2018. *Assembling the Tropics: Science and Medicine in Portugal's Empire, 1450–1700*. Cambridge.

Caldwell, J. C. 1986. "Routes to Low Mortality in Poor Countries." *Population and Development Review* 12: 171–220.

Caldwell, J. C., P. Reddy, and P. Caldwell. 1988. *The Causes of Demographic Change: Experimental Research in South India*. Madison.

Calisher, C. H., et al. 2006. "Bats: Important Reservoir Hosts of Emerging Viruses." *Clinical Microbiology Reviews* 19: 531–45.

Callahan, G. N. 2007. *Infection: The Uninvited Universe*. New York.

Calvignac-Spencer, S., et al. 2012. "Wild Great Apes as Sentinels and Sources of Infectious Disease." *Clinical Microbiology and Infection* 18: 521–27.

Cambier, C. J., S. Falkow, and L. Ramakrishnan. 2014. "Host Evasion and Exploitation Schemes of *Mycobacterium tuberculosis*." *Cell* 159: 1497–509.

Cambier, C. J., et al. 2014. "Mycobacteria Manipulate Macrophage Recruitment through Coordinated Use of Membrane Lipids." *Nature* 505: 218–22.

Cameron, A. 1985. *Procopius and the Sixth Century*. Berkeley.

Cameron, C. M., P. Kelton, and A. C. Swedlund, eds. 2015. *Beyond Germs: Native Depopulation in North America*. Tucson.

Campbell, B. M. S. 2016. *The Great Transition: Climate, Disease and Society in the Late Medieval World*. Cambridge.

Camus, A. 1948. *The Plague*. Translated by S. Gilbert. New York.

Cao, A., and R. Galanello. 2010. "Beta-thalassemia." *Genetics in Medicine* 12: 61–76.

Capitanio, J. P. 2012. "Social Processes and Disease in Nonhuman Primates: Introduction to the Special Section." *American Journal of Primatology* 74: 491–96.

Cappers, R. 2006, *Roman Foodprints at Berenike: Archaeobotanical Evidence of Subsistence and Trade in the Eastern Desert of Egypt*. Los Angeles.

Carlson, C. C., G. J. Armelagos, and A. L. Magennis. 1992. "Impact of Disease on the Precontact and Early Historic Populations of New England and the Maritimes." In *Disease and Demography in the Americas*, edited by J. Verano and D. Ubelaker, 141–53. Washington, DC.

Carlson, C. J., et al. 2019. "Global Estimates of Mammalian Viral Diversity Accounting for Host Sharing." *Nature Ecology & Evolution* 3: 1070–75.

Carlton, J. M., A. Das, and A. A. Escalante. 2013. "Genomics, Population Genetics and Evolutionary History of *Plasmodium vivax*." *Advances in Parasitology* 81: 203–22.

Carmichael, A. 1986. *Plague and the Poor in Renaissance Florence*. Cambridge.

———. 1993. "Diphtheria." In *The Cambridge World History of Human Disease*, edited by K. Kiple, 680–83. Cambridge.

———. 1998. "Epidemics and State Medicine in Fifteenth-Century Milan." In *Medicine from the Black Death to the French Disease*, edited by R. French, J. Arrizabalaga, and A. Cunningham, 221–47. Aldershot.

———. 2014. "Plague Persistence in Western Europe: A Hypothesis." *Medieval Globe* 1: 157–91.

Carmichael, A., and A. Silverstein. 1987. "Smallpox in Europe before the Seventeenth Century: Virulent Killer or Benign Disease?" *Journal of the History of Medicine* 42: 147–68.

Carmody, R. 2017 "Evolution of the Human Dietary Niche: Quest for High Quality." In *Chimpanzees and Human Evolution*, edited by M. Muller, R. Wrangham, and D. Pilbeam, 311–38. Cambridge.

Carotenuto, F., et al. 2016. "Venturing Out Safely: The Biogeography of *Homo erectus* Dispersal out of Africa." *Journal of Human Evolution* 95: 1–12.

Carpenter, S. J., and W. J. LaCasse. 1974. *Mosquitoes of North America*. Berkeley.

Carrasco, D. 2012. *The Aztecs: A Very Short Introduction*. Oxford.

Carrillo-Esper, R., et al. 2018. "Opera Medicinalia. The First Book of Medicine at American Continent Written by Dr. Francisco Bravo and Printed in 1570 at Novohispana Capital." *Medicinia Interna de México* 34: 113–26.

Carter, H. R. 1931. *Yellow Fever: An Epidemiological and Historical Study of Its Place of Origin*. Baltimore.

Carter, R., and K. N. Mendis. 2002. "Evolutionary and Historical Aspects of the Burden of Malaria." *Clinical Microbiology Reviews* 15: 564–94.

Carter, S. B. 2006. *Historical Statistics of the United States*. Cambridge.

Carver, C. 2017. *Immune: How Your Body Defends and Protects You*. London.

Casadevall, A. 2012. "The Future of Biological Warfare." *Microbial Biotechnology* 5: 584–87.

Casals, F., et al. 2011. "Genetic Adaptation of the Antibacterial Human Innate Immunity Network." *BMC Evolutionary Biology* 11: 1–11.

Casanova, J.-L., and L. Abel. 2018. "Human Genetics of Infectious Diseases: Unique Insights into Immunological Redundancy." *Seminars in Immunology* 36: 1–12.

Casanova, J.-L., L. Abel, and L. Quintana-Murci. 2013. "Immunology Taught by Human Genetics." *Cold Spring Harbor Symposia on Quantitative Biology* 78: 157–72.

Cashdan, E. 2014. "Biogeography of Human Infectious Disease: A Global Historical Analysis." *PLoS One* 9: e106752.

Casson, L. 1989. *The Periplus Maris Erythraei: Text with Introduction, Translation, and Commentary*. Princeton.

Cathey, J. T., and J. S. Marr. 2014. "Yellow Fever, Asia and the East African Slave Trade." *Transactions of the Royal Society of Tropical Medicine and Hygiene* 108: 252–57.

CDC (Centers for Disease Control and Prevention). 2012. *Principles of Epidemiology in Public Health Practice: An Introduction to Applied Epidemiology and Biostatistics*. 3rd ed. Atlanta.

———. 2021. "HIV: Basic Statistics." Accessed February 1, 2021. https://www.cdc.gov/hiv/basics/statistics.html.

Chadwick, E. 1965. *Report on the Sanitary Condition of the Labouring Population of Great Britain*. Edited by M. W. Flinn. Edinburgh. First published 1842.

Chakrabarti, P. 2010. *Materials and Medicine: Trade, Conquest and Therapeutics in the Eighteenth Century*. New York.

Chalmers, L. 1776. *An Account of the Weather and Diseases of South-Carolina*. London.

Chan, L.-J., et al. 2020. "*Plasmodium vivax* Reticulocyte Binding Proteins for Invasion into Reticulocytes." *Cellular Microbiology* 22: e13110.

Chandler, T. 1987. *Four Thousand Years of Urban Growth: An Historical Census*. Lewiston.

Chandra, S., G. Kuljanin, and J. Wray. 2012. "Mortality from the Influenza Pandemic of 1918–1919: The Case of India." *Demography* 49: 857–65.

Chaney, E. 2018. "Medieval Origins: A Review Essay on Campbell's *The Great Transition*." *Journal of Economic Literature* 56: 643–56.

Chang, C.-F. 1996. "Aspects of Smallpox and Its Significance in Chinese History." PhD diss., School of Oriental and African Studies, University of London.

———. 2002. "Disease and Its Impact on Politics, Diplomacy, and the Military: The Case of Smallpox and the Manchus (1613–1795)." *Journal of the History of Medicine and Allied Sciences* 57: 177–97.

Chapman, J. 2019. "The Contribution of Infrastructure Investment to Britain's Urban Mortality Decline 1861–1900." *Economic History Review* 72: 233–59.

Chapman, S. J., and A. V. S. Hill. 2012. "Human Genetic Susceptibility to Infectious Disease." *Nature Reviews: Genetics* 13: 175–88.

Chatterjee, H. N. 1953. "Control of Vomiting in Cholera and Oral Replacement of Fluid." *Lancet* 262: 1063.

Chen, C., and X.-P. Dong. 2016. "Epidemiological Characteristics of Human Prion Diseases." *Infectious Diseases of Poverty* 5: 47.

Chen, S., and J. K. Kung. 2016. "Of Maize and Men: The Effect of a New World Crop on Population and Economic Growth in China." *Journal of Economic Growth* 21: 71–99.

Cherian, P. J. 2011. *Pattanam Excavations: Fifth Season Field Report*. Trivandrum.

Chernin, E. 1983. "Sir Patrick Manson's Studies on the Transmission and Biology of Filariasis." *Reviews of Infectious Diseases* 5: 148–66.

Cherry, J., and T. Leppard. 2015. "Experimental Archaeology and the Earliest Seagoing: The Limitations of Inference." *World Archaeology* 47: 740–55.

Chesnais, J. C. 1992. *The Demographic Transition: Stages, Patterns, and Economic Implications: A Longitudinal Study of Sixty-Seven Countries Covering the Period 1720–1984*. Oxford.

Childe, V. G. 1936. *Man Makes Himself*. London.

Chippaux, J., and A. Chippaux. 2018. "Yellow Fever in Africa and the Americas: A Historical and Epidemiological Perspective." *Journal of Venomous Animals and Toxins Including Tropical Diseases* 24: 1–14.

Chisholm, R. H., et al. 2016. "Controlled Fire Use in Early Humans Might Have Triggered the Evolutionary Emergence of Tuberculosis." *Proceedings of the National Academy of Sciences* 113: 9051–56.

Choi, J. Y., et al. 2017. "The Rice Paradox: Multiple Origins but Single Domestication in Asian Rice." *Molecular Biology and Evolution* 34: 969–79.

Chouin, G. 2018. "Reflections on Plague in African History (14th–19th c.)." *Afriques. Débats, méthodes et terrains d'histoire* 9.

Christakos, G., et al. 2005. *Interdisciplinary Public Health Reasoning and Epidemic Modelling: The Case of the Black Death.* Berlin.

Christian, D. 2011. *Maps of Time: An Introduction to Big History.* Berkeley.

Christie, J. 1876. *Cholera Epidemics in East Africa: An Account of the Several Diffusions of the Disease in That Country from 1821 till 1872, with an Outline of the Geography, Ethnology, and Trade Connections of the Regions through Which the Epidemics Passed.* London.

Chritz, K., et al. 2015. "Environments and Trypanosomiasis Risks for Early Herders in the Later Holocene of the Lake Victoria Basin, Kenya." *Proceedings of the National Academy of Sciences* 112: 3674–79.

Ciccarelli, C., and J. Weisdorf. 2018. "Pioneering into the Past: Regional Literacy Developments in Italy before Italy." *European Review of Economic History* 23: 329–64.

Cieza de León, P. 1998. *The Discovery and Conquest of Peru: Chronicles of the New World Encounter.* Durham.

Cipolla, C. 1969. *Literacy and Development in the West.* Harmondsworth.

———. 1981. *Fighting the Plague in Seventeenth-Century Italy.* Madison.

Clark, G. 2007. *A Farewell to Alms: A Brief Economic History of the World.* Princeton.

Clark, P. 2009. *European Cities and Towns: 400–2000.* Oxford.

Cliff, A. D., and P. Haggett. 1985. *The Spread of Measles in Fiji and the Pacific: Spatial Components in the Transmission of Epidemic Waves through Island Communities.* Canberra.

Cliff, A. D., P. Haggett, and M. Smallman-Raynor. 1993. *Measles: An Historical Geography of a Major Human Viral Disease: From Global Expansion to Local Retreat, 1840–1990.* Oxford.

Clinton, C., and D. Sridhar. 2017. *Governing Global Health: Who Runs the World and Why?* Oxford.

Clodfelter, M. 2017. *Warfare and Armed Conflicts: A Statistical Encyclopedia of Casualty and Other Figures, 1492–2015.* 4th ed. Jefferson.

Close, F. 1865. *The Cattle Plague, Viewed in the Light of Holy Scripture. A Sermon, Etc.* London.

Cloudsley-Thompson, J. 1977. *Insects and History.* London.

Clouston, S. A. P., et al. 2016. "A Social History of Disease: Contextualizing the Rise and Fall of Social Inequalities in Cause-Specific Mortality." *Demography* 53: 1631–56.

Coale, A. J. 1984. *Rapid Population Change in China, 1952–1982.* Washington, DC.

Coburn, B., G. A. Grassl, and B. B. Finlay. 2007. "Salmonella, the Host and Disease: A Brief Review." *Immunology and Cell Biology* 85: 112–18.

Cockburn, A. 1967. *Infectious Diseases: Their Evolution and Eradication.* Springfield.

————. 1971. "Infectious Diseases in Ancient Populations." *Current Anthropology* 12: 45–62.

Coclanis, P. A. 1989. *The Shadow of a Dream: Economic Life and Death in the South Carolina Low Country, 1670–1920.* New York.

Coelho, P. R. P., and R. A. McGuire. 1999. "Biology, Diseases, and Economics: An Epidemiological History of Slavery in the American South." *Journal of Bioeconomics* 1: 151–90.

Cogolludo, D. L. 1868. *Historia de Yucatan.* Merida.

Cohen, M. N. 1989. *Health and the Rise of Civilization.* New Haven.

Cohen, M. N., G. J. Armelagos, and C. S. Larsen, eds. 1984. *Paleopathology at the Origins of Agriculture.* Orlando.

Cohen, M. N., and G. Crane-Kramer. 2007. *Ancient Health: Skeletal Indicators of Agricultural and Economic Intensification.* Gainesville.

Cohen, R. 1995. *The Cambridge Survey of World Migration.* West Nyack.

Cohn, S. K. 2002. *The Black Death Transformed: Disease and Culture in Early Renaissance Europe.* London.

Colangelo, P., et al. 2015. "Mitochondrial Phylogeography of the Black Rat Supports a Single Invasion of the Western Mediterranean Basin." *Biological Invasions* 17: 1859–68.

Colby, D., and S. Prusiner. 2011. "Prions." *Cold Spring Harbor Perspectives in Biology* 3: a006833.

Coldham, P. 1984. *English Adventurers and Emigrants, 1609–1660: Abstracts of Examinations in the High Court of Admiralty with Reference to Colonial America.* Baltimore.

Coleman, M., et al. 2017. "Developing Global Maps of Insecticide Resistance Risk to Improve Vector Control." *Malaria Journal* 16: 86.

Coleman, W. 1982. *Death Is a Social Disease: Public Health and Political Economy in Early Industrial France.* Madison.

Colley, D., et al. 2014. "Human Schistosomiasis." *Lancet* 383: 2253–64.

Coluzzi, M. 1999. "The Clay Feet of the Malaria Giant and Its African Roots: Hypotheses and Inferences about Origin, Spread and Control of *Plasmodium falciparum.*" *Parassitologia* 41: 277–83.

Comas, I., et al. 2013. "Out-of-Africa Migration and Neolithic Coexpansion of *Mycobacterium tuberculosis* with Modern Humans." *Nature Genetics* 45: 1176–82.

Connelly, M. J. 2008. *Fatal Misconception: The Struggle to Control World Population.* Cambridge.

Connor, T. R., et al. 2015. "Species-Wide Whole Genome Sequencing Reveals Historical Global Spread and Recent Local Persistence in *Shigella flexneri.*" *Elife* 4: e07335.

Conrad, L. 1981. "The Plague in the Early Medieval Near East." PhD diss., Princeton University.

Cook, C. H. 1889. "A Study of Malarial Fever in Eastern Massachusetts." *Boston Medical and Surgical Journal* 121: 356–59.

Cook, F. 1894. "Medical Observations among the Esquimaux." *Transactions of the New York Obstetrical Society* 3: 282–89.

Cook, M. 2015. "The Centrality of Islamic Civilization." In *Expanding Webs of Exchange and Conflict, 500 CE–1500 CE,* edited by B. Z. Kedar and M. Wiesner-Hanks, 385–414. Vol. 5 of *The Cambridge World History.* Cambridge.

Cook, M. T. 1913. *The Diseases of Tropical Plants.* London.

Cook, N. D. 1981. *Demographic Collapse: Indian Peru, 1520–1620.* Cambridge.

———. 1993. "Disease and the Depopulation of Hispaniola, 1492–1518." *Colonial Latin American Review* 2: 213–45.

———. 1998. *Born to Die: Disease and New World Conquest, 1492–1650.* Cambridge.

Cook, N. D., and W. G. Lovell, eds. 1991. *Secret Judgments of God: Old World Disease in Colonial Spanish America.* Norman.

Cook, S. F., and W. Borah. 1960. *The Indian Population of Central Mexico 1531–1610.* Berkeley.

Cook, S. F. 1955. *The Epidemic of 1830–1833 in California and Oregon.* Berkeley.

———. 1973. "The Significance of Disease in the Extinction of the New England Indians." *Human Biology* 45: 485–508.

———. 1976. *The Indian Population of New England in the Seventeenth Century.* Berkeley.

Cooper, N., J. Kamilar, and C. Nunn. 2012. "Host Longevity and Parasite Species Richness in Mammals." *PLoS One* 7: e42190.

Cooper, N., and C. Nunn. 2013. "Identifying Future Zoonotic Disease Threats: Where Are the Gaps in Our Understanding of Primate Infectious Diseases?" *Evolution, Medicine, and Public Health* 2013: 27–36.

Cordey, S., et al. 2010. "Rhinovirus Genome Evolution during Experimental Human Infection." *PLoS One* 5: 10588.

Cordingley, M. G. 2017. *Viruses: Agents of Evolutionary Invention.* Cambridge.

Corfield, P. J. 1982. *The Impact of English Towns: 1700–1800.* Oxford.

Cornélio, A. M., et al. 2016. "Human Brain Expansion during Evolution Is Independent of Fire Control and Cooking." *Frontiers in Neuroscience* 10: 167.

Corradi, A. 1865–94. *Annali delle epidemie occorse in Italia dalle prime memorie fino al 1850.* 5 vols. Bologna.

Corti, P. 1984. "Malaria e società contadina nel Mezzogiorno." In *Storia d'Italia. Annali 7. Malattia e medicina*, edited by F. Della Peruta, 635–78. Turin.

Cosma, C. L., D. R. Sherman, and L. Ramakrishnan. 2003. "The Secret Lives of the Pathogenic Mycobacteria." *Annual Review of Microbiology* 57: 641–76.

Côté, I. M., and R. Poulin. 1995. "Parasitism and Group Size in Social Animals: A Meta-Analysis." *Behavioral Ecology* 6: 159–65.

Cowan, A. 1998. *Urban Europe, 1500–1700.* London.

Cowan, C. W., and P. J. Watson. 1992. *The Origins of Agriculture: An International Perspective.* Tuscaloosa.

Cowan, G. O. 2016. *The Most Fatal Distemper: Typhus in History.* Tullibody.

Cowman, A. F., et al. 2017. "The Molecular Basis of Erythrocyte Invasion by Malaria Parasites." *Cell Host & Microbe* 22: 232–45.

Cox, F. E. G. 2004. "History of Sleeping Sickness (African Trypanosomiasis)." *Infectious Disease Clinics of North America* 18: 231–45.

Crawford, D. H. 2007. *Deadly Companions: How Microbes Shaped Our History.* Oxford.

———. 2009. *The Invisible Enemy: A Natural History of Viruses.* Oxford.

Crawford, J., et al. 2017. "Population Genomics Reveals That an Anthropophilic Population of *Aedes aegypti* Mosquitoes in West Africa Recently Gave Rise to American and Asian Populations of This Major Disease Vector." *BMC Biology* 15: 1–16.

Crawford, M. J. 2014. "An Empire's Extract: Chemical Manipulations of Cinchona Bark in the Eighteenth-Century Spanish Atlantic World." *Osiris* 29: 215–29.

———. 2016. *The Andean Wonder Drug: Cinchona Bark and Imperial Science in the Spanish Atlantic, 1630–1800.* Pittsburgh.

Crayen, D., and J. Baten. 2010. "New Evidence and New Methods to Measure Human Capital Inequality before and during the Industrial Revolution: France and the US in the Seventeenth to Nineteenth Centuries." *Economic History Review* 63: 452–78.

Creighton, C. 1891–94. *A History of Epidemics in Britain from A.D. 664 to the Extinction of Plague.* 2 vols. Cambridge.

Crellen, T., et al. 2016. "Whole Genome Resequencing of the Human Parasite *Schistosoma mansoni* Reveals Population History and Effects of Selection." *Scientific Reports* 6: 20954.

Cromwell, E., et al. 2020. "The Global Distribution of Lymphatic Filariasis, 2000–18: A Geospatial Analysis." *Lancet Global Health* 8: e1186–94.

Cronon, W. 1991. *Nature's Metropolis: Chicago and the Great West.* New York.

Crook, T. 2016. *Governing Systems: Modernity and the Making of Public Health in England, 1830–1910.* Berkeley.

Crosby, A. W. 1967. "Conquistador y Pestilencia: The First New World Pandemic and the Fall of the Great Indian Empires." *Hispanic American Historical Review* 47: 321–37.

———. 1972. *The Columbian Exchange: Biological and Cultural Consequences of 1492.* Westport.

———. 1996. *Ecological Imperialism: Biological Expansion of Europe, 900–1900.* Cambridge.

———. 2003. *America's Forgotten Pandemic: The Influenza of 1918.* 2nd ed. Cambridge.

———. 2006. *Children of the Sun: A History of Humanity's Unappeasable Appetite for Energy.* New York.

Crowther, A., et al. 2018. "Subsistence Mosaics, Forager-Farmer Interactions, and the Transition to Food Production in East Africa." *Quaternary International* 489: 101–20.

Croxen, M. A., et al. 2013. "Recent Advances in Understanding Enteric Pathogenic *Escherichia coli.*" *Clinical Microbiology Reviews* 26: 822–80.

Crutzen, P., and E. Stoermer. 2000. "Anthropocene." *IGBP Newsletter* 41: 17–18.

Cruz-Cárdenas, C. I., et al. 2019. "Wild Relatives of Maize." In *Important Species* edited by S. L. Greene et al., 3–39. Vol. 2 of *North American Crop Wild Relatives.* Cham.

Cucina, A., et al. 2006. "The Necropolis of Vallerano (Rome, 2nd–3rd Century AD): An Anthropological Perspective on the Ancient Romans in the Suburbium." *International Journal of Osteoarchaeology* 16: 104–17.

Cui, Y., et al. 2013. "Historical Variations in Mutation Rate in an Epidemic Pathogen." *PNAS* 110: 577–82.

Cummins, N. 2017. "Lifespans of the European Elite, 800–1800." *Journal of Economic History* 77: 406–39.

Cummins, N., M. Kelly, and C. Ó Gráda. 2016. "Living Standards and Plague in London, 1560–1665." *Economic History Review* 69: 3–34.

Cunningham, A., and R. K. French, eds. 1990. *The Medical Enlightenment of the Eighteenth Century.* Cambridge.

Curtin, P. D. 1964. *The Image of Africa: British Ideas and Action, 1780–1850.* Madison.

————. 1989. *Death by Migration: Europe's Encounter with the Tropical World in the Nineteenth Century.* Cambridge.

————. 1990. *The Rise and Fall of the Plantation Complex: Essays in Atlantic History.* Cambridge.

————. 1993. "Disease Exchange across the Tropical Atlantic." *History and Philosophy of the Life Sciences* 15: 329–56.

————. 1994. "Malarial Immunities in Nineteenth-Century West Africa and the Caribbean." *Parassitologia* 36: 69–82.

————. 1998. *Disease and Empire: The Health of European Troops in the Conquest of Africa.* Cambridge.

Cutbush, M., and P. L. Mollison. 1950. "The Duffy Blood Group System." *Heredity* 4: 383–89.

Cutler, D., A. Deaton, and A. Lleras-Muney. 2006. "The Determinants of Mortality." *Journal of Economic Perspectives* 20: 97–120.

Cutler, D., et al. 2010. "Early-Life Malaria Exposure and Adult Outcomes: Evidence from Malaria Eradication in India." *American Economic Journal: Applied Economics* 2: 72–94.

Cutler, S. J. 2010. "Relapsing Fever—A Forgotten Disease Revealed." *Journal of Applied Microbiology* 108: 1115–22.

Dabbagh, A., et al. 2018. "Progress toward Regional Measles Elimination—Worldwide, 2000–2017." *Morbidity and Mortality Weekly Report* 67: 1323–29.

Dalby, T. 1690. *An Historical Account of the Rise and Fall of the West-India Colonies and of the Great Advantages They Are to England in Respect to Trade.* London.

Dalrymple, U., B. Mappin, and P. W. Gething. 2015. "Malaria Mapping: Understanding the Global Endemicity of Falciparum and Vivax Malaria." *BMC Medicine* 13: 140.

Damgaard, P., et al. 2018. "137 Ancient Human Genomes from across the Eurasian Steppes." *Nature* 557: 369–74.

D'Andrea, A. C., et al. 2007. "Early Domesticated Cowpea (*Vigna unguiculata*) from Central Ghana." *Antiquity* 81: 686–98.

Daniele, V., and N. Ostuni. 2013. "The Burden of Disease and the IQ of Nations." *Learning and Individual Differences* 28: 109–18.

Darby, A. C., et al. 2007. "Intracellular Pathogens Go Extreme: Genome Evolution in the Rickettsiales." *TRENDS in Genetics* 23: 511–20.

Darwin, C. 1959. *The Voyage of the Beagle.* New York.

————. 2001. *Charles Darwin's Beagle Diary.* Edited by R. D. Keynes. Cambridge.

————. 2017. *The Correspondence of Charles Darwin.* Edited by F. Burkhardt. Vol. 25. Cambridge.

Darwin, J. 2007. *After Tamerlane: The Global History of Empire.* London.

Das, A., et al. 2012. "Malaria in India: The Center for the Study of Complex Malaria in India." *Acta Tropica* 121: 267–73.

Das, K., and S. Ganguly. 2014. "Evolutionary Genomics and Population Structure of *Entamoeba histolytica.*" *Computational and Structural Journal* 12: 26–33.

Das Gupta, P. 1971. "Estimation of Demographic Measures for India, 1881–1961, Based on Census Age Distributions." *Population Studies* 25: 395–414.

Daub, J. T., et al. 2013. "Evidence for Polygenic Adaptation to Pathogens in the Human Genome." *Molecular Biology and Evolution* 30: 1544–58.

Dauer, C. C. 1938. "Studies on the Epidemiology of Poliomyelitis." *Public Health Reports* 53: 1003–20.

Davenport, R. 2013. "Year of Birth Effects in the Historical Decline of Tuberculosis Mortality: A Reconsideration." *PLoS One* 8: 81797.

———. 2015. "The First Stage of the Epidemiological Transition in British Cities: A Comparison of Infant Mortality in Manchester and London, 1750–1820." University of Cambridge Repository.

———. 2017. "The First Stages of the Mortality Transition in England: A Perspective from Evolutionary Biology." University of Cambridge Repository.

———. 2020. "Urbanization and Mortality in Britain, c. 1800–50." *Economic History Review* 73: 455–85.

Davenport, R., J. Boulton, and L. Schwarz. 2016. "Urban Inoculation and the Decline of Smallpox Mortality in Eighteenth-Century Cities—a Reply to Razzell." *Economic History Review* 69: 188–214.

Davenport, R., L. Schwarz, and J. Boulton. 2011. "The Decline of Adult Smallpox in Eighteenth-Century London." *Economic History Review* 64: 1289–314.

David, P. A., S. R. Johansson, and A. Pozzi. 2010. "The Demography of an Early Mortality Transition: Life Expectancy, Survival and Mortality Rates for Britain's Royals, 1500–1799." Oxford Discussion Papers in Economic and Social History no. 83.

Davies, J., and D. Davies. 2010. "Origins and Evolution of Antibiotic Resistance." *Microbiology and Molecular Biology Reviews* 74: 417–33.

Davies, K. G. 1975. "The Living and the Dead: White Mortality in West Africa, 1684–1732." In *Race and Slavery in the Western Hemisphere: Quantitative Studies*, edited by S. Engerman and E. Genovese, 83–98. Princeton.

Davis, K. 1951. *The Population of India and Pakistan*. New York.

———. 1956. "The Amazing Decline of Mortality in Underdeveloped Areas." *American Economic Review* 46: 305–18.

Davis, M. 2001. *Late Victorian Holocausts: El Niño Famines and the Making of the Third World*. London.

De Jesus, N. H. 2007. "Epidemics to Eradication: The Modern History of Poliomyelitis." *Virology Journal* 4: 70.

De Ligt, L. 2012. *Peasants, Citizens and Soldiers: Studies in the Demographic History of Roman Italy 225 BC–AD 100*. Cambridge.

De Romanis, F., and A. Tchernia, eds. 1997. *Crossings: Early Mediterranean Contacts with India*. New Delhi.

De Tocqueville, A. 1958. *Journeys to England and Ireland*. New Haven.

De Toro, L. 1564. *De febris epidemicae et novę, quae Latine puncticularis, vulgo tavardillo, et pintas dicitur, natura, cognitione, & medela*. Burgis.

De Villalba, J. 1802. *Epidemiologia española: O, historia cronológia de las pestes, contagios, epidemias y epizootias que han acaecido en España desde la venida de los cartagineses hasta el año 1801*. Madrid.

———. 1984. *Epidemiología española*. Facsimile edition. Málaga.

De Vries, J. 1984. *European Urbanization, 1500–1800*. Cambridge.

———. 2008. *The Industrious Revolution: Consumer Behavior and the Household Economy, 1650 to the Present*. Cambridge.

———. 2009. "The Economic Crisis of the Seventeenth Century after Fifty Years." *Journal of Interdisciplinary History* 40: 151–94.

Dean, K. R., et al. 2018. "Human Ectoparasites and the Spread of Plague in Europe during the Second Pandemic." *Proceedings of the National Academy of Sciences of the United States of America* 115: 1304–9.

Deaton, A. 2013. *The Great Escape: Health, Wealth, and the Origins of Inequality*. Princeton.

Debo, A. 1940. *And Still the Waters Run*. Princeton.

Decaro, N., et al. 2020. "COVID-19 from Veterinary Medicine and One Health Perspectives: What Animal Coronaviruses Have Taught Us." *Research in Veterinary Science* 131: 21–23.

Degroot, D. 2018. *The Frigid Golden Age: Climate Change, the Little Ice Age, and the Dutch Republic, 1560–1720*. Cambridge.

Dehority, W. 2020. "Infectious Disease Outbreaks, Pandemics, and Hollywood—Hope and Fear across a Century of Cinema." *JAMA* 323: 1878–80.

DeLacy, M. 2017. *Contagionism Catches On: Medical Ideology in Britain, 1730–1800*. Cham.

Delaporte, F. 1986. *Disease and Civilization: The Cholera in Paris, 1832*. Cambridge.

Del Panta, L. 1980. *Le epidemie nella storia demografica Italian (secoli XIV–XIX)*. Turin.

Del Panta, L., and M. Livi Bacci. 1977. "Chronologie, intensité et diffusion des crises de mortalité en Italie: 1600–1850." *Population* 32: 401–46.

Demeure, C. E., et al. 2019. "*Yersinia pestis* and Plague: An Updated View on Evolution, Virulence Determinants, Immune Subversion, Vaccination, and Diagnostics." *Genes & Immunity* 20: 357–70.

Denevan, W. M. 1992. *The Native Population of the Americas in 1492*. 2nd ed. Madison.

Deng, K. G. 2004. "Unveiling China's True Population Statistics for the Pre-modern Era with Official Census Data." *Population Review* 43: 32–69.

Denham, T. 2011. "Early Agriculture and Plant Domestication in New Guinea and Island Southeast Asia." *Current Anthropology* 52: S379–95.

———. 2013. "Early Farming in Island Southeast Asia: An Alternative Hypothesis." *Antiquity* 87: 250–7.

Denham, T., et al. 2020. "The Domestication Syndrome in Vegetatively Propagated Field Crops." *Annals of Botany* 125: 581–97.

Dennell, R. 2003. "Dispersal and Colonisation, Long and Short Chronologies: How Continuous Is the Early Pleistocene Record for Hominids outside East Africa?" *Journal of Human Evolution* 45: 421–40.

———. 2010. "The Colonization of 'Savannahstan': Issues of Timing(s) and Patterns of Dispersal across Asia in the Late Pliocene and Early Pleistocene." In *Asian Paleoanthropology: From Africa to China and Beyond*, edited by C. J. Norton and D. R. Braun, 7–30. Dordrecht.

Dennison, T., and S. Ogilvie. 2014. "Does the European Marriage Pattern Explain Economic Growth?" *Journal of Economic History* 74: 651–93.

Desprès, L., et al. 1992. "Molecular Evidence Linking Hominid Evolution to Recent Radiation of Schistosomes (Platyhelminthes: Trematoda)." *Molecular Phylogenetics and Evolution* 1: 295–304.

Détroit, F., et al. 2019. "A New Species of *Homo* from the Late Pleistocene of the Philippines." *Nature* 568: 181–86.

Devault, A. M., et al. 2014. "Second-Pandemic Strain of Vibrio Cholerae from the Philadelphia Cholera Outbreak of 1849." *New England Journal of Medicine* 370: 334–40.

Devaux, C. A. 2013. "Small Oversights That Led to the Great Plague of Marseille (1720–1723): Lessons from the Past." *Infection, Genetics and Evolution* 14: 169–85.

Dewan, K. K., and E. T. Harvill. 2019. "Did New Transmission Cycles in Anthropogenic, Dense, Host Populations Encourage the Emergence and Speciation of Pathogenic *Bordetella*?" *PLoS Pathogens* 15: 107600.

DeWitte, S. N. 2014. "Mortality Risk and Survival in the Aftermath of the Medieval Black Death." *PLoS One* 9: e96513.

Diamond, J. 1987. "The Worst Mistake in the History of the Human Race." *Discovery*, 64–66.

———. 1997. *Guns, Germs, and Steel: The Fates of Human Societies*. New York.

Diavatopoulos, D. A., et al. 2005. "*Bordetella pertussis*, the Causative Agent of Whooping Cough, Evolved from a Distinct, Human-Associated Lineage of *B. Bronchiseptica*," *PLoS Pathogens* 1: e45.

Dickens, C. 1865. *The Life and Adventures of Nicholas Nickleby*. London.

———. 1873. *All the Year Round*. London.

———. 1911. *The Works of Charles Dickens*. Vol. 2. New York.

Dickson, R. P., J. R. Erb-Downward, and G. B. Huffnagle. 2014. "Towards an Ecology of the Lung: New Conceptual Models of Pulmonary Microbiology and Pneumonia Pathogenesis." *Lancet Respiratory Medicine* 2: 238–46.

Di Cosmo, N. 2010. "Black Sea Emporia and the Mongol Empire: A Reassessment of the Pax Mongolica." *Journal of the Economic and Social History of the Orient* 53: 83–108.

Dillehay, T., et al. 2007. "Preceramic Adoption of Peanut, Squash, and Cotton in Northern Peru." *Science* 316: 1890–93.

Dinānah, T. 1927. "Die Schrift von Abī Ǧaʿfar Aḥmed ibn ʿAlī ibn Moḥammed ibn ʿAlī ibn Ḥātimah aus Almeriah über die Pest." *Archiv für Geschichte der Medizin* 1: 27–81.

Diop, A., D. Raoult, and P. Fournier. 2018. "Rickettsial Genomics and the Paradigm of Genome Reduction Associated with Increased Virulence." *Microbes and Infection* 20: 401–9.

Disney, A. R. 2009. *A History of Portugal and the Portuguese Empire: From Beginnings to 1807*. Cambridge.

Dobson, A. 2009. "Food-Web Structure and Ecosystem Services: Insights from the Serengeti." *Philosophical Transactions of the Royal Society B: Biological Sciences* 364: 1665–82.

Dobson, A. P. 2005. "What Links Bats to Emerging Infectious Diseases?" *Science* 310: 628–29.

Dobson, M. 1980. "'Marsh Fever'—The Geography of Malaria in England." *Journal of Historical Geography* 6: 357–89.

———. 1989. "Mortality Gradients and Disease Exchanges: Comparisons from Old England and Colonial America." *Social History of Medicine* 2: 259–97.

———. 1997. *Contours of Death and Disease in Early Modern England*. Cambridge.

Dobyns, H. F. 1963. "An Outline of Andean Epidemic History to 1720." *Bulletin of the History of Medicine* 37: 493–515.

———. 1966. "Estimating Aboriginal American Population." *Current Anthropology* 7: 395–416.

————. 1983. *Their Number Become Thinned: Native American Population Dynamics in Eastern North America*. Knoxville.

Dobzhansky, T. 1973. "Nothing in Biology Makes Sense Except in the Light of Evolution." *American Biology Teacher* 35: 125–29.

Dols, M. W. 1977. *The Black Death in the Middle East*. Princeton.

Domingo, E., and C. Perales. 2019. "Viral Quasispecies." *PLoS Genetics* 15: e1008271.

Donoghue, H., et al. 2015. "A Migration-Driven Model for the Historical Spread of Leprosy in Medieval Eastern and Central Europe." *Infection, Genetics and Evolution* 31: 250–56.

————. 2018. "The Distribution and Origins of Ancient Leprosy." In *Hansen's Disease: The Forgotten and Neglected Disease*, edited by W. Ribón. London.

Donohue, K. 2011. *Darwin's Finches: Readings in the Evolution of a Scientific Paradigm*. Chicago.

Doolan, D. L., C. Dobaño, and J. K. Baird. 2009. "Acquired Immunity to Malaria." *Clinical Microbiology Reviews* 22: 13–36.

Dóró, R., et al. 2015. "Zoonotic Transmission of Rotavirus: Surveillance and Control." *Expert Review of Anti-infective Therapy* 13: 1337–50.

Dos Anjos, B. C. 2016. "Single Treaty on the Pestilential Constitution of Pernambuco: First Description of the 'Males' by João Ferreira da Rosa in the XVII Century." *Temporalidades* 8: 11–36.

Downey, S. S., W. R. Haas, and S. J. Shennan. 2016. "European Neolithic Societies Showed Early Warning Signals of Population Collapse." *Proceedings of the National Academy of Sciences* 113: 9751–56.

Drake, A., and M. Oxenham. 2013. "Disease, Climate and the Peopling of the Americas." *Historical Biology* 25: 565–97.

Drake, D. 1850. *A Systematic Treatise, Historical, Etiological and Practical, on the Principal Diseases of the Interior Valley of North America: As They Appear in the Caucasian, African, Indian, and Esquimaux Varieties of Its Population*. Cincinnati.

Drancourt, M., L. Houhamdi, and D. Raoult. 2006. "*Yersinia pestis* as a Telluric, Human Ectoparasite-Borne Organism." *Lancet Infectious Diseases* 6: 234–41.

Drancourt, M., et al. 1998. "Detection of 400-Year-Old *Yersinia pestis* DNA in Human Dental Pulp: An Approach to the Diagnosis of Ancient Septicemia." *Proceedings of the National Academy of Sciences* 95: 12637–40.

Drevets, D. A., P. J. M. Leenen, and R. A. Greenfield. 2004. "Invasion of the Central Nervous System by Intracellular Bacteria." *Clinical Microbiology Reviews* 17: 323–47.

Drexler, J. F., et al. 2012. "Bats Host Major Mammalian Paramyxoviruses." *Nature Communications* 3: 1–13.

Du, Z., and X. Wang. 2016. "Pathology and Pathogenesis of *Yersinia pestis*." In *Yersinia pestis: Retrospective and Perspective*, edited by R. Yang and A. Anisimov, 193–222. Dordrecht.

Dubisch, J. 1985. "Low Country Fevers: Cultural Adaptations to Malaria in Antebellum South Carolina." *Social Science & Medicine* 21: 641–49.

Dubos, R. J. 1951. *Louis Pasteur: Free Lance of Science*. London.

Dubos, R. J., and J. Dubos. 1952. *The White Plague; Tuberculosis, Man and Society*. Boston.

Dubyanskiy, V., and A. Yeszhanov. 2016. "Ecology of *Yersinia pestis* and the Epidemiology of Plague." In *Yersinia pestis: Retrospective and Perspective*, edited by R. Yang and A. Anisimov, 101–70. Dordrecht.

Duchêne, S., et al. 2020. "The Recovery, Interpretation and Use of Ancient Pathogen Genomes." *Current Biology* 30: R1215–31.

Duffy, J. 1953. *Epidemics in Colonial America*. Baton Rouge.

———. 1990. *The Sanitarians: A History of American Public Health*. Urbana.

Duffy, S., L. Shackelton, and E. Holmes. 2008. "Rates of Evolutionary Change in Viruses: Patterns and Determinants." *Nature Reviews Genetics* 9: 267–76.

Duggan, A. T., et al. 2016. "17th Century Variola Virus Reveals the Recent History of Smallpox." *Current Biology* 26: 3407–12.

Dull, R. A., et al. 2010. "The Columbian Encounter and the Little Ice Age: Abrupt Land Use Change, Fire, and Greenhouse Forcing." *Annals of the Association of American Geographers* 100: 755–71.

Duncan, C. J., and S. Scott. 2004. "What Caused the Black Death?" *Postgraduate Medical Journal* 81: 315–20.

Duncan, S. R., S. Scott, and C. J. Duncan. 2000. "Modelling the Dynamics of Scarlet Fever Epidemics in the 19th Century." *European Journal of Epidemiology* 16: 619–26.

Duncan-Jones, R. 1996. "The Impact of the Antonine Plague." *Journal of Roman Archaeology* 9: 108–93.

———. 2018. "The Antonine Plague Revisited." *Arctos* 52: 41–72.

Dunlap, T. R. 1981. *DDT: Scientists, Citizens, and Public Policy*. Princeton.

Dunn, O., and J. E. Kelly. 1989. *The Diary of Christopher Columbus' First Voyage to America, 1492–1493*. Norman.

Dunn, R. 1972. *Sugar and Slaves: The Rise of the Planter Class in the English West Indies, 1624–1713*. Chapel Hill.

———. 1977. "A Tale of Two Plantations: Slave Life at Mesopotamia in Jamaica and Mount Airy in Virginia, 1799 to 1828." *William and Mary Quarterly* 34: 32–65.

———. 2014. *A Tale of Two Plantations: Slave Life and Labor in Jamaica and Virginia*. Cambridge.

Dunn, R. R., et al. 2010. "Global Drivers of Human Pathogen Richness and Prevalence." *Proceedings of the Royal Society B: Biological Sciences* 277: 2587–95.

Dunstan, H. 1975. "The Late Ming Epidemics: A Preliminary Survey." *Ch'ing-Shih Wen-t'i* 3: 1–59.

Durey, M. 1979. *The Return of the Plague: British Society and the Cholera, 1831–2*. Dublin.

Durliat, J. 1989. "La peste du VIe siècle. Pour un nouvel examen des sources byzantines." In *IVe—VIIe siècle*, 107–19. Vol. 1 of *Hommes et richesses dans l'empire byzantin*, edited by J. Lefort and J. Morrisson. Paris.

Du Tertre, J. B. 1667. *Histoire générale des Antilles habitées par les François*. Paris.

Düx, A., et al. 2020. "Measles Virus and Rinderpest Virus Divergence Dated to the Sixth Century BCE." *Science* 368: 1367–70.

Dyson, T. 2010. *Population and Development*. London.

———. 2018. *A Population History of India: From the First Modern People to the Present Day*. Oxford.

Earle, C. 1979. "Environment, Disease and Mortality in Early Virginia." *Journal of Historical Geography* 5: 365–90.

Early, J. D., and T. N. Headland. 1998. *Population Dynamics of a Philippine Rain Forest People: The San Ildefonso Agta*. Gainesville.

Easterlin, R. 1981. "Why Isn't the Whole World Developed?" *Journal of Economic History* 41: 1–19.

———. 1995. "Industrial Revolution and Mortality Revolution: Two of a Kind?" *Journal of Evolutionary Economics* 5: 393–408.

———. 1996. *Growth Triumphant: The Twenty-First Century in Historical Perspective.* Ann Arbor.

———. 1999. "How Beneficent Is the Market? A Look at the Modern History of Mortality." *European Review of Economic History* 3: 257–94.

Easton, A., et al. 2020. "Molecular Evidence of Hybridization between Pig and Human *Ascaris* Indicates an Interbred Species Complex Infecting Humans." *eLife* 9: e61562.

Ecclestone, M. 1999. "Mortality of Rural Landless Men before the Black Death: The Glastonbury Head-Tax Lists." *Local Population Studies* 63: 6–29.

Echenberg, M. 2002. "*Pestis* Redux: The Initial Years of the Third Bubonic Plague Pandemic, 1894–1901." *Journal of World History* 13: 429–49.

———. 2007. *Plague Ports: The Global Urban Impact of Bubonic Plague, 1894–1901.* New York.

———. 2011. *Africa in the Time of Cholera: A History of Pandemics from 1817 to the Present.* Cambridge.

Eckert, E. A. 1996. *The Structure of Plagues and Pestilences in Early Modern Europe: Central Europe, 1560–1640.* Basel.

———. 2000. "The Retreat of Plague from Central Europe, 1640–1720: A Geomedical Approach." *Bulletin of the History of Medicine* 74: 1–28.

Eckstein, A. 2006. *Mediterranean Anarchy, Interstate War, and the Rise of Rome.* Berkeley.

Eder, J. 1987. *On the Road to Tribal Extinction: Depopulation, Deculturation, and Adaptive Well-Being among the Batak of the Philippines.* Berkeley.

Edwards, J., and S. Ogilvie. 2018. "Did the Black Death Cause Economic Development by 'Inventing' Fertility Restriction?" CESifo working paper 7016. Munich.

Edwards, T., and P. Kelton. 2020. "Germs, Genocides, and America's Indigenous Peoples." *Journal of American History* 107: 52–76.

Ehrlich, P. R., and A. H. Ehrlich. 2009. *The Dominant Animal: Human Evolution and the Environment.* Washington, DC.

Elias, P. M. 2007. "The Skin Barrier as an Innate Immune Element." *Seminars in Immunopathology* 29: 3.

Elliott, C. 2016. "The Antonine Plague, Climate Change and Local Violence in Roman Egypt." *Past & Present* 231: 3–31.

Ellis, H. 1921. *Impressions and Comments.* London.

Else, K., et al. 2020. "Whipworm and Roundworm Infections." *Nature Reviews Disease Primers* 6: 1–23.

Elvin, M. 1973. *The Pattern of the Chinese Past.* Stanford.

———. 2004. *The Retreat of the Elephants: An Environmental History of China.* New Haven.

Engel, J. 2006. *The Epidemic: A Global History of AIDS.* New York.

Engelmann, L., and C. Lynteris. 2020. *Sulphuric Utopias: A History of Maritime Fumigation.* Cambridge.

Engmann, E. V. T. 1986. *Population of Ghana, 1850–1960.* Accra.

Enoki, K. 1959. "On the Nationality of the Ephthalites." *Memoirs of the Research Department of the Toyo Bunko* 18: 1–58.

Eppig, C., C. L. Fincher, and R. Thornhill. 2010. "Parasite Prevalence and the Worldwide Distribution of Cognitive Ability." *Proceedings of the Royal Society B: Biological Sciences* 277: 3801–8.

Eriksen, A. 2020. "Smallpox Inoculation: Translation, Transference and Transformation." *Palgrave Communications* 6: 1–9.

Erlandson, J. M., and T. J. Braje. 2015. "Coasting out of Africa: The Potential of Mangrove Forests and Marine Habitats to Facilitate Human Coastal Expansion via the Southern Dispersal Route." *Quaternary International* 382: 31–41.

Ermus, C. 2015. "The Plague of Provence: Early Advances in the Centralization of Crisis Management." *Arcadia* 9.

———. 2016. "The Spanish Plague That Never Was: Crisis and Exploitation in Cádiz During the Peste of Provence." *Eighteenth-Century Studies* 49: 167–93.

Eroshenko, G. A., et al. 2017. "*Yersinia pestis* Strains of Ancient Phylogenetic Branch 0.ANT Are Widely Spread in the High-Mountain Plague Foci of Kyrgyzstan." *PLoS One* 12: e0187230.

Escalante, A. A., et al. 2005. "A Monkey's Tale: The Origin of *Plasmodium vivax* as a Human Malaria Parasite." *Proceedings of the National Academy of Sciences* 102: 1980–85.

Escobar-Páramo, P., et al. 2003. "The Evolutionary History of *Shigella* and Enteroinvasive *Escherichia coli* Revised." *Journal of Molecular Evolution* 57: 140–48.

Espinosa, M. 2014. "The Question of Racial Immunity to Yellow Fever in History and Historiography." *Social Science History* 38: 437–53.

Etemad, B. 2007. *Possessing the World: Taking the Measurements of Colonisation from the Eighteenth to the Twentieth Century.* New York.

Evans, B. 1991. "Death in Aymaya of Upper Peru, 1580–1623." In *Secret Judgments of God: Old World Disease in Colonial Spanish America*, edited by N. D. Cook and W. G. Lovell, 142–58. Norman.

Evans, R. J. 1987. *Death in Hamburg: Society and Politics in the Cholera Years.* New York.

———. 1988. "Epidemics and Revolutions: Cholera in Nineteenth-Century Europe." *Past & Present* 120: 123–46.

Ewald, P. W. 1991. "Transmission Modes and the Evolution of Virulence: With Special Reference to Cholera, Influenza, and AIDS." *Human Nature* 2: 1–30.

———. 1994. *Evolution of Infectious Disease.* Oxford.

Fagan, B. M. 2017. *Fishing: How the Sea Fed Civilization.* New Haven.

Fages, A., et al. 2019. "Tracking Five Millennia of Horse Management with Extensive Ancient Genome Time Series." *Cell* 177: 1419–35.

———. 2020. "Horse Males Became Over-Represented in Archaeological Assemblages during the Bronze Age." *Journal of Archaeological Science: Reports* 31: 102364.

Farag, T. H., et al. 2013. "Housefly Population Density Correlates with Shigellosis among Children in Mirzapur, Bangladesh: A Time Series Analysis." *PLoS Neglected Tropical Diseases* 7: 2280.

Faria, N. R., et al. 2014. "The Early Spread and Epidemic Ignition of HIV-1 in Human Populations." *Science* 346: 56–61.

Farley, J. 1991. *Bilharzia: A History of Imperial Tropical Medicine.* Cambridge.

———. 2004. *To Cast Out Disease: A History of the International Health Division of the Rockefeller Foundation (1913–1951).* Oxford.

Farrell, J. M. 2006. "'This Horrible Spectacle': Visual and Verbal Sketches of the Famine in Skibbereen." In *Rhetorics of Display*, edited by L. Prelli, 66–89. Columbia.

Farris, W. W. 1985. *Population, Disease, and Land in Early Japan, 645–900*. Cambridge.

Faust, E. C. 1949. "Malaria Incidence in North America." In *Malariology: A Comprehensive Survey of All Aspects of This Group of Diseases from a Global Standpoint*, edited by M. F. Boyd, vol. 1, 749–63. Philadelphia.

Fauvelle, F.-X. 2018. *The Golden Rhinoceros: Histories of the African Middle Ages*. Translated by T. Tice. Princeton.

Federmann, N. 1859. *N. Federmanns und H. Stades Reisen in Südamerica 1529 bis 1555*. Stuttgart.

Feinberg, H. M. 1974. "New Data on European Mortality in West Africa: The Dutch on the Gold Coast, 1719–1760." *Journal of African History* 15: 357–71.

Feldman, M., et al. 2016. "A High-Coverage *Yersinia pestis* Genome from a Sixth-Century Justinianic Plague Victim." *Molecular Biology and Evolution* 33: 2911–23.

Felice, E. 2007. "I divari regionali in Italia sulla base degli indicatori sociali (1871–2001)." *Rivista di politica economica* 97: 359–405.

Fenn, E. A. 2001. *Pox Americana: The Great Smallpox Epidemic of 1775–82*. New York.

Fenner, F., et al., eds. 1989. *Smallpox and Its Eradication*. Geneva.

Ferretti, J. J., D. L. Stevens, and V. A. Fischetti. 2017. *Streptococcus pyogenes: Basic Biology to Clinical Manifestations*. Oklahoma City.

Field, Y., et al. 2016. "Detection of Human Adaptation during the Past 2000 Years." *Science* 354: 760–64.

Fiers, W., et al. 1976. "Complete Nucleotide Sequence of Bacteriophage MS2 RNA: Primary and Secondary Structure of the Replicase Gene." *Nature* 260: 500–7.

Findlay, R., and K. O'Rourke. 2007. *Power and Plenty: Trade, War, and the World Economy in the Second Millennium*. Princeton.

Fischer, D. H. 1991. *Albion's Seed: Four British Folkways in America*. Oxford.

Fitak, R., et al. 2015. "The *de novo* Genome Assembly and Annotation of a Female Domestic Dromedary of North African Origin." *Molecular Ecology Resources* 16: 314–24.

———. 2020. "Genomic Signatures of Domestication in Old World Camels." *Communications Biology* 3: 1–10.

Flajnik, M. F. 2018. "A Cold-Blooded View of Adaptive Immunity." *Nature Reviews Immunology* 18: 438–53.

Fleagle, J., et al., eds. 2010. *Out of Africa I: The First Hominin Colonization of Eurasia*. Dordrecht.

Flemming, R. 2019. "Galen and the Plague." In *Galen's Treatise Περὶ Ἀλυπίας (De indolentia) in Context*, edited by C. Petit, 219–44. Leiden.

Flinn, M. W. 1981. *The European Demographic System, 1500–1820*. Baltimore.

Flint, J., et al. 1998. "The Population Genetics of the Haemoglobinopathies." *Baillière's Clinical Haematology* 11: 1–51.

Flint, S., et al. 2015. *Principles of Virology*. 2 vols. Washington, DC.

Floud, R., et al. 2011. *The Changing Body: Health, Nutrition, and Human Development in the Western World since 1700*. Cambridge.

Fogel, R. W. 2004. *The Escape from Hunger and Premature Death, 1700–2100: Europe, America, and the Third World*. Cambridge.

Fontaine, R. E., A. E. Najjar, and J. S. Prince. 1961. "The 1958 Malaria Epidemic in Ethiopia." *American Journal of Tropical Medicine and Hygiene* 10: 795–803.

Ford, J. 1971. *Role of the Trypanosomiases in African Ecology: A Study of the Tsetse Fly Problem.* Oxford.

Foreman-Peck, J. 2011. "The Western European Marriage Pattern and Economic Development." *Explorations in Economic History* 48: 292–309.

Foreman-Peck, J., and P. Zhou. 2018. "Late Marriage as a Contributor to the Industrial Revolution in England." *Economic History Review* 71: 1073–99.

Formenty, P., et al. 2003. "Infectious Diseases in West Africa: A Common Threat to Chimpanzees and Humans." In *Status Survey and Conservation Action Plan: West African Chimpanzees,* edited by R. Kormos, 169–74. Cambridge.

Forni, D., et al. 2017. "Molecular Evolution of Human Coronavirus Genomes." *Trends in Microbiology* 25: 35–48.

———. 2020. "Recent Out-of-Africa Migration of Human Herpes Simplex Viruses." *Molecular Biology and Evolution* 37: 1259–71.

Foster, E. A. 1950. *Translation of Historia de los indios de la Nueva España.* Berkeley.

Foucault, M. 1975. *Surveiller et punir.* Paris.

Foulke, W. D. 1907. *History of the Langobards.* Philadelphia. Translation of Paul the Deacon, *Historia Langobardorum.*

Fracastoro, G. 1930. *Hieronymi fracastorii de contagione et contagiosis morbis et eorum curatione libri III.* New York.

France, M. M., and J. R. Turner. 2017. "The Mucosal Barrier at a Glance." *Journal of Cell Science* 130: 307–14.

Frank, S. 1996. "Models of Parasite Virulence." *Quarterly Review of Biology* 71: 37–78.

Franklin, B. 1751. "Observations Concerning the Increase of Mankind." In vol. 4 of *The Papers of Benjamin Franklin,* edited by L. W. Labaree, 225–34. New Haven.

Frankopan, P. 2016. *The Silk Roads: A New History of the World.* London.

———. 2019. "Why We Need to Think about the Global Middle Ages." *Journal of Medieval Worlds* 1: 5–10.

Frantz, L., et al. 2020. "Animal Domestication in the Era of Ancient Genomics." *Nature Reviews Genetics* 21: 449–60.

Frazer, J. G. 1930. *Myths of the Origin of Fire: An Essay.* London.

Friedrichs, C. R. 1995. *The Early Modern City, 1450–1750.* New York.

Frier, B. W. 2000. "Demography." In *The High Empire, A.D. 70–192,* edited by P. Garnsey, D. Rathbone, and A. K. Bowman, 787–816. Vol. 11 of *The Cambridge Ancient History.* Cambridge.

Fu, Q., et al. 2016. "The Genetic History of Ice Age Europe." *Nature* 534: 200–205.

Fuks, D., et al. 2020. "The Rise and Fall of Viticulture in the Late Antique Negev Highlands Reconstructed from Archaeobotanical and Ceramic Data." *Proceedings of the National Academy of Sciences* 117: 19780–91.

Fumagalli, M., et al. 2011. "Signatures of Environmental Genetic Adaptation Pinpoint Pathogens as the Main Selective Pressure through Human Evolution." *PLoS Genetics* 7: 1002355.

Furuse, Y., A. Suzuki, and H. Oshitani. 2010. "Origin of Measles Virus: Divergence from Rinderpest Virus between the 11th and 12th Centuries." *Virology Journal* 7: 52.

Fusco, I. 2007. *Peste, demografia e fiscalità nel regno di Napoli del XVII secolo*. Milan.

——. 2009. "La peste del 1656–58 nel Regno di Napoli: Diffusione e mortalità." *Popolazione e storia* 2: 115–38.

Gage, K., et al. 2008. "Climate and Vectorborne Diseases." *American Journal of Preventive Medicine* 35: 436–50.

Gage, K. L., and M. Y. Kosoy. 2005. "Natural History of Plague: Perspectives from More Than a Century of Research." *Annual Review of Entomology* 50: 505–28.

Gage, T., and S. DeWitte. 2009. "What Do We Know about the Agricultural Demographic Transition?" *Current Anthropology* 50: 649–55.

Gale, G. 2011. *Dying on the Vine: How Phylloxera Transformed Wine*. Berkeley.

Galinski, M., E. Meyer, and J. Barnwell. 2013. "*Plasmodium vivax*: Modern Strategies to Study a Persistent Parasite's Life Cycle." *Advances in Parasitology* 81: 1–26.

Gallagher, D. E., and S. A. Dueppen. 2018. "Recognizing Plague Epidemics in the Archaeological Record of West Africa." *Afriques: Débats, méthodes et terrains d'histoire* 9.

Gallup, J. L., and J. D. Sachs. 2001. "The Economic Burden of Malaria." *American Journal of Tropical Medical Hygiene* 64: 85–96.

Gallup-Diaz, I. 2005. *The Door of the Seas and Key to the Universe: Indian Politics and Imperial Rivalry in the Darién, 1640–1750*. Rev. ed. New York.

Gal-Mor, O., et al. 2014. "Same Species, Different Diseases: How and Why Typhoidal and Non-typhoidal *Salmonella enterica* Serovars Differ." *Frontiers in Microbiology* 5: 391.

Galois, R. M. 1996. "Measles, 1847–1850: The First Modern Epidemic in British Columbia." *BC Studies* 109: 31–43.

Galor, O. 2011. *Unified Growth Theory*. Princeton.

Gamble, C. 1993. *Timewalkers: The Prehistory of Global Colonization*. Cambridge.

Gao, F., et. al. 1999. "Origin of HIV-1 in the Chimpanzee *Pan troglodytes troglodytes*." *Nature* 397: 436–41.

Gardyner, G. 1651. *A Description of the New World, or, America, Islands and Continent: And by What People Those Regions Are Now Inhabited, and What Places Are There Desolate and without Inhabitants, and the Bays, Rivers, Capes, Forts, Cities and Their Latitudes, the Seas on Their Coasts, the Trade, Winds, the North-West Passage, and the Commerce of the English Nation, as They Were All in the Year 1649*. London.

Garrett, L. 1994. *The Coming Plague: Newly Emerging Diseases in a World out of Balance*. New York.

Gat, A. 2000a. "The Human Motivational Complex: Evolutionary Theory and the Causes of Hunter-Gatherer Fighting. Part I. Primary Somatic and Reproductive Causes." *Anthropological Quarterly* 73: 20–34.

——. 2000b. "The Human Motivational Complex: Evolutionary Theory and the Causes of Hunter-Gatherer Fighting, Part II. Proximate, Subordinate, and Derivative Causes." *Anthropological Quarterly* 73: 74–88.

Gaunitz, C., et al. 2018. "Ancient Genomes Revisit the Ancestry of Domestic and Przewalski's Horses." *Science* 360: 111–14.

Gautam, R., et al. 2015. "Full Genomic Characterization and Phylogenetic Analysis of a Zoonotic Human G8P[14] Rotavirus Strain Detected in a Sample from Guatemala." *Infection, Genetics and Evolution* 33: 206–11.

Geisel, T. 2005. *Theodor Seuss Geisel: The Early Works of Dr. Seuss*. Miamisburg.

Geison, G. L. 1995. *The Private Science of Louis Pasteur*. Princeton.

Gelabert, P., et al. 2017. "Malaria Was a Weak Selective Force in Ancient Europeans." *Scientific Reports* 7: 1377.

Geltner, G. 2019a. "In the Camp and on the March: Military Manuals as Sources for Studying Premodern Public Health." *Medical History* 63: 44–60.

———. 2019b. *Roads to Health: Infrastructure and Urban Wellbeing in Later Medieval Italy*. Philadelphia.

———. 2020. "The Path to Pistoia: Urban Hygiene before the Black Death." *Past & Present* 246: 3–33.

Gensini, G. F., A. A. Conti, and D. Lippi. 2007. "The Contributions of Paul Ehrlich to Infectious Disease." *Journal of Infection* 54: 221–24.

Ghawar, W., et al. 2017. "Insight into the Global Evolution of Rodentia Associated Morbilli Related Paramyxoviruses." *Scientific Reports* 7: 1–12.

Gheorgiu, M. 2011. "Antituberculosis BCG Vaccine: Lessons from the Past." In *History of Vaccine Development*, edited by S. Plotkin, 47–55. New York.

Giannecchini, M., and J. Moggi-Cecchi. 2008. "Stature in Archeological Samples from Central Italy: Methodological Issues and Diachronic Changes." *American Journal of Physical Anthropology* 135: 284–92.

Giffin, K., et al. 2020. "A Treponemal Genome from an Historic Plague Victim Supports a Recent Emergence of Yaws and Its Presence in 15th Century Europe." *Scientific Reports* 10: 1–13.

Gifford-Gonzalez, D. 2000. "Animal Disease Challenges to the Emergence of Pastoralism in Sub-Saharan Africa." *African Archaeological Review* 17: 95–139.

Gilabert, A., et al. 2018. "*Plasmodium vivax*-Like Genome Sequences Shed New Insights into *Plasmodium vivax* Biology and Evolution." *PLoS Biology* 16: e2006035.

Gilberg, R. 1976. *The Polar Eskimo Population, Thule District*. Copenhagen.

———. 1984. "Polar Eskimo." In *Arctic*, edited by D. Damas, 577–94. Vol. 5 of *Handbook of the North American Indian*. Washington, DC.

Gilbert, J., et al. 2018. "Current Understanding of the Human Microbiome." *Nature Medicine* 24: 392–400.

Gilbert, T., et al. 2004. "Absence of *Yersinia pestis*-Specific DNA in Human Teeth from Five European Excavations of Putative Plague Victims." *Microbiology* 150: 341–54.

Gillespie, T. R., et al. 2010. "Demographic and Ecological Effects on Patterns of Parasitism in Eastern Chimpanzees (*Pan troglodytes schweinfurthii*) in Gombe National Park, Tanzania." *American Journal of Physical Anthropology* 143: 534–44.

Gilliam, J. F. 1961. "The Plague under Marcus Aurelius." *American Journal of Philology* 94: 225–51.

Gillings, M. R., and I. T. Paulsen. 2014. "Microbiology of the Anthropocene." *Anthropocene* 5: 1–8.

Glaeser, E. L., et al. 2004. "Do Institutions Cause Growth?" *Journal of Economic Growth* 9: 271–303.

Glynn, I., and J. Glynn. 1994. *The Life and Death of Smallpox*. New York.

Go, S., and P. Lindert. 2007. "The Curious Dawn of American Public Schools." National Bureau of Economic Research working paper 13335. Cambridge.

———. 2010. "The Uneven Rise of American Public Schools to 1850." *Journal of Economic History* 70: 1–26.

Goldberg, A., A. M. Mychajliw, and E. A. Hadly. 2016. "Post-invasion Demography of Prehistoric Humans in South America." *Nature* 532: 232–35.

Goldin, C. 2016. "Human Capital." In *Handbook of Cliometrics*, edited by C. Diebolt and M. Haupert, 55–86. Heidelberg.

Goldstone, J. A. 1991. *Revolution and Rebellion in the Early Modern World*. Berkeley.

———. 2002. "Efflorescences and Economic Growth in World History: Rethinking the 'Rise of the West' and the Industrial Revolution." *Journal of World History* 13: 323–89.

Gomez, M. A. 2018. *African Dominion: A New History of Empire in Early and Medieval West Africa*. Princeton.

Gómez, N. W. 2008. *The Tropics of Empire: Why Columbus Sailed South to the Indies*. Cambridge.

Goodyear, J. 1978. "The Sugar Connection: A New Perspective on the History of the Yellow Fever." *Bulletin of the History of Medicine* 52: 5–21.

Gordon, R. J. 2016. *The Rise and Fall of American Growth: The U.S. Standard of Living since the Civil War*. Princeton.

Goring-Morris, N., and A. Belfer-Cohen. 2010. "'Great Expectations,' or the Inevitable Collapse of the Early Neolithic in the Near East." In *Becoming Villagers: Comparing Early Village Societies*, edited by M. S. Brandy and J. R. Fox, 62–80. Tucson.

Goudsblom, J. 1992. *Fire and Civilization*. London.

———. 2015. "Fire and Fuel in Human History." In vol. 1 of *The Cambridge World History*, edited by D. Christian, 185–207. Cambridge.

Gould, S. J. 1988. *An Urchin in the Storm: Essays about Books and Ideas*. New York.

———. 1996. *Full House: The Spread of Excellence from Plato to Darwin*. New York.

Gourevitch, D. 2009. *Limos kai Loimos: A Study of the Galenic Plague*. Paris.

Gowland, R., and P. Garnsey. 2010. "Skeletal Evidence for Health, Nutrition and Malaria in Rome and the Empire." In *Roman Diasporas: Archaeological Approaches to Mobility and Diversity in the Roman Empire*, edited by H. Eckardt, 131–56. Portsmouth.

Gradmann, C. 2009. *Laboratory Disease: Robert Koch's Medical Bacteriology*. Baltimore.

Gradoni, L., and F. Bruschi. 2018. *The Leishmaniases: Old Neglected Tropical Diseases*. Cham.

Gragg, L. D. 1993. "A Puritan in the West Indies: The Career of Samuel Winthrop." *William and Mary Quarterly* 50: 768–86.

———. 1995. "'To Procure Negroes': The English Slave Trade to Barbados, 1627–60." *Slavery and Abolition* 16: 65–84.

———. 2003. *Englishmen Transplanted: The English Colonization of Barbados 1627–1660*. Oxford.

Grant, A. 2019. *Globalisation of Variolation: The Overlooked Origins of Immunity for Smallpox in the 18th Century*. London.

Grant, P., and B. Grant. 1996. "Speciation and Hybridization in Island Birds." *Philosophical Transactions of the Royal Society of London. Series B: Biological Sciences* 351: 765–72.

Gray, J. 1962. *History of Zanzibar, from the Middle Ages to 1856*. London.

Green, M. 2014. "Taking 'Pandemic' Seriously: Making the Black Death Global." *Medieval Globe* 1: 27–61.

————, ed. 2015. *Pandemic Disease in the Medieval World: Rethinking the Black Death*. Kalamazoo.

————. 2017. "The Globalisations of Disease." In *Human Dispersal and Species Movement: From Prehistory to the Present*, edited by N. Boivin, R. Crassard, and M. D. Petraglia, 494–520. Cambridge.

————. 2018. "Putting Africa on the Black Death Map: Narratives from Genetics and History." *Afriques: Débats, méthodes, et terrains d'histoire* 9.

————. 2020. "The Four Black Deaths." *American Historical Review* 125: 1601–31.

Green, M., and L. Jones. 2020. "The Evolution and Spread of Major Human Diseases in the Indian Ocean World." In *Disease Dispersion and Impact in the Indian Ocean World*, edited by G. Campbell and E.-M. Knoll, 25–57. Cham.

Green, T. 2019. *A Fistful of Shells: West Africa from the Rise of the Slave Trade to the Age of Revolution*. Chicago.

Greenberg, B. 1965. "Flies and Disease." *Scientific American* 213: 92–99.

————. 1971. *Flies and Disease*. 2 vols. Princeton.

Greenberg, J. 2003. "Plagued by Doubt: Reconsidering the Impact of a Mortality Crisis in the 2nd c. A.D.," *Journal of Roman Archaeology* 16: 413–25.

Greenblatt, C. L., and M. Spigelman. 2003. *Emerging Pathogens: The Archaeology, Ecology, and Evolution of Infectious Disease*. Oxford.

Greenhill, W., trans. 1847. *A Treatise on the Smallpox and Measles*. By Rhazes. London.

Greenwood, D. 2008. *Antimicrobial Drugs: Chronicle of a Twentieth Century Medical Triumph*. Oxford.

Greenwood, M. 1937. *Epidemics and Crowd-Diseases: An Introduction to the Study of Epidemiology*. London.

Greer, M., W. D. Mignolo, and M. Quilligan. 2007. *Rereading the Black Legend: The Discourses of Religious and Racial Difference in the Renaissance Empires*. Chicago.

Griffin, R. H., and C. L. Nunn. 2012. "Community Structure and the Spread of Infectious Disease in Primate Social Networks." *Evolutionary Ecology* 26: 779–800.

Griffiths, A. 1884. *The Chronicles of Newgate*. Vol. 1. London.

Grignolio, A. 2018. "A Brief History of Anti-vaccination Movements." In *Vaccines: Are They Worth a Shot?*, edited by A. Grignolio, 25–40. Cham.

Grimmelshausen, H. J. C. von. 2018. *The Adventures of Simplicius Simplicissimus*. Translated by J. A. Underwood. London. First published 1668.

Gripp, E., et al. 2011. "Closely Related *Campylobacter jejuni* Strains from Different Sources Reveal a Generalist Rather Than a Specialist Lifestyle." *BMC Genomics* 12: 1–21.

Grivet, L., et al. 2004. "A Review of Recent Molecular Genetics Evidence for Sugarcane Evolution and Domestication." *Ethnobotany Research & Applications* 2: 9–17.

Grmek, M. D. 1989. *Diseases in the Ancient Greek World*. Baltimore.

Grob, G. N. 2002. *The Deadly Truth: A History of Disease in America*. Cambridge.

Gross, M. 2015. *Farewell to the God of Plague: Chairman Mao's Campaign to Deworm China*. Oakland.

Groucutt, H. S., et al. 2015. "Rethinking the Dispersal of *Homo sapiens* out of Africa." *Evolutionary Anthropology* 24: 149–64.

————. 2018. "*Homo sapiens* in Arabia by 85,000 Years Ago." *Nature Ecology & Evolution* 2: 800–809.

Grubb, F. 1990. "Growth of Literacy in Colonial America: Longitudinal Patterns, Economic Models, and the Direction of Future Research." *Social Science History* 14: 451–82.

Gruhn, R. 2020. "Evidence Grows That Peopling of the Americas Began More Than 20,000 Years Ago." *Nature* 584: 47–48.

Grützmacher, K., et al. 2018. "Human Quarantine: Toward Reducing Infectious Pressure on Chimpanzees at the Taï Chimpanzee Project, Côte d'Ivoire." *American Journal of Primatology* 80: e22619.

Gubser, N. J. 1965. *The Nunamiut Eskimos, Hunters of Caribou*. New Haven.

Guernier, V., M. Hochberg, and J.-F. Guégan. 2004. "Ecology Drives the Worldwide Distribution of Human Diseases." *PLoS Biology* 2: 740–46.

Guerra, F. 1968. "Aleixo de Abreu [1568–1630], Author of the Earliest Book on Tropical Medicine Describing Amoebiasis." *Journal of Tropical Medicine and Hygiene* 71: 55–69.

———. 1988. "The Earliest American Epidemic: The Influenza of 1493." *Social Science History* 12: 305–25.

———. 1999. "Origen y efectos demográficos del tifo en el México colonial." *Colonial Latin American Historical Review* 8: 273–319.

Guinnane, T. 2011. "The Historical Fertility Transition: A Guide for Economists." *Journal of Economic Literature* 49: 589–614.

Gunn, B., et al. 2011. "Independent Origins of Cultivated Coconut (*Cocos nucifera* L.) in the Old World Tropics." *PLoS One* 6: e21143.

Gupta, A., et al. 2012. "*Mycobacterium tuberculosis*: Immune Evasion, Latency and Reactivation." *Immunobiology* 217: 363–74.

Gupta, J. N. 1911. *Life and Work of Romesh Chunder Dutt*. London.

Gupta, K. R. L. 1987. *Madhava nidana: Ayurvedic System of Pathology*. Delhi.

Gurven, M., and C. Gomes. 2017. "Mortality, Senescence, and the Life Span." In *Chimpanzees and Human Evolution*, edited by M. Muller, R. Wrangham, and D. Pilbeam, 181–216. Cambridge.

Gurven, M., and H. Kaplan. 2007. "Longevity among Hunter-Gatherers: A Cross-Cultural Examination." *Population and Development Review* 33: 321–65.

Gutmann, M. P. 1980. *War and Rural Life in the Early Modern Low Countries*. Princeton.

Györy, T. 1901. *Morbus Hungaricus; eine medico-historische Quellenstudie zugleich ein Beitrag zur Geschichte der Türkenherrschaft in Ungarn*. Jena.

Hacker, J. D. 1997. "Trends and Determinants of Adult Mortality in Early New England: Reconciling Old and New Evidence from the Long Eighteenth Century." *Social Science History* 21: 481–519.

Hackett, L. W. 1937. *Malaria in Europe; an Ecological Study*. London.

Haensch, S., et al. 2010. "Distinct Clones of *Yersinia pestis* Caused the Black Death." *PLoS Pathogens* 6: e1001134.

Haeusler, M., et al. 2013. "Evidence for Juvenile Disc Herniation in a *Homo erectus* Boy Skeleton." *Spine* 38: E123.

Haines, M. R. 2001. "The Urban Mortality Transition in the United States, 1800–1940." *Annales de demographie historique* 101: 33–64.

Haines, R., and R. Shlomowitz. 1998. "Explaining the Modern Mortality Decline: What Can We Learn from Sea Voyages?" *Social History of Medicine* 11: 15–48.

Hajnal, J. 1965. "European Marriage Patterns in Perspective." In *Population in History: Essays in Historical Demography*, edited by D. V. Glass, 101–43. Chicago.

———. 1982. "Two Kinds of Preindustrial Household Formation System." *Population and Development Review* 8: 449–94.

Hamilton, M., et al. 2007. "The Complex Structure of Hunter-Gatherer Social Networks." *Proceedings of the Royal Society B: Biological Sciences* 274: 2195–203.

Hamlin, C. 1998. *Public Health and Social Justice in the Age of Chadwick: Britain, 1800–1854.* Cambridge.

———. 2009. *Cholera: The Biography.* Oxford.

———. 2011. "Public Health." In *The Oxford Handbook of the History of Medicine*, edited by M. Jackson, 411–28. Oxford.

———. 2015. *More than Hot: A Short History of Fever.* Baltimore.

Hammer, P., ed. 2017. *Warfare in Early Modern Europe 1450–1660.* Milton Park.

Han, B. A., A. M. Kramer, and J. M. Drake. 2016. "Global Patterns of Zoonotic Disease in Mammals." *Trends in Parasitology* 32: 565–77.

Han, B. A., et al. 2015. "Rodent Reservoirs of Future Zoonotic Diseases." *Proceedings of the National Academy of Sciences* 112:7039–44.

Han, X., and F. Silva. 2014. "On the Age of Leprosy." *PLoS Neglected Tropical Diseases* 8: e2544.

Hanks, B. K., and K. M. Linduff. 2009. *Social Complexity in Prehistoric Eurasia: Monuments, Metals and Mobility.* Cambridge.

Hanley, S. 1987. "Urban Sanitation in Preindustrial Japan." *Journal of Interdisciplinary History* 18: 1–26.

Hanson, J. W. 2016. *An Urban Geography of the Roman World, 100 BC to AD 300.* Oxford.

Harari, Y. N. 2014. *Sapiens: A Brief History of Humankind.* London.

Harbach, R. E. 2013. *Mosquito Taxonomic Inventory.* Accessed August 2020. http://mosquito -taxonomic-inventory.info/.

Hardy, A. 1988. "Urban Famine or Urban Crisis? Typhus in the Victorian City." *Medical History* 32: 401–25.

———. 1993a. *The Epidemic Streets: Infectious Disease and the Rise of Preventive Medicine, 1856– 1900.* Oxford.

———. 1993b. "Scarlet Fever." In *The Cambridge World History of Human Disease*, edited by K. Kiple, 990–92. Cambridge.

Harpending, H. and L. Wandsnider. 1982. "Population Structures of Ghanzi and Ngamiland !Kung." *Current Developments in Anthropological Genetics* 2: 29–50.

Harper, K. 2016. "Reply to John Brooke, on Civilization, Climate, and Malthus." *Journal of Interdisciplinary History* 46: 579–84.

———. 2017. *The Fate of Rome: Climate, Disease, and the End of an Empire.* Princeton.

———. 2020. "Germs, Genes, and Global History in the Age of COVID-19." *Journal of Global History* 15: 350–62.

Harper, K. N., and G. J. Armelagos. 2013. "Genomics, the Origins of Agriculture, and Our Changing Microbe-scape: Time to Revisit Some Old Tales and Tell Some New Ones." *American Journal of Physical Anthropology* 57: 135–52.

Harris, B. 2004. "Public Health, Nutrition, and the Decline of Mortality: The McKeown Thesis Revisited." *Social History of Medicine* 17: 379–407.

Harris, W. 1693. *An Exact Enquiry into, and Cure of the Acute Diseases of Infants*. London.

Harris, W. V. 1985. *War and Imperialism in Republican Rome, 327–70 BC*. Oxford.

Harrison, G. 1978. *Mosquitoes, Malaria, and Man: A History of the Hostilities since 1880*. New York.

Harrison, M. 1994. *Public Health in British India: Anglo-Indian Preventive Medicine, 1859–1914*. Cambridge.

———. 2012. *Contagion: How Commerce Has Spread Disease*. New Haven.

———. 2015. "A Global Perspective: Reframing the History of Health, Medicine, and Disease." *Bulletin of the History of Medicine* 89: 639–89.

———. 2020. "A Dreadful Scourge: Cholera in Early Nineteenth-Century India." *Modern Asian Studies* 54: 502–53.

Harvey, S. A. 1990. *Asceticism and Society in Crisis: John of Ephesus and the Lives of the Eastern Saints*. Berkeley.

Haseyama, K. L. F., et al. 2015. "Say Goodbye to Tribes in the New House Fly Classification: A New Molecular Phylogenetic Analysis and an Updated Biogeographical Narrative for the Muscidae (Diptera)." *Molecular Phylogenetics and Evolution* 89: 1–12.

Hassan, F. A. 1981. *Demographic Archaeology*. New York.

Hatcher, J. 1977. *Plague, Population and the English Economy, 1348–1530*. London.

———. 2003. "Understanding the Population History of England 1450–1750." *Past & Present* 180: 83–130.

Hawash, M., et al. 2016. "Whipworms in Humans and Pigs: Origins and Demography." *Parasites & Vectors* 9: 37.

Hay, S. I., et al. 2010. "Developing Global Maps of the Dominant Anopheles Vectors of Human Malaria." *PLoS Medicine* 7: 1000209.

Hayakawa, T., et al. 2008. "Big Bang in the Evolution of Extant Malaria Parasites." *Molecular Biology and Evolution* 25: 2233–39.

Hayman, D. T. S. 2016. "Bats as Viral Reservoirs." *Annual Review of Virology* 3: 77–99.

Haynes, D. 2001. *Imperial Medicine: Patrick Manson and the Conquest of Tropical Disease*. Philadelphia.

Hays, J. N. 1998. *The Burdens of Disease: Epidemics and Human Response in Western History*. New Brunswick.

———. 2005. *Epidemics and Pandemics: Their Impacts on Human History*. Santa Barbara.

Hazen, T. H., et al. 2016. "Investigating the Relatedness of Enteroinvasive *Escherichia coli* to Other *E. coli* and *Shigella* Isolates by Using Comparative Genomics." *Infection and Immunity* 84: 2362–71.

Headland, T. 1988. "Ecosystemic Change in a Philippine Tropical Rainforest and Its Effect on a Negrito Foraging Society." *Tropical Ecology* 29: 121–35.

Headrick, D. R. 1981. *The Tools of Empire: Technology and European Imperialism in the Nineteenth Century*. New York.

Heberden, W. 1813. "Some Observations on the Scurvy." *Medical Transactions of the Royal College of Physicians* 4: 70.

Hemingway, J., L. Field, and J. Vontas. 2002. "An Overview of Insecticide Resistance." *Science* 298: 96–97.

Hemingway, J., and H. Ranson. 2000. "Insecticide Resistance in Insect Vectors of Human Disease." *Annual Review of Entomology* 45: 371–91.

Hemingway, J., et al. 2004. "The Molecular Basis of Insecticide Resistance in Mosquitoes." *Insect Biochemistry and Molecular Biology* 34: 653–65.

Hemming, J. 1978. *Red Gold: The Conquest of the Brazilian Indians*. Cambridge.

———. 2006. "Romance and Reality: The First European Vision of Brazilian Indians." In *Human Impacts on Amazonia: The Role of Traditional Ecological Knowledge in Conservation and Development*, edited by D. Posey and M. Balick, 5–16. New York.

Henderson, J. 1992. "The Black Death in Florence: Medical and Communal Responses." In *Death in Towns: Urban Responses to the Dying and the Dead, 100–1600*, edited by S. Bassett, 136–50. London.

———. 2006. *The Renaissance Hospital: Healing the Body and Healing the Soul*. New Haven.

Hendrickson, R. 1983. *More Cunning than Man: A Social History of Rats and Men*. New York.

Henige, D. P. 1998. *Numbers from Nowhere: The American Indian Contact Population Debate*. Norman.

Herbert, E. 1975. "Smallpox Inoculation in Africa." *Journal of African History* 16: 539–59.

Herlihy, D. 1997. *The Black Death and the Transformation of the West*. Cambridge.

Hersh, J., and H. J. Voth. 2009. "Sweet Diversity: Colonial Goods and the Rise of European Living Standards after 1492." Center for Economic Policy Research discussion paper no. DP7386.

Hershberg, R., et al. 2008. "High Functional Diversity in *Mycobacterium tuberculosis* Driven by Genetic Drift and Human Demography." *PLoS Biology* 6: e311.

Hershkovitz, I., et al. 2018. "The Earliest Modern Humans outside Africa." *Science* 359: 456–59.

Hewitt, C. G. 1914. *The House-Fly: Its Structure, Habits, Development, Relation to Disease and Control*. Cambridge.

Hidalgo, D. R. 2001. "To Get Rich for Our Homeland: The Company of Scotland and the Colonization of the Isthmus of Darien." *Colonial Latin American Historical Review* 10: 311–50.

Higginson, F. 1908. *New-Englands Plantation: With the Sea Journal and Other Writings*. Salem. First published 1630.

Higman, B. W. 2000. "The Sugar Revolution." *Economic History Review* 53: 213–36.

———. 2011. *A Concise History of the Caribbean*. New York.

Hill, E. M., M. J. Tildesley, and T. House. 2017. "Evidence for History-Dependence of Influenza Pandemic Emergence." *Scientific Reports* 7: 43623.

Hill, K. 2001. "Mortality Rates among Wild Chimpanzees." *Journal of Human Evolution* 40: 437–50.

Hill, K., and A. M. Hurtado. 1996. *Ache Life History: The Ecology and Demography of a Foraging People*. Somerset.

Hill, K., A. M. Hurtado, and R. S. Walker. 2007. "High Adult Mortality among Hiwi Hunter-Gatherers: Implications for Human Evolution." *Journal of Human Evolution* 52: 443–54.

Hill, K. R. 1953. "Non-specific Factors in the Epidemiology of Yaws." *Bulletin of the World Health Organization* 8: 17–47.

Hin, S. 2013. *The Demography of Roman Italy: Population Dynamics in an Ancient Conquest Society, 201 BCE—14 CE*. Cambridge.

Hinman, A., et al. 1983. "Impact of Measles in the United States." *Reviews of Infectious Diseases* 5: 439–44.

Hinnebusch, B. J., I. Chouikha, and Y.-C. Sun. 2016. "Ecological Opportunity, Evolution, and the Emergence of Flea-Borne Plague." *Infection and Immunity* 84: 1932–40.

Hinnebusch, B. J., C. O. Jarrett, and D. M. Bland. 2017. "'Fleaing' the Plague: Adaptations of *Yersinia pestis* to Its Insect Vector That Lead to Transmission." *Annual Review of Microbiology* 71: 215–32.

Hirsch, A. 1883. *Acute Infectious Diseases*. Vol. 1 of *Handbook of Geographical and Historical Pathology*. London.

Hirschfeld, K. 2020. "Microbial Insurgency: Theorizing Global Health in the Anthropocene." *Anthropocene Review* 7: 3–18.

Hirth, F., and W. W. Rockhill. 1911. *Chau Ju-Kua: His Work on the Chinese and Arab Trade in the Twelfth and Thirteenth Centuries, Entitled Chu Fan Chï*. St. Petersburg.

Hiyoshi, H., et al. 2018. "Typhoidal Salmonella Serovars: Ecological Opportunity and the Evolution of a New Pathovar." *FEMS Microbiology Reviews* 42: 527–41.

Hlubik, S., et al. 2017. "Researching the Nature of Fire at 1.5 Mya on the Site of FxJj20 AB, Koobi Fora, Kenya, Using High-Resolution Spatial Analysis and FTIR Spectrometry." *Current Anthropology* 58: 243–57.

Ho, S., et al. 2005. "Time Dependency of Molecular Rate Estimates and Systematic Overestimation of Recent Divergence Times." *Molecular Biology and Evolution* 22: 1561–68.

Hobsbawm, E. J. 1954. "The General Crisis of the European Economy in the 17th Century." *Past & Present* 5: 33–53.

Hodder, I. 1990. *The Domestication of Europe: Structure and Contingency in Neolithic Societies*. Oxford.

Hodgson, D. 1991. "Benjamin Franklin on Population: From Policy to Theory." *Population and Development Review* 17: 639–61.

Hofman, C., and C. Warinner. 2019. "Ancient DNA 101: An Introductory Guide in the Era of High-Throughput Sequencing." *SAA Archaeological Record* 19: 18–25.

Hohenberg, P. M., and L. H. Lees. 1985. *The Making of Urban Europe, 1000–1950*. Cambridge.

Hohmann, G. 2009. "The Diets of Non-human Primates: Frugivory, Food Processing, and Food Sharing." In *The Evolution of Hominin Diets: Integrating Approaches to the Study of Palaeolithic Subsistence*, edited by J. J. Hublin, 1–14. Dordrecht.

Hollingsworth, T. 1977. "Mortality in the British Peerage Families since 1600." *Population* 32: 323–52.

Holmes, C., and N. Standen. 2018. "Introduction: Towards a Global Middle Ages." *Past & Present* 238: 1–44.

Holmes, F. 2003. *The Sickly Stuarts: The Medical Downfall of a Dynasty*. Stroud.

Holmes, O. W. 1838. *Prize Dissertations for the Years 1836 and 1837*. Boston.

Holt, K. E., et al. 2008. "High-Throughput Sequencing Provides Insights into Genome Variation and Evolution in *Salmonella typhi*." *Nature Genetics* 40: 987–93.

———. 2012. "*Shigella sonnei* Genome Sequencing and Phylogenetic Analysis Indicate Recent Global Dissemination from Europe." *Nature Genetics* 44: 1056–59.

Honap, T., et al. 2018. "*Mycobacterium leprae* Genomes from Naturally Infected Nonhuman Primates." *PLoS Neglected Tropical Diseases* 12: e0006190.

Hong, S. C. 2007. "The Burden of Early Exposure to Malaria in the United States, 1850–1860: Malnutrition and Immune Disorders." *Journal of Economic History* 67: 1001–35.

Honigsbaum, M. 2014. *A History of the Great Influenza Pandemics: Death, Panic, and Hysteria, 1830–1920*. London.

Hopkins, D. R. 2002. *The Greatest Killer: Smallpox in History, with a New Introduction.* Chicago.

Hopkins, J. F. P., and N. Levtzion. 1981. *Corpus of Early Arabic Sources for West African History.* Cambridge.

Hopkins, K. 2018. *Sociological Studies in Roman History.* Edited by C. Kelly. Cambridge.

Horden, P. 2005. "Mediterranean Plague in the Age of Justinian." In *The Cambridge Companion to the Age of Justinian,* edited by M. Maas, 134–60. Cambridge.

Horn, J., and P. D. Morgan. 2005. "Settlers and Slaves: European and African Migrations to Early Modern British America." In *The Creation of the British Atlantic World,* edited by E. Mancke and C. Shammas, 19–44. Baltimore.

Horrox, R. 1994. *The Black Death.* Manchester.

Hotez, P. J. 2005. "Hookworm: 'The Great Infection of Mankind.'" *PLoS Medicine* 2: 67.

———. 2013. *Forgotten People, Forgotten Diseases: The Neglected Tropical Diseases and Their Impact on Global Health and Development.* 2nd ed. Washington, DC.

Hotez, P. J., et al. 2006. "The Neglected Tropical Diseases: The Ancient Afflictions of Stigma and Poverty and the Prospects for Their Control and Elimination." In *Hot Topics in Infection and Immunity in Children III,* edited by A. J. Pollard and A. Finn, 23–33. Boston.

———. 2020. "What Constitutes a Neglected Tropical Disease?" *PLoS Neglected Tropical Diseases* 14: e0008001.

Houldcroft, C. J. 2019. "Human Herpesvirus Sequencing in the Genomic Era: The Growing Ranks of the Herpetic Legion." *Pathogens* 8: 186.

Houldcroft, C. J., and S. J. Underdown. 2016. "Neanderthal Genomics Suggests a Pleistocene Time Frame for the First Epidemiologic Transition." *American Journal of Physical Anthropology* 160: 379–88.

Houston, A. 2003. "Population Politics: Benjamin Franklin and the Peopling of North America." Center for Comparative Immigration Studies working paper 88. University of California, San Diego. La Jolla.

Houston, R. A. 2014. *Literacy in Early Modern Europe.* 2nd ed. New York.

Howard, J. 1777. *The State of the Prisons in England and Wales: With Preliminary Observations, and an Account of Some Foreign Prisons.* London.

Howard, R. 1994. "Eighteenth Century West Indian Pharmaceuticals." *Harvard Papers in Botany* 1: 69–91.

Howard-Jones, N. 1975. *The Scientific Background of the International Sanitary Conferences, 1851–1938.* Geneva.

Howell, N. 1979. *Demography of the Dobe !Kung.* New York.

Howes, R., et al. 2011. "The Global Distribution of the Duffy Blood Group." *Nature Communications* 2: 266.

———. 2013. "Spatial Distribution of G6PD Deficiency Variants across Malaria-Endemic Regions." *Malaria Journal* 12: 1–15.

———. 2016. "Global Epidemiology of *Plasmodium vivax.*" *American Journal of Tropical Medicine and Hygiene* 95: 15–34.

Howitt-Marshall, D., and C. Runnels. 2016. "Middle Pleistocene Sea-Crossings in the Eastern Mediterranean?" *Journal of Anthropological Archaeology* 42: 140–53.

Hu, D., et al. 2016. "Origins of the Current Seventh Cholera Pandemic." *Proceedings of National Academy of Sciences* 113: 7730–39.

Huber, V. 2006. "The Unification of the Globe by Disease? The International Sanitary Conferences on Cholera, 1851–1894." *Historical Journal* 49: 453–76.

Hudson, G., ed. 2007. *British Military and Naval Medicine, 1600–1830*. Amsterdam.

Huffman, M. A., and C. A. Chapman. 2009. *Primate Parasite Ecology: The Dynamics and Study of Host-Parasite Relationships*. Cambridge.

Hufthammer, A., and L. Walløe. 2013. "Rats Cannot Have Been Intermediate Hosts for *Yersinia pestis* during Medieval Plague Epidemics in Northern Europe." *Journal of Archaeological Science* 40: 1752–59.

Hughes, G. 1872. *Amoy and the Surrounding Districts: Compiled from Chinese and Other Records*. Hong Kong.

Hugo, W. B. 1991. "A Brief History of Heat and Chemical Preservation and Disinfection." *Journal of Applied Bacteriology* 71: 9–18.

Hume, J. C. C., E. J. Lyons, and K. P. Day. 2003. "Human Migration, Mosquitoes and the Evolution of *Plasmodium falciparum*." *Trends in Parasitology* 19: 144–49.

Humphreys, M. 1992. *Yellow Fever and the South*. New Brunswick.

———. 2006. "A Stranger to Our Camps: Typhus in American History." *Bulletin of the History of Medicine* 80: 269–90.

Huysecom, E., et al. 2009. "The Emergence of Pottery in Africa during the Tenth Millennium Cal BC: New Evidence from Ounjougou (Mali)." *Antiquity* 83: 905–17.

Hymes, R. H. 2014. "Epilogue: A Hypothesis on the East Asian Beginnings of the *Yersinia pestis* Polytomy." *Medieval Globe* 1: 285–308.

Ibn Khaldūn. 1967. *The Muqaddimah: An Introduction to History*. 2nd ed. 3 vols. Translated by F. Rosenthal. Princeton.

Igler, D. 2004. "Diseased Goods: Global Exchanges in the Pacific Basin, 1770–1850." *American Historical Review* 109: 699–716.

———. 2013. *The Great Ocean: Pacific Worlds from Captain Cook to the Gold Rush*. New York.

Iles, J. C., et al. 2014. "Phylogeography and Epidemic History of Hepatitis C Virus Genotype 4 in Africa." *Virology* 464–65: 233–43.

Iliffe, J. 2006. *The African AIDS Epidemic: A History*. Athens.

———. 2017. *Africans: The History of a Continent*. Cambridge.

Imbert, J., and M. Mollat. 1982. *Histoire des hôpitaux en France*. Toulouse.

Inoue, H., et al. 2015. "Urban Scale Shifts since the Bronze Age: Upsweeps, Collapses, and Semiperipheral Development." *Social Science History* 39: 175–200.

Iraola, G., et al. 2014. "Genomic Evidence for the Emergence and Evolution of Pathogenicity and Niche Preferences in the Genus *Campylobacter*." *Genome Biology and Evolution* 6: 2392–405.

———. 2017. "Distinct *Campylobacter fetus* Lineages Adapted as Livestock Pathogens and Human Pathobionts in the Intestinal Microbiota." *Nature Communications* 8: 1367.

Iriemenam, N. C., et al. 2008. "Dracunculiasis—the Saddle Is Virtually Ended." *Parasitology Research* 102: 343–47.

Isenberg, D. 2020. *The Destruction of the Bison: An Environmental History, 1750–1920*. 20th anniversary edition. Cambridge.

Islam, M. T., M. Alam, and Y. Boucher. 2017. "Emergence, Ecology and Dispersal of the Pandemic Generating *Vibrio cholerae* Lineage." *International Microbiology* 20: 106–15.

Jablonski, D., et al. 2017. "Shaping the Latitudinal Diversity Gradient: New Perspectives from a Synthesis of Paleobiology and Biogeography." *American Naturalist* 189: 1–12.

Jackson, J. 1835. *Memoir of James Jackson*. Boston.

Jackson, P. 2014. *The Mongols and the West: 1221–1410*. 2nd ed. New York.

Jamieson, B. G. M. 2016. *Schistosoma: Biology, Pathology and Control*. Boca Raton.

Jannetta, A. B. 1987. *Epidemics and Mortality in Early Modern Japan*. Princeton.

———. 2007. *The Vaccinators: Smallpox, Medical Knowledge, and the 'Opening' of Japan*. Stanford.

Jansen, H. J., et al. 2014. "Biological Warfare, Bioterrorism, and Biocrime." *Clinical Microbiology and Infection* 20: 488–96.

Jarcho, S. 1993. *Quinine's Predecessor: Francesco Torti and the Early History of Cinchona*. Baltimore.

Jartti, T., et al. 2012. "New Respiratory Viral Infections." *Current Opinion in Pulmonary Medicine* 18: 271–78.

Jay, F. 1997. *Historia Eclesiástica Indiana: A Franciscan's View of the Spanish Conquest of Mexico*. Lewiston.

Jedwab, R., N. Johnson, and M. Koyama. 2020. "The Economic Impact of the Black Death." Center for Economic Policy Research discussion paper no. DP15132.

Jenner, E. 1800. *An Inquiry into the Causes and Effects of the Variolae Vaccinae*. London.

Jensen, P. 2014. "Behavior Genetics and the Domestication of Animals." *Annual Review of Animal Biosciences* 2: 85–104.

Jiang, P., et al. 2007. "Evidence for Emergence of Diverse Polioviruses from C-Cluster Coxsackie A Viruses and Implications for Global Poliovirus Eradication." *Proceedings of the National Academy of Sciences* 104: 9457–62.

Jin, L., et al. 2015. "Genomic Diversity of Mumps Virus and Global Distribution of the 12 Genotypes." *Reviews in Medical Virology* 25: 85–101.

Johansson, S. R. 2010. "Medics, Monarchs and Mortality, 1600–1800: Origins of the Knowledge-Driven Health Transition in Europe." Available at SSRN: https://ssrn.com/abstract=1661453.

Johnson, A. L. 2014. "Exploring Adaptive Variation among Hunter-Gatherers with Binford's Frames of Reference." *Journal of Archaeological Research* 22: 1–42.

Johnson, N. P., and J. Mueller. 2002. "Updating the Accounts: Global Mortality of the 1918–1920 'Spanish' Influenza Pandemic." *Bulletin of the History of Medicine* 76: 105–15.

Johnston, H. 1894. *Report by Commissioner Johnston of the First Three Years' Administration of the Eastern Portion of British Central Africa, Dated March 31, 1894*. London.

Jones, C. I. 2005. "Growth and Ideas." In *Handbook of Economic Growth*, edited by P. Aghion and S. Durlauf, 1063–111. Amsterdam.

Jones, C. P. 2005. "Ten Dedications 'To the Gods and Goddesses' and the Antonine Plague." *Journal of Roman Archaeology* 18: 293–301.

———. 2006. "Addendum to JRA 18 (2005): Cosa and the Antonine Plague?" *Journal of Roman Archaeology* 19: 368–69.

Jones, D. 2003. "Virgin Soils Revisited." *William and Mary Quarterly* 60: 703–42.

Jones, E. E., and S. N. DeWitte. 2012. "Using Spatial Analysis to Estimate Depopulation for Native American Populations in Northeastern North America, AD 1616–1645." *Journal of Anthropological Archaeology* 31: 83–92.

Jones, K. E., et al. 2008. "Global Trends in Emerging Infectious Diseases." *Nature* 451: 990–93.

Jongman, W. M., J. P. A. M. Jacobs, and G. M. Klein Goldewijk. 2019. "Health and Wealth in the Roman Empire." *Economics and Human Biology* 34: 138–50.

Jonsson, F. A. 2014. "The Origins of Cornucopianism: A Preliminary Genealogy." *Critical Historical Studies* 1: 151–68.

Juhas, M. 2015. "Horizontal Gene Transfer in Human Pathogens." *Critical Reviews in Microbiology* 41: 101–8.

Junqueira, A. C. M., et al. 2016. "Large-Scale Mitogenomics Enables Insights into Schizophora (Diptera) Radiation and Population Diversity." *Scientific Reports* 6: 21762.

Kaldellis, A. 2004. *Procopius of Caesarea: Tyranny, History, and Philosophy at the End of Antiquity.* Philadelphia.

———. 2007. "The Literature of Plague and the Anxieties of Piety in Sixth-Century Byzantium." In *Piety and Plague: From Byzantium to the Baroque*, edited by F. Mormando and T. Worcester, 1–22. Kirksville.

———. 2014. *The Wars of Justinian.* Indianapolis. Translation of Procopius, *De bellis*, by H. B. Dewing, revised and modernized.

Kamiya, T., et al. 2014. "What Determines Species Richness of Parasitic Organisms? A Meta-Analysis across Animal, Plant and Fungal Hosts." *Biological Reviews* 89: 123–34.

Kantar, M. B., et al. 2017. "The Genetics and Genomics of Plant Domestication." *BioScience* 67: 971–82.

Karimkhani, C., et al. 2017. "Global Burden of Cutaneous Leishmaniasis." *Lancet Infectious Diseases* 17: 264.

Karlen, A. 1995. *Man and Microbes: Disease and Plagues in History and Modern Times.* New York.

Karlsson, E. K., D. P. Kwiatkowski, and P. C. Sabeti. 2014. "Natural Selection and Infectious Disease in Human Populations." *Nature Reviews: Genetics* 15: 379–93.

Karunaweera, N. D., et al. 1992. "Dynamics of Fever and Serum Levels of Tumor Necrosis Factor Are Closely Associated during Clinical Paroxysms in *Plasmodium vivax* Malaria." *Proceedings of the National Academy of Sciences* 89: 3200–3.

———. 2003. "The Paroxysm of *Plasmodium vivax* Malaria." *Trends in Parasitology* 19: 188–93.

Kaspari, M., and J. Powers. 2016. "Biogeochemistry and Geographical Ecology: Embracing All Twenty-Five Elements Required to Build Organisms." *American Naturalist* 188: 62–73.

Kay, G. L., et al. 2015. "Eighteenth-Century Genomes Show That Mixed Infections Were Common at Time of Peak Tuberculosis in Europe." *Nature Communications* 6: 6717.

Kazadi, W. M. 2014. "Epidemiology of Yaws: An Update." *Clinical Epidemiology* 6: 119–28.

Kearns, G. 1988. "The Urban Penalty and the Population History of England." In *Society, Health and Population during the Demographic Transition*, edited by A. Brändström and L.-G. Tedebrand, 213–36. Stockholm.

Keeling, D. 2013. "Atlantic Historical Migrations, 1500–1965." In *The Encyclopedia of Global Human Migration.* Hoboken.

Keeling, M. J., and C. A. Gilligan. 2000a. "Bubonic Plague: A Metapopulation Model of a Zoonosis." *Proceedings of the Royal Society B* 267: 2219–30.

———. 2000b. "Metapopulation Dynamics of Bubonic Plague." *Nature* 407: 903–6.

Keller, M., et al. 2019. "Ancient *Yersinia pestis* Genomes from across Western Europe Reveal Early Diversification during the First Pandemic (541–750)." *Proceedings of the National Academy of Sciences* 116: 12363–72.

Kelley, F. 1915. "Children in the Cities." *National Municipal Review* 4: 197–203.

Kelly, M., J. Mokyr, and C. Ó Gráda. 2014. "Precocious Albion: A New Interpretation of the British Industrial Revolution." *Annual Review of Economics* 6: 363–89.

Kelly, R. L. 2013. *The Lifeways of Hunter-Gatherers: The Foraging Spectrum.* 2nd ed. Cambridge.

Kelton, P. 2007. *Epidemics and Enslavement: Biological Catastrophe in the Native Southeast, 1492–1715.* Lincoln.

Kenny, C. 2021. *The Plague Cycle.* New York.

Kerem, Z., et al. 2007. "Chickpea Domestication in the Neolithic Levant through the Nutritional Perspective." *Journal of Archaeological Science* 34: 1289–93.

Kerner, G., et al. 2021. "Human Ancient DNA Analyses Reveal the High Burden of Tuberculosis in Europeans over the Last 2,000 Years." *American Journal of Human Genetics* 108: 517–24.

Kerpel, D. 2014. *The Colors of the New World: Artists, Materials, and the Creation of the Florentine Codex.* Los Angeles.

Keusch, B. 2009. "Shigellosis." In *Bacterial Infections of Humans: Epidemiology and Control,* edited by P. Brachman and E. Abrutyn, 4th ed., 699–742. Boston.

Key, F. M., et al. 2020. "Emergence of Human-Adapted *Salmonella enterica* Is Linked to the Neolithization Process." *Nature Ecology & Evolution* 4: 324–33.

Keynes, R. 2001. *Annie's Box: Charles Darwin, His Daughter, and Human Evolution.* London.

Khalil, I. A., et al. 2018. "Morbidity and Mortality Due to *Shigella* and Enterotoxigenic *Escherichia coli* Diarrhoea: The Global Burden of Disease Study 1990–2016." *Lancet Infectious Diseases* 18: 1229–40.

Khan, E. 2013. "Visitations of Plague in Mughal India." *Proceedings of the Indian History Congress* 74: 305–12.

Khan, S., and D. Huremović. 2019. "Psychology of the Pandemic." In *Psychiatry of Pandemics: A Mental Health Response to Infection Outbreak,* edited by D. Huremović, 37–44. Cham.

Kheraj, S. 2018. "The Great Epizootic of 1872–73: Networks of Animal Disease in North American Urban Environments." *Environmental History* 23: 495–521.

Kidgell, C., et al. 2002. "*Salmonella typhi,* the Causative Agent of Typhoid Fever, Is Approximately 50,000 Years Old." *Infection, Genetics and Evolution* 2: 39–45.

Killgrove, K. 2010. *Migration and Mobility in Imperial Rome.* PhD diss., University of North Carolina.

———. 2014. "Bioarchaeology in the Roman Empire." In *Encyclopedia of Global Archaeology,* edited by C. Smith, 876–82. New York.

Kim-Farley, R. 1993. "Mumps." In *The Cambridge World History of Human Disease,* edited by K. Kiple, 887–89. Cambridge.

Kinch, M. S. 2018. *Between Hope and Fear: A History of Vaccines and Human Immunity.* New York.

King, C. H. 2015. "It's Time to Dispel the Myth of 'Asymptomatic' Schistosomiasis." *PLoS Neglected Tropical Diseases* 9: e0003504.

Kinkela, D. 2011. *DDT and the American Century: Global Health, Environmental Politics, and the Pesticide That Changed the World.* Chapel Hill.

Kiple, K. F. 1984. *The Caribbean Slave: A Biological History.* Cambridge.

———. 1987. *The African Exchange: Toward a Biological History of Black People.* Durham.

———, ed. 1993. *The Cambridge World History of Human Disease.* Cambridge.

————. 1999. *Plague, Pox & Pestilence: Disease in History.* London.

————. 2001. "Response to Sheldon Watts, 'Yellow Fever Immunities in West Africa and the Americas in the Age of Slavery and Beyond: A Reappraisal.'" *Journal of Social History* 34: 969–74.

————. 2007. *A Moveable Feast: Ten Millennia of Food Globalization.* Cambridge.

Kiple, K. F., and B. T. Higgins. 1992. "Yellow Fever and the Africanization of the Caribbean." In *Disease and Demography in the Americas,* edited by J. Verano and D. Ubelaker, 237–48. Washington, DC.

Kirsch, D. R., and O. Ogas. 2016. *The Drug Hunters: The Improbable Quest to Discover New Medicines.* La Vergne.

Klebanoff, S. 2005. "Myeloperoxidase: Friend and Foe." *Journal of Leukocyte Biology* 77: 598–625.

Klein, H. S. 2010. *The Atlantic Slave Trade.* 2nd ed. Cambridge.

Klein, I. 1973. "Death in India, 1871–1921." *Journal of Asian Studies* 32: 639–59.

————. 2001. "Development and Death: Reinterpreting Malaria, Economics and Ecology in British India." *Indian Economic and Social History Review* 38: 147–79.

Klein Goldewijk, K., et al. 2011. "The HYDE 3.1 Spatially Explicit Database of Human Induced Global Land Use Change over the Past 12,000 Years." *Global Ecology & Biogeography* 20: 73–86.

————. 2017. "Anthropogenic Land Use Estimates for the Holocene—HYDE 3.2." *Earth System Science Data* 9: 927–53.

Kleivan, H. 1966. *The Eskimos of Northeast Labrador.* Oslo.

Klenerman, P. 2017. *The Immune System: A Very Short Introduction.* Oxford.

Klimpel, S., and H. Mehlhorn, eds. 2014. *Bats (Chiroptera) as Vectors of Diseases and Parasites: Facts and Myths.* Berlin.

Knaysi, G. 1930. "Disinfection: I. The Development of Knowledge of Disinfection." *Journal of Infectious Diseases* 47: 293–302.

Knottnerus, O. S. 2002. "Malaria around the North Sea: A Survey." In *Climate Development and History of the North Atlantic Realm,* edited by G. Wefer, 339–53. Berlin.

Koch, A., et al. 2019. "Earth System Impacts of the European Arrival and Great Dying in the Americas after 1492." *Quaternary Science Reviews* 207: 13–36.

Köndgen, S., et al. 2008. "Pandemic Human Viruses Cause Decline of Endangered Great Apes." *Current Biology* 18: 260–64.

Konkola, K. 1992. "More Than a Coincidence? The Arrival of Arsenic and the Disappearance of Plague in Early Modern Europe." *Journal of the History of Medicine and Allied Sciences* 47: 186–209.

Kotloff, K. L., et al. 2013. "Burden and Aetiology of Diarrhoeal Disease in Infants and Young Children in Developing Countries (The Global Enteric Multicenter Study, GEMS): A Prospective, Case-Control Study." *Lancet* 382: 209–22.

Kotsakiozi, P., et al. 2018. "*Aedes aegypti* in the Black Sea: Recent Introduction or Ancient Remnant?" *Parasites & Vectors* 11: 396.

Kotti, B. K., and M. V. Zhilzova. 2020. "The Significance of Fleas (Siphonaptera) in the Natural Plague Foci." *Entomological Review* 100: 191–99.

Kouam, E. B., et al. 2012. "Genetic Structure and Mating System of Wild Cowpea Populations in West Africa." *BMC Plant Biology* 12: 113.

Krause, J., and S. Pääbo. 2016. "Genetic Time Travel." *Genetics* 203: 9–12.

Krebs, C. J. 2013. *Population Fluctuations in Rodents*. Chicago.

Kroeber, A. L. 1934. "Native American Population." *American Anthropologist* 36: 1–25.

———. 1939. *Cultural and Natural Areas of Native North America*. Berkeley.

Krönig, B., and T. Paul. 1897. "Die chemischen Grundlagen der Lehre von der Giftwirkung und Desinfection." *Zeitschrift für Hygiene und Infektionskrankheiten* 25: 1–112.

Krzywinski, J., and N. J. Besansky. 2003. "Molecular Systematics of *Anopheles*: From Subgenera to Subpopulations." *Annual Review of Entomology* 48: 111–39.

Kugeler, K., et al. 2015. "Epidemiology of Human Plague in the United States, 1900–2012." *Emerging Infectious Diseases* 21: 16–22.

Kuhlwilm, M., et al. 2016. "Ancient Gene Flow from Early Modern Humans into Eastern Neanderthals." *Nature* 530: 429–33.

Kuhn, D. 2009. *The Age of Confucian Rule: The Song Transformation of China*. Cambridge.

Kukla, J. 1986. "Kentish Agues and American Distempers: The Transmission of Malaria from England to Virginia in the Seventeenth Century." *Southern Studies* 25: 135–47.

Kulikoff, A. 1986. *Tobacco and Slaves: The Development of Southern Cultures in the Chesapeake, 1680–1800*. Chapel Hill.

Kulikowski, M. 2016. *The Triumph of Empire: The Roman World from Hadrian to Constantine*. Cambridge.

Kumari, A., et al. 2005. "Physical and Psychosocial Burden Due to Lymphatic Filariasis as Perceived by Patients and Medical Experts." *Tropical Medicine & International Health* 10: 567–73.

Kunz, T. H., and M. B. Fenton. 2003. *Bat Ecology*. Chicago.

Kupperman, K. 1984. "Fear of Hot Climates in the Anglo-American Colonial Experience." *William and Mary Quarterly* 41: 213–40.

Kurbanov, A. 2013. "The Hephthalite Numismatics." *Tyragetia* 7: 369–380.

Kuris, A. 2012. "The Global Burden of Human Parasites: Who and Where Are They? How Are They Transmitted?" *Journal of Parasitology* 98: 1056–64.

Kuroda, A. 2009. "The Eurasian Silver Century, 1276–1359: Commensurability and Multiplicity." *Journal of Global History* 4: 245–69.

La Berge, A. 1992. *Mission and Method: The Early Nineteenth-Century French Public Health Movement*. Cambridge.

Labisch, A. 1992. *Homo Hygienicus: Gesundheit und Medizin in der Neuzeit*. Frankfurt.

La Croix, S. 2019. *Hawai'i: Eight Hundred Years of Political and Economic Change*. Chicago.

Ladurie, E. 1973. "Un concept: l'unification microbienne du monde (XIVe–XVIIe siècles)." *Schweizerische Zeitschrift für Geschichte* 23: 627–94.

Laksono, B. M., et al. 2016. "Measles Virus Host Invasion and Pathogenesis." *Viruses* 8: 210.

Lammert, G. 1890. *Geschichte der Seuchen, Hungers- und Kriegsnoth zur Zeit des dreissigjährigen Krieges*. Wiesbaden.

Landers, J. 1987. "Mortality and Metropolis: The Case of London 1675–1825." *Population Studies* 41: 59–76.

———. 1993. *Death and the Metropolis: Studies in the Demographic History of London, 1670–1830.* Cambridge.

Landers, J., and V. Reynolds, eds. 1990. *Fertility and Resources.* Cambridge.

Larner, A. J. 2019. "Retrospective Diagnosis: Pitfalls and Purposes." *Journal of Medical Biography* 27: 127–28.

Larsen, C. S. 1994. "In the Wake of Columbus: Native Population Biology in the Postcontact Americas." *Yearbook of Physical Anthropology* 37: 109–54.

———. 2006. "The Agricultural Revolution as Environmental Catastrophe: Implications for Health and Lifestyle in the Holocene." *Quaternary International* 150: 12–20.

———. 2018. "The Bioarchaeology of Health Crisis: Infectious Disease in the Past." *Annual Review of Anthropology* 47: 295–313.

———. 2019. "Bioarchaeology of Neolithic Çatalhöyük Reveals Fundamental Transitions in Health, Mobility, and Lifestyle in Early Farmers." *Proceedings of the National Academy of Sciences* 116: 12615–23.

Larsen, C. S., et al. 1992. "Population Decline and Extinction in La Florida." In *Disease and Demography in the Americas,* edited by J. Verano and D. Ubelaker, 25–39. Washington, DC.

———. 2018. *The Backbone of Europe: Health, Diet, Work and Violence over Two Millennia.* Cambridge.

Las Casas, B. de. 1876. *Historia de las Indias.* Madrid.

Latham, R., and W. Matthews, eds. 1971. *The Diary of Samuel Pepys.* 10 vols. London.

Latham, R. G. 1850. *The Works of Thomas Sydenham, M.D.* 2 vols. London.

Latour, B. 1993. *The Pasteurization of France.* Cambridge.

Launaro, A. 2011. *Peasants and Slaves: The Rural Population of Roman Italy (200 BC to AD 100).* Cambridge.

Laurence, B. R. 1970. "The Curse of Saint Thomas." *Medical History* 14: 352–63.

Laval, G., et al. 2019. "Recent Adaptive Acquisition by African Rainforest Hunter-Gatherers of the Late Pleistocene Sickle-Cell Mutation Suggests Past Differences in Malaria Exposure." *American Journal of Human Genetics* 104: 553–61.

Lavely, W., and R. B. Wong. 1998. "Revising the Malthusian Narrative: The Comparative Study of Population Dynamics in Late Imperial China." *Journal of Asian Studies* 57: 714–48.

Lawson, J. 1967. *A New Voyage to Carolina.* Chapel Hill. First published 1709.

Lawton, S., et al. 2011. "Genomes and Geography: Genomic Insights into the Evolution and Phylogeography of the Genus *Schistosoma.*" *Parasites & Vectors* 4: 131.

Lay, P. 2020. *Providence Lost: The Rise & Fall of Cromwell's Protectorate.* London.

Lazaridis, I., et al. 2016. "Genomic Insights into the Origin of Farming in the Ancient Near East." *Nature* 536: 419–24.

Leach, H. M. 2003. "Human Domestication Reconsidered." *Current Anthropology* 44: 349–68.

Lean, G., D. Hinrichsen, and A. Markham. 1990. *Atlas of the Environment.* London.

Le Bailly, M., and F. Bouchet. 2006. "Paleoparasitology and Immunology: The Case of *Entamoeba hystolytica.*" *Revue d'Archéométrie* 30: 129–35.

Le Bailly, M., C. Maicher, and B. Dufour. 2016. "Archaeological Occurrences and Historical Review of the Human Amoeba, *Entamoeba hystolytica,* over the Past 6,000 Years." *Infection, Genetics and Evolution* 42: 34–40.

Lederberg, J., R. E. Shope, and S. C. Oaks Jr. 1992. *Emerging Infections: Microbial Threats to Health in the United States.* Washington, DC.

Lee, J. Z., and W. Feng. 2009. *One Quarter of Humanity: Malthusian Mythology and Chinese Realities, 1700–2000.* Cambridge.

Lee, K. H., A. Gordon, and B. Foxman. 2016. "The Role of Respiratory Viruses in the Etiology of Bacterial Pneumonia: An Ecological Perspective." *Evolution, Medicine, and Public Health* 2016: 95–109.

Lee, R. B. 1979. *The Dobe !Kung.* New York.

Lee, R. D. 1987. "Population Dynamics of Humans and Other Animals." *Demography* 24: 443–65.

Leendertz, F. H., et al. 2006. "Pathogens as Drivers of Population Declines: The Importance of Systematic Monitoring in Great Apes and Other Threatened Mammals." *Biological Conservation* 131: 325–37.

Leisner, J. J. 2020. "The Diverse Search for Synthetic, Semisynthetic and Natural Product Antibiotics from the 1940s and up to 1960 Exemplified by a Small Pharmaceutical Player." *Frontiers in Microbiology* 11: 976.

Lenger, F. 2012. *European Cities in the Modern Era, 1850–1914.* Leiden.

Lesch, J. E. 2007. *The First Miracle Drugs: How the Sulfa Drugs Transformed Medicine.* Oxford.

Levine, M., et al. 2012. "The Global Enteric Multicenter Study (GEMS): Impetus, Rationale, and Genesis." *Clinical Infectious Diseases* 55: S215–24.

Levine, O. S., and M. M. Levine. 1991. "Houseflies (*Musca domestica*) as Mechanical Vectors of Shigellosis." *Reviews of Infectious Diseases* 13: 688–96.

Levtzion, N., and J. Spaulding. 2003. *Medieval West Africa: Views from Arab Scholars and Merchants.* Princeton.

Lewis, K. 2013. "Platforms for Antibiotic Discovery." *Nature Reviews Drug Discovery* 12: 371–87.

Lewis, M. E. 2009a. *China between Empires: The Northern and Southern Dynasties.* Cambridge.
———. 2009b. *China's Cosmopolitan Empire: The Tang Dynasty.* Cambridge.

Lewis-Rogers, N., J. Seger, and F. R. Adler. 2017. "Human Rhinovirus Diversity and Evolution: How Strange the Change from Major to Minor." *Journal of Virology* 91: 01659–716.

Li, C., et al. 2006. "Rice Domestication by Reducing Shattering." *Science* 311: 1936–39.

Li, K., et al. 2016. "Identification of Novel and Diverse Rotaviruses in Rodents and Insectivores, and Evidence of Cross-Species Transmission into Humans." *Virology* 494: 168–77.

Li, Y., and Z. Yang. 2017. "Adaptive Diversification between Yellow Fever Virus West African and South American Lineages: A Genome-Wide Study." *American Journal of Tropical Medicine and Hygiene* 96: 727–34.

Li, Y.-H., et al. 2013. "Molecular Footprints of Domestication and Improvement in Soybean Revealed by Whole Genome Re-sequencing." *BMC Genomics* 14: 579.

Liebmann, M. J., et al. 2016. "Native American Depopulation, Reforestation, and Fire Regimes in the Southwest United States, 1492–1900 CE." *Proceedings of the National Academy of Sciences* 113: E696–704.

Ligon, R. 1673. *A True and Exact History of the Island of Barbadoes.* London.

Lilly, W., and E. Ashmole. 1774. *The Lives of Those Eminent Antiquaries Elias Ashmole, Esquire, and Mr. Lilly.* London.

Lind, J. 1771. *An Essay on Diseases Incidental to Europeans in Hot Climates with the Methods of Preventing Their Fatal Consequences.* London.

Lindemann, M. 2013. *Medicine and Society in Early Modern Europe.* 2nd ed. Cambridge.

Lindenfors, P., et al. 2007. "Parasite Species Richness in Carnivores: Effects of Host Body Mass, Latitude, Geographical Range and Population Density." *Global Ecology and Biogeography* 16: 496–509.

Linder, F. E., and R. D. Grove. 1947. *Vital Statistics Rates in the United States 1900–1940.* Washington, DC.

Lindo, J., et al. 2016. "A Time Transect of Exomes from a Native American Population before and after European Contact." *Nature Communications* 7: 13175.

———. 2018. "The Genetic Prehistory of the Andean Highlands 7,000 Years BP through European Contact." *Science Advances Anthropology* 4: 49821.

Lindqvist, C., and O. P. Rajora, eds. 2019. *Paleogenomics: Genome-Scale Analysis of Ancient DNA.* Cham.

Lindsay, S. W., and C. J. Thomas. 2000. "Mapping and Estimating the Population at Risk from Lymphatic Filariasis in Africa." *Transactions of the Royal Society of Tropical Medicine and Hygiene* 94: 37–45.

Linz, B., et al. 2016. "Acquisition and Loss of Virulence-Associated Factors during Genome Evolution and Speciation in Three Clades of *Bordetella* Species." *BMC Genomics* 17: 767.

Lipsitch, M., and A. O. Sousa. 2002. "Historical Intensity of Natural Selection for Resistance to Tuberculosis." *Genetics* 161: 1599–607.

Lipson, M., et al. 2017. "Parallel Palaeogenomic Transects Reveal Complex Genetic History of Early European Farmers." *Nature* 551: 368–72.

———. 2018. "Ancient Genomes Document Multiple Waves of Migration in Southeast Asian Prehistory." *Science* 361: 92–95.

Little, L., ed. 2007a. "Life and Afterlife of the First Plague Pandemic." In *Plague and the End of Antiquity: The Pandemic of 541–750,* 2–32. New York.

———. 2007b. *Plague and the End of Antiquity: The Pandemic of 541–750.* New York.

Littman, R. J., and M. L. Littman. 1973. "Galen and the Antonine Plague." *American Journal of Philology* 94: 243–55.

Liu, W., et al. 2014. "African Origin of the Malaria Parasite *Plasmodium vivax.*" *Nature Communications* 5: 3346.

Liu, W.-Q., et al. 2009. "*Salmonella paratyphi* C: Genetic Divergence from *Salmonella choleraesuis* and Pathogenic Convergence with *Salmonella typhi.*" *PLoS One* 4: 4510.

Livi Bacci, M. 1990. *Population and Nutrition: An Essay on European Demographic History.* Cambridge.

———. 2008. *Conquest: The Destruction of the American Indios.* Cambridge.

———. 2012. *A Concise History of World Population.* 5th ed. Chichester.

Livingstone, F. B. 1958. "Anthropological Implications of Sickle Cell Gene Distribution in West Africa." *American Anthropologist* 60: 533–62.

Lo Cascio, E. 1994. "The Size of the Roman Population: Beloch and the Meaning of the Augustan Census Figures." *Journal of Roman Studies* 84: 23–40.

———. 2009. *Crescita e declino: Studi di storia dell'economia romana.* Rome.

———, ed. 2012. *L'impatto della "peste Antonina".* Bari.

Lo Cascio, E., and Malanima, P. 2005. "Cycles and Stability. Italian Population before the Demographic Transition (225 BC–AD 1900)." *Rivista di storia economica* 21: 5–40.

Locey, K. J., and J. T. Lennon. 2016. "Scaling Laws Predict Global Microbial Diversity." *Proceedings of the National Academy of Sciences* 113: 5970–75.

Lockridge, K. A. 1974. *Literacy in Colonial New England; an Enquiry into the Social Context of Literacy in the Early Modern West*. New York.

Lombardo, U., et al. 2020. "Early Holocene Crop Cultivation and Landscape Modification in Amazonia." *Nature* 581: 190–93.

Long, C. A., and F. Zavala. 2017. "Immune Responses in Malaria." *Cold Spring Harbor Perspectives in Medicine* 7: a025577.

Long, E. 1764. 1774. *The History of Jamaica: Or, General Survey of the Antient and Modern State of the Island: With Reflections on Its Situation Settlements, Inhabitants, Climate, Products, Commerce, Laws, and Government*. 3 vols. London.

Loosjes, F. E. 1956. "Is the Brown Rat (*Rattus norvegicus* Berkenhout) Responsible for the Disappearance of Plague from Western Europe?" *Documenta de medicina geographica et tropica* 8: 175–78.

Lopez, B., et al. 2017. "Treponemal Disease in the Old World? Integrated Palaeopathological Assessment of a 9th–11th Century Skeleton from North-Central Spain." *Anthropological Science* 125: 101–14.

López, S., L. van Dorp, and G. Hellenthal. 2015. "Human Dispersal out of Africa: A Lasting Debate." *Evolutionary Bioinformatics* 11: 57–68.

López Losa, E., and S. Piquero Zarauz. 2020. "Spanish Subsistence Wages and the Little Divergence in Europe, 1500–1800." *European Review of Economic History* 25: 59–84.

Lordkipanidze, D., et al. 2005. "The Earliest Toothless Hominin Skull." *Nature* 434: 717–18.

Lorentzen, P., J. McMillan, and R. Wacziarg. 2008. "Death and Development." *Journal of Economic Growth* 13: 81–124.

Louca, S., et al. 2019. "A Census-Based Estimate of Earth's Bacterial and Archaeal Diversity." *PLoS Biology* 17: e3000106.

Louis, P. 1829. *Recherches anatomiques, pathologiques et thérapeutiques sur la maladie connue sous les noms de gastro-entérite, fièvre putride, adynamique, ataxique, typhoïde, etc.* Paris.

Loukas, A., et al. 2016. "Hookworm Infection." *Nature Reviews Disease Primers* 2: 16088.

Lovell, G. 1991. "Disease and Depopulation in Early Colonial Guatemala." In *Secret Judgments of God: Old World Disease in Colonial Spanish America*, edited by N. D. Cook and W. G. Lovell, 49–83. Norman.

Loy, D. E., et al. 2017. "Out of Africa: Origins and Evolution of the Human Malaria Parasites *Plasmodium falciparum* and *Plasmodium vivax*." *International Journal for Parasitology* 47: 87–97.

———. 2018. "Evolutionary History of Human *Plasmodium vivax* Revealed by Genome-Wide Analyses of Related Ape Parasites." *Proceedings of the National Academy of Sciences* 115: 8450–59.

Lu, H., et al. 2009. "Earliest Domestication of Common Millet (*Panicum miliaceum*) in East Asia Extended to 10,000 Years Ago." *Proceedings of the National Academy of Sciences of the United States of America* 106: 7367–72.

Lucas, A. M. 2010. "Malaria Eradication and Educational Attainment: Evidence from Paraguay and Sri Lanka." *American Economic Journal: Applied Economics* 2: 46–71.

Lucas, R. E. 1988. "On the Mechanics of Economic Development." *Journal of Monetary Economics* 22: 3–42.

Luis, A. D., et al. 2013. "A Comparison of Bats and Rodents as Reservoirs of Zoonotic Viruses: Are Bats Special?" *Proceedings of the Royal Society B: Biological Sciences* 280: 20122753.

Luo, T., et al. 2015. "Southern East Asian Origin and Coexpansion of *Mycobacterium tuberculosis* Beijing Family with Han Chinese." *Proceedings of the National Academy of Sciences* 112: 8136–41.

Lupi, O., and S. K. Tyring. 2003. "Tropical Dermatology: Viral Tropical Diseases." *Journal of the American Academy of Dermatology* 49: 979–1000.

Lupi, O., et al. 2006. "Tropical Dermatology: Bacterial Tropical Diseases." *Journal of the American Academy of Dermatology* 54: 559–78.

Lutz, W., W. P. Butz, and S. KC. 2017. *World Population & Human Capital in the Twenty-First Century: An Overview*. Oxford.

Lutz, W., and S. KC. 2010. "Dimensions of Global Population Projections: What Do We Know about Future Population Trends and Structures?" *Philosophical Transactions of the Royal Society B: Biological Sciences* 365: 2779–91.

Lynteris, C. 2016. "The Epidemiologist as Culture Hero: Visualizing Humanity in the Age of 'the Next Pandemic.'" *Visual Anthropology* 29: 36–53.

Lysenko, A. J., and I. N. Semashko. 1968. "Geography of Malaria. A Medico-geographic Profile of an Ancient Disease." *Itogi Nauki: Medicinskaja Geografija* 25: 25–146.

MacArthur, W. P. 1956. "Medical History of the Famine." In *The Great Famine: Studies in Irish History 1845–52*, edited by R. D. Edwards and T. D. Williams, 263–315. New York.

Macaulay, T. B. M. 1856. *The History of England from the Accession of James II.* 5 vols. London.

MacHugh, D. E., G. Larson, and L. Orlando. 2017. "Taming the Past: Ancient DNA and the Study of Animal Domestication." *Annual Review of Animal Biosciences* 5: 329–51.

Mack, R. 1970. "The Great African Cattle Plague Epidemic of the 1890's." *Tropical Animal Health and Production* 2: 210–19.

MacNamara, C. N. 1876. *A Treatise on Asiatic Cholera*. London.

MacPhee, R. 2019. *End of the Megafauna: The Fate of the World's Hugest, Fiercest, and Strangest Animals*. New York.

MacPherson, K. L. 1998. "Cholera in China, 1820–1930." In *Sediments of Time: Environment and Society in Chinese History*, edited by M. Elvin and T. Liu, 487–519. New York.

Maddison, A. 2007a. *Chinese Economic Performance in the Long Run: 960–2030 AD*. Paris.

———. 2007b. *Contours of the World Economy, 1–2030 AD: Essays in Macro-economic History*. Oxford.

Madley, B. 2015. "Reexamining the American Genocide Debate: Meaning, Historiography, and New Methods." *American Historical Review* 120: 89–139.

———. 2016. *An American Genocide: The United States and the California Indian Catastrophe, 1846–1873*. New Haven.

Madsen, J. B. 2016. "Barriers to Prosperity: Parasitic and Infectious Diseases, IQ, and Economic Development." *World Development* 78: 172–87.

Mahajan, M. 2019. "The IHME in the Shifting Landscape of Global Health Metrics." *Global Policy* 10: 110–20.

Majander, K., et al. 2020. "Ancient Bacterial Genomes Reveal a High Diversity of *Treponema pallidum* Strains in Early Modern Europe." *Current Biology* 30: 1–16.

Malthus, T. R. 1798. *An Essay on the Principle of Population*, 1st ed. London.

———. 2018. *An Essay on the Principle of Population: The 1803 Edition*. New Haven.

Mandell, L., et al. 2006. *Respiratory Infections*. London.

Manela, E. 2010. "A Pox on Your Narrative: Writing Disease Control into Cold War History." *Diplomatic History* 34: 299–323.

———. 2015. "The Politics of Smallpox Eradication." In *Production, Destruction and Connection, 1750–Present*, edited by J. R. McNeill and K. Pomeranz, 7:258–82. Vol. 7 of *The Cambridge World History*. Cambridge.

Manguin, S. 2008. *Biodiversity of Malaria in the World*. Montrouge.

Mann, C. C. 2005. *1491: New Revelations of the Americas before Columbus*. New York.

———. 2011. *1493: Uncovering the New World Columbus Created*. New York.

Manning, P. 2010. "African Population." In *The Demographics of Empire: The Colonial Order and the Creation of Knowledge*, edited by K. Ittmann, D. D. Cordell, and G. H. Maddox, 245–75. Athens.

Manson, P. 1883. *The Filaria sanguinis hominis and Certain New Forms of Parasitic Disease in India, China, and Warm Countries*. London.

Manzi, G. 1999. "Discontinuity of Life Conditions at the Transition from the Roman Imperial Age to the Early Middle Ages: Example from Central Italy Evaluated by Pathological Dento-Alveolar Lesions." *American Journal of Human Biology* 11: 327–41.

Manzoni, A. 1924. *The Betrothed (I promessi sposi): A Milanese Story of the Seventeenth Century*. Translated by D. J. Connor. New York. First published 1840–42.

Marchisio, A., ed. 2016. *Relatio de mirabilibus orientalium tatarorum: Edizione critica*. Florence.

Marciniak, S., and H. Poinar. 2018. "Ancient Pathogens through Human History: A Paleogenomic Perspective." In *Paleogenomics*, edited by C. Lindqvist and O. Rajora, 115–38. Cham.

Marciniak, S., et al. 2016. "*Plasmodium falciparum* Malaria in 1st–2nd Century CE Southern Italy." *Current Biology* 26: R1205–25.

Marcone, A. 2002, "La peste antonina: Testimonianze e interpretazioni," *Rivista storica italiana* 114: 803–19.

Marcus, J., et al. 2020. "Genetic History from the Middle Neolithic to Present on the Mediterranean Island of Sardinia." *Nature Communications* 11: 939.

Marinucci, M. 1982. "Hemoglobinopathies in Italy." *Hemoglobin* 6: 247–55.

Mark, C., and Rigau-Pérez, J. G. 2009. "The World's First Immunization Campaign: The Spanish Smallpox Vaccine Expedition, 1803–1813." *Bulletin of the History of Medicine* 83: 63–94.

Markov, P. V., et al. 2009. "Phylogeography and Molecular Epidemiology of Hepatitis C Virus Genotype 2 in Africa." *Journal of General Virology* 90: 2086–96.

———. 2012. "Colonial History and Contemporary Transmission Shape the Genetic Diversity of Hepatitis C Virus Genotype 2 in Amsterdam." *Journal of Virology* 86: 7677–87.

Marks, R. 1998. *Tigers, Rice, Silk, and Silt: Environment and Economy in Late Imperial South China*. Cambridge.

———. 2012. *China: Its Environment and History*. Lanham.

Marlowe, F. W. 2005. "Hunter-Gatherers and Human Evolution." *Evolutionary Anthropology: Issues, News, and Reviews* 14: 54–67.

Marr, J. S., and J. T. Cathey. 2010. "New Hypothesis for Cause of Epidemic among Native Americans, New England, 1616–1619." *Emerging Infectious Diseases* 16: 281–86.

Marriott, A. L., and C. K. Rachlin. 1968. *American Indian Mythology*. New York.

Marshall, J. 1832. *Mortality of the Metropolis: A Statistical View of the Number of Persons Reported to Have Died of Each of More than 100 Kinds of Disease and Casualties within the Bills of Mortality, in Each of the Two Hundred and Four Years, 1629–1831*. London.

Marshall, S. A. 2012. *Flies: The Natural History & Diversity of Diptera*. Richmond Hill.

Martella, V., et al. 2010. "Zoonotic Aspects of Rotaviruses." *Veterinary Microbiology* 140: 246–55.

Martin, D. L., and A. J. Osterholtz. 2015. *Bodies and Lives in Ancient America: Health before Columbus*. Abingdon.

Martin, M. D., et al. 2015. "Genomic Characterization of a South American *Phytophthora* Hybrid Mandates Reassessment of the Geographic Origins of *Phytophthora infestans*." *Molecular Biology and Evolution* 33: 478–91.

Martino, D., et al. 2005. "Tracing Sydenham's Chorea: Historical Documents from a British Paediatric Hospital." *Archives of Disease in Childhood* 90: 507–11.

Masters, W., and M. McMillan. 2001. "Climate and Scale in Economic Growth." *Journal of Economic Growth* 6: 167–86.

Mather, C. 1708. *Diary of Cotton Mather: 1681–1708*. Boston.

Mathieson, I., et al. 2018. "The Genomic History of Southeastern Europe." *Nature* 555: 197–210.

Mattingly, D., ed. 2003. *The Archaeology of the Fazzān*. London.

———. 2006. *An Imperial Possession: Britain in the Roman Empire, 54 BC–AD 409*. London.

Maxcy, K. F. 1923. "The Distribution of Malaria in the United States as Indicated by Mortality Reports." *Public Health Reports* 38: 1125–38.

McArthur, N. 1967. *Island Populations of the Pacific*. Canberra.

McBryde, F. W. 1940. "Influenza in America during the Sixteenth Century (Guatemala: 1523, 1559–62, 1576)." *Bulletin of the History of Medicine* 8: 296–302.

McCaa, R. 1995. "Spanish and Nahuatl Views on Smallpox and Demographic Catastrophe in Mexico." *Journal of Interdisciplinary History* 25: 397–431.

———. 1997. "The Peopling of Mexico from Origins to Revolution." In *A Population History of North America*, edited by M. R. Haines and R. H. Steckel, 241–304. New York.

McCandless, P. 2011. *Slavery, Disease, and Suffering in the Southern Lowcountry*. Cambridge.

McCook, S. 2006. "Global Rust Belt: *Hemileia vastatrix* and the Ecological Integration of World Coffee Production since 1850." *Journal of Global History* 1: 177–95.

———. 2019. *Coffee Is Not Forever: A Global History of the Coffee Leaf Rust*. Athens.

McCormick, M. 1998. "Bateaux de vie, bateaux de mort. Maladie, commerce, transports annonaires et le passage économique du bas-empire au moyen âge." *Settimane di studio—Centro Italiano di studi alto medioevo* 45: 35–118.

———. 2001. *Origins of the European Economy: Communications and Commerce, AD 300–900*. Cambridge.

———. 2003. "Rats, Communications, and Plague: Toward an Ecological History." *Journal of Interdisciplinary History* 34: 1–25.

———. 2015. "Tracking Mass Death during the Fall of Rome's Empire (I)." *Journal of Roman Archaeology* 28: 325–57.

———. 2016. "Tracking Mass Death during the Fall of Rome's Empire (II): A First Inventory of Mass Graves." *Journal of Roman Archaeology* 29: 1008–46.

———. 2021. "Gregory of Tours on Sixth-Century Plague and Other Epidemics." *Speculum* 96: 38–96.

McDonald, S. K., et al. 2020. "'TB or Not TB': The Conundrum of Pre-European Contact Tuberculosis in the Pacific." *Philosophical Transactions of the Royal Society B: Biological Sciences* 375: 20190583.

McEvedy, C., and R. Jones. 1978. *Atlas of World Population History*. Harmondsworth.

McGoey, L. 2015. *No Such Thing as a Free Gift: The Gates Foundation and the Price of Philanthropy*. New York.

McGrew, R. E. 1960. "The First Cholera Epidemic and Social History." *Bulletin of the History of Medicine* 34: 61–73.

———. 1965. *Russia and the Cholera, 1823–1832*. Madison.

McGuire, M. 2013. *The Chlorine Revolution Water Disinfection and the Fight to Save Lives*. Denver.

McGuire, R. A., and P. R. P. Coelho. 2011. *Parasites, Pathogens, and Progress: Diseases and Economic Development*. Cambridge.

McKenna, M. 2017. *Big Chicken: The Incredible Story of How Antibiotics Created Modern Agriculture and Changed the Way the World Eats*. Washington, DC.

McKenzie, F. E., and W. H. Bossert. 2005. "An Integrated Model of *Plasmodium falciparum* Dynamics." *Journal of Theoretical Biology* 232: 411–26.

McKenzie, F. E., et al. 2001. "Seasonality, Parasite Diversity, and Local Extinctions in *Plasmodium falciparum* Malaria." *Ecology* 82: 2673–81.

McKeown, A. 2004. "Global Migration, 1846–1940." *Journal of World History* 15: 155–89.

McKeown, T. 1976. *The Modern Rise of Population*. New York.

———. 1988. *The Origins of Human Disease*. Oxford.

McKeown, T., R. G. Brown, and R. G. Record. 1972. "An Interpretation of the Modern Rise of Population in Europe." *Population Studies* 26: 345–82.

McLaughlin, R. 2010. *Rome and the Distant East: Trade Routes to the Ancient Lands of Arabia, India and China*. London.

McManus, K. F., et al. 2017. "Population Genetic Analysis of the DARC Locus (Duffy) Reveals Adaptation from Standing Variation Associated with Malaria Resistance in Humans." *PLoS Genetics* 13: 1006560.

McMichael, A. J. 2017. *Climate Change and the Health of Nations: Famines, Fevers, and the Fate of Populations*. New York.

McMillen, C. W. 2008. "'The Red Man and the White Plague': Rethinking Race, Tuberculosis, and American Indians, ca. 1890–1950." *Bulletin of the History of Medicine* 82: 608–45.

———. 2016. *Pandemics*. Oxford.

McNally, A., et al. 2016. "'Add, Stir and Reduce': *Yersinia* Spp. as Model Bacteria for Pathogen Evolution." *Nature Reviews Microbiology* 14: 177.

McNeill, J. R. 2000. *Something New under the Sun: An Environmental History of the Twentieth-Century World*. New York.

———. 2010. *Mosquito Empires: Ecology and War in the Greater Caribbean, 1620–1914*. New York.

———. 2015. "Energy, Population, and Environmental Change since 1750: Entering the Anthropocene." In *Production, Destruction and Connection, 1750–Present*, edited by J. R. McNeill and K. Pomeranz, 51–82. Vol. 7 of *The Cambridge World History*. Cambridge.

———. forthcoming. "Disease Environments of the Caribbean to 1850: A Tale of Two Syndemics." In *Sea and Land: An Environmental History of the Early Caribbean*, edited by P. Morgan et al. Oxford.

McNeill, J. R., and P. Engelke. 2016. *The Great Acceleration: An Environmental History of the Anthropocene since 1945*. Philadelphia.

McNeill, J. R., and W. H. McNeill. 2003. *The Human Web: A Bird's-Eye View of World History*. New York.

McNeill, W. H. 1976. *Plagues and Peoples*. Harmondsworth.

———. 1989. *The Age of Gunpowder Empires, 1450–1800*. Washington, DC.

———. 1999. "How the Potato Changed the World's History." *Social Research* 66: 67–83.

McVety, A. K. 2018. *The Rinderpest Campaigns: A Virus, Its Vaccines, and Global Development in the Twentieth Century*. New York.

Medawar, P. B., and J. S. Medawar. 1983. *Aristotle to Zoos: A Philosophical Dictionary of Biology*. Cambridge.

Meerburg, B. G., G. R. Singleton, and A. Kijlstra. 2009. "Rodent-Borne Diseases and Their Risks for Public Health." *Critical Reviews in Microbiology* 35: 221–70.

Meier, M. 2003. *Das andere Zeitalter Justinians: Kontingenzerfahrung und Kontingenzbewältigung im 6. Jahrhundert n. Chr.* Göttingen.

———. 2005. "'Hinzu kam auch noch die Pest . . .' Die sogenannte Justinianische Pest und ihre Folgen." In *Pest—Die Geschichte eines Menschheitstraumas*, edited by M. Meier, 86–107, 396–400. Stuttgart.

———. 2016. "The 'Justinianic Plague': The Economic Consequences of the Pandemic in the Eastern Roman Empire and Its Cultural and Religious Effects." *Early Medieval Europe* 24: 267–92.

———. 2020. "The 'Justinianic Plague': An 'Inconsequential Pandemic'? A Reply." *Medizinhistorisches Journal* 55: 172–99.

Melosi, M. V. 2008. *The Sanitary City: Urban Infrastructure in America from Colonial Times to the Present*. Baltimore.

Membrebe, J. V., et al. 2019. "Bayesian Inference of Evolutionary Histories under Time-Dependent Substitution Rates." *Molecular Biology and Evolution* 36: 1793–803.

Menard, R. R. 2006. *Sweet Negotiations: Sugar, Slavery, and Plantation Agriculture in Early Barbados*. Charlottesville.

Mendes, M., et al. 2020. "The History behind the Mosaic of the Americas." *Current Opinion in Genetics & Development* 62: 72–77.

Mercer, A. 1990. *Disease, Mortality, and Population in Transition: Epidemiological-Demographic Change in England since the Eighteenth Century as Part of a Global Phenomenon*. Leicester.

———. 2014. *Infections, Chronic Disease, and the Epidemiological Transition: A New Perspective*. Suffolk.

———. 2018. "Updating the Epidemiological Transition Model." *Epidemiology and Infection* 146: 680–87.

Merhej, V., and D. Raoult. 2011. "Rickettsial Evolution in the Light of Comparative Genomics." *Biological Reviews* 86: 379–405.

Merrens, H. 1969. "The Physical Environment of Early America: Images and Image Makers in Colonial South Carolina." *Geographical Review* 59: 530–56.

Merrens, H., and G. Terry. 1984. "Dying in Paradise: Malaria, Mortality, and the Perceptual Environment in Colonial South Carolina." *Journal of Southern History* 50: 533–50.

Messenger, A. M., A. N. Barnes, and G. C. Gray. 2014. "Reverse Zoonotic Disease Transmission (Zooanthroponosis): A Systematic Review of Seldom-Documented Human Biological Threats to Animals." *PLoS One* 9: e89055.

Migliano, A., L. Vinicius, and M. Lahr. 2007. "Life History Trade-offs Explain the Evolution of Human Pygmies." *Proceedings of the National Academy of Sciences* 104: 20216–19.

Miller, G. 1981. "Putting Lady Mary in Her Place: A Discussion of Historical Causation." *Bulletin of the History of Medicine* 55: 2–16.

Miller, L., et al. 1976. "The Resistance Factor to *Plasmodium vivax* in Blacks." *New England Journal of Medicine* 295: 302–4.

———. 2002. "The Pathogenic Basis of Malaria." *Nature* 415: 673–79.

Milner, G. 1992. "Disease and Sociopolitical Systems in Late Prehistoric Illinois." In *Disease and Demography in the Americas*, edited by J. Verano and D. Ubelaker, 103–16. Washington, DC.

Mintz, S. W. 1985. *Sweetness and Power: The Place of Sugar in Modern History*. New York.

Mira, A., R. Pushker, and F. Rodríguez-Valera. 2006. "The Neolithic Revolution of Bacterial Genomes." *TRENDS in Microbiology* 14: 200–206.

Mitchell, B. R. 1998a. *International Historical Statistics: Europe, 1750–1993*. 4th ed. London.

———. 1998b. *International Historical Statistics: The Americas, 1750–1993*. 4th ed. London.

———. 2007. *International Historical Statistics. Africa, Asia and Oceania 1750–2005*. 5th ed. Basingstoke.

———. 2011. *British Historical Statistics*. Cambridge.

Mitchell, P. D. 2011. "Retrospective Diagnosis and the Use of Historical Texts for Investigating Disease in the Past." *International Journal of Paleopathology* 1: 81–88.

Mitchell, P. 2018a. "The Constraining Role of Disease on the Spread of Domestic Mammals in Sub-Saharan Africa: A Review." *Quaternary International* 471: 95–110.

———. 2018b. *The Donkey in Human History: An Archaeological Perspective*. Oxford.

Mitchell, S. 2015. *A History of the Later Roman Empire, AD 284–641*. 2nd ed. Malden.

Mithen, S. J. 2003. *After the Ice: A Global Human History, 20,000–5000 BC*. London.

Mitjà, O., K. Asiedu, and D. Mabey. 2013. "Yaws." *Lancet* 381: 763–73.

Mitterauer, M. 2010. *Why Europe? Medieval Origins of Its Special Path*. Translated by G. Chapple. Chicago.

Modell, B., and M. Darlison. 2008. "Global Epidemiology of Haemoglobin Disorders and Derived Service Indicators." *Bulletin of the World Health Organization* 86: 480–87.

Modelski, G. 2003. *World Cities: –3000 to 2000*. Washington, DC.

Mokyr, J. 1990. *The Lever of Riches: Technological Creativity and Economic Progress*. New York.

———. 1999. "The Second Industrial Revolution, 1870–1914." In *Storia dell'economia mondiale*, edited by V. Castronovo, 219–45. Rome.

———. 2000. "Why 'More Work for Mother?' Knowledge and Household Behavior, 1870–1945." *Journal of Economic History* 60: 1–41.

———. 2017. *A Culture of Growth: The Origins of the Modern Economy*. Princeton.

Mokyr, J., and C. Ó Gráda. 2002. "What Do People Die of During Famines: The Great Irish Famine in Comparative Perspective." *European Review of Economic History* 6: 339–63.

Molina-Cruz, A., et al. 2016. "Mosquito Vectors and the Globalization of *Plasmodium falciparum* Malaria." *Annual Review of Genetics* 50: 447–65.

Monaghan, E. J. 2005. *Learning to Read and Write in Colonial America: Literacy Instruction and Acquisition in a Cultural Context*. Worcester.

Monath, T. P. 1988. *The Arboviruses: Epidemiology and Ecology*. Boca Raton.

———. 2001. "Yellow Fever: An Update." *Lancet Infectious Diseases* 1: 11–20.

Monecke, S., H. Monecke, and J. Monecke. 2009. "Modelling the Black Death. A Historical Case Study and Implications for the Epidemiology of Bubonic Plague." *International Journal of Medical Microbiology* 299: 582–93.

Monteiro, K., et al. 2019. "Mitochondrial DNA Reveals Species Composition and Phylogenetic Relationships of Hookworms in Northeastern Brazil." *Infections, Genetics and Evolution* 68: 105–12.

Mooney, G. 2007. "Infectious Diseases and Epidemiologic Transition in Victorian Britain? Definitely." *Social History of Medicine* 20: 595–606.

———. 2015. *Intrusive Interventions: Public Health, Domestic Space, and Infectious Disease Surveillance in England, 1840–1914*. Rochester.

Moore, A., et al. 2000. *Village on the Euphrates: From Foraging to Farming at Abu Hureyra*. New York.

Moore, R. 2016. "A Global Middle Ages?" In *The Prospect of Global History*, edited by J. Belich, 80–92. Oxford.

Moorhead, R. 2002. "William Budd and Typhoid Fever." *Journal of the Royal Society of Medicine* 95: 561–64.

Moran, M., and M. Stevenson. 2013. "Illumination and Innovation: What Philanthropic Foundations Bring to Global Health Governance." *Global Society* 27: 117–37.

Morand, S. 2000. "Wormy World: Comparative Tests of Theoretical Hypotheses on Parasite Species Richness." In *Evolutionary Biology of Host-Parasite Relationships: Theory Meets Reality*, edited by R. Poulin, S. Morand, and A. Skorping, 63–79. Cambridge.

Mordechai, L., et al. 2019. "The Justinianic Plague: An Inconsequential Pandemic?" *Proceedings of the National Academy of Sciences* 116: 25546–54.

Morelli, G., et al. 2010. "*Yersinia pestis* Genome Sequencing Identifies Patterns of Global Phylogenetic Diversity." *Nature Genetics* 42: 1140–43.

Moreno-Estrada, A., et al. 2013. "Reconstructing the Population Genetic History of the Caribbean." *PLoS Genetics* 9: e1003925.

Morens, D. M. 1998. "Measles in Fiji, 1875: Thoughts on the History of Emerging Infectious Diseases." *Pacific Health Dialog* 5: 119–28.

Morens, D. M., and A. S. Fauci. 2007. "The 1918 Influenza Pandemic: Insights for the 21st Century." *Journal of Infectious Diseases* 195: 1018–28.

———. 2020. "Emerging Pandemic Diseases: How We Got to COVID-19." *Cell* 182: 1077–92.

Morens, D. M., G. K. Folkers, and A. S. Fauci. 2009. "What Is a Pandemic?" *Journal of Infectious Diseases* 200: 1018–21.

Morens, D. M., and J. K. Taubenberger. 2010a. "An Avian Outbreak Associated with Panzootic Equine Influenza in 1872: An Early Example of Highly Pathogenic Avian Influenza?" *Influenza and Other Respiratory Viruses* 4: 373–77.

———. 2010b. "Historical Thoughts on Influenza Viral Ecosystems, or Behold a Pale Horse, Dead Dogs, Failing Fowl, and Sick Swine." *Influenza and Other Respiratory Viruses* 4: 327–37.

———. 2018. "The Mother of All Pandemics Is 100 Years Old (and Going Strong)!" *American Journal of Public Health* 108: 1449–54.

Morgan, J. A. T., et al. 2005. "Origin and Diversification of the Human Parasite *Schistosoma mansoni.*" *Molecular Ecology* 14: 3889–902.

Morony, M. G. 2007. "'For Whom Does the Writer Write?': The First Bubonic Plague Pandemic according to Syriac Sources." In *Plague and the End of Antiquity: The Pandemic of 541–750*, edited by L. K. Little, 58–86. New York.

Morrell, P. L., and M. T. Clegg. 2007. "Genetic Evidence for a Second Domestication of Barley (*Hordeum vulgare*) East of the Fertile Crescent." *Proceedings of the National Academy of Sciences* 104: 3289–94.

Morris, G. P., et al. 2013. "Population Genomic and Genome-Wide Association Studies of Agroclimatic Traits in Sorghum." *Proceedings of the National Academy of Sciences* 110: 453–58.

Morris, I. 2010. *Why the West Rules—for Now: The Patterns of History, and What They Reveal about the Future.* New York.

———. 2013. *The Measure of Civilization: How Social Development Decides the Fate of Nations.* Princeton.

Morris, I., and W. Scheidel, eds. 2009. *The Dynamics of Ancient Empires: State Power from Assyria to Byzantium.* New York.

Morris, R. J. 1976. *Cholera, 1832: The Social Response to an Epidemic.* New York.

Morton, V., and T. Staub. 2008. "A Short History of Fungicides." *APSnet Features* 10: 0308.

Moss, W. J. 2017. "Measles." *Lancet* 390: 2490–502.

Motolinia, T. de. 1970. *Memoriales e historia de los indios de la Nueva España.* Madrid.

Mouahid, G., et al. 2012. "A New Chronotype of *Schistosoma mansoni*: Adaptive Significance." *Tropical Medicine and International Health* 17: 727–32.

Mounier, A., and M. M. Lahr. 2019. "Deciphering African Late Middle Pleistocene Hominin Diversity and the Origin of Our Species." *Nature Communications* 10: 3406.

Mühlemann, B., et al. 2020. "Diverse Variola Virus (Smallpox) Strains Were Widespread in Northern Europe in the Viking Age." *Science* 369: eaaw8977.

Mukherjee, S. 2017. "Emerging Infectious Diseases: Epidemiological Perspective." *Indian Journal of Dermatology* 62: 459–67.

Mulhall, J. 2019. "Plague before the Pandemics: The Greek Medical Evidence for Bubonic Plague before the Sixth Century." *Bulletin of the History of Medicine* 93: 151–79.

Muller, M., et al. 2017. *Chimpanzees and Human Evolution.* Cambridge.

Müller, M. J. 1863. "Ibnulkhatîbs Bericht über die Pest." *Sitzungsberichte der Königl. Akademie der Wissenschaften zu München* 2: 1–33.

Muller, M. N., and R. W. Wrangham. 2018. "Morality Rates among Kenyawara Chimpanzees." *Journal of Human Evolution* 66: 107–14.

Muller, R. 1971. "Dracunculus and Dracunculiasis." *Advances in Parasitology* 9: 73–151.

Murchison, C. 1884. *A Treatise on the Continued Fevers of Great Britain*. London.

Murdoch, W. 1994. "Population Regulation in Theory and Practice." *Ecology* 75: 271–87.

Murphey, R. 1999. *Ottoman Warfare, 1500–1700*. New Brunswick.

Murphy, J., and A. Blank. 2012. *Invincible Microbe: Tuberculosis and the Never-Ending Search for a Cure*. Boston.

Murray, C. J. L. 1994. *The Global Burden of Disease in 1990*. Washington, DC.

Murray, C. J. L., and A. D. Lopez. 1996. *The Global Burden of Disease: A Comprehensive Assessment of Mortality and Disability from Diseases, Injuries, and Risk Factors in 1990 and Projected to 2020: Summary*. Washington, DC.

Murray, G. G. R., et al. 2016. "The Phylogeny of Rickettsia Using Different Evolutionary Signatures: How Tree-Like Is Bacterial Evolution?" *Systematic Biology* 65: 265–79.

Murray, K. A., et al. 2015. "Global Biogeography of Human Infectious Diseases." *Proceedings of the National Academy of Sciences* 112: 12746–51.

Nairz, M., and G. Weiss. 2020. "Iron in Infection and Immunity." *Molecular Aspects of Medicine* 75: 100864.

Namouchi, A., et al. 2018. "Integrative Approach Using *Yersinia pestis* Genomes to Revisit the Historical Landscape of Plague during the Medieval Period." *Proceedings of the National Academy of Sciences* 115: 11790–97.

Naphy, W. G. 2002. *Plagues, Poisons, and Potions: Plague-Spreading Conspiracies in the Western Alps, c. 1530–1640*. Manchester.

Nash, T. A. M. 1969. *Africa's Bane: The Tsetse Fly*. London.

Nasser, W., et al. 2014. "Evolutionary Pathway to Increased Virulence and Epidemic Group A *Streptococcus* Disease Derived from 3,615 Genome Sequences." *Proceedings of the National Academy of Sciences* 111: 1768–76.

Nathanson, N., and O. M. Kew. 2010. "From Emergence to Eradication: The Epidemiology of Poliomyelitis Deconstructed." *American Journal of Epidemiology* 172: 1213–29.

Nathanson, N., and J. R. Martin. 1979. "The Epidemiology of Poliomyelitis: Enigmas Surrounding Its Appearance, Epidemicity, and Disappearance." *American Journal of Epidemiology* 110: 672–92.

Navarrete, A., C. P. van Schaik, and K. Isler. 2011. "Energetics and the Evolution of Human Brain Size." *Nature* 480: 91–93.

Nédélec, Y., et al. 2016. "Genetic Ancestry and Natural Selection Drive Population Differences in Immune Responses to Pathogens." *Cell* 167: 657–69.

Needham, J. 2000. *Science & Civilisation in China*. Edited by N. Sivin. Vol. 6. Cambridge.

Nejsum, P., et al. 2017. "Ascaris Phylogeny Based on Multiple Whole mtDNA Genomes." *Infection, Genetics and Evolution* 48: 4–9.

Nelson, C. A., et al. 2020. "Antimicrobial Treatment of Human Plague: A Systematic Review of the Literature on Individual Cases, 1937–2019." *Clinical Infectious Diseases* 70: S3–10.

Nelson, M. I., and E. C. Holmes. 2007. "The Evolution of Epidemic Influenza." *Nature Reviews Genetics* 8: 196–205.

Nelson, M. I., and M. Worobey. 2018. "Origins of the 1918 Pandemic: Revisiting the Swine 'Mixing Vessel' Hypothesis." *American Journal of Epidemiology* 187: 2498–502.

Neubauer, S., J.-J. Hublin, and P. Gunz. 2018. "The Evolution of Modern Human Brain Shape." *Science Advances* 4: eaao5961.

Neven, M. 1997. "Epidemiology of Town and Countryside: Mortality and Causes of Death in East Belgium, 1850–1910." *Revue belge d'histoire contemporaine* 27: 39–82.

Newfield, T. P. 2009. "A Cattle Panzootic in Early Fourteenth-Century Europe." *Agricultural History Review* 57: 155–90.

———. 2012. "A Great Carolingian Panzootic: The Probable Extent, Diagnosis and Impact of an Early Ninth-Century Cattle Pestilence." *Argos* 46: 200–10.

———. 2013. "Early Medieval Epizootics and Landscapes of Disease: The Origins and Triggers of European Livestock Pestilences, 400–1000 CE." In *Landscapes and Societies in Medieval Europe East of the Elbe: Interactions between Environmental Settings and Cultural Transformations*, edited by S. Kleingärtner et al., 73–113. Toronto.

———. 2015. "Human-Bovine Plagues in the Early Middle Ages." *Journal of Interdisciplinary History* 46: 1–38.

———. 2017. "Malaria and Malaria-Like Disease in the Early Middle Ages." *Early Medieval Europe* 25: 251–300.

Newitt, M. D. D. 2005. *A History of Portuguese Overseas Expansion, 1400–1668*. London.

Newsholme, A. 1910. *The Prevention of Tuberculosis*. Methuen.

Newson, L. 1991. "Old World Epidemics in Early Colonial Ecuador." In *Secret Judgments of God: Old World Disease in Colonial Spanish America*, edited by N. D. Cook and W. G. Lovell, 84–112. Norman.

———. 1995. *Life and Death in Early Colonial Ecuador*. Norman.

———. 2006. "The Demographic Impact of Colonization." In *The Cambridge Economic History of Latin America*, edited by V. Bulmer-Thomas, J. Coatsworth, and R. Cortés Conde, 143–84. Cambridge.

Ngabonziza, J., et al. 2020. "A Sister Lineage of the *Mycobacterium tuberculosis* Complex Discovered in the African Great Lakes Region." *Nature Communications* 11: 1–11.

Nguyen-Hieu, T., et al. 2010. "Evidence of a Louse-Borne Outbreak Involving Typhus in Douai, 1710–1712 during the War of Spanish Succession." *PLoS One* 5: 15405.

Nichols, W. G., et al. 2008. "Respiratory Viruses Other than Influenza Virus: Impact and Therapeutic Advances." *Clinical Microbiology Reviews* 21: 274–90.

Nielsen, R., et al. 2017. "Tracing the Peopling of the World through Genomics." *Nature* 541: 302–10.

Nikiforov, V., et al. 2016. "Plague: Clinics, Diagnosis and Treatment." In *Yersinia pestis: Retrospective and Perspective*, edited by R. Yang and A. Anisimov, 293–312. Dordrecht.

Noreña, C. 2011. *Imperial Ideals in the Roman West*. Cambridge.

North, D. C., and R. P. Thomas. 1973. *The Rise of the Western World: A New Economic History*. Cambridge.

Noymer, A., and B. Jarosz. 2008. "Causes of Death in Nineteenth-Century New England: The Dominance of Infectious Disease." *Social History of Medicine* 21: 573–78.

Nozaki, T., and A. Bhattacharya, eds. 2015. *Amebiasis: Biology and Pathogenesis of Entamoeba*. Tokyo.

Nunn, C., and S. Altizer. 2006. *Infectious Diseases in Primates: Behavior, Ecology and Evolution.* Oxford.

Nunn, C. L., et al. 2003. "Comparative Tests of Parasite Species Richness in Primates." *American Naturalist* 162: 597–614.

———. 2005. "Latitudinal Gradients of Parasite Species Richness in Primates." *Biodiversity Research* 11: 249–56.

———. 2012. "Primate Disease Ecology in Comparative and Theoretical Perspective." *American Journal of Primatology* 74: 497–509.

———. 2015. "Infectious Disease and Group Size: More than Just a Numbers Game." *Philosophical Transactions of the Royal Society B: Biological Sciences* 370: 20140111.

Nunn, N., and N. Qian. 2010. "The Columbian Exchange: A History of Disease, Food, and Ideas." *Journal of Economic Perspectives* 24: 163–88.

———. 2011. "The Potato's Contribution to Population and Urbanization: Evidence from a Historical Experiment." *Quarterly Journal of Economics* 126: 593–650.

Nutall, G. H. F., and G. S. Graham-Smith, eds. 1908. *The Bacteriology of Diphtheria.* Cambridge.

Nutton, V. 1990. "The Reception of Fracastoro's Theory of Contagion: The Seed That Fell among Thorns?" *Osiris* 6: 196–234.

Nützenadel, A. 2008. "A Green International? Food Markets and Transnational Politics c. 1850–1914." In *Food and Globalization: Consumption, Markets and Politics in the Modern World,* edited by A. Nützenadel and F. Trentmann, 153–72. Oxford.

Oberg, B., ed. 2006. *The Papers of Thomas Jefferson.* Vol. 33. Princeton.

O'Connor, T. 2014. *Animals as Neighbors: The Past and Present of Commensal Animals.* East Lansing.

O'Driscoll, C. A., and J. C. Thompson. 2018. "The Origins and Early Elaboration of Projectile Technology." *Evolutionary Anthropology: Issues, News, and Reviews* 27: 30–45.

Ó Gráda, C. 1995. *The Great Irish Famine.* Cambridge.

Ó Gráda, C., E. Vanhaute, and R. Paping, eds. 2007. *When the Potato Failed: Causes and Effects of the Last European Subsistence Crisis, 1845–1850.* Turnhout.

Ohm, J., et al. 2018. "Rethinking the Extrinsic Incubation Period of Malaria Parasites." *Parasites & Vectors* 11: 178.

Oldstone, M. B. A. 1998. *Viruses, Plagues, and History.* Oxford.

Olival, K., et al. 2016. "Host and Viral Traits Predict Zoonotic Spillover from Mammals." *Nature* 546: 646–50.

Olivarius, K. M. M. 2016. *Necropolis: Yellow Fever, Immunity, and Capitalism in the Deep South, 1800–1860.* PhD diss., University of Oxford.

Oliveira, A., et al. 2017. "Insight of Genus *Corynebacterium*: Ascertaining the Role of Pathogenic and Non-Pathogenic Species." *Frontiers in Microbiology* 8: 1937.

Olmstead, A. L., and P. W. Rhode. 2008. *Creating Abundance: Biological Innovation and American Agricultural Development.* New York.

———. 2015. *Arresting Contagion: Science, Policy, and Conflicts over Animal Disease Control.* Cambridge.

Olsen, L., et al., eds. 2011. *Fungal Diseases: An Emerging Threat to Human, Animal, and Plant Health.* Washington, DC.

Omran, A. 1971. "The Epidemiologic Transition: A Theory of the Epidemiology of Population Change." *Milbank Memorial Fund Quarterly* 49: 509–38.

O'Neill, M. B., et al. 2019. "Lineage Specific Histories of *Mycobacterium tuberculosis* Dispersal in Africa and Eurasia." *Molecular Ecology* 28: 3241–56.

Oppenheimer, S. 2004. *Out of Africa's Eden: The Peopling of the World.* Johannesburg.

Orme, N., and M. Webster. 1995. *The English Hospital 1070–1570.* New Haven.

O'Shea, T. J., and M. A. Bogan, eds. 2003. *Monitoring Trends in Bat Populations of the United States and Territories: Problems and Prospects.* Fort Collins.

Oshinsky, D. M. 2006. *Polio: An American Story.* New York.

Ossa, A., M. E. Smith, and J. Lobo. 2017. "The Size of Plazas in Mesoamerican Cities and Towns: A Quantitative Analysis." *Latin American Antiquity* 28: 457–75.

Osterhammel, J. 2005. *Globalization: A Short History.* Princeton.

———. 2014. *The Transformation of the World: A Global History of the Nineteenth Century.* Princeton.

Osterholm, M. T., and M. Olshaker. 2017. *Deadliest Enemy: Our War against Killer Germs.* New York.

Otter, C. 2008. *The Victorian Eye: A Political History of Light and Vision in Britain, 1800–1910.* Chicago.

———. 2013. "Planet of Meat: A Biological History." In *Challenging (the) Humanities,* edited by T. Bennett, 33–49. Canberra.

Ottesen, E. A. 2006. "Lymphatic Filariasis: Treatment, Control and Elimination." *Advances in Parasitology* 61: 395–441.

Otto, K. F. 2003. *A Companion to the Works of Grimmelshausen.* Rochester.

Otto, T. D., et al. 2018. "Genomes of All Known Members of a Plasmodium Subgenus Reveal Paths to Virulent Human Malaria." *Nature Microbiology* 3: 687–97.

———. 2019. "Evolutionary Analysis of the Most Polymorphic Gene Family in Falciparum Malaria." *Wellcome Open Research* 4.

Oueslati, T., et al. 2020. "1st Century BCE Occurrence of Chicken, House Mouse and Black Rat in Morocco: Socio-economic Changes around the Reign of Juba II on the Site of Rirha." *Journal of Archaeological Science: Reports* 29: 102162.

Outram, Q. 2001. "The Socio-economic Relations of Warfare and the Military Mortality Crises of the Thirty Years' War." *Medical History* 45: 151–84.

———. 2002. "The Demographic Impact of Early Modern Warfare." *Social Science History* 26: 245–72.

Pääbo, S. 2015. "The Diverse Origins of the Human Disease Pool." *Nature Reviews Genetics* 16: 313–14.

Pacheco, J. F., et al. 1864. *Colección de documentos inéditos relativos al descubrimiento, conquista y colonización de las posesiones españolas en América y Oceanía.* 42 vols. Madrid.

Packard, R. M. 2007. *The Making of a Tropical Disease.* Baltimore.

———. 2016. *A History of Global Health: Interventions into the Lives of Other Peoples.* Baltimore.

Paixão, E. S., M. G. Teixeira, and L. C. Rodrigues. 2018. "Zika, Chikungunya and Dengue: The Causes and Threats of New and Re-emerging Arboviral Diseases." *BMJ Global Health* 3: e000530.

Pajer, P., et al. 2017. "Characterization of Two Historic Smallpox Specimens from a Czech Museum." *Viruses* 9: 200.

Pakendorf, B., et al. 2011. "Molecular Perspectives on the Bantu Expansion: A Synthesis." *Language Dynamics and Change* 1: 50–88.

Palmer, S. P. 2010. *Launching Global Health: The Caribbean Odyssey of the Rockefeller Foundation.* Ann Arbor.

Pamuk, S. 2007. "The Black Death and the Origins of the 'Great Divergence' across Europe, 1300–1600." *European Review of Economic History* 11: 289–317.

Pamuk, S., and M. Shatzmiller. 2014. "Plagues, Wages, and Economic Change in the Islamic Middle East, 700–1500." *Journal of Economic History* 74: 196–229.

Panagiotakopulu, E., and P. C. Buckland. 2017. "A Thousand Bites—Insect Introductions and Late Holocene Environments." *Quaternary Science Reviews* 156: 23–35.

———. 2018. "Early Invaders: Farmers, the Granary Weevil and Other Uninvited Guests in the Neolithic." *Biological Invasions* 20: 219–33.

Panter-Brick, C., R. Layton, and P. Rowley-Conwy. 2001. *Hunter-Gatherers: An Interdisciplinary Perspective.* Cambridge.

Panum, P. 1940. *Observations Made during the Epidemic of Measles on the Faroe Islands in the Year 1846.* Translated by A. S. Hatcher. New York.

Panzac, D. 1985. *La Peste dans l'Empire Ottoman: 1700–1850.* Leuven.

Park, Y. H., et al. 2020. "Ancient Familial Mediterranean Fever Mutations in Human Pyrin and Resistance to *Yersinia pestis.*" *Nature Immunology* 21: 857–67.

Parker, G. 1996. *The Military Revolution: Military Innovation and the Rise of the West, 1500–1800.* 2nd ed. New York.

———. 1997. *The Thirty Years' War.* Florence.

———. 2013. *Global Crisis: War, Climate Change and Catastrophe in the Seventeenth Century.* New Haven.

Parker, G., and L. M. Smith. 1997. *The General Crisis of the Seventeenth Century.* 2nd ed. New York.

Parkhill, J., et al. 2003. "Comparative Analysis of the Genome Sequences of *Bordetella pertussis, Bordetella parapertussis* and *Bordetella bronchiseptica.*" *Nature Genetics* 35: 32–40.

Parmakelis, A., et al. 2008. "Historical Analysis of a Near Disaster: *Anopheles gambiae* in Brazil." *American Journal of Tropical Medicine and Hygiene* 78: 176–78.

Parola, P., et al. 2013. "Update on Tick-Borne Rickettsioses around the World: A Geographic Approach." *Clinical Microbiology Reviews* 26: 657–702.

Parry, C. M. 2006. "Epidemiological and Clinical Aspects of Human Typhoid Fever." In *Salmonella Infections: Clinical, Immunological and Molecular Aspects,* edited by P. Mastroeni and D. Maskell, 1–17. Cambridge.

Parthasarathi, P. 2011. *Why Europe Grew Rich and Asia Did Not: Global Economic Divergence, 1600–1850.* Cambridge.

Patel, M. K., et al. 2019. "Progress toward Regional Measles Elimination—Worldwide, 2000–2018." *Morbidity and Mortality Weekly Report* 68: 1105–11.

Patrono, L. V., and F. Leendertz. 2019. "Acute Infectious Diseases Occurring in the Taï Chimpanzee Population: A Review." In *The Chimpanzees of the Taï Forest: 40 Years of Research,* edited by C. Boesch et al., 385–93. Cambridge.

Patrono, L. V., et al. 2018. "Human Coronavirus OC43 Outbreak in Wild Chimpanzees, Côte d'Ivoire, 2016." *Emerging Microbes & Infections* 7: 1–4.

Patterson, G. 2009. *The Mosquito Crusades: A History of the American Anti-mosquito Movement from the Reed Commission to the First Earth Day.* New Brunswick.

Patterson, K. D. 1981. *Health in Colonial Ghana: Disease, Medicine, and Socio-economic Change, 1900–1955.* Waltham.

———. 1986. *Pandemic Influenza 1700–1900: A Study in Historical Epidemiology.* Totowa.

———. 1992. "Yellow Fever Epidemics and Mortality in the United States, 1693–1905." *Social Science & Medicine* 34: 855–65.

Patterson, K. D., and G. F. Pyle. 1983. "The Diffusion of Influenza in Sub-Saharan Africa during the 1918–1919 Pandemic." *Social Science & Medicine* 17: 1299–307.

———. 1991. "The Geography and Mortality of the 1918 Influenza Pandemic." *Bulletin of the History of Medicine* 65: 4–21.

Paul, J. R. 1971. *A History of Poliomyelitis.* New Haven.

Pearce, J. M. S. 2012. "Brain Disease Leading to Mental Illness: A Concept Initiated by the Discovery of General Paralysis of the Insane." *European Neurology* 67: 272–78.

Peary, R. E. 1898a. "Journeys in North Greenland." *Geographical Journal* 11: 213–40.

———. 1898b. *Northward over the Great Ice: A Narrative of Life and Work along the Shores and upon the Interior Ice-Cap of Northern Greenland in the Years 1886 and 1891–1897.* New York.

Pechous, R. D., et al. 2016. "Pneumonic Plague: The Darker Side of *Yersinia pestis.*" *Trends in Microbiology* 24: 190–97.

Peck, J. J. 2009. *The Biological Impact of Culture Contact: A Bioarchaeological Study of Roman Colonialism in Britain.* PhD diss., Ohio State University.

Pedersen, A. B., et al. 2005. "Patterns of Host Specificity and Transmission among Parasites of Wild Primates." *International Journal for Parasitology* 35 (6): 647–57.

Pennington, T. H. 1995. "Listerism, Its Decline and Its Persistence: The Introduction of Aseptic Surgical Techniques in Three British Teaching Hospitals, 1890–99." *Medical History* 39: 35–60.

Pepin, J. 2011. *The Origins of AIDS.* Cambridge.

Pepperell, C. S., et al. 2013. "The Role of Selection in Shaping Diversity of Natural *M. Tuberculosis* Populations." *PLoS Pathogens* 9: 1003543.

Percoco, M. 2013. "The Fight against Disease: Malaria and Economic Development in Italian Regions." *Economic Geography* 89: 105–25.

Pérez Moreda, V. 1980. *Las crisis de mortalidad en la España interior (siglos XVI–XIX).* Madrid.

Perrenoud, A. 1975. "L'Inegalite Sociale Devant La Mort à Genève Au XVIII Siècle." *Population* 30: 221–43.

———. 1991 "The Attenuation of Mortality Crises and the Decline of Mortality." In *The Decline of Mortality in Europe,* edited by R. Schoefield, D. Reher, and A. Bideau, 18–37. Oxford.

Pfister, U., and G. Fertig. 2010. "The Population History of Germany: Research Strategy and Preliminary Results." Max-Planck-Institut Für Demografische Forschung working paper WP 2010-035. Rostock.

Philbrick, N. 2006. *Mayflower: A Story of Courage, Community, and War.* New York.

Phillips, C., and C. Lancelotti. 2014. "Chimpanzee Diet: Phytolithic Analysis of Feces." *American Journal of Primatology* 76: 757–73.

Phoofolo, P. 1993. "Epidemics and Revolutions: The Rinderpest Epidemic in Late Nineteenth-Century Southern Africa." *Past & Present* 138: 112–43.

Pickrell, J. K., et al. 2009. "Signals of Recent Positive Selection in a Worldwide Sample of Human Populations." *Genome Research* 19: 826–37.

Pickstone, J. V. 1992. "Dearth, Dirt, and Fever Epidemics: Rewriting the History of British 'Public Health,' 1780–1950." In *Epidemics and Ideas: Essays on the Historical Perception of Pestilence*, edited by T. Ranger and P. Slack, 125–48. Cambridge.

Piel, F. B., et al. 2010. "Global Distribution of the Sickle Cell Gene and Geographical Confirmation of the Malaria Hypothesis." *Nature Communications* 1: 1–7.

Pimenoff, V., C. Mendes de Oliveira, and I. Bravo. 2017. "Transmission between Archaic and Modern Human Ancestors during the Evolution of the Oncogenic Human Papillomavirus 16." *Molecular Biology and Evolution* 34: 4–19.

Pinhasi, R., and J. T. Stock, eds. 2011. *Human Bioarchaeology of the Transition to Agriculture.* Chichester.

Pinto, G. 1996. "Dalla tarda antichità alla metà del XVI secolo." In *La populazione italiana dal medioevo a oggi*, edited by L. Del Panta et al., 15–71. Bari.

Pinto, G., and E. Sonnino. 1997. "L'Italie." In *Histoires des populations de l'Europe: I. Des origines aux prémices de la révolution démographique*, edited by J.-P. Bardet and J. Dupâquier, 485–508. Paris.

Piperno, D. R., and T. D. Dillehay. 2008. "Starch Grains on Human Teeth Reveal Early Broad Crop Diet in Northern Peru." *Proceedings of the National Academy of Sciences* 105: 19622–27.

Piperno, D. R., and K. V. Flannery. 2001. "The Earliest Archaeological Maize (*Zea mays* L.) from Highland Mexico: New Accelerator Mass Spectrometry Dates and Their Implications." *Proceedings of the National Academy of Sciences of the United States of America* 98: 2101–3.

Pittarello, O., et al., eds. 2017. *Statuti di Padova di età carrarese.* Rome.

Plotkin, S. A., ed. 2011. *History of Vaccine Development.* New York.

Plowright, R. K., et al. 2015. "Ecological Dynamics of Emerging Bat Virus Spillover." *Proceedings of the Royal Society B: Biological Sciences* 282: 20142124.

Plowright, W. 1982. "The Effects of Rinderpest and Rinderpest Control on Wildlife in Africa." *Symposia of the Zoological Society of London* 50: 1–28.

Poespoprodjo, J. R., et al. 2009. "Vivax Malaria: A Major Cause of Morbidity in Early Infancy." *Clinical Infectious Diseases* 48: 1704–12.

Pollitzer, R. 1954. *Plague.* Geneva.

———. 1959. *Cholera.* Geneva.

Pomeranz, K. 2000. *The Great Divergence: China, Europe, and the Making of the Modern World Economy.* Princeton.

Pontremoli, C., et al. 2020. "Possible European Origin of Circulating Varicella Zoster Virus Strains." *Journal of Infectious Diseases* 221: 1286–94.

Pontzer, H. 2017. "The Crown Joules: Energetics, Ecology, and Evolution in Humans and Other Primates." *Evolutionary Anthropology* 26: 12–24.

Pontzer, H., et al. 2016. "Metabolic Acceleration and the Evolution of Human Brain Size and Life History." *Nature* 533: 390–93.

Pormann, P. E., and E. Savage-Smith. 2010. *Medieval Islamic Medicine.* Edinburgh.

Porter, A. 1994. *European Imperialism, 1860–1914*. London.

Porter, D. 1999. *Health, Civilization, and the State: A History of Public Health from Ancient to Modern Times*. London.

Porter, R. 1995. *Disease, Medicine, and Society in England, 1550–1860*. 2nd ed. Cambridge.

———. 1998. *The Greatest Benefit to Mankind: A Medical History of Humanity*. New York.

Post, J. D. 1984. "Climatic Variability and the European Mortality Wave of the Early 1740s." *Journal of Interdisciplinary History* 15: 1–30.

Potter, C. W. 2001. "A History of Influenza." *Journal of Applied Microbiology* 91: 572–79.

Potts, D. 2018. "Sasanian Iran and Its Northeastern Frontier: Offense, Defense, and Diplomatic Entente." In *Empires and Exchanges in Eurasian Late Antiquity: Rome, China, Iran, and the Steppe, ca. 250–750*, edited by N. Di Cosmo and M. Maas, 287–301. Cambridge.

Poulin, R. 2007. *Evolutionary Ecology of Parasites*. 2nd ed. Princeton.

Poulin, R., and S. Morand. 2000. "The Diversity of Parasites." *Quarterly Review of Biology* 75: 277–93.

Powell, J. R. 2016. "New Contender for Most Lethal Animal." *Nature* 540: 525.

———. 2018. "Mosquito-Borne Human Viral Diseases: Why *Aedes aegypti*?" *American Journal of Tropical Medicine and Hygiene* 98: 1563–65.

Powell, J. R., A. Gloria-Soria, and P. Kotsakiozi. 2018. "Recent History of *Aedes aegypti*: Vector Genomics and Epidemiology Records." *BioScience* 68: 854–60.

Powłowska, K. 2014. "The Smells of Neolithic Çatalhöyük, Turkey: Time and Space of Human Activity." *Journal of Anthropological Archaeology* 36: 1–11.

Prebble, J. 1968. *The Darien Disaster*. London.

Prem, H. 1991. "Disease Outbreaks in Central Mexico during the Sixteenth Century." In *Secret Judgments of God: Old World Disease in Colonial Spanish America*, edited by N. D. Cook and G. W. Lovell, 20–48. Norman.

Preston, S. H. 1975. "The Changing Relation between Mortality and Level of Economic Development." *International Journal of Epidemiology* 36: 484–90.

———. 1976. *Mortality Patterns in National Populations: With Special Reference to Recorded Causes of Death*. New York.

———. 1980. "Causes and Consequences of Mortality Declines in Less Developed Countries during the Twentieth Century." In *Population and Economic Change in Developing Countries*, edited by R. Easterlin, 289–360. Chicago.

Preston, S. H., and V. E. Nelson. 1974. "Structure and Change in Causes of Death: An International Summary." *Population Studies* 28: 19–51.

Price, R., J. K. Baird, and S. I. Hay. 2012. *The Epidemiology of* Plasmodium vivax: *History, Hiatus and Hubris*. San Diego.

Price-Smith, A. T. 2009. *Contagion and Chaos: Disease, Ecology and National Security in the Era of Globalization*. Cambridge.

Pringle, J. 1750. *Observations on the Nature and Cure of Hospital and Jayl-Fevers*. London.

———. 1753. *Observations on the Diseases of the Army, in Camp and Garrison. In Three Parts. With an Appendix, Containing Some Papers of Experiments, Read at Several Meetings of the Royal Society*. London.

———. 1764. *Observations on the Diseases of the Army*. 4th ed. London.

Prinzing, F. 1916. *Epidemics Resulting from Wars*. Oxford.

Pritchett, J. B. 1995. "Strangers' Disease: Determinants of Yellow Fever Mortality during the New Orleans Epidemic of 1853." *Explorations in Economic History* 32: 517–39.

Priuli, G. 1938. *I Diarii*. In *Rerum Italicarum Scriptores*, edited by R. Cessi, 24.4. Bologna.

Prowse, T. 2016. "Isotopes and Mobility in the Ancient Roman World." In *Migration and Mobility in the Early Roman Empire*, edited by L. de Ligt and L. E. Tacoma, 205–33. Leiden.

Prowse, T., et al. 2004. "Isotopic Paleodiet Studies of Skeletons from the Imperial Roman-Age Cemetery of Isola Sacra, Rome, Italy." *Journal of Archaeological Science* 31: 259–72.

———. 2007. "Isotopic Evidence for Age-Related Immigration to Imperial Rome." *American Journal of Physical Anthropology* 132: 510–19.

———. 2008. "Isotopic and Dental Evidence for Infant and Young Child Feeding Practices in an Imperial Roman Skeletal Sample." *American Journal of Physical Anthropology* 137: 294–308.

Prugnolle, F., et al. 2013. "Diversity, Host Switching and Evolution of *Plasmodium vivax* Infecting African Great Apes." *Proceedings of the National Academy of Sciences* 110: 8123–28.

Puckett, E., D. Orton, and J. Munshi-South. 2020. "Commensal Rats and Humans: Integrating Rodent Phylogeography and Zooarchaeology to Highlight Connections between Human Societies." *Bioessays* 42: 1900160.

Purcell, N. 2016. "Unnecessary Dependences: Illustrating Circulation in Pre-modern Large-Scale History." In *The Prospect of Global History*, edited by J. Belich et al., 65–79. Oxford.

Pybus, O. G., and J. Thézé. 2016. "Hepacivirus Cross-Species Transmission and the Origins of the Hepatitis C Virus." *Current Opinion in Virology* 16: 1–7.

Pyle, G. F. 1986. *The Diffusion of Influenza: Patterns and Paradigms*. Totowa.

Pyle, G. F., and K. D. Patterson. 1984. "Influenza Diffusion in European History: Patterns and Paradigms." *Ecology of Disease* 2: 173–84.

Quammen, D. 2012. *Spillover: Animal Infections and the Next Human Pandemic*. New York.

Quétel, C. 1990. *History of Syphilis*. Baltimore.

Quigley, E. M. M. 2013. "Gut Bacteria in Health and Disease." *Gastroenterology & Hepatology* 9: 560–69.

———. 2017. *The Gut Microbiome*. Philadelphia

Quinn, M. J. 1926. "Malaria in New England." *Boston Medical and Surgical Journal* 194: 244–47.

Quintana-Murci, L. 2019. "Human Immunology through the Lens of Evolutionary Genetics." *Cell* 177: 184–99.

Rabbani, G. H., and W. B. Greenough. 1992. "Pathophysiology and Clinical Aspects of Cholera." In *Cholera*, edited by D. Barua and W. Greenough, 209–28. Boston.

Raccianello, V. 2012. "What Is a Virus?" Course material, Columbia University. http://www.virology.ws/w3310/001_W3310_12.pdf.

Radivojević, M., and B. W. Roberts. forthcoming. "Early Balkan Metallurgy: Origins, Evolution and Society (c. 6200–3200 BCE)." *Journal of World Prehistory*.

Raghavan, M. 2015. "Genomic Evidence for the Pleistocene and Recent Population History of Native Americans." *Science* 349: 3884.

Rahuma, N., et al. 2005. "Carriage by the Housefly (*Musca domestica*) of Multiple-Antibiotic-Resistant Bacteria That Are Potentially Pathogenic to Humans, in Hospital and Other Urban Environments in Misurata, Libya." *Annals of Tropical Medicine & Parasitology* 99: 795–802.

Raina, B. L. 1991. *Introduction to Malaria Problem in India: Vedic Period to Early 1950's*. New Delhi.

Rambaut, A., et al. 2008. "The Genomic and Epidemiological Dynamics of Human Influenza A Virus." *Nature* 453: 615–19.

Ramenofsky, A. F. 1987. *Vectors of Death: The Archaeology of European Contact.* 1st ed. Albuquerque.

Ranjel, R. 1922. *Narratives of the Career of Hernando de Soto in the Conquest of Florida: As Told by a Knight of Elvas and in a Relation by Luys Hernandez de Biedma, Factor of the Expedition; Translated by Buckingham Smith, together with an Account of de Soto's Expedition Based on the Diary of Rodrigo Ranjel, His Private Secretary Translated from Oviedo's Historia General y Natural de Las Indias.* 2 vols. New York.

Ransford, O. 1983. *"Bid the Sickness Cease": Disease in the History of Black Africa.* London.

Raoult, D., et al. 2000. "Molecular Identification by 'Suicide PCR' of *Yersinia pestis* as the Agent of Medieval Black Death." *Proceedings of the National Academy of Sciences* 97: 12800–3.

———. 2004. "The History of Epidemic Typhus." *Infectious Disease Clinics of North America* 18: 127–40.

Raschke, M. G. 1978. "New Studies in Roman Commerce with the East." *Aufstieg und Niedergang der römischen Welt* 2.9.2: 604–1361.

Rascovan, N., et al. 2019. "Emergence and Spread of Basal Lineages of *Yersinia pestis* during the Neolithic Decline." *Cell* 176: 295–305.

Rasmussen, S., et al. 2015. "Early Divergent Strains of *Yersinia pestis* in Eurasia 5,000 Years Ago." *Cell* 163: 571–82.

Rassi, A., A. Rassi, and J. Marin-Neto. 2010. "Chagas Disease." *Lancet* 375: 1388–402.

Raudzens, G. 1997. "In Search of Better Quantification for War History: Numerical Superiority and Casualty Rates in Early Modern Europe." *War & Society* 15: 1–30.

Rawcliffe, C. 2013. *Urban Bodies: Communal Health in Late Medieval English Towns and Cities.* Woodbridge.

Rawcliffe, C., and C. Weeda, eds. 2019. *Policing the Urban Environment in Premodern Europe.* Amsterdam.

Ray, A. 1976. "Diffusion of Diseases in the Western Interior of Canada, 1830–1850." *Geographical Review* 66: 139–57.

Razzell, P. E. 2003. *The Conquest of Smallpox: The Impact of Inoculation on Smallpox Mortality in Eighteenth Century Britain.* Firle.

———. 2007. *Population and Disease: Transforming English Society, 1550–1850.* London.

Reba, M., F. Reitsma, and K. Seito. 2016. "Spatializing 6,000 Years of Global Urbanization from 3700 BC to AD 2000." *Scientific Data* 3: 160034.

Rebellato, L., W. I. Woods, and E. G. Neves. 2009. "Pre-Columbian Settlement Dynamics in the Central Amazon." In *Amazonian Dark Earths: Wim Sombroek's Vision,* edited by W. I. Woods et al., 15–31. Dordrecht.

Recker, M., et al. 2011. "Antigenic Variation in *Plasmodium falciparum* Malaria Involves a Highly Structured Switching Pattern." *PLoS Pathogens* 7: e1001306.

Redfern, R. C., and S. N. DeWitte. 2011a. "A New Approach to the Study of Romanization in Britain: A Regional Perspective of Cultural Change in Late Iron Age and Roman Dorset Using the Siler and Gompertz–Makeham Models of Mortality." *American Journal of Physical Anthropology* 144: 269–85.

————. 2011b. "Status and Health in Roman Dorset: The Effect of Status on Risk of Mortality in Post-Conquest Populations." *American Journal of Physical Anthropology* 146: 197–208.

Redfern, R. C., et al. 2015. "Urban-Rural Differences in Roman Dorset, England: A Bioarchaeological Perspective on Roman Settlements." *American Journal of Physical Anthropology* 157: 107–20.

Reff, D. T. 1991. *Disease, Depopulation, and Culture Change in Northwestern New Spain, 1518–1764.* Salt Lake City.

Reher, D. S. 2001. "In Search of the 'Urban Penalty': Exploring Urban and Rural Mortality Patterns in Spain during the Demographic Transition." *International Journal of Population Geography* 7: 105–27.

Reich, D. 2018. *Who We Are and How We Got Here: Ancient DNA and the New Science of the Human Past.* New York.

Renfrew, C. 2008. *Prehistory: The Making of the Human Mind.* New York.

Rénia, L., and Y. S. Goh. 2016. "Malaria Parasites: The Great Escape." *Frontiers in Immunology* 7: 463.

Renny-Byfield, S., et al. 2016. "Independent Domestication of Two Old World Cotton Species." *Genome Biology and Evolution* 8: 1940–47.

Reubi, D. 2018. "Epidemiological Accountability: Philanthropists, Global Health and the Audit of Saving Lives." *Economy and Society* 47: 83–110.

Reuter, J. A., D. V. Spacek, and M. P. Snyder. 2015. "High-Throughput Sequencing Technologies." *Molecular Cell* 58: 586–97.

Reynolds, S. C., R. J. Clarke, and K. A. Kuman. 2007. "The View from the Lincoln Cave: Mid- to Late Pleistocene Fossil Deposits from Sterkfontein Hominid Site, South Africa." *Journal of Human Evolution* 53: 260–71.

Richards, J. 2003. *The Unending Frontier: An Environmental History of the Early Modern World.* Berkeley.

Richardson, B. W. 1876. *Hygeia: A City of Health.* London.

Richardson, G. 2019. "The Vulnerability of New Orleans' Black and Foreign-Born Populations in the 1878 Yellow Fever Outbreak: A Reassessment." *GeoJournal* 84: 1465–80.

Rielly, K. 2010. "The Black Rat." In *Extinctions and Invasions. A Social History of British Fauna,* edited by T. O'Connor and N. Sykes, 134–45. Oxford.

Rifkin, J., C. L. Nunn, and L. Garamszegi. 2012. "Do Animals Living in Larger Groups Experience Greater Parasitism? A Meta-analysis." *American Naturalist* 180: 70–82.

Riley, C. V. 1891. *Reports of the United States Commissioners to the Universal Exposition of 1889 at Paris.* Vol. 5. Washington, DC.

Riley, J. C. 1981. "Mortality on Long-Distance Voyages in the Eighteenth Century." *Journal of Economic History* 41: 651–56.

————. 1986. "Insects and the European Mortality Decline." *American Historical Review* 91: 833–58.

————. 1987. *The Eighteenth-Century Campaign to Avoid Disease.* New York.

————. 2001. *Rising Life Expectancy: A Global History.* Cambridge.

————. 2005a. "Bibliography of Works Providing Estimates of Life Expectancy at Birth and Estimates of the Beginning Period of Health Transitions in Countries with a Population in 2000 of at Least 400,000." https://www.lifetable.de/RileyBib.pdf.

———. 2005b. "Estimates of Regional and Global Life Expectancy, 1800–2001." *Population and Development Review* 31: 537–43.

———. 2005c. *Poverty and Life Expectancy: The Jamaica Paradox.* New York.

———. 2005d. "The Timing and Pace of Health Transitions around the World." *Population and Development Review* 31: 741–64.

———. 2008. *Low Income, Social Growth, and Good Health: A History of Twelve Countries.* Berkeley.

Rimas, A., and E. Fraser. 2008. *Beef: The Untold Story of How Milk, Meat, and Muscle Shaped the World.* New York.

Rio, A. 2020. *Slavery after Rome, 500–1000.* Oxford.

Rios, L., et al. 2017. "Deciphering the Emergence, Genetic Diversity and Evolution of Classical Swine Fever Virus." *Scientific Reports* 7: 1–18.

Ripamonti, G. 1841. *La Peste di Milano del 1630.* Milan. First published 1640.

Risse, G. B. 1985. "'Typhus' Fever in Eighteenth-Century Hospitals: New Approaches to Medical Treatment." *Bulletin of the History of Medicine* 59: 176–95.

———. 1986. *Hospital Life in Enlightenment Scotland: Care and Teaching at the Royal Infirmary of Edinburgh.* Cambridge.

Rival, L., and D. McKey. 2008. "Domestication and Diversity in Manioc (*Manihot esculenta* Crantz ssp. *esculenta, Euphorbiaceae*)." *Current Anthropology* 49: 1119–28.

Roberts, B. W. 2011. "Ancient Technology and Archaeological Cultures: Understanding the Earliest Metallurgy in Eurasia." In *Investigating Archaeological Cultures: Material Culture, Variability, and Transmission,* edited by B. W. Roberts and M. Vander Linden, 137–50. New York.

Roberts, B. W., and M. Radivojević. 2015. "Invention as a Process: Pyrotechnologies in Early Societies." *Cambridge Archaeological Journal* 25: 299–306.

Roberts, B. W., C. P. Thornton, and V. C. Pigott. 2009. "Development of Metallurgy in Eurasia." *Antiquity* 83: 1012–22.

Roberts, C. A. 2015. "Old World Tuberculosis: Evidence from Human Remains with a Review of Current Research and Future Prospects." *Tuberculosis* 95: S117–21.

Roberts, C. A., and J. E. Buikstra. 2003. *The Bioarchaeology of Tuberculosis: A Global View on a Reemerging Disease.* Gainesville.

Roberts, L. 2020. "Global Polio Eradication Falters in the Final Stretch." *Science* 367: 14–15.

Roberts, M. 1956. *The Military Revolution, 1560–1660: An Inaugural Lecture Delivered before the Queen's University of Belfast.* Belfast.

Roberts, M. B. V. 1986. *Biology: A Functional Approach.* 4th ed. Cheltenham.

Robertson, J. C. 1996. "Reckoning with London: Interpreting the 'Bills of Mortality' before John Graunt." *Urban History* 23: 325–50.

Robertson, W. 1817. *The Works of William Robertson.* London.

Robinson, M. 2009. "Plague and Humiliation: The Ecclesiastical Response to Cattle Plague in Mid-Victorian Britain." *Journal of Scottish Historical Studies* 29: 52–71.

Roe, T. 1740. *The Negociations . . . in His Embassy to the Ottoman Porte from the Year. 1621–28 Inclusive. Now First Publ. from the Originals.* London.

Roeder, P., J. Mariner, and R. Kock. 2013. "Rinderpest: The Veterinary Perspective on Eradication." *Philosophical Transactions of the Royal Society B: Biological Sciences* 368: 20120139.

Rogers, A. R., et al. 2020. "Neanderthal-Denisovan Ancestors Interbred with a Distantly Related Hominin." *Science Advances* 6: eaay5483.

Rogers, C., ed. 2018. *The Military Revolution Debate: Readings on the Military Transformation of Early Modern Europe*. Boulder.

Rolleston, J. D. 1928. "The History of Scarlet Fever." *British Medical Journal* 2: 926–29.

Romano, T. 1997. "The Cattle Plague of 1865 and the Reception of 'The Germ Theory' In Mid-Victorian Britain." *Journal of the History of Medicine and Allied Sciences* 52: 51–80.

Rose, R., et al. 2013. "Viral Evolution Explains the Associations among Hepatitis C Virus Genotype, Clinical Outcomes, and Human Genetic Variation." *Infection, Genetics and Evolution* 20: 418–21.

Rosen, G. 1974. *From Medical Police to Social Medicine: Essays on the History of Health Care*. New York.

———. 1993. *A History of Public Health*. Expanded ed. Baltimore.

Rosenberg, C. E. 1962. *The Cholera Years: The United States in 1832, 1849, and 1866*. Chicago.

Rosenkrantz, B. 1994. *From Consumption to Tuberculosis: A Documentary History*. New York.

Ross, J. 1819. *A Voyage of Discovery*. London.

Rota, M., and J. Weisdorf. 2020. "Italy and the Little Divergence in Wages and Prices: New Data, New Results." Center for Economic Policy Research discussion paper no. DP14295.

Rothenberg, G. E. 1973. "The Austrian Sanitary Cordon and the Control of the Bubonic Plague: 1710–1871." *Journal of the History of Medicine and Allied Sciences* 28: 15–23.

Roumagnac, P., et al. 2006. "Evolutionary History of *Salmonella typhi*." *Science* 314: 1301–4.

Rowe, W. T. 2009. *China's Last Empire: The Great Qing*. Cambridge.

Roy, T. 2000. *The Economic History of India: 1857–1947*. Oxford.

Ruddiman, W. F. 2003. "The Anthropogenic Greenhouse Era Began Thousands of Years Ago." *Climatic Change* 61: 261–93.

Ruffino, L., and E. Vidal. 2010. "Early Colonization of Mediterranean Islands by *Rattus rattus*: A Review of Zooarcheological Data." *Biological Invasions* 12: 2389–94.

Ruiz-Tiben, E., and D. R. Hopkins. 2006. "Dracunculiasis (Guinea Worm Disease) Eradication." *Advances in Parasitology* 61: 275–309.

Rumsey, H. 1789. "An Account of an Epidemic Sore Throat Which Appeared at Chesham, In Buckinghamshire, In the Year 1788." *London Medical Journal* 10 (Pt 1): 7–39.

Rush, B. 1818. *Medical Inquiries and Observations*. Philadelphia.

Rusnock, A. A. 2008. *Vital Accounts: Quantifying Health and Population in Eighteenth-Century England and France*. Cambridge.

Russell, E. 2001. *War and Nature: Fighting Humans and Insects with Chemicals from World War I to Silent Spring*. Cambridge.

Rutman, D. B., and A. H. Rutman. 1976. "Of Agues and Fevers: Malaria in the Early Chesapeake." *William and Mary Quarterly* 33: 31–60.

Sabin, A. B. 1949. "Epidemiologic Patterns of Poliomyelitis in Different Parts of the World." In *Poliomyelitis: Papers and Discussions Presented at the First International Poliomyelitis Conference. Compiled and Edited for the International Poliomyelitis Congress*, 3–33. Philadelphia.

Sabin, S., et al. 2020. "A Seventeenth-Century *Mycobacterium tuberculosis* Genome Supports a Neolithic Emergence of the *Mycobacterium tuberculosis* Complex." *Genome Biology* 21: 201.

Sachs, J. 2012. "Reply to Acemoglu and Robinson's Response to My Book Review." https://www
.jeffsachs.org/journal-articles/z37yfg9bcx9k8atat8wez48aebtnzp.

———. 2020. *The Ages of Globalization: Geography, Technology, and Institutions*. New York.

Sackton, T. B., B. P. Lazzaro, and A. G. Clark. 2017. "Rapid Expansion of Immune-Related Gene
Families in the House Fly, *Musca domestica*." *Molecular Biology and Evolution* 34: 857–72.

Sahl, J. W., et al. 2015. "Defining the Phylogenomics of *Shigella* Species: A Pathway to Diagnostics." *Journal of Clinical Microbiology* 53: 951–60.

Sahlins, M. 1972. *Stone Age Economics*. Chicago.

Saif, L. J. 2010. "Bovine Respiratory Coronavirus." *Veterinary Clinics: Food Animal Practice* 26:
349–64.

Sallares, R. 2002. *Malaria and Rome: A History of Malaria in Ancient Italy*. Oxford.

Salley, A. S., ed. 1916. *Commissions and Instructions from the Lords Proprietors of Carolina to Public
Officials of South Carolina*. Columbia.

Salmond, G., and M. Welch. 2008. "Antibiotic Resistance: Adaptive Evolution." *Lancet* 372:
S97–103.

Samie, A., A. ElBakri, and R. AbuOdeh. 2012. "Amoebiasis in the Tropics: Epidemiology and
Pathogenesis." In *Current Topics in Tropical Medicine*, edited by A. J. Rodriguez-Morales,
201–26. Rijeka.

Sanderson, S. K. 1990. *Social Evolutionism: A Critical History*. Cambridge.

Sandosham, A. A. 1970. "Malaria in Rural Malaya." *Medical Journal of Malaya* 24: 221–26.

Sangal, V., and P. A. Hoskisson. 2016. "Evolution, Epidemiology and Diversity of *Corynebacterium diphtheriae*: New Perspectives on an Old Foe." *Infection, Genetics and Evolution* 43:
364–70.

Sanjuán, R., et al. 2010. "Viral Mutation Rates." *Journal of Virology* 84: 9733–48.

Sankara, D., et al. 2016. "Dracunculiasis (Guinea Worm Disease)." In *Neglected Tropical
Diseases—Sub-Saharan Africa*, edited by J. Gyapong and B. Boatin, 45–61. Cham.

Sankararaman, S., et al. 2012. "The Date of Interbreeding between Neandertals and Modern
Humans." *PLoS Genetics* 8: e1002947.

———. 2014. "The Genomic Landscape of Neanderthal Ancestry in Present-Day Humans."
Nature 507: 354–57.

Sano, K., et al. 2019. "The Earliest Evidence for Mechanically Delivered Projectile Weapons in
Europe." *Nature Ecology & Evolution* 3: 1409–14.

Sarabian, C., B. Ngoubangoye, and A. MacIntosh. 2017. "Avoidance of Biological Contaminants
through Sight, Smell and Touch in Chimpanzees." *Royal Society Open Science* 4: 170968.

Sariyeva, G., et al. 2019. "Marmots and *Yersinia pestis* Strains in Two Plague Endemic Areas of
Tien Shan Mountains." *Frontiers in Veterinary Science* 6: 207.

Sarris, P. 2002. "The Justinianic Plague: Origins and Effects." *Continuity and Change* 17:
169–82.

———. 2020. "Climate and Disease." In *A Companion to the Global Early Middle Ages*, edited by
E. Hermans, 511–38. Leeds.

Sasa, M. 1976. *Human Filariasis: A Global Survey of Epidemiology and Control*. Baltimore.

Sasaki, T., M. Kobayashi, and N. Agui. 2000. "Epidemiological Potential of Excretion and Re-
gurgitation by *Musca domestica* (Diptera: Muscidae) in the Dissemination of *Escherichia coli*
O157: H7 to Food." *Journal of Medical Entomology* 37: 945–49.

Saunders-Hastings, P. R., and D. Krewski. 2016. "Reviewing the History of Pandemic Influenza: Understanding Patterns of Emergence and Transmission." *Pathogens* 5: 66.

Saville, A. C., et al. 2016. "Historic Late Blight Outbreaks Caused by a Widespread Dominant Lineage of *Phytophthora infestans* (Mont.) de Bary." *PLoS One* 11: 0168381.

Schamiloglu, U. 2016. "The Plague in the Time of Justinian and Central Eurasian History: An Agenda for Research." In *Central Eurasia in the Middle Ages: Studies in Honour of Peter B. Golden*, edited by I. Zimonyi and O. Karatay, 293–311. Wiesbaden.

Scheidel, W. 1999. "Emperors, Aristocrats, and the Grim Reaper: Towards a Demographic Profile of the Roman Élite." *Classical Quarterly* 49: 254–81.

———. 2001. *Death on the Nile: Disease and the Demography of Roman Egypt*. Leiden.

———. 2002. "A Model of Demographic and Economic Change in Roman Egypt after the Antonine Plague." *Journal of Roman Archaeology* 15: 97–114.

———. 2014. "The Shape of the Roman World: Modelling Imperial Connectivity." *Journal of Roman Archaeology* 27: 7–32.

———. 2015. "Death and the City: Ancient Rome and Beyond." https://ssrn.com/abstract =2609651.

———. 2019. *Escape from Rome: The Failure of Empire and the Road to Prosperity*. Princeton.

Scheutz, M., et al., eds. 2008. *Europäisches Spitalwesen: institutionelle Fürsorge in Mittelalter und früher Neuzeit (Hospitals and Institutional Care in Medieval and Early Modern Europe)*. Vienna.

Schiess, R., et al. 2014. "Revisiting Scoliosis in the KNM-WT 15000 *Homo erectus* Skeleton." *Journal of Human Evolution* 67: 48–59.

Schlich, T. 2012. "Asepsis and Bacteriology: A Realignment of Surgery and Laboratory Science." *Medical History* 56: 308–34.

Schmid, B. V., et al. 2015. "Climate-Driven Introduction of the Black Death and Successive Plague Reintroductions into Europe." *Proceedings of the National Academy of Sciences* 112: 3020–25.

Schmid-Hempel, P. 2013. *Evolutionary Parasitology: The Integrated Study of Infections, Immunology, Ecology, and Genetics*. Oxford.

———. 2017. "Parasites and Their Social Hosts." *Trends in Parasitology* 33: 453–62.

Schmitz-Cliever, V. E. 1954. "History of Morbus Hungaricus (Spotted Fever)." *Archiv für Hygiene und Bakteriologie* 138: 445–49.

Schoepf, J. D. 1911. *Travels in the Confederation*. Vol. 1. Philadelphia.

Schofield, R., and D. Reher. 1991. "The Decline of Mortality in Europe." In *The Decline of Mortality in Europe*, edited by R. Schoefield, D. Reher, and A. Bideau, 1–17. Oxford.

Schofield, R., D. Reher, and A. Bideau, eds. 1991. *The Decline of Mortality in Europe*. Oxford.

Schrago, C. G. 2014. "The Effective Population Sizes of the Anthropoid Ancestors of the Human-Chimpanzee Lineage Provide Insights on the Historical Biogeography of the Great Apes." *Molecular Biology and Evolution* 31: 37–47.

Schroeder, H., et al. 2018. "Origins and Genetic Legacies of the Caribbean Taino." *Proceedings of the National Academy of Sciences* 115: 2341–46.

Schuenemann, V. J., et al. 2011. "Targeted Enrichment of Ancient Pathogens Yielding the pPCP1 Plasmid of *Yersinia pestis* from Victims of the Black Death." *Proceedings of the National Academy of Sciences* 108: e746-e752.

———. 2013. "Genome-Wide Comparison of Medieval and Modern *Mycobacterium leprae*." *Science* 341: 179–183.

———. 2018a. "Ancient Genomes Reveal a High Diversity of *Mycobacterium leprae* in Medieval Europe." *PLoS Pathogens* 14: e1006997.

———. 2018b. "Historic *Treponema pallidum* Genomes from Colonial Mexico Retrieved from Archaeological Remains." *PLoS Neglected Tropical Diseases* 12: 0006447.

Schwartz, R. B. 1983. *Daily Life in Johnson's London*. Madison.

Scott, D. 1965. *Epidemic Disease in Ghana, 1901–1960*. Oxford.

Scott, G. R. 1990. "Rinderpest Virus." *Virus Infections of Ruminants* 3: 341–54.

Scott, H. G., and K. S. Littig. 1962. *Flies of Public Health Importance and Their Control*. Insect Control Series, part V. Atlanta.

———. 1970. "Training Guide." In *Flies of Public Health Importance and Their Control*. Atlanta.

Scott, J., trans. 1828. *On the Disinfecting Properties of Labarraque's Preparations of Chlorine*. By Antoine Germain Labarraque. London.

Scott, J. C. 2017. *Against the Grain: A Deep History of the Earliest States*. New Haven.

Scott, J. G., et al. 2014. "Genome of the House Fly, *Musca domestica* L., a Global Vector of Diseases with Adaptations to a Septic Environment." *Genome Biology* 15: 466.

Scully, E. J., et al. 2018. "Lethal Respiratory Disease Associated with Human Rhinovirus C in Wild Chimpanzees, Uganda, 2013." *Emerging Infectious Diseases* 24: 267–74.

Sedivy, E. J., et al. 2017. "Soybean Domestication: The Origin, Genetic Architecture and Molecular Bases." *New Phytologist* 214: 539–53.

Seidelman, R. 2020. *Under Quarantine: Immigrants and Disease at Israel's Gate*. New Brunswick.

Seifert, L., et al. 2016. "Genotyping *Yersinia pestis* in Historical Plague: Evidence for Long-Term Persistence of *Y. pestis* in Europe from the 14th to the 17th Century." *PLoS One* 11: e0145194.

Seland, E. 2014. "Archaeology of Trade in the Western Indian Ocean, 300 BC–AD 700." *Journal of Archaeological Research* 22: 367–402.

Selwyn, S. 1966. "Sir John Pringle: Hospital Reformer, Moral Philosopher and Pioneer of Antiseptics." *Medical History* 10: 266–74.

Sender, R., S. Fuchs, and R. Milo. 2016. "Revised Estimates for the Number of Human and Bacteria Cells in the Body." *PLoS Biology* 14: e1002533.

Sepkowitz, K. A. 2001. "AIDS—The First 20 Years." *New England Journal of Medicine* 344: 1764–72.

Sepúlveda, N., et al. 2017. "Malaria Host Candidate Genes Validated by Association with Current, Recent, and Historical Measures of Transmission Intensity." *Journal of Infectious Diseases* 216: 45–54.

Serruys, H. 1980. "Smallpox in Mongolia during the Ming and Ching Dynasties." *Zentralasiatische Studien* 14: 41–63.

Seth, S. 2018. *Difference and Disease: Medicine, Race, and the Eighteenth-Century British Empire*. Cambridge.

Shah, S. 2010. *The Fever: How Malaria Has Ruled Humankind for 500,000 Years*. New York.

———. 2016. *Pandemic: Tracking Contagions, from Cholera to Ebola and Beyond*. New York.

Shahraki, A. H., E. Carniel, and E. Mostafavi. 2016. "Plague in Iran: Its History and Current Status." *Epidemiology and Health* 38: e2016033.

Shanks, G., et al. 2014. "Measles Epidemics of Variable Lethality in the Early 20th Century." *American Journal of Epidemiology* 179: 413–22.

Sharman, J. C. 2019. *Empires of the Weak: The Real Story of European Expansion and the Creation of the New World Order*. Princeton.

Sharp, P. M., and B. H. Hahn. 2008. "Prehistory of HIV-1." *Nature* 7213: 605–6.

———. 2011. "Origins of HIV and the AIDS Pandemic." *Cold Spring Harbor Perspectives in Medicine* 1: a006841.

Sharp, P. M., L. J. Plenderleith, and B. Hahn. 2020. "Ape Origins of Human Malaria." *Annual Reviews in Microbiology* 74: 39–63.

Shaw-Taylor, L. 2020. "An Introduction to the History of Infectious Diseases, Epidemics and the Early Phases of the Long-Run Decline in Mortality." *Economic History Review* 73: e1–19.

Shennan, S. 2018. *The First Farmers of Europe: An Evolutionary Perspective*. Cambridge.

Shennan, S., et al. 2013. "Regional Population Collapse Followed Initial Agriculture Booms in Mid-Holocene Europe." *Nature Communications* 4: 2486.

Sheppard, S. K., and M. C. J. Maiden. 2015. "The Evolution of *Campylobacter jejuni* and *Campylobacter coli*." *Cold Spring Harbor Perspectives in Biology* 7: 018119.

Sheridan, R. B. 1974. *Sugar and Slavery: an Economic History of the British West Indies, 1623–1775*. Baltimore.

Shi, T., et al. 2017. "Global, Regional, and National Disease Burden Estimates of Acute Lower Respiratory Infections Due to Respiratory Syncytial Virus in Young Children in 2015: A Systematic Review and Modelling Study." *Lancet* 390: 946–58.

Shiels, A. B., et al. 2014. "Biology and Impacts of Pacific Island Invasive Species. 11. *Rattus rattus*, the Black Rat (Rodentia: Muridae)." *Pacific Science* 68: 145–84.

Shors, T. 2013. *Understanding Viruses*. 2nd ed. Burlington.

Shrewsbury, J. F. D. 1970. *A History of Bubonic Plague in the British Isles*. Cambridge.

Shulman, S. T., D. L. Shulman, and R. H. Sims. 2009. "The Tragic 1824 Journey of the Hawaiian King and Queen to London: History of Measles in Hawaii." *Pediatric Infectious Disease Journal* 28: 728–33.

Sibly, R. M. 2005. "On the Regulation of Populations of Mammals, Birds, Fish, and Insects." *Science* 309: 607–10.

Sidebotham, S. E. 2011. *Berenike and the Ancient Maritime Spice Route*. Berkeley.

Sigerist, H. 1941. "The People's Misery: Mother of Diseases, an Address, Delivered in 1790 by Johann Peter Frank, Translated from the Latin." *Bulletin of the History of Medicine* 9: 81–100.

Sigurdson, C. J., J. C. Bartz, and M. Glatzel. 2019. "Cellular and Molecular Mechanisms of Prion Disease." *Annual Review of Pathology: Mechanisms of Disease* 14: 497–516.

Silberbauer, G. B. 1965. *Report to the Government of Bechuanaland on the Bush Man Survey*. Gaberones.

Silva, C. 2011. *Miraculous Plagues: An Epidemiology of Early New England Narrative*. Oxford.

Silva, J. C., et al. 2015. "A New Method for Estimating Species Age Supports the Coexistence of Malaria Parasites and Their Mammalian Hosts." *Molecular Biology and Evolution* 32: 1354–64.

Silver, L. L. 2011. "Challenges of Antibacterial Discovery." *Clinical Microbiology Reviews* 24: 71–109.

Silvestroni, E., and I. Bianco. 1975. "Screening for Microcytemia in Italy: Analysis of Data Collected in the Past 30 Years." *American Journal of Human Genetics* 27: 198–212.

Simpson, J. 2011. *Creating Wine: The Emergence of a World Industry, 1840–1914*. Princeton.

Singer, D. W. 1949. "Sir John Pringle and His Circle. Part I. Life." *Annals of Science* 6: 127–80.

———. 1950. "Sir John Pringle and His Circle. Part II. Public Health." *Annals of Science* 6: 229–47.

Singer, R. 1960. "Some Biological Aspects of the Bushman." *Zeitschrift für Morphologie und Anthropologie* 51: 1–6.

Singla, L. D., et al. 2008. "Rodents as Reservoirs of Parasites in India." *Integrative Zoology* 3: 21–26.

Sinka, M. E., et al. 2010. "The Dominant Anopheles Vectors of Human Malaria in Africa, Europe and the Middle East: Occurrence Data, Distribution Maps and Bionomic Précis." *Parasites and Vectors* 3: 117.

———. 2012. "A Global Map of Dominant Malaria Vectors." *Parasites and Vectors* 5: 69.

Sisk, M. L., and J. J. Shea. 2011. "The African Origin of Complex Projectile Technology: An Analysis Using Tip Cross-Sectional Area and Perimeter." *International Journal of Evolutionary Biology* 2011: 968012.

Sistrom, M., et al. 2014. "Comparative Genomics Reveals Multiple Genetic Backgrounds of Human Pathogenicity in the *Trypanosoma brucei* Complex." *Genome Biology and Evolution* 6: 2811–19.

Sitkiewicz, I. 2018. "How to Become a Killer, or Is It All Accidental? Virulence Strategies in Oral Streptococci." *Molecular Oral Microbiology* 33: 1–12.

Skaff, J. K. 1998. "Sasanian and Arab-Sasanian Silver Coins from Turfan: Their Relationship to International Trade and the Local Economy." *Asia Major* 11: 67–115.

Skaggs, J. M. 1986. *Prime Cut: Livestock Raising and Meatpacking in the United States, 1607–1983*. College Station.

Skoglund, P., et al. 2017. "Reconstructing Prehistoric African Population Structure." *Cell* 171: 59–71.

Sköld, P. 1996. *The Two Faces of Smallpox: A Disease and Its Prevention in Eighteenth- and Nineteenth-Century Sweden*. Umeå.

Slack, P. 1981. "The Disappearance of Plague: An Alternative View." *Economic History Review* 34: 469–76.

———. 1985. *The Impact of Plague in Tudor and Stuart England*. London.

———. 1988. *Poverty and Policy in Tudor and Stuart England*. London.

———. 2012. *Plague: A Very Short Introduction*. Oxford.

Slavin, P. 2012. "The Great Bovine Pestilence and Its Economic and Environmental Consequences in England and Wales, 1318–50." *Economic History Review* 65: 1239–66.

———. 2019. "Death by the Lake: Mortality Crisis in Early Fourteenth-Century Central Asia." *Journal of Interdisciplinary History* 50: 59–90.

Sloane, B. 2013. *Black Death in London*. Stroud.

Smail, D. L. 1996. "Accommodating Plague in Medieval Marseille." *Continuity and Change* 11: 11–41.

———. 2005. "In the Grip of Sacred History." *American Historical Review* 110: 1337–61.

———. 2008. *On Deep History and the Brain*. Berkeley.

Small, S. T., D. J. Tisch, and P. A. Zimmerman. 2014. "Molecular Epidemiology, Phylogeny and Evolution of the Filarial Nematode *Wuchereria bancrofti*." *Infection, Genetics and Evolution* 28: 33–43.

Small, S. T, et al. 2019. "Human Migration and the Spread of the Nematode Parasite *Wuchereria bancrofti*." *Molecular Biology and Evolution* 36: 1931–41.

Smallman-Raynor, M. R., and A. Cliff. 2004. *War Epidemics: An Historical Geography of Infectious Diseases in Military Conflict and Civil Strife, 1850–2000*. Oxford.

Smil, V. 2005. *Creating the Twentieth Century: Technical Innovations of 1867–1914 and Their Lasting Impact*. Oxford.

———. 2015. *Harvesting the Biosphere: What We Have Taken from Nature*. Cambridge.

———. 2017. *Energy and Civilization: A History*. Cambridge.

Smith, A. F. 2015. *Sugar: A Global History*. London.

Smith, A. R., et al. 2015. "The Significance of Cooking for Early Hominin Scavenging." *Journal of Human Evolution* 84: 62–70.

Smith, B. D. 2014. "The Domestication of *Helianthus annuus* L. (Sunflower)." *Vegetation History and Archaeobotany* 23: 57–74.

Smith, B. G. 2013. *Ship of Death: A Voyage That Changed the Atlantic World*. New Haven.

Smith, D. 1978. "Mortality and Family in the Colonial Chesapeake." *Journal of Interdisciplinary History* 8: 403–27.

Smith, D. C. 1980. "Gerhard's Distinction between Typhoid and Typhus and Its Reception in America." *Bulletin of the History of Medicine* 54: 368–85.

———. 1981. "Medical Science, Medical Practice, and the Emerging Concept of Typhus in Mid-Eighteenth-Century Britain." *Medical History Supplement* 1: 121–34.

Smith, J. 1631. *Advertisements for the Unexperienced Planters of New-England, or Any Where*. London.

Smith, K., and J.-F. Guegan. 2010. "Changing Geographic Distributions of Human Pathogens." *Annual Review of Ecology, Evolution, and Systematics* 41: 231–50.

Smith, K. F., et al. 2007. "Globalization of Human Infectious Disease." *Ecology* 88: 1903–10.

Smith, M. E. 2005. "City Size in Late Postclassic Mesoamerica." *Journal of Urban History* 31: 403–34.

Smith, O., and T. P. Gilbert. 2019. "Ancient RNA." In *Paleogenomics*, edited by C. Lindqvist and O. Rajora, 53–74. Cham.

Smith, P. 1991. "The Dental Evidence for Nutritional Status in the Natufians." In *The Natufian Culture in the Levant*, edited by O. Bar-Yosef and F. Valla, 425–33. Ann Arbor.

Smith, P. D., et al. 2020. *Principles of Mucosal Immunology*. Boca Raton.

Snodgrass, J. J., W. R. Leonard, and M. L. Robertson. 2009. "The Energetics of Encephalization in Early Hominids." In *The Evolution of Hominin Diets: Integrating Approaches to the Study of Palaeolithic Subsistence*, edited by J. J. Hublin, 15–29. Dordrecht.

Snow, D., and K. Lanphear. 1988. "European Contact and Indian Depopulation in the Northeast: The Timing of the First Epidemics." *Ethnohistory* 35: 15–33.

Snowden, F. M. 1995. *Naples in the Time of Cholera, 1884–1911*. Cambridge.

———. 1999. "'Fields of Death': Malaria in Italy." *Modern Italy* 4: 25–57.

———. 2006. *The Conquest of Malaria: Italy, 1900–1962*. New Haven.

———. 2019. *Epidemics and Society: From the Black Death to the Present.* New Haven.

Soares, R. R. 2007. "On the Determinants of Mortality Reductions in the Developing World." *Population and Development Review* 33: 247–87.

Soltow, L. 1981. *The Rise of Literacy and the Common School in the United States: A Socioeconomic Analysis to 1870.* Chicago.

Somervail, A. 1823. "On the Medical Topography and Diseases of a Section of Virginia." *Philadelphia Journal of the Medical and Physical Sciences* 6: 276–89.

Sompayrac, L. 2016. *How the Immune System Works.* 5th ed. Oxford.

Sonenshine, D. E., et al. 1978. "Epizootiology of Epidemic Typhus (*Rickettsia prowazekii*) in Flying Squirrels." *American Journal of Tropical Medicine and Hygiene* 27: 339–49.

Soppelsa, P., and A. Rodgers. 2019. "Origins of the Flyswatter." *Technology and Culture* 60: 886–95.

Sorensen, C., et al. 2008. "Charles V. Riley, France, and Phylloxera." *American Entomologist* 54: 134–49.

———. 2019. *Charles Valentine Riley: Founder of Modern Entomology.* Tuscaloosa.

Soumana, I. H., B. Linz, and E. T. Harvill. 2017. "Environmental Origin of the Genus *Bordetella*." *Frontiers in Microbiology* 8: 28.

Specht, J. 2019. *Red Meat Republic: A Hoof-to-Table History of How Beef Changed America.* Princeton.

Spielman, A., and M. D'Antonio. 2001. *Mosquito: A Natural History of Our Most Persistent and Deadly Foe.* New York.

Spier, F. 2010. *Big History and the Future of Humanity.* Chichester.

Spierenburg, P. C. 1995. "The Body and the State: Early Modern Europe." In *The Oxford History of the Prison: The Practice of Punishment in Western Society*, edited by N. Morris and D. J. Rothman, 49–77. Oxford.

———. 2007. *The Prison Experience: Disciplinary Institutions and Their Inmates in Early Modern Europe.* Amsterdam.

Spikins, P., et al. 2019. "Living to Fight Another Day: The Ecological and Evolutionary Significance of Neanderthal Healthcare." *Quaternary Science Reviews* 217: 98–118.

Spinage, C. A. 2003. *Cattle Plague: A History.* New York.

———. 2012. *African Ecology—Benchmarks and Historical Perspectives.* Berlin.

Spooner, D., et al. 2005. "A Single Domestication for Potato Based on Multilocus Amplified Fragment Length Polymorphism Genotyping." *Proceedings of the National Academy of Sciences* 102: 14694–99.

Spreeuwenberg, P., M. Kroneman, and J. Paget. 2018. "Reassessing the Global Mortality Burden of the 1918 Influenza Pandemic." *American Journal of Epidemiology* 187: 2561–67.

Spruill, J. C. 1936. "Women in the Founding of the Southern Colonies." *North Carolina Historical Review* 13: 202–18.

Spyrou, M., et al. 2016. "Historical *Y. pestis* Genomes Reveal the European Black Death as the Source of Ancient and Modern Plague Pandemics." *Cell Host & Microbe* 19: 874–81.

———. 2018. "Analysis of 3,800-Year-Old *Yersinia pestis* Genomes Suggests Bronze Age Origin for Bubonic Plague." *Nature Communications* 9: 1–10.

———. 2019a. "Ancient Pathogen Genomics as an Emerging Tool for Infectious Disease Research." *Nature Reviews Genetics* 20: 323–40.

———. 2019b. "Phylogeography of the Second Plague Pandemic Revealed through Analysis of Historical *Yersinia pestis* Genomes." *Nature Communications* 10: 4470.

Squicciarini, M. P., and N. Voigtländer. 2015. "Human Capital and Industrialization: Evidence from the Age of Enlightenment." *Quarterly Journal of Economics* 130: 1825–83.

Stahl, P. W. 2008. "Animal Domestication in South America." In *The Handbook of South American Archaeology*, edited by H. Silverman and W. H. Isbell, 121–30. New York.

Stanaway, J. D., and G. Roth. 2015. "The Burden of Chagas Disease: Estimates and Challenges." *Global Heart* 10: 139–44.

Stanaway, J. D., et al. 2016. "The Global Burden of Dengue: An Analysis from the Global Burden of Disease Study 2013." *Lancet Infectious Diseases* 16: 712–23.

Standley, C. J., et al. 2012. "Zoonotic Schistosomiasis in Non-human Primates: Past, Present and Future Activities at the Human-Wildlife Interface in Africa." *Journal of Helminthology* 86: 131–40.

Stathakopoulos, D. 2004. *Famine and Pestilence in the Late Roman and Early Byzantine Empire: A Systematic Survey of Subsistence Crisis and Epidemics*. Burlington.

Steckel, R. H., and J. C. Rose, eds. 2002. *The Backbone of History: Health and Nutrition in the Western Hemisphere*. Cambridge.

Steen, K. 2014. *The American Synthetic Organic Chemicals Industry: War and Politics, 1910–1930*. Chapel Hill.

Steere-Williams, J. 2020. *The Filth Disease: Typhoid Fever and the Practices of Epidemiology in Victorian England*. Rochester.

Stein, C., et al. 2003. "The Global Burden of Measles in the Year 2000—A Model That Uses Country-Specific Indicators." *Journal of Infectious Diseases* 187: S8–14.

Stenborg, P. 2016. "Towards a Regional History of Pre-Columbian Settlements in the Santarém and Belterra Regions, Pará, Brazil." In *Beyond Waters: Archaeology and Environmental History of the Amazonian Inland*, edited by P. Stenborg, 9–20. Gothenburg.

Stenseth, N. C., et al. 2008. "Plague: Past, Present, and Future." *PLoS Medicine* 5: e3.

Stephens, P., et al. 2016. "The Macroecology of Infectious Diseases: A New Perspective on Global-Scale Drivers of Pathogen Distributions and Impacts." *Ecology Letters* 19: 1159–71.

Stephenson, J. Z. 2018. "'Real' Wages? Contractors, Workers, and Pay in London Building Trades, 1650–1800." *Economic History Review* 71: 106–132.

Steverding, D. 2008. "The History of African Trypanosomiasis." *Parasites & Vectors* 1: 3.

Stewart, K. M. 1994. "Early Hominid Utilisation of Fish Resources and Implications for Seasonality and Behavior." *Journal of Human Evolution* 27: 229–45.

Stodder, A., and D. Martin. 1992. "Health and Disease in the Southwest before and after Spanish Contact." In *Disease and Demography in the Americas*, edited by J. W. Verano and D. H. Ubelaker, 55–73. Washington, DC.

Stone, A. C., et al. 2009. "Tuberculosis and Leprosy in Perspective." *Yearbook of Physical Anthropology* 52: 66–94.

Strauss, J. H., and E. G. Strauss. 2008. *Viruses and Human Disease*. 2nd ed. Amsterdam.

Streusand, D. E. 2010. *Islamic Gunpowder Empires: Ottomans, Safavids, and Mughals*. Boulder.

Strindberg, S., et al. 2018. "Guns, Germs, and Trees Determine Density and Distribution of Gorillas and Chimpanzees in Western Equatorial Africa." *Science Advances* 4: 2964.

Stringer, C. 2016. "The Origin and Evolution of *Homo sapiens.*" *Philosophical Transactions of the Royal Society B: Biological Sciences* 371: 20150237.

Stucki, D., et al. 2016. "*Mycobacterium tuberculosis* Lineage 4 Comprises Globally Distributed and Geographically Restricted Sublineages." *Nature Genetics* 48: 1535–43.

Stukenbrock, E. H., and B. A. McDonald. 2008. "The Origins of Plant Pathogens in Agroecosystems." *Annual Review of Phytopathology* 46: 75–100.

Styles, J. 2007. *The Dress of the People: Everyday Fashion in Eighteenth-Century England.* New Haven.

Subrahmanyam, S. 2012. *The Portuguese Empire in Asia, 1500–1700: A Political and Economic History.* Chichester.

Sullivan, R. 2004. *Rats: Observations on the History and Habitat of the City's Most Unwanted Inhabitants.* New York.

Sun, Y.-C., et al. 2014. "Retracing the Evolutionary Path That Led to Flea-Borne Transmission of *Yersinia pestis.*" *Cell Host & Microbe* 15: 578–86.

Sundararaman, S., et al. 2016. "Genomes of Cryptic Chimpanzee Plasmodium Species Reveal Key Evolutionary Events Leading to Human Malaria." *Nature Communications* 7: 11078.

Sundstrom, L. 1997. "Smallpox Used Them Up: References to Epidemic Disease in Northern Plains Winter Counts, 1714–1920." *Ethnohistory* 44: 305–43.

Suntsov, V. V. 2017. "Recent Speciation of Plague Microbe *Yersinia pestis* in the Heterothermal (Heteroimmune) Environment of Marmot–Flea (*Marmota sibirica–Oropsylla silantiewi*): Biogeocenotic Preconditions and Preadaptations." *Biology Bulletin Reviews* 7: 299–311.

Susser, M., and Z. Stein. 2009. *Eras in Epidemiology: The Evolution of Ideas.* Oxford.

Sussman, G. D. 2011. "Was the Black Death in India and China?" *Bulletin of the History of Medicine* 85: 319–55.

Swedlund, A. C., and G. J. Armelagos. 1990. *Disease in Populations in Transition: Anthropological and Epidemiological Perspectives.* New York.

Swellengrebel, N. H., and A. D. Buck. 1938. *Malaria in the Netherlands.* Amsterdam.

Szreter, S. 1988. "The Importance of Social Intervention in Britain's Mortality Decline c.1850–1914: A Re-interpretation of the Role of Public Health." *Social History of Medicine* 1: 1–37.

———. 2002. "Rethinking McKeown: The Relationship between Public Health and Social Change." *American Journal of Public Health* 92: 722–25.

———. 2005. *Health and Wealth: Studies in History and Policy.* Rochester.

Taagepera, R. 1978a. "Size and Duration of Empires: Growth-Decline Curves, 3000 to 600 BC." *Social Science Research* 7: 180–97.

———. 1978b. "Size and Duration of Empires: Systematics of Size." *Social Science Research* 7: 108–27.

———. 1979. "Size and Duration of Empires: Growth-Decline Curves, 600 BC to 600 AD." *Social Science History* 3: 115–38.

Tahara, M., et al. 2016. "Measles Virus Hemagglutinin Protein Epitopes: The Basis of Antigenic Stability." *Viruses* 8: v8080216.

Takken, W., and N. Verhulst. 2012. "Host Preferences of Blood-Feeding Mosquitoes." *Annual Review of Entomology* 58: 433–53.

Talbi, M. 2012. "Ibn Khaldūn." *Encyclopaedia of Islam, Second Edition.* Leiden.

Tallavaara, M., et al. 2015. "Human Population Dynamics in Europe over the Last Glacial Maximum." *Proceedings of the National Academy of Sciences* 112: 8232–37.

Tallavaara, M., J. T. Eronen, and M. Luoto. 2018. "Productivity, Biodiversity, and Pathogens Influence the Global Hunter-Gatherer Population Density." *Proceedings of the National Academy of Sciences* 115: 1232–37.

Tallett, F. 1992. *War and Society in Early-Modern Europe, 1495–1715.* London.

Talty, S. 2009. *The Illustrious Dead: The Terrifying Story of How Typhus Killed Napoleon's Greatest Army.* New York.

Tanaka, J. 1980. *The San: Hunter-Gatherers of the Kalahari: A Study in Ecological Anthropology.* Tokyo.

Tanno, K., and G. Willcox. 2006. "How Fast Was Wild Wheat Domesticated?" *Science* 311: 1886.

Tannous, J. 2018. *The Making of the Medieval Middle East: Religion, Society, and Simple Believers.* Princeton.

Taubenberger, J. K., and D. M. Morens. 2018. "Influenza Cataclysm." *New England Journal of Medicine* 379: 2285–87.

———. 2019. "The 1918 Influenza Pandemic and Its Legacy." *Cold Spring Harbor Perspectives in Medicine*: a038695.

Taubenberger, J. K., et al. 1997. "Initial Genetic Characterization of the 1918 'Spanish' Influenza Virus." *Science* 275: 1793–96.

———. 2005. "Characterization of the 1918 Influenza Virus Polymerase Genes." *Nature* 437: 889–93.

Taylor, L. H., S. M. Latham, and M. Woolhouse. 2001. "Risk Factors for Human Disease Emergence." *Philosophical Transactions of the Royal Society of London. Series B: Biological Sciences* 356: 983–89.

Taylor, M. W. 2014. "Influenza." In *Viruses and Man: A History of Interactions,* edited by M. W. Taylor, 191–209. Cham.

Taylor-Mulneix, D. L., et al. 2017. "Evolution of Bordetellae from Environmental Microbes to Human Respiratory Pathogens: Amoebae as a Missing Link." *Frontiers in Cellular and Infection Microbiology* 7: 510.

Temin, P. 2012. *The Roman Market Economy.* Princeton.

The, H. C., et al. 2016. "The Genomic Signatures of *Shigella* Evolution, Adaptation and Geographical Spread." *Nature Reviews Microbiology* 14: 235–50.

Therborn, G. 2000. "Globalizations: Dimensions, Historical Waves, Regional Effects, Normative Governance." *International Sociology* 15: 151–79.

Thomas, F., F. Renaud, and J.-F. Guégan. 2005. *Parasitism and Ecosystems.* Oxford.

Thomas, S., ed. 2016. *Rickettsiales: Biology, Molecular Biology, Epidemiology, and Vaccine Development.* Cham.

Thompson, J. N. 2013. *Relentless Evolution.* Chicago.

Thompson, M. G. 1997. *The Polden Hill Manors of Glastonbury Abbey: Land and People circa 1260 to 1351.* PhD diss., University of Leicester.

Thonemann, P. forthcoming. *Lucian, Alexander or the False Prophet.* Oxford.

Thornton, R. 1987. *American Indian Holocaust and Survival: A Population History since 1492.* Norman.

———. 1997. "Aboriginal North American Population and Rates of Decline, ca. AD 1500–1900." *Current Anthropology* 38: 310–15.

Thwaites, R. G. 1898. *The Jesuit Relations and Allied Documents.* 73 volumes. Cleveland.

Tibbs, C. J. 1997. "Tropical Aspects of Viral Hepatitis." *Transactions of the Royal Society of Tropical Medicine and Hygiene* 91: 121–24.

Tierney, J., P. deMenocal, and P. Zander. 2017. "A Climactic Context for the Out-of-Africa Migration." *Geological Society of America* 45: 1023–26.

Tiffany, N. M. 1900. *Pilgrims and Puritans: The Story of the Planting of Plymouth and Boston.* Boston.

Tilly, C. 1975. "Reflections on the History of European Statemaking." In *The Formation of National States in Western Europe,* edited by C. Tilly, 3–83. Princeton.

Timberg, C., and D. Halperin. 2013. *Tinderbox: How the West Sparked the AIDS Epidemic and How the World Can Finally Overcome It.* New York.

Timmermann, A. 2020. "Quantifying the Potential Causes of Neanderthal Extinction: Abrupt Climate Change versus Competition and Interbreeding." *Quaternary Science Reviews* 238: 106331.

Tognotti, E. 2009. "The Rise and Fall of Syphilis in Renaissance Europe." *Journal of Medical Humanities* 30: 99–113.

Tomalin, C. 2002. *Samuel Pepys: The Unequalled Self.* Westminster.

Tomber, R. 2008. *Indo-Roman Trade: From Pots to Pepper.* London.

———. 2012. "From the Roman Red Sea to beyond the Empire: Egyptian Ports and Their Trading Partners." *British Museum Studies in Ancient Egypt and Sudan* 18: 201–15.

Tomes, N. 1998. *The Gospel of Germs: Men, Women, and the Microbe in American Life.* Cambridge.

Torfing, T. 2015. "Neolithic Population and Summed Probability Distribution of 14C-Dates." *Journal of Archaeological Science* 63: 193–98.

Toribio Polo, J. 1913. *Apuntes sobre las epidemias en el Perú.* Lima.

Townsend, C. 2019. *Fifth Sun: A New History of the Aztecs.* New York.

Trevor-Roper, H. R. 1959. "The General Crisis of the 17th Century." *Past & Present* 16: 31–64.

Troesken, W. 2015. *The Pox of Liberty: How the Constitution Left Americans Rich, Free, and Prone to Infection.* Chicago.

Trofa, A. F., et al. 1999. "Dr. Kiyoshi Shiga: Discoverer of the Dysentery Bacillus." *Clinical Infectious Diseases* 29: 1303–6.

Tröhler, U. 2011. "The Introduction of Numerical Methods to Assess the Effects of Medical Interventions during the 18th Century: A Brief History." *Journal of the Royal Society of Medicine* 104: 465–74.

Trost, E., et al. 2012. "Pangenomic Study of *Corynebacterium diphtheriae* That Provides Insights into the Genomic Diversity of Pathogenic Isolates from Cases of Classical Diphtheria, Endocarditis, and Pneumonia." *Journal of Bacteriology* 194: 3199–215.

Trueba, G., and M. Dunthorn. 2012. "Many Neglected Tropical Diseases May Have Originated in the Paleolithic or Before: New Insights from Genetics." *PLoS Neglected Tropical Diseases* 6: e1393.

Truman, R. 2005. "Leprosy in Wild Armadillos." *Leprosy Review* 76: 198–208.

Tsiamis, C., E. Poulakou-Rebelakou, and E. Petridou. 2009. "The Red Sea and the Port of Clysma: A Possible Gate of Justinian's Plague." *Gesnerus* 66: 209–17.

Tuchman, B. W. 1978. *A Distant Mirror: The Calamitous 14th Century*. New York.

Turchin, P. 2003. *Complex Population Dynamics: A Theoretical/Empirical Synthesis*. Princeton.

———. 2009. "Long-Term Population Cycles in Human Societies." *The Year in Ecology and Conservation Biology* 1162: 1–17.

———. 2018. *Historical Dynamics: Why States Rise and Fall*. Princeton.

Turchin, P., and S. A. Nefedov. 2011. *Secular Cycles*. Princeton.

Turmelle, A. S., and K. J. Olival. 2009. "Correlates of Viral Richness in Bats (Order Chiroptera)." *EcoHealth* 6: 522–39.

Turner, J. R. 2009. "Intestinal Mucosal Barrier Function in Health and Disease." *Nature Reviews Immunology* 9: 799–809.

Tuttle, M. D. 2015. *The Secret Lives of Bats: My Adventures with the World's Most Misunderstood Mammals*. Boston.

Twigg, G. 1984. *The Black Death: A Biological Reappraisal*. New York.

Twitchett, D. 1979. "Population and Pestilence in T'ang China." In *Studia Sino-Mongolica: Festschrift fur Herbert Franke*, edited by W. Bauer, 35–68. Wiesbaden.

Twohig, K. A., et al. 2019. "Growing Evidence of *Plasmodium vivax* across Malaria-Endemic Africa." *PLoS Neglected Tropical Diseases* 13: e0007140.

Tworek, H. J. S. 2019. "Communicable Disease: Information, Health, and Globalization in the Interwar Period." *American Historical Review* 124: 813–42.

Ubelaker, D. 1992. "North American Indian Population Size: Changing Perspectives." In *Disease and Demography in the Americas*, edited by J. W. Verano and D. H. Ubelaker, 169–76. Washington, DC.

Underdown, S. J., K. Kumar, and C. Houldcroft. 2017. "Network Analysis of the Hominin Origins of Herpes Simplex Virus 2 from Fossil Data." *Virus Evolution* 3: vex026.

United Nations. 2018. *The World's Cities in 2018*. New York.

———. 2020. *Progress toward the Sustainable Development Goals: Report of the Secretary-General*. New York.

Urban, J., et al. 2016. "The Effect of Habitual and Experimental Antiperspirant and Deodorant Product Use on the Armpit Microbiome." *PeerJ* 4: e1605.

Vågene, A. J. 2018. "Genomic Insights into Pre- and Post-contact Human Pathogens in the New World." PhD diss., Eberhard-Karls Universität Tübingen.

Vågene, A. J., et al. 2018. "*Salmonella enterica* Genomes from Victims of a Major Sixteenth-Century Epidemic in Mexico." *Nature Ecology & Evolution* 2: 520–28.

Vainio, J., and F. Cutts. 1998. *Yellow Fever*. Geneva.

Vale, T. C., and F. Cardoso. 2015. "Chorea: A Journey through History." *Tremor and Other Hyperkinetic Movements* 5: 1–6.

Valenčius, C. B. 2000. "Histories of Medical Geography." *Medical History* 44: 3–28.

Valleron, A.-J., et al. 2010. "Transmissibility and Geographic Spread of the 1889 Influenza Pandemic." *Proceedings of the National Academy of Sciences* 107: 8778–81.

Vallès, X., et al. 2020. "Human Plague: An Old Scourge That Needs New Answers." *PLoS Neglected Tropical Diseases* 14: e0008251.

Valtueña, A. A., et al. 2017. "The Stone Age Plague and Its Persistence in Eurasia." *Current Biology* 27: 3683–91.

Van Arsdale, P. 1978. "Population Dynamics among Asmat Hunter-Gatherers of New Guinea: Data, Methods, Comparisons." *Human Ecology* 6: 435–67.

Van Ginkel, J. J. 1995. *John of Ephesus: A Monophysite Historian in Sixth-Century Byzantium*, PhD diss., University of Groningen.

Vanhaute, E., R. Paping, and C. Ó Gráda. 2006. "The European Subsistence Crisis of 1845–1850: A Comparative Perspective." UCD Centre for Economic Research working paper WP06/09. University College Dublin.

Van Roosbroeck, F., and A. Sundberg. 2017. "Culling the Herds? Regional Divergences in Rinderpest Mortality in Flanders and South Holland, 1769–1785." *Tijdschrift voor Sociale en Economische Geschiedenis* 14: 31–55.

Van Ruysbroeck, W. 2009. *The Mission of Friar William of Rubruck: His Journey to the Court of the Great Khan Möngke, 1253–1255*. Indianapolis.

Van Zanden, J. L. 2009. *The Long Road to the Industrial Revolution: The European Economy in a Global Perspective, 1000–1800*. Leiden.

Van Zanden, J. L., S. Carmichael, and T. de Moor. 2019. *Capital Women: The European Marriage Pattern, Female Empowerment and Economic Development in Western Europe 1300–1800*. New York.

Varlik, N. 2015. *Plague and Empire in the Early Modern Mediterranean World: The Ottoman Experience, 1347–1600*. New York.

———. 2020. "The Plague That Never Left: Restoring the Second Pandemic to Ottoman and Turkish History in the Time of COVID-19." *New Perspectives on Turkey* 63: 176–89.

Vázquez-Espinosa, E., C. Laganá, and F. Vazquez. 2020. "John Donne, Spanish Doctors and the Epidemic Typhus: Fleas or Lice?" *Revista Española de Quimioterapia* 33: 87–93.

Velmet, A. 2020. *Pasteur's Empire: Bacteriology and Politics in France, Its Colonies, and the World*. New York.

Verano, J. W. 1992. "Prehistoric Disease and Demography in the Andes." In *Disease and Demography in the Americas*, edited by J. W. Verano and D. H. Ubelaker, 15–24. Washington, DC.

Verano, J. W., and D. H. Ubelaker, eds. 1992. *Disease and Demography in the Americas*. Washington, DC.

Verga, G. 1928. *Little Novels of Sicily*. Translated by D. H. Lawrence. London. First published 1883.

Verne, J. 2005. *The Begum's Millions*. Translated by S. L. Luce. Middletown. First published 1879.

Verran, J., and X. A. Reyes. 2018. "Emerging Infectious Literatures and the Zombie Condition." *Emerging Infectious Diseases* 24: 1774–78.

Viganó, C., et al. 2017. "2,000 Year Old β-Thalassemia Case in Sardinia Suggests Malaria Was Endemic by the Roman Period." *American Journal of Physical Anthropology* 164: 362–70.

Vijgen, L., et al. 2005. "Complete Genomic Sequence of Human Coronavirus OC43: Molecular Clock Analysis Suggests a Relatively Recent Zoonotic Coronavirus Transmission Event." *Journal of Virology* 79: 1595–604.

———. 2006. "Evolutionary History of the Closely Related Group 2 Coronaviruses: Porcine Hemagglutinating Encephalomyelitis Virus, Bovine Coronavirus, and Human Coronavirus OC43." *Journal of Virology* 80: 7270–74.

Villermé, L.-R. 1830. *De la mortalité dans les divers quartiers de la ville de Paris, et des causes qui la rendent trés différente dans plusieurs d'entre eux, ainsi que dans les divers quartiers de beaucoup de grande villes.* Paris.

Visaria, L., and P. Visaria. 1982. "Population (1757–1947)." In vol. 2 of *The Cambridge Economic History of India*, edited by D. Kumar, 463–532. Cambridge.

———. 1995. "India's Population in Transition." *Population Bulletin* 50: 1–51.

Voigtländer, N., and H.-J. Voth. 2013a. "How the West 'Invented' Fertility Restriction." *American Economic Review* 103: 2227–64.

———. 2013b. "The Three Horsemen of Riches: Plague, War, and Urbanization in Early Modern Europe." *Review of Economic Studies* 80: 774–811.

Volkman, S. K., et al. 2001. "Recent Origin of *Plasmodium falciparum* from a Single Progenitor." *Science* 293: 482–84.

Voroshilova, M. K. 1989. "Potential Use of Nonpathogenic Enteroviruses for Control of Human Disease." *Progress in Medical Virology* 36: 191–202.

Vries, P. H. H. 2013. *Escaping Poverty: The Origins of Modern Economic Growth.* Göttingen.

Vynnycky, E., and P. E. Fine. 1999. "Interpreting the Decline in Tuberculosis: The Role of Secular Trends in Effective Contact." *International Journal of Epidemiology* 28: 327–34.

Wachsmuth, K., P. A. Blake, and Ø. Olsvik. 1994. *Vibrio Cholerae and Cholera: Molecular to Global Perspectives.* Washington, DC.

Wagner, D. M., et al. 2014. "*Yersinia pestis* and the Plague of Justinian 541–543 AD: A Genomic Analysis." *Lancet Infectious Diseases* 14: 319–26.

Wain, J., et al. 2015. "Typhoid Fever." *Lancet* 385: 1136–45.

Waite, J. L., et al. 2019. "Exploring the Lower Thermal Limits for Development of the Human Malaria Parasite, *Plasmodium falciparum*." *Biology Letters* 15: 20190275.

Walker, R. S., L. Sattenspiel, and K. R. Hill. 2015. "Mortality from Contact-Related Epidemics among Indigenous Populations in Greater Amazonia." *Scientific Reports* 5: 14032.

Wallace, A. R. 1899. *The Wonderful Century: Its Successes and Its Failures.* New York.

Wallerstein, I. 1974. *The Modern World-System.* New York.

Walløe, L. 2008. "Medieval and Modern Bubonic Plague: Some Clinical Continuities." *Medical History* 52 (S27): 59–73.

Walter, J., and R. Schofield, eds. 1989. *Famine, Disease, and the Social Order in Early Modern Society.* Cambridge.

Wamai, R., et al. 2020. "Visceral Leishmaniasis: A Global Overview." *Journal of Global Health Science* 2: e3.

Wang, L., and D. E. Anderson. 2019. "Viruses in Bats and Potential Spillover to Animals and Humans." *Current Opinion in Virology* 34: 79–89.

Ward, W. P. 2019. *The Clean Body: A Modern History.* Montreal.

Wardeh, M., et al. 2015. "Database of Host-Pathogen and Related Species Interactions, and Their Global Distribution." *Scientific Data* 2: 1–11.

Waring, J. I. 1964. *A History of Medicine in South Carolina, 1670–1825.* Columbia.

Warinner, C., et al. 2012. "Disease, Demography, and Diet in Early Colonial New Spain: Investigation of a Sixteenth-Century Mixtec Cemetery at Teposcolula Yucundaa." *Latin American Antiquity* 23: 467–89.

Warren, H. 1741. *A Treatise Concerning the Malignant Fever in Barbados and the Neighbouring Islands*. London.

Warrick, G. 2008. *A Population History of the Huron-Petun, AD 500–1650*. Cambridge.

———. 2010. "European Infectious Disease and Depopulation of the Wendat-Tionontate (Huron-Petun)." *World Archaeology* 35: 258–75.

Wasik, B., and M. Murphy. 2012. *Rabid: A Cultural History of the World's Most Diabolical Virus*. New York.

Watson, S. 2006. "The Origins of the English Hospital." *Transactions of the Royal Historical Society* 16: 75–94.

Watts, D. 1987. *The West Indies: Patterns of Development, Culture, and Environmental Change since 1492*. Cambridge.

Watts, S. 1997. *Epidemics and History: Disease, Power, and Imperialism*. New Haven.

———. 2001. "Yellow Fever Immunities in West Africa and the Americas in the Age of Slavery and Beyond: A Reappraisal." *Journal of Social History* 34: 955–67.

Wazer, C. G. 2017. *Salus Patriae: Public Health and the State in the Early Roman Empire*. PhD diss., Columbia University.

Weatherall, J. D. 2004. "J. B. S. Haldane and the Malaria Hypothesis." In *Infectious Disease and Host-Pathogen Evolution*, edited by K. R. Dronamraju, 18–36. Cambridge.

Weaver, S., et al. 2016. *Virus Evolution: Current Research and Future Directions*. Norfolk.

Weaver, S. C., et al. 2018. "Zika, Chikungunya, and Other Emerging Vector-Borne Viral Diseases." *Annual Review of Medicine* 69: 395–408.

Webb, J. L. A. 2006. "Ecology and Culture in West Africa." In *Themes in West Africa's History*, edited by E. K. Akyeampong, 33–51. Athens.

———. 2009. *Humanity's Burden: A Global History of Malaria*. Cambridge.

———. 2014. *The Long Struggle against Malaria in Tropical Africa*. New York.

———. 2019. *The Guts of the Matter: A Global History of Human Waste and Infectious Intestinal Disease*. Cambridge.

Webster, B. L., V. R. Southgate, and D. T. J. Littlewood. 2006. "A Revision of the Interrelationships of Schistosoma Including the Recently Described *Schistosoma guineensis*." *International Journal for Parasitology* 36: 947–55.

Webster, R. G., et al. 1992. "Evolution and Ecology of Influenza A Viruses." *Microbiology and Molecular Biology Reviews* 56: 152–79.

Weedall, G. D., and N. Hall. 2011. "Evolutionary Genomics of Entamoeba." *Research in Microbiology* 162: 637–45.

Weedall, G. D., et al. 2012. "Genomic Diversity of the Human Intestinal Parasite *Entamoeba histolytica*." *Genome Biology* 13: 38.

Weidenhammer, E. 2016. "Patronage and Enlightened Medicine in the Eighteenth-Century British Military: The Rise and Fall of Dr. John Pringle, 1707–1782." *Social History of Medicine* 29: 21–43.

Weil, D. N. 2007. "Accounting for the Effect of Health on Economic Growth." *Quarterly Journal of Economics* 122: 1265–306.

———. 2014. "Health and Growth." In vol. 2B of *Handbook of Economic Growth*, edited by P. Aghion and S. Durlauf, 623–82. Burlington.

————. 2015. "A Review of Angus Deaton's *The Great Escape: Health, Wealth, and the Origins of Inequality.*" *Journal of Economic Literature* 53: 102–14.

Weiner, J. 1994. *The Beak of the Finch: A Story of Evolution in Our Time.* New York.

Weiss, R. A. 2001. "The Leeuwenhoek Lecture 2001: Animal Origins of Human Infectious Disease." *Philosophical Transactions of the Royal Society of London. Series B: Biological Sciences* 356: 957–77.

Wertheim, J., et al. 2014. "Evolutionary Origins of Human Herpes Simplex Viruses 1 and 2." *Molecular Biology and Evolution* 31: 2356–64.

Wesseling, H. L. 1996. *Divide and Rule: The Partition of Africa, 1880–1914.* Westport.

Whitaker, J. 2007. *Christ, the Settlement of Unsettled Times.* Coconut Creek.

White, N. J. 2011. "Determinants of Relapse Periodicity in *Plasmodium vivax* Malaria." *Malaria Journal* 10: 297.

White, S. 2010. "Rethinking Disease in Ottoman History." *International Journal of Middle East Studies* 42: 549–67.

————. 2011. *The Climate of Rebellion in the Early Modern Ottoman Empire.* Cambridge.

Whiteside, A. 2008. *HIV/AIDS: A Very Short Introduction.* Oxford.

Whittaker, C. R. 1994. *Frontiers of the Roman Empire: A Social and Economic Study.* Baltimore.

Whyte, R. 2015. "Disinfection in the Laboratory: Theory and Practice in Disinfection Policy in Late C19th and Early C20th England." *Endeavour* 39: 35–43.

Wiet, G. 1962. "La grande peste noire en Syrie et en Égypte." In *Etudes d'orientalisme dédiées à la mémoire de Lévi-Provençal,* edited by E. G. Gomez, 367–84. Paris.

Wilder-Smith, A., and P. Byass. 2016. "The Elusive Global Burden of Dengue." *Lancet Infectious Diseases* 16: 629–31.

Wilkening, R. V., and M. J. Federle. 2017. "Evolutionary Constraints Shaping *Streptococcus pyogenes*–Host Interactions." *Trends in Microbiology* 25: 562–72.

Williams, K. J. 2009. "The Introduction of 'Chemotherapy' Using Arsphenamine—The First Magic Bullet." *Journal of the Royal Society of Medicine* 102: 343–48.

Willoughby, U. E. 2017. *Yellow Fever, Race, and Ecology in Nineteenth-Century New Orleans.* Baton Rouge.

Wilmhurst, J., J. Fryxell, and P. Colucci. 1999. "What Constrains Daily Intake in Thomson's Gazelles?" *Ecology* 80: 2338–47.

Wilschut, L., et al. 2015. "Spatial Distribution Patterns of Plague Hosts: Point Pattern Analysis of the Burrows of Great Gerbils in Kazakhstan." *Journal of Biogeography* 42: 1281–92.

Wilson, E. O. 1999. *Consilience: The Unity of Knowledge.* New York.

————. 2014. *The Meaning of Human Existence.* New York.

Wilson, L. G. 1990. "The Historical Decline of Tuberculosis in Europe and America: Its Causes and Significance." *Journal of the History of Medicine and Allied Sciences* 45: 366–96.

————. 2005. "Commentary: Medicine, Population, and Tuberculosis." *International Journal of Epidemiology* 34: 521–24.

Wilson, P. H. 2011. *The Thirty Years War: Europe's Tragedy.* Cambridge.

Wilson, P. J. 1988. *The Domestication of the Human Species.* New Haven.

Winthrop, J. 1908. *Winthrop's Journal: "History of New England," 1630–1649.* Edited by J. K. Hosmer. New York. First published 1647.

Wirth, T., et al. 2008. "Origin, Spread and Demography of the *Mycobacterium tuberculosis* Complex." *PLoS Pathogens* 4: e1000160.

Wisecup, K. 2011. "African Medical Knowledge, the Plain Style, and Satire in the 1721 Boston Inoculation Controversy." *Early American Literature* 46: 25–50.

Witakowski, W., trans. 1996. *Pseudo-Dionysius of Tel-Mahre, Chronicle: Known Also as the Chronicle of Zuqnin. Part III*. Liverpool.

Wlasiuk, G., and M. W. Nachman. 2010. "Promiscuity and the Rate of Molecular Evolution at Primate Immunity Genes." *Evolution: International Journal of Organic Evolution* 64: 2204–20.

Wohl, A. 1977. *The Eternal Slum: Housing and Social Policy in Victorian London*. Montreal.

Wolfe, N. 2013. *The Viral Storm: The Dawn of a New Pandemic Age*. London.

Wolfe, N., C. Dunavan, and J. Diamond. 2007. "Origins of Major Human Infectious Diseases." *Nature Reviews* 447: 279–83.

Wolff, G., and J. Riffell. 2018. "Olfaction, Experience and Neural Mechanisms Underlying Mosquito Host Preference." *Journal of Experimental Biology* 221: jeb157131.

Wolfson, L. J., et al. 2009. "Estimates of Measles Case Fatality Ratios: A Comprehensive Review of Community-Based Studies." *International Journal of Epidemiology* 38: 192–205.

Wong, S., and K.-Y. Yuen. 2012. "*Streptococcus pyogenes* and Re-emergence of Scarlet Fever as a Public Health Concern." *Emerging Microbes and Infections* 1: 1–10.

———. 2018. "The Comeback of Scarlet Fever." *EBioMedicine* 28: 7–8.

Wood, B., and I. Gilby. 2017. "From *Pan* to Man the Hunter: Hunting and Meat Sharing by Chimpanzees, Humans, and Our Common Ancestor." In *Chimpanzees and Human Evolution*, edited by M. Muller, R. Wrangham, and D. Pilbeam, 339–82. Cambridge.

Wood, B. M. 2017. "Favorable Ecological Circumstances Promote Life Expectancy in Chimpanzees Similar to That of Human Hunter-Gatherers." *Journal of Human Evolution* 105: 41–56.

Wood, P. H. 1975. *Black Majority: Negroes in Colonial South Carolina from 1670 through the Stono Rebellion*. New York.

Woods, R. 2000. *The Demography of Victorian England and Wales*. Cambridge.

———. 2003. "Urban-Rural Mortality Differentials: An Unresolved Debate." *Population and Development Review* 29: 29–46.

Woods, R., and N. Shelton. 1997. *An Atlas of Victorian Mortality*. Liverpool.

Woods, R., and N. Williams. 1995. "Must the Gap Widen Before It Can Be Narrowed? Long-Term Trends in Social Class Mortality Differentials." *Continuity and Change* 10: 105–37.

Woolf, G. 1998. *Becoming Roman: The Origins of Provincial Civilization in Gaul*. Cambridge.

———. 2020. *The Life and Death of Ancient Cities*. Oxford.

Worboys, M. 2000. *Spreading Germs: Disease Theories and Medical Practice in Britain, 1865–1900*. Cambridge.

———. 2007. "Was There a Bacteriological Revolution in Late Nineteenth-Century Medicine?" *Studies in History and Philosophy of Biological and Biomedical Sciences* 38: 20–42.

World Bank. 1993. *World Development Report 1993: Investing in Health*. New York.

Worster, D. 2017. "The Good Muck: Toward an Excremental History of China." *Rachel Carson Center Perspectives* 5: 1–54.

Wrangham, R W. 2009. *Catching Fire: How Cooking Made Us Human*. New York.

———. 2017. "Control of Fire in the Paleolithic: Evaluating the Cooking Hypothesis." *Current Anthropology* 58: S303–13.

Wright, W. C. 1930. *Contagion, Contagious Diseases and Their Treatment*. New York.

Wrigley, E. A. 1967. "A Simple Model of London's Importance in Changing English Society and Economy 1650–1750." *Past & Present* 37: 44–70.

———. 1988. *Continuity, Chance and Change: The Character of the Industrial Revolution in England*. Cambridge University Press.

Wrigley, E. A., and R. S. Schofield. 1981. *The Population History of England, 1541–1871: A Reconstruction*. Cambridge.

Wylie, J. 1987. *The Faroe Islands: Interpretations of History*. Lexington.

Ximénez, C., et al. 2009. "Reassessment of the Epidemiology of Amebiasis: State of the Art." *Infection, Genetics and Evolution* 9: 1023–32.

Xiong, H., et al. 2016. "Genetic Diversity and Population Structure of Cowpea (*Vigna unguiculata* L. Walp)." *PLoS One* 11: e0160941.

Yang, J., et al. 2007. "Revisiting the Molecular Evolutionary History of *Shigella* Spp." *Journal of Molecular Evolution* 64: 71–79.

Yang, R., and A. Anisimov, eds. 2016. *Yersinia pestis: Retrospective and Perspective*. Netherlands.

Yang, Z., and B. Rannala. 2012. "Molecular Phylogenetics: Principles and Practice." *Nature Reviews Genetics* 13: 303–14.

Yap, P., and K. Thong. 2017. "*Salmonella typhi* Genomics: Envisaging the Future of Typhoid Eradication." *Tropical Medicine and International Health* 22: 918–25.

Yeoman, T. H. 1848. *Consumption of the Lungs, or, Decline: The Causes, Symptoms, and Rational Treatment*. London.

Yi, B. X., et al. 2016. "Chinese National Income: ca. 1661–1933." *Australian Economic History Review* 57: 368–93.

Yong, E. 2016. *I Contain Multitudes: The Microbes within Us and a Grander View of Life*. London.

Yoshida, K., et al. 2013. "The Rise and Fall of the *Phytophthora infestans* Lineage That Triggered the Irish Potato Famine." *Elife* 2: 00731.

You, Y., et al. 2018. "Scarlet Fever Epidemic in China Caused by *Streptococcus pyogenes* Serotype M12: Epidemiologic and Molecular Analysis." *EBioMedicine* 28: 128–35.

Young, A. D. and J. P. Gillung. 2020. "Phylogenomics—Principles, Opportunities and Pitfalls of Big-Data Phylogenetics." *Systematic Entomology* 45: 225–47.

Yule, H. 1866. *Cathay and the Way Hither*. 2 vols. London.

Zahid, H. J., E. Robinson, and R. L. Kelly. 2016. "Agriculture, Population Growth, and Statistical Analysis of the Radiocarbon Record." *Proceedings of the National Academy of Sciences* 113: 931–35.

Zalasiewicz, J., et al., eds. 2019. *The Anthropocene as a Geological Time Unit: A Guide to the Scientific Evidence and Current Debate*. Cambridge.

Zehender, G., et al. 2018. "Bayesian Reconstruction of the Evolutionary History and Cross-Species Transition of Variola Virus and Orthopoxviruses." *Journal of Medical Virology* 90: 1134–41.

Zelener, Y. 2003. "Smallpox and the Disintegration of the Roman Economy after 165 AD." Ph.D. diss., Columbia University.

Zhang, Y., and E. C. Holmes. 2020. "A Genomic Perspective on the Origin and Emergence of SARS-CoV-2." *Cell* 181: 223–27.

Zhou, Z., et al. 2018. "Pan-Genome Analysis of Ancient and Modern *Salmonella enterica* Demonstrates Genomic Stability of the Invasive Para C Lineage for Millennia." *Current Biology* 28: 2420–28.

Ziegler, P. 1969. *The Black Death*. London.

Zimmer, C. 2015. *A Planet of Viruses*. 2nd ed. Chicago.

Zinsser, H. 1935. *Rats, Lice and History: Being a Study in Biography, Which, after Twelve Preliminary Chapters Indispensable for the Preparation of the Lay Reader, Deals with the Life History of Typhus Fever*. Boston.

Zohary, D., M. Hopf, and E. Weiss. 2012. *Domestication of Plants in the Old World: The Origin and Spread of Domesticated Plants in Southwest Asia, Europe, and the Mediterranean Basin*. 4th ed. Oxford.

Zondervan, N. A., et al. 2018. "Regulation of the Three Virulence Strategies of *Mycobacterium tuberculosis*: A Success Story." *International Journal of Molecular Sciences* 19: 347.

Zuckerkandl, E., and L. Pauling. 1965. "Molecules as Documents of Evolutionary History." *Journal of Theoretical Biology* 8: 357–66.

INDEX

Abbasid Caliphate, 218

Abreu, Aleixo de, 311

Abu Hureyra, 133–34

Accra, 494

Ache people, 89

Adams, Henry, 398, 417, 422, 460

Adams, John, 417

adenoviruses, 141, 172, 457, 485

Adriatic Sea, 367

Aedes, 107, 287, 298, 306–8, 319

Aeta people, 89

Africa, 6, 7, 8, 11, 156, 161, 165–66, 169, 191–92, 204, 208, 218, 236, 245–46, 251–53, 272, 275, 277, 279, 303–4, 328, 341, 449, 458, 462–64, 491, 493–94; *Aedes aegypti*, 306–7, 319; cholera in, 433–35; domestications (of animals/plants), 125–27, 163; AIDS, 500–502; eastern, 68, 74, 89, 110, 156, 163, 176–77, 192, 196, 224, 229, 310, 433, 435, 443; human evolution, 4–5, 49, 63, 66, 79–82; leishmaniasis in, 113; lymphatic filariasis in, 108; malaria in, 102–3, 179–84, 323; northern, 127, 191, 208, 218, 228, 230, 233–34, 462; plague in, 210, 228–30, 443; rinderpest, 420, 454; schistosomiasis in, 72–74; sleeping sickness in, 31, 109–11; smallpox in, 195–96, 362–63, 407; southern, 86, 110, 454, 502; sub-Saharan, 110, 161, 165, 228, 463, 494, 501–2; tuberculosis in, 175–77; western, 50, 102, 110, 256, 284–300, 310, 317, 323, 407, 425, 437, 493, 500; whipworm in, 91; yaws in, 256; yellow fever in, 310–12, 314–17, 437

Agra, 356

Agta people, 86–90, 113, 531

AIDS, 4, 5, 21, 27, 40, 43, 254, 469, 491, 499–502

Aka people, 89

Akyeampong, Emmanuel, 463

Alaska, 283

Alexandria, 191, 212, 215, 226, 229–30

Alfani, Guido, 359

alpacas, 125, 127, 246

Alps, 215, 234, 353, 355

Altizer, Sonia, 58

Amazon River, 249, 261, 275, 327

Amoy. *See* Xiamen

Amsterdam, 338, 341

Anatolia, 156, 215, 234, 355

Andes Mountains, 126, 247, 249, 253, 261, 264, 275, 327, 406, 447

Angola, 311

Anne, Queen, 360

Anopheles, 94, 97–100, 103, 107, 138, 180–81, 203, 296, 318–19, 499; *arabiensis*, 180, 296; *atroparvus*, 100, 318; *coluzzi*, 180, 296; *funestus*, 180, 296; *gambiae*, 180–81, 296, 319; *quadrimaculatus*, 319–20

Anthropocene, 469, 504–5, 507

antibiotics, 1, 13, 300, 397, 440, 483–84, 505, 506; and mortality decline, 380, 384, 481, 483–84, 493, 494, 495, 497; period before, 139, 151, 204, 256, 346, 397, 440; resistance to, 13, 505–6, 579

antibodies, 36, 38, 142, 489

Antioch, 191, 215

THE PRINCETON ECONOMIC HISTORY
OF THE WESTERN WORLD

Joel Mokyr, Series Editor

Recent titles